A HISTORY OF RUSSIAN PHILOSOPHY 1830–1930

The great age of Russian philosophy spans the century between 1830 and 1930 – from the famous Slavophile–Westernizer controversy of the 1830s and 1840s, through the "Silver Age" of Russian culture at the beginning of the twentieth century, to the formation of a Russian "philosophical emigration" in the wake of the Russian Revolution. This volume is a major new history and interpretation of Russian philosophy in this period. Eighteen chapters (plus a substantial introduction and afterword) discuss Russian philosophy's main figures, schools, and controversies, while simultaneously pursuing a common central theme: the development of a distinctive Russian tradition of philosophical humanism focused on the defense of human dignity. As this volume shows, the century-long debate over the meaning and grounds of human dignity, freedom, and the just society involved thinkers of all backgrounds and positions, transcending easy classification as "religious" or "secular." The debate still resonates strongly today.

G.M. HAMBURG is the Otho M. Behr Professor of History at Claremont McKenna College. He has written, translated and edited many books in Russian history, including *Politics of the Russian Nobility, 1881–1905* (1984), *Boris Chicherin and Early Russian Liberalism, 1828–1866* (1992), *Liberty, Equality, and the Market: Selected Essays of Boris Chicherin* (1998), and *Russian–Muslim Confrontation in the Caucasus: Alternative Visions of the Conflict between Imam Shamil and the Russians, 1830–1859* (2004) (with J. Thomas Sanders and Ernest Tucker).

RANDALL A. POOLE is Associate Professor of History at the College of St. Scholastica. He has translated and edited *Problems of Idealism: Essays in Russian Social Philosophy* (2003) and written numerous articles and book chapters in Russian intellectual history and philosophy.

D1103649

A History of Russian Philosophy
1830–1930

Faith, Reason, and the Defense of Human Dignity

EDITED BY

G.M. HAMBURG AND RANDALL A. POOLE

CAMBRIDGE
UNIVERSITY PRESS

CAMBRIDGE UNIVERSITY PRESS
Cambridge, New York, Melbourne, Madrid, Cape Town,
Singapore, São Paulo, Delhi, Mexico City

Cambridge University Press
The Edinburgh Building, Cambridge CB2 8RU, UK

Published in the United States of America by Cambridge University Press, New York

www.cambridge.org
Information on this title: www.cambridge.org/9781107612785

First published 2010
First paperback edition 2013

A catalogue record for this publication is available from the British Library

ISBN 978-0-521-88450-1 Hardback
ISBN 978-1-107-61278-5 Paperback

To George L. Kline

CONTENTS

CONTRIBUTORS

MARTIN BEISSWENGER recently received his Ph.D. in history at the University of Notre Dame, where he is at present Sorin Postdoctoral Fellow. His dissertation, written under the direction of Gary Hamburg, is a study of P.N. Savitskii and Eurasianism. His publications include *Petr Nikolaevich Savitskii (1895–1968): A Bibliography of his Published Works* (2008) and several articles.

ROBERT BIRD is Associate Professor in the Departments of Slavic Languages and Literatures and Cinema and Media Studies at the University of Chicago. He is the author of *The Russian Prospero: The Creative Universe of Viacheslav Ivanov* (2006), translator of Viacheslav Ivanov's *Selected Essays* (2001), and editor of several works of Russian religious philosophy. Author of two books on film-maker Andrei Tarkovsk, including *Andrei Tarkovsky: Elements of Cinema* (2008), he has also published essays on Russian philosophy, theology, and aesthetic theory.

STEVEN CASSEDY is Professor of Slavic and Comparative Literature and Associate Dean of Graduate Studies at the University of California at San Diego. His books include *Flight from Eden: The Origins of Modern Literary Criticism and Theory* (1990); *To the Other Shore: The Russian Jewish Intellectuals who Came to America* (1997); *Building the Future: Jewish Immigrant Intellectuals and the Making of Tsukunft* (1999); and *Dostoevsky's Religion* (2005). In addition, he has published many essays in Russian and European intellectual history and philosophy.

CARYL EMERSON is A. Watson Armour III University Professor of Slavic Languages and Literatures at Princeton University, where she chairs the Slavic Department with a co-appointment in Comparative Literature. A translator and critic of Mikhail Bakhtin, she has also published widely on nineteenth-century Russian literature (Pushkin, Dostoevskii, Tolstoi), on the history and relevance of literary criticism, and on Russian opera and vocal music. Recent projects include *The Cambridge Introduction to Russian Literature* (2008) and the adaptation of Russian literary classics to the Stalinist-era musical stage.

STUART FINKEL is Associate Professor of History at the University of Florida. He is the author of *On the Ideological Front: The Russian Intelligentsia and the Making of the Soviet Public Sphere* (2007) and several articles on the Russian intelligentsia and Soviet power. His current project focuses on Ekaterina Peshkova and the "Political Red Cross," which lobbied on behalf of political prisoners in the Soviet Union during the 1920s and 1930s.

VICTORIA S. FREDE is Assistant Professor of History at the University of California, Berkeley. She has published articles on the history of the Russian intelligentsia and is currently completing a book project, *"If God Does Not Exist . . . ": Educated Russians and Unbelief, 1780–1870.*

PHILIP T. GRIER is Thomas Bowman Professor of Philosophy and Religion at Dickinson College in Carlisle, Pennsylvania. He is the author of *Marxist Ethical Theory in the Soviet Union* (1978), editor of *Dialectic and Contemporary Science: Essays in Honor of Errol E. Harris* (1989), editor of *Identity and Difference: Studies in Hegel's Logic, Philosophy of Spirit, and Politics* (2007), and translator and editor of Ivan Il'in's *Hegel's Philosophy as a Theory of the Concreteness of God and Humanity* (2010). In addition, he has written many articles and book chapters on Hegelianism, Marxism, Russian philosophy, ethics, and other topics in philosophy.

G.M. HAMBURG is Otho M. Behr Professor of European History at Claremont McKenna College. He has written, translated, and edited many books in Russian history, including *Politics of the Russian Nobility, 1881–1905* (1984); *Boris Chicherin and Early Russian Liberalism, 1828–1866* (1992), the first of a projected two-volume study; and *Russian–Muslim Confrontation in the Caucasus: Alternative Visions of the Conflict between Imam Shamil and the Russians, 1830–1859*, co-authored with J. Thomas Sanders and Ernest Tucker (2004). He has also translated and edited *Liberty, Equality and the Market: Selected Essays of Boris Chicherin* (1998). His current book projects include *A History of Russian Political Thought*.

SERGEY HORUJY, a preeminent Russian philosopher, is Professor at the Institute of Philosophy, Russian Academy of Sciences, and Research Director at the Center for Synergetic Anthropology, State University Higher School of Economics, Moscow. His many works include *Opyty iz russkoi dukhovnoi traditsii* (2005); *O starom i novom* (2000); *K fenomenologii askezy* (1998); and *Posle pereryva: puti russkoi filosofii* (1994).

JUDITH DEUTSCH KORNBLATT is Professor of Slavic Languages and Literatures at the University of Wisconsin. She is the author of *The Cossack Hero in Russian Literature: A Study in Cultural Mythology* (1992); *Doubly Chosen: Jewish Identity, the Soviet Intelligentsia, and the Russian Orthodox Church* (2004); *Divine Sophia: The Wisdom Writings of Vladimir Solovyov* (2009); and essays on Vladimir Solov'ëv and Russian religious philosophy. In addition, she has co-edited *Russian Religious Thought* (1996).

PATRICK LALLY MICHELSON received his Ph.D. in history from the University of Wisconsin, Madison, where he is at present Honorary Associate Fellow at the Center for Russia, East Europe, and Central Asia.

THOMAS NEMETH has been an Alexander von Humboldt Fellow and a post-doctoral fellow at the University of Melbourne. He is the author of *Gramsci's Philosophy: A Critical Study* (1980) and translator of Gustav Shpet's *Appearance and Sense* (1991). He has written articles on Russian philosophy for journals and reference works, including a major series of articles on "Kant in Russia."

FRANCES NETHERCOTT is Lecturer in Modern History at the University of St. Andrews. Her major publications include *Une rencontre philosophique: Bergson en Russie (1907–1917)* (1995); *Russia's Plato: Plato and the Platonic Tradition in Russian Education, Science and Ideology, 1840–1930* (2000); and *Russian Legal Culture Before and After Communism: Criminal Justice, Politics, and the Public Sphere* (2007).

DEREK OFFORD is Professor of Russian Intellectual History in the Department of Russian Studies at the University of Bristol. He is a specialist in eighteenth- and nineteenth-century Russian history, thought, and literature. His books include *Portraits of Early Russian Liberals: A Study of the Thought of T.N. Granovsky, V.P. Botkin, P.V. Annenkov, A.V. Druzhinin and K.D. Kavelin* (1985, 2009); *The Russian Revolutionary Movement in the 1880s* (1986); and *Journeys to a Graveyard: Perceptions of Europe in Classical Russian Travel Writing* (2006). He has edited or co-edited four other books and is also the author of two widely used books on the modern Russian language.

RANDALL A. POOLE is Associate Professor of History at the College of St. Scholastica. He has translated and edited *Problems of Idealism: Essays in Russian Social Philosophy* (2003) and written numerous articles and book chapters in Russian intellectual history and philosophy. He is currently completing a book, *Autonomy, Dignity, Perfectibility: Idealism and Liberalism in Russia, 1885–1922*.

BERNICE GLATZER ROSENTHAL is Professor of History at Fordham University. Her works in Russian intellectual history include, as author, *D.S. Merezhkovsky and the Silver Age: The Development of a Revolutionary Mentality* (1975) and *New Myth, New World: From Nietzsche to Stalinism* (2002); and, as editor and contributor, *Nietzsche in Russia* (1986); *A Revolution of the Spirit: Crisis of Value in Russia, 1890–1924* (1990); *Nietzsche and Soviet Culture: Ally and Adversary* (1994); and *The Occult in Russian and Soviet Culture* (1997).

JAMES P. SCANLAN is Professor Emeritus of Philosophy at The Ohio State University. He has written and edited many books in Russian philosophy, including the three-volume classic *Russian Philosophy* (1965, 1976); *Marxism in the USSR: A Critical Survey of Current Soviet Thought* (1986); *Russian Thought After Communism: The Recovery of a Philosophical Heritage* (1994); and *Dostoevsky the Thinker* (2002).

PHILIP J. SWOBODA is Professor of History at Sarah Lawrence College. He has published several articles on Semën Frank and is currently completing a book, *Confidence in Being: The Philosophical Odyssey of S.L. Frank*.

PAUL VALLIERE is Professor of Religion and McGregor Professor in the Humanities at Butler University, Indianapolis. His books include the major study *Modern Russian Theology: Bukharev, Soloviev, Bulgakov – Orthodox Theology in a New Key* (2000). He is currently completing a book manuscript on conciliarism in comparative and ecumenical perspective.

ANDRZEJ WALICKI is O'Neill Family Professor Emeritus of History at the University of Notre Dame. An eminent historian of ideas, his most important works in English are *The Slavophile Controversy: History of a Conservative Utopia in Nineteenth-Century Russian Thought* (1975); *A History of Russian Thought from the Enlightenment to Marxism* (1979); *Philosophy and Romantic Nationalism: The Case of Poland* (1982); *Legal Philosophies of Russian Liberalism* (1987); *Stanislaw Brzozowski and the Polish Beginnings of "Western Marxism"* (1989); and *Marxism and the Leap to the Kingdom of Freedom: The Rise and Fall of the Communist Utopia* (1995).

ACKNOWLEDGMENTS

This volume was preceded by a research conference on the history of Russian philosophy, held at Claremont McKenna College, in April 2008. Major funding for the conference was provided by Claremont McKenna College, Claremont, California (Gould Center for Humanistic Studies and William F. Podlich Fund) and The College of St. Scholastica, Duluth, Minnesota (Office of the President). The editors are grateful for this financial support and for the honor of working with the distinguished group of scholars whose work constitutes this volume.

Introduction

THE HUMANIST TRADITION
IN RUSSIAN PHILOSOPHY

G.M. HAMBURG AND RANDALL A. POOLE

This book is a history of Russian philosophy from roughly 1830 to 1930, that is, from the genesis of a distinctively Russian philosophical humanism during the Slavophile–Westernizer controversy of the 1830s and 1840s to the formation of a Russian "philosophical emigration" in the wake of the Russian Revolution. This century – call it Russian philosophy's "long nineteenth century" – confronts scholars with a vast, unusually forbidding intellectual terrain, its ground demarcated by a deep chasm between idealist and materialist thinkers, pockmarked by political disagreements, and riven by strife between amateur and professional philosophers.

Previous students of Russian philosophy have tried to traverse this terrain by sticking to accustomed pathways: the development of religious philosophy,[1] or appearance of historical materialism;[2] the symbiotic relationship between philosophy and literature,[3] or between philosophy and social thought;[4] the

---

[1] Probably the best-known essay on Russian religious philosophy is Nicolas Berdyaev, *The Russian Idea* (R.M. French (trans.), London: Geoffrey Bles, 1947). Since perestroika and the disintegration of the Soviet Union, much of the corpus of nineteenth- and twentieth-century Russian religious philosophy has been reprinted in new editions, in most cases for the first time since the Revolution. The new Russian scholarship on the history of religious philosophy is also remarkable, including, to take two prominent examples, Sergei Khoruzhii [Horujy], *O starom i novom* (St. Petersburg: Aleteiia, 2000), which connects Russian religious thought in the "long nineteenth century" to its Byzantine and Orthodox roots, and P.P. Gaidenko, *Vladimir Solov'ëv i filosofiia Serebrianogo veka* (Moscow: Progress-Traditsiia, 2001).

[2] The standard work from the late Soviet period is V.E. Evgrafov *et al.* (eds.), *Istoriia filosofii v SSSR*, 5 vols. (Moscow: Nauka, 1968–1988).

[3] Among the many books in this genre, see the classic Thomas Garrigue Masaryk, *The Spirit of Russia: Studies in History, Literature and Philosophy*, 2nd edn., 2 vols. (Eden and Cedar Paul (trans.), London: George Allen and Unwin, 1955). A recent sophisticated consideration is Edith W. Clowes, *Fiction's Overcoat: Russian Literary Culture and the Question of Philosophy* (Ithaca, NY: Cornell University Press, 2004).

[4] Here the classic works are Andrzej Walicki, *A History of Russian Thought from the Enlightenment to Marxism* (Hilda Andrews-Rusiecka (trans.), Stanford University Press, 1979), which has recently appeared in a revised and expanded Polish edition, *Zarys myśli rosyjskiej od oświecenia do renesansu religijno-filozoficznego* (Cracow: Wydawnictwo Uniwersytetu Jagiellońskiego, 2005); and Andrzej Walicki, *Legal Philosophies of Russian Liberalism* (Oxford University Press, 1987).

dialectical relationship between Russian "national" philosophy and western cosmopolitan influences;[5] or the self-transformation of philosophy into an academic discipline situated mainly in universities.[6] Intrepid scholars have sometimes explored several of these pathways in the same book, though there has been a tendency to exaggerate the significance of Marxism and its forerunners while underestimating the importance of idealist philosophical approaches – for understandable historical reasons.

We have learned much from our predecessors' achievements. We think that no reductive approach to the history of Russian philosophy can succeed in communicating the richness of the subject; that a proper appreciation of Russian philosophy must take into account its profound connections both with Russian literature (both narrative fiction and poetry) and Russian politics (the populist, social-democratic and liberal traditions alongside the Byzantine or Russian Orthodox discourse on politics and human nature); and that professional academic philosophy, which appeared in inchoate form in the universities by the 1870s and matured in the first decade of the twentieth century, never displaced the robust "amateur" philosophizing that was typical of the early period from 1830 to 1870 but was also largely characteristic of "Silver Age" culture from 1890 to 1920. Consequently, we decided to undertake a book that would foreground the formal and conceptual complexities of our subject, without neglecting the peculiarities of Russia's changing historical context. To execute our plan, we solicited contributions from intellectual historians, philosophers, and literary critics, each of them expert on a particular feature of the philosophical landscape.

The present volume, in spite of its chronological sweep and thematic breadth, does not pretend to be an encyclopedic history of modern Russian philosophy, but it does aim to comprehend what we think is most characteristic and best

---

[5] See, e.g., Nicholas V. Riasanovsky, *Russia and the West in the Teaching of the Slavophiles: A Study of Romantic Ideology* (Cambridge, MA: Harvard University Press, 1952); and Andrzej Walicki, *The Slavophile Controversy: History of a Conservative Utopia in Nineteenth-Century Russian Thought* (Hilda Andrews-Rusiecka (trans.), Oxford: Clarendon Press, 1975).

[6] This transformation is one of the main themes in two standard histories of Russian philosophy: Nicholas O. Lossky, *History of Russian Philosophy* (New York: International Universities Press, 1951), and V.V. Zenkovsky, *A History of Russian Philosophy*, 2 vols. (George L. Kline (trans.), New York: Columbia University Press, 1953). More recently, see the remarkable reference work by V.F. Pustarnakov, *Universitetskaia filosofiia v Rossii. Idei. Personalii. Osnovnye tsentry* (St. Petersburg: Izdatel'stvo Russkogo Khristianskogo gumanitarnogo instituta, 2003). Other good reference works include M.A. Maslin (ed.), *Russkaia filosofiia: Slovar'* (Moscow: Respublika, 1995); A.I. Abramov et al. (eds.), *Russkaia filosofiia: Malyi entsiklopedicheskii slovar'* (Moscow: Nauka, 1995); and P.F. Alekseev (ed.), *Filosofy Rossii XIX–XX stoletii: Biografii, idei, trudy*, 3rd edn. (Moscow: Akademicheskii Proekt, 1999).

about Russian philosophy in this period: its humanist tradition.[7] A few philosophical thinkers, such as the panslavist theorist Nikolai Danilevskii and the Byzantine enthusiast Konstantin Leont'ev, clearly do not belong to that tradition and are not considered here.[8] Nor are certain other Russian philosophers who worked mainly in specialized areas such as epistemology, logic, and philosophy of science: for example, the critical positivist Vladimir Lesevich, neo-Kantians such as Aleksandr Vvedenskii and Sergei Hessen, the Hegelian logician Nikolai Debol'skii, and scientist-philosophers such as Vladimir Vernadskii.[9] Finally, some figures relevant to Russian philosophical humanism were excluded or given relatively little attention because of considerations of space: they include the conservative critic Nikolai Strakhov,[10] the Christian naturalist Nikolai Fëdorov,[11] the "concrete" idealist Sergei Trubetskoi,[12] the religious existentialist Lev Shestov,[13] and the religious, moral, and social philosopher Boris

[7] The prominent British historian of ideas Aileen M. Kelly has written two volumes on important aspects of Russian philosophical humanism: *Toward Another Shore: Russian Thinkers Between Necessity and Chance* (New Haven: Yale University Press, 1998) and *Views from the Other Shore: Essays on Herzen, Chekhov, and Bakhtin* (New Haven, CT: Yale University Press, 1999).

[8] See Robert E. MacMaster, *Danilevsky: A Russian Totalitarian Philosopher* (Cambridge, MA: Harvard University Press, 1967); on Leont'ev, see Nicolas Berdyaev, *Leontiev* (George Reavey (trans.), London: Geoffrey Bles, Centenary Press, 1940), and George L. Kline's classic study, *Religious and Anti-Religious Thought in Russia* (University of Chicago Press, 1968), pp. 35–54.

[9] On these thinkers see *Studies in East European Thought* 47, nos. 3–4 (1995), special issue devoted to "Neo-Kantianism in Russian Thought" (Bernice Glatzer Rosenthal (ed.)); Thomas Nemeth, "Debol'skij and Lesevič on Kant: Two Russian Philosophies in the 1870s," *Studies in East European Thought* 45, no. 4 (1993), 282–305; Andrzej Walicki, *Legal Philosophies of Russian Liberalism*, ch. 7 (on Hessen, whose significance, as Walicki shows, goes well beyond neo-Kantian epistemology and value theory); Kendall E. Bailes, *Science and Russian Culture in an Age of Revolutions: V.I. Vernadsky and His Scientific School, 1863–1945* (Bloomington, IN: Indiana University Press, 1990); and Randall A. Poole, "Vernadskii, Vladimir Ivanovich (1863–1945)" in Edward Craig (ed.), *Routledge Encyclopedia of Philosophy* (London: Routledge, 1998–), online version (2002).

[10] Linda Gerstein, *Nikolai Strakhov: Philosopher, Man of Letters, Social Critic* (Cambridge, MA: Harvard University Press, 1971).

[11] George M. Young, Jr., *Nikolai Fedorov: An Introduction* (Belmont, MA: Nordland, 1979); Irene Masing-Delic, *Abolishing Death: A Salvation Myth of Russian Twentieth-Century Literature* (Stanford University Press, 1992), pp. 76–104; and Michael Hagemeister, *Nikolaj Fedorov: Studien zu Leben, Werk und Wirkung* (Munich: Verlag Otto Sagner, 1989).

[12] Martha Bohachevsky-Chomiak, *Sergei N. Trubetskoi: An Intellectual Among the Intelligentsia in Prerevolutionary Russia* (Belmont, MA: Nordland, 1976), and Randall A. Poole, "Trubetskoi, Sergei Nikolaevich (1862–1905)" in Edward Craig (ed.), *Routledge Encyclopedia of Philosophy* (London: Routledge, 1998–), online version (2002).

[13] Shestov is briefly considered in chapter 11. See Louis J. Shein, *The Philosophy of Lev Shestov (1866–1938): A Russian Religious Existentialist* (Lampeter, NY: E. Mellen Press, 1991); Andrius Valevičius, *Lev Shestov and His Times: Encounters with Brandes, Tolstoy, Dostoevsky, Chekhov, Ibsen, Nietzsche, and Husserl* (New York: Peter Lang, 1993); Clowes, *Fiction's Overcoat*, ch. 5; Kline, *Religious and Anti-Religious Thought in Russia*, pp. 73–90; and A.A. Kudishina, *Ekzistentsializm i gumanizm v Rossii: Lev Shestov i Nikolai Berdiaev* (Moscow: Akademicheskii proekt, 2007). The bibliography at the end of this volume lists Shestov's works in translation.

Vysheslavtsev.[14] Even a large volume such as this one cannot avoid a degree of selectivity. Nonetheless, we believe that "philosophical humanism" constitutes an inclusive, powerful framework for a new, interpretive history of Russian philosophy. Our goal has been to treat the most important thinkers and developments in some depth, rather than trying to survey everything.

The central theme of our book is that Russian philosophers in the long nineteenth century concerned themselves almost obsessively with the importance of human dignity, conceived either as an intrinsic property of the individual or as a project to be realized as the final goal of social development. At some risk of oversimplifying, we would claim that Russian philosophy as a whole constitutes an extended dialogue on human dignity, with many philosophers defending it against those political institutions and ideas that were not adverse to reducing human beings to mere instruments, that is, to means for achieving large political or social objectives. These philosophical thinkers either regarded human beings as ends-in-themselves, and thus as precious, autonomous beings endowed with inviolable rights, or (and these were not necessarily incompatible positions, though sometimes there was tension between them) as creative beings possessing the capacity to shape the world through the free exercise of will.

This picture of Russian philosophy may at first seem counterintuitive to some readers who may understand Russian thought as a congenial locus of social utopias or dystopias.[15] Here the Slavophiles' fabrication of Old Russia as a "golden age," Vladimir Odoevskii's dystopian fantasy *Russian Nights* (1844), the Petrashevskii circle's embrace of French utopian socialism in the late 1840s, Nikolai Chernyshevskii's landmark novel of the early 1860s *What Is To Be Done?*, the Bolshevik Aleksandr Bogdanov's propagandistic science fiction novel *Red Star* (1908), and Lenin's treatise *State and Revolution* (1917) may come to mind as examples of the utopian genre in Russia. Our contention, however, is that utopian literature can be properly understood only as part of a cultural dialogue about human dignity in which Russian utopian writers made or responded to claims about how to achieve a just society in which human beings may live a dignified existence and realize their full potential.

---

[14] B.P. Vysheslavtsev, *The Eternal in Russian Philosophy* (Penelope V. Burt (trans.), Grand Rapids, MI: William B. Eerdmans Publishing Company, 2002).

[15] Lately, we have benefited from the first systematic surveys of utopianism in Russian thought. See Léonid Heller and Michel Niqueux, *Histoire de l'utopie en Russie* (Paris: Presses Universitaires de France, 1995), translated into Russian as Leonid Geller, Mishel' Nike, *Utopiia v Rossii* (St. Petersburg: Giperion, 2003); and the marvelous B.F. Egorov, *Rossiiskie utopii. Istoricheskii putevoditel'* (St. Petersburg: Iskusstvo and SPB, 2007). Also, T.V. Artem'eva, *Ot slavnogo proshlogo k svetlomu budushchemu: Filosofiia istorii i utopiia v Rossii epokhi Prosveshcheniia* (St. Petersburg: Aleteiia, 2005).

As we shall demonstrate, the deepest and broadest current in Russian philosophy was the Russian humanist tradition, whose best representatives recognized that individual human beings are absolute in value and that there are no higher ends – social, political, historical, or religious – for which they could be sacrificed or treated merely as means. The core of the Russian humanist tradition is the idea of *lichnost'*, which can mean person, personality, individual, or self.[16] Its richest philosophical meaning is personhood, a term emphasizing the absolute value and dignity that make human beings persons or, in Kant's terminology, ends-in-themselves. In the Russian humanist tradition, personhood and human dignity are closely related concepts, for personhood implies the capacity to recognize one's own dignity and that of others.

Certain thinkers in the Russian humanist tradition, perhaps most notably Alexander Herzen, resisted drawing metaphysical conclusions from the dignity of the individual; in fact, Herzen feared that metaphysical systems pose a danger to moral autonomy and responsibility. Other Russian humanists, beginning with the Slavophiles, thought that the moral idea of personhood entails a theistic conception of human nature. In 1909, Semën Frank called this second current in Russian thought "religious humanism."[17] This phrase may seem paradoxical, given the common tendency to think of humanism as privileging human values over the absolute claims of religion and metaphysics. Frank and other Russian idealist philosophers believed, however, that the very idea of being human (that is, possessing reason, free will, and the capacity for morality) leads to certain general theistic or metaphysical conclusions. For them, "religious humanism" was a just a fuller expression of the term "humanism."

RELIGIOUS HUMANISM IN THE RENAISSANCE AND IN RUSSIA

The humanism of the European Renaissance was also religious. In his classic study *In Our Image and Likeness: Humanity and Divinity in Italian Humanist Thought*, Charles Trinkaus argues that Genesis 1:26 – "And God said, 'Let us make man in our image, after our likeness'" – was the critical text in the development of Renaissance humanism.[18] Following a wide range of Hebrew, Greek, and Latin sources, Italian humanist thinkers gave the Genesis text a

---

[16] See Derek Offord, "*Lichnost'*: Notions of Individual Identity" in Catriona Kelly and David Shepherd (eds.), *Constructing Russian Culture in the Age of Revolution: 1881–1940* (Oxford University Press, 1998), pp. 13–25.

[17] S.L. Frank, "The Ethic of Nihilism: A Characterization of the Russian Intelligentsia's Moral Outlook" in Marshall S. Shatz and Judith E. Zimmerman (eds. and trans.), *Vekhi/Landmarks: A Collection of Articles about the Russian Intelligentsia* (Armonk, NY: M.E. Sharpe, 1994), p. 155.

[18] Charles Trinkaus, *In Our Image and Likeness: Humanity and Divinity in Italian Humanist Thought*, 2 vols. (University of Chicago Press, 1970; University of Notre Dame Press, 1995).

dynamic, synergetic interpretation: human beings are graciously created in God's image, but we must assimilate to God's likeness by our own efforts, through moral striving and self-realization. Trinkaus stresses that man's "similitude" to God "connoted the dynamic process of becoming like God, or Platonic 'assimilation.'"[19] According to Marsilio Ficino (1433–1499), the leading figure in the Florentine revival of Platonism, human beings are rational, free, and therefore responsible for progressively realizing God's likeness in themselves. In the view of Ficino and other Renaissance humanists, salvation cannot be attained without human participation. Salvation itself was increasingly understood not merely as a divine gift to depraved humankind, as in the Augustinian framework, but as the self-realization of our divine-human potential – as deification, or, in the Greek patristic expression, *theosis*. This new emphasis on human freedom, agency, and responsibility formed the core of the Renaissance idea of human dignity. The two main themes of Ficino's philosophy – "the dignity of man in his pursuit of deification, and the universality of all human traditions in this pursuit" – were central, Trinkaus believes, to Renaissance culture as a whole.[20]

The importance of these themes can be seen in Giovanni Pico della Mirandola's splendid oration, *De hominis dignitate* (1486), often regarded as the manifesto of the Italian Renaissance. In it Pico recounts how God made man a "creature of indeterminate nature" and said to him:

The nature of all other beings is limited and constrained within the bounds of laws prescribed by Us. Thou, constrained by no limits, in accordance with thine own free will, in whose hand We have placed thee, shalt ordain for thyself the limits of thy nature . . . We have made thee neither of heaven nor of earth, neither mortal nor immortal, so that with freedom of choice and with honor, as though the maker and molder of thyself, thou mayest fashion thyself in whatever shape thou shalt prefer. Thou shalt have the power to degenerate into the lower forms of life, which are brutish. Thou shalt have the power, out of thy soul's judgment, to be reborn into the higher forms, which are divine.[21]

Ernst Cassirer wrote in a seminal essay on Pico that this idea of man as a free "maker and molder" of himself, with the power to ascend to divine heights, "adds a new element to the basic religious notion of 'likeness to God.' . . . The

---

[19] Charles Trinkaus, "Renaissance Idea of the Dignity of Man" in *Dictionary of the History of Ideas: Studies of Selected Pivotal Ideas*, 4 vols. (New York: Charles Scribner's Sons, 1973), vol. 4, p. 137; Trinkaus, *In Our Image and Likeness*, vol. 1, pp. 181–188.

[20] Trinkaus, "Renaissance Idea of the Dignity of Man," p. 144; on Ficino's idea of deification, see Trinkaus, *In Our Image and Likeness*, vol. 2, pp. 487–498. More generally, see Paul Oskar Kristellar, "Renaissance Concepts of Man," part 4 of his *Renaissance Thought and Its Sources* (Michael Mooney (ed.), New York: Columbia University Press, 1979), pp. 165–210, esp. ch. 9, "The Dignity of Man."

[21] Giovanni Pico della Mirandola, "Oration on the Dignity of Man," E.L. Forbes (trans.), in Ernst Cassirer, Paul Oskar Kristeller, and John Herman Randall, Jr. (eds.), *The Renaissance Philosophy of Man* (University of Chicago Press, 1948), pp. 223–227.

likeness and resemblance to God is not a gift bestowed on man to begin with, but an achievement for him to work out: it is to be brought about by man himself."[22] Pico believed that freedom, the capacity for self-determination, exalts human beings above not only "beasts" but also above purely "spiritual beings," to whom perfection had been granted at the creation. Since human perfection must be freely achieved, Pico apparently thought it to be of a higher order than one that is bestowed.[23] For Pico, Cassirer suggests, our likeness to God consists in freedom and the perfectibility that it makes possible.[24] Through freedom, we are not only related to God, "but actually one with Him. For human *freedom* is of such a kind that any increase in its meaning or value is impossible . . . Thus when Pico ascribes to man an independent and innate creative power, he has in this one fundamental respect made man equal to Divinity."[25]

In short, for Pico, the source of human dignity is the capacity for self-determination and perfectibility. As he puts it, the human condition is that "we can become what we will." Cassirer notes the striking contrast between the medieval worldview, which valued what is immutable and eternal, and the new world of the Renaissance. "Here," in the world of human freedom, "there is an independent setting of a goal: man *chooses* the form he will bring forth . . . Thus man is not merely subject to a passive becoming; he rather determines his own goal and realizes it in free activity."[26] Almost exactly three centuries after Pico's oration, Immanuel Kant published his *Groundwork of the Metaphysics of Morals* (1785). In it he derives human dignity from autonomy or self-determination,[27] just as Pico had done – a fact that the neo-Kantian philosopher Cassirer could not have failed to appreciate.

Ficino, Pico, and other Renaissance humanists were convinced that faith and reason were compatible. At the beginning of *De hominis dignitate* Pico refers to man as "a great miracle." This was no mere rhetorical flourish. Human freedom and creativity, the ability to pose ideals and realize them, transforming ourselves and the world, were for Pico the grounds not only of human dignity but also

---

[22] Ernst Cassirer, "Giovanni Pico della Mirandola: A Study in the History of Renaissance Ideas," *Journal of the History of Ideas* 3, nos. 2–3 (1942), 123–144, 319–346 (here, 320–321).

[23] Cassirer "Giovanni Pico della Mirandola," 323.

[24] Thus it is not surprising that "Pico reaffirms the basic Pelagian thesis" against original sin and the dogma that salvation is possible only through God's grace (Cassirer, "Giovanni Pico della Mirandola," 329). Tzvetan Todorov, *Imperfect Garden: The Legacy of Humanism* (Princeton University Press, 2002), p. 43, writes that "humanism takes up the tradition attributed to the name Pelagius, for whom the salvation of men is in their own hands." Todorov considers Pico in his second chapter, "The Declaration of Autonomy."

[25] Cassirer, "Giovanni Pico della Mirandola," 336.   [26] *Ibid.* 332.

[27] Immanuel Kant, *Groundwork of the Metaphysic of Morals* (H.J. Paton (trans.), New York: Harper & Row, 1964). "*Autonomy*," Kant writes, "is . . . the ground of the dignity of human nature and of every rational nature" (p. 103).

of faith in divine reality. The direction of movement here was characteristic: the humanists tended to proceed from the human up to the divine (by reason), rather than from the divine down to the human (by revelation). For them, the very presence of the free, creative human spirit in the physical world implied God's existence. Their faith was justified by a natural theology of the "great miracle" of man. Since the humanist approach to faith was premised on and affirmed human autonomy and dignity, it logically excluded coercion. Pico's views are again characteristic. For him, Cassirer writes, "any compulsion in the things of faith is . . . not only to be rejected on moral and religious grounds: it is also ineffective and futile."[28]

These Renaissance themes – human dignity in self-determination and per-fectibility, ultimately culminating in deification, and the compatibility of faith and reason – were also central to Russian philosophical humanism, as our volume will show.

One of the sources of Renaissance humanism was Greek patristic theology. Werner Jaeger, at the end of his book *Early Christianity and Greek Paideia*, emphasizes the Greek influence: "From the Renaissance the line leads straight back to the Christian humanism of the [Greek] fathers of the fourth century A.D. and to their idea of man's dignity . . . With the Greeks who emigrated after the fall of Constantinople (1453) there came to Italy the whole literary tradition of the Byzantine East, and the works of the Greek fathers were its choicest part."[29] If Byzantine theology helped to shape the development of Italian humanism, then we might expect the Greek impact to have been even stronger on Russian humanism, given the cultural preeminence of Eastern Orthodoxy in Russia.

Patrick Lally Michelson makes this very argument in his 2007 essay, "In the Image and Likeness of God: The Patristic Tradition of Human Dignity and Freedom in Nineteenth-Century Russia."[30] He notes that the Greek monk Maximos (Michael) Trivolis (c. 1470–1556), known in Russia as Maksim the Greek and remembered for his Slavonic translations of *Psalms* and his liturgical reforms, studied with Pico in Ficino's Platonic Academy in Florence. Maksim was a learned exponent of the Greek patristic anthropology of "image and likeness" (in its hesychastic, ascetic interpretation).[31] He propagated these ideas in Muscovy until 1525, when he was accused of heresy by a Russian church

---

[28] Cassirer, "Giovanni Pico della Mirandola," 328.

[29] Werner Jaeger, *Early Christianity and Greek Paideia* (Cambridge, MA: Harvard University Press, 1961), pp. 100–101. Also see, more generally, Kristellar, "Renaissance Thought and Byzantine Learning," part 3 of his *Renaissance Thought and Its Sources*, pp. 135–163.

[30] The essay is the first chapter of his excellent doctoral dissertation, *"The First and Most Sacred Right": Religious Freedom and the Liberation of the Russian Nation, 1825–1905* (Madison: University of Wisconsin, 2007), pp. 29–92. His account is informed by the works of Trinkaus, Cassirer, and Jaeger, among many others.

[31] On hesychasm, see chapter 1.

council. After Maksim, patristic and other theological texts of the Eastern Orthodox tradition were known to other Russian churchmen and intellectual elites, but the texts did not enter the Russian public sphere until the nineteenth century, when they were finally translated into vernacular Russian.[32]

The translations were undertaken at the empire's four theological academies. (The theological academies laid the foundation for the growth of university philosophy in the nineteenth century, and also played an important role in the Russian reception of Kant.[33]) In 1821, the St. Petersburg Theological Academy began to translate various writings of the fourth-century Cappadocian Fathers Basil of Caesarea, Gregory of Nazianzus, and Gregory of Nyssa.[34] The youngest and most philosophical of the Cappadocians, and the one who probably exercised the most influence on Italian humanism,[35] was Gregory of Nyssa. In 1840, one of his essential exegeses of Genesis 1:26 was published in Russian translation. "For the first time in Russian history," Michelson avers, "members of educated society unfamiliar with ancient Greek, Latin, or Church Slavonic could read in contemporary vernacular that Orthodox believers were personally responsible for aspiring to the likeness of God, a concept that implied sanctity of the individual."[36]

Three years later the Moscow Theological Academy began to publish *Works of the Holy Fathers in Russian Translation*, a massive project that eventually comprised forty-eight volumes.[37] By the 1860s, Russian theological studies, including several on Gregory himself, were advancing a moral-philosophical (rather than strictly mystical) understanding of *theosis*: a "theological anthropology of moral perfectibility, human dignity, and theocentric freedom," in Michelson's formulation.[38] These studies were greatly facilitated by the translation projects, which over several decades had introduced educated Russians to patristic anthropology and had played an important role in the birth and development of Russian philosophical humanism.[39]

THE NINETEENTH CENTURY

Russian philosophy's long nineteenth century began with the patristic translation projects and the reception of German philosophical romanticism and idealism. The eminent Russian philosopher Sergey Horujy opens Part I of our

---

[32] Michelson, "*The First and Most Sacred Right*," pp. 48–52.
[33] A.I. Abramov, "Kant v russkoi dukhovno-akademicheskoi filosofii" in Z.A. Kamenskii and V.A. Zhuchkov (eds.), *Kant i filosofiia v Rossii* (Moscow: Nauka, 1994), pp. 81–113.
[34] Michelson, "*The First and Most Sacred Right*," p. 61.
[35] Trinkaus, "Renaissance Idea of the Dignity of Man," p. 137.
[36] Michelson, "*The First and Most Sacred Right*," p. 62.   [37] *Ibid.* pp. 62–63.
[38] *Ibid.* pp. 79, 84, 73–92 passim.   [39] *Ibid.* p. 63.

book with his chapter on the Slavophile–Westernizer controversy. This seminal debate formulated some of the basic positions in Russian philosophy of history, national identity, social and political thought, and religious philosophy. As Horujy shows, the problem of personhood (*lichnost'*) was central to the whole discussion. His overall framework of analysis is synergetic anthropology, which he has done much to revive in post-Soviet Russian philosophy.

The problem of "Russia and the West" was first given powerful philosophical formulation by Pëtr Chaadaev. His eight *Philosophical Letters*, written in French between 1828 and 1830, helped to set the terms of the debate between the future Slavophiles and Westernizers. In 1836, the first letter was published in the Russian journal *Teleskop*, the only letter published during Chaadaev's lifetime. *Les lettres philosophiques* outline a religious philosophy of history, according to which Christianity is the source of universal historical development and the western church is the embodiment of human unity. Chaadaev believed that divine reason acts through the church, that the church was guiding humanity to the Kingdom of God, and that the Kingdom of God had already been partly established in the West. Unfortunately, Russia had derived its Christianity from "miserable, despised Byzantium"; its "religious separatism" had thus closed the country off from universal historical development. "Isolated in the world," Chaadaev wrote in his first letter, "we [Russians] have given nothing to the world, we have taught nothing to the world; we have not added a single idea to the mass of human ideas; we have contributed nothing to the progress of the human spirit. And we have disfigured everything we have touched of that progress."[40] For these views the Russian government declared Chaadaev insane. His response was *Apology of a Madman* (1837), in which he claimed that Russia's lack of history could turn out to be an advantage. Russia was a type of *tabula rasa*; without the burdens of the past, nothing held the country back from rapid progress. Russians could learn from European history, avoid its mistakes, and rationally create a better future not only for themselves but for all of Europe.

Chaadaev's ideas spurred the formation of two groups of thinkers who would soon view themselves as Slavophiles and Westernizers. The excitement was captured by a contemporary (and Westernizer), Pavel Annenkov, who called the period between 1838 and 1848 a "marvelous decade" in Russian intellectual life.[41] The main Slavophile thinkers were Ivan Kireevskii, Aleksei Khomiakov, Konstantin Aksakov, and Iurii Samarin. As a group, they retained Chaadaev's

---

[40] Pëtr Chaadaev, "Philosophical Letters" in James M. Edie, James P. Scanlan, and Mary-Barbara Zeldin (eds.), with the collaboration of George L. Kline, *Russian Philosophy*, 3 vols. (Chicago: Quadrangle Books, 1965; Knoxville: University of Tennessee Press, 1976), vol. 1, pp. 117, 116.

[41] *The Extraordinary Decade: Literary Memoirs by P. V. Annenkov* (Irwin R. Titunik (trans.), Arthur P. Mendel (ed.), Ann Arbor, MI: University of Michigan Press, 1968).

religious conception of history, but inverted his categories: for them, Russia's Byzantine heritage was not a curse but a blessing, the source of true Russian spirituality. They celebrated Russia's distinct historical development, for it had spared the country the rationalistic, atomistic aspects of Roman law and civilization. Instead of the implicitly antagonistic principles of Western legalism, Russian social principles, according to the Slavophiles, were rooted in Christian love and harmony, embodied in the peasant commune and Orthodox church.[42]

The Slavophiles' social philosophy and philosophy of history rested on their concern for the integrity or inner wholeness of the human person. The Slavophiles developed their conception of "integral personhood" (*tsel'naia lichnost'*) within what Horujy calls the "theocentric personological paradigm" of Eastern Christianity, but they were far from completing their philosophical project. "That task was inherited from them," Horujy writes, "by Russian philosophy of the Silver Age." Nonetheless, Ivan Kireevskii, for Horujy the "most powerful philosophical mind of his generation," clearly pointed the way in his essay "On the Necessity and Possibility of New Principles in Philosophy" (1856).[43] Here the Slavophile philosopher laid out his concept of the "integral consciousness of believing reason," which reconciles faith and reason. Unlike European rationalism, Orthodox "believing reason," according to Kireevskii, is capable of bringing the subject and object of knowledge together in an immediate, concrete intuition. It is a kind of revelation or immediate apprehension that penetrates to the ontological essence of reality, ultimately to God, thus grounding the self in the divine source of all being.[44] The Slavophile theory of personhood was not new; Kireevskii proudly pointed to his continuity with the Greek church fathers, whose works he studied and translated at the Optina Monastery.[45]

The Westernizers (Mikhail Bakunin, Vissarion Belinskii, Timofei Granovskii, Alexander Herzen, and others) articulated their ideas within the philosophical framework of Hegelianism, in direct opposition to Slavophile romanticism.

---

[42] An excellent concise exposition of Slavophilism can be found in Andrzej Walicki, *A History of Russian Thought*, pp. 92–114.

[43] Ivan Kireevskii, "On the Necessity and Possibility of New Principles in Philosophy" in Robert Bird and Boris Jakim (eds. and trans.), *On Spiritual Unity: A Slavophile Reader* (Hudson, NY: Lindisfarne Books, 1998), pp. 233–273.

[44] *Ibid.* pp. 257–273; Walicki, *A History of Russian Thought*, pp. 99–103.

[45] See Abbott Gleason, *European and Muscovite: Ivan Kireevsky and the Origins of Slavophilism* (Cambridge, MA: Harvard University Press, 1972), pp. 236–257. Walicki has emphasized Kireevskii's debt to European romanticism, especially the later Schelling's philosophy of revelation (*Philosophie der Offenbarung*), in opposition to Hegel, in whom both Schelling and the Slavophiles saw the culmination of European rationalism. Walicki, *The Slavophile Controversy*, pp. 121–178.

They were united by a general belief that Russia should develop along west-ern, European lines; in this respect they shared the universalism of Chaadaev's philosophy of history, though not his religious formulation of it. The West-ernizers were also united in their defense of "autonomous personhood" – of the free, self-contained individual who realizes him or herself through con-scious action in history and work toward progress. Their conception, sharply different from the Slavophile philosophy of "integral personhood," belongs to what Horujy terms the "anthropocentric personological paradigm" of western philosophy. However, according to Horujy, Westernism never fully elaborated a concept of personhood; in his apt formulation, personhood was not studied as a philosophical problem, but was rather treated as a solution to other problems (typically social ones). He modifies this judgment in the case of Herzen, whose approach was more philosophical. Herzen thought that self-realization is the necessary task of personality, a task accomplished through action. In Herzen's words, only in "rational, morally free and passionately energetic action" do human beings attain "the reality of personhood." As Horujy observes, Herzen based his ethics on the principles of freedom and dignity. His credo, "action is personality itself," may echo Pico's and Kant's idea that human dignity consists in self-determination.

Alexander Herzen receives detailed consideration in chapter 2, by Derek Offord. Until the late 1840s, Herzen retained a generalized Hegelian belief in historical progress. This belief did not survive his emigration to the West, where he witnessed the defeat of western European socialists in the 1848 revolutions. Over the next several years he expounded his concept of "Russian socialism" as an alternative vision of Russia's future, based on values he imputed (follow-ing the Slavophiles) to the peasantry. He laid his hopes for Russian socialism on a voluntaristic philosophy of history directed against teleological systems of historical necessity. Herzen set out his new philosophy in *From the Other Shore* (1850), a work often seen, in Offord's words, as "the classic exposition of Herzen's philosophy of history and his thinking on liberty." Offord deals can-didly with what he calls the "limitations of Herzen's defense of personhood," especially the Russian thinker's disregard of legal, institutional, and political safeguards of individual liberty and rights.

The Slavophiles had manifested similar limitations, as Horujy indicates. True, Konstantin Aksakov's distinction between "Land" and "State" was based on the idea of "freedom from politics" and on the inviolability of the inner life of the spirit. Hence the Slavophiles' defense of freedom of conscience and expression. These and other liberal elements of Slavophile thought enable Horujy to remark that, "the pathos for freedom, dignity, and the rights of personhood was in no way a monopoly of the Westernizers." But, like Herzen, the Slavophiles did not recognize that these rights must be firmly guaranteed by law. Aksakov declared: "Guarantees are unnecessary. They are an evil!" With his approach, albeit an extreme one, "juridical standards are completely repudiated," Horujy writes. "The opposition between ethics and rights, between 'inner truth' and 'external truth,' is sharpened to the point of legal nihilism." The examples of the Slavophiles and Herzen (and they are far from the only ones) make clear that Russian humanism was not necessarily liberal in its applications. Liberalism requires not only a humanist focus on the person and human dignity, but also recognition of the value of law. By this measure and others, neither the Slavophiles nor Herzen were liberals.

Alexander II's succession to the throne in 1855 marked the beginning of a new period in Russian intellectual history. This period, usually called the "sixties," is sometimes named the second Russian "enlightenment" (*prosveshchenie*), a description that suggests a certain similarity between its ideas and eighteenth-century rationalist and naturalist notions of human perfectibility. New currents of Russian radicalism arose as the hopes of the Great Reforms turned to frustration and disappointment. Thinkers such as Nikolai Chernyshevskii, Nikolai Dobroliubov, and Dmitrii Pisarev adopted a perspective comprising various elements of materialism, utilitarianism, realism, and "rational egoism." Their outlook, frequently referred to as "nihilism," was notoriously embodied by Bazarov, the hero of Ivan Turgenev's novel *Fathers and Children*.

Whatever its philosophical flaws, the worldview of the radical intelligentsia, the subject of chapter 3, by Victoria Frede, was surely charged with humanist pathos. These philosophical flaws were significant, however. Frede shows that the materialists' denial of free will prevented them from dealing successfully with the problem of human dignity. Their most formidable critic was the philosopher Pamfil Iurkevich, a professor at the Kiev Theological Academy. Frede notes that his refutation of materialism combined philosophical idealism (Kantianism) with Orthodox Christian theology, a combination that was to be characteristic of Russian religious philosophy of the late nineteenth and early twentieth centuries.[46] (Vladimir Solov'ëv studied with Iurkevich, who moved to Moscow University in 1861.) Part of Iurkevich's critique focused specifically on human dignity. He believed, according to Frede, that human beings are created in the image of God and are born with innate ideas, "which are manifestations of their 'godlike' (*bogopodobnyi*) souls." Dignity is one of these ideas, and it can only be realized by willing the good: "a philosophical system that denies free will thus excludes dignity," in Frede's summation.

[46] Thomas Nemeth, "Karpov and Jurkevič on Kant: Philosophy in Service to Orthodoxy?," *Studies in East European Thought* 45, no. 3 (1993), 169–211.

Positivism formed the general climate of progressive opinion in Russia down to the twentieth century. In its most reductive forms, it took a naturalistic view of the world, asserting that the only reality, or at least the only one that we can know, is the empirical world of positively given sense data. Yet the dominance of positivism was never complete, as Thomas Nemeth shows in chapter 4. Already by the 1870s there was a reaction against "objectivist," deterministic theories of progress and a renewed "subjectivist" defense of the role of the individual in history. This shift took place with the elaboration of Russian populism (*narodnichestvo*). The populists' "subjective method" (or "subjective sociology") helped to rehabilitate human will, purposiveness, and moral values as real factors in the historical process. To some extent it thus anticipated the turn to ethical idealism and the "revolt against positivism" at the end of the century.[47]

By then, as Nemeth indicates, another current of Russian social thought had gone further in this direction: the revisionist movement within Russian Marxism. The Russian revisionists or "legal Marxists," led by Pëtr Struve, attempted to use neo-Kantianism to bolster the philosophical foundations of Marxism. In the process they partially recovered the Kantian distinction between "what is" (*das Sein*) and "what ought to be" (*das Sollen*) – a distinction that positivism by definition collapses – and so contributed to the critique of positivism even before their full conversion to idealism and liberalism. Their conversion was completed by 1902, when they contributed to the large volume *Problems of Idealism*, a milestone in the development of Russian philosophy of the Silver Age, as the early twentieth-century Russian cultural renaissance has come to be known.[48]

Russian literature also played an essential role in preserving and deepening the Russian humanist tradition in the second half of the nineteenth century. From the perspective of the future development of Russian philosophy, Dostoevskii was the most important figure. Already at the age of seventeen, he had committed himself to solving what he called "the mystery of man," and he devoted his life's work to the task.[49] For him the mystery was not only that human

---

[47] The classic account of the broader European revolt against positivism is H. Stuart Hughes, *Consciousness and Society: The Reorientation of European Social Thought*, revised edn. (New York: Vintage Books, 1977).

[48] Randall A. Poole (ed. and trans.), *Problems of Idealism: Essays in Russian Social Philosophy* (New Haven: Yale University Press, 2003).

[49] James P. Scanlan, *Dostoevsky the Thinker* (Ithaca, NY: Cornell University Press, 2002), p. 9. The focus of Scanlan's excellent study is Dostoevskii's conception of humanity or his philosophical anthropology. Gary Saul Morson has also emphasized Dostoevskii's philosophical significance. See his *Narrative and Freedom: The Shadows of Time* (New Haven, CT: Yale University Press, 1994) and, for a good overview, "Dostoevskii, Fëdor Mikhailovich (1821–81)" in Edward Craig (ed.), *Routledge Encyclopedia of Philosophy*, 10 vols. (London: Routledge, 1998), vol. 3, pp. 114–119.

beings combine in themselves both human and divine elements, but that the realization of the divine depends on human freedom. The human realization of the divine involves tortuous inner struggle, since the human element is inclined toward the physical world while called toward the spiritual. For Dostoevskii's Grand Inquisitor, the burden of this struggle is so great that to impose it on human beings is inhumane. For Dostoevskii, *not* to impose it is inhumane, since without freedom (especially freedom of conscience) humanity cannot realize its highest, divine potential.

Dostoevskii thought freedom the ground of genuine faith. He believed that faith must come from within each person, on "the evidence of things not seen" (Hebrews 11:1), not externally through the Grand Inquisitor's instruments of "miracle, mystery, and authority." But freedom entails the possibility (and abundant historical reality) of moral evil, the ultimate justification of which is beyond human understanding. Dostoevskii's anguish over the problem of evil led to his messianic vision of a universal Christian brotherhood united by Russia, the one "God-bearing" nation. Utopianism aside (and sometimes not), the genius with which Dostoevskii explored the inscrutable "mystery of man" had a deep impact on Russian philosophy of the Silver Age, especially through his close friend Vladimir Solov'ëv,[50] but also through (among the figures considered in this book) Sergei Bulgakov, Nikolai Berdiaev, and Dmitrii Merezhkovskii.

Lev Tolstoi also contributed powerfully to Russian anti-positivism. His major novels, *War and Peace, Anna Karenina,* and *Resurrection,* all valued the goal of individual inner self-perfection over the objective of political reform. In his philosophical tract, *On Life* (1888), Tolstoi made the case that every human being should cultivate "rational consciousness," a principle of personal economy ordering the passions or "appetites."[51] In the same tract, he attacked positivists under the label of modern-day "Scribes," for ruling out any questions about life beyond those pertaining to the "animal existence" of human beings.[52] In his defense of religious anarchism, *The Kingdom of God is Within You* (1893), Tolstoi elaborated a three-stage theory of history asserting that human beings have moved from an initial period of individualism, through an intermediate stage of social collectivism, to a final period of "divine consciousness" characterized by faith in "the source of eternal, undying life – God."[53] This theory of history was a deliberate repudiation of August Comte's positivist scheme, which imagined

[50] Marina Kostalevsky, *Dostoevsky and Soloviev: The Art of Integral Vision* (New Haven, CT: Yale University Press, 1997).

[51] L.N. Tolstoi, *O zhizni,* in *Polnoe sobranie sochinenii,* 90 vols. (Moscow: Gosudarstvennoe izdatel'stvo khudozhestvennoi literatury, 1928–1964), vol. 26, pp. 379–380.

[52] Tolstoi, *O zhizni,* pp. 326–338.

[53] Tolstoi, *Tsarstvo bozhie vnutri vas,* in *Polnoe sobranie sochinenii,* vol. 28, pp. 69–70.

historical progress as a move away from "primitive" religious and metaphysical consciousness. Tolstoi's anti-positivism made him, along with Dostoevskii, a hero to Berdiaev, Bulgakov, Frank, and Struve, who in the 1909 *Landmarks* (*Vekhi*) anthology celebrated his independence from the irreligious intelligentsia.

METAPHYSICAL IDEALISM: CHICHERIN, SOLOV'ËV, AND THE RUSSIAN PANPSYCHISTS

By the end of the nineteenth century, the revolt against positivism that could be detected in certain currents of Russian social thought and literature was well under way in Russian philosophy proper, as Part II of our book shows. The reaction began as early as the 1870s in the metaphysical idealism of Boris Chicherin and Vladimir Solov'ëv, the most prominent philosophers of nineteenth-century Russia. Both were vitally concerned to defend human dignity, and both did so on the Kantian foundations of moral autonomy and self-determination.

Chicherin, Russia's greatest Hegelian philosopher and liberal theorist, was the living link between the "philosophical epoch" of the 1840s and the neo-idealist revival of the Silver Age. Among his works, *Science and Religion* (1879) and *Philosophy of Law* (1900) were the most influential in this revival. Both volumes are wide-ranging and profound. In them Chicherin presents his mature philosophical conceptions of human nature, religion, society, politics, and history, exploring, along the way, the relationship between God and man, faith and reason, individual and society, and law and liberty. In chapter 5, Gary Hamburg reconstructs Chicherin's philosophy of history, showing how it achieved a powerful synthesis of Kant's conception of human dignity and Hegel's conception of history as the progressive realization of the Absolute. This synthesis largely reinterpreted Hegel in the spirit of classical liberalism, based on the inviolability of persons. Hamburg pays close attention to Chicherin's *Philosophy of Law*, the definitive statement of his liberal theory and, arguably, one of the great works of European social thought. It demonstrates that Chicherin, unlike many Russian humanists who also exalted the principle of personhood, had a deep appreciation of the need for its protection under the rule of law.

In 1874, Vladimir Solov'ëv defended his master's thesis, *The Crisis in Western Philosophy: Against the Positivists*. Within twenty-five years he would be Russia's greatest religious philosopher. Randall Poole, in chapter 6, focuses on the central concept of Solov'ëv's philosophy, Godmanhood (*bogochelovechestvo*), also translated as "divine humanity" or the "humanity of God." Godmanhood refers to humanity's divine potential and vocation, the ideal of our divine self-realization in and union with God. Human beings, created in the image of God, are called to realize the divine likeness through positively working for the Kingdom of

God, for universal transformation in the "unity of all" (*vsëedinstvo*), in which all will be one in God. Since Godmanhood depends on autonomous human activity and self-development, it is, as Nikolai Berdiaev remarked, humanistic in its very conception.[54] At many points Solov'ëv's thought recalls the religious humanism of the Renaissance. In 1891, Solov'ëv delivered a lecture, "On the Reasons for the Collapse of the Medieval Worldview," before the Moscow Psychological Society.[55] On this occasion he condemned as "monstrous" the medieval doctrine that the only path to salvation is faith in church dogma, and as "cheap" the idea of "salvation through dead faith and works of piety – *works* and not *work*."[56] True salvation requires, rather, the hard work of self- and social transformation, of assimilating to God's likeness and achieving deification.

During this period other Russian metaphysical idealists also advanced challenging theories of personhood, but on somewhat different foundations than Chicherin and Solov'ëv. The neo-Leibnizian tradition of Russian panpsychism, examined masterfully in chapter 7 by James Scanlan, was founded by Aleksei Kozlov (himself not a personalist) and developed by Lev Lopatin and Nikolai Losskii. All three philosophers advanced a spiritualistic metaphysics that conceived reality as a multiplicity of individual spiritual (or psychic) substances at different stages of development, all grounded in and striving toward the supreme substance, God.

Lopatin designated his system "concrete spiritualism" to emphasize its personalism. Like Kozlov, he criticized Solov'ëv for conflating philosophy and religion; he thought faith has no role in philosophy and that reason alone discloses the truth about ultimate reality. In his metaphysics, Lopatin returned to the rationalism of Descartes and Leibniz. Kant had feared that this type of rationalist metaphysics (like Newtonian science) risks infringing upon free will. His system of transcendental idealism reconceptualized nature as empirical experience (transcendentally conditioned by the *a priori* forms of space

---

[54] Berdyaev, *The Russian Idea*, p. 91.

[55] Despite its name, the Psychological Society was the first and most important center of the growth of Russian philosophy over the some thirty-seven years of its existence (1885–1922), which roughly coincided with the broader Silver Age. A key factor in its success was its journal, *Questions of Philosophy and Psychology* (1889–1918), Russia's first regular, specialized journal in philosophy. The society was led (and its journal was edited) by the idealist philosophers Nikolai Grot, Lev Lopatin, Sergei Trubetskoi, and Solov'ëv. Grot was chair from 1888 until his death in 1899; then Lopatin took over until 1919, a year before his own death. Ivan Il'in chaired the society in its remaining few years. On it, see the editor's introduction to Poole, *Problems of Idealism*, pp. 1–78, and Randall A. Poole, "Moscow Psychological Society" in Edward Craig (ed.), *Routledge Encyclopedia of Philosophy* (London: Routledge, 1998–), online version (2002).

[56] V.S. Solov'ëv, "O prichinakh upadka srednevekovogo mirosozertsaniia" in *Sochineniia v dvukh tomakh* (Moscow, 1989), vol. 2, pp. 344–355. There is an English translation in *A Solovyov Anthology* (S.L. Frank (ed.), Natalie Duddington (trans.), London: SCM Press, 1950; reissued, London: Saint Austin Press, 2001), pp. 60–71, here pp. 67, 65.

and time) in order to permit a transcendent or noumenal sphere beyond those limits, although it also thereby ruled out theoretical knowledge of that sphere. "I . . . found it necessary to deny *knowledge*," Kant wrote, "in order to make room for *faith*" – in freedom, immortality, and God.[57] Lopatin's solution to the problem of free will and determinism was his doctrine of "creative causality," which imputed, on the basis of human psychic experience, freedom and creativity to all reality. In other words, he rejected mechanistic determinism in order to save both human free will and his own pre-Kantian metaphysics. It is striking, however, that his system seems to have been built on the premise of Kantian ethics – that dignity consists in self-determination. Thus Lopatin could write of the "infinite dignity of everything spiritual" because he stipulated the "free creativity" of spirit.[58]

RUSSIAN RELIGIOUS PHILOSOPHY AFTER SOLOV'ËV: BULGAKOV, FLORENSKII, AND FRANK

Part III of our book turns to three major religious philosophers of twentieth-century Russia. In recent years Paul Valliere has done a great deal to advance our understanding of Russian religious philosophy. His subject here, in chapter 8, is Sergei Bulgakov. Bulgakov's conversion from Marxism to idealism was brought about by his recognition that faith is a basic human need, and that it cannot be satisfied by positivist ideologies. (In chapter 11, Bernice Glatzer Rosenthal shows that Dmitrii Merezhkovskii's Christian humanism was based on a similar recognition.) Bulgakov found that Solov'ëv's metaphysics of the "unity of all," inspired by Schelling, could do justice to the human need for faith by vindicating its object as transcendent and yet as related to the world. This doctrine was not a form of pantheism, but of panentheism. Bulgakov was most attracted to Solov'ëv's idea of Sophia: the Divine Wisdom by which God created the world, the creative principle in God, the unity and divinity of creation. Bulgakov's sophiology took the form of a "cosmodicy," or a demonstration of "the pervasiveness of testimony to God in the world," as Valliere expresses it. "Cosmodicy," he writes, "is a distinctively modern project in its affirmation of the freedom and dignity of the world."

The idea of Sophia is also essential to Pavel Florenskii's thought, as Steven Cassedy shows in his fascinating and wide-ranging discussion in chapter 9. "So powerfully did Florenskii believe in the venerability of God's creation and

---

[57] Immanuel Kant, *Critique of Pure Reason* (Norman Kemp Smith (trans.), New York: St. Martin's, 1965), p. 29.
[58] L.M. Lopatin, "Teoreticheskie osnovy soznatel'noi nravstvennoi zhizni," *Voprosy filosofii i psikhologii* 2:1, book 5 (1890), 34–83, here 66–67, emphasis omitted.

specifically of humanity that," Cassedy writes, "he gave us a fourth Person of the Trinity to represent them" – Sophia. Very much like Solov'ëv and Bulgakov, Florenskii thought that "God reveals his divinity through his very creation." Thus, for Florenskii, "to be a humanist is not to abandon faith but to embrace it." He shared with Pico the conviction that God's creatures constitute "an eternal divine miracle."

In chapter 10, Philip J. Swoboda presents a compelling interpretation of Semën Frank's philosophy as "expressivist humanism." The expressivist vision of man, according to Swoboda, "affirms the infinite value of each human person as a potential vehicle for the manifestation of unique spiritual content." In certain respects, however, Frank's expressivism was, especially in his émigré period, "incompatible with the assumptions of liberal humanism," most obviously in his ambivalence toward the idea of law. Frank, Bulgakov, and Florenskii all championed the idea of human dignity, but they arrived at no consensus about what type of social philosophy might best promote human freedom, dignity, and the realization of human potential.

RELIGIOUS HUMANISM IN THE RUSSIAN SILVER AGE

In general, as Part IV of our book suggests, the Silver Age was divided between defenders of individual freedom under the rule of law and proponents of one or another vision of human transformation through "positive freedom," that is, between liberal and radical religious humanists, as Bernice Glatzer Rosenthal calls them in her rich survey of the period (chapter 11). Most of the Silver Age humanists dealt with in this book were indeed "religious" in one sense or another, even Marxist "God-builders" such as Maksim Gor'kii and Anatolii Lunacharskii (see chapters 13 and 15).[59]

The liberal religious humanists are the subject of chapter 12, by Frances Nethercott. They believed that the ideal of human perfectibility rests on *self-realization*, which requires a sphere of personal autonomy (freedom from external interference) guaranteed by legally enforced human rights. Three outstanding liberal theorists of the period, Pavel Novgorodtsev, Evgenii Trubetskoi, and Sergei Kotliarevskii, were neo-idealist philosophers whose recognition of the value of law stemmed from a theistic conception of human dignity and destiny. Their work, as Nethercott demonstrates, was shaped by the powerful double legacy of Chicherin and Solov'ëv. For the liberal humanists, law was an essential *spiritualizing force*: by removing people from the state of nature and limiting the

[59] For a pioneering and highly influential account of Gor'kii and Lunacharskii as "God-builders," see Kline, *Religious and Anti-Religious Thought in Russia*, ch. 4.

power of one person over another, it normalized human relations and placed them on the basis of equality. It enabled people to develop as persons and ultimately to realize their divine potential. At the same time (and this is one of Nethercott's main themes) the liberal philosophers maintained that the rule of law itself rests on the *spiritual force* of a highly developed civic consciousness built through "cultural endeavor."

The "radical" religious humanists formed a larger group, more representative of the Silver Age as a whole. Here were the poets, artists, philosophers, and visionaries whose insight into human creative powers often led to a certain Prometheanism that neglected or denigrated the value of law and incremental progress. These cultural figures, many iconic, are emphasized in Rosenthal's account, and are the subject of chapter 13 by Robert Bird. Bird takes us on an exciting tour of the main venues and attractions of the period's "new religious consciousness." Along the way we encounter, for example, the Marxist Aleksandr Bogdanov's powerful images of a future society as a single super-human being, and we hear him proclaiming, "Man has not yet arrived, but he is . . . on the horizon." Bird remarks that this faith in the "untapped potential of human imagination" traversed the ideological spectrum; it was a faith in the power of image alone to transform reality. Marxists and modernists alike longed for the total realization of collective human potential, typically through some external agent or event (an *eschaton*). Perfectibility was not so much an individual autonomous process, as a collective totalizing eschatology. Art, the proletariat, the Russian nation, technology, even sex were all given salvific roles.

The confrontation between these two competing notions of freedom and of human perfectibility, between what might be called liberal and illiberal humanism, was a critical part of Silver Age philosophical and cultural history. It reflected the complex legacy of Vladimir Solov'ëv, whose influence on the Silver Age was vast and multifaceted, largely because his syncretic thought could appeal to very different types of thinkers. As Judith Deutsch Kornblatt shows in chapter 14, in a carefully constructed and considered argument, Solov'ëv's legacy involves two opposing conceptions of faith and salvation. One, which Kornblatt argues was Solov'ëv's own through the end of his life, is faith in humanity and its own salvific power; salvation is our individual responsibility and cannot be achieved without active human participation. The other conception is faith in salvation through external intervention, faith in apocalypse and eschatology, which displaces human agency and responsibility to an external salvific force and awaits redemption. Solov'ëv's Silver Age heirs (Kornblatt focuses on the Symbolist poets Valerii Briusov and Aleksandr Blok) imputed the second conception to him on the basis of their pessimistic and apocalyptic readings of the philosopher's "Short Tale of the Antichrist," written in the last year of his life.

It is easy to see how the tale could be read as Solov'ëv's repudiation of his earlier faith in humanity, but Kornblatt herself, in a revisionist interpretation, argues that it does not represent a dramatic departure from his lifelong commitment to optimistic humanism. Its overriding message is hope in the "truth and goodness of human interaction."

CODA

Not the least fateful development of the "positive," collectivist direction of freedom and perfectibility in Russian humanism was Russian Marxism, the subject of chapter 15 by the eminent Polish historian of ideas Andrzej Walicki. His chapter opens Part V of our book, "Russian Philosophy in Revolution and Exile." In an incisive analysis that covers complex developments over a sixty-year period, Walicki explains how the "Marxian dream of the total realization of collective human potential, envisioning a totally regenerated human species," was transformed into the reality of an ideology that "proved deeply inimical to its own humanist ideals."

Philip T. Grier, in chapter 16, deals with the efforts of three Russian philosophers to combine Hegelian dialectic and Husserlian phenomenology – purely philosophical pursuits in an environment that was rapidly turning deadly for philosophical inquiry. These three philosophical projects succeeded, but at great personal cost to their creators: Ivan Il'in was exiled in 1922, Aleksei Losev was imprisoned and sent to the camps (1930–1933), Gustav Shpet was executed in 1937. Losev had been secretly tonsured as a monk in 1929. In his fealty to the Orthodox mystical tradition of hesychasm, he was a modern Slavophile. Shpet, by contrast, was a modern Westernizer. In Grier's telling, Shpet swam against the ideological current of his day by advocating the pursuit of philosophy as objective knowledge, "not as morality, not as preaching, not as 'worldviews.'" He hoped this disinterested philosophical enterprise would help bring about a Russian Renaissance. Yet there was something similar to the Promethean outlook of Bolshevism in Shpet's attributing to philosophers and artists the historical power to reconstitute or revivify actuality (in the form of social being). In his hermeneutics of discourse, he upheld the dignity of the intellectual as seer, a notion fully compatible with that of the Italian humanists.

Il'in was among the nearly one hundred prominent intellectuals, including most of Russia's major philosophers, who were forcibly deported from the country in 1922. In chapter 17, Stuart Finkel follows the trajectory of exiled philosophers from Soviet Russia to émigré life in Europe. As Finkel observes, the philosophers tended to view the 1917 Revolution as a spiritual catastrophe, an apocalyptic moment of destruction foretold by Dostoevskii and limned by

Oswald Spengler's *Decline of the West*. They disagreed bitterly over whether to persist in political opposition to the Soviet regime (Struve and Il'in) or to concentrate on the "spiritual tasks" of self-perfection (Berdiaev and Frank). This debate, Finkel argues, continued the one begun by the *Vekhi* collection in 1909.

Some of the Russian émigrés formed Eurasianism, an intellectual movement usually associated with the assertion of Russian cultural uniqueness and geopolitical might. Martin Beisswenger, in chapter 18, reconceptualizes Eurasianism by demonstrating that religious–philosophical ideas of personhood were central to it. By the mid-1920s, leading Eurasianists actively speculated on the humanist task of affirming the image and likeness of God in both individuals and collective "persons" (e.g., nation, state, church). Lev Karsavin's concept of Eurasia held out hope for the "ecclesiastization" of the state and the world in general. This hope had Byzantine and Muscovite roots, in the concept of the "symphonic relationship" of church and state. It also resembled the idealized view of society articulated by the Elder Zosima in *The Brothers Karamazov*. But it raised serious issues about the protection of individual rights against collective or symphonic "persons," issues that were at the forefront of Eurasianism's further development. The tensions within Eurasianism, so ably identified by Beisswenger, testify both to the tensions inherent in Russian philosophical humanism and to the protean vitality of that tradition.

In his landmark 1994 book *Posle pereryva* (*After the Break*), Sergei Horujy put on the post-Soviet philosophical agenda the task of recovering from the Russian emigration the philosophical legacy suppressed by the Bolshevik Revolution, and of reintroducing into the secularized philosophical discourse of the 1990s the rich resources of Orthodox theology. To a remarkable degree and in a relatively short time, Horujy and other Russian philosophers have succeeded in rekindling within Russia academic interest in Russian idealism and religious philosophy. We hope the present volume will augment that interest and spread it in the West, where the history of Russian philosophy has been studied and fully appreciated mainly by specialists. In addition, we hope our book makes clear the degree of fruitful interaction between reason and faith, western-rooted and eastern-oriented humanism, characteristic of Russian philosophy during its "long nineteenth century." Finally, we hope our book conveys the excellence of the philosophical questions asked by Russian thinkers about the nature of human beings, our intrinsic value, our rights before one another and the state, and our historical lot. No one should expect from Russian philosophy final answers to such questions, even though the answers provided by Russian philosophers are as intelligent as any in identifying the dangers consequent on ignoring or diminishing human dignity. If nothing else, Russian philosophy teaches us, in Horujy's words, that "history and the cosmos are open," and "this radical openness is truth itself."[60]

---

[60] Khoruzhii [Horujy], *Posle pereryva. Puti russkoi filosofii* (St. Petersburg: Izdatel'stvo "Aleteiia," 1994), p. 12. Horujy adds that "the ultimate meaning of history is being decided at every instant between God and us."

PART I

THE NINETEENTH CENTURY

I

SLAVOPHILES, WESTERNIZERS, AND THE BIRTH OF RUSSIAN PHILOSOPHICAL HUMANISM

SERGEY HORUJY

TRANSLATED BY PATRICK LALLY MICHELSON

INTRODUCTION

The purpose of this chapter is to analyze the philosophical significance of the famous dispute between the Westernizers and Slavophiles that occurred in the decade from the late 1830s to the late 1840s. The immediate pretext for this dispute was the 1836 publication of a "philosophical letter" by Pëtr Chaadaev (1794–1856), a thinker who argued that Russia had never belonged either to the West or to the East, that it lacked the traditions of these other civilizations, and that therefore "we [Russians] have not been touched by the universal education of the human race."[1] The young Aleksandr Herzen described Chaadaev's letter as a "pistol shot resounding in the dead of night," a "pitiless cry of pain and reproach to Petrine Russia."[2] By the late 1830s, largely in response to Chaadaev's provocative letter, two intellectual parties took shape, each holding a different view of the historical-cultural differences between Russia and the West. After a time, these parties came to be known as the "Westerners" or "Westernizers" (zapadniki) and the "Slavophiles" (slavianofily). The Westernizers considered the differences between Russia and the West to be manifestations of Russia's cultural backwardness; they thought the paradigm of western civilization universal, and believed Russia's task was to adopt completely the western paradigm and to assimilate European culture along with it. By contrast, the Slavophiles held that the historical-cultural differences between Russia and the West indicated Russia's superiority and the radically different nature of Russian society and history. Leading figures in the Westernizer camp were Vissarion Belinskii (1811–1848), Aleksandr Herzen (1812–1870), and Timofei Granovskii (1813–1855).

---

[1] P.Ia. Chaadaev, "Lettres philosophiques adressées à une dame [1829–1830]. Lettre première" in Z.A. Kamenskii (ed.), *Polnoe sobranie sochinenii i izbrannye pis'ma*, 2 vols. (Moscow: Nauka, 1991), vol. 1, p. 89.
[2] A.I. Gertsen [Herzen], "Byloe i dumy" in *Sobranie sochinenii*, 30 vols. (Moscow: Izdatel'stvo Akademii nauk SSSR, 1954–1965), vol. 9, pp. 139–140.

The leading Slavophiles were Aleksei Khomiakov (1804–1860), Ivan Kireevskii (1806–1856), and Konstantin Aksakov (1817–1860).

The essay will also comment on the complex historical relationship between the Westernizer–Slavophile dispute and the genesis of Russian philosophy. Very often, the Westernizer–Slavophile debate is analyzed against the background of the importation of German philosophical romanticism and idealism into Russia, with the intellectual indebtedness of the various participants in the debate being traced to specific thinkers, such as Hegel and Schelling. The approach taken here is to treat Slavophilism less in relation to modern western philosophy and more in relation to Eastern Orthodox religious thinking about the nature of human community and about the relationship between God and human nature. In order to set the stage for this discussion, let us begin with a structural analysis of Russian self-consciousness and of Russia's spiritual and cultural tradition.[3]

THE GENESIS OF PHILOSOPHY IN RUSSIA

Starting in the fourth century, eastern Christianity (Orthodoxy) began to develop a distinctive system of discourse – a semiotic process with its own methods of signifying meaning and its own language for assimilating reality. This discourse system provided the spiritual, conceptual, and epistemological foundation for Byzantine culture, and subsequently for Russian *mentalité* and culture. The discourse of Eastern Christianity took shape in response to the Orthodox experience of aspiring to and uniting with Christ, the experience of Christocentric communion with God. The attainment, preservation, and dissemination of this experience were considered to be Orthodoxy's principal tasks, whereas in the Latin West the primary tasks were understood to be the definitive statement of church doctrine and the construction of a viable ecclesiastical organization.

The primacy of experiencing communion with God led the Orthodox to develop a special practice dedicated to the cultivation of such an experience. The mystical-ascetic pursuit of hesychasm (from the Greek *hesychia*, meaning solitary and silent peace) originated as early as the fourth century, and, over the course of many centuries, it developed into a classical system of *spiritual practice*: a step–by–step process of ascending toward holistic self-transformation and actual ontological self-transcending. The goal (*telos*) of this spiritual process, understood in Orthodoxy as the complete unity of the practitioner's energies with the Divine energies, is called deification, or *theosis*. Deification is the

---

[3] Our framework of analysis will be synergetic anthropology. See S.S. Khoruzhii [Horujy], *Opyty iz russkoi dukhovnoi traditsii* (Moscow: Parad, 2005).

generative and constitutive element of hesychast prayer, which usually occurs in small, dedicated ascetic communities separated from society as a whole. But because the Orthodox see deification as the highest goal of human existence, hesychasm may exert a deep, persistent, and sometimes decisive influence on the particular society or *Sozium* in which it is practiced.[4]

The spiritual practice of hesychasm and its paradigm of deification constitute the core components of Eastern Christian spiritual discourse. From these core components came a certain way of thinking about personality (or personhood) and human identity. The Greek fathers of the fourth century and the first ecumenical church councils conceived personality first and foremost in theological terms: for them, the model personality is to be found in the Divine *Hypostasis* ("person"): in the perfect combination of human and divine natures in Christ and in the "communion" among the three *Hypostases* or persons of the Trinity. According to this conception, the Divine Hypostasis is the ontological modus of perfect Divine being, constituted through love and communion. As a logical extension of this paradigm, the Eastern Christian church fathers held that empirical man, by his nature created and fallen, possesses neither personality nor self-identity, but that he can (and must) acquire them through communion with God, that is, through sharing or participating in Divine being. Such participation is only attainable in our ascent toward deification. In this view, hesychast practice constitutes the path by which we attain personhood and form our true self. This Orthodox way of thinking about the human personality can be described as a *theocentric* personological paradigm. Obviously, it differs sharply from the *anthropocentric* personological paradigm developed in classical European metaphysics, which holds that individual men and women are persons by virtue of their status as empirical human beings.

Emphasis on the primacy of spiritual experience had profound implications for the destiny of philosophy in Eastern Christianity. During the initial period of church history from the first through the third centuries, stoic and platonic philosophy provided Christians with a framework for understanding Christian truth. But, as we have seen, a new discourse arose beginning in the fourth century, under the influence of the Greek church fathers. This new discourse – "dogmatic theology" – differs sharply from philosophy, since it is based on two specific kinds of experience, both cultivated by Christianity and both non-philosophical: the collective "conciliary" experience, which is the source of

---

[4] Translator's note: Throughout this chapter, the author employs the word *sotsium* to designate a socially connected system of interacting subgroups that reside in a broader social milieu. *Sotsium* is derived from the German *Sozium*, which is how I translate the Russian. In the current Russian usage, *sotsium* is practically synonymous to *obshchestvo*, or society.

the dogmatic formulas arrived at by the church councils; and the individual experience of communion with God, rooted in ascetic (hesychast) practice.

In Eastern Christianity the term "theology" means not "theoretical discourse about God," but rather a direct rendering or expression of the experience of human ascent to God. The Orthodox theology of spiritual experience (both conciliary and personal) had always been the dominant discourse of Byzantine thought. It raised much stronger obstacles to the development of philosophy than did the kind of theology cultivated in the West. Thus, Byzantium had nothing like Scholasticism; indeed, it was not until the fourteenth century, just a century before Byzantium's collapse, that vigorous intellectual controversy over the nature of hesychast experience created an opening for the development of Eastern Christianity's own original philosophy. This opening was exploited by certain Eastern Christian thinkers, but only to a minimal extent.

Russian culture, which took its initial shape in the transference of Eastern Christian discourse from Byzantium to Rus', inherited these special features of the situation of philosophy in the East. In fact, in Russia, there were additional barriers to the development of philosophy that did not exist in Byzantium. For example, in early Russia, since Greek was almost an unknown language, classical Greek philosophy was rarely studied. Moreover, Russian religious consciousness, which was mostly dominated by ethical and ascetic motifs, paid little attention to the theological and even less to the philosophical content of the Eastern Christian discourse. Thus, the systematic formation of philosophical thought in Russia began only in the context of the westernized culture that gradually emerged in the country during the seventeenth and especially the eighteenth centuries. Even then, however, Russian thought never became wholly westernized: from the time of its birth during the dispute between the Slavophiles and Westernizers, modern Russian philosophy always saw itself as confronting a dilemma – whether to adopt the western philosophical or the Eastern Christian discourse – and its content has always reflected this conflict.

Russian philosophy gradually developed in the first decades of the nineteenth century, and in the 1830s it entered a period of remarkable development. Perhaps the chief force behind this development was the appearance of so-called "circles" (*kruzhki*): small groups of intellectuals connected by friendly relations and meeting regularly to discuss matters of culture. Most circles focused on literature and politics, but at least two circles in Moscow contributed to the genesis of Russian philosophy: the Lovers of Wisdom in the 1820s, and the circle that formed around Nikolai Stankevich in the 1830s. The Stankevich circle is especially important because it included many future leaders of Russian thought; figures such as the anarchist Mikhail Bakunin, the literary critic Vissarion Belinskii, the historian Timofei Granovskii, the Slavophile publicist

Konstantin Aksakov, and the journalist Mikhail Katkov. The Stankevich circle was the first venue in Russia where Hegel's philosophy was studied and hotly debated.

The awakening of philosophical reflection was further stimulated by the writing of Pëtr Chaadaev, a solitary yet influential "private thinker" rather than a public intellectual. He produced an outline of a Christian philosophy of history and culture, in the form of a cycle of eight "Philosophical Letters." The publication of Chaadaev's first letter in 1836, as noted at the beginning of this chapter, was one of the most significant episodes in the intellectual life of Nicholas I's reign. The letter struck its readers by its harsh, nihilistic repudiation of the value and meaning of Russian history, and by its assertions that everything in the West was created by Christianity and that "in a certain sense the Kingdom of God has actually been realized" there.[5] It is difficult to imagine a more powerful stimulus to historical reflection! The letter galvanized the formation of both Westernism and Slavophilism.

Yet another stimulating factor was the influence of official government ideology, based on Count Sergei Uvarov's principles of "Orthodoxy, Autocracy, Nationality." Most of educated society treated Uvarov's formulation of official ideology coldly or negatively, but nevertheless it represented a well-defined conceptual model that sometimes affected people's outlooks even against their will. Thus, Uvarov's triad and especially the idea of "nationality" also contributed to the genesis of Russian philosophy; indeed, the first philosophical doctrines in Russia crystallized around the discussion of subjects very close to the theme of "nationality."

By the late 1830s, two parties had already formed, with opposing views of the historical-cultural differences between Russia and the West. In the winter of 1838–1839 the Slavophiles produced their first programmatic texts, "On the Old and the New" by Khomiakov, and "In Response to A.S. Khomiakov" by Kireevskii. Between 1839 and 1842, the Slavophile and Westernizer camps elaborated their doctrines and then, finally, the decisive battles began. They took place from 1842 to 1844 in the form of regular, highly emotional disputes in the salons of the Moscow nobility. Gradually the divergences between the two sides became completely irreconcilable. By early 1845 all discussion between them ceased, and a complete rupture in personal relations ensued. From that time forward, as Aleksandr Herzen recalled, both groups "mercilessly tormented each other in print."[6] Yet for the history of Russian consciousness, this negative outcome bore positive fruit. The rise of these two intellectual camps, fully

---

[5] Chaadaev, "Lettres philosophiques," vol. 1, pp. 103, 336.   [6] Gertsen, "*Byloe i dumy*," p. 171.

constituted and mutually demarcated in the realm of ideas, undoubtedly marked the "birth of a new intelligentsia that was unofficial and free."[7]

REFLECTIONS OF THE RUSSIAN JANUS

Herzen depicted the two camps of Westernizers and Slavophiles as grown inseparably together, but two-headed like the Roman God Janus. Now we must relate what the two heads of this Russian Janus were thinking. Although their debates eventually touched all the principal domains of their respective worldviews, a few key subjects were always at the center of their polemics: the theme of Russia, of its history and nationality (*narodnost'*); and the theme of personhood, especially personhood in relation to society.

THE SLAVOPHILES AND THE THEME OF RUSSIA

Regarding the problem of Russia, the positions of both Slavophiles and Westernizers were based on the common assumption that Russia and Europe were antithetical to one another. Essentially, this assumption constituted an ideological postulate that could not be proven but nevertheless became embedded in public consciousness in the 1840s, thanks chiefly to the influence of Chaadaev and Uvarov. Having accepted this postulate, the two camps jointly created two ideological constructs, an "image of Russia" and an "image of Europe." Russia was understood to be a patriarchal, conventional culture, alive but ahistorical, static, and oriented toward traditional values and collective consciousness. The West was thought to be a world of dynamism, development, perfectibility, which aspired toward the future and preached individualism. Moreover, the two groups developed a theory that Russian history and European history had originated from antithetical sources. This theory powerfully influenced how the Slavophiles imagined the entire process of historical development in Russia and the West.

The "Slavic" or "Slavophile" conception was the first to be formulated. Unlike the one developed later by the Westernizers, it was philosophically grounded, in principles articulated by Aleksei Khomiakov. In this conception, we find a general thesis that assigns a particular, constitutive role to the origin of the historical process. "The law of social development," Khomiakov declared, "resides in its embryo."[8] It is clear that Khomiakov's thesis is the direct

---

[7] G.G. Shpet, *Ocherk razvitiia russkoi filosofii*, part 1 (Petrograd: Kolos, 1922), p. 281.

[8] A.S. Khomiakov, "Mnenie russkikh ob inostrantsakh" in *Polnoe sobranie sochinenii*, 3rd edn. (Moscow: Univ. tip., 1900), vol. 1, p. 68.

expression of a definite type of philosophical thinking – *archaeological* thinking – that is richly represented in European thought, from the Greeks to Heidegger. In particular, "organic philosophy," which presents being (*bytie*) in an organic paradigm, belongs to this type of thinking. And it is to organic philosophy that Slavophile philosophy belongs. Thus, for the Slavophiles, the original source of society is primary and constitutive. If, at its very source, Khomiakov tells us, a particular *Sozium* is peaceful and harmonious, then it generates an organic unity, "a living and organic community [*obshchina*]," that advances in the course of its entire historical existence via the path of consensus and agreement. If, however, the *Sozium* is initially organized by force and conquest, it generates a society composed of an "arbitrary aggregate of individual people," which can only be ruled through coercion. According to Khomiakov, the two different social models, one a peaceful association of tribes and the other a conflict-ridden aggregation of individuals, are represented in world history by Russia and Western Europe. Thus, two starkly different historical sources gave rise to two diametrically opposed types of *Sozium* and of historical development.

According to the Slavophiles, Russia's *Sozium* embodies the principles of harmony and concord, an embodiment facilitated by the existence within it of a peculiar social formation: the commune (*obshchina*) or peasant community (*mir*). The Slavophiles commonly asserted that this type of peasant community constituted a unique feature of Rus', a feature that was absent in the West and even unknown to western scholarship. The commune was based upon "a natural and moral fraternity [among Russians] and on an inner truth." Thus, it possessed certain "communal virtues . . . that were unlikely to find their equivalents elsewhere in the history of the world: genuine humility, meekness combined with spiritual strength, inexhaustible tolerance, a disposition toward self-sacrifice, honesty before courts of law and deep respect for justice, [and] strong family ties."[9]

The cult of the commune was a cornerstone of Slavophile ideology, revealing many of its most important aspects. First, Slavophilism was a typical example of conservative, traditionalist thought, which always tended to idealize peasant society and peasant life "unspoiled by the city." Furthermore, Slavophile writings about the commune brought to the surface exaggerated elements in their ethical thinking. For example, their view of the morally ideal nature of the communal order made it superfluous for them to advocate the legal rights of individuals. Because members of the commune were allegedly *moral*, both the decisions made by the peasant assembly and the personal agreements made

---

[9] A.S. Khomiakov, "Po povodu stat'i I.V. Kireevskogo 'O kharaktere prosveshcheniia Evropy i o ego otnoshenii k prosveshcheniiu Rossii'" in *Polnoe sobranie sochinenii*, vol. 1, p. 242.

among its members were regarded by the Slavophiles as sufficient to regulate legal and economic life. Like many other Slavophile ideas, this *opposition between ethics and rights* (an opposition that is undoubtedly attractive to Russian consciousness), was taken by Konstantin Aksakov to an extreme that bordered on the absurd. "[Legal] guarantees [of individual rights] are unnecessary," Aksakov declared. "They are an evil! Wherever a guarantee is required, nothing good exists . . . All strength resides in moral convictions . . . [Russia] has always believed in them and never relied on contracts."[10] Finally, Slavophile writings about the commune asserted the primacy of society over the individual, an issue that we shall examine more fully below.

In Slavophile teaching, the West developed from a morally corrupt source, in which there was division instead of unity, that is, from a conflict between the victors and the vanquished. According to Khomiakov, this corrupt source could not generate a living organism. Instead, it produced an alternative type of society, whose principle of existence was not life, but mechanistic "stagnation." With dogmatic determination, Khomiakov introduced this opposition into every aspect of his analysis of Russia and the West, so that the image of Europe ("the West") that he portrayed was decisively negative. All European norms, principles, and relationships were characterized by Khomiakov as artificial and formal. Each relationship was supposedly based on a "conditional contract," as opposed to a "true brotherhood." Rights in Europe were allegedly nothing more than "dead justice," "external, formal legality," as opposed to the inner recognition of the moral law that obtained in Russia; or western rights were based on "negative liberty," which manifested itself in dissension, as opposed to "positive liberty," which is identical to unity and manifests itself in unanimity.[11] According to Khomiakov, the state in Europe was centralized and thus stood in the way of the "flourishing of local life and regional centers." The western state was also organized as a bureaucratic mechanism, which Khomiakov saw as a principal cause of social and moral stagnation.

It is pointless to discuss the relation of this image, which was simply an ideological construct, to reality. The binary logic of Khomiakov's thought required an opposing counterpart for Russia. In Khomiakov's historical thinking, the image of the West played a role that was not independent, but auxiliary: the real object of Khomiakov's thought was Russia. Therefore, what was important for him was not the West as it actually was, but rather how the West had influenced (i.e., westernized) Russia.

[10] K.S. Aksakov, "Ob osnovnykh nachalakh russkoi istorii" in *Polnoe sobranie sochinenii*, 2nd edn. (Moscow: Univ. tip., 1889), vol. 1, p. 18.

[11] It is instructive to compare the concepts of negative and positive freedom in Khomiakov with the same concepts in western political philosophy from Isaiah Berlin to John Rawls.

After the idea of the commune, western influence was the next key subject in the Slavophile conceptualization of Russia, and Khomiakov also provided it with a philosophical foundation, which he easily constructed within the parameters of his general "organic philosophy." He believed that the life of a social organism is based upon a full-blooded connection with its original source. Obviously, external influences may disrupt and violate the connection with the original source. If these external intrusions are powerful and sustained, there is a good chance that the very nature of the *Sozium* will change. And this is exactly what had happened in Russia as a result of the Petrine reforms. The positing of a radical opposition between pre-Petrine or "old" Russia and Petrine or "modern" Russia was another cornerstone of Slavophilism. According to Khomiakov, the change in the Russian *Sozium* took the form of division and schism. The upper social estates accepted western norms and structures, subordinating education and culture, administration, the state system, and so forth to these norms. The lower estates, the *narod*, remained the carriers of Russia's primordial norms and structures. Thus, a deep "chasm in the intellectual and spiritual life of Russia" appeared, a chasm that divided the people's "authentic way of life" from the Europeanized elite's artificially "grafted enlightenment."[12]

The Slavophiles' organic paradigm demanded that they regard the "new" Russia as an inferior, artificial, non-organic society. If organic life implies unity, then non-organic social life implies disunity and stagnation. But the stagnation in modern Russia was not like that in Europe. It was something else. Thus, the Slavophiles found it necessary to analyze the nature of Russia's shortcomings, to offer a diagnosis of Russia's ailment. Indeed, this was exactly how the Slavophiles saw their mission. Having extolled ancient Rus', they described contemporary Russia as suffering from a "deep-seated disease," from a "deep wound," etc. According to Khomiakov's diagnosis, the disease most adversely affecting modern Russia was *imitation*, its habit of following foreign models. This diagnosis also derived from the organic paradigm. A healthy organism draws its life and being entirely from its source, and the organism's life unfolds from what it receives from this source. If, however, an organism seeks sustenance from some foreign source, it weakens and loses its connection with its original source. It thereby harms its own life; it becomes ill. "The introduction of non-organic elements into an organic body," Khomiakov insisted, "is soon followed by an internal disorder."[13] By this logic, the influence of western culture on Russia could only be negative: according to Khomiakov, "the influence of western education distorted the very structure of Russian life."[14]

---

[12] Khomiakov, "Mnenie russkikh ob inostrantsakh," p. 33.   [13] *Ibid.* p. 61.
[14] A.S. Khomiakov, "Poslanie k serbam" in *Polnoe sobranie sochinenii*, vol. 1, p. 381.

This conclusion is what the Slavophiles' dogma dictated; and, obeying it, the Slavophiles denied the most evident reality: the outstanding achievements of the "Russian synthesis," the Europeanization of Russia's culture. It was inconvenient, even impossible for the Slavophiles to acknowledge that cultural creativity can be synthetic, and that cross-cultural contacts may be fruitful.

Having made their diagnosis of Russia's malaise, the Slavophiles offered a remedy for this illness: return to the primordial condition that had existed in the country prior to the "introduction of non-organic principles," a condition that was presumed to be authentic and healthy precisely because it was primordial. "The restoration of our spiritual strength," Khomiakov concluded, "depends on establishing a living union with ancient, but nevertheless to us contemporary, Russian life," for it was this life, which kept a full-blooded connection with the original source, that would provide sustenance to contemporary Russia.[15] Of course, the Slavophiles did not call for a literal return to the past, but rather, as Khomiakov explained in "On the Old and the New," a dialectical return in which "ancient Rus' will revive, but now conscious of itself." Khomiakov made it clear that for the country to attain the requisite self-consciousness, the light of Christianity would have to penetrate into every aspect of Russian life. Only in this manner could Rus' "realize its supreme vocation."

The Slavophile idea of Russia corresponds to a well-known type of thinking about society, *retrospective utopianism*. A retrospective utopia is a social model that locates a social ideal somewhere in the distant past, representing it as a kind of Golden Age. It is quite typical for retrospective utopias to be combined with the mythologem of the Fall, the event of expulsion from an ideal, paradisiacal way of life into the "fallen world." The Slavophiles' Golden Age was pre-Mongol Rus'; in their doctrine, the "Fall" had been brought about by the Petrine reforms and westernization.

THE WESTERNIZERS AND THE THEME OF RUSSIA

The principal Westernizer response to the Slavophile conception of Russian history is usually considered to be Konstantin Kavelin's "An Examination of Ancient Russia's Juridical Life" (1847), an article based on a series of lectures delivered at Moscow University. Although he was to some degree obviously influenced by Hegel's philosophy of history, Kavelin made no attempt to provide his historical analysis with a rigorous philosophical underpinning. Nevertheless,

---

[15] A.S. Khomiakov, "O vozmozhnosti russkoi khudozhestvennoi shkoly" in *Polnoe sobranie sochinenii*, vol. 1, p. 97.

he tried to answer all the fundamental questions concerning the genesis of Russia, its condition and the principles of its social being. Like the Slavophiles, Kavelin juxtaposed old Russia to the West. The ancient social structure of Rus' was understood to be strictly familial and patriarchal, whereas in the West the social structure was hierarchical and martial (*druzhinnyi*). But it was at this point that the Slavophiles and Westernizers parted ways. If Khomiakov saw the western knighthood (*druzhina*) as the carrier of "stagnation," then the Westernizers saw it as the cradle of personhood. Nor did the Westernizers follow the Slavophiles in thinking Russia a living organism and the West a dead mechanism. Instead, the Westernizers saw Russian society as suffering from the absence or suppression of personhood, whereas western society was the locus of the free development of personhood. The governing principle of the Westernizers' discourse was completely different from that of the Slavophiles: the Westernizers replaced the Slavophiles' cult of the commune with their own cult of personhood.

From this point onward, the Westernizers viewed the historical process through the prism of personhood. "Ancient Russia," Kavelin declared, "was organized around life in clans. Personhood... had not yet been developed; it was being suppressed by clan blood relations."[16] The absence of personhood in ancient Rus' was the central thesis of the Westernizer conception of history, its persistent leitmotif. The absence of personhood in old Russia implied that the peasant commune had been a detrimental factor in Russian history. Moreover, the Westernizers did not think of personhood as a trait peculiar to some societies but not others; instead they saw it as a necessary precondition for each people to participate fully in the course of world history. "Existence," Kavelin concluded, "is not possible for peoples [*narody*] who are called to world-historical action without the element of personhood... Personhood, conscious of its infinite, unconditional value, is the necessary condition for a people's spiritual development."[17] The inherent goal and meaning of Russian history were now clear. Russia had to overcome its clan-based society and bring about "the gradual formation and manifestation of the principle of personhood." Once again, Russia was opposed to Europe. "The task of history for the Russian-Slavic tribes was distinct from that of the Germanic tribes. The German tribes were assigned the task of developing historical personhood, [a principle] which was inherent to them from their origins. However, we [Russians] had to create

---

[16] K.D. Kavelin, "Vzgliad na iuridicheskii byt drevnei Rossii" in *Nash umstvennyi stroi: Stat'i po filosofii russkoi istorii i kul'tury* (Moscow: Pravda, 1989), pp. 50–51.

[17] *Ibid.* p. 22.

personhood [ex nihilo]."[18] In a private letter Kavelin emphasized the difficulty of Russia's task: "The Russian state crushed personhood at every level of social development . . . Had we been an Asiatic people, we would have rotted to death in such a condition. But we possess the capability of development. And that is why the principle of personhood, or individuality [individual'nost'], had to be expressed and gradually won its rights."[19]

According to Kavelin, Peter the Great had successfully solved Russia's historical problem. Before Peter, Russia "did not possess the principle of personhood," but, from the "eighteenth century onward, it was cultivated and made active."[20] Kavelin extolled Peter for this monumental achievement. "Peter . . . was a great man, our hero and demigod, our hope."[21] It is worthwhile to compare Kavelin's assessment of Peter with that of the Slavophiles, who believed that Peter had violated the Russian state's unwritten agreement with the common people and had "seduced Rus' into following the western path." Of course, Westernizers turned this "seduction" on its head. In their estimation, westernization was not only useful, but also necessary for the creation of personhood in Russia. "The individual," Kavelin argued, "could begin to think and act only under some foreign influence. Such influence was necessary and beneficial for him."[22]

At this point, however, one must express a caveat. The Westernizer scheme of history, which concluded optimistically that Russia had been "Europeanized" and had "entered the universal life [of nations]," was embraced only by those Westernizers who had come to think of themselves as liberals. But as early as 1845–1846 the Westernizers split into two factions: a liberal faction, including such thinkers as Kavelin and Granovskii; and a radical faction, including Belinskii, Herzen, and Bakunin. Joining Chaadaev, the radical Westernizers did not see in Russian reality any signs of "entering the universal life [of nations]." Herzen declared that in Russia "the individual has always been crushed and devoured . . . Slavery has increased hand in hand with education."[23] "The history of Russia," Herzen wrote elsewhere, "is the history of the development of autocracy and power, whereas the history of Europe is that of the development of freedom and rights."[24]

---

[18] *Ibid.* p. 23.
[19] Letter to Baroness E.F. Rahden, 26 May 1864, in *Russkaia mysl'* 12 (1899), 14.
[20] Kavelin, "Vzgliad na iuridicheskii byt," p. 66.
[21] K.D. Kavelin, "Kratkii vzgliad na russkuiu istoriiu" in *Nash umstvennyi stroi* (Moscow, 1989), p. 164.
[22] Kavelin, "Vzgliad na iuridicheskii byt," p. 59.
[23] A.I. Gertsen, "S togo berega," *Polnoe sobranie sochinenii*, vol. 6, p. 319.
[24] A.I. Gertsen, "Razvitie revoliutsionnykh idei v Rossii," *Polnoe sobranie sochinenii*, vol. 7, p. 244.

THE WESTERNIZERS AND THE THEME OF PERSONHOOD

As we have noted, the theme of personhood constitutes the red thread that runs through the discourse of Westernism, comprising both its pathos and its *raison d'être*. Every Westernizer affirmed the primacy of the principle of personhood in history and in social life, as well as the autonomy, value, and liberty of the individual. Nevertheless, what we might call the doctrine of Westernism never fully developed a philosophical notion of personhood. Granted, Herzen outlined such a concept or, at least, its core. But this concept, which was not given any systematic formulation, was instead part of his own philosophical worldview rather than a doctrine common to all Westernizers. And since the main interests of the Westernizers lay in social life, they never sought to clarify philosophically the meaning of personhood. In other words, the Westernizers did not study personhood as a philosophical problem, but instead considered it a solution to a social problematic. When personhood is only an element of *social* philosophy (or merely a topic in public rhetoric), then even if it is declared to be the highest of values, it is not analyzed: it constitutes a mere axiom or postulate. Thus, the Westernizers generally treated the concept of personhood as the object of a cult, rather than as a subject of philosophical reflection.

If the Westernizers' "discourse of personhood" did not lead to a conceptual analysis of the phenomenon, but instead strongly emphasized the need for its development and its ultimate value in the unconditional protection of legal rights, then this discourse was not so much a personalist discourse but an ethical one. In this sense, Westernizers exalted the concept of personhood as an ethical principle, much as the Slavophiles had exalted the commune.

Among the Westernizers, Belinskii most clearly and explicitly expressed this moral pathos regarding personhood. In an 1841 letter to Vasilii Botkin, Belinskii lodged a famous moral protest against Hegel's philosophy:

The fate of the subject, the individual, the person is more important than the fate of the entire world... and of the Hegelian *Allgemeinheit*. I humbly bow before you, Georg Friedrich [Hegel]..., but even if I climbed to the highest rung of the ladder of development, I would all the same ask you to give me an account of all the victims of life and history. Otherwise, I would throw myself down from the highest rung of the ladder. I do not want happiness, if I cannot be sure about the fate of all my brothers.[25]

In this reckless ethical maximalism, Belinskii resembled Konstantin Aksakov, who declared that legal guarantees of individual rights were harmful. In fact, Belinskii and Aksakov had been friends since their days together in Stankevich's

---

[25] V.G. Belinskii, *Polnoe sobranie sochinenii*, 13 vols. (Moscow: Izdatel'stvo Akademii nauk SSSR, 1953–1959), vol. 12, p. 22.

circle. This hypertrophied ethics proved to be an implicit motivation behind both Westernism and Slavophilism, and, consequently, behind the foundation of Russian consciousness at that time. Such ethical maximalism was inevitably fraught with risks; paradoxically, it may well be among the factors causing the *atrophy* of ethics visible now in Russia. And in the 1840s, ethical maximalism and a desire for free personhood naturally attracted radical Westernizers to socialism, an ideology to which they gave an ethical coloration. Socialism was considered to offer a practical solution to the problem of personhood and, as such, it easily acquired a religious dimension. These conceptual links were well expressed by Bakunin: "What must arrive after all religions is *socialism*. Understood in a religious sense, socialism is belief in man's ability to fulfill his destiny on earth."[26]

Only very rarely can one find Westernizers asking the question, "What is personhood?" And it is even rarer to find in Westernizer discourse any attempts at conceptual analysis defining the scope and limits of this notion. A careful examination shows that Westernizer discourse conflates the elements of two different paradigms of personhood, the Christian and the secular paradigm. And this conflation speaks to the philosophical immaturity of Westernism.

Herzen, however, proved an exception to the rule. His way of thinking, beginning with his youthful affinity for Saint-Simonianism, never lost its focus on the living unity of human beings. One of his earliest works was titled "Regarding Man's Place in Nature" (1832). In it, he opposed the idea of man as a living totality to the concept of "dualism," which he saw as the dominant trait and main deficiency of European thought. Dualism, according to Herzen, was "Christianity turned into stark logic, severed from its tradition, from mysticism. Its primary technique is to divide into false opposition that which is not really divisible, such as body and spirit. For fifteen hundred years everything was imbued with dualism . . . [which] perverted the most basic concepts."[27]

Hegel helped Herzen, as well as all of Europe, to overcome dualism. Herzen's relationship to Hegel's thought, however, was not that of a simple follower. Hegel's system did not have an anthropological orientation. In fact, it contained elements that were essentially "anti-anthropological."[28] Gustav Shpet, who deeply studied the "Herzen and Hegel" theme, has argued that Herzen assimilated Hegel only very partially: like many philosophically gifted Russians, Herzen sacrificed the pursuit of genuine philosophy for the sake of social activism. "It was not the content of Hegel's philosophy," Shpet observed,

---

[26] M.A. Bakunin, "Mezhdunarodnoe tainoe obshchestvo osvobozhdeniia chelovechestva" in *Izbrannye filosofskie sochineniia i pis'ma* (Moscow: Mysl', 1987), p. 265.

[27] Gertsen, "S togo berega," pp. 126–127.

[28] See S.S. Horujy, "Anti-antropologiia klassicheskogo nemetskogo idealizma," *Voprosy filosofii* 6–7 (2007), 114–129.

"that captivated Herzen, but rather the general character of this philosophy . . . Herzen was fascinated, first, by the scientific aspect of Hegel's philosophy, and, second, by the fact that the final end of this philosophy was reality as such."[29] Therefore, after having mastered Hegelian discourse and language, Herzen made them serve his own view of human nature; with their help, he outlined his conception of personhood. These moves by Herzen may also remind us of Feuerbach, another thinker who was hostile to dualism; indeed, Herzen's philosophy was long treated as a type of "Feuerbachianism." Yet Shpet proves that this interpretation was incorrect, and that Herzen as a thinker was essentially independent of Feuerbach.

By simple syllogisms in the Hegelian mode, Herzen constructed the basis of his conception of personhood. Universality and reason possess an internal necessity and demand for individualization. They are capable of generating the transformation from genus to species and from species to the individual and to personality. In turn, the task of self-realization becomes necessary for personality. And the quintessence of Herzen's conception is hidden in the way in which personhood solves this problem. Here again it was necessary to overcome dualism. On the one hand was the task of thinking and theorizing; on the other was the task of acting and doing. Herzen stressed the second task, which had been slighted or ignored in speculative philosophy. "Forgotten by science," Herzen declared, "personality demanded its own rights, it demanded to live . . . which [demand] could only be satisfied by creative, free action." Herzen demonstrated that the key to the constitution of personality principally resided in action. "Action is personality itself . . . In rational, morally free, and passionately energetic action man actualizes the reality of his personality."[30] For it is in such action, "free, rational, and conscious" action, Herzen repeatedly stated, that theory is translated into life and the division between theory and practice, as well as every type of dualism, is overcome. On this basis, the theory of personality was then developed in many concrete ways: Herzen outlined his ethics based on principles of freedom and dignity, discussed the dependence of personality upon its milieu and epoch, and so on.

Herzen's primary contribution to the notion of personhood resides in his concept of the active nature of personality. In itself, such a thesis may seem trite, but Herzen understood both personality and its active nature in terms of Hegel's concept of "reality" (*Wirklichkeit*). Herzen emphasized the importance of personality's role in historically transformative rational action. Personality

---

[29] G.G. Shpet, *Filosofskoe mirovozzrenie Gertsena* (Petrograd: Kolos, 1921), p. 12.

[30] A.I. Gertsen, "Diletantizm v nauke. Pis'mo III: Diletantizm i tsekh uchenykh" cited in Shpet, *Filosofskoe mirovozzrenie Gertsena*, p. 22.

itself appeared in Herzen's thought to be a unique crucible in which, to quote Shpet, "all reality is smelted so that, having purified it of slag and 'chance' rubbish, one could pour it, now pure and precious, into the forms of rationality."[31] As Shpet says, in this conception Hegelian "reality started speaking with the voice of personality." Today we can find affinities here with many philosophical phenomena of the twentieth century, such as personalism, neo-Marxism, and the influential "reflexive activity approach" in late Soviet philosophy. One can hardly doubt that Herzen's conception of personality is the apex of the anthropological and personological thought of the Westernizers.

THE SLAVOPHILES AND THE THEME OF PERSONHOOD

Aspiring to maintain a sense of objectivity in his polemics, Herzen wrote about the relationship between personhood and the peasant commune: "The commune is our great legacy . . . I highly value it, but the element of personhood is inadequately represented in it."[32] The judgment of other Westernizers was even more severe. They usually asserted not just personhood's "inadequate representation" within the commune, but personhood's complete absence within it. If we examine how the Slavophiles attempted to answer Herzen's accusation, we shall find a rather poor and vague response. Although Konstantin Aksakov formulated, as he always did, an explicit and clear-cut position, in this case his answer bordered on the utopian.

Aksakov presented a radical solution to the problem of personhood and the commune, offering his own definition of the commune.

The commune is a union of people, who have renounced their egoism, their own personality . . . This is action based on love, a supreme Christian action . . . The commune is a moral choir in which no one loses his voice . . . Thus personality is not lost in the commune, but, having abandoned its exclusivity for the general concord, it finds itself in a more purified form, in a concord of equally self-sacrificing persons . . . In this moral accord, each person is heard, not as a solitary voice but in harmony with others, and this represents the supreme manifestation of a harmonious totality of the being of rational creatures.[33]

According to Aksakov, the constitutive principle of the commune is unanimity, or the "free moral concord of all." Of course, under conditions of actual life, the permanent maintenance of the commune's unanimity was unlikely, as Aksakov himself acknowledged. "Unanimity," he observed, "is difficult to

---

[31] Shpet, *Filosofskoe mirovozzrenie Gertsena*, p. 24.   [32] Gertsen, "S togo berega," p. 319.
[33] K.S. Aksakov, "Kratkii istoricheskii ocherk Zemskikh Soborov" in *Polnoe sobranie sochinenii*, vol. 1, pp. 279–280.

maintain, but every moral achievement is difficult." In fact, for Aksakov, all forces that constituted and held the commune together were of a moral nature. He emphasized this point by declaring that the "Slavic commune was a union of people that was founded upon a moral principle . . . When these people formed a commune, then the universal, inner moral law stood out as the ordering principle of communal life . . . The only [viable] foundation of society is a common moral conviction."[34] In Aksakov's thinking, all aspects of communal life, aside from moral ones, become secondary; juridical standards are completely repudiated. The opposition between ethics and rights, between "inner truth" and "external truth," is sharpened to the point of legal nihilism. According to Aksakov, the "Slavs lived under the conditions of inner truth . . . The triumph of external truth is the death of inner truth, the only genuine and free truth."[35] In this interpretation, the commune was no longer a real rural community, but some sort of purely ethical construct, the utopian character of which was reinforced by the fact that its ethic of love and concord remained secret and mysterious. Where could the Slavs have acquired such a marvelous ethic?

This dubious conception of the commune gave rise to a no less dubious description of the Russian *Sozium* as a union of "Land" (that is, all communes conceived as one big commune) and "State." The principles of this union were rooted in the notion that "the unlimited right to action and law belongs to the State, while the complete right of opinion and speech belongs to the Land . . . ; unlimited power belongs to the tsar, complete freedom of life and spirit belong to the common people [*narod*] . . . The right of spiritual freedom . . . the freedom of thought and words is the inalienable right of the Land. But, having this right, the Land does not desire political rights of any kind; it has granted unlimited political authority to the State."[36] The contradictory and utopian character of such a construct is obvious, but, nevertheless, this understanding of the common people's relationship to state and politics was accepted by all Slavophiles. They fervently believed that the common people did not want to intrude into these spheres: the people considered them as sinful and therefore delegated political authority to the tsar and to his agents. At the same time, however, the *narod* wanted to preserve its free and inviolable "internal life," i.e., its religion, customs, and way of life.

Aksakov's description of the Russian people hardly corresponded to the really existing *narod*, but his description proved that the Slavophiles had a profound intuition of the Christian tradition. The attitude toward politics imputed to the

---

[34] K.S. Aksakov, "Neskol'ko slov o russkoi istorii, vozbuzhdennykh istorieiu g. [S.M.] Solov'ëva" in *Polnoe sobranie sochinenii*, vol. 1, pp. 58, 55.
[35] Aksakov, "Kratkii istoricheskii ocherk Zemskikh Soborov," p. 287.   [36] *Ibid.* p. 284.

Russian people by Aksakov corresponded exactly to the attitude of the early
Christians toward politics, as described, for example, by Hannah Arendt: "The
Christian concept of political freedom... arose out of the early Christians'
suspicion of and hostility against the public realm as such, from whose concerns
they demanded to be absolved in order to be free."[37] According to Arendt,
this attitude was based on the "definition of political freedom as potential
freedom from politics"; and she traces a definite line in the history of political
thought that follows this interpretation of freedom and political rights. It is to
this school of thought that the political philosophy of the Slavophiles belongs.
Since the Slavophiles interpreted the inviolable sphere of the "freedom of life
and spirit" very broadly, their philosophy, while affirming the necessity of
autocracy, paradoxically embraced political theories that sought to curtail the
prerogatives of state. Ivan Aksakov expressed this position in a letter to Countess
A.D. Bludova: "The Russian people are not political... They are a social people
that have made the inner life, the life of the land, their goal. Their ideal is not
the perfection of state, but the creation of a Christian society. Our primary
interest is that the state should permit the maximum degree of freedom to inner
life, while understanding its own jurisdiction and shortcomings."[38]

Returning to the issue of personhood, we can see that although Aksakov's
"Land" is again an idealized, purely ethical construct, his conception also contains important ideas about the rights of personhood. According to the doctrine
of the Slavophiles, these rights have nothing to do with politics per se. Instead,
they relate to the "inner life," to the sphere of the Land, and, as such, are
inalienable and inviolable. In other words, attachment to freedom, dignity, and
the rights of personhood was in no way a monopoly of the Westernizers. The
Slavophiles actively pressed for the establishment of free thought and free speech
in Russia, and their declarations and actions were no less radical than those of the
Westernizers. Whereas Belinskii voiced his criticism in a private letter to Nikolai Gogol, Konstantin Aksakov expressed his frustrations in a memorandum to
Alexander II. "Russia's contemporary condition is marked by internal discord,
which is concealed by shameless falsehoods... Lies have engulfed everything,
deceit is everywhere... It is our oppressive system of government that generates all the misfortunes [of our country]... If it could, this system would turn
every man into an animal that obeys without thinking."[39] Konstantin's younger
brother Ivan, in the editorial of the first issue of the newspaper *Day*, founded

[37] H. Arendt, "What is Freedom?" in *Between Past and Future* (New York: Viking, 1961), pp. 150–151.
[38] Cited in *Rannie slavianofily*, compiled by N.L. Brodskii (Moscow: Tip. T-va I.D. Sytina, 1910),
pp. liv–lv. The letter is dated January 15, 1862.
[39] K.S. Aksakov, "Zapiska o vnutrennem sostoianii Rossii" in *Rannie slavianofily*, pp. 89–91.

by him, made a proposal to include in the Russian Collection of Laws, as the very first chapter, the following rule: "Freedom of the printed word is the inviolable right of each subject of the Russian empire, without regard to social standing."[40]

Nevertheless, Aksakov's conception of personhood is quite fantastic. As we have already seen, according to his theory, personhood was not absent from the Russian *Sozium*, but it took a very specific and unrealizable form. Aksakov understood man as a self-sacrificing member of the commune, who has renounced not only egoism but even his very personality in order to attain a higher and purer type of personhood that resides in a "moral choir." Such a conception of human nature is a purely ethical construct, positing an entirely ethicized man, and is therefore nothing more than a utopian vision of human nature. But we could add that Aksakov himself, by all accounts, very closely resembled this "non-existing" type of man.

Other Slavophiles understood communal and rural institutional structures, as well as the type of personhood that resided in them, more realistically. Although Khomiakov first formulated the Slavophile doctrine on the commune, he did not construct an ethical utopia as Konstantin Aksakov did. "Personal virtues," Khomiakov insisted, "have not developed in rural communes to the same degree as have communal virtues."[41] In his opinion, "high levels of personal virtue in [Russian] rural life" were only "beautiful exceptions to the rule," whereas western knighthood "possessed indisputably higher personal virtues." His vision of the problem of "personhood and commune" did not differ much from that of the Westernizers. Nevertheless the main body of his teaching on personhood was very far from Westernizers' positions. The reason is that this body of ideas belongs not to his conception of the commune, but to a quite different theory that he developed toward the end of his life: the famous doctrine of *sobornost'* ("catholicity" or "conciliarity").

Khomiakov's doctrine of *sobornost'* and Kireevskii's historical-philosophical ideas constitute the two main religious-philosophical products of Slavophilism. They were mostly formulated in the 1850s and, as such, were no longer oriented around the debates of the 1830s and 1840s, which had focused on the commune and on national history. Instead, they concentrated on a more purely religious problematic. This shift in Slavophile thinking is especially important for its implications regarding the problem of personhood. The Slavophile vision of personhood had religious roots, and without reflection on these roots it could not hope to lay solid foundations.

---

[40] I.S. Aksakov, "Peredovaia gazety *Den'*, 19 maia 1862" in *Rannie slavianofily*, p. 129.
[41] Khomiakov, "Po povodu stat'i I.V. Kireevskogo" in *Polnoe sobranie sochinenii*, vol. 1, p. 243.

In retrospect, the positions of Westernizers and Slavophiles regarding the problem of personhood do not appear to be that complex. As noted above, the Westernizer conception of a "free, rational, conscious person" corresponds to the anthropocentric paradigm, in which personhood is understood to be an autonomous, self-contained *individuum*, related closely to the Cartesian subject. Contrary to this notion of personhood, the Slavophiles adhered to the theocentric paradigm, which states that the fullness of personal being belongs to God, not man. The human person is said to be constituted in the process of striving toward, and in being in communion with, the Divine Person; this human connection with God is thought to be not only spiritual but integral and holistic, that is, to encompass man's entire being. Wholeness and integrity are, therefore, the primary predicates of human personhood. This concept of the "integral person," which represents a coherent unity among all the levels and capabilities of human beings, and which is open to union with God, forms the basis of the Slavophile discourse regarding personhood. However, the Slavophiles did not succeed in developing a consistent personalistic philosophy or theology based on this concept. That task was inherited from them by Russian philosophy of the Silver Age, and then by Orthodox theology of personhood.

In its initial stages, Khomiakov's thought was principally a social philosophy that concentrated on describing a definite type of human community characterized by a whole array of ideal qualities, or "communal virtues." Two dominant features marked this philosophy. First, the specific nature of this perfect community was expressed in the language and concepts of an organic paradigm. Secondly, it was assumed that this type of community had been realized in history in the form of the Russian commune. But, unlike Konstantin Aksakov, Khomiakov did not think in a utopian way, and hence he had to conclude that the commune had not and could not come to embody a perfectly organic community. A new stage of his philosophy was born when this negative conclusion was accompanied by a positive thesis, namely, that the actual, and only adequate realization of a perfect community, is the *church*.

At the basis of Khomiakov's fundamental reorientation is simple logic. Because of its ideal qualities, a perfect community cannot exist in any purely empirical society. A perfect community must be supra-empirical, and only the church, as opposed to an ordinary *Sozium*, possesses supra-empirical characteristics. Then, still at the "communal" stage of his philosophical path, Khomiakov determined the set of principal predicates of perfect community. The main predicate among them was a harmonious combination of, or even identity between, complete unity and complete freedom. These predicates could not be found in the commune, but Khomiakov soon discovered that they are present in the church. This conceptualization of ecclesiastic being came about through a detailed analysis of a specific characteristic of the church, which, according to the Nicene Creed, it undoubtedly possesses: the property of *sobornost'*. To be more precise, the Creed includes the term "catholic church" (*sobornaia Tserkov'*). Khomiakov derived the neologism "*sobornost'*" from the adjective *sobornaia* ("sobornal"), which has ever since occupied an important place in both Russian, and more broadly Christian, religious and social thought.

Sobornaia is the third of four attributes assigned to the church, and it was expressed in the original Greek by the term *catholicos*, meaning "universal," "whole," "all-embracing." An important feature of the Russian term, absent in the Greek original, is the connection with the notion of a church council, or gathering of believers (*sobor*). Exploiting this connection to the utmost, Khomiakov developed a doctrine of *sobornost'* as "conciliar unity," a unique kind of unity, in which the fullness of unity and the fullness of freedom are not only compatible, but presuppose one another. Khomiakov asserted that it is this synthesis of freedom and unity that constitutes the essential nature of the church. "The Church," he declared, "is freedom in unity,"[42] and "the unity of the Church is nothing but the concord of personal freedoms."[43]

But Khomiakov did not apply the word "synthesis" or any other speculative description to this combination of two principles. As Georges Florovsky has emphasized, Khomiakov's discourse on *sobornost'* unfolded through personal witness: it is an *experiential* discourse, which renders the profound experience of his own life in the church. And in the horizon of this experience, the combination of freedom and unity in the church is not dialectical, but *gracious*, that is, achieved with the help of God's grace, or Divine energy. Khomiakov's notion of conciliar unity implies that freedom assumes a unique form, conciliar freedom, "freedom illuminated by grace," whereas conciliar unity itself is created by "the grace of God," not by human effort. Since the Divine energy or grace emanates from the Divine essence, i.e., from an ontological horizon of Divine being, *sobornost'* by its very nature belongs to this horizon too. Florovsky, arguably the most authoritative scholar on the doctrine of *sobornost'*, neatly captured Khomiakov's intent: "*Sobornost'*, as Khomiakov understood it, is not a human characteristic, but a Divine characteristic."[44] This important thesis

---

[42] A.S. Khomiakov, "Neskol'ko slov pravoslavnogo khristianina o zapadnykh veroispovedaniiakh. Po povodu odnogo okruzhnogo poslaniia Parizhskogo arkhiepiskopa" in *Sochineniia*, 2 vols. (Moscow: Medium, 1994), vol. 2, p. 66.

[43] A.S. Khomiakov, "Neskol'ko slov pravoslavnogo khristianina o zapadnykh veroispovedaniiakh. Po povodu raznykh sochinenii latinskikh i protestantskikh o predmetakh very" in *Sochineniia*, vol. 2, p. 209.

[44] Georgii Florovskii, *Puti russkogo bogosloviia*, 3rd edn. (Paris: YMCA Press, 1983), p. 277.

makes it necessary to reject each of the numerous attempts to exploit *sobornost'*
as a social or national ideal, relating it to empirical social being.

It is clear that in his doctrine of *sobornost'* Khomiakov entered into the realm
of ontology, and, doing so, he did not adopt Hegelianism or any other type
of western metaphysics. Instead, Khomiakov followed an original course that,
although partly philosophical, was essentially theological. This move was an
important step in the development of Russian thought. Several new philosophical and theological perspectives issued from Khomiakov's innovation, the three
most important of which occurred in (1) ontology, in connection with the
concept of the unity of all (*vsëedinstvo*); (2) epistemology, in certain ontological
approaches to the theory of knowledge; and (3) social philosophy, most notably
in attempts to use *sobornost'* as a principle of social organization.[45]

The development of a theological doctrine of *sobornost'* was cut short by
Khomiakov's death. It is clear that this development would inevitably have led to
the displacement of the organic paradigm. Organic discourse, with its biological
connotations and narrow empirical horizon, inevitably comes into conflict with
ontological discourse. In his later works, it must be noted, Khomiakov became
more cautious and restrained in applying organic categories to the study of the
church and its life; he increasingly foregrounded the principles of personhood,
love, and community, all of which were supra-organic. Khomiakov's discourse
of *sobornost'* evolved toward a *theology of personhood* and thus advanced toward
the theocentric personological paradigm characteristic of Eastern Christianity.
The decisive step toward overcoming organicism would have required that
Khomiakov recognize the notions of personhood and Divine Hypostasis as
identical. But such a move also would have required that he shift his main themes
from ecclesiology to Christology, a shift he only started to make. In addition,
the doctrine of *sobornost'*, having strenuously underlined the constitutive role
of grace in the church, had also to evolve toward a *theology of Divine energies*,
a theology belonging at the center of Eastern Christian discourse, but nearly
forgotten in Khomiakov's day. These two theological directions were actively
pursued with the development of the doctrine of *sobornost'* in twentieth-century
Orthodox thought – a development that was an integral part of the renaissance
of Eastern Christian discourse.

Kireevskii's thought was an important prologue to this later renaissance. The
very concept of an Eastern Christian discourse began to take shape in his later
writings, especially in the posthumously published "On the Possibility and

---

[45] For a discussion of the reception of the doctrine of *sobornost'* in Russian philosophy, see S.S.
Horujy, "Aleksei Khomiakov i ego delo," part 2, sections 6–7, in *Opyty iz russkoi dukhovnoi traditsii*,
pp. 169–204.

Necessity of New Principles for Philosophy" (1856). It was in this latter work that the problem of creating an authentic philosophy, which was to be based not on European metaphysics but on the principles of Eastern Christian discourse, was first raised and analyzed. With great philosophical insight, Kireevskii, who is considered by many, including this author, to be the most powerful philosophical mind of his generation, established the ideational context of such a philosophy and also defined its contours. As Kireevskii stressed, this philosophy should not be a new conceptual system that subordinates itself (as Scholasticism did) to the dogmas of faith as to external demands. Instead, it should present a new way of thinking capable of providing an adequate expression of spiritual experience, thus creating a new philosophical discourse. He demonstrated that Eastern Christian discourse, unlike western thought, had assigned a leading role to spiritual experience of the hesychast type. (He established active contacts with the monastery Optina Pustyn', the principal hesychast center in Russia.) "The distinctive feature of Orthodox thought, which issues from reason's particular relationship to faith, should determine . . . the direction of our unique type of education," he wrote.[46]

In a historical-philosophical context, Kireevskii thought, this type of philosophy should be able to unite two poles: it should necessarily be topical, "responding to questions of the day," while at the same time the "philosophy of the holy fathers of the Orthodox Church" should serve as its "life-giving embryo and light-giving guide." Thus, the task of this new philosophy was to correlate "all the principles of contemporary culture with the tradition of the holy fathers." By underlining the immanent, never obsolete role of Greek patristics, which can and must stimulate creative solutions to "questions of the day" (rather than merely rehearsing archaic or conservative formulas), Kireevskii directly anticipated Father Florovsky's neopatristic synthesis. Kireevskii pointed precisely in the direction followed by Russian thought in the twentieth century to overcome the key conflict in Russian culture, the opposition between the spiritual tradition and cultural tradition.

Nevertheless, neither Kireevskii nor Khomiakov was able to create the type of philosophy toward which they both aspired: a contemporary philosophy that was built upon the distinctive foundations of Russia's spiritual tradition and that was therefore distinct from classical European metaphysics. Khomiakov's doctrine of *sobornost'* developed within the parameters of public debate; it was more theological than philosophical, very fragmentary and frequently polemical. Kireevskii's complex of ideas, however, constituted a convincing,

---

[46] I.V. Kireevskii, "O vozmozhnosti i neobkhodimosti novykh nachal dlia filosofii" in *Izbrannye stat'i* (Moscow: Sovremennik, 1984), p. 262.

well-conceived project, even though the author did not even start realizing it. Although the renewal of Russian thought had begun with the Slavophiles, the task of creating a Russian philosophy remained in the future.

CONCLUSION

The image of Slavophilism and Westernism in Russian cultural consciousness has heretofore tended to be a *symmetrical stereotype*: the two systems have been perceived as phenomena of the same type, despite their different ideological positions. In reality, however, they were not at all symmetrical. They interpreted differently the pressing needs of Russian thought and society and, as a result, developed different goals. The Westernizers emphasized the development and emancipation of both social and, especially, personal consciousness, which compelled them to support the cultivation of unfettered personhood. The Slavophiles, on the other hand, emphasized the self-determination of Russian consciousness, which, they thought, had to reflect on its own foundations, appreciate its own principles, and comprehend its unique historical and spiritual experience. Clearly, these goals were of a different order. The Westernizers adopted ready-made western concepts relating to personhood and social justice, and they focused chiefly on problems such as how to enlighten the country's uneducated common people. The approach and vision of the Slavophiles led them to investigate self-consciousness and its development, deeply philosophical matters by their very nature. That is why Gustav Shpet, though his own views were completely Westernist, could unambiguously assert that "Slavophile problems . . . are the only original problems of Russian philosophy."[47] Among the Westernizers, only Herzen was considered by Shpet as having some philosophical weight. Westernizer thought was inspired by social and civic pathos, by the "religion of a great social transformation," in Herzen's words. That is why it was common for Westernizers to abandon philosophy for social action, journalistic writing, and politics. For their part, the Slavophiles never ignored social issues, but their thought was nourished by a philosophical source and, thus, they could never abandon the *topos* of Russian self-consciousness.

As a result of these differences, a "division of labor" in the intellectual life and culture of Russia took shape. Slavophile tendencies predominated in the philosophical process, in the sphere of creative thought, whereas the Westernizers' ideas were more influential in social processes and in shaping popular consciousness. Most Westernizers made only superficial contributions to philosophy, while the Slavophiles were never able to "captivate the masses" or offer

---

[47] Shpet, *Ocherk razvitiia russkoi filosofii*, p. 37.

society a realistic social program. The artificiality of both doctrines, which were based on conditional ideological constructs, manifested itself clearly over time. Understood as dogma, each of these doctrines displayed obvious incongruities, and each was shown to be unsound and archaic. It is not without reason that the finest intellectual achievements of both camps (Khomiakov's doctrine of *sobornost'*, Kireevskii's philosophical project, Herzen's conception of personhood) belonged neither to "canonical" Slavophilism nor to Westernism. But at the same time, each current proved not to be entirely archaic, but rather a permanent and necessary orientation in Russian thought, in its capacity as one element among others in Russian cultural strategies.

The misfortune of Russian history, however, resides in the fact that neither doctrine could or would understand itself as a necessary but partial moment in the self-realization of a cultural organism, as part of a living whole that cannot be encompassed by any dogma. To use an ancient saying, the one did not wish to recognize the other's truth. Neither the Slavophiles nor the Westernizers removed their ideological blinders, accepted the relativity of their own dogmas, and achieved "synergy" or coordination and cooperation with their counterparts in the opposing camp. (It was only fleetingly that the elements of such a synergy arose in the culture of the Silver Age and glittered in the idea of a Slavic renaissance.) The further polarization of social consciousness was the order of the day, something that was easily foreseen and inevitably came to pass.

2

ALEXANDER HERZEN

DEREK OFFORD

RUSSIAN WESTERNISM AND THE CONCEPT OF PERSONHOOD

"Because they like symmetry," Richard Pipes observed long ago, "historians
have created a foil for the Slavophiles, a party they call 'Westerners,' but it is difficult to perceive among the opponents of Slavophile theories any unity except
that of a negative kind."[1] And indeed it is true that the Westernizers, as I shall
call them, held few beliefs that they shared for very long save that the Slavophiles'
claims about the peculiarly Christian spirit and peaceable character of the Russian people, and about the organic nature of the people's pre-Petrine community,
were mistaken and utopian. For Westernism was a broad church in the 1840s
and 1850s. On the one hand, it embraced moderate, relatively dispassionate
men who might be classified as in some sense liberal, liberal-conservative, or
even Tory. In this category we find the historian Timofei Granovskii, the jurist
Konstantin Kavelin, the maturing imaginative writer Ivan Turgenev, and also
like-minded dilettanti and aesthetes such as Pavel Annenkov and Vasilii Botkin.
On the other hand, Westernism also embraced more impassioned spirits who
came to be attracted to radical, even revolutionary ideas. Among these men we
should include the literary critic Vissarion Belinskii ("furious Vissarion"), the
instinctive rebel and revolutionary agitator Mikhail Bakunin, and the subject of
this chapter, the novelist, social and political thinker, and eventual political exile,
journalist and autobiographer, Alexander Ivanovich Herzen (1812–1870).[2]

---

[1] Richard Pipes, *Russia under the Old Regime* (Harmondsworth: Penguin, 1977), p. 268.
[2] There is a large literature on Herzen. See especially, in alphabetical order by author: Edward
Acton, *Alexander Herzen and the Role of the Intellectual Revolutionary* (Cambridge University Press,
1979); Isaiah Berlin, "Herzen and Bakunin on Individual Liberty" and "Alexander Herzen" in
Henry Hardy and Aileen Kelly (eds.), *Russian Thinkers*, revised 2nd edn. (London: Penguin, 2008),
pp. 93–129 and pp. 212–239 respectively (for an encomium to Herzen the libertarian see especially
pp. 98–115); Aileen M. Kelly, *Toward Another Shore: Russian Thinkers Between Necessity and Chance*
(New Haven and London: Yale University Press, 1998) and *Views from the Other Shore: Essays on
Herzen, Chekhov, and Bakhtin* (New Haven and London: Yale University Press, 1999); E. Lampert,
Studies in Rebellion (London: Routledge and Kegan Paul, 1957); Martin Malia, *Alexander Herzen and
the Birth of Russian Socialism, 1812–1855* (Cambridge, MA: Harvard University Press, 1961).

Nevertheless it is not impossible, *pace* Pipes, to find some factors that lent coherence to the thought of the so-called Westernizers. First, the culture that the Westernizers wished to develop in Russia was secular. That is not to say that all the Westernizers followed Belinskii and Herzen in embracing Ludwig Feuerbach, who in his *Essence of Christianity* had rejected belief in God as a being with an objective existence outside human consciousness; but they did not follow the Slavophiles in conceiving of a utopian society in which every aspect of life was informed by spiritual priorities. Secondly, the Westernizers had been profoundly affected in the late 1830s by German philosophy, plunging "head first into 'the German sea,'" to use Turgenev's expression.[3] Granovskii, Turgenev, and Bakunin had all studied in Berlin in the late 1830s or early 1840s. They had been devotees of Hegel, whose works, as Herzen recalled in his autobiography *My Past and Thoughts*, were feverishly debated and on whose philosophy every available publication was sought out and read and re-read until it fell apart.[4]

From Hegel, or from his disciples the Left or Young Hegelians, the Westernizers drew ideas that continued to affect them deeply even after they thought they had disavowed him: ideas about the nature of certain civilizations and their rise and fall, the supposed ascent of humanity toward the realization of some goal, and the positive value of negation of an apparently outmoded way of life. Hegel nourished in them a belief in the possibility of a future better than the reality of Russia under Nicholas I. Faith in the future, Herzen wrote in 1843 at the end of an essay saturated with Hegelian terminology, "will save us in trying moments from despair."[5] Most importantly, perhaps, the Westernizers, and Russian thinkers more broadly, acquired from Hegel a certain cast of mind, a taste for a schematic, dialectical mode of thinking of the sort that inspires the opening words of the third essay in Herzen's early cycle *Dilettantism in Science* (1842–1843). "At all times in the long life of humanity," Herzen confidently asserts, "two opposing movements can be seen; the development of one determines the emergence of the other, along with struggle and the destruction of the first" (III, p. 43).

A third factor that lent coherence to Westernism was the Westernizers' apparent respect for the individual human person, for *lichnost'*. Now for the

---

3 "Literaturnye i zhiteiskie vospominaniia" in I.S. Turgenev, *Polnoe sobranie sochinenii i pisem*, 28 vols. (Moscow and Leningrad: Izdatel'stvo Akademii nauk SSSR, 1961–1968), vol. 14, p. 9.

4 Alexander Herzen, *My Past and Thoughts: The Memoirs of Alexander Herzen*, 4 vols. (Constance Garnett (trans.), revised by Humphrey Higgens, London: Chatto and Windus, 1968), vol. 2, p. 398.

5 A.I. Gertsen [Herzen], *Sobranie sochinenii*, 30 vols. (Moscow: Izdatel'stvo Akademii nauk SSSR, 1954–1965), vol. 3, p. 88. Future references to this edition will be cited parenthetically in the text of this chapter.

Slavophiles, and for later Russian romantic conservatives such as Dostoevskii, the highest form of self-expression to which the human could aspire was efface-ment of individuality through self-sacrifice for the common good, after the example of Christ. For the Westernizers, on the other hand, the distinctive autonomous personality became a value as important as secularism. Belinskii famously upheld it in the letters to Botkin that chart his rejection of Hegel in 1840–1841 and mark the end of his period of reconciliation with the autocratic state.[6] Granovskii, for his part, measured historical progress by the degree to which members of the mass became differentiated from it, enlightened, and individualized.[7] The subject of personality was also explored by Kavelin in his "Brief Survey of the Juridical Way of Life of Ancient Russia" (1847), which was warmly welcomed by other Westernizers such as Belinskii and Herzen. From the period of the Tatar yoke, the clan or kinship principle that had under-pinned ancient Russian society, Kavelin claimed, began to be broken down by the Muscovite princes as they asserted the interests of the state over those of the family. Accordingly the notion of personal worth, which had been lacking in ancient Russia, gained ground as a criterion for social status and political influence, and in due course Peter the Great supposedly created the conditions in which the autonomous individual could flourish.[8]

Herzen was also interested in the historical development of the notion of personhood. In the ancient world, he asserted in his *Dilettantism in Science*, the private individual was subordinate to the public citizen, who himself was but an atom in the city state (III, p. 30). In the modern age, though, the time had come for the individual to find full self-expression; this might happen if thought and action were in harmony, if self-conscious understanding ("science," properly conceived) were brought to bear on "life," that is to say on humans' practical activity in this vale of tears (III, p. 69). Herzen's search for a synthesis of opposites, such as "universality" and "singularity" (III, p. 83), has a Hegelian character, but it was with the Young Hegelians that he aligned himself as he rejected the reconciliation with reality to which many had been led by a conservative interpretation of Hegel. For only in "rational, morally free and passionately energetic action [*deianii*]" do human beings attain "the reality of personhood" and immortalize themselves in the world of events (III, p. 71). Again, the

[6] See the letter of October 4, 1840 in V.G. Belinskii, *Polnoe sobranie sochinenii*, 13 vols. (Moscow: Izdatel'stvo Akademii nauk SSSR, 1953–1959), vol. 11, p. 556, and also his letter of March 1, 1841 (vol. 12, p. 22).
[7] T.N. Granovskii, *Sochineniia*, 4th edn. (Moscow: Tovarishchestvo Tipografii A.I. Mamontova, 1900), p. 445.
[8] See K.D. Kavelin, *Sobranie sochinenii*, 4 vols. (St. Petersburg: Tipografiia M.M. Stasiulevicha, 1897–1900), vol. 1, cols. 5–66.

something of one's own that humans tried to salvage from the "vortex of contingencies," Herzen wrote in 1843 in an article entitled "Some Observations on the Historical Development of Honour," was precisely a "sense of one's own worth and an aspiration to preserve the moral independence [*samobytnost'*] of one's person." This sense of worth, manifested in devotion first to the clan, custom, and tradition (as it still was, according to Herzen, in the contemporary Orient) and then to the state (as in the ancient Greek and Roman worlds), led in the Middle Ages to the development of the concept of honour and personal dignity, which found expression in the institution of knight-errantry (II, pp. 154–156, 162–169).

Yet it is difficult to accept the Westernizers' assurances that they respected the sanctity of the person; or at least the terms or contexts in which they offered such assurances raise fresh problems. Belinskii's defense of the individual, for example, is hard to recognize from within the Anglophone discourse on liberty. His "love of freedom and the independence of the human personality," he confessed to Botkin, are "wild, frenzied, fanatical." They involved much human sacrifice to thirsty gods. "Human personality has become an obsession which I fear will drive me insane," he wrote. "I am beginning to love mankind after the fashion of Marat: in order to make the smallest part of it happy I think I would be prepared to destroy the rest of it with fire and sword."[9] Even among the moderate, liberal Westernizers (and it should be noted that the term "liberal" needs to be used with caution in the Russian context), respect for the individual sat uncomfortably with the pronounced *étatisme* of their historiography.[10] Kavelin, for instance, extolled Ivan the Terrible, as did Belinskii, treating him as a "noble and worthy" representative of the idea of the state, a misunderstood genius who buckled under the strain of his attempt to introduce the principle of "personal merit" into patriarchal Muscovy.[11] Granovskii, while admiring the enlightened jurist or ruler who tried to instill moral principles and a sense of law into the medieval feudal state,[12] also revered ruthless absolute rulers such as Alexander the Great.[13] In the face of such "great men of history," who in Granovskii's judgment are called upon to fulfill some providential design, the individual was likely to be trampled underfoot, like "poor Evgenii" as he is pursued in

---

9 Letter of June 28, 1841 in Belinskii, *Polnoe sobranie sochinenii*, vol. 12, pp. 51–52.
10 Respect for the strong, centralized state goes back through Nikolai Karamzin, who is in a sense a forerunner of the Westernizers of the 1840s, to eighteenth-century admirers of Peter the Great, such as Vasilii Tatishchev and Mikhail Lomonosov.
11 Kavelin, *Sobranie sochinenii*, cols. 46–53. See also Belinskii, *Polnoe sobranie sochinenii*, vol. 7, p. 593, vol. 10, p. 195, vol. 12, p. 267.
12 "Abbat Sugerii" in Granovskii, *Sochineniia*, pp. 173–240, especially pp. 180–182, 225; "Chetyre istoricheskie kharakteristiki: Liudovik IX" in *Sochineniia*, pp. 264–276, especially pp. 272–274.
13 "Chetyre istoricheskie kharakteristiki: Aleksandr Velikii" in Granovskii, *Sochineniia*, pp. 250–264.

his imagination by the statue of Peter the Great on his charger in Pushkin's narrative poem "The Bronze Horseman."

Even Herzen, who from the early 1840s attached particular importance to individual liberty, succumbed to notions or ways of thinking that might be regarded as inconsistent to some degree with his libertarianism. I shall pursue this claim with reference to Herzen's writings in the early years of his emigration, 1847–1854, especially his cycle of essays *From the Other Shore* (the first Russian edition of which was published in 1855), since this work is usually taken as the classic exposition of Herzen's philosophy of history and his thinking on liberty.

HERZEN'S MAIN ARGUMENTS IN *FROM THE OTHER SHORE*

The first argument that Herzen advances in *From the Other Shore*, and the premise that underlies the cycle, is that the "old world" is dying. By the "old world" Herzen meant the "Catholic-feudal" civilization of western Europe (VI, p. 51) and the contemporary order that had arisen out of it, particularly in France, in which capitalism was the dominant economic system and the bourgeoisie the ascendant social force. Herzen's skeptic puts forward the idea in the opening pages of the dialogic essay with which the cycle begins, "Before the Storm." "The world in which we live," he says with an air of expectancy (VI, p. 22; Budberg, pp. 22–23):

is dying – that is the forms in which life manifests itself; no medicine will have any more effect on its decayed body. In order that the heirs may breathe freely, the body should be interred, but people insist on trying to cure it and delay its death. You must have known the numbing sadness, the lingering nervous uncertainty that pervades a house where someone is dying. Despair is fortified by hope, everyone's nerves are taut, the sounds grow sick, things are at a standstill. The death of the sick man lifts the burden from the souls of those who remain.[14]

The suppression of the Parisian insurrection in June 1848, on which Herzen reflected with dismay in the second essay of the cycle, "After the Storm," seems only to have strengthened his conviction that the old world was dying. The age in which Paris had served as the lodestar for other peoples, he writes, has now passed (VI, p. 47).

Time and again in *From the Other Shore*, Herzen buttressed his claim that contemporary European civilization was drawing to a close by alluding to the collapse of the Roman Empire a millennium and a half earlier. Rome, he

---

[14] In inset quotations from the cycle *From the Other Shore* I have used the translation by Moura Budberg in Alexander Herzen, *"From the Other Shore" and "The Russian People and Socialism,"* with an introduction by Isaiah Berlin (London: Weidenfeld and Nicolson, 1956).

argues, had been undermined initially by the early Christians, whom Herzen compares as a group whose time had arrived with the socialists of his own day (VI, pp. 31, 58, 137, 140–141), and then by the barbarian Germanic tribes, who foreshadowed the emerging Slav peoples. The fact that three of the eight essays in *From the Other Shore* bear a Latin title strengthens this analogy. The notion of the impending death of the old world, moreover, is quite in keeping with the taste of the Romantic age in which Herzen grew up for melancholy reflection on the loss of past grandeur. Gibbon, to whom Herzen refers in "Before the Storm" (VI, p. 38) and whose musings among the Roman ruins gave rise to his monumental late eighteenth-century history of the decline and fall of the Roman Empire, may have been inspirational in this respect.

The second major argument that Herzen advances in *From the Other Shore* is one against the notion that there is purpose or design in human life and history. He tries to demonstrate that life and history have no ultimate ends by having his idealist in "Before the Storm" repeatedly adopt a teleological position for his skeptic to refute. The idealist, pained by his social conscience, would like to be able to conceive of his generation (or rather the privileged members of it, as we shall see) as surveyors who are erecting the landmarks of a new world. He has faith in the future (or at least he would like to have it, but the skeptic is destroying it): some time after their death, the idealist hopes, the house for which they have cleared the ground will be built, and people will be comfortable in it. Without such a sense that the future belongs to them the lives of his generation would seem to have no meaning (VI, pp. 25–26). He cannot reconcile himself to the possibility that while in nature everything seems so purposive, human civilization emerges "as if by accident, drops out of life and fades away, leaving behind only a dim memory," or that history, as Shakespeare's Macbeth would have it, is a tale told by an idiot, signifying nothing (VI, p. 30).[15] The idealist therefore has to believe that in the last analysis there is a thread of "progress" running through all the changes and confusions of history, binding it into a single whole (VI, p. 33). Herzen's skeptic, on the other hand, sees no reason to believe that the future house will be built according to any plan laid down by previous generations (VI, p. 27). Life and history have no libretto. He prefers to think of human experience as an end attained rather than a means to something else. What, after all, is the purpose of the flower's ephemeral bloom and fragrance, or of the singer's song, other than people's pleasure in its notes as it is sung? The aim of each generation, then, is not to serve as a means to the attainment of the distant harmony that some future generation might enjoy, but to live its own life to the full (VI, pp. 31–36).

---

[15] Herzen's reference is to *Macbeth*, V, 5.

It follows from Herzen's argument against teleology (and this is the third of the arguments that I want to tease out of Herzen's cycle) that there is no historical inevitability. Humans have freedom, within certain limits, to affect the course of their history. Nothing in human affairs is predestined, his skeptical doctor avers (VI, p. 92). This resistance to the doctrine of historical inevitability is to some extent emotional. For Herzen's skeptics would find it intolerable to have to live with the knowledge that there was no history, only logic; or at least history, such as it was, would lose all interest for them (VI, p. 36). Again, if the ends that the idealist seeks were "a programme," "a command," something inevitable, then we should have to consider ourselves "puppets," "wheels in a machine," rather than "morally free beings" (VI, p. 33). However, Herzen's skeptic in "Before the Storm," besides objecting instinctively to teleology, does also believe that human beings, by exercising their wills, can lend "unexpected, dramatic dénouements and *coups de théâtre*" to history (VI, p. 32). History has "no frontiers, no itineraries," he contends; "all is improvization, all is will, all is *ex tempore*"; there is an "eternal challenge to the fighters to try their strength, to go where they will, where there is a road; and where there is none, genius will blast a path" (VI, p. 36).

It is true, as Herzen admitted through his authorial persona in a later essay in the cycle, "Omnia mea mecum porto" ("I Carry with Me All that is Mine"), that our conduct is strongly affected by factors outside our control, such as physiology, heredity, education, and attachment to our time and native place. Nonetheless we are freer than is commonly believed, he argues here: a large part of our destiny lies in our own hands (VI, pp. 118–120). And in the closing essay of the cycle, "Donoso Cortés, Marqués de Valdegamas, and Julian, Roman Emperor," he still took the view, even after the severe disappointments of 1848–1849, that history lacks "the strict, unalterable, predetermined quality" that Catholics and philosophers had attributed to it, but is affected by many variables, first and foremost the will and power of the individual (VI, p. 137). Herzen's anti-teleological argument, developed in *From the Other Shore* with great poetic power, represents a repudiation of the Hegelian view of history as an apparently inevitable spiral progression toward the realization of an Idea of which only a few individuals are conscious instruments.

Not all humans, however, have the capacity to affect the course of history (and here we come to a fourth argument in *From the Other Shore*), but only a small minority, a social, intellectual, and moral elite. Herzen drew a sharp distinction between the cultivated minority and the masses. Whilst minorities represent the conscious thought of an age, the masses, according to Herzen's skeptic in the fourth essay, "Vixerunt" ("They have lived") (VI, p. 80; Budberg, p. 92):

are elemental, they are oceanic, their path is the path of nature: they are her nearest heirs, they are led by dark instincts, unaccountable passions, they cling obstinately to what they have achieved, even if it is bad; hurled into motion, they sweep irresistibly with them or crush underfoot everything in their way, even if it is good . . . It is absurd to blame the people – they are right because they conform to the circumstances of their past life. They bear no responsibility for good or evil; they are facts, like good or bad harvests, like an oak tree, or a blade of grass.

A further skeptical character, the doctor in the fifth essay, "Consolatio," continues in a similar vein, doubting whether the "aspiration to freedom and independence" is as powerful a drive as hunger for most of humanity at most times. He accepts that "some strata of society, developed under peculiarly fortunate circumstances, have certain tendencies towards freedom," though not very strong ones. It is true that the existence of the educated minority (VI, pp. 95–96; Budberg, 110):

who soar triumphantly above the heads of others and from century to century hand down their thoughts and aspirations which the masses, teeming below, have nothing to do with, is a shining testimony to how far human nature can develop, what a tremendous fund of strength exceptional circumstances can call forth; but all this has nothing to do with the masses, with mankind. The beauty of an Arab horse, bred over twenty generations, does not give us the slightest right to expect the same qualities in all horses.

The fully developed independent person, then, represents "that excellence which everything that is free, gifted and strong is striving to achieve." The masses, on the other hand, are characterized by their impersonality (VI, p. 102). They "are indifferent to individual freedom, to freedom of speech," and they "love authority" (VI, p. 124).

Clearly the creator of *From the Other Shore* regarded himself as one of the "exceptional" individuals "for whom constraint is burdensome," not one of the majority whose yearning for freedom is weak, and "who gives a constant *démenti* to these martyrs" (VI, p. 94). One senses here, on the personal level, Herzen's overweening self-belief and also the elitist persona of the wealthy aristocrat. Herzen was after all a lord, or *barin*, who in 1847 urged his representative in Russia, while he still owned an estate there, to ensure that his serfs paid their dues on time so that he could fund his revolutionary tourism (XXIII, p. 44) and who later objected to his son's marriage to an Italian girl on the grounds that she was too plebeian.[16] On the intellectual plane, we glimpse the difficulty of reconciling the different sorts of liberation to which Herzen aspired: full

---

[16] E.H. Carr, *The Romantic Exiles: A Nineteenth-Century Portrait Gallery* (Harmondsworth: Peregrine Books, 1968; first published by Victor Gollancz, 1933), p. 237.

self-realization of the enlightened individual, on the one hand, and emancipation of the lower classes from economic servitude, on the other.

Unfortunately, the elite minority, who alone were potentially free and capable of self-development, all too compliantly and all too often surrendered their freedom. This they did (and here is Herzen's fifth main argument in *From the Other Shore*) by succumbing to values or doctrines that were no less oppressive in their way than authoritarian political regimes of the sort experienced at first hand by the Russian intelligentsia. It may be the historical disease of "idealism" (VI, p. 35) or the "dualism" afflicting human consciousness, Herzen believed, that causes people to enslave themselves. For "dualism" divides man into something ideal and something animal, posits a struggle between the conscience and the passions, and breeds a morality that requires of people "constant sacrifice, continuous exploit, continuous self-renunciation" (VI, p. 127). The fundamental errors of "contempt for the earth and the temporal" and "lack of respect for individuals and worship of the state" give rise to all those maxims like *salus populi suprema lex* ("the well-being of the people is the supreme law") that "have a terrible smell of burnt flesh, of blood, inquisition, torture, and in general *the triumph of order*" (VI, p. 140).

In the political sphere (and this point was particularly topical in 1848–1849) self-enslavement, Herzen believed, is a vice characteristic of liberals, whom he assails in *From the Other Shore* and also in his contemporaneous *Letters from France and Italy*, which consist of essays published over the period 1847–1854. The French liberals of 1848, for example, were deluded Don Quixotes who believed in things that could never come to be. They had foolishly sought to liberate others before liberating themselves, but in conceiving of a republic that is "an abstract and unrealizable notion," "the apotheosis of the existing state order," they merely clung to the dying world, of which their dream was the last "poetic delirium" (VI, p. 50). They created a new political religion, with the people as its idol, although the people as imagined by liberals were an *a priori* notion derived from things that have been read, characters dressed up "in a Roman toga or a shepherd's garb" (VI, p. 82). In general, human beings, including the would-be liberators of 1848, were prone in Herzen's eyes to accept conventional phrases which may appear "moral and good" but which in fact constrain their thinking and subjugate them (VI, p. 99). In thrall to ideology (though Herzen did not use this term), human beings sacrifice the individual, who is "the true, real monad of society," to "some general concept, some collective noun, some banner or other," "to society, the people, humanity, an idea" (VI, pp. 125–126).

Nevertheless (and this is the sixth and last of the arguments put forward in *From the Other Shore* that I want to identify) humans can and should liberate themselves from the irrational beliefs of the moribund "old world." In fact, paradoxical as it might seem, it is more important for humanity as a whole, Herzen contended, that free independent individuals should attempt to liberate themselves than that they should seek to liberate their fellow humans. For these individuals will be better able in due course to liberate others if they themselves have succeeded in jettisoning false values (VI, p. 119). Herzen compared the self-liberation that the elite should undertake to a voyage across an unknown ocean, like the voyage of discovery made by Christopher Columbus, a "genius" whose example Herzen invokes in the first and third essays of his cycle (VI, pp. 36, 51). The need for such a voyage is the most important point that Herzen wished to press upon his readers. Indeed the title of his cycle implies that the author, who appears to speak to his readers from the new world across the ocean, has already made it to the other shore.

However, to accomplish the crossing to the new world, it was not enough literally to emigrate, for North America was merely a neat emended edition of an old feudal-Christian text (VI, pp. 28, 68). Rather the free individual had to become a new type of personality. He (I say "he" because it is not obvious that Herzen envisaged women playing this role) had mercilessly to arraign all illusions before the tribunal of reason (VI, pp. 44–46). (Herzen deliberately deploys the imagery of revolutionary justice.) He had to discard all outmoded beliefs and call upon people "to execute institutions, destroy beliefs, take away reliance on the past, break prejudices, and make no concessions to any previous objects of worship or show them any mercy" (VI, p. 85). Herzen required his "new people" to be fearless seekers after truth and always to utter it, no matter how unpalatable it might be (VI, p. 100). It is doubtful, though, whether he considered his contemporaries, including erstwhile friends, capable of living up to such expectations. In his despondent "Epilogue 1849," the seventh essay of the cycle, he spoke with shame and pessimism about men of his generation, portraying them in terms that related them to the Russian literary type of the enervated "superfluous man," exemplified by the character Bel'tov in his own novel *Who Is To Blame?* (1845–1846) (VI, p. 109).

The difficulty confronting superfluous men living in such a transitional epoch is explored in more detail in "Omnia mea mecum porto." In periods when the forms of social life have become obsolete and are slowly perishing (VI, p. 121), the activity of free individuals, who by definition eschew the seductive ideologies of the age, may be modest and introspective. Such individuals will do well (so it now seemed to Herzen, after the failure of the revolutions of 1848) to follow the example of those Romans of the early Christian era who, faced with the demise of their world, "vanished from the scene completely" (VI, pp. 122–123; Budberg, 131–132):

They scattered along the shores of the Mediterranean Sea, disappeared for the others in the silent grandeur of their grief – but for themselves they did not disappear. And fifteen centuries later we must admit that they in fact were the conquerors, they the sole, the free, the powerful representatives of the independent human personality and dignity. They were *human beings*, they could not be counted like heads of cattle, they did not belong to the herd, and not wishing to lie, and having nothing in common with the herd – they withdrew. (original emphasis)[17]

By now Herzen's posture, far from being revolutionary, resembled that of the Stoic sage, who seeks inner tranquillity through cultivation of personal virtue, which is conceived partly in negative terms. Herzen wished not to quarrel with the world, not to do violence to others or to waste himself, but "to begin an independent, original life of [his] own [*samobytnuiu zhizn'*]." He strove to attain personal salvation even if (the thought is absurd, for Herzen appeared to intend no irony) the whole world around him were to perish (VI, p. 131).

LIMITATIONS OF HERZEN'S DEFENSE OF PERSONHOOD

In a farewell message of March 1, 1849 to his friends in Russia, which he embedded in his introduction to the first Russian edition of *From the Other Shore*, Herzen implicitly instructed readers to receive his cycle of essays as a defense of the free person. He had decided to remain in the West, he explained, in spite of the fact that he found no happiness, rest or even certain refuge there, because in the West there was free speech and it was taken for granted that the individual should be recognized (VI, p. 15). Russia had nothing similar, only "monstrous despotism from which there was no escape" (VI, p. 15; Budberg, 13):

With us the individual has always been crushed, absorbed, he has never even tried to emerge. Free speech with us has always been considered insolence, independence – subversion; man was engulfed in the State, dissolved in the community. The revolution of Peter the Great replaced the obsolete squirearchy of Russia with a European bureaucracy; everything that could be copied from the Swedish and German codes, everything that could be taken over from the free municipalities of Holland into our half-communal, half-absolutist country, was taken over; but the unwritten, the moral check on power, the instinctive recognition of the rights of man, of the rights of thought, of truth, could not be and were not imported.

Herzen's opposition to the Russian autocratic state and his rejection of the conservative interpretation of Hegel, according to which the state in a certain form is mankind's highest goal, make it plausible to argue that he was an

---

[17] I have slightly modified Budberg's translation.

advocate of "negative freedom" as defined by Isaiah Berlin in his well-known series of essays on the concept of liberty. Advocates of negative freedom, Berlin explained, are concerned with the question "How much am I governed?" and they "want to curb authority as such." Despotism, he contended, is "the kind of evil" against which the concept of negative liberty has usually been directed. Advocates of "positive freedom," on the other hand, are concerned with the question "By whom am I governed?" and seek to place power in their own hands. They envisage the "realization of the real self not so much in individual men" as through the supposed incarnation of the individual "in institutions, traditions, forms of life wider than the empirical spatio-temporal existence of the finite individual."[18] Therefore "positive freedom" may easily turn into an oppressive doctrine of the sort about which Herzen expressed apprehensions even before he wrote *From the Other Shore*, for example in his essay of 1843 on the concept of honour, where he rued the fact that the French Revolution, having taken the "inviolable sanctity of the individual" as its starting-point, had ended by subordinating the individual to the republic (II, p. 174).

Nonetheless we may wonder whether Herzen, as he expressed himself in the influential writings of the early years of his emigration, may be so easily accommodated within this model of types of liberty. It is questionable, for example, whether he altogether discarded the doctrine of historical inevitability, which Berlin considers essential to repudiate if we are truly to accord humans free will, moral responsibility, and dignity. In this connection a passage about Hegel and Marx in Berlin's essay on historical inevitability seems curiously applicable to Herzen too. "Great social forces are at work of which only the acutest and most gifted individuals are even aware," wrote Berlin, summarizing the Hegelian and Marxian positions:

From time to time the real forces – impersonal and irresistible – which truly govern the world develop to a point where a new historical advance is "due." Then (as both Hegel and Marx notoriously believed) the crucial moments of advance are reached; these take the form of violent, cataclysmic leaps, destructive revolutions which, often with fire and sword, establish a new order upon the ruins of the old. Inevitably the foolish, obsolete, purblind, home-made philosophies of the denizens of the old establishment are knocked over and swept away together with their possessors.[19]

When the cataclysmic moment arrives, Berlin wrote with Hegel and Marx still in mind, "the two great prophets of destruction are in their element; they enter into their inheritance; they survey the conflagration with a defiant, almost Byronic, irony and disdain. To be wise is to understand the direction in which

[18] I. Berlin, *Four Essays on Liberty* (Oxford University Press, 1969), pp. xliii, xlv–xlvi, 166.
[19] *Ibid.* pp. 60–61.

the world is inexorably moving, to identify oneself with the rising power which ushers in the new world."[20]

Precisely so, readers of *From the Other Shore* may feel. For although Herzen insisted that history has no ends, that the will of free human beings is a factor that helps to determine history's course, and that "ideals, theoretical constructions, never materialize in the form in which they float in our minds" (VI, p. 78), nevertheless at certain points he made the destruction of the current order seem historically inevitable. It is not just that in "Epilogue 1849" he invokes Vico's theory of ever-recurring historical motion, the "eternal play of life," as Herzen puts it, "pitiless as death, irresistible as birth, the *corsi e ricorsi* of history, the *perpetuum mobile* of the pendulum" (VI, p. 110). It is also that Herzen too, like Hegel, envisaged periodic cataclysmic struggles between old worlds, whose animating principles he thought he could identify, and new worlds, which he perceived as antitheses developing in the womb of the old. To him, it seemed beyond human power to prevent the resultant transformations. "Neither Metternich with his intellect, nor Cavaignac with his soldiers, nor the republicans with their lack of understanding," Herzen wrote in "Year LVII of the Republic," "can actually stop the stream, whose current is so sharply defined" (VI, p. 55). The collapse of the old world that he observed in the middle of the nineteenth century was but a stage in an ineluctable process: "the development of the middle class, a constitutional order," one of his voices declares, "are nothing but transitory forms linking the feudal-monarchic world with the social republican one" (VI, p. 60). Even after his arrival in England in 1852 he still struck a teleological note when it suited him. Nicholas I had acted instinctively, he wrote in 1854, at the time of the Crimean War, "for, ultimately, he too is the bearer of a *Destiny*: he continues, without understanding it, to fulfil the inner designs of history" (XII, p. 165). Thus Herzen seemed trapped between the rational claim central to his philosophy of history, that there was no necessity, and the emotional assertion, inspired by his yearning for individual liberty and social justice, that indeed there was necessity of a sort.[21]

We might also wonder whether Herzen's representations of the common people are always consistent with the demand that he expressed so powerfully in *From the Other Shore*, that the individual who aspires to freedom repudiate all the abstractions that humans are said to idealize and to which advocates of positive freedom have recourse. For the author who censured liberals for elevating the common people to the status of an idol was himself in the habit of illuminating the struggle that he perceived between the old and new worlds by contrasting with the mercenary western bourgeoisie his own idealized examples

---

[20] *Ibid.* pp. 61–62.   [21] This point, in essence, is made by Acton, *Alexander Herzen*, p. 36.

of certain social classes and races. Thus, in the *Letters from France and Italy* he portrayed French workers as models of peaceable sociality (V, p. 150) and Italian peasants as noble and graceful in appearance and demeanour (V, pp. 103, 108–109). He also repeatedly extolled the Slav character in these *Letters* and in his essays on "Russian socialism," in which he envisaged the possibility that Russia might follow a different path of economic and social development from that taken by the western nations (e.g., V, p. 74; VII, pp. 25, 68–69; XII, p. 154). Most strikingly, he characterized the Russian peasant as a being of handsome countenance and lively mind (VI, pp. 162–163), strong, vivacious, beautiful in a virile way (VI, p. 172), refreshingly averse to private property and legal contracts, and endowed instead with collectivist instincts that found expression in the rural commune, the *obshchina* or *mir* (V, p. 14; VI, p. 173; VII, pp. 10, 286–287). Turgenev, a more consistently liberal Westernizer, took Herzen to task for the Slavophilic complexion of these views and even for what seemed to him a continuing Germanic mode of thought: Herzen still thought in abstractions, doing obeisance to the Russian sheepskin coat, as Turgenev unkindly put it in a letter of 1862.[22]

It is also worth noting that while he described freedom of the individual as that greatest thing of all, the cornerstone of self-respect and the only thing on which "the real will of the people" could grow (VI, p. 14), Herzen did not hold up for emulation any contemporary western European institutions which might have helped to protect it. He did not see any necessary connection, for example, between individual liberty and parliamentary democracy, however broad the franchise. On the contrary, in the early years of his emigration he mounted a bitter assault on democracy, as well as on liberals who prized it. Even the National Constituent Assembly elected in France in April 1848 by universal manhood suffrage seemed to Herzen indefensible per se, because it did not implement policies of which he approved (VI, p. 47). In any case, political representation in general, Herzen believed, was "a cunning device" by means of which the bourgeoisie sought "to transmute social needs and a readiness to take energetic action into words and endless arguments" (VI, p. 74). In a still broader historical perspective, democracy, as viewed by Herzen's skeptic in "Vixerunt," is an ephemeral political phenomenon, a "purifying flame which will burn up all the obsolete forms and will of course die down when all is consumed." It "can create nothing" and "will become meaningless after the death of its last enemy." It stands "on the Christian shore" from which Herzen intended to set sail and had no place in his brighter future (VI, pp. 77–78).

---

[22] Letter of September 26, 1862 (New Style) in Turgenev, *Polnoe sobranie sochinenii i pisem. Pis'ma*, vol. 5, pp. 51–52.

Nor does democracy fare any better in Herzen's *Letters from France and Italy*. The French Constituent Assembly was pusillanimous, a bordello, a second-hand market, he scoffed here (V, pp. 135, 137). The Provisional Government would have done better, he mused, to postpone elections until socialists had had sufficient time "to prepare the people somewhat, especially the peasants," who might then have voted differently (V, p. 163). Or better still, it could have invested itself with dictatorial powers, like the Jacobin Committee of Public Safety of 1793–1794, whose "faith and energy" Herzen admired (V, p. 159). (Elsewhere Herzen endorsed the view of the Decembrist Pavel Pestel', that Russia should be ruled by a revolutionary dictatorship for at least a decade (XIII, p. 133).) In private correspondence Herzen was even more forthright on the subject of democracy: universal suffrage, he told the liberal Westernizers from whom he was growing apart in 1848, was "the last vulgar commonplace of the formal political world"; it had "enfranchized the orang-utans," who made up "four-fifths of France as a whole and four-and-three-quarter-fifths of Europe as a whole" (XXIII, p. 111). Such sentiments may be partly explained by a belief that, as Herzen expressed it later, democracy and republican government would not suffice to ensure liberty and independence if a people were not mature enough for them (XIV, p. 9), but no doubt they were also due in large measure to the elitism in Herzen's thought, his aristocratic disdain for the bourgeoisie and the masses. In any event it is plain that the question asked by advocates of positive liberty "By whom am I governed?" could sometimes take precedence for Herzen over the question posed by advocates of negative liberty, "How much am I governed?"

It is true that Herzen's skeptical attitude toward democracy was not exceptional among western thinkers in his time and that in this respect, as in others, he resembled one of the classical nineteenth-century champions of negative liberty, John Stuart Mill, whose famous essay on the subject Herzen himself invoked in this connection.[23] His attitude toward temporal law and its application, though, raises further doubts as to whether he concerned himself sufficiently with means of protecting individuals' rights. One might expect Russian thinkers living under a regime characterized (as they often lamented) by *proizvol*, the arbitrariness of autocracy and its officialdom, to have been attracted by the notion of law as a general norm that was applied without caprice or discrimination. And yet Herzen took a distinctly relativistic view of the application of laws. He looked with equanimity, for example, on the lawlessness of the Parisian populace when it broke into the Constituent Assembly on May 15, 1848. The

---

[23] On Herzen's affinity with Mill, see Aileen Kelly, "Historical Diffidence: A New Look at an Old Russian Debate," *Common Knowledge* 8, no. 3 (2002), 496–515, especially 507–509.

assembly had been properly elected in a formal sense, Herzen conceded in the *Letters from France and Italy*; but when the people ceased, just three weeks after the election in which they had taken part, to regard this representative body as legitimate, he claimed that there was another "higher justice" on their side, irrespective of their guilt in law (V, pp. 172–173).

Moreover, his standard for judging the legitimacy of the use of force by governments plainly varied with historical circumstances and from tribunal to tribunal and victim to victim. While in the *Letters* he deplored the reactionary "terror" during the June Days of 1848, as he also did in *From the Other Shore* (VI, pp. 40–48), he took a comparatively benign view of the terror unleashed in 1793 by the Committee of Public Safety. "The terror of '93," he wrote:

never went so far as the terror now . . . Many heads fell on the guillotine, many innocent ones, there is no doubt of that, we know them by name. But whom did they shoot [in 1848] . . . Who passed judgment on these people, who pronounced them guilty, and what was the need for these bloody crimes? Why the secrecy, why were the people robbed of their right to know their martyrs? Did the Committee of Public Safety conceal its measures? The slaughter of the September Days took place in broad daylight, and the lists were examined quite attentively . . . But who examined the lists for these executions [in 1848] at dead of night, and who produced them? Who dared to take upon himself such a bloody responsibility? . . . The will of the bourgeoisie – there's the culprit. No, my worthy petty bourgeois, enough talk of the *red* republic [i.e., the period of the National Convention and Jacobin dictatorship] and of bloodthirstiness; when it shed blood it believed it was impossible to do otherwise, doomed itself to this tragic fate and cut off heads with a clear conscience, whereas you just took vengeance, took vengeance meanly, safely, on the quiet.

In comparison to 1848, the terror of 1793 was, Herzen concludes in a memorable phrase, "majestic in its somber relentlessness" (V, pp. 154–155; see also 185–186).

The Jacobins, then, as Herzen portrays them here, are to be applauded for the transparency of their decision-making, their proper scrutiny of the death sentences that they meted out, and their courageous assumption of a heavy responsibility that they could not shirk. It is hard to reconcile this perception of the Jacobin terror with the sympathy that Herzen expresses in *From the Other Shore* for the victims of Moloch, the false god who mocks the multitudes sacrificed to him with the assurance "that after their death things will be beautiful on earth" (VI, p. 34).

CONCLUSION

Herzen is a figure of great importance in the history of Russian thought. He left a rich legacy for later thinkers to consider, especially in the essays that he wrote in the early years after his arrival in the West. His "new people," capable of liberating humans from their mental shackles and regenerating society, were reborn as rational egoists in Nikolai Chernyshevskii's novel, *What Is To Be Done?* (1863), as members of the "critically thinking minority" in Pëtr Lavrov's *Historical Letters* (1868), and, in different incarnations again, as the questing heroes and antiheroes of Dostoevskii's fiction. In his writings on "Russian socialism" he laid the foundations for the revolutionary populism of the 1870s. Most importantly from our present point of view, Herzen insisted on the importance of freedoms of conscience, association, and expression in a civilized society and deplored the sacrifice of individual human beings for the sake of some imagined higher purpose. He is a leading early exponent of the tradition of skeptical humanism that is identified in this volume as one of the elements in the Russian philosophical paradigm, an element that may be set against the tradition of utopian speculation about universal salvation. For these reasons he was inspirational not only to later pre-revolutionary thinkers but also to thinkers trying to come to terms in the early Soviet years with Bolshevik totalitarianism.

And yet alongside this libertarian thinker, who is generally admired in western (especially British) scholarship for his "remarkably prescient insights into the self-deceptions of self-confident ideological thought,"[24] there is a socialist thinker who occupied a prominent position in the Soviet pantheon. This latter Herzen, from whom the "poor heroic" Parisian workers will hear no reproach (V, p. 153), conceived of the Russian peasantry as a Rousseauesque abstraction and commended their commune (in which it is hard to believe the individual would have primacy) as a model for a collectivist utopia. He was a critic of the *laissez-faire* economic attitudes that in western societies were associated with the extension of personal and political rights. He persistently predicted that western civilization was about to die and devoutly wished that it would. He tended, in the crucial works on which I have focused in this chapter, to undermine rather than to promote respect among his compatriots for such notions as parliamentary democracy, the rule of law, and contractual exchange. He declined unequivocally to condemn revolutionary violence or to advertise the benefits of political stability. Indeed it is arguable, finally, that his attack on liberalism, which reverberates in later Russian radical thought, helped to weaken the Russian branch of a political current whose representatives were themselves concerned to promote the very liberties and respect for human dignity that Herzen so eloquently advocated.

[24] *Ibid.* 498.

3

MATERIALISM AND THE RADICAL
INTELLIGENTSIA: THE 1860S

VICTORIA S. FREDE

Materialism, or the philosophical proposition that the world consists entirely of matter, has existed since the ancient Greeks. The implications of this proposition, however, have changed considerably over time. In Russia in the late 1850s and early 1860s, radicals were principally interested in the consequences of materialism for theories of the way the mind operates. Contradicting Christian conceptions, they argued that there is no such thing as an immortal soul, responsible for all thoughts and decisions and capable of exercising free will. Nor, they claimed, are there any innate ideas. All thoughts are the results of sensory stimuli, formed into perceptions and ideas inside an entirely material mind.

These assertions were based on scientific theories that were still controversial in the mid-nineteenth century. Even so, Russian radical journalists elevated materialism to the status of a worldview that contained the answers to the country's most pressing political and social problems. The sweeping nature of their claims led the conservative critic Mikhail Katkov (1818–1887) to denounce materialism as a new "religion" in 1861, a view famously repeated by the philosopher Nikolai Berdiaev in the early twentieth century.[1]

From 1858, the two leading radical journals, *The Contemporary* and *The Russian Word*, became synonymous with materialism. It was not long, however, before some radical writers began to voice significant doubts about their religion. Indeed, materialism's postulates were never entirely stable. Articles by its most famous representatives, Nikolai Chernyshevskii (1828–1889), Nikolai Dobroliubov (1836–1861), Maksim Antonovich (1835–1919), and Dmitrii Pisarev (1840–1868), had an experimental quality and were not free of contradictions. These journalists were (sometimes ineptly) trying to settle highly

---

[1] [M.N. Katkov], "Starye bogi i novye bogi," *Russkii vestnik* 31 (1861), 891–904; N.A. Berdiaev, "Filosofskaia istina i intelligentskaia pravda" in *Vekhi. Intelligentsiia v Rossii* (Moscow: Molodaia gvardiia, 1991), pp. 24–42, here pp. 32–33.

complex philosophical questions.[2] Fearless as they were in attacking their liberal and conservative opponents, they were just as frequently on the defensive, testing new ground as they attempted to refute criticisms that had been leveled at them. One of the thorniest objections they faced was their failure to take into account the principle of human dignity. This was a problem materialists were not successfully able to resolve.

MATERIALISM IN THE ERA OF REFORMS

In the mid-nineteenth century, materialism emerged in tandem with recent discoveries in the natural sciences: physics, chemistry, geology, and biology. Physiology was of special interest, as research conducted in France and Germany during the 1830s transformed the way the operation of the nervous system and brain was understood. In Germany of the 1840s and 1850s three talented writers, all trained as natural scientists, stepped forward to popularize new discoveries: Carl Vogt (1817–1895), Jacob Moleschott (1822–1893), and Ludwig Büchner (1824–1899). They did more than just summarize the latest research, however, but used it to advance political, social, and religious claims.

Their most famous slogan was "Keine Kraft ohne Stoff": no force without matter, a statement that held sharply anti-Christian implications.[3] God and the immortal soul could be excluded from scientific studies. Vogt, Moleschott, and Büchner found philosophical grounds for their anti-religious zeal in *The Essence of Christianity* (1841) and *Lectures on the Essence of Religion* (1848), by the Left Hegelian philosopher Ludwig Feuerbach (1804–1872).[4] Religions, according to Feuerbach, were the inventions of primitive societies. Ignorance had led people to explain incomprehensible features of the natural world by attributing them to fictitious deities. They eagerly dedicated themselves to carrying out their gods' wishes, but forgot to take care of their own needs. Denigrating themselves, they projected their best attributes onto their gods. Humanity must now learn to see the "divine" in human nature and commit itself to living in accordance with

[2] Evgenii Lampert found Chernyshevskii's views contradictory and poorly thought through: for example, he never defined what he meant by "matter." E. Lampert, *Sons Against Fathers: Studies in Russian Radicalism and Revolution* (Oxford: Clarendon Press, 1965), p. 144. Similar accusations were leveled against the German materialists of the nineteenth century by Friedrich Albert Lange, *Geschichte des Materialismus und Kritik seiner Bedeutung in der Gegenwart*, 8th edn., 2 vols. (Leipzig, 1908), vol. 2, pp. 89–105, especially pp. 98–101.

[3] Ludwig Büchner, *Kraft und Stoff. Empirisch-naturphilosophische Studien* (Frankfurt am Main, 1855), p. 2. Like many of their slogans, this one circulated among the three: Moleschott and Vogt used it as well.

[4] Feuerbach did not consider himself a strict materialist. See Hermann Braun, "Materialismus-Idealismus" in Otto Brunner (ed.), *Geschichtliche Grundbegriffe: Historisches Lexicon*, 8 vols. (Stuttgart: Klett-Cotta, 1972–1997), vol. 3, pp. 977–1019, here pp. 1002–1003.

that nature. To Vogt, Moleschott, and Büchner, the study of physiology became a means of rehabilitating the "dignity of matter."[5]

There was a political agenda behind the materialists' provocative advocacy of atheism: all three were opponents of monarchy. Moleschott and Büchner sympathized with the republicanism of the 1848 revolutions, while Vogt directly participated in them. Their attacks on religion were intended to facilitate a future revolution by undermining the religious ideology on which conservative German states based their power.[6] But the three also had an egalitarian social agenda. Physiology could prove the innate equality of human beings by showing that disparities in intelligence and physical strength were merely the result of unequal material circumstances and education. They could be eradicated through a more even distribution of goods. By making new discoveries available to "the German people," Moleschott, Vogt, and Büchner sought to disseminate science more equally.[7] Needless to say, their writings met significant resistance among natural scientists, philosophers, and clergymen. Disputes came to a head in 1854 during the so-called *Materialistenstreit*, in which it became almost impossible to distinguish political and religious arguments from ones that were scientific or philosophical.[8]

Conservatives in Russia were well aware how powerful this blend of science and politics could be. When revolutions broke out abroad in 1848, Nicholas I responded by tightening censorship at home and banning the instruction of philosophy at universities. After 1850, only clerics at seminaries and theological academies were permitted to teach subjects like logic and psychology.[9] As a result, idealism was formally defended only by philosophers trained at theological academies, who came from a clerical background. Nicholas I's censorship may have delayed the arrival of the new materialism into Russia, but it probably radicalized the terms of the debate when materialism did arrive. Idealism's association with the church would later make it an easier target for proponents of materialism like Chernyshevskii.

The conservatism of Nicholas I's regime was discredited by Russia's humiliating defeat in the Crimean War (1854–1856). When Alexander II came to power, he was forced, *nolens volens*, to commit himself to sweeping reforms, including the long-awaited peasant emancipation, promulgated in 1861. He

---

[5] Büchner, *Kraft und Stoff*, p. 25.
[6] Frederick Gregory, *Scientific Materialism in Nineteenth-Century Germany* (Dordrecht: D. Reidel, 1977), p. 1.
[7] Gregory, *Scientific Materialism*, pp. 88, 71.
[8] Braun, "Materialismus-Idealismus," pp. 1008–1011; Gregory, *Scientific Materialism*, pp. 29–48.
[9] Nicholas V. Riasanovsky, *Nicholas I and Official Nationality in Russia, 1825–1855* (Berkeley, CA: University of California Press, 1959), pp. 218–219.

also relaxed censorship, making the late 1850s and early 1860s golden years for the Russian press. Despite his displays of liberalism, however, Alexander II remained committed to autocracy and firm social hierarchy and made no less use of Orthodox ritual than his father had.[10] His vacillations helped give rise to radicalism, as some educated Russians became convinced that far-reaching change in Russia would not come from above.

Radicals were also troubled by Russia's persistently rigid social stratification.[11] Nikolai Chernyshevskii, a priest's son from Saratov, sensed this keenly in the 1840s and 1850s as he moved to St. Petersburg and attempted to establish himself in the nobility-dominated world of journalism. He suffered from his lack of social refinement, and his noble colleagues at *The Contemporary* did little to allay his fears; privately, they referred to him as "that bedbug-stinking gentleman."[12] This was not unrequited disdain. Chernyshevskii, together with his younger colleagues (and fellow seminarians) Dobroliubov and Antonovich, no doubt returned the noblemen's scorn with the same ardor.[13]

In this strained atmosphere, the arrival of German materialism was well timed. Educated Russians had been watching scientific developments in western Europe closely since the 1840s, when thick journals like *The Contemporary* began to publish large numbers of translations of the latest in popular science.[14] Now, in the 1850s, science promised to vindicate the "seminarians'" demands for respect, providing them with a seemingly objective basis for their defense of human equality.

BODY, MIND, AND FREE WILL

Materialism also helped Chernyshevskii and his followers establish grounds for a new system of morality outside of Christian ethics, one which could in turn be used to justify sweeping social reforms. All this hinged on an argument over the relationship between mind and body: individuals' actions were regulated from

---

[10] Richard S. Wortman, *Scenarios of Power: Myth and Ceremony in Russian Monarchy*, 2 vols. (Princeton University Press, 1995, 2000), vol. 2, pp. 19–91.

[11] On the limitations of social mobility for educated Russians, see Daniel Brower, *Training the Nihilists: Education and Radicalism in Tsarist Russia* (Ithaca, NY: Cornell University Press, 1975), pp. 51–68, especially p. 56.

[12] Irina Paperno, *Chernyshevsky and the Age of Realism: A Study in the Semiotics of Behavior* (Stanford University Press, 1988), p. 77.

[13] Laurie Manchester argues that enmity toward the nobility helped cement the "collective identity" of priests' sons. Laurie Manchester, *Holy Fathers, Secular Sons: Clergy, Intelligentsia, and the Modern Self in Revolutionary Russia* (DeKalb, IL: Northern Illinois University Press, 2008), pp. 38–67.

[14] Alexander Vucinich, *Science in Russian Culture*, 2 vols. (Stanford University Press, 1963, 1970), vol. 1, pp. 348–349, 371, 379.

within by an instinctual, physical understanding of what was good for them, not by a soul that recognized good and evil by virtue of its connection to God.

The debate about the relationship between body and mind has always tended to center on two positions. Ideas may be formed in an immaterial soul; or, as materialists insist, they are produced by the body ("matter"). In the nineteenth century, discoveries about the operation of the nervous system and brain gave materialists new confidence. Moleschott, Vogt, and Büchner used them to back up their slogan, "no force without matter." Thoughts are caused, directly or indirectly, by physical stimuli conveyed by the nerves and processed by the brain. The extrasensory has no place in explanations of the functioning of the mind, and the notion of an immaterial soul can be dismissed as invalid. From this vantage point, Moleschott, Vogt, and Büchner also rejected the Christian doctrine of free will. There is no higher instance in the mind that regulates its operations. Thought processes are entirely subject to natural laws that determine their outcome. An individual's mental habits are largely the product of upbringing; moods and dispositions are attributable to environmental and nutritional influences on brain chemistry. The materialists did not deny that people have will, but maintained that its exercise is entirely determined by environment and circumstances.[15]

Nikolai Dobroliubov first brought these views to the Russian reading public in the pages of *The Contemporary* from February to May 1858. Drawing on the work of Moleschott, he argued that there can be no "spirit" without "material attributes," no thoughts, ideas, impulses, or memories that do not involve some activity of the brain and nervous system. A properly functioning mind depends on a healthy brain. Education and upbringing play a part in mental function: the content of a person's thoughts depends on impressions he or she receives from early childhood on. Together, physical health and upbringing determine whether those thoughts and feelings tend toward the bad or the good.[16] Dobroliubov claimed that there is no such thing as an immortal soul or a free will. The impulse to act comes from the body, more specifically, from the brain and the nerves, which always guide the person to pursue pleasant sensations.[17] Religious beliefs and experiences, even the sensation

---

[15] Carl Vogt, *Bilder aus dem Thierleben* (Frankfurt am Main, 1852), pp. 422–452; Jacob Moleschott, *Der Kreislauf des Lebens. Physiologische Antworten auf Liebig's Chemische Briefe* (Mainz, 1852), pp. 403–434; Büchner, *Kraft und Stoff*, pp. 251–258.

[16] N.A. Dobroliubov, "Organicheskoe razvitie cheloveka v sviazi s ego umstvennoi i nravstvennoi deiatel'nost'iu" in *Polnoe sobranie sochinenii* (*PSS*), 6 vols. (Leningrad: GIKhL, 1934–1941), vol. 3, pp. 90–113, here pp. 95, 102–104, 109. Compare Moleschott, *Der Kreislauf des Lebens*, pp. 364, 370–373.

[17] N.A. Dobroliubov, "Fiziologichesko-psikhologicheskii sravntitel'nyi vzgliad na nachalo i konets zhizni" in *PSS*, vol. 3, pp. 342–349, here p. 345; "Organicheskoe razvitie," pp. 110–111.

of communing with God, are nothing but the combined product of external influences: culture, geography, physical health, nourishment.[18]

Summarized in this way, Dobroliubov's views would have been too radical to publish.[19] This may be why he left it to his mentor, Chernyshevskii, to expound the social and ethical implications of the new materialist theories. Chernyshevskii had been skeptical of the principle of free will ever since his student days.[20] He began to challenge this and other Christian notions of morality in his essay "Russian Man at a *Rendez-Vous*" (1858).[21] Two years later he more fully elaborated his ideas in one of his best-known works, "The Anthropological Principle in Philosophy," published anonymously in *The Contemporary*.

The article was framed as an attack on Pëtr Lavrov (1823–1900), a liberal, member of the nobility, and perfect target for Chernyshevskii. Lavrov later became famous as a populist, but at the time he was mainly known for his philosophical erudition and eclecticism. His article "Notes on Questions of Practical Philosophy" (1859) provoked Chernyshevskii by taking a cautiously idealist position. Lavrov emphasized the importance of "dignity," arguing that it is the product of ethical self-awareness. Every person, Lavrov claimed, has an inner being, or self, which consists of two parts. One is the "real" self, the sum of a person's impulses, feelings, wishes, and moods. The other is the "ideal" self, which serves to master the changing impulses of the real self, judging them in accordance with the person's fixed norms of dignity. Dignity, then, consists in an ethical decision-making process. It is neither subject to the body nor mind alone, but to the will.[22]

In "The Anthropological Principle in Philosophy,"[23] Chernyshevskii countered that the notion of two selves, and indeed any distinction between mind, body, and will, is nonsensical. People's decisions are the result of a chain of thought responses and as such are subject to the laws of cause and effect. Mind and body are not separate, but governed by the same "law," presumably a natural one.[24] And thoughts are nothing but the product of sensations and impressions,

---

[18] N.A. Dobroliubov, "Zhizn' Magometa," *PSS*, vol. 3, pp. 334–339, here pp. 337–338.

[19] He claimed, improbably, that his views on the soul were "compatible with the higher Christian view." Dobroliubov, "Organicheskoe razvitie," p. 96.

[20] Paperno, *Chernyshevsky*, p. 108.

[21] Chernyshevskii, too, was forced to make some concessions to censorship: "Russian Man at a *Rendez-Vous*" was not published in *The Contemporary*, but in the more obscure *Athenaeum* (*Atenei*). N.G. Chernyshevskii, "Russkii chelovek na rendez-vous," *Polnoe sobranie sochinenii* (*PSS*), 16 vols. (Moscow: GIKhL, 1939–1953), vol. 5, pp. 156–174.

[22] P.L. Lavrov, "Ocherki voprosov prakticheskoi filosofii" in I.S. Knizhnik-Vetrov (ed.), *Filosofiia i sotsiologiia. Izbrannye proizvedeniia*, 2 vols. (Moscow: Mysl', 1965), vol. 1, pp. 339–461, here pp. 377–381, 384.

[23] N.G. Chernyshevskii, "Antropologicheskii printsip v filosofii" in *PSS*, vol. 7, pp. 222–295.

[24] *Ibid.* pp. 240, 283, 293.

gathered and formulated through the nervous system.[25] They are not arbitrary, nor can they be understood as the result of a will that stands above or outside of a chain of thought.[26]

Three points seemed especially important to Chernyshevskii as he formulated the ethical consequences of rejecting free will in "Russian Man at a *Rendez-Vous*" and "The Anthropological Principle in Philosophy." All three points corresponded closely to the theories of the German materialists Büchner, Moleschott, and Vogt. One was that materialist physiology effaced the notion of innate mental and moral differences between people. All human beings are innately the same. Circumstances and environment dictate what they become as adults. In this regard members of the nobility were at a particular disadvantage: their upbringing not only conditioned them to look down on members of lower orders, but prepared them only for flaccid inactivity as adults. By nature, however, all people are equal, even if there are undoubtedly better or worse adults.[27]

A second point made by Chernyshevskii was that the rejection of free will undermines good and evil as absolute categories. According to Chernyshevskii (and Büchner), these categories are not fixed but extremely unstable concepts, often applied by people in contradictory ways to a wide range of behaviors.[28] Consistency can only be introduced by making these categories measures of judgment about the utility of actions.[29] To determine the utility of an action, in turn, one must judge the extent to which it fulfills human needs: the needs of the individual, a given community, or humanity at large. The greater the number of people who benefit, the better the action is.[30] Chernyshevskii hoped that these calculations would permit mathematical precision in resolving ethical questions and thus free people from having to rely on Christian ethical values.

Thirdly, according to Chernyshevskii, the materialist denial of free will legitimated social reform while undermining the principle of individual moral and

---

[25] *Ibid.* pp. 277–280.   [26] *Ibid.* pp. 260–261.

[27] Chernyshevskii, "Russkii chelovek," pp. 164, 165, 168, 170–171; "Antropologicheskii printsip," pp. 264, 274.

[28] Chernyshevskii, "Antropologicheskii printsip," pp. 260, 256. Compare Büchner, *Kraft und Stoff*, pp. 245–246, 248.

[29] This is why Chernyshevskii posits the pursuit of pleasure and avoidance of pain as the primary motivating factor in all human action and calls this "egoism." Chernyshevskii, "Antropologicheskii printsip," pp. 282–285. A comparable passage, including the word "egoist," can be found in Büchner, *Kraft und Stoff*, p. 249. For an overview of Chernyshevskii's "rational egoism," see N.G.O. Pereira, *The Thought and Teachings of N.G. Černyševskij* (The Hague: Mouton, 1975), pp. 35–39.

[30] Chernyshevskii, "Antropologicheskii printsip," pp. 286–287. Compare Moleschott, *Der Kreislauf des Lebens*, pp. 427–428.

legal culpability. If all decisions result from thought processes over which people have little or no control, then they cannot be held accountable for their
actions.[31] Indeed, it is hypocritical for one person to condemn another for
harmful behavior. Since human beings are physiologically the same, and all
respond to circumstances in the same way, the judge would behave no differently than the judged under the same conditions.[32] Moral condemnation is in
any case misplaced: society and material circumstance are the cause of harmful behavior, not the individual. If society is to reduce harmful behavior, it
must change the circumstances in which people live.[33] To Chernyshevskii, the
most pressing priority was to abolish the grossest manifestation of inequality in
Russia – serfdom.[34]

In sum, Chernyshevskii sought to rule out free will because he wanted
to make ethical and social deliberation less arbitrary and less personal. Harmful
behavior is not the result of an individual's free choice to do wrong. If bureaucrats
are corrupt and peasants violent, it is because upbringing and environment
induce them to act this way. Likewise, helpful behavior cannot be attributed to
an individual's free choice to do good. If journalists like Chernyshevskii called
for social reform, they did so as a result of their upbringing and environment,
which left them in a better position to understand their true interests.

IURKEVICH'S FIRST CRITIQUE AND ANTONOVICH'S RESPONSE

Chernyshevskii's views were roundly attacked, in fiction, philosophy, and literary criticism. Philosophically, his most formidable adversary was another priest's
son only one and a half years his senior: Pamfil Iurkevich (1827–1874), professor
at the Kiev Theological Academy. In 1860, Iurkevich published "The Science of
the Human Spirit," a refutation of materialism, in *Studies of the Kiev Theological*

---

[31] Vogt, *Bilder aus dem Thierleben*, pp. 445–446; Büchner, *Kraft und Stoff*, pp. 250, 256–257; Moleschott,
Der Kreislauf des Lebens, pp. 428–429. Not everyone who looked for the origin of thought in physio-
logical processes believed that this cancelled out moral liability. See Monika Ritzer, "Physiologische
Anthropologien. Zur Relation von Philosophie und Naturwissenschaft um 1850" in Andreas Arndt
and Walter Jaeschke (eds.), *Materialismus und Spiritualismus. Philosophie und Wissenschaften nach 1848*
(Hamburg: Felix Meiner, 2000), pp. 113–140, here pp. 121–124.

[32] Chernyshevskii, "Russkii chelovek," pp. 164–166.

[33] Chernyshevskii, "Antropologicheskii printsip," pp. 265–266; "Russkii chelovek," pp. 165–166.
In the latter passage, Chernyshevskii admitted that some acts of violence (a tiny minority) were
egregious and could not be accounted for by material circumstance alone.

[34] Chernyshevskii, "Russkii chelovek," pp. 172–174. He did not explicitly mention emancipation in
these pages (journals were forbidden to discuss it in any detail at this time), but contemporaries and
scholars read them this way. See A.I. Batiuto, "Turgenev, Chernyshevskii, Dobroliubov, Annenkov"
in *Izbrannye trudy* (St. Petersburg: Nestor-Istoriia, 2004), pp. 712–759, here p. 721.

Academy.[35] The article, which combined philosophical idealism with Orthodox Christian theology, sharply criticized Chernyshevskii's "Anthropological Principle in Philosophy." The conservative critic Mikhail Katkov was so pleased by the article that he republished it in 1861 in his widely-read journal, *The Russian Herald.* Iurkevich was further rewarded that year by being promoted to a professorship in philosophy at Moscow University.

Iurkevich began from an idealist perspective by critiquing Chernyshevskii's materialist claim that thoughts are produced by matter. This proposition could not be proven by natural science, because ideas are not tied to sensory experience; no physiologist and no microscope will ever demonstrate that nerves and the brain beget ideas. Ideas are only subject to the kind of internal observation conducted by psychologists and philosophers.[36] Further, perceptions can only be explained by taking into account the individual self that perceives them, and this self can make choices about how and what to perceive.[37] Materialism, by contrast, denies the individual the freedom to determine his or her own thoughts.

Chernyshevskii dismissed Iurkevich's review out of hand,[38] but his protégés Antonovich and Dobroliubov responded to it in some detail. Maksim Antonovich, one of the youngest of the *popovichi* at *The Contemporary,* had always been interested in natural science. Having graduated from the St. Petersburg Theological Academy (in 1861), he was also in a very good position to appreciate the theological and philosophical foundations of Iurkevich's views. (Both Chernyshevskii and Dobroliubov had ended their theological education at the seminary level.) In 1861 and 1862, Antonovich published three articles refuting idealism in *The Contemporary.* He first focused on Lavrov, but his main targets were Iurkevich and other philosophers trained at Russia's theological academies.[39] Antonovich had no patience with their attempts to integrate idealist philosophy with Orthodox Christian teachings on the soul, which resulted, he claimed, only in obscure and "unnatural" theories of the operation of the mind.[40]

---

[35] P.D. Iurkevich, "Iz nauki o chelovecheskom dukhe" in A.I. Abramov and I.V. Borisova (eds.), *Filosofskie proizvedeniia* (Moscow: Pravda, 1990), pp. 104–192.

[36] *Ibid.* pp. 110–112, 115.   [37] *Ibid.* pp. 128, 131.

[38] N.G. Chernyshevskii, "Polemicheskie krasoty" in *PSS,* vol. 7, pp. 707–774, here pp. 725–726, 762–763, 769–773.

[39] Specifically, S.S. Gogotskii, graduate of the Kiev Theological Academy and teacher at Kiev University, and V.N. Karpov, graduate of the Kiev Theological Academy and teacher at the St. Petersburg Theological Academy.

[40] M.A. Antonovich, "Sovremennaia filosofiia," *Sovremennik* 85 (1861), 249–280, here 261–262, 268–269; "Dva tipa sovremennykh filosofov" in V.S. Kruzhkov (ed.), *Izbrannye filosofskie sochineniia* (Moscow: OGIZ, 1945), pp. 18–91, here pp. 23–29.

Antonovich further displayed the weakness of quasi-idealist Christianity by highlighting the strength of physiological accounts of mental phenomena. He detailed the process by which the nervous system transfers sensory stimuli to the brain to form impressions and ideas. When such impressions accumulate, they eventually give rise to more abstract ideas, knowledge, and consciousness. The entire process is "purely material," a point Antonovich did not tire of emphasizing. The nervous system acts as a "conductor," and the transformation of impressions to ideas is "purely mechanical." It is thus "involuntary," taking place by "physiological necessity." There is no part of the mind that observes the thought process as if from outside and assents to or denies the impact of impressions on it. Instead, ideas develop "freely," as if by themselves.[41] Here, Antonovich went considerably further than Chernyshevskii. While denying free will, Chernyshevskii continued to speak of a will actively intervening in a person's thought processes.[42] Antonovich, by contrast, described thought processes in the passive voice and tended to use organic metaphors, arguing that individuals have little ability to intervene in the formation of their own ideas.[43] He used some lurid examples to prove that seemingly voluntary, goal-oriented actions do not depend on the brain, much less on the soul, and have nothing at all to do with free will. Experiments on frogs had shown that a living organism remains capable of activity even when the brain is cut out. Indeed, frogs that have been deprived of their brains are capable of goal-oriented action through reflexes that come from the spinal cortex. In responding to certain stimuli, they behave in exactly the same way a human being would.[44]

Antonovich did seem to recognize that people make important philosophical choices, for example, in preferring materialism over idealism or philosophical eclecticism. In describing how or why people commit themselves to materialism, however, he deliberately avoided terms like choice or decision. Materialism, he claimed, is more than an intellectual option; rather, it fulfills a human need. The individual "needs" a coherent, "decisive," "definite" philosophy to "bring order into his head," to resolve all of those "persistent and pressing" questions

---

[41] Antonovich, "Dva tipa," pp. 48–52; "Sovremennaia filosofiia," 265, 267, 270–271; "Sovremennaia fiziologiia i filosofiia," *Sovremennik* 91 (1862), 227–266, here 255, 260–263. This was ostensibly a review of George Henry Lewes, *The Physiology of Common Life* (1859–1860). Antonovich's description of the nervous system as a "conductor" (*Leitung*) that relayed sensory stimuli to the brain probably came from Moleschott, *Der Kreislauf des Lebens*, pp. 409–410.

[42] Chernyshevskii, "Antropologicheskii printsip," p. 277. Here, he claimed that the mind can "choose" to focus on certain impressions over others, using "*vybrat'*" and "*vybor*" three times in one sentence.

[43] Antonovich, "Dva tipa," p. 48: "Our inner world is formed, it grows out of the external, so to speak, it is the fruit, of which the roots are the feelings, and the nourishing, formative sources are the phenomena of the external world."

[44] Antonovich, "Sovremennaia fiziologiia," 256.

that bother him.[45] He described Orthodox Christianity as too confusing and unnatural to meet this need; it evokes doubts rather than certainty in the most sincere people and threatens doubters with damnation. Materialism, by contrast, offers not only certainty, but courage, the courage to think for oneself and try new things. To Antonovich, becoming a materialist was an act of "spiritual liberation," a veritable "rebirth."[46]

This was an important part of Antonovich's argument, because it addressed a further criticism Iurkevich had leveled against materialism. Iurkevich had pointed out that materialism makes any kind of individual decision-making pointless. If everything in the world (including human behavior) were predetermined by natural laws, it would be useless to attempt to change the status quo.[47] Antonovich must have had this criticism in mind when he claimed that materialism, far from leading people to despair, gives them courage. Yet here Antonovich's empiricist rhetoric and denial of free will broke down. In Orthodox Christianity, "rebirth" is what happens when an individual chooses to live in Christ, casting off his or her old, sinful nature. As Antonovich knew, such rebirth is an exercise of free will.[48] This may only have been a rhetorical lapse on Antonovich's part, but it was ironic, given that it was precisely through philosophical rigor and the empirical evidence furnished by the natural sciences that he hoped to defeat Iurkevich. The lapse serves to demonstrate how difficult it was even for him to uphold the logic of his own materialism. Subsequent developments would prove that fellow radicals had even more trouble with the rejection of free will than he.

DIGNITY: IURKEVICH'S SECOND CRITIQUE AND DOBROLIUBOV'S REBUTTAL

Antonovich may have thought he had finished Iurkevich off, but there was a second line of argument in Iurkevich's "The Science of the Human Spirit" that Antonovich had entirely failed to address. This portion of Iurkevich's article concerned human dignity. Chernyshevskii had advanced an ethical system in which free will played no role at all. People, he said, are instinctively driven to pursue their own interests, and the actions that result are good when their outcome benefits not only the individual actor, but a maximum number of

---

[45] Antonovich, "Dva tipa," pp. 77–78.   [46] *Ibid.* pp. 30–33.

[47] P.D. Iurkevich, "Materializm i zadachi filosofii" in *Filosofskie proizvedeniia*, pp. 193–244, here pp. 196, 197–198.

[48] See, e.g., Makarii (Bulgakov), *Pravoslavno-dogmaticheskoe bogoslovie*, 5th edn., 2 vols. (Moscow: Golike, 1895), vol. 2, p. 294. Originally printed in 1856–1857, this work would have been available to Antonovich.

other people. Iurkevich argued that intention, not outcome, has to be taken into account in judging people's actions. And in evaluating intentions, people invariably refer to human dignity. Here, Iurkevich drew on theology: human beings are formed in the image of God and are born with innate ideas and feelings, which are manifestations of their "godlike" (*bogopodobnyi*) souls. Dignity is one of these innate ideas: it is what people try to preserve or secure by their actions, and it is the measure they use to judge one another's behavior. Dignity can only be realized by willing the good; a philosophical system that denies free will thus excludes dignity.[49]

Dignity was indeed a term that materialists rarely made use of, perhaps because it was widely associated with Kantian metaphysics.[50] To make it serviceable, materialists would have to show that dignity is not an attribute of the mind or soul, but of the body. Feuerbach had suggested such an approach in *The Essence of Christianity*: human beings might honor dignity in God, but this dignity was in fact a human attribute that had been projected onto an imaginary God. Further, Feuerbach claimed, dignity is not a mental trait, derived from human reason. Rather, it consists of the recognition that the self is embedded in a body made of flesh, and that this fleshly body must be respected.[51]

While Chernyshevskii and Antonovich were silent about dignity, Dobroliubov used the term while pursuing a line of reasoning much like Feuerbach's in literary reviews he wrote in the last year of his life. Most notably, he defended the dignity of the flesh in "A Ray of Light in the Kingdom of Darkness" (October 1860), a review of Aleksandr Ostrovskii's play, *The Storm* (1860). The article was an encomium to the play's heroine, Katerina Kabanova; in Dobroliubov's rendition, she rebelled against the stifling atmosphere in her home by committing adultery and then suicide. From an Orthodox Christian perspective, both acts represent sheer immorality, the weakness of a body overcome by passion. To Dobroliubov, however, these acts were manifestations of strength: a strong person is one who will always seek to satisfy her natural and physical needs. Katerina, a woman of the people, had no education, no capacity for theorizing, but she did not need learning or theory. She was an empiricist: she acted

---

[49] Iurkevich, "Iz nauki," pp. 165–169, 172–173.

[50] Kant famously claimed that dignity is the chief attribute separating human beings from animals: humans are different in the sense that they cannot be judged only in terms of their utility, or treated only as a means to an end. On the contrary, every human being has dignity by virtue of being a rational person. Immanuel Kant, *The Metaphysics of Morals* (Mary Gregor (trans.), Cambridge University Press, 1991), pp. 230, 255. Materialists (including Moleschott, Vogt, and Büchner, but also Chernyshevskii) stressed that human beings *are* just another kind of animal, acting according to the same natural laws. No special status should be accorded to them on the basis of higher mental capacities.

[51] Ludwig Feuerbach, *Das Wesen des Christentums* (Stuttgart: Reclam, 1994), p. 520.

"on the basis of living impressions" and in response to "life's facts." Katerina also acted on reflex: she was driven by "instinct" to fulfill "a need that arises from the depths of her whole organism"; she allowed "nature to guide her." Dobroliubov implied that there was nothing undignified in acting on instinct, in responding to the needs of one's organism. Those "ideas," "prejudices," and "artificial combinations" (by which Dobroliubov meant religious values) that had been imposed upon Katerina could do nothing but confuse her and pervert what was truly "lawful and holy" in her, namely her feelings.[52]

According to Dobroliubov, then, dignity does not consist in acting according to religious ideals. Religiously-motivated behavior involves the subordination of one individual to the will of another – a subordination that Dobroliubov thought *deprives* a person of dignity.[53] On the contrary, dignity is to be measured by the degree to which one acts on one's own initiative.[54]

Dobroliubov extrapolated on this claim in "Downtrodden People," his September 1861 review of Dostoevskii's works. In his latest novel, *The Downtrodden and Humiliated* (1861), Dostoevskii had warned that the radicals' system of ethics "risked unleashing forces in the human personality over which Utilitarian reason had no control."[55] So much the better, said Dobroliubov. People were constantly being treated with contempt under the existing order. The only force that could redeem them was the "divine spark" inherent in all human beings, which prompts them to defend their humanity by rebelling against the status quo. The instinct to rebel was indeed frightening, above all to people who felt it stirring inside themselves. This was why most refused to act on it. Instead, they responded by justifying their humiliation to themselves: there was some higher order, divinely ordained, that demanded that they occupy their lowly position and accept it without complaint.[56] To Dobroliubov, this cultivation of humility was the ultimate crime perpetrated by humanity against itself: it meant the "inner suppression of one's human nature, the sincere admission that one was something far lower than a human being." To demand such resignation was to expect a person "to transform himself entirely into a machine." Instinct was the only guarantor that dignity would eventually prevail: the "divine spark" must lead the person to recognize his unhappiness and rebel.[57]

---

52 N.A. Dobroliubov, "Luch sveta v temnom tsarstve" in *PSS*, vol. 2, pp. 310–366, here pp. 349, 351, 356, 357–358, 361–362.

53 Dobroliubov spelled this out in another review of Ostrovskii's works: "Temnoe tsarstvo" in *PSS*, vol. 2, pp. 36–139, here p. 133.

54 N.A. Dobroliubov, "Zabitye liudi" in *PSS*, vol. 2, pp. 367–405, here p. 397.

55 Joseph Frank, *Dostoevsky: The Stir of Liberation, 1860–1865* (Princeton University Press, 1986), p. 125.

56 Dobroliubov, "Zabitye liudi," pp. 398, 390, 384–387.   57 *Ibid.* pp. 380, 396, 398.

Iurkevich, too, had spoken of a "spark" in the human being: a "spark of goodness" or "spark of good will" that prompts feelings of altruism. He viewed this as a manifestation of the divine in the individual, the image of God imparted to humanity at the moment of creation.[58] By contrast, when Dobroliubov used the term "divine," he was gesturing in the opposite direction, at Feuerbach, who had argued that God's attributes are in fact human traits that people project onto an imagined, higher being. The "divine spark," as Dobroliubov understood it, was the opposite of what Iurkevich meant. Dobroliubov's spark dictated that people preserve their own fleshly and individual nature, not sacrifice themselves for others; it is a manifestation of the instinct to defend one's personality and assert one's rights in a world that stifles the human impulse for freedom.

TURGENEV'S CRITIQUE

The debate over the proper role of natural inclinations entered its next stage with the publication of Turgenev's famous novel, *Fathers and Children*, in March 1862.[59] Ivan Turgenev (1818–1883) had decided to publish it in Katkov's conservative journal *The Russian Messenger* after quitting *The Contemporary* in anger over some negative reviews of his work by Chernyshevskii and Dobroliubov. Some readers, including Chernyshevskii, viewed *Fathers and Children* as a personal attack on Dobroliubov.[60] Though this was undoubtedly a one-sided interpretation, the novel did point to a key flaw in Dobroliubov's understanding of natural human inclinations; namely, that acting on them had little to do with materialism. Indeed, the materialists in the novel are the characters least capable of coming to grips with their inclinations.

The hero of the novel, Bazarov, was Turgenev's version of a radical materialist. He was, like Chernyshevskii and Dobroliubov, a *raznochinets*, the grandson of a priest, and the offspring of a country doctor. Bazarov was training to be a doctor and natural scientist; he spent every morning in pursuit of frogs on which to perform experiments. Nominally, then, Bazarov was an empiricist. As he told some boys he met on one of his frog-hunting expeditions, he would dissect a frog in order to "see what goes on inside it, and since you and I are the same as frogs, only we walk on our legs, I will also know what goes on inside us."[61]

---

[58] Iurkevich, "Iz nauki," pp. 179, 185, 182, 140.

[59] Ivan Turgenev, *Ottsy i deti*, in *Sochineniia*, 12 vols. (Moscow: Nauka, 1978–1986), vol. 7, pp. 7–188.

[60] V. Evgen'ev-Maksimov, *"Sovremennik" pri Chernyshevskom i Dobroliubove* (Leningrad: GIKhL, 1936), pp. 544–546; David Lowe, *Turgenev's Fathers and Sons* (Ann Arbor: Ardis, 1983), pp. 90–93.

[61] Turgenev, *Ottsy i deti*, pp. 21–22.

Figure 3.1 Illustration from A.M. Volkov, *Ottsy i deti. Karikaturnyi roman* (St. Petersburg, 1869), p. 7.

In claiming that there is no essential difference between humans and animals, Bazarov mirrored Antonovich and Chernyshevskii, and there were other points of correspondence, too. He asserted that all people are inherently the same. Though there are differences between "good and evil" people, such differences are not attributable to free will. Rather, bad behavior is usually a sign of "moral illnesses" stemming from a person's irrational upbringing and difficult social circumstances.[62] Bazarov and his acolyte, Arkadii Kirsanov, called for radical social change in Russia. They asserted that all existing authorities and institutions must be overturned. Arkadii claimed to reject "all principles," and Bazarov denied the very existence of principles, stating that all mental processes come down to "sensation." Their rejection of principles dumfounded Arkadii's uncle,

---

[62] *Ibid.* pp. 78–79.

Pavel Petrovich, and led him to wonder, "Let's see how you will exist in empty space, in a vacuum."[63]

Reading *Fathers and Children*, some of Turgenev's contemporaries noted a disjuncture between Bazarov's materialist philosophy and the way his mind operated: in everyday life, he was not much of an empiricist.[64] The critic Nikolai Strakhov (1828–1896) noted that Bazarov was more of a "theoretician." Bazarov did not seem to develop gradually in response to sense impressions, as an empiricist should, but resisted them. Indeed, he was an "ascetic" who avoided anything that might influence him unduly, and stood "aloof from life" itself. Yet Bazarov was also a sincere, passionate person; he had attempted to bury himself in theory, but he could not help but respond to "the forces of life."[65] If Bazarov acted on his natural inclinations, he did so despite himself.

Returning to *Fathers and Children*, one may observe that Bazarov's materialist associates are even more inclined to suppress their inclinations than he is. In Bazarov's presence, Arkadii constantly hides feelings of which he himself seems only dimly to be aware. Arkadii suppresses tears, buries his joy, and forces himself to laugh at Bazarov's jokes. The narrator makes it clear that this was no accident: "he viewed it as his duty to hide feelings. Not for nothing was he a nihilist!"[66] The same traits stand out even more markedly in the character Avdot'ia Nikitishna Kukshina, who has changed her name to "Eudoxie." She is at once the novel's most willfully progressive and most unnatural character. Her chief trait is "awkwardness," a trait her radical associate, Sitnikov, shares. His only real pleasure, the narrator explains, is feeling and expressing contempt, and contempt seems to be the only emotion he evokes in others. His fellow materialists Arkadii and Bazarov are constantly putting him down.[67]

Turgenev showed, then, that materialism did not necessarily heighten respect for dignity in other people; still less did it enable people to manifest the "divine spark" of their own humanity. Indeed, there was a general discordance between materialists' principles, their experiences, and their actions. By pointing out

---

[63] *Ibid.* pp. 25, 48–49, 121.

[64] The arch-conservative Mikhail Katkov noted that Bazarov's negating stance and rejection of "phrases" was not motivated by concern for the truth, but was itself a phrase and form of dogmatism. M.N. Katkov, "O nashem nigilizme po povodu romana Turgeneva," in *Kritika 60-kh godov XIX veka* (Moscow: Astvel', 2003), pp. 143–169, here pp. 150–165.

[65] N.N. Strakhov, "I.S. Turgenev, 'Ottsy i deti,'" in L.I. Sobol'ev (ed.), *Kritika 60-kh godov XIX veka* (Moscow: Astrel', 2003), pp. 65–109, here pp. 78, 96, 98, 105. Strakhov may have been paraphrasing a remark Dostoevskii made about Dobroliubov: Dobroliubov was a "theoretician" whose knowledge of "reality is often poor." F.M. Dostoevskii, "G-n –bov i vopros ob iskusstve" in *Polnoe sobranie sochinenii*, 30 vols. (Leningrad, 1972–1990), vol. 18, pp. 70–103, here p. 81.

[66] Turgenev, *Ottsy i deti*, pp. 57, 94, 102, 105.   [67] *Ibid.* pp. 61–63, 65, 67, 100–101, 103.

these discrepancies, Turgenev had opened a breach in the materialists' defenses. It was up to radical journalists to plug it.

ANTONOVICH AND PISAREV RESPOND

Fathers and Children infuriated many a radical reader, but few can have been angrier than the intensely partisan Antonovich. His review, "The Asmodeus of our Time," published in *The Contemporary* immediately upon the appearance of Turgenev's novel, was so vituperative that it embarrassed many of his contemporaries. Antonovich repudiated Bazarov for being a poor caricature of the young generation. Turgenev's treatment of Bazarov was "hateful," and Turgenev himself was as "incapable of enthusiasm," as "cold" and "unfeeling," as Bazarov. But Turgenev had misrepresented the radical position more generally by accusing his young heroes of denying "all principles," of rejecting "everything," including art, poetry, "and . . ." (God, it is implied). By doing so, Antonovich wrote, Turgenev falsified the radical position. The young generation did have its principles, and its selection of those principles was not arbitrary, or "without cause." Here, Antonovich relied upon the quasi-scientific language of cause and effect. Young people held beliefs, but those beliefs "resulted from some foundation that resides in the very person." Young people recognized only one "authority," namely themselves; they accepted only those principles that "satisfied" their individual "nature" and that cohered with the "inner motives" of their personality and level of development.[68] Radicals' principles followed naturally from their experiences. Once again, Antonovich was trying to argue that a person could adopt materialism as a principle without that adoption involving an act of choice.

Antonovich did not, however, speak for all radicals. In the same month that his review of *Fathers and Children* appeared in *The Contemporary*, a very different interpretation was published in the radical journal *The Russian Word*. Its author was Dmitrii Pisarev. Unlike Antonovich, Pisarev was not the son of a priest, but came from a noble family of limited means. His career with *The Russian Word* had begun in 1861, at the same time Antonovich had started writing for *The Contemporary*.

Like Antonovich, Pisarev was a materialist and had devoted several reviews to works by the German materialists.[69] Unlike Antonovich, however, he praised

---

[68] M.A. Antonovich, "Asmodei nashego vremeni" in V. Evgen'ev-Maksimov (ed.), *Izbrannye stat'i. Filosofiia. Kritika. Polemika* (Leningrad: GIKhL, 1938), pp. 141–202, here pp. 144, 148, 160, 189.

[69] Pisarev reviewed works by Vogt, Moleschott, and Büchner in "Protsess zhizni," "Fiziologicheskie eskizy Moleshotta," and "Fiziologicheskie kartiny." See D.I. Pisarev in *Polnoe sobranie sochinenii* (*PSS*), 12 vols. (F.F. Kuznetsov *et al.* (eds.), Moscow: Nauka, 2000–), vols. 3 and 4.

Turgenev's novel. In "Bazarov" (March 1862), he celebrated the hero as a "pure empiricist." Pisarev's Bazarov was such an empiricist that he found himself responding involuntarily to outward stimuli. No external "regulator" could be detected in him, "no moral law, and no principle" guiding his actions. This did not mean that Bazarov was incapable of calculated decision-making (*raschet*), but as a proper materialist, he based his calculations on his natural inclinations. Bazarov always acted in accordance with his nature, driven by "taste" and "unlimited impulse." Admittedly, Bazarov occasionally failed to take feeling properly into account. He tended toward a "despotism of the mind" that led him "arbitrarily" to reject natural inclinations in himself and other people. But this tendency was only caused by the circumstances in which Bazarov had been raised; these circumstances had bred in him a kind of extremism that would have softened, given time.[70]

Turgenev had provoked materialists by claiming that their theories were only scantly connected to empirical realities and that materialism seemed to prevent them from acting on their natural inclinations. Pisarev and Antonovich, coming from different angles, thought they had refuted him. Having answered this criticism, however, they unwittingly opened a new gap in their defenses – this one among radicals themselves over the very merit of scientific empiricism.

THE SCHISM OF THE NIHILISTS

The journals for which Antonovich and Pisarev wrote had never entirely seen eye to eye on the capacity of the natural sciences to solve the country's social problems. Antonovich and his colleagues at *The Contemporary* were enthusiastic about materialism, but they did not view it as the *only* possible source of progress in Russia: they believed that even uneducated people had a role to play in bringing about social change. Pisarev and his fellows at *The Russian Word*, by contrast, believed that meaningful change would only occur thanks to scientific advances and the spread of education. Peasants were too backward to contribute meaningfully toward social progress.[71]

The tensions between the two journals could be observed in Antonovich's and Pisarev's continuing dispute over *Fathers and Children*. Antonovich was appalled by what he considered to be Bazarov's indifference to the fate of the

---

[70] Pisarev, "Bazarov," *PSS*, vol. 4, pp. 164–201, here pp. 166–168, 179–182, 191, 192, 196, 199.

[71] The debate between the two journals is explained in great detail in Daniel Philip Todes, *From Radicalism to Scientific Convention: Biological Psychology in Russia from Sechenov to Pavlov* (Doctoral Dissertation, University of Pennsylvania, 1981), pp. 15–67.

Russian peasant.[72] Pisarev, by contrast, thought this indifference entirely natural: Bazarov and the peasants had nothing in common.[73] The same disagreement would be played out in 1864 as Antonovich and Pisarev reconsidered Ostrovskii's play, *The Storm*. In 1860, Dobroliubov had praised Ostrovskii's uneducated heroine Katerina for her rebelliousness. Antonovich continued to celebrate her "primitive," "instinctual" protest.[74] Pisarev, by contrast, found little to admire in Katerina: she might be virtuous, but since her mind was weak, she could benefit neither herself nor others. To lead a meaningful life, people must be able to think independently and systematically, and this was an ability they could only acquire by engaging directly in scientific study.[75]

Having repudiated Katerina, Pisarev went on in his article "Realists" (1864) to repudiate instinct more generally.[76] People cannot base their actions exclusively on instinct, inclination, or feeling, because they do not always know what their true instincts and feelings are. These are not necessarily spontaneous responses to external stimuli, but often reflect culturally learned preferences. Worse yet, even if one's impulses are spontaneous, acting on them may lead one to become the passive instrument of changing external events and circumstances. People need to examine what they think and why they act in the way they do. They need a "large" aim in life, and acquiring such an aim involves choice: they must "choose a specific form of activity" for themselves, one that will be morally satisfying and useful to society.[77] This was exactly the opposite of the position Pisarev had taken in earlier years, when he had followed Chernyshevskii in trumpeting the dominating influence of "circumstances" over the volitional life of the individual.[78] As if he had not signaled his change of heart strongly enough, Pisarev now dismissed the philosophy of Büchner and Feuerbach as "childish."[79]

Pisarev was not the only radical to call into question core tenets of materialism. *The Contemporary*, too, was gradually edging away from materialism. Partly, this was caused by a growing sense of desperation among radicals: a wave of state repression, with tightened censorship and countless arrests, set in during summer

---

[72] Antonovich, "Asmodei," p. 190. See also M.A. Antonovich, "Promakhi" in *Izbrannye stat'i*, pp. 431–484, here pp. 470, 472.

[73] Pisarev, "Bazarov," p. 195; see also Pisarev, "Motivy russkoi dramy," *PSS*, vol. 5, pp. 359–388, here pp. 384–385.

[74] Antonovich, "Promakhi," pp. 444–445.   [75] Pisarev, "Motivy," pp. 363, 375, 385.

[76] Pisarev, "Realisty," *PSS*, vol. 6, pp. 222–353.   [77] *Ibid.* pp. 274–276, 241, 244, 299, 280–281.

[78] Prior to this, Pisarev had accorded "will" an important role, not in making free choices, but in maintaining self-discipline. Bazarov, for example, had an usually strong "will." It prompted him to act on his inclinations, to work hard, and think things through. (Pisarev, "Bazarov," pp. 193, 176, 170; "Motivy," p. 380.) But it was not involved in making choices. The term "choice" does not figure in these earlier articles.

[79] Pisarev, "Realisty," p. 249.

1862. Radical journalists, fearful that their young adherents would abandon the cause under these adverse circumstances, felt the need to remind them of their moral duty to work for political and social change. They also wanted to reassure readers that change was possible. In other words, journalists behaved as if the political environment were subject to their influence. Amidst these calls to action, the old criticism that materialism bred an attitude of passivity proved an embarrassment.[80]

By 1865, *The Contemporary* was prepared to give the floor to Lavrov, whose idealist leanings had been the subject of Chernyshevskii's attacks five years earlier. Lavrov now dismissed as a waste of time journal articles that popularized science. In "On Journalist-Popularizers and on Natural Science," he claimed that principles deduced from the study of the natural world cannot tell people how to organize their social relations. Moreover, he wrote, materialist determinism promotes a kind of passivity that is out of keeping with the radical spirit of social activism.[81] In making this last point, Lavrov was implicitly siding with Iurkevich against Chernyshevskii, Dobroliubov, and Antonovich. Remarkably, far from alienating radical readers, Lavrov gained a following among them that was to make him a leader of the intelligentsia for the next decade (see Thomas Nemeth in chapter 4). The materialist era in Russian radicalism was (for the time being) over.

THE END OF A DEBATE

Three reasons may be given for the relative decline of materialism in the mid-1860s. One I have already mentioned was the atmosphere of renewed political repression, which made the deterministic aspect of materialism unattractive. A second was that materialism had been undermined by disagreements among its most prominent proponents. In the early 1860s, radical journalists had touted materialism for its ability to provide unambiguous and precise answers to the country's most pressing social problems. Yet the vehement disagreements between Pisarev and Antonovich showed that certainty was illusive. Disputes between *The Contemporary* and *The Russian Word* over key issues struck a blow to materialism's mystique of objectivity.

A third and more complex reason has to do with materialists' changing attitude toward idealists. Friedrich Albert Lange observed that materialism

---

[80] Todes, *From Radicalism to Scientific Convention*, pp. 66–67.
[81] P.L. Lavrov, "O publitsistakh-populiarizatorakh i o estestvoznanii" in I.S. Knizhnik-Vetrov (ed.), *Izbrannye sochineniia na sotsial'no-politicheskie temy*, 4 vols. (Moscow: Obshchestvo politkatorzhan, 1934–1935), vol. 1, pp. 134–160, here pp. 148–152, 155.

flourishes where there is a healthy spirit of debate,[82] and this was especially true of Russia in the late 1850s. At that time, materialists might have viewed idealists as enemies, but they took them seriously enough to enter into polemics with them. Why else would Antonovich seek to vanquish Iurkevich? Radical ardor on this score seems to have dampened, however, as a result of the political polarization that accompanied state reaction in the mid-1860s: radicals were now more inclined to dismiss men like Iurkevich as political reactionaries unworthy of being taken seriously as adversaries.

Materialism returned to intellectual prominence in the late nineteenth and early twentieth centuries, thanks to theorists like Georgii Plekhanov and Vladimir Lenin. By this time, however, German idealism, especially Kantianism and neo-Kantianism, were finding new adherents in Europe and Russia. Plekhanov and Lenin were driven to take up the pen not only by their loyalty to Marx's materialism, but by their anger at peers who had drifted off in the wrong direction. The resurgence of idealism lent materialism new energy.

[82] Lange, *Geschichte des Materialismus*, vol. 2, p. 71.

4

RUSSIAN ETHICAL HUMANISM: FROM POPULISM TO NEO-IDEALISM

THOMAS NEMETH

Russia's desultory performance in the Crimean War against the western powers in the 1850s demonstrated to government and educated society the efficient power of an industrial economy as well as the inflexibility of a serf army. The following years, known as the era of great reforms, saw the emancipation of the peasants and other measures, including the 1864 judicial reform, which introduced the principle of equality before the law. Revised university statutes led to soaring student enrollment. Many university students and some recent graduates now looked to the burgeoning natural sciences for answers to pressing social problems. However, some Russians viewed an unbridled positivism with caution, even alarm. They were concerned above all with the human and moral implications of an outlook that seemed to submerge the individual in a mechanistic world. This chapter will focus first on the ethical humanism of the two greatest theorists of Russian populism, Pëtr Lavrov and Nikolai Mikhailovskii. It will then explore how these figures were themselves eclipsed at the turn of the century by philosophical thinkers of a younger generation, whose critique of positivism took them from revisionist Marxism to neo-idealism in search of the true nature of ethical values.

LAVROV'S ETHICS

The son of a former colonel, Pëtr Lavrovich Lavrov (1823–1900) was educated at the Mikhailovskii Artillery School, where, after graduating, he taught mathematics. Somewhat incongruously, perhaps, given his profession and military rank, Lavrov also began writing poetry and articles on pedagogy. However, it was due to his lengthy philosophical articles from the late 1850s that he burst on the Russian intellectual scene. Like many at the time, Lavrov had been deeply influenced by Auguste Comte's positivism, with its unflinching faith in scientific progress, but Lavrov argued that scientific knowledge of the external world cannot exhaust the scope of human inquiry and aspiration, which also include the search for beauty and justice. In one of his earliest philosophical writings,

"Sketch of a Theory of the Human Individual" (1859), Lavrov argued that the individual (*lichnost'*), through self-consciousness, distinguishes himself or herself from the external world.[1] Self-consciousness is the preeminent distinctive characteristic of human beings, but it arises in us only in the wake of enjoyment or suffering. The desire for pleasure and avoidance of pain lies behind the pursuit of knowledge and creativity, and it also constitutes, in Lavrov's opinion, the basis for morality and practical philosophy.

Of course, the very notion of morality presupposes the possibility of choosing among alternative actions and responsibility for the course chosen. Although enamored with the theoretical progress science had made, Lavrov realized that it provided facts and only facts. When its object is human individuals, science can tell us only what we are and what we are doing, not what we should be or what we ought to do. Physical science can neither prove nor disprove freedom of the will. That is, it cannot establish that the will is essentially free, free "in itself," even though we certainly believe we are free. No philosophical argument can dispel our immediate sense that, whatever we do, we could do otherwise. Accordingly, we must accept responsibility for the consequences of our actions.

Lavrov's sympathy for a broadly utilitarian ethic was part of his genetic account of a humanistic morality. He believed that, in striving to fulfill material and intellectual desires, we posit ideals, foremost among which is an ideal mental representation of the self, i.e., of our personal human dignity. Historically, we first represent the ideal self in primitive egoistic terms, with self-perfection and personal freedom being all that matters to us. In time, through interaction with people, an individual's notion of dignity broadens and is extended to others. Our idea of justice – the recognition that others also have a corresponding dignity – develops in tandem with our own self-consciousness. Just as I see myself as having ideals, dignity, and rights, so, too, with my emerging recognition of the dignity and equality of others, do I demand respect for them in the form of obligations and rights. According to Lavrov, a moral infraction against another is eventually seen as an infraction against oneself. That some individuals do not try to act upon or even acknowledge this basic sense of justice is due to a psychological weakness or simply a lack of knowledge of their own best interest. However, Lavrov had no doubt that a conception of justice, whereby all of us are aware that we must act towards others in a manner commensurate with dignity, is a constant in human nature. Thus, the behavioral rules by which I live and by which I want others to treat me become generalized into a code decreeing that everyone should act on their basis.

---

[1] "Ocherk teorii lichnosti" in P.L. Lavrov, *Filosofiia i sotsiologiia. Izbrannye proizvedeniia v dvukh tomakh* (Moscow: Mysl', 1965), vol. 1, pp. 339–461.

Lavrov acknowledged that Immanuel Kant had correctly identified the universally applicable form a moral rule must assume.[2] Nevertheless, Lavrov refrained from explicitly supporting Kant's categorical imperative or even addressing the reasoning behind it. Like Proudhon, Lavrov saw morality as arising in time, as a mutual recognition among members of society of each other's dignity. Morality needed no external buttresses such as the church or the state, since morality is rooted in our nature as social beings. In fact, Lavrov explicitly disavowed any appeal to religion as a source of morality. He alleged that, in Christianity, moral actions are not truly based on a sense of obligation or connection between people but on devotion to God.

A year later, in October 1860, Lavrov attempted to give another exposition of his philosophical position, now labeled simply "anthropology," a term the radical literary critic Chernyshevskii was then using to designate his own philosophy.[3] In this long essay, "What is Anthropology?" Lavrov reiterated his interest in the human individual, particularly in the relationship between the psyche and body.[4] And it is here that he found the usual scientific methods, based on external observations, deficient, for only reflection or self-observation can grasp the nuances of our internal conscious processes. Although Lavrov discerned no logical basis for rejecting solipsism, he also held that there is no basis for denying the existence of an external world. Indeed, all conscious processes count in favor of its acceptance. In fact, he wrote, there is no reason to think that our own consciousness is not the product of non-conscious processes in an independently existing world. For Lavrov, the important point is that one cannot logically draw ontic claims from our subjective representations of exteriority independent of consciousness. From these bare considerations, Lavrov drew three principles that form the basis of his metaphysics. First, the existence of consciousness and its associated phenomena, e.g., dreams and abstractions, are indubitable, or, in Lavrov's terminology, "actual." Secondly, the existence of the external, real world with its associated facts and entities carries real conviction, albeit that not all facts and entities carry the same degree of conviction. These two principles are distinct and non-reducible, which leads to Lavrov's third metaphysical principle, that we cannot resolve whether consciousness and conscious processes are the result of really existing beings or vice versa.

Lavrov found moral philosophy to be based on two principles, corresponding to the first two metaphysical ones above. The first principle expresses the

[2] Thomas Nemeth, "Kant in Russia: Lavrov in the 1860s – A New Beginning?" *Studies in Soviet Thought* 43, no. 1 (1992), 1–36.

[3] Lavrov later designated his general outlook "anthropologism." See his "Biografiia-ispoved' 1885–1889" in Lavrov, *Filosofiia i sotsiologiia*, vol. 2, p. 632.

[4] "Chto takoe antropologiia?" in Lavrov, *Filosofiia i sotsiologiia*, vol. 1, pp. 465–491.

independence of the individual from externality; that is, individuals cognize themselves as free and responsible for their own actions. The second moral principle, the principle of ideal creation, sets the actual, practical person against ideals, just as the second, theoretical principle sets consciousness against the real world.[5] Here we find the basis of all human activity, the motivation for doing anything. All human individuals seek enjoyments of some kind that they imagine they do not have at a given moment. This principle places human beings squarely within the real world. However, through our creative faculty we construct ideals that extend beyond our immediate satisfaction, ideals that belong to the moral, political, and social spheres. Lavrov had enunciated much of this already in "Sketch of a Theory of the Human Individual." In "What is Anthropology?" he attempted a systemization of his general humanist outlook, connecting the defense of his ethical philosophy with his object-language phenomenalism and an abjuration of ontological claims about an ultimate reality.

There are two branches of theoretical philosophy: philosophy of nature and philosophy of spirit. Whether we follow the one or the other depends upon whether we prioritize the real world or actual consciousness. So, too, when speaking of human activity, we can prioritize either the form or the content embodied in that form. In the first case, we have philosophy of art, the ideal of which is a beautiful creation, and in the second the philosophy of life, which seeks the ideal of human dignity through ethical activity.

The final element of "anthropology" as a philosophical system is the philosophy of history, which, Lavrov wrote, includes both theoretical and practical philosophy from the perspective of their developmental processes. The philosophy of history outlines the laws of human development. That such a process of development exists, Lavrov had no doubt. Humanity as a whole is passing gradually to an ever-greater awareness of itself, of its abilities and its limitations. In our theoretical activity, we strive to proceed from faith to knowledge, from myths to the deliberate construction of philosophical systems, with science (*nauka*) as the ultimate goal. The philosophy of history reveals that philosophy has historically been striving for a harmonious, complete integration of all knowledge. Philosophies are not detached ivory-tower abstractions, but are based on all aspects of the life of society. The philosopher's entire intellectual, social, and cultural development is embodied in his or her philosophical system.

Such is the essence of Lavrov's thought as it stood in late 1860. In November of that year, he had the opportunity to deliver three lectures on "the contemporary

---

[5] *Ibid.* p. 485.

significance of philosophy."[6] Dressed in an officer's uniform adorned with medals and awards, Lavrov reiterated many of the themes he had covered in his articles, but in his third lecture he turned to the importance of human dignity as the moral ideal. However moderate the tone of these lectures and however reassuring to officialdom was his dress, his association with those politically to his Left did not endear Lavrov to the government. When two more politically and philosophically radical figures attacked him in print for his alleged ambiguity and idealism, he replied that, although they had misunderstood him owing to their own philosophical naivety, they all agreed on practical goals. Lavrov himself genuinely believed that, despite his differences with the radicals on metaphysical and epistemological issues, moral issues were paramount and could be addressed separately.[7] Lavrov's declaration of a common cause with the radicals surely contributed in 1861 to the government's rejection of his application to fill the St. Petersburg University philosophy professorship that he coveted. Despite support from the historian Konstantin Kavelin, who thought him merely a fellow liberal, others, such as the literature professor Aleksandr Nikitenko, found him a dangerous radical.[8]

Lavrov was kept under police surveillance in the coming years, though he was not arrested for the time being. During the mid-1860s, he continued writing, but his literary output failed to attract the attention he had hoped, perhaps due to his scholarly manner. He vehemently defended the role of individuals in history, especially the role of the educated minority in formulating moral ideals and defending human dignity. With his personal life in disrepair and with the government's crackdown following Dmitrii Karakozov's assassination attempt on the tsar in 1866, Lavrov was briefly arrested, and then, in February 1867, sent into internal exile in Vologda province, approximately 500 kilometers north of Moscow. Among his numerous writings in exile was a long essay entitled "The Tasks of Positivism and Their Solution," published in 1868.[9] In it, Lavrov reaffirmed his esteem for the sciences, both natural and social, and for positivism as a philosophical reflection on them. He asked, however, "Where do we find the 'beautiful,' the 'ought,' the 'useful'?" In Lavrov's opinion, positivism's reductionism, its refusal to accept a phenomenon as it presents itself, is its ultimate shortcoming. Positivism has no way to deal with or even address the

---

[6] "Tri besedy o sovremennom znachenii filosofii" in Lavrov, *Filosofiia i sotsiologiia*, vol. 1, pp. 511–573. A quarter century later, Lavrov remarked that these lectures were "the first public words on philosophy by a secular person in Russia outside a theological institution since Nicholas I closed the university philosophy departments [in 1850]." *Filosofiia i sotsiologiia*, vol. 2, p. 619.

[7] P.L. Lavrov, "Moim kritikam," *Russkoe slovo*, 6 (June 1861), 48–69, here 68.

[8] Aleksandr Nikitenko, *Diary of a Russian Censor* (Helen Saltz Jacobson (trans.), Amherst, MA: University of Massachusetts Press, 1975), p. 313.

[9] "Zadachi positivizma i ikh reshenie" in Lavrov, *Filosofiia i sotsiologiia*, vol. 1, pp. 577–634.

practical questions of life. Positivists claimed that we must turn to sociology to chart the future, but Lavrov noted that sociology concerns itself with the classification of facts, not with the "best" course of action. The only option for positivism was to adopt the "subjective method" of analyzing choices.[10] In order to understand the subjective factors underlying a given human choice, we must know the intended aim or purpose of the action. "But what is this goal?" Lavrov asked. "It is something desired, pleasant, useful, something that ought to be. All these categories are purely subjective as well as comprehensible to all individuals. Consequently, these phenomena, being part of the investigation, necessitate the use of the subjective method as well as allow this to be done in a fully scientific manner."[11]

There is yet another aspect to the "scientific" resolution of practical questions through the subjective method that has no correlate in the metaphysical realm. As human individuals, we often choose among possible courses of action based on a particular course's moral worth. This determination is necessarily subjective, in Lavrov's eyes, in that the morally preferable choice is something only the individual can know. Implicit in the conceptual transition from thought to action is the possibility of choice. Thus, the subjective method supposes not only the individual's free will, but that his or her moral sense plays a decisive role in determining the chosen course of action. Just as we must conceive the world as mechanically ordered, so too must practical philosophy be conceived as based on "free choice."[12] For example, an individual's physical movement can be objectively observed and stated in terms of mechanics. However, it can also be explained subjectively in terms of moral theory, as the result of a choice determined by the individual's understanding of what he or she ought to do (e.g., enter a burning building to rescue someone).

Lavrov's essays from this period contain an extended defense of his philosophy, contrasting it to what he took to be the prevailing objectivist trend in positivism. While his philosophical essays may not have gained him a large popular following, this was to change dramatically with the appearance of his *Historical Letters*. Originally published in fifteen installments between 1868 and 1869, the *Letters* appeared as a single volume in 1870.[13] Reading them today it is, perhaps, hard to imagine the excitement they aroused among Russia's youth. But the book proved enormously popular, enjoyed a wide circulation, and was

---

[10] *Ibid.* p. 606.   [11] *Ibid.* p. 609.   [12] *Ibid.* p. 628.

[13] A second edition was published in Geneva in 1891, reprinted in Lavrov, *Filosofiia i sotsiologiia*, vol. 2, pp. 7–295. There is a masterful English edition: Peter Lavrov, *Historical Letters* (James P. Scanlan (ed. and trans.), Berkeley and Los Angeles, CA: University of California Press, 1967). The English edition includes an introductory study by J.P. Scanlan, "Peter Lavrov: An Intellectual Biography," pp. 1–65.

taken by youthful revolutionaries as a gospel of what had to be done in Russia there and then. Its essential message was that a distinct social minority historically had held and continued to hold all the privileges, while the vast majority of people lived a life of misery and unceasing labor. The framing of this thesis in strictly ethical, not political, terms helped Lavrov get the censor's approval for his book. He urged the privileged minority to recognize and repay its moral debt to the unfortunate majority. It took time for this idea to percolate through the youthful Left. When it did, in the summers of 1873 and 1874, masses of university students poured into the countryside with no fixed ideology, only the intent to serve the peasants and to learn from them how to work.

The result of this "going to the people" was in many cases a personal disaster for the individual students. Many peasants whom they intended to help and learn from were perplexed by and suspicious of the students from the outset, and so informed the police, who were already on the look-out for subversives. Nevertheless, although the revolutionary students failed to strike a responsive chord among the peasantry, they did occasionally find a safe harbor among members of the gentry and local officials, who provided the material means for the dissemination of the radicals' message. The central authorities in St. Petersburg noticed this and concluded that the revolutionary movement had to be eliminated.

What in the *Historical Letters* could evoke such a response? Scholars generally agree that the book was chiefly directed against the "nihilism" of Dmitrii Pisarev, whose unabashed faith in the natural sciences to solve all human problems entailed a sharp diminution of the importance of religion, metaphysics, and moral values in human progress.[14] Lavrov asked which questions are more relevant to our everyday lives and vital interests: those posed by the natural sciences or those posed by sociology and economics? Clearly, the latter are intrinsically more important, since they deal with our "inner world, the problems of human consciousness."[15] Lavrov singled out the study of history as the discipline which specifically deals with these problems. He described the methods employed by the natural sciences as inadequate to explain the subjective problems of life and the processes of social evolution. While not deriding the value of the sciences, he claimed that serious study of them is impossible without concern for history, for science, as one of humanity's intellectual activities, can only be fully understood when seen in its interdependence with history. Science is a product of our personal and social life, whose laws are illuminated through the study of history.

---

[14] See, e.g., Franco Venturi, *Roots of Revolution: A History of the Populist and Socialist Movements in Nineteenth-Century Russia* (Francis Haskell (trans.), University of Chicago Press, 1960), p. 449.
[15] Lavrov, *Historical Letters*, p. 81.

Certainly, the historian investigates the conscious aims of the principal actors and figures of an age, but the interpretation of these aims cannot be divorced from the investigator's own moral ideals. The historian cannot help but interpret the facts from the vantage point of ideals, asking whether a given act promoted or hindered the realization of these moral ideals. In Lavrov's opinion, a historian cannot legitimately speak of historical progress in the abstract, for nature knows nothing of good and bad, beneficial and harmful. Moral judgments apply only to human beings, not to the passionless realm of nature. Lavrov did not suppose that there must be as many moral ideals as there are people; indeed he held that individual moral ideals may converge into a single moral ideal upon which the progress of society may be judged. He formulated this ideal as "the physical, intellectual, and moral development of the individual, and the incorporation of truth and justice in social institutions."[16]

Leaving aside the ambiguity of this grand formulation, Lavrov held that, in order for truth and justice to be so incorporated, certain conditions had to be met. First, individuals would have to develop the ability to express scientific conclusions and philosophical convictions. Secondly, they would have to acquire a sufficient minimum of public education. Thirdly, they would have to have the freedom to discuss and change social institutions, if necessary. He argued that a civilization progresses to the extent that it realizes these conditions, and it stagnates or collapses when they are not realized. Even in the best circumstances, however, the growth of scientific knowledge and moral development cannot be uniform among all members of a society. In most societies, a distinct minority enjoys such benefits, but only due to the arduous labor of the majority. Although the advantages of the minority appear as a natural law of social development, Lavrov held that the cultivated minority bears a profound moral debt to the toiling masses for its advantages. Admittedly, there have been societies in which this debt was not recognized, but these societies have historically fallen along the wayside. Modern civilization has inherited both the achievements of past elites and their unpaid obligations to previous toiling majorities. The cultivated minorities today cannot rectify past injustices, but they can and morally should act to reduce evils in the present and future. Their knowledge should be put to the service of the moral ideal, especially the development of the human individual.

Such was the moral, essentially humanistic, message Russian students carried to the countryside in 1874. By this time, Lavrov had long escaped Russia to France. After witnessing the Paris Commune in 1871 and now freed from Russian censorship, he wrote not only more explicitly of political revolution, but he also revised his view of the role of the intelligentsia in effecting radical social

---

[16] *Ibid*. p. 111, translation slightly modified, italics omitted.

change. Displaying, in the words of one eminent scholar, a "limited evolution toward Marxism,"[17] he now decided that the masses could make revolution on their own, and he accorded a new primacy to economics in explaining social formations. Nevertheless, his basic humanistic orientation remained unaltered. Even in his later years, he reiterated his fundamental belief that human thought and action presuppose both a phenomenal world, subject to causal laws, and a free choice of goals as we pose and understand them, whatever they may be "in themselves." "Consequently," Lavrov wrote, "the fundamental starting point of any philosophical construction is the human being, who evaluates himself theoretically and practically and who develops in society."[18] History is made by individuals who, realizing its inevitable march, understand progress as an ethical commitment necessitating action, even struggle and pain. Lavrov believed that the central concepts of ethics were human dignity, development, critical conviction, and justice, concepts that remained at the center of all his philosophical and literary activity.

MIKHAILOVSKII'S ETHICS

A second ethical humanist, often linked with Lavrov in discussions of "critical populism" and the "subjective method" in sociology, was Nikolai Konstantinovich Mikhailovskii (1842–1904). Despite their similarities, there were substantial intellectual and political differences between them. Whereas Lavrov had a mathematical background and considered physics the paradigmatic natural science, Mikhailovskii was fascinated by biology. Like Lavrov, Mikhailovskii placed the highest value on the all-round development of the individual. In January 1878, he articulated, arguably, the most succinct statement of his fundamental belief: "The individual, sacred and inviolable, must never be sacrificed."[19] The chief enemy of the individual is society, which "progresses" to greater and greater heterogeneity at the expense of the individual. In his 1869 essay "What is Progress?" Mikhailovskii concluded:

Progress is the gradual approach to the integral individual, to the fullest possible and the most diversified division of labor among man's organs and the least possible division of labor among people. Everything that impedes this advance is immoral, unjust, pernicious, and unreasonable. Everything that diminishes the heterogeneity of society and thereby increases the heterogeneity of its members is moral, just, reasonable, and beneficial.[20]

[17] Scanlan, "Peter Lavrov: An Intellectual Biography," p. 58.
[18] Lavrov, *Filosofiia i sotsiologiia*, vol. 2, pp. 633–634.
[19] N.K. Mikhailovskii, *Sochineniia* (St. Petersburg: Tip. N.N. Klobukova, 1906), vol. 4, p. 452.
[20] James M. Edie, James P. Scanlan, Mary-Barbara Zeldin, and George L. Kline (eds.), *Russian Philosophy*, 3 vols. (Knoxville, TN: University of Tennessee Press, 1976), vol. 2, p. 187.

Like Lavrov, Mikhailovskii started with the conviction that self-development is the goal of progress. In this, he took exception to the social Darwinists and their belief that the strongest individuals are those who survive the test of adapting to society. For Mikhailovskii, such adaptation demonstrated weakness. In his own intellectual endeavors he conceived himself as a striking example of one who could not be labeled simply a literary critic, a sociologist, a philosopher, or whatever. He claimed he had nothing in common with those members of the intelligentsia dedicated to pure science or pure art or with those in Russia who sought to defend such notions as abstract justice.[21] Mikhailovskii's opposition to specialization extended even to the division between intellectual and physical labor, a division he associated with the emergence of rulers and subjects. Mikhailovskii did not condemn this differentiation per se. What he objected to was that some individuals lived off the toil of others without acknowledging their debt. The ultimate injustice here lay not in the minority's lack of gratitude for the majority's labor, but in the one-sidedness of the lives everyone led. He felt this injustice was doubly galling because it was unnecessary, as Lev Tolstoi had also recognized.[22]

Mikhailovskii did not idealize the peasantry. He saw clearly their ignorance, barbarism, crudeness, and filth. Nevertheless, recognizing civilization's debt to them and that their suffering need not extend into the indefinite future, he believed it incumbent on educated Russians to repay this debt. Doing so would not completely relieve peasants of their burden, but it would help develop them to the highest level presently attainable, while retaining their freedom and equality. Mikhailovskii believed that the Russian peasant, despite his deficiencies, enjoyed with his peers a sense of mutual equality and a sense of cooperation not found under western capitalism. Unlike the historically privileged classes, the peasants had never exploited others; they went about their routines with a clear conscience.[23] Thus, the way forward for Russia was to base social life on the traditional village commune, the *obshchina*, which retained egalitarianism and common ownership of the land. If this vision of a social transformation in Russia were accomplished, the country would be able to avert the evils, particularly the loss of individuality, attendant on western capitalist industrialization. Western technology might then be introduced gradually into Russia without destroying the country's social fabric, whereas in the West the "struggle for individuality" could succeed only through a revolution in its basic values.

---

[21] Mikhailovskii, *Sochineniia*, vol. 5, p. 539.   [22] *Ibid.* vol. 6, p. 410, from a July 1886 essay.
[23] *Ibid.* vol. 6, p. 394.

Mikhailovskii shared Lavrov's epistemic phenomenalism, opposing the introduction of metaphysics into natural science: "We do not and cannot know
noumena, things in themselves. We know only phenomena in their succession
and coexistence."[24] Therefore, according to Mikhailovskii, all knowledge of
the world is only relative knowledge, knowledge in relation to the cognizing
subject. There is no absolute truth, only truth for us, truth as it appears to
human beings with our limited faculties. Just as the cognizing subject can and
does change, so too truth can and does change. Mikhailovskii proceeded a step
further, asserting that truth (and not merely what is considered to be true) is
what satisfies human cognitive needs.[25] To inquire into the essence of the world
is a futile endeavor, he thought. There cannot be a definitive answer accessible
to us. Nevertheless, truth is not a purely individual matter: Mikhailovskii did
not posit that you have your truth and I have mine. Although the cognitive
process is an individual matter, we are all members of a society and we all share
the same world, which sets the same limits on us all. Regrettably, Mikhailovskii
failed to amplify these cursory remarks.

Mikhailovskii, again like Lavrov, rejected outright the possibility of *a priori*
epistemic conditions and allowed for only *a posteriori* knowledge. That did
not mean, however, that he granted existence only to what is, in principle,
intersubjectively accessible. After all, there is the human will and the human
consciousness with its ideals and goals. These can be experienced and thereby
known only from the first-person perspective, i.e., by the individual who has
them. Without a belief in freedom of the will, the individual loses a sense of
responsibility and also loses motivation for intervening in the world. On the
other hand, Mikhailovskii always remained convinced, even more than Lavrov,
in the reign of determinism: he thought nature is governed by objective, strict,
and precise laws. Likewise, Mikhailovskii never doubted that history unfolds in
accordance with laws, but he did stipulate that the individual, admittedly shaped
by society but also acting on the basis of ideals, is the principal moving force
in history. "The living individual [*lichnost'*], with all his thoughts and feelings,
becomes the responsible maker of history. He, and not some mystical force, sets
historical goals and moves events."[26] Unlike Marx, Mikhailovskii did not see
the economic base of society as the determining force in history. Nor did he
agree with the nihilist assertion that science alone is responsible for the progress
of civilization. While proclaiming that he was not totally opposed to scientific
specialization, he urged scientists not to forget their role in society: their pursuits
must serve the society of which they are an intimate part. Rather than divide
society further, scientific progress can and should promote the realization of

[24] *Ibid.* vol. 4, p. 97.   [25] *Ibid.* vol. 3, pp. 533–534.   [26] *Ibid.* vol. 3, p. 448.

common human ideals, including the spread of democracy and the equalization of social classes. Thus, both freedom and necessity, tempering each other, found a role in Mikhailovskii's outlook, although the inherent contradiction in this position was never clearly resolved, a tension that his opponents would use to their own advantage in the years ahead.

Like Lavrov, Mikhailovskii is best known for his advocacy of a distinctive method of investigation in the social sciences. He had no quarrel with the traditional conception of the scientific method employed in the natural sciences, which studies facts "objectively" and takes no account of the investigator. As mentioned, Mikhailovskii was convinced that purely physical phenomena behave according to regular, precise laws. There is nothing behind nature actively directing it one way or another. Yet in the social sciences, investigators must take into account human desires and motivations, because here the object and subject of the investigation are identical.[27] For this reason, the sociologist must employ a subjective method that includes an explanation of how the investigator understands the phenomenon being studied. The sociologist can only attain knowledge of his or her subjects once he or she has become one with them, sharing their interests and life experiences. Mikhailovskii labeled this methodology the "subjective method."[28] Thus, sharply countering the positivism of the Russian nihilists, Mikhailovskii held that social scientific methodology fundamentally differs from the methodology of the natural sciences. He made much of the Russian word "*pravda,*" which combines the epistemic notion of truth as relating to that which objectively is and the moral notion of truth as justice, that which ought to be. The historian and the sociologist must not only gather facts, but also place them in a perspective arising from the individual investigator's ideals. These ideals are not arbitrary biases, but values shared with the subjects under investigation. In this way, Mikhailovskii defended the vital role of the individual not just as the object, but also as the subject in the social sciences. A sound sociological analysis looks to the concrete activities of people and to the moral aims motivating them. In this way, the social scientist unravels the true laws of history and society.

RUSSIAN ETHICAL HUMANISM AFTER THE POPULISTS

Unlike Lavrov, Mikhailovskii was never imprisoned and never abandoned Russia for exile abroad. As the chief editor of the journals *Otechestvennye zapiski* (*Notes of the Fatherland*) (for fifteen years) and then *Russkoe bogatstvo* (*Russian Wealth*),

---

[27] *Ibid.* vol. 2, p. 12.   [28] *Ibid.* vol. 3, p. 402.

he made his living as a literary critic and social theorist, not a professional philosopher. In this capacity, Mikhailovskii in the 1890s entered into a number of exchanges, often quite polemical, with Marxist theoreticians of the two emerging camps: the revolutionary Marxists (Georgii Plekhanov) and the so-called Legal Marxists (Pëtr Struve and Mikhail Tugan-Baranovskii). Despite their differences, both camps emphatically rejected the populists' social-scientific methodology and their position that truth is subjective. For Plekhanov (1856–1918), the leading Russian Marxist theorist, a correct methodology is one that accurately depicts social relations: it has nothing to do with the social scientist's personal ideals, beliefs, or values. While not dismissing the role of the individual in history, Plekhanov admonished his readers to remember that the actions of individuals are only effective when the socio-economic conditions are ripe. Individuals can be agents of historical change if they consciously coordinate their actions with the objective laws of social evolution. Similarly, Tugan-Baranovskii (1865–1919), who at this time defended the universal applicability of Marxist economic doctrine, wrote that capitalist economies follow unvarying laws of development. As for the individual, he reiterated the classic Marxist refrain "it is not consciousness that determines human existence, but, vice versa, social existence that determines human social consciousness."[29] Mikhailovskii responded, in turn, that "economic materialism" is not an all-encompassing philosophical system. It has, for example, nothing philosophical to say about nature. Moreover, its attempt to explain societal relations in terms of economics was wrongheaded and simplistic: "History is too complex and multifaceted to be built on any monochromatic foundation."[30] According to Mikhailovskii, the Marxists erred in describing society's functioning in terms of laws that took on a metaphysical quality.

The other principal figure among the Legal Marxists at this time, Struve (1870–1944), had already by the mid-1890s accepted Mikhailovskii's contention, contrary to Plekhanov, that Marxism was not a complete philosophical system. Nonetheless, in his first major book Struve held that individuals are but an expression of the social group to which they belong, apart from which they amount to nothing.[31] He agreed with Plekhanov that individuals are free when they act in accordance with the laws of history and economic development. Nonetheless, within a few years, Struve moved significantly closer to Mikhailovskii's stand, writing that goal-seeking actions require a psychological

[29] M.I. Tugan-Baranovskii, *Russkaia fabrika v proshlom i nastoiashchem* (St. Petersburg: Izd. L.F. Pantelieeva, 1898), vol. 1, p. iv.
[30] N.K. Mikhailovskii, "Literatura i zhizn'," *Russkoe bogatstvo* (February 1894), 154.
[31] P.B. Struve, *Kriticheskie zametki k voprosu ob ekonomicheskom razvitii Rossii* (St. Petersburg: Izd. N. Skorokhodova, 1894), pp. 31, 40.

feeling of personal freedom that contradicts the acceptance of the universal causality that underlies the possibility of scientific knowledge.[32] Only through metaphysics can the contradiction between personal freedom and universal causality be resolved, a path Struve was not yet, in the mid-1890s, willing to take. Without admitting an increasing affinity to Mikhailovskii's positions, Struve uncovered numerous inconsistencies in those of Kant. He dismissed the noumenal realm, finding individual freedom to be a fundamentally inescapable psychological illusion, an illusion that made the positing of ideals and goals possible. In other words, he recognized a contradiction within our everyday consciousness between a recognition of the causal necessity of objective events and the feeling of freedom to act as we choose, a contradiction that at this time he could not satisfactorily resolve.

In 1900, in a lengthy preface to a book-length critique of Mikhailovskii by a young philosopher, Nikolai Berdiaev, Struve made a dramatic volte-face. He now not only rejected Mikhailovskii's epistemic phenomenalism with its talk of truths as purely relative to the cognizing subject, but even Mikhailovskii's ethical subjectivism. According to Struve, there is neither a subordination of epistemology to ethics nor the opposite. We recognize the eternal moral law not by experience or by logic. Indeed, the absolute good, just like absolute truth and beauty, is not given empirically even though we know that there is such a thing.[33] The realization of human potential and the creation of a new society can only be accomplished through willing the absolute good, in the free fulfillment of our duty. From the standpoint of the absolute good, the individual person is the highest moral value. However, it is not the empirical or phenomenal aspects of the individual, but his or her ideal essence that is the source of moral autonomy and fundamental human equality. These essentially metaphysical claims no longer struck Struve as peculiar. Although no logical or empirical proof can establish the existence of a personal God, he thought that viewing the world as a rationally ordered whole entailed theism. Having no proof of the objectivity of morality but nonetheless a firm belief in it, Struve explicitly conceded that he was left with the metaphysical postulate of a moral world-order independent of subjective consciousness.[34]

---

[32] P.B. Struve, "Svoboda i istoricheskaia neobkhodimost'" in *Na raznye temy (1893–1901 gg.)* (St. Petersburg: Tip. A.E. Kolpinskogo, 1902), pp. 487–488.

[33] P.B. Struve, "Predislovie" in N.A. Berdiaev (ed.), *Sub''ektivizm i individualizm v obshchestvennoi filosofii: Kriticheskii etiud o N.K. Mikhailovskom* (Moscow: Kanon, 1999), p. 59.

[34] *Ibid.* p. 51. An activist like Struve could hardly have been content with Kantian abstractions even in the moral realm. In another essay from 1900, he rejected Eduard Bernstein's cry "Back to Lange!" with the cry "Back to Lassalle, which means in a certain sense back to Hegel and even more to Fichte." P.B. Struve, "F. Lassalle" in *Na raznye temy*, p. 266.

Struve's intellectual development did not stop with ethical idealism. He increasingly moved toward a wholehearted endorsement of a metaphysical or religious idealism, though his surviving philosophical utterances are general and wholly undogmatic. His evolving convictions centered on the Kantian ideas of moral duty (autonomy) and the absolute value of the human person (dignity), but he appreciated that these ideas had religious roots in Christian teachings about the human soul as an eternal and self-determining substance.[35]

Like Struve, Berdiaev (1874–1948) in his early years inclined towards social-ism, even Marxism, but then dramatically veered away from his former beliefs. Within a relatively short period he embraced a more radical form of idealism that would eventually bear scant resemblance to Kantianism. But at the begin-ning of the twentieth century, Berdiaev, in contrast to Struve with his Kantian dualism, clung to a monism deeply indebted to Marxist historical materialism. Yet in his critique of Mikhailovskii, mentioned above, Berdiaev rejected the populists' subjectivism by appealing to the Kantian conception of the objective as that which is universally valid. If we deny the universal validity of concepts outright, leaving them as merely psychologically valid, as do the empiricists, we logically arrive at skepticism. Such reasoning applies equally both to the logical and to the moral realm, and such a conclusion is unconscionable. For Berdiaev, "there must exist some kind of *objective* standard, which would place one subjective ideal above another and point out to us *the obligatory truth in the moral sphere*."[36] The moral law is neither a subjective, psychological illusion nor, for that matter, something reducible to elements in any non-moral sphere. As in epistemology, so in ethics Berdiaev turned to Kant, particularly to the German philosopher's second formulation of the categorical imperative, which prohibits treating any person merely as a means to an end.[37]

Berdiaev saw the basic principles of morality as objective and, as such, not subject to alteration. This is one facet of his claim (and Struve's) that there is only one postulate of practical reason, that of a moral world-order. The specific content of morality does, however, change over time; nevertheless, the moral order is not ethereal but concrete – something that is being realized in the historical process. And moral progress does occur in history: this is the other facet of Berdiaev's claim. While morality is not a psychological or even strictly speaking a sociological matter, its development, according to Berdiaev, is his-torically linked with the most progressive social class of the time (the proletariat in Berdiaev's time). He thought he could witness the moral development of humanity as it approached the absolute moral good through the elimination

[35] P.B. Struve, "K voprosu o morali" in *Na raznye temy*, p. 520.
[36] Berdiaev, *Sub''ektivizm i individualizm v obshchestvennoi filosofii*, p. 130.   [37] *Ibid.* p. 140.

of (populist) subjectivism. Here again we see Berdiaev's debt to the historical materialism from which he was still distancing himself.[38] He wanted to augment Marxism with Kantian ethics, especially Kant's notion that the criterion for judging progress is the regulative idea of always treating persons as ends-in-themselves. Berdiaev understood that the validity of this idea can no more be proven than can the universal applicability of causality to appearances. However, without the latter we would be epistemically blind, and without the former we would be morally blind.

Berdiaev agreed with Mikhailovskii and Struve that freedom is a prerequisite for morality, but the agreement stopped there. Berdiaev found their dualism, their desire to uphold a psychological belief in freedom of the will and a belief in the physical world as rigorously determined, to be philosophically impoverished and logically untenable. In fact, Kant's own pronouncements in this matter are far from his most astute. Part of the problem is that Kant did not consistently distinguish between the epistemological and the psychological. For Berdiaev, there was no contradiction: freedom and necessity belong to two distinct categories, the psychological and epistemological, respectively. To say that the will is free does not mean that its decisions are totally uncaused. Rather, the will can be caused, but by inner (psychic or moral) causes as opposed to forces external to it. Were the will completely undetermined, without rhyme or reason, its decisions would be quite capricious, rendering moral responsibility impossible.

Although at this point in his intellectual development Berdiaev realized the philosophical deficiencies of Marxism, he still found an important psychological truth in its statement of the relationship between freedom and necessity. He thought we could observe their conceptual identity in the social class whose aspirations harmonized with the developmental path of historical societies. This path, according to Berdiaev, was heading toward the progressive victory of human freedom, power and consciousness. Only those within the progressive class whose will is in harmony with progressive social demands could recognize themselves as free, as being able to act as they choose.[39] And what were these demands? They were to be found in our struggle to control nature, to master its elemental forces so that we can develop our humanity. Such a victory over nature is what the Marxists, despite their philosophical anemia, meant by the leap from the kingdom of necessity to that of freedom. To speak of the progressive ascendancy of humanity over nature as the telos of history presupposes the human being as the objective end of history, which Berdiaev defined as the realization of the kingdom of humanity, not as Kant thought in some postulated,

---

[38] *Ibid.* p. 144.   [39] *Ibid.* p. 177.

noumenal realm but in the real world around us. Berdiaev acknowledged that Mikhailovskii's ideals were largely identical with his: that is, a just social order in which all individuals are equal and which fosters the cultural and intellectual development of each person. However, whereas for Mikhailovskii the human being was merely a subjective moral end, for Berdiaev the individual was an objective end, a formal norm that remained constant even as the material ends of humanity changed over time.

CONCLUSION

While the figures examined here were the vanguard of the attack on positivism and moral subjectivism, they were by no means alone. In a few short years, others joined the attack, defending "the principle of the absolute significance of personhood."[40] However, the Russian neo-idealists certainly were not of one mind. The allegiance of some, most strikingly typified by Berdiaev, to monism and to the rejection of science grew stronger in the coming years, as they turned instead to religion and irrationalism. Yet already as early as the 1902 anthology *Problems of Idealism*, Berdiaev affirmed that, even though for him human beings are ends-in-themselves, what he had in mind are ideal, spiritual beings, not individuals of flesh and blood. The everyday person on the street often fails to embody the ideal human essence, or ideal spiritual state, that has absolute value.[41] The aim of ethics is neither the happiness of the individual nor even of the species, but the cultivation of the spirit that is the ground of absolute human value.

Other Russian neo-idealists were more steadfast in their support of both scholarship and liberal democratic ideals. A notable example is Bogdan Kistiakovskii (1868–1920), a product of the Baden School of German neo-Kantianism. His defense of the rule of law and the "inviolability of the person"[42] is taken up by Frances Nethercott in chapter 12 of this volume. Kistiakovskii's liberalism was closely related to his critique of scientism, which, unlike Berdiaev's increasingly religious and even mystical outlook, was strictly methodological. Kistiakovskii rejected the positivist reduction of sociological concepts to physiological ones, yet admitted that we cannot discount *a priori* the

---

[40] P.I. Novgorodtsev, "Foreword to the Russian Edition" in Randall A. Poole (ed. and trans.), *Problems of Idealism: Essays in Russian Social Philosophy* (New Haven, CT: Yale University Press, 2003), p. 83.

[41] N.A. Berdiaev, "The Ethical Problem in the Light of Philosophical Idealism" in *Problems of Idealism*, pp. 170–171.

[42] Bogdan Kistiakovskii, "In the Defense of Law: The Intelligentsia and Legal Consciousness" in Marshall S. Shatz and Judith E. Zimmerman (eds. and trans.), *Vekhi/Landmarks: A Collection of Articles about the Russian Intelligentsia* (Armonk, NY: M.E. Sharpe, 1994), p. 96.

applicability in the social sciences of models used in the natural sciences.[43] He had no doubt about the importance of science, its ability to disclose objective truth, and its ability to improve everyday life. Even after Berdiaev's treatise on Mikhailovskii, Kistiakovskii thought it worthwhile to criticize the famous populist in his contribution to *Problems of Idealism*.[44] Like his friend Max Weber, he respected religion and the values it upheld, while refusing to follow Berdiaev in devaluing natural and historical existence.

For a pivotal historical moment at the turn of the century, all the Russian idealists supported liberal freedoms and the absolute value of the individual. The emergence of philosophical and political differences among them would occur over the next several years as Russia entered its age of revolution.

---

[43] B. Kistiakovskii, "Kategorii neobkhodimosti i spravedlivosti pri issledovanii sotsial'nykh iavlenii," *Zhizn'* (May 1900), 288.

[44] B. Kistiakovksii, "The 'Russian Sociological School' and the Category of Possibility in the Solution of Social-Ethical Problems" in *Problems of Idealism*, pp. 325–355.

PART II

RUSSIAN METAPHYSICAL IDEALISM IN DEFENSE OF HUMAN DIGNITY

5

BORIS CHICHERIN AND HUMAN DIGNITY IN HISTORY

G.M. HAMBURG

The assertion that human beings possess inherent value, an innate dignity, is an old one, dating at least as far back as the book of *Genesis,* in which God declared: "We have made you in our own image and likeness." The idea was spiritualized by Augustine in his great treatise on *The Trinity* (written 400–416), which argued that the human faculties of memory, intellect, and will are in the image of the three persons of the Trinity, who embody divine being, divine intellect, and divine will. In his biblical commentaries, Thomas Aquinas associated the image of God strictly with mind, not the body. Yet whether the idea of human dignity was understood in a literal, spiritual, or intellectual sense, it lacked firm roots in the political realm until the Italian Renaissance, when the Italian humanist Lorenzo Valla (1406–1457) linked it with the transformation of secular history through human will.[1] Once Valla's successors began to think about the problem of dignity in history, they confronted the empirical truth that most human beings live in a squalor scarcely suited to sustain a dignified life; moreover, these thinkers faced the terrible moral reality that powerful men often choose to oppose the just life or harbor visions of justice that radically contradict the idea of universal dignity. The tension between dignity as an inherent metaphysically grounded trait of human nature and dignity as a historical project therefore lay at the heart of European philosophy from the Renaissance until the era of Kant and Hegel.

A LIBERAL PHILOSOPHER IN NINETEENTH-CENTURY RUSSIA

In Russia, no thinker worked more systematically in the defense of human dignity than the liberal philosopher Boris Nikolaevich Chicherin (1828–1904). As a public intellectual, Chicherin was Russia's foremost advocate of liberty of

---

[1] This is the argument of Charles Trinkaus, *"In Our Image and Likeness": Humanity and Divinity in Italian Humanist Thought,* 2 vols. (University of Chicago Press, 1970), vol. 1, pp. 103–170.

conscience, a freedom he called in an 1856 essay "the first and most sacred right
of a citizen."[2] In various works before 1861 he championed the abolition of
serfdom as a step toward healing the "inner corruption" of the Russian character
and as a means of restoring the "moral worth" of the peasantry.[3] In the 1860s
he urged the government to adopt a series of liberal reforms (his motto was
"strong government, liberal measures") designed to guarantee freedom under
law, especially civil rights. In 1866, 1870–1871, in 1878, and again in 1900, he
debated whether conditions in Russia were right for the introduction of political rights and representative government. Throughout his life he considered a
genuine *Rechtsstaat*, founded on individual freedom and designed to harmonize
the conflicting desires of citizens in Russia's pluralistic society, to be the ultimate goal of all "healthy-minded" citizens. The effort to secure human dignity
through rational political change and the rule of law informed Chicherin's practical activity over four decades in zemstvo assemblies in Tambov province and
in his eighteen-month term (from 1881 to 1883) as mayor of Moscow. Indeed,
the central government dismissed Chicherin from his position as mayor because
it suspected him of supporting a constitution.[4]

Chicherin did not arrive at his political philosophy at one step or by dint of
wholesale borrowing from this or that isolated thinker. As a student at Moscow
University in the 1840s, he fell under the influence of moderate Westernizers such as Konstantin Kavelin, Timofei Granovskii, and Sergei Solov'ëv. They
posited that history advances in the direction of personal freedom: Kavelin spoke
of the reign of personhood (*lichnost'*) and Granovskii of "the gradual development of all facets of the human spirit."[5] Like many other Europeans of the day,
they constructed their theories of historical progress at least in part on Hegelian
foundations. Chicherin himself studied Hegel's political philosophy and logic
for several months, so intensively that fellow students nicknamed him "Hegel."[6]
His own early essays show unmistakable traces of Hegelian ideas, and his commitment to Hegelianism was a key factor in his bitter debate with Aleksandr

---

[2] See B.N. Chicherin, "Sovremennye zadachi russkoi zhizni" in *Golosa iz Rossii* (London, 1857),
   book 4, p. 112. English translation: "Contemporary Tasks of Russian Life" in *Liberty, Equality, and
   the Market: Essays by B.N. Chicherin* (G.M. Hamburg (ed. and trans.), New Haven, CT and London:
   Yale University Press, 1998), pp. 110–140, here p. 134.
[3] This argument can be found in his essay "O krepostnom sostoianii" in *Golosa iz Rossii* (London,
   1856), book 2, pp. 127–154. English translation: "On Serfdom" in *Liberty, Equality, and the Market*,
   pp. 69–109.
[4] See *Vospominaniia Borisa Nikolaevicha Chicherina. Zemstvo i Moskovskaia duma* (Moscow: Koopera-
   tivnoe izdatel'stvo "Sever," 1934), pp. 167–266.
[5] *Vospominaniia Borisa Nikolaevicha Chicherina. Moskva sorokovykh godov* (Moscow: Izdanie M. i S.
   Sabashnikovykh, 1929), p. 14.
[6] *Ibid.* pp. 73–74.

Herzen over the future political direction of Russia.[7] However, Chicherin's
fascination with Hegel soon yielded to wide reading of classical Greek philosophers and also of post-Renaissance philosophers, especially Montesquieu, Adam
Smith, the radical French *philosophes*, and contemporary socialists. Thus, over
time his initial allegiance to Hegel gave way to an appreciation of the entire
legacy of western political thought. This legacy he explored further in the early
1860s when he taught public law at Moscow University; he also wrote about
it in his sprawling five-volume *History of Political Ideas* (1869–1902), a work
that made his reputation as perhaps the most erudite Russian humanist of his
day. Chicherin's mature political philosophy was an eclectic mixture based on
his life-long exploration of ideas: a Russian variant of *juste-milieu* liberalism,
Manchesterite political philosophy, and German metaphysical idealism.

FORMATION OF CHICHERIN'S PHILOSOPHY OF HISTORY

Chicherin's first books showed that he had internalized the view that the
achievement of human dignity is a viable historical project. His master's thesis, *Regional Institutions of Russia in the Seventeenth Century* (1856), rested on
the assumption that Russian development had followed the general pattern
of western European evolution from clan society, through private law to the
modern state, with the crucial differences that, in western Europe, modern
governments were less centralized than in Russia and western citizens enjoyed
a greater share of rights.[8] Implicit in the argument of this book was the belief
that, with Peter the Great, Russia had entered a new period in its history whose
goals were popular enlightenment and the gradual growth of individual liberty.
In *On Popular Representation* (1866) Chicherin defended liberty under representative institutions as the concrete goal of every law-abiding society, although
he emphasized that representative governments can only operate successfully in
societies mature enough to provide for them a solid foundation. He contended
that a proper foundation for representative institutions includes a tradition of
civil rights, responsible public opinion and responsible political parties, plus a
strong, centralized state devoted to the nurturing and protection of civil society.[9]
On Popular Representation reflected Chicherin's preoccupation with the problem
of the preconditions of constitutional government, but it also showed his deepening interest in the provision of civil rights, a matter that he now explicitly
linked with full human self-realization.

---

[7] On this debate see G.M. Hamburg, *Boris Chicherin and Early Russian Liberalism, 1828–1866* (Stanford
University Press, 1992), pp. 194–201.
[8] B.N. Chicherin, *Oblastnye uchrezhdeniia Rossii v XVII veke* (Moscow: Tipografiia A. Semena, 1856).
[9] B.N. Chicherin, *O narodnom predstavitel'stve* (Moscow: Tipografiia Gracheva, 1866).

By the late 1860s Chicherin was trying to formulate his own philosophy of history. In the first volume of *History of Political Ideas* (1869) he sketched out the elements of this philosophy. He argued that humanity's point of departure was a condition of "primitive unity" found in the ancient polis, wherein politics encompassed all aspects of citizens' lives and activities. This condition of unity could not be long maintained, for two reasons: first, the polis was based on the labor of slaves, and therefore was predicated on the exclusion of bondsmen from its deliberations; secondly, the polis was subject to criticism from within by citizens who sought for themselves a measure of autonomy from its demands. Eventually, under internal and external pressure, the ancient world order collapsed, giving way to a dialectical tension between civil society (based on private law and individual rights) and the church (based on the ethical and religious elements of community). This tension, characteristic of western European feudalism, was eventually transcended by the modern state, which protects both the civil freedoms developed within civil society and the ethical authority of the church. The modern state brings an end to slavery of every sort and upholds the rights of citizens to maintain a sphere of inner liberty outside the control of state officials. Chicherin clearly believed that human dignity can be realized in a benign *Rechtsstaat*. He described this dispensation, this new, pluralistic and harmonious polity, as "unity aspiring to supreme harmony."[10] He connected this unity with a movement of political philosophy he called "syncretism" or "universalism," which aimed at a synthesis of deductive reason and empiricism.[11] He classified German idealism as the preeminent form of universalistic thinking. Thus, by his reckoning, the concrete realization of human dignity in the future *Rechtsstaat* was to come about, at least in part, through the agency of idealist political philosophy.

A decade later, in *Science and Religion* (1879), Chicherin added to his interpretation of history an explicitly religious dimension. He did so in part because he had undergone a slow religious conversion between 1865 and 1874 and in part because he now felt that human dignity could not be effectively defended in the absence of religious belief. *Science and Religion* consists of three books. The first is an analysis of reason focusing on its limits, achievements, and religious implications; the second is an analysis of faith in its philosophical, aesthetic, moral, and institutional dimensions; the third discusses human history by highlighting the transformation of religious belief over time and concludes with a statement of the "laws of human development."

[10] B.N. Chicherin, *Istoriia politicheskikh uchenii*, 5 vols. (Moscow, 1869–1902), vol. 1, *Drevnost' i srednie veka* (Moscow: Tipografiia Gracheva, 1869), p. 11.
[11] *Ibid.* p. 9.

Through the volume Chicherin struggled to reconcile the idea of human liberty with obedience to the laws of history. In the first book, for example, he complained that any attempt to understand human nature purely through natural science inevitably reduces humanity to "one contingent object among other contingent objects." On such a theory, "the individual becomes the plaything of blind forces."[12] He rejected in principle all theories analyzing human nature exclusively in naturalistic or empirical terms; he claimed that human beings have an irreducible spiritual dimension, and that they, as sentient and rational beings, will seek to connect themselves with the Absolute (p. 9). In his opinion, God created human beings not as blind instruments of the divine will, but rather as free moral agents: therefore, he declared, "the human soul is the arena of freedom" (p. 101). Chicherin dismissed the notion of a Supreme Reason that had foreseen and predetermined the entire chain of causes and effects we know as human history, for such a notion leaves no room for individual liberty: "Consistent spiritualism [Chicherin's code for Leibnizian monism] inevitably leads to determinism, to the negation of liberty" (p. 117).

Chicherin's conception of human nature as rational, religious, and free was closely bound up with his postulate that human dignity can be realized in history. In Book Three of *Science and Religion* he argued that history had begun with a "first synthetic epoch" dominated by naturalistic religions and by early philosophical religions. It was succeeded by a "first analytical epoch" characterized by the development of Greek philosophy, which in turn yielded to a "second synthetic epoch" (the medieval and modern age of faith) and a "second analytical epoch" (the enlightenment and age of philosophical realism). The end of the historical process would be the appearance of a "final synthesis" or "age of universalism." In it materialist philosophy would yield to a new, more advanced metaphysics; materialist politics based on utilitarian or egalitarian premises would yield first to liberal democracy, and then to a rule-of-law state governed by technical experts. If the first synthetic epoch had worshipped the God of Might, and the second synthetic epoch had adored the God of the Word, the third epoch would adore the "God of Spirit." In this final age, the Spirit would reveal itself fully and "lead humanity to its ultimate goal, to complete harmony" (p. 370). In this age, Christianity would not be replaced since it was already "the perfect moral religion"; instead it would be "brought to fulfillment by a new revelation of other aspects of the divine being" (p. 367). Here Chicherin elaborated a religious–political utopia, based on his adaptation of Hegel's dialectical logic of history.

---

[12] B.N. Chicherin, *Nauka i religiia* (Moscow: Tipografiia Marynova & Ko., 1879), p. 3. Subsequent page references cited parenthetically in text.

To his credit, Chicherin was troubled by two possible objections to his scheme. The first objection had to do with the implication that we can only enjoy our liberty by obeying the laws of the dialectic. He tried to parry this objection by restating it in favorable terms (pp. 449–450):

Freedom does not consist in creating laws, but rather in carrying them out... Our duty is simply to follow the moral law. By the same token, in history, the recognition of a law code does not annihilate human liberty, for the law can only be observed by means of liberty. An individual is shown a path, but the methods of traversing the path depend upon his or her free will. The individual may shorten or lengthen stride, choose instruments of war or peace, deviate from the goal and return to it again after vainly expending energies on the deviant course.

In restating the objection, Chicherin sought to preserve the cardinal principle of individual free will and simultaneously to identify historically efficacious choice with obedience to the laws of history. His tactic did not succeed because *Science and Religion* laid more stress on the imperatives of reason and historical logic than it did on individual volition. This was an error that Chicherin would seek to correct in *Philosophy of Law*.

The second objection was that the realization of human dignity in some future age could not repair the devastating indignities suffered by past generations. Chicherin registered this objection in Book One, when he observed: "Even if we assume that, at the end of historical time, the individual will be able to attain his or her full potential, that will not change the lot of the many millions who have perished on the way. Shall we claim they were instruments of humanity's highest aspirations and their purpose consisted in playing the role of tools?" He answered: "The demand that full human potential be achieved must apply equally to past and future generations, for human nature is the same in all" (pp. 167–168). For this reason, he declared, we are logically bound to accept the existence of the afterlife, with a system of rewards in it, for only then can past injustices be righted. In effect, Chicherin's utopian postulate of a coming age of the Spirit drove him to seek in recognition of the afterlife a supra-historical solution to the problem of human dignity. The difficulty of this posture was that it rendered superfluous the necessity of realizing dignity through historical change: if all tears are to be wiped clean in the afterlife, why should human beings strive mightily to build the kingdom of God on earth? Chicherin would decide in *Philosophy of Law* to drop the element of utopianism in his religious philosophy and to reject the possibility of achieving the kingdom of God on earth. This decision did not entirely resolve the dilemma he had created for himself in posing human dignity as inherent human property and as historical project, but it made that dilemma less acute.

ORIGINS OF CHICHERIN'S *PHILOSOPHY OF LAW*

Late in his life, in the 1880s and 1890s, Chicherin grasped that the idealist tradition of philosophy, which had dominated the Russian academy in his youth, had fallen out of favor with young people and academic philosophers. Accordingly, he did his best to revive that tradition in books such as *Positive Philosophy and the Unity of Science* (1892), a critique of Comtean positivism, and in his masterpiece *Philosophy of Law* (serialized 1898–1899, published as a book in 1900). The latter book contains his mature views on metaphysics and ethics, two branches of philosophy he insisted are connected. In it we find his teaching on human dignity, on the relationship between the individual and society, on the proper roles of church and state in the modern world, and, finally, on the relationship between freedom and law. Because the book is so rich and its arguments so intricate (Andrzej Walicki called it "masterly" and took it as the fullest presentation of the "old liberal" or "classical" liberal philosophy of law in Russia[13]) its origins and content deserve careful exposition.

Chicherin began to write *Filosofiia prava* (*Philosophy of Law*) in late summer/ early fall 1898. The immediate impulse for the book was his unhappiness with the young jurist Leon Petrażycki's *Die Lehre vom Einkommen. Vom Standpunkt des gemeinen Civilrechts*,[14] a book containing a view of civil rights that Chicherin found "utterly perverse."[15] Chicherin was also driven to record his legal philosophy by Kiev University Professor Nikolai Karlovich Rennenkampf, whose 1898 newspaper articles in *Kievlianin* seemed to Chicherin to justify discrimination against Poles and Jews.[16] Aside from the desire to answer Petrażycki and Rennenkampf, Chicherin was motivated to put pen to paper by irritation over the latest philosophical works of Sergei Trubetskoi and Vladimir Solov'ëv. He found Trubetskoi's recent series of articles, "Foundations of Idealism" (1896),[17] closer to materialism than to idealism, vague, and philosophically

[13] Andrzej Walicki, *Legal Philosophies of Russian Liberalism* (Oxford: Clarendon Press, 1987), pp. 117, 130–155.

[14] L. Petrażycki, *Die Lehre vom Einkommen. Vom Standpunkt des gemeinen Civilrechts*, 2 vols. (Berlin: Müller, 1893–1895).

[15] ROBL/RORGB (Rukopis'nyi otel Rossiiskoi gosudarstvennoi biblioteki) fond 334 (fond Chicherina), ed. khr. 6, "Pis'ma Borisa Nikolaevicha Chicherina k Aleksandru Vasil'evichu Stankevichu, 1896–1898," ll. 72–72 verso, letter of June 27, 1898.

[16] Three open letters to Chicherin appeared in issues 158, 159, 160, 162, 163, 164, and 165. They were collected in a short pamphlet, N.K. Rennenkampf, *Pol'skie i evreiskie voprosy (Otkrytye pis'ma N.K. Rennenkampfa B.N. Chicherinu)* (Berlin: Rosenthal & Co., 1901). Chicherin's reply to Rennenkampf was published anonymously in Berlin by his brother Sergei Nikolaevich, under the title *Pol'skie i evreiskie voprosy. Otvet na otkrytye pis'ma N.K. Rennenkampfa* (Berlin: Izdanie Hugo Steinitz, 1899).

[17] S.N. Trubetskoi, "Osnovaniia idealizma," *Voprosy filosofii i psikhologii* 7:1–5, books 31–35 (1896); reprinted in *Sobranie sochinenii Kn. Sergeia Nikolaevicha Trubetskogo*, 6 vols. (Moscow, 1907–1912), vol. 2, pp. 161–284. On Trubetskoi and his philosophical system of "concrete idealism," see Martha

naive.[18] He thought Solov'ëv's great meditation *Justification of the Good* lacking in proper metaphysical foundations, and thus an attempt "to philosophize without philosophy."[19] According to Chicherin, Solov'ëv had accepted Kant's approach to the problem of practical reason without considering recent objections to it or to the underlying ideas of Kant's critique of pure reason. Furthermore, Solov'ëv had constructed his own moral philosophy without thinking through freedom of will. Indeed, Chicherin contended, Solov'ëv had tried "to banish the question of freedom of the will from the sphere of moral activity" (p. 592). By so doing, Solov'ëv had discarded an idea that Kant had considered "an essential postulate of moral philosophy" (p. 593).[20] Solov'ëv's undertheorized ethical system was, in general, "full of concepts that had to be accepted on faith, concepts of unknown origins and bearing arbitrary significance" (p. 594).

Solov'ëv based his ethical system on three "psychological facts": the shame we feel in the face of our lower, material nature; the pity or compassion we feel toward other human beings; and the reverence we feel toward social superiors and toward God. Chicherin found nothing convincing in this psychological perspective on ethics. He saw no reason to follow Solov'ëv's Christian prudery in classifying sexual relations as inherently shameful, and he found appalling Solov'ëv's attempt to explain conscience as an elaboration of the shame instinct (pp. 608–609). In Chicherin's opinion, conscience is not a sophisticated version of shame, but a "manifestation of the inner freedom of human beings . . . In conscience, a human being is a self-determining and therefore a moral being. Here the unbreakable tie between ethics and inner freedom reveals itself fully. But for Solov'ëv that tie does not exist at all" (pp. 608–609).

Solov'ëv's idea that human beings relate to one another through pity or compassion also seemed one-sided to Chicherin. In particular, Chicherin dismissed Solov'ëv's conclusion that altruism is nothing but "recognition of others' rightful significance − of [their] right to existence and right to prosperity or well-being [*vozmozhnoe blagopoluchie*]" (pp. 614–615). He accused Solov'ëv of "propagating a strange concept of rights":

Bohachevsky-Chomiak, *Sergei N. Trubetskoi: An Intellectual Among the Intelligentsia in Prerevolutionary Russia* (Belmont, MA: Nordland Publishing Co., 1976), and Randall A. Poole, "Trubetskoi, Sergei Nikolaevich (1862–1905)" in Edward Craig (ed.), *Routledge Encyclopedia of Philosophy* (London: Routledge, 1998–), online version.

[18] B.N. Chicherin, "Sushchestvo i metody idealizma," *Voprosy filosofii i psikhologii* 8:2, book 37 (1897), 185–235, here 191.

[19] B.N. Chicherin, "O nachalakh etiki," *Voprosy filosofii i psikhologii* 8:4, book 39 (1897), 586–701, here 588. Subsequent page references cited parenthetically in the text.

[20] These criticisms should be compared to Solov'ëv's actual treatment of Kant. See Randall Poole in chapter 6.

What is this right to well-being? The right not to suffer? Not to be ill? Not to lose one's loved ones to illness? To possess a beloved woman? To have sufficient means to realize one's desires? Everyone certainly wants all this for himself, but between desire and right there is a huge difference. I may desire to have a fine house, but I have no right to it whatsoever: I have to buy or build it, and that requires money, which no one is obliged to supply to me. (pp. 616–617)

Solov'ëv's muddled idea concerning the right to well-being was a symptom of a deeper confusion about personal rights, responsibility, injury, and insult. In Solov'ëv's opinion, not to assist a needy person was to insult that person; not to show compassion was to be heartless. In Chicherin's view, however, justice toward others has nothing to do with others' purported "right" to well-being, for justice consists solely of giving to each person that which legally belongs to him or her. Showing charity to the needy must be a free moral choice; charity cannot be required by law, for it is a moral act going beyond the legal imperative to render justice to others (pp. 618–619).

Concerning Solov'ëv's contention that human beings feel natural reverence toward superior beings (for example, toward their parents and God) Chicherin objected that not everyone shows respect toward his or her parents, and that love of parents is in any case a different order of emotion than religious reverence. Chicherin insisted that worship of God must not be reduced to the false analogue of filial piety (pp. 622–624). He also pointed out that not every human being has toward God the inner feeling experienced by Solov'ëv (pp. 627–628).

These objections were very important, because they pointed to the flaw in Solov'ëv's theory of history, which aimed at nothing less than the construction of the kingdom of God on earth. Solov'ëv hoped for a human future resting on the perfected shame instinct (conscience), compassion (in the form of compulsory altruism), and Christian self-perfection (in the name of reverence to God). This hope, Chicherin believed, could never be realized; worse, it presented a "broad field for every kind of fantasy" (p. 635). According to Chicherin, the coming of the kingdom of God could never be achieved except by state coercion, that is, "by the complete rejection of freedom" (p. 640). He likened Solov'ëv to a modern Torquemada, who saw a universal community as the realization of every person's desire for justice in the construction of "organized good." In Chicherin's opinion, the construction of this "organized good" would entail the end of human freedom and of the autonomy of conscience. It would inevitably lead to the jailing of heretics and of apostates (pp. 645–646).

PHILOSOPHY OF LAW: PERSON, SOCIETY, AND RIGHT

In the first book of *Philosophy of Law* Chicherin outlined the theoretical relationship between the individual and society. He described the individual as the "cornerstone of the social edifice," because "not society, but individuals think, feel and desire; everything issues from and returns to them." For him, personhood was based less on physiology than on "the entire spiritual world, whose source is reason and will."[21] Chicherin argued that an essential attribute of human personhood is freedom of will. He censured those philosophers who denied this freedom when they suggested that human acts are determined by external causes or directed by mechanical responses to physical stimuli. According to Chicherin, these philosophers erred by treating human personhood as "an empty vessel, wherein various sensations and representations collide" (p. 59). In reality, a human subject "is an active force, whose actions, to the degree they are determined by inner self-consciousness, depend on volition" (p. 60). Because humans are unique, spiritual, free beings, they possess an inherent dignity (*dostoinstvo*) demanding the respect of others. In Chicherin's thinking, human beings must always be regarded as ends, never as means or instruments to an end, for treating them as instruments "is a diminution of their dignity" (p. 76). Chicherin's radical insistence on freedom of will aligned him closely with Kant but also with Dostoevskii, a thinker with whom otherwise he had large differences. Since the establishment of rules for social conduct inevitably limits individual liberty, Chicherin believed that living in society entails "the mutual limitation of freedom under a common code of law" (p. 81). Yet even in society, individuals are irreducible units, "the fundamental and necessary element of any community." "Where the human personality lacks recognition," he wrote, "there can be no genuinely human community" (pp. 86–87).

Chicherin argued that human societies evolve "through [changes in] consciousness and will" (p. 93). Since human beings consciously determine their goals and since this process follows a logic according to which each idea is realized gradually, human history itself has a logic corresponding to "the law of the evolution of reason" (p. 94). Sometimes, as in certain Oriental states, this logic reaches a dead-end, but in Christian societies the unfolding of historical logic had been continuous. Chicherin came close to Pëtr Chaadaev when he argued that "a nationality acquires universal significance when it partakes in this collective process [of development] and assimilates the fruits of universal human enlightenment" (pp. 97–98). If living in community enables individuals to contribute to and benefit from the gradual realization of reason in history, then, Chicherin appeared to suggest, the dignity of personhood has two functions. First, it endows individuals with an irreducible value quite apart from the social

---

[21] B.N. Chicherin, "*Filosofiia prava. Kniga pervaia. Lichnost' i obshchestvo*," *Voprosy filosofii i psikhologii* 10:1, book 46 (1899), 46–104, here 46–47. Subsequent page references cited parenthetically in the text.

status they may possess at a given stage of historical development. Secondly, it enables individuals to make rational choices leading to the institutional recognition and protection of that dignity. Thus, metaphysically free beings can, over time, construct free societies governed by representative bodies; that is, they can realize the fullness of human dignity in history.

In the second book of *Philosophy of Law* Chicherin analyzed the problem of right (*pravo*); that is, of "liberty defined by statutory law."[22] Among Russian thinkers, Chicherin was perhaps the most consistent in distinguishing sharply between morality and law. Thus, he argued that morality must never be enforced by coercion, whereas right always entails a measure of coercion. Furthermore, he maintained, these two concepts pertain to different spheres of human life: morality has to do with self-regulation of one's inner impulses, right with the limitation of external actions affecting others (pp. 220–221). Since morality and right belong to different spheres, the general rule should be that "the moral sphere should not be subordinated to statutory law" (p. 222).

According to Chicherin, the concept of right is inextricably related to the principle of equity or justice (*pravda* or *spravedlivost'*) in the treatment of society's members. A society that wishes to treat its members justly need not establish mechanical equality amongst them; indeed, any objective observer will discover that, in most cases, individuals are unequal to each other in physical, intellectual, and moral capacities. In Chicherin's opinion, "inequality predominates in human communities" (p. 227). He thought this inequality to some degree rooted in nature, in the different endowments of human beings, but he recognized it was also a product of freedom of choice. Since this was so, he thought, social inequality should be considered a logical consequence of freedom. That being the case, he argued, equality and freedom are contradictory and incommensurable goals (p. 228). Since freedom of the will underlies any rational conception of justice, recognition of social inequality is "an inevitable consequence of justice" (p. 229).

Yet Chicherin did not think that material inequality should preclude equal treatment under the law, for, as sentient beings, humans possess an irreducible dignity that the law must respect. He included amongst the civil rights that should be enjoyed by all: the right to move one's domicile; the right to choose one's occupation; the right to enter freely into civil contracts; and the right freely to express one's ideas and feelings. This last right included freedom of conscience, freedom of religious assembly, and freedom to convert from one faith to another. It also included freedom of thought, that is, freedom of

---

[22] B.N. Chicherin, "*Filosofiia prava. Kniga vtoraia. Pravo,*" *Voprosy filosofii i psikhologii* 10:2, book 47 (1899), 214–249, here 214. Subsequent page references cited parenthetically in the text.

self-expression in the public sphere. Chicherin understood these civil freedoms to be protected from government intrusion (pp. 239–246).

His top priority was freedom of conscience. He hoped immediately to persuade the Russian government to stop discriminating against Jews, Old Believers, and other religious minorities, and so he reminded the government that articles 44 and 45 of the imperial code of laws guaranteed subjects freedom of religious practice (p. 242).

Chicherin defined property as "the first manifestation of liberty in the external world."[23] He claimed that property is the result of an act of appropriation whereby an individual applies his or her will to nature and subjugates it, yet the individual holds the appropriated thing not by physical right but by virtue of the act of will involved in the appropriation. Right "is not a physical, but rather a spiritual principle." To Chicherin, the notion of the communal ownership of property by all humanity was either a "fantasy" or an "empty phrase," because humanity has no will apart from the sum of individual wills composing it (p. 384).

This rejection of communal property was a crucial move in Chicherin's theory of right, because it gave him leverage to deflect the socialist attack on private property. He wrote: "The fruits of labor belong to the laborer. This is a completely obvious rule of equity and is also an unshakable foundation of private property, for the individual, not society, toils. This completely obvious truth is rejected by socialists" (p. 388). If this was so, then it followed that private property should be defended "as a manifestation of liberty so long as it does not conflict with the rights of others" (p. 390).

On this foundation Chicherin constructed his theory of inheritance rights and also a broad justification for capitalism. He acknowledged that the capitalist system generates social inequality, but he reminded readers that "freedom, by its nature, leads to inequality. In the sphere of property this rule shows itself fully operative, yet one cannot destroy this inequality without destroying its root – that is, human liberty – and consequently without infringing on the source of all right" (p. 397).

At the end of Book Two, Chicherin turned to the problem of punishment for crime. He dismissed those who justify punishment as a measure designed to protect society by deterring future criminals, for the theory of deterrence had led to "disproportionate punishments." "It had generated torture and inhuman executions" (p. 415). He also dismissed those who justify punishment on therapeutic grounds, as a means morally to correct and rehabilitate the criminal. He

---

[23] B.N. Chicherin, "*Filosofiia prava*. Prodolzhenie," *Voprosy filosofii i psikhologii* 10:3, book 48 (1899), 382–425, here 383. Subsequent page references cited parenthetically in the text.

regarded the hope of rehabilitation as unjustified in important criminal cases. Furthermore, he found the entire theory of deterrence to have a pedagogical flavor, for it posits that the criminal be treated not as a willful adult malefactor but as a child wanting in discipline (p. 417).

Instead, Chicherin defended a theory of punishment based on reciprocal deprivation of rights: if a criminal attacks another person or steals someone's property, the criminal deprives the victim of the enjoyment of a right, and thus may be deprived of his or her right in return. This logic led Chicherin directly to defend capital punishment as a just punishment, "the taking of something that had been taken [from someone else]" (pp. 419–420). In Chicherin's view, only a theory of punishment rooted in a metaphysical understanding of rights can constitute an appropriate basis for the defense of human dignity.

This theory of punishment, with its counterintuitive justification of capital punishment, sat at odds with Bentham's and Mill's utilitarian theories of punishment, and with Solov'ëv's impassioned call for an end to retributive justice. The editors of *Problems of Philosophy and Psychology* made clear in a footnote their rejection of Chicherin's views of capital punishment, "both on juridical and moral grounds" (p. 425). To us, perhaps, what is most disturbing about Chicherin's theory may be his willingness to ascribe to the death penalty a role, even a mechanical role, in upholding human dignity: there can be, it would seem, nothing dignified in death at the executioner's hand. Yet, according to Chicherin, a criminal who knowingly takes another person's life forfeits at that moment his or her own. Chicherin regarded freedom of will not only as a precious thing, but also as a frightening responsibility. He hinted that we actually show respect to the murderers as bearers of rights by executing them.

PHILOSOPHY OF LAW: MORALITY

In Book Three of *Philosophy of Law* Chicherin presented his ethical theory.[24] He took the view that our sense of right and wrong appeared *before* the historical foundation of religions, and that ethical theory is therefore the property of all rational human beings, regardless of their religious affiliations. He rejected the utilitarians' effort to ground morality on the individual's desire to maximize pleasure and to minimize pain: he found their standard of judgment entirely subjective and egoistic, but also philosophically barren. According to Chicherin, a far better way to think about morality is to posit that every human being has a conscience informed by reason and by knowledge of moral law. Here he

---

[24] B.N. Chicherin, "*Filosofiia prava. Kniga tret'ia. Nravstvennost'*," *Voprosy filosofii i psikhologii* 10:4, book 49 (1899), 479–539, here 480. Page references cited parenthetically in the text.

followed Kant's idea of the categorical imperative as a guide to conduct standing above egoistic calculations. To rebut the objection that the categorical imperative is itself based on selfishness, Chicherin interpreted the imperative – "act as if the rule guiding your actions should be a law for every sentient being"[25] – as a simultaneous recognition of one's own and others' dignity. From the recognition of human dignity there followed the philosophical rule: "a rational being should be for you an end not a means" (pp. 487–488).[26] Each individual should show respect to other individuals, and this respect entails treating others as members of a community with common values. If we discriminate against others, we effectively exclude them from our community, and thus violate what Chicherin called the "law of love" (pp. 488–489).

Since the love we owe to others is an unconditional moral imperative, a demand of absolute reason, we are bound by our own recognition of human dignity to acknowledge the universal bearer of the Absolute Idea – namely, God. By Chicherin's reasoning, therefore, our innate knowledge of moral law leads us to accept the divine source of reason itself. Thus, for Chicherin, moral philosophy and the religious impulse are closely linked.

But if reason leads human beings both to value community and to believe in God, then why did Chicherin not insist that the laws of community and religious law be identical? Why did he distinguish statutory from moral law? Here Chicherin returned to Kant's distinction between external actions and inner impulses. Statutory law imposes rules on external acts, and therefore should not concern itself with inner impulses except insofar as these impulses express themselves in a given action. Meanwhile, the inner world of moral calculation should be free of external compulsion, for a precondition of fulfilling one's moral obligations is that one have freedom of will. By this theory, human beings should carry out their legal responsibilities because they are bound by statutory law to do so, but they should discharge their moral duties freely.

To these general observations about ethics, Chicherin added concrete discussions clarifying the distinction between statutory law and morality. He argued that positive law may forbid certain actions, but it is also a framework permitting a broad range of actions. For example, statutory law recognizes an individual's right to property and thus the right freely to dispose of that property. Thus,

---

[25] Chicherin's paraphrase; for Kant's formulation, see Immanuel Kant, *Groundwork of the Metaphysic of Morals* (H.J. Paton (trans.), New York: Harper & Row, 1964), p. 88. Chicherin does not specifically acknowledge Kant's great work. However, fifteen years earlier, in an essay on Kant in *History of Political Ideas*, Chicherin gave a remarkably sympathetic account of the *Groundwork* (and *Critique of Practical Reason*), with citations to the German text. See *Istoriia politicheskikh uchenii*, vol. 3 (Moscow, 1874), pp. 330–336.

[26] Chicherin's paraphrase of Kant's second formula of the categorical imperative (Kant, *Groundwork*, p. 96).

the law creates a framework in which individual property owners may exercise their discretion over their property's disposition; the law must not tell that individual whether to use that property in this way or that, morally or immorally. For example, positive law must not force an individual to be charitable to the poor: the imperative to aid the poor is a moral demand, not a legal imperative, and therefore a property owner should be left free to show charity or not. The German socialists' notion that the principle of "coerced sacrifice" should be incorporated into statutory law struck Chicherin as "essentially immoral" (pp. 504–505).

Likewise, Chicherin argued, positive law should recognize the individual's right to freedom of conscience "as the cornerstone of human freedom and therefore of human dignity." In Chicherin's opinion, a state should never hinder the free exercise of religion by religious dissenters (*inovertsy*). Not only is state interference with religious practice a violation of the individual's freedom of conscience, it is an act that dissolves the responsibility of the individual to obey the government's dictates (p. 508). Here Chicherin asserted, without elaboration or emphasis, a right of passive resistance to intrusive government. Chicherin understood that the exercise of freedom of conscience leads in practice to religious pluralism in society. In general, he maintained that statutory law should function to create a protected arena within which individuals may exercise their freedom of ethical choice.

Chicherin did not object to government efforts to promote virtuous conduct among its subjects. Indeed, he thought that morally informed dispositions of the will – courage, a sense of proportion or moderation, equity, self-respect, gratitude toward the Creator, and love of the common good – constitute solid foundations for dutiful moral action in private life and in the public realm as well. He was not worried that the possession of these virtues by everyone in society might lead to the homogenization of the citizenry and thus to uniformity in the social order. In fact, he argued, cultivating virtue is a way of building a pluralistic society, because virtuous citizens will exercise their inner freedom in different ways (pp. 510–519). Moreover, living virtuously does not require an individual to treat all other individuals identically. One may love this person more than that one; one may respect a righteous person more than an unrighteous one. Virtuous people observe the rule that justice consists in offering to each individual what that person deserves, but what one person deserves may be different than what his or her neighbor deserves (pp. 520–522).

The danger comes when a government enlists the universal moral imperative to love others as one loves oneself as a justification for statutes compelling one citizen to help another. By such "juridical charity," Chicherin thought, the government actually undercuts virtue. "Under the surface [of such an enterprise as 'juridical charity']," Chicherin wrote, "lurk those perverse doctrines that, under the guise of universal brotherhood, demand complete suppression of individual personhood" (p. 525). In the end, no system of coercion should be allowed to order an individual's ethical life: righteous conduct depends on the free voice of conscience, on virtue, on "inner free self-determination" (p. 530).

Given a well-developed knowledge of virtue, can a society attain the moral ideal? Is it possible to achieve the Kingdom of God on earth? As we noted above, Chicherin thought such an achievement impossible. To be sure, moral perfection is a goal toward which every individual ought to strive, but the hard fact is that "the overwhelming majority of men stand on a very unlofty moral plane" (p. 529). If they do not fall further into vice each day, the reason is their adherence to religious beliefs, especially to Christianity with its doctrine of the afterlife. Following Kant, Chicherin argued that "the future life, with its rewards and punishments, is a necessary postulate of the moral law. Without the afterlife, it [the moral law] remains incomplete and impotent" (p. 533). Here again, Chicherin agreed with Dostoevskii in rejecting utilitarian notions of reward and punishment on earth as being sufficient inducements to live a virtuous life. Only belief in God and in the afterlife can sustain human beings in the face of temptation and tragedy (pp. 533–535). Yet even with the prospect of the afterlife, human beings remain imperfect in their conduct. "The kingdom of God is unrealizable," Chicherin wrote, "for it presupposes perfected humanity, but on the earth there are and can be no perfect people" (p. 537). To imagine that all individuals will voluntarily follow the moral law without deviating from it "is nothing but an idle fantasy" (p. 538).

In describing perfection as beyond the reach of human beings, Chicherin felt no reason to despair about the human prospect. He maintained that imperfect people can successfully live a public life "informed by moral principles," because such an ambition "does not require that all people be virtuous, rather it demands only the establishment of a system of institutions that harmonize with the moral law and facilitate its affirmation." He called this public sphere where morality encounters law, where inner liberty operates simultaneously with external liberty, the sphere of "objective morality" and "objective law" (p. 539). It was to this sphere of activity that he devoted Book Four of *Philosophy of Law*.

PHILOSOPHY OF LAW: SOCIAL INSTITUTIONS

In Book Four, Chicherin sketched out a theory of social institutions. He argued that, although every society ultimately rests on individuals, it necessarily contains at least four human associations: family, civil society, church, and state.

Each of these associations has a distinctive ethos and function, and it is imperative for society not to permit these associations to collapse into one another.
For example, he regarded the promotion of economic activity as a central goal
of civil society that should be largely free from interference by church and
state. He argued that the church should be stripped of all property except that
necessary for its survival, even if the seizure of property be a revolutionary
act. The church's status as a separate legal estate should be abolished – this to
preserve the separation between church and civil society.[27] Naturally, he argued
in favor of separating church and state, but strangely he did not think this separation need be airtight. He defended a combination of three different systems
of church–state relations: that is, he thought it possible to combine an established church (for example, Russian Orthodoxy) with legal recognition of other
confessions (Roman Catholicism and mainline Protestant churches) and with
toleration (extended in Russia to Protestant sects, Judaism, Islam, and Buddhism)
(pp. 113–114).

Implicit in this complex scheme of church–state relations was a defense of
religious pluralism. Chicherin rejected the contemporary movement toward
unification of the Christian community (a movement joined by Vladimir
Solov'ëv) because he thought the existence of different confessions satisfies
the multiple dimensions of the human soul. He even argued that "if Protes-
tantism were to disappear, then for those people who value the free search for
[spiritual] truth, there would remain no recourse but unbelief [*neverie*]." He
saw the difference among Christian confessions as "a difference over many secondary dogmas, over ritual and sacraments," not over essential matters of belief.
He said that a single church government applied across the world would result in
"the complete moral enslavement of humanity" (pp. 108–110). Thus, his view
of the church's place in society and in the state was, by late nineteenth-century
standards, liberal, even radical. Within the Russian Orthodox Church, he stood
in the modernist camp.

At Book Four's end, Chicherin arrived at the subject of the state, the human
association that "forms a united, permanent and autonomous whole." Here,
law and morality finally come together in synthesis. Yet in Chicherin's opinion
this unity "is not physical but spiritual"; that is, it is based on an "ideal form,"
on a "metaphysical principle" (pp. 114–115). Since the state rests on an ideal,
its existence is not inconsistent with the preservation within it of other human
associations – family, civil society, and church. Indeed, the state's chief objectives
are to protect these other associations against attack, to codify and preserve their

---

[27] B.N. Chicherin, "*Filosofiia prava,*" *Voprosy filosofii i psikhologii* 11:1, book 51 (1900), 101–149, here
111–112. Subsequent page references cited parenthetically in the text.

rights, and to harmonize their interests. In the pursuit of these goals the state may establish laws and institutions in the common interest, that is, it may print money, collect taxes, build roads, and establish schools. But these activities must not be allowed to destroy human liberty (pp. 116–118).

Chicherin distinguished sharply between personal liberty and public liberty, or perhaps more accurately, between civil rights and political rights. For him, as we have seen, personal or civil rights include: the right to move one's domicile, to change one's occupation, to enter into contracts, and to express one's ideas. Political rights guarantee civil rights through the establishment of a law limiting the prerogatives of government and through the establishment of an independent court system to preserve them (pp. 123–124). Political rights also include the right to participate in public affairs. Although Chicherin dared not say so explicitly, his notion of political rights pointed to a constitutional charter and some form of representative government.

This simple distinction between civil and political rights was a cardinal issue for Chicherin. He apparently thought of civil rights as those rights that flow most immediately from human dignity, from our status as free sentient beings. Therefore, we should not surrender these rights as a precondition of participation in public life, as Rousseau had proposed in *Du contrat social*. In fact, Chicherin believed, the abolition of civil rights for any reason leads to monstrous despotism (p. 122). Political rights, although rooted in human beings' metaphysical liberty, appeared historically only after civil rights had established themselves, that is, in sophisticated modern states. Therefore, he seemed to hint, political rights are more distantly related to our status as free sentient beings: they constitute the culmination of dignity's trajectory in human history.

CONCLUSION

Chicherin's *Philosophy of Law* was distinguished by the author's determination to revitalize German idealist modes of thinking about morality, law, the individual, and the state. This determination took concrete form in an attempt to combine Kant's teaching about moral duty with Hegel's approach to right and to the state. Chicherin defined human nature metaphysically, as Kant had done. He endorsed Kant's basic position on individual self-determination and moral autonomy, and he accepted Kant's categorical imperative as the best guide to moral action. He followed Kant's logic in vindicating freedom of conscience and in opposing state coercion in matters of religious belief. He was strongly influenced by Kant's thinking about human dignity.

Like Hegel, Chicherin saw history as an evolutionary process whose logic represented the unfolding of an absolute idea in time due to human beings' gradual recognition of the Absolute. He agreed with Hegel's emphasis on volition as an earmark of human nature and as a crucial element in political action. He shared Hegel's view that proper understanding of criminal law and of political rights depends upon one's estimate of the importance of human willfulness in fixing responsibility for crime and in defining citizens' duties. Chicherin's *Philosophy of Law* used Hegelian categories as the building blocks of political theory, and it even assigned those categories similar functions in the elaboration of legal philosophy. Finally, Chicherin followed Hegel in seeing the state as sovereign authority, as the symbol and guarantor of social unity, and as the agency responsible for enforcing freedom under the law. Coercion, in Chicherin's opinion, was built into the very fabric of the state, which required force to maintain the rule of law.

Chicherin's intentions in combining Kantian and Hegelian thinking in *Philosophy of Law* are obvious. Kant's analysis (of the metaphysical grounding of human dignity and freedom, of the importance of recognizing individual moral autonomy, and of protecting freedom of conscience) was connected to Hegel's thinking (about freedom of the will, about state authority and divided government, and about the harmony between individual liberty and the individual's subordination to the laws of history) to produce a powerful synthesis pointing to the possibility of upholding individual freedom and dignity alongside an externally powerful, internally divided state authority. Chicherin used Kantian teaching about human dignity as a cat's paw against utilitarian and utopian socialist thinking, which debased human dignity by undercutting the individual's metaphysical nature and which undercut human liberty by aiming at mechanical equality. He used Hegel's *Philosophy of Right* to outline a fruitful way to combine individual liberty with state power and to suggest how, concretely, individual freedom might be reconciled with obedience to the laws of history.

Chicherin's *Philosophy of Law* had three important results in the decade following its publication. First, it served as a foundation for his telling practical criticisms of the Russian state in *Russia on the Eve of the Twentieth Century.*[28] Secondly, it contributed significantly to Pëtr Struve's transformation into a "conservative liberal"[29] and to Pavel Novgorodstev's neo-idealist thinking about law and morality.[30] It may also have influenced Novgorodtsev's attempt in *On the Social Ideal* to think through more carefully than Chicherin had done the

[28] Russkii patriot [B.N. Chicherin], *Rossiia nakanune dvadtsatogo stoletiia*, 3rd edn. (Berlin: Hugo Steinitz, 1901).
[29] Richard Pipes, *Struve: Liberal on the Right* (Cambridge, MA: Harvard University Press, 1980), pp. 375–376; Walicki, *Legal Philosophies of Russian Liberalism*, p. 107.
[30] See Walicki, *Legal Philosophies of Russian Liberalism*, pp. 310–311.

relationship between the Absolute and history.[31] Finally, in a general way *Philosophy of Law* served as the soundest ideological foundation for the moderate wing of the constitutionalist movement in Russia before 1905.

Judging only by *Philosophy of Law*, Chicherin's contributions to Russian liberal thought and politics were of such magnitude and intellectual distinction that we can scarcely accept Aileen Kelly's judgment that he belongs in the company of such twentieth-century types "who were able calmly and dispassionately to recommend the mass slaughter of human beings, secure in the belief that they were history's instruments and, if necessary its executioners."[32] Indeed, on the basis of his consistent denunciation of the nineteenth-century predecessors of these types, a sounder view would hold him to be a prescient opponent of the coming historical disaster.

That said, one cannot leave the subject of Chicherin's philosophy without remarking on the characteristic tension within it between his ideal of human liberty and his ideological commitment to the realization of that freedom through obedience to historical laws. At bottom, as we have seen, this is a tension between a belief in the metaphysical fact of freedom of the will and the empirical fact that freedom in history can only be fully achieved if one believes that its achievement corresponds to the hidden nature of things. According to Chicherin, our belief in human liberty as a metaphysical reality and our willing collaboration with historical laws are justified, because, as sentient beings, we must logically believe in the possibility of realizing our inner dignity in the external world before we can actually build free institutions. This conviction of Chicherin helps account for his brave attempt to move beyond Kant's confusion of inner liberty with external liberty. Chicherin may have been mistaken in his thinking, but, if he erred, his mistake was neither characteristic of blind fanaticism nor of fantasy. We should think better of him and better of the German metaphysical tradition in which he invested such hope.

---

[31] See P.I. Novgorodtsev, *Ob obshchestvennom ideale*, 3rd edn. (Berlin: Izdatel'stvo "Slovo," 1921), pp. 9–34.

[32] Aileen Kelly, "The Rational Reality of Boris Chicherin" in *Toward Another Shore: Russian Thinkers Between Necessity and Chance* (New Haven, CT and London: Yale University Press, 1998), p. 244.

6

VLADIMIR SOLOV'ËV'S PHILOSOPHICAL ANTHROPOLOGY: AUTONOMY, DIGNITY, PERFECTIBILITY

RANDALL A. POOLE

Vladimir Solov'ëv is widely regarded as Russia's greatest philosopher, certainly its greatest religious philosopher.[1] The focus of this chapter is the essential humanism of his core philosophical concept, Godmanhood (*bogochelovechestvo*), which incorporates human dignity as a constituent and inviolable principle.[2] Solov'ëv believed that personhood entails both consciousness of the absolute and the capacity to determine oneself according to that consciousness, i.e., according to absolute ideals. This conception of human nature, or philosophical anthropology, is deeply indebted to Kant. Solov'ëv develops it in his three most important philosophical works: *Lectures on Godmanhood*, *Critique of Abstract Principles*, and *Justification of the Good*.[3]

LIFE, WORKS, CONCEPTS

Vladimir Sergeevich Solov'ëv was born in Moscow in 1853, the son of Sergei Solov'ëv, the leading Russian historian of his generation. In November 1874 he defended his master's thesis, *The Crisis of Western Philosophy: Against the Positivists*,

---

[1] Semën Frank called him "unquestionably the greatest of Russian philosophers." See his introduction to S.L. Frank (ed.), *A Solovyov Anthology* (Natalie Duddington (trans.), London: SCM Press, 1950; London: Saint Austin Press, 2001), p. 9.

[2] Frank stressed Solov'ëv's Christian humanism: *A Solovyov Anthology*, pp. 30–31. In Paul Valliere's apt evaluation, "the concept of *bogochelovechestvo* was the vehicle for a principled and profound Orthodox Christian humanism." See his major study *Modern Russian Theology. Bukharev, Soloviev, Bulgakov: Orthodox Theology in a New Key* (Grand Rapids, MI: William B. Eerdmans Publishing Company, 2000), p. 12. Valliere has also written an excellent essay-length treatment of the Russian philosopher: "Vladimir Soloviev (1853–1900)" in John Witte, Jr. and Frank S. Alexander (eds.), *The Teachings of Modern Christianity on Law, Politics, and Human Nature*, 2 vols. (New York: Columbia University Press, 2006), vol. 1, pp. 533–575.

[3] Different versions of this essay have appeared as "The Greatness of Vladimir Solov'ëv: A Review Essay," *Canadian Slavonic Papers* 50, nos. 1–2 (2008), 201–223, and "Human Dignity and the Kingdom of God: A Russian Theological Perspective (Vladimir Solov'ëv)," *Listening/Journal of Religion and Culture* 42, no. 3 (2007), 33–54. I am grateful to Caryl Emerson, Gary Hamburg, Judith Deutsch Kornblatt, James Scanlan and Paul Valliere for their help with this chapter.

his first book.[4] He began lecturing at Moscow University, but in June 1875 went abroad for research on gnosticism and mysticism at the British Museum. There he had a mystical vision of Sophia, the Divine Wisdom, who directed him to travel to Egypt; in the desert he saw her again. Returning to Moscow in the summer of 1876, Solov'ëv resumed teaching and wrote his second book, *Philosophical Principles of Integral Knowledge* (1877).[5] Within a year he moved to St. Petersburg to take a position in the Ministry of Public Education. In early 1878 he delivered his famous *Lectures on Godmanhood* to audiences of nearly a thousand that included Dostoevskii.[6] In April 1880 the young philosopher defended a brilliant doctoral dissertation, *Critique of Abstract Principles*, and began teaching at St. Petersburg University.[7] He was 27 years old.

These early works, all highly theoretical, advance the main outlines of Solov'ëv's philosophical system – a metaphysics of the "unity of all" (*vsëedinstvo*), which conceives the cosmos as the manifestation of the divine absolute in the process of its own becoming or self-realization.[8] The unity of all, the return of (perfected) creation to the creator, is to be achieved through Godmanhood, the ideal of humanity's divine self-realization in and union with God (deification or *theosis*). Achievement of this ideal requires that human beings work toward "free unity" among the three spheres of life: "free theurgy" in creativity, "free theosophy" in knowledge, and "free theocracy" in social practice.[9] Another key element of Solov'ëv's metaphysics of cosmic redemption is Sophia, the subject of his mystical experiences.[10] Sophia is the Divine Wisdom by which God created the world, the unity and divinity of creation. Since humanity is the point where creation most reflects its creator, Sophia can be described as ideal humanity, humanity as it ought to be, as conceived by God. Our task, according to Solov'ëv, is to perfect ourselves and thus to transfigure the world by embodying the divine, Sophic essence. Indeed, the great theme of his philosophy is human perfectibility.[11]

Compared to the theoretical focus of his first four books, Solov'ëv's work in the 1880s took a somewhat different direction. On March 1, 1881, Emperor

---

[4] *Krizis zapadnoi filosofii (Protiv pozitivistov)* in S.M. Solov'ëv and E.L. Radlov (eds.), *Sobranie sochinenii Vladimira Sergeevicha Solov'ëva*, 2nd edn., 10 vols. (St. Petersburg, 1911–1914), vol. 1, pp. 27–170.

[5] *Filosofskie nachala tsel'nogo znaniia* in *Sobranie sochinenii*, vol. 1, pp. 250–406.

[6] *Chteniia o Bogochelovechestve* in *Sobranie sochinenii*, vol. 3, pp. 1–181.

[7] *Kritika otvlechënnykh nachal* in *Sobranie sochinenii*, vol. 2, pp. v–xvi, 1–397.

[8] Solov'ëv distinguishes between two poles of the absolute. The first is self-subsistent (God), the second is in the process of becoming (man), "and the full truth can be expressed by the word 'Godmanhood.'" *Kritika otvlechënnykh nachal*, pp. 315–324 (quotation at p. 323).

[9] *Filosofskie nachala tsel'nogo znaniia*, pp. 286–287.

[10] Judith Deutsch Kornblatt, *Divine Sophia: The Wisdom Writings of Vladimir Solovyov* (Ithaca, NY: Cornell University Press, 2008).

[11] It is the first of Solov'ëv's "central teachings" identified by Jonathan Sutton in his *The Religious Philosophy of Vladimir Solovyov: Towards a Reassessment* (New York: St. Martin's Press, 1988).

Alexander II was assassinated by terrorists. Later that month, Solov'ëv gave a public speech in which he appealed to the new tsar, Alexander III, to spare the regicides who had killed his father the death penalty, which Solov'ëv regarded as an unconscionable violation of human dignity.[12] Solov'ëv's plea was poorly received by both his audience and Alexander III, who, when he heard of the speech, ordered the philosopher to "refrain for a certain time" from lecturing in public.[13] This was a mild measure, but Solov'ëv felt it necessary to resign his positions at the Ministry of Public Education and St. Petersburg University. Thenceforth he lived as an independent scholar and public intellectual, devoting himself to his writings.

In the 1880s his works focused on various aspects of his project for establishing a worldwide "free theocracy" in preparation for the Kingdom of God on earth.[14] Disappointment with Russia, which he had imagined to be the messianic agent of universal theocracy, and more generally with the external forms of his theocratic ideal, led Solov'ëv to return to philosophy proper in the 1890s. This period culminated with *Justification of the Good* (1897), his magnum opus.[15] His final work was *Three Dialogues on War, Progress and the End of World History, with a Brief Tale of the Anti-Christ* (1899–1900).[16] He died on July 31, 1900 at the age of 47.

GODMANHOOD AND THE MEANING OF ABSOLUTE HUMAN VALUE

The central idea of Solov'ëv's philosophy is *bogochelovechestvo* – a term variously translated as Godmanhood, divine humanity, or the humanity of God.[17] The concept's meaning, as conveyed by the teaching of St. Athanasius and

---

[12] Solov'ëv was a lifelong opponent of capital punishment. He wrote devastating critiques of it in his long essay *Law and Morality: Essays in Applied Ethics* (1897) and in a shorter one, "Retribution (On the Spanish-American War)" (1898), a remarkable piece that also deals with another of his abiding concerns: freedom of conscience. Both are included in Vladimir Wozniuk (ed. and trans.), *Politics, Law, and Morality: Essays by V.S. Soloviev* (New Haven, CT: Yale University Press, 2000), pp. 111–123, 171–184.

[13] On Solov'ëv's speech and its reception see Marina Kostalevsky, *Dostoevsky and Soloviev: The Art of Integral Vision* (New Haven, CT: Yale University Press, 1997), pp. 78–80.

[14] His works of the period include *Dukhovnye osnovy zhizni* (*The Spiritual Foundations of Life*) (1882–1884); "Velikii spor i khristianskaia politika" ("The Great Schism and Christian Politics") (1883); "Evreistvo i khristianskii vopros" ("The Jews and the Christian Problem") (1884); *Istoriia i budushchnost' teokratii* (*The History and Future of Theocracy*) (1887); *L'Idée russe* (1888); *La Russie et l'Église universelle* (1889); and *Natsional'nyi vopros v Rossii* (*The National Question in Russia*), 2 vols. (1888, 1891).

[15] *Opravdanie dobra: nravstvennaia filosofiia* in *Sobranie sochinenii*, vol. 8, pp. 3–516.

[16] *Tri razgovora o voine, progresse i kontse vsemirnoi istorii, so vkliucheniem kratkoi povesti ob antikhriste i s prilozheniiami* in *Sobranie sochinenii*, vol. 10, pp. 81–221.

[17] See the "note on translation" in Valliere, *Modern Russian Theology*, pp. 11–15.

other church fathers, is that "God became man so that man might become God."[18] The formula consists of two key elements: *kenosis* (the humanization of God in the incarnation) and *theosis* (the deification of man). For Solov'ëv, *bogochelovechestvo* meant both the humanity of God and the (potential) divinity of humanity.[19] The term "Godmanhood," perhaps better than either the "humanity of God" or "divine humanity," suggests Solov'ëv's conception of God and man as ultimately one absolute, divine-human being: divinity that is also human (intrinsically and not only in the incarnation) and humanity that is also divine (by origin and vocation). Crucially, it also conveys the idea of a condition that is to be achieved.

Godmanhood was not an initial dogmatic premise for Solov'ëv, but rather the logical conclusion of sound philosophical method. His point of departure was not God but man, specifically human consciousness and morality. He believed that morality – our consciousness of absolute ideals and the capacity to act on them – is not only the most distinctive property of human beings but also our primary testimony to the ultimate nature of reality. He therefore made it the basis of his philosophy.[20] In this respect he followed Kant, whose epistemology (transcendental idealism) was designed to validate moral experience and to demonstrate the possibility of the metaphysical "postulates" he drew from it: God, freedom, and immortality.[21]

---

[18] One of the places Solov'ëv quotes St. Athanasius's formula is his 1883 "Note in Defense of Dostoevskii against the Charge of a 'New' Christianity," where he argues (against Konstantin Leont'ev) that Dostoevskii's humanism was truly Christian, that his belief in humanity meant "believing in its *capacity for deification*, believing according to the words of Saint Athanasius the Great, that in Christ God became man in order to make man god." This "Note" is included in Vladimir Wozniuk (ed. and trans.), *The Heart of Reality: Essays on Beauty, Love, and Ethics by V.S. Soloviev* (University of Notre Dame Press, 2003), pp. 199–204 (quotation at p. 202). Solov'ëv knew well the work of the Eastern church fathers, especially Maximus the Confessor. See Richard Gustafson's seminal essay, "Soloviev's Doctrine of Salvation," in Judith Deutsch Kornblatt and Richard F. Gustafson (eds.), *Russian Religious Thought* (Madison, WI: University of Wisconsin Press, 1996), pp. 31–48.

[19] Konstantin Mochul'skii, *Vladimir Solov'ëv. Zhizn' i uchenie* (Paris: YMCA Press, 1951), p. 10, uses these two phrases together to gloss "*bogochelovechestvo.*"

[20] E.N. Trubetskoi's classic two-volume study of his friend and philosophical mentor emphasizes the primacy of ethics in his philosophy. *Mirosozertsanie Vl. S. Solov'ëva*, 2 vols. (Moscow, 1913), vol. 1, pp. 107, 121.

[21] Kant held that duty and the capacity to act on it (free will or self-determination) indicated that natural necessity was not the sufficient determining cause of every event. He believed that morality was thus grounds for thinking that nature was not "coextensive with the real," as he put it in the preface to the second edition of the *Critique of Pure Reason*. The problem was to show how nature might not extend "everywhere," as in the Newtonian conception. Kant's solution was transcendental idealism, which, by reconceptualizing space and time as *a priori* forms of sensibility or representation (empirical experience) rather than properties of "objective reality" (Kant's term), left room for a supra-sensible (and thus also theoretically unknowable or "noumenal") metaphysical reality beyond those limits (nature). Immanuel Kant, *Critique of Pure Reason* (Norman Kemp Smith (trans.), unabridged edn., New York: St. Martin's Press, 1965), pp. 465–466, 26, 89. I develop

Solov'ëv's method, proceeding up to the divine from analysis of the human, is brilliantly deployed from the beginning of *Lectures on Godmanhood*. The first three lectures introduce important aspects of his philosophical anthropology by examining the rise of secular humanism in modern European history. Insofar as modern humanist ideologies such as socialism and positivism proclaim the principle of human dignity, they are right, according to Solov'ëv; but they are wrong, he says, in supposing that human beings can be absolute in value while also being only facts among a multitude of other facts.[22] Thus Solov'ëv's main criticism of secular humanists is that, in Paul Valliere's formulation, they do not appreciate the implications of their basic assumption.[23] Solov'ëv draws out these implications and concludes that the very capacity to conceive ourselves as absolute in value entails the reality of the absolute, i.e., a theistic metaphysics.

The Russian philosopher distinguishes between two aspects of our self-conception. The first is "negative absoluteness," which "consists in the ability to transcend every finite, limited content," never to be satisfied with such content and constantly to strive for more (p. 17). Negative absoluteness describes the nature of consciousness, which is to transcend facts, evaluate everything according to ideals, and strive in our thought and action toward those ideals – morality in the broad sense. It is the basis for human perfectibility or infinite development. Negative absoluteness presupposes a positive end toward which the whole process of infinite development tends; this is "positive absoluteness," the fullness of being or "unity of all." Secular humanists stop at negative absoluteness, since they fail to recognize that the capacity for infinite striving and development – their (and Solov'ëv's) precious ideal of human perfectibility – implies the reality of the positive absolute. From this logic Solov'ëv draws a striking conclusion: "Belief in oneself, belief in the human person, is at the same time belief in God" (p. 23).[24]

The reasoning behind this conclusion (that negative entails positive absoluteness) is that there is something "unnatural" about our self-conception and human consciousness in general. The idea of "absolute," present in our thought

---

Kant's argument in my essay "The Neo-Idealist Reception of Kant in the Moscow Psychological Society," *Journal of the History of Ideas* 60, no. 2 (April 1999), 319–343. I did not discuss Solov'ëv in detail there, but he embraced Kant's approach, as I will try to show here.

[22] Vladimir Solovyov, *Lectures on Divine Humanity* (Peter P. Zouboff (trans.), Boris Jakim (rev. and ed.), Hudson, NY: Lindisfarne Press, 1995), pp. 18–19. Subsequent references to this work will be cited parenthetically in the text. I have at points modified the translation in accordance with the Russian text (see note 6).

[23] *Modern Russian Theology*, p. 147.

[24] Solov'ëv retained the basic idea behind positive and negative absoluteness, but reformulated it in his later works. In *Justification of the Good* he refers to it simply as consciousness of absolute perfection (God) and our capacity for perfectibility according to that consciousness (see below).

at all levels whether we consciously recognize it or not, is a striking anomaly in an empirical world of relative facts. Even such evaluations (the world as "empirical" and facts as "relative") demonstrate the inevitability of the absolute perspective of consciousness. It is the nature of the mind to evaluate, and in doing so we rely on absolute, ideal norms. As Solov'ëv writes, "the simple, universally clear, and, one might say, trivial distinction of good from evil, truth from falsehood, beauty from ugliness, already in itself presupposes recognition of the objective and absolute principle in these three spheres of spiritual life" (p. 30). The upshot is that our capacity to evaluate – and to value and perfect ourselves as absolute – when experience confronts us with only facts starkly contradicts the naturalistic (i.e., atheistic) worldview.

The "objective and absolute principle" presupposed by our intellectual, moral, and aesthetic evaluations, toward which we strive in our "negative absoluteness," is, in its highest unity, God. Although Solov'ëv does not refer to Kant, he clearly has in mind the "ideal of pure reason," which the German philosopher, too, called God.[25] According to Solov'ëv, neither the existence of God nor of the external world in general can be proved – it must be taken on faith. Solov'ëv says this for the same reason Kant did: we know only phenomena, not things in themselves, and the forms and concepts of our knowledge are inadequate to establish the actual existence of things apart from our representations of them (pp. 30–31). Solov'ëv does not indicate, as did Kant, that transcendental idealism justifies such faith.[26]

There is another aspect to Solov'ëv's understanding of absolute human value, one that goes to the heart of his concept of Godmanhood. Solov'ëv insists that Godmanhood cannot be achieved without human autonomy: "The divine content," he said in his 1880 inaugural lecture in philosophy at St. Petersburg University, "must be appropriated by a human being *from within himself*, consciously and freely."[27] Godmanhood can only be a free union between man and God, as he emphasizes in a key passage of *Lectures on Godmanhood* (p. 17):

Such a union would be impossible if the divine principle were purely external to humanity, if it were not rooted in human personhood itself. If it were not so rooted, our relationship to the divine principle could be only one of involuntary, fateful subordination. The free inner union between the absolute, divine principle and the human person

[25] Kant, *Critique of Pure Reason*, pp. 485–495.
[26] Kant's argument is that space and time naturalize or phenomenalize whatever they encompass and so, were they "transcendentally real," would preclude a sure ground of being by turning everything into "mere illusion" (*Critique of Pure Reason*, p. 89). Transcendental idealism, by contrast, makes possible "faith" in being apart from phenomena (nature), although it also rules out theoretical knowledge (which, according to Kant, depends on the forms of space and time) of such being.
[27] "Istoricheskie dela filosofii" in *Sobranie sochinenii*, vol. 2, p. 410.

is possible only because the latter also has absolute significance. The human person can unite with the divine principle freely, from within, only because the person is in a certain sense divine, or more precisely, participates in Divinity.

The human person "is in a certain sense divine" because our divinity is an intrinsic potential that must be freely, *humanly* realized, and this would be impossible without divine–human equality – the meaning of absolute human value.[28]

THE THREE PRINCIPLES OF HUMAN NATURE

Solov'ëv calls human consciousness of the (positive) absolute the divine, religious, or mystical principle in man. It is one of three principles in his overall conception of human nature. The other two are the material principle, by which human beings are part of the natural world, and rational freedom or autonomy (reason and morality), which is the distinctively human principle, the middle principle between the divine and material (p. 158). The human principle is the capacity for self-determination in the direction of either the material or the divine, the capacity to "become" more (or less) than we presently are, to perfect (or degrade) ourselves (p. 142). Solov'ëv sees the capability to "become" as distinctively human. Non-rational beings do not "become," they can only "be" what they are by nature; their natural capacities are realized over the course of their life by instinct, not self-determination. God, too, according to Solov'ëv, can only "be," in that he is already perfect. Only human beings (and in principle other free rational beings) are capable of "becoming" and therefore of self-perfection.[29] The autonomous human element, as noted above, is an indispensable component of Godmanhood.

CRITIQUE OF ABSTRACT PRINCIPLES: RATIONAL AUTONOMY AND FREE THEOCRACY

The conception of human nature (divine–human–natural) that Solov'ëv introduced in *Lectures on Godmanhood* forms the basic philosophical framework of his

[28] Compare to Ernst Cassirer's characterization of Pico della Mirandola's idea of freedom, quoted in the Introduction to this volume: "Thus when Pico ascribes to man an independent and innate creative power, he has in this one fundamental respect made man equal to Divinity."

[29] He stresses this human capacity to "become" in many of his works. In *Justification of the Good* he calls it the "essentially human attribute." See Vladimir Solovyov, *The Justification of the Good: An Essay on Moral Philosophy* (Natalie A. Duddington (trans.), Boris Jakim (ed. and annot.), Grand Rapids, MI: William B. Eerdmans Publishing Company, 2005), p. lv. Also see *The Meaning of Love* (1892–1894), included in Wozniuk (ed.), *The Heart of Reality*, pp. 83–133, especially p. 92; and "The Idea of a Superman" in Wozniuk (ed.), *Politics, Law, and Morality*, pp. 255–263.

subsequent works. *Critique of Abstract Principles*, written concurrently with *Lectures on Godmanhood*, is an indispensable exposition of the philosopher's whole system. An "abstract principle" is one that is abstracted from and mistaken for the whole, whether the whole is person, society, or, ultimately, the "unity of all." Solov'ëv shows how the material, human, and divine principles can each be abstracted or put in place of the whole. Even so, he was much less concerned with the dangers of rational autonomy (the human principle) being an abstract principle than of it not being firmly included in the whole, between the material and divine principles. Indeed, in many respects the *Critique* is a defense of human autonomy. Solov'ëv demonstrates that autonomy is the essence of true morality and law, which must themselves be relatively autonomous parts of any social order or whole. The vision of the ideal society that he laid out in the *Critique* is "free theocracy," "free" because it purports to respect human autonomy.

The first half of the *Critique* is devoted to morality and to the social conditions for its realization and development (to pure or "subjective" ethics and to applied or "objective" ethics). Solov'ëv dealt with ethics (practical philosophy) before epistemology and metaphysics (theoretical philosophy) because he thought theory should explicate what moral experience immediately discloses about reality. Later, in *Justification of the Good*, he defended this approach as the "autonomy of morality" (see below). In the *Critique*, he indicated that the task of theoretical philosophy, which occupies him in the book's second part (beyond the scope of this essay), is to demonstrate the objective ontological reality of what Kant called the postulates of practical reason. He says that ethics is thus directly dependent on metaphysics (in the sense of the metaphysical reality of the postulates) and that this was Kant's own point of view, but, like many other Russian idealists, Solov'ëv was ambivalent about whether Kant held that the postulates are metaphysical truths or merely subjective claims.[30] In any case, he had far more confidence in their theoretical certainty than Kant did.

Solov'ëv's overall emphasis on the primacy of ethics is Kantian, as is his specific conception of the nature of morality. He begins his account with a critique of empiricist theories of ethics (hedonism, eudaemonism, altruism), which seek to derive the end or aim of moral activity from the data of sense experience, i.e., from observable human behavior.[31] These ethical theories (altruism in particular) may explain the psychological origins or motives of a moral act, but, according to Solov'ëv, they cannot account for what is specifically moral about it, for its quality of being normative or obligatory, since this can only be determined *a priori* by pure reason. Hence the psychological or "material"

---

[30] *Kritika otvlechënnykh nachal* in *Sobranie sochinenii*, vol. 2, pp. 190–191.   [31] *Ibid.* pp. 15–37.

principle in morality must be brought under the rational principle, and empirical morality must be supplemented by rational ethics.[32]

The rational principle in morality, the distinctively human one, is what gives a moral act its specifically moral quality. Solov'ëv's conception of rational ethics relies wholly on Kant, whose *Groundwork of the Metaphysic of Morals* he closely paraphrased at length.[33] Kant's central idea is the autonomy of the will, the will's self-determination by duty or the moral law ("ought," *das Sollen*), which it recognizes as its own. Heteronomy, by contrast, is the will's determination by sources (or objects) external to the moral law, such as ordinary natural impulses and inclinations. "In that case," Kant writes, "the will does not give itself the law, but the object does so in virtue of its relation to the will."[34] Solov'ëv embraced Kant's conception, declaring the autonomy of the will to be the "essence of morality."[35] He continues that "only through the concept of duty does morality cease to be an instinct," as with empiricist theories, "and become a rational conviction."[36] Here he paraphrased Kant's proposition that "duty is the necessity to act out of reverence for the law."[37]

The moral law holds, Kant says, not only for human beings but for all rational beings as such.[38] There may be rational beings whose will is determined solely by reason and its apprehension of the good; human beings are not among them, since our will is also subject to empirical determination (it may be either autonomous or heteronomous).[39] For us, therefore, the moral law takes the form of a command or imperative, specifically the categorical imperative: "Act only on that maxim through which you can at the same time will that it should become a universal law."[40]

Kant formulates the categorical imperative not only in terms of the form but also in terms of the ends or objects of morality. These ends are the same rational beings whose will ought to and can be self-determined by the moral law. He defines these rational beings as *persons* or ends-in-themselves. They are absolute values in themselves, "for unless this is so, nothing at all of *absolute* value would

---

[32] *Ibid.* pp. 37–46, 62–64.

[33] *Ibid.* pp. 44–62. In fact, much of what he presents as a paraphrase of Kant is a direct translation of key passages from the *Groundwork*.

[34] Immanuel Kant, *Groundwork of the Metaphysic of Morals* (H.J. Paton (trans.), New York: Harper & Row, 1964), p. 108.

[35] *Kritika*, p. 44.   [36] *Ibid.* p. 47.

[37] *Groundwork*, p. 68; *Kritika*, p. 49. Although Solov'ëv, like Kant, regards duty as necessary for morality, he does not think that only acts done solely from duty have moral worth (a view he attributes to Kant). Duty and natural inclination may coincide in the same act, he says, and this not only does not diminish but increases its moral value (*Kritika*, p. 65). In this way he tries to reconcile the natural feeling of compassion (altruism) with the categorical imperative.

[38] *Groundwork*, p. 76.   [39] *Ibid.* pp. 80–81.   [40] *Ibid.* p. 88, italics omitted; *Kritika*, p. 55.

be found anywhere."[41] These words Solov'ëv clearly took to heart in writing about the meaning of absolute human value in *Lectures on Godmanhood*. He also quotes, in the *Critique*, Kant's famous second formulation of the categorical imperative: "Act in such a way that you always treat humanity, whether in your own person or in the person of any other, never simply as a means, but always at the same time as an end."[42] Kant's third formulation is "the Idea of the will of every rational being as a will which makes universal law."[43]

The categorical imperative leads to Kant's "very fruitful concept" of the kingdom of ends,[44] which Solov'ëv calls the ultimate aim of all moral action.[45] Citizens of the kingdom of ends are self-legislating in that their will mandates only universal laws, to which they themselves are, of course, subject. Autonomy, Kant stresses, is the ground of their intrinsic value or dignity.[46] The kingdom of ends made a deep impression on Solov'ëv. "If every subject is a moral agent," he writes, "and everyone else as an end-in-itself is the object of its action, then the general result of the moral activity of all subjects will be their organic unity in the kingdom of ends."[47] Kant's kingdom of ends closely resembles Solov'ëv's own vision of the ideal society (free theocracy), which in the preface to the *Critique* he describes as the practical "unity of all" (*vseedinstvo*), "by virtue of which all are the end . . . for each and each for all."[48]

It is clear that Solov'ëv's concept of rational autonomy – the middle, distinctively human principle in his overall conception of human nature – is deeply indebted to Kant's ethics, in two ways. First, Kant's idea of the autonomy of the will is the core notion of human freedom that Solov'ëv adopts in his own work.[49] Secondly, Kant's idea that human dignity consists in rational autonomy, that is, in self-determination by consciousness of "ought" (the moral law) – as Kant directly puts it, morality "is the only thing which has dignity"[50] – is Solov'ëv's basic understanding as well. For Solov'ëv, the divine or religious

---

[41] *Groundwork*, p. 96; *Kritika*, p. 58.

[42] *Groundwork*, p. 96, italics omitted; *Kritika*, p. 58. Solov'ëv argues that Kant's distinction between rational and non-rational beings is artificial and may not be valid from the noumenal point of view, and that therefore all beings, whether we recognize them as rational or not, ought to be treated as ends-in-themselves. Accordingly he reformulates Kant's second principle as follows: "Act in such a way that all beings are the end and not only the means of your activity" (*Kritika*, pp. 69–70).

[43] *Groundwork*, p. 98, italics omitted; *Kritika*, p. 59.

[44] The quoted phrase is Kant's (*Groundwork*, p. 100), but Solov'ëv presents it as his own.

[45] *Kritika*, pp. 70, 114, 116.   [46] *Groundwork*, pp. 100–103.

[47] *Kritika*, p. 70.   [48] *Ibid.* p. viii.

[49] Kant treated autonomy and free will synonymously, writing that "a free will and a will under moral laws are one and the same." *Groundwork*, p. 114. Solov'ëv devotes two chapters to the problem of free will and Kant's solution, again presenting his direct translations of Kant (in this case *Critique of Pure Reason* and *Critique of Practical Reason*) as a paraphrase (*Kritika*, pp. 89–110).

[50] *Groundwork*, pp. 102–103, 106–107.

principle in human nature is not, by itself, the source of human dignity. The real source is the human principle of autonomy, or self-determination according to our consciousness of the absolute or divine. In *Lectures on Godmanhood*, Solov'ëv affirms absolute human value, human divinity, and divine-human equality, but the core of human dignity is autonomy, the capacity for the self-realization of our intrinsic divine potential – the capacity to realize God within ourselves, to *become* divine (theosis).[51] Were this realization externally rather than internally determined (heteronomously rather than autonomously), human dignity would be deprived of its basis. "Salvation" apart from free will, by external divine agency (grace), as in mainstream Christian understandings of salvation since Augustine, would violate human dignity or at any rate be accomplished past it.[52] For this reason, the source of human dignity, according to Solov'ëv, is not God but Godmanhood. This is the humanist thread that runs through his philosophy.

We know that both Kant and Solov'ëv held consciousness of moral duty, of the absolute principle(s) by which the will is self-determining, to be grounds for theistic belief: the German philosopher referred to the metaphysical postulates and the Russian to the "positive absolute." It is important to appreciate the direction of their argument. Both philosophers thought that our moral ideals suppose a higher metaphysical reality, and that the very presence of these ideals and their hold over us are sure testimony to that reality. While neither philosopher could conceive of human dignity without God, both maintained that the idea of God is entailed by (or follows from) human dignity, and both insisted on that logical sequence. Solov'ëv was a mystic whose life and thought were full of divine presence, yet he was no less concerned than Kant to prevent autonomy (and hence human dignity) from being overwhelmed by God. This is an intricate point.

Kant makes it in a striking passage, which Solov'ëv quotes, in the *Groundwork of the Metaphysic of Morals*. Kant is writing that morality cannot, of course, be derived from examples:

---

[51] This connection between human dignity and theosis is most explicit in *Justification of the Good* (see below).

[52] Orthodox theology in general has not drawn the sharp opposition between (human) nature and grace that has characterized much of western Christian thought. See Valliere, "Introduction to the Modern Orthodox Tradition" and "Vladimir Soloviev" in *The Teachings of Modern Christianity on Law, Politics, and Human Nature*, vol. 1, pp. 508, 554. For Solov'ëv, "grace" comes as human beings freely perfect themselves and is a result of that process. See, for example, *Istoriia i budushchnost' teokratii* in *Sobranie sochinenii*, vol. 4, pp. 337–342.

Even the Holy One of the gospel must first be compared with our ideal of moral perfection before we can recognize him to be such. He [Jesus] also says of himself: "Why callest thou me (whom thou seest) good? There is none good (the archetype of the good) but one, that is, God (whom thou seest not)." But where do we get the concept of God as the highest good? Solely from the *Idea* of moral perfection, which reason traces *a priori* and conjoins inseparably with the concept of a free will. Imitation has no place in morality.[53]

These lines powerfully capture the distinction between autonomy and heteronomy. The moral law or the good must be recognized from within if human autonomy and dignity are to be preserved. For this reason, God must not be "seen," as in the claims of miracle or revelation, but rather experienced from within, through faith.

Solov'ëv leaves Kant's passage without comment, but the reasoning underlying it was integral to his thought. The principle of autonomy led him to downplay or reconceptualize the role of miracle, revelation, and dogma in religion, all of which, he feared, risked undermining true faith by purporting to manifest the divine as if it were something external and knowable as a positive fact.[54] Like Dostoevskii, Solov'ëv understood that miracles can enslave, impairing the free, human realization of the divine. This understanding decisively shaped Solov'ëv's Christology. In *Lectures on Godmanhood* he writes that "strictly speaking, the incarnation of Divinity is not miraculous, that is, it is not alien to the general order of being" (p. 157). In his 1891 speech "The Collapse of the Medieval Worldview," he comments on Luke 9: 49–56 as follows: "James and John did not know the spirit of Christ, and they did not know it just because they believed above all in His external miraculous power. Such power there was, but it was not the essential thing."[55] The Russian philosopher closest to Solov'ëv, Evgenii Trubetskoi, expressed the spirit of Solov'ëv's Christology by writing: "Christ's complete sacrifice saves man not as sorcery from outside, but as spiritual influence *liberating him from inside* and transforming his nature only on the condition of the *autonomous* self-determination of his will."[56]

Autonomy is the essence of morality, but morality cannot be realized in a vacuum, by the autonomous subject on his or her own. The moral will must have an object or end, which for Kant is other persons and for Solov'ëv all living

---

[53] *Groundwork*, p. 76; *Kritika*, p. 51. Solov'ëv does not quote the last sentence. The biblical verses Kant quotes are in the Synoptic Gospels (with slight differences among them): Mark 10:18; Matthew 19:17; and Luke 18:19.

[54] One of the many places Solov'ëv specifies his view that true faith cannot be coerced but rests on "the evidence of things not seen" (Hebrews 11:1) is his essay "The Jews and the Christian Problem" (1884), which is translated in part in Frank (ed.), *A Solovyov Anthology* (here, p. 112).

[55] The speech is translated in *A Solovyov Anthology* (quotation at p. 62).

[56] E.N. Trubetskoi, *Smysl zhizni* (Berlin: Slovo, 1922), p. 204 (1st edn., Moscow, 1918).

beings, treated as ends-in-themselves. Morality thus presupposes society, ideally the kingdom of ends; thus Solov'ëv passes from "subjective" to "objective" ethics. He always insisted that human dignity and potential are realized in society and develop in history. The task is to clarify the social ideal, a vision of the normative society adequate to the ever fuller realization of human dignity.[57]

In trying to meet this task, social philosophy is as prone to abstractions as pure ethics is. In both cases Solov'ëv concentrates, first, on what happens when the material principle is abstracted and taken for the whole. In "subjective ethics" the result, as we have seen, is empiricist theories that miss the essence of morality. In "objective ethics" the result is "abstract economism," either economic individualism (capitalism or "plutocracy") or economic collectivism (socialism).[58] "Both standpoints," in Walicki's summary, "are equally immoral because both reduce man to *homo economicus*, instead of giving him the status of a person."[59] In social philosophy no less than in pure ethics Solov'ëv emphasized the importance of subordinating the material principle to the human principle.

In Solov'ëv's social philosophy, the principle of rational autonomy takes the form of law, based on recognition that human beings are persons, ends-in-themselves, and bearers of rights.[60] In Valliere's felicitous expression, "law is grounded in metaphysical personhood (freedom and reason), the inalienable glory of the human being."[61] The virtue of law, according to Solov'ëv, is that it makes possible the realization of all higher potentials of human nature, for it is the very condition of civilized life and peaceful society. By removing people from the state of nature, where the strong brutalize the weak and themselves in the process, law equalizes human relations and enables people to develop as persons.[62] This was Solov'ëv's ultimate justification of law and, more generally, of "objective ethics."

Law is an essential but not the highest principle of Solov'ëv's social philosophy. Its domain is the means by which people pursue their ends, but not the ends themselves. In the *Critique*, he writes that the equality of all before the law actually means that "all are equally *limited* by law, or all equally limit each other; this means there is no inner or positive unity among them, only their

---

[57] *Kritika*, pp. 116, 120.   [58] *Kritika*, pp. 126–134.

[59] Andrzej Walicki, *Legal Philosophies of Russian Liberalism* (Oxford University Press, 1987), pp. 182–183.

[60] *Kritika*, pp. 139–140.

[61] "Vladimir Soloviev," p. 546. A comprehensive account of Solov'ëv's legal philosophy can be found in Andrzej Walicki, *Legal Philosophies of Russian Liberalism*, pp. 165–212. Solov'ëv's essay *Law and Morality: Essays in Applied Ethics* serves as a good overall statement of his philosophy of law (Wozniuk (ed.), *Politics, Law, and Morality*, pp. 131–212).

[62] *Dukhovnye osnovy zhizni* in *Sobranie sochinenii*, vol. 3, p. 340.

correct division and demarcation."[63] Only the divine or mystical principle in human nature – "by virtue of which all members of society are not limits for each other, but rather internally fulfill each other in the free unity of spiritual love" – can provide inner, positive unity among people. This principle is realized in the church. "Thus the normative society," according to Solov'ëv, "has as its foundation a spiritual union or the church, which defines its absolute ends."[64] But the realization of the divine principle in society must be approached freely and consciously; it cannot be based on clerical authority or blind faith; and it must fully respect the human principle of rational autonomy, both in morality (where it takes the form of freedom of conscience, which Solov'ëv consistently championed) and law. "Thus the true, normative society must be defined as free theocracy."[65] This was Solov'ëv's social ideal, the way to the realization of humanity's divine potential (Godmanhood).[66]

The meaning of Solov'ëv's theocratic ideal has long vexed scholars.[67] A society freely united in love of God, all of whose members seek to fulfill each other in that love, is one that has attained a vastly higher level of moral development than any in Solov'ëv's day or ours. The Russian philosopher may have wanted to suggest that the Kingdom of God would not be possible until, at least, "free theocracy" was.[68] In any case, Solov'ëv believed that the establishment of free theocracy – the Christianization of life culminating in the final triumph of the Kingdom of God – rested on the reunification of the church.[69] Solov'ëv devoted himself to this cause (ecumenism, as it would come to be called) in the 1880s. He even had an operational plan to make his vision a reality: Christendom was to be reunited by an alliance between the Russian emperor, Alexander III, and Pope Leo XIII. Nowhere, perhaps, is it more clear that

---

[63] *Kritika*, p. 167. Interestingly this closely recalls Marx's critique of the French Declaration of the Rights of Man and Citizen. See "On the Jewish Question" in Robert C. Tucker (ed.), *The Marx-Engels Reader*, 2nd edn. (New York: W.W. Norton, 1978), p. 42.

[64] *Kritika*, pp. viii–ix.   [65] *Kritika*, p. ix.

[66] The most sophisticated and sensitive treatment of Solov'ëv's ideal of free theocracy can be found in Paul Valliere's works, *Modern Russian Theology*, especially pp. 127–137, and "Vladimir Soloviev," pp. 547–551.

[67] The first of whom was Boris Chicherin, whose *Mistitsizm v nauke* (1880) is a book-length critique of Solov'ëv's dissertation.

[68] Kostalevsky, *Dostoevsky and Soloviev*, p. 115. Valliere proposes that "theonomy" may be a better name than "theocracy" for Solov'ëv's ideal ("Vladimir Soloviev," pp. 550–551).

[69] His first and most important work laying out his conception of the church and ideal of church unity is "The Great Schism and Christian Politics" (1883), translated in part in Frank (ed.) *A Solovyov Anthology*, pp. 75–101. In it he applies his tripartite model of human nature to the church. Eastern Christianity represents the divine element and western Christianity the human, but the historical development of each has been one-sided or "abstract." The ideal of the church, in contrast to these historical distortions, is the free inner union of both the divine and human elements.

Solov'ëv, the mystic, had difficulty distinguishing between this world and the next one.

JUSTIFICATION OF THE GOOD: MORAL EXPERIENCE AND ITS AUTONOMY

In the 1890s Solov'ëv grew disillusioned with his practical (or so he had imagined) plans for theocracy, though never with the ideal itself. He returned to the type of philosophical work that had engaged him a decade earlier. By common consensus, his *Justification of the Good*, which appeared in 1897, is the most important Russian work of moral philosophy.[70] Arguably it is one of the great modern works of ethics and religious philosophy. In it we find Solov'ëv's most powerful defense of human dignity.

Justification of the Good is divided into three parts, "The Good in Human Nature," "The Good from God," and "The Good through Human History." In the first part Solov'ëv applies the three principles of human nature to an analysis of moral experience. He identifies three "primary data of morality": shame, compassion, and reverence. Shame corresponds to the material principle in human nature, compassion to the purely human, and reverence to the divine. Shame indicates that human beings are not merely material beings, but something other and higher, since we could not be ashamed of our material nature were we identical with it. As Solov'ëv puts it, "*I am ashamed, therefore I exist*" (p. 27). He believed shame to be the root of morality and the source of conscience. Compassion is the feeling of solidarity with other animate beings. It is the basis of the moral relation of equality and the rational principle of justice. Reverence is the moral basis of religion.

Solov'ëv calls shame, compassion, and reverence the "primary data of morality" because they are immediately given in moral experience and are irreducible. In moral experience we are directly conscious of ourselves as supra-material beings, of fellow persons, and of God. These are not representations or phenomena but actual realities (pp. 140–143). Solov'ëv insists that we cannot doubt the reality of what is given in moral experience, despite theoretical arguments against the existence of God, other selves, and the external world. He took such arguments seriously on their own terms; critical philosophy had demonstrated the difficulty of proving the reality behind sense phenomena.[71] Solov'ëv held

---

[70] Conceived as a new edition of *Critique of Abstract Principles*, the project grew into a new book. Page references will be cited parenthetically in the text to Jakim (ed.), *The Justification of the Good*. At points I have modified the translation in accordance with the Russian text (see note 15).

[71] Solov'ëv's views on this point changed somewhat between *Lectures on Godmanhood* and *Justification of the Good*. In the first work he held that the existence of both God and the external world could

that moral experience discloses reality in a more reliable way than empirical experience or theoretical philosophy: hence the importance of the autonomy of morality.

Solov'ëv thought that moral experience is our primary guide to the nature of reality, but he assigned reason an indispensable role in working moral data into general, indeed universal and necessary, principles. This role is perhaps most obvious in ethics itself (pp. 35–36). In Walicki's apt formulation of Solov'ëv's position, "It is only possible to speak of ethics when reason deduces the inner ethical content from the natural data and confirms it as a categorical imperative independent of its psychological foundations."[72] Since the primary material of reason in the development of ethics is moral experience, not revealed religion or theoretical metaphysics, Solov'ëv defended the autonomy of ethics relative to them.[73] But in a real sense he held that moral experience, as he broadly defined it, is the foundation not only of ethics but also of religion and metaphysics; here as well reason works with the primary data of morality, which includes religious experience (reverence) or, as he also called it, consciousness of the absolute. Reason in these spheres, theology and metaphysics, may be more or less adequate to moral-religious experience, or it may lose the experience altogether, but "the most false and absurd theological doctrine cannot prevent anyone from experiencing the Divine, nor cause anyone to doubt the reality of what is given in experience" (p. 142).

The autonomy of morality is a concept most often associated with Kant. By it the German philosopher meant, as we have seen, the autonomy of the will, its self-determination by the moral law. Solov'ëv embraced Kant's conception in *Justification of the Good* no less than in *Critique of Abstract Principles*, writing in the later work that it "is one of the greatest achievements of the human mind" (p. 135). At the same time, the Russian philosopher stressed that the moral law rests on metaphysical premises, Kant's postulates of practical reason. Solov'ëv claimed that the postulates are undermined by transcendental idealism and so are arbitrary elements of Kant's system. He offered his own concept of moral autonomy as a remedy: "God and the soul are not the postulates of the moral

---

be taken only on faith (p. 32). By faith in the external world he meant the assumption that it is real beyond the phenomena of our sense experience. This use of the term "faith" could not strictly apply to God since God is not a phenomenon. In *Justification of the Good* Solov'ëv adopts the approach that the data of moral experience are immediately given (that is, not mediated by space and time) and therefore do not need to be taken on faith – we can be more sure of their reality than of empirical data, which are so mediated.

[72] Walicki, *Legal Philosophies of Russian Liberalism*, p. 194.

[73] His introduction to *Justification of the Good* is entitled "Moral Philosophy as an Independent Science." Here he refers to the authority of St. Paul, who wrote that people can do good regardless of their religion because the moral or natural law is "written in their hearts" (Romans 2:14–15).

law, but the direct creative forces of moral reality," ones that are immediately given in moral experience and therefore need not be merely "postulated" (p. 138).[74]

JUSTIFICATION OF THE GOOD: HUMAN PERFECTIBILITY IN THE IMAGE AND LIKENESS OF GOD

Solov'ëv regarded religious experience (reverence) as a very important component of moral experience, so much so that his overall conception is really moral-religious experience. Part II of *Justification of the Good*, "The Good from God," develops this aspect of his moral philosophy. Throughout he emphasizes the immediacy and authenticity of religious experience. "The reality of the divine is not a *deduction* from religious experience but the *content* of it . . . *God is in us, therefore He is*" (p. 144). This conviction in the veracity of moral-religious experience as testimony to the ultimate nature of reality is, as I have stressed, the foundation of his whole philosophy.

Solov'ëv divides the content of religious experience into three constituent elements: consciousness of God as absolute perfection, consciousness of our own imperfection, and conscious striving toward divine perfection. Our consciousness of divine perfection is the "image of God" in us; our striving to perfect ourselves according to that image is our "likeness" to God (p. 145). This type of dynamic, synergetic interpretation of the "image and likeness" verses had been advanced by Christian humanists since the Eastern church fathers (see the Introduction to this volume). In *Justification of the Good*, Solov'ëv also refers to Matthew 5:48 ("Be perfect even as your Father in heaven is perfect") but explains that the command can only be accomplished by the *process of becoming perfect* (perfectibility), so that "be perfect" actually means "become perfect" (p. 147).

In a remarkable statement that ties together several strands of his argument, Russia's greatest religious philosopher declares (p. 151):

> The concept of God that reason deduces from what is given in true religious experience is so clear and definite that we always can know, if we wish to, what God wants from us. In the first place, God wants us to be conformable to and like Him. We must manifest our inner kinship with the divine, our power and determination to attain free perfection. This idea can be expressed in the form of the following rule: *Have God in you.*

Solov'ëv now explicitly defines human dignity as consisting in our consciousness of absolute perfection (the image of God) and in our striving to perfect

---

[74] I believe Solov'ëv drew too sharp an opposition here between his position and Kant's.

ourselves (the likeness of God) (p. 152). He calls the image of God the power of representation (of absolute perfection) and the likeness of God the power of striving (to achieve it). This "double infinity" belongs to every person. "It is in this that the absolute significance, dignity, and worth of human person-hood consist, and this is the basis of its inalienable rights" (p. 176). Further, the human person contains an element of intrinsic value, "which can never be merely a means – namely, the possibility, inherent in it, of infinite perfection through apprehending and assimilating [*vospriiatie i usvoenie*] the absolute fullness of being" (p. 196). And in perhaps the most capacious lines from *Justification of the Good*, Solov'ëv writes, "The absolute value of man is based . . . upon the *possibility* inherent in his reason and his will of infinitely approaching perfection or, according to the patristic expression, the possibility of becoming divine (*theosis*)" (p. 296).

Human autonomy, dignity, and perfectibility are the conditions of Godman-hood or the Kingdom of God. Solov'ëv insists that the Kingdom of God is a human project: it cannot be expected by the immediate action of God, for "God has never acted immediately" – a striking comment meant to reinforce the necessity of free human participation in God's work. "In man's conscious-ness and his freedom is the inner possibility for each human being to stand in an independent relation to God," Solov'ëv writes, "and therefore to be His direct end [*tsel'*], to be a citizen possessed of full rights in the kingdom of ends" (p. 150). The "kingdom of ends" is a very significant reference in this context. It is Kant's "very fruitful concept," which Solov'ëv explicated and embraced as his own in *Critique of Abstract Principles*. In *Justification of the Good*, Solov'ëv's point is that the Kingdom of God can be achieved only through the kingdom of ends. "Universal history is the realization of this possibility for everyone," he declares. "Man who takes part in it attains to actual perfection through his own experience, through his interaction with other human beings. This perfection attained by himself, this full, conscious, and free union with the Divine, is precisely that which God ultimately wants – the unconditional good" (p. 150). Solov'ëv's premise throughout is that an achieved perfection is greater than one that is bestowed.[75]

The gradual realization of human potential in history, the process of human perfectibility and striving toward Godmanhood, is called progress. It is the subject of Part III of *Justification of the Good*, "The Good through Human History." The fundamental principle of Solov'ëv's social philosophy is human dignity, the "moral norm of social life," as he calls one of his chapters. The just

---

[75] Sutton, *The Religious Philosophy of Vladimir Solovyov*, pp. 74–75, demonstrates that Solov'ëv was indebted to Schelling on this central point.

society ought to recognize that each of its members has the right to a dignified or worthy existence, and it ought to materially provide, where necessary, for this right (pp. 296–298, 306). In this belief that the state ought to guarantee a certain minimum welfare for its members, in his protest against dehumanizing social conditions and his concern for the poor and urban working classes, Solov'ëv was a modern "new" liberal.[76] His views on criminal justice, including his devastating critique of the death penalty, are also quite modern and entirely consistent with the "moral norm" of human dignity.

Progress appears to be the very concept of the "justification of the good" and to explain why humanity was not created perfect, why the Kingdom of God is our task rather than God's gift. "Perfection," according to Solov'ëv, "is not a thing which one person can make a gift of to another; it is an inner condition attainable through one's own experience alone" (pp. 150–151). That Godmanhood is an ideal to be achieved can only mean that perfectibility is itself the highest good and that it is God's justification for permitting (or enabling) the whole process.[77] If so, then Solov'ëv's "justification of the good" is a type of theodicy.[78] In his own formulation: on the one hand, God permits evil since to do otherwise would violate freedom and be a greater evil, "for it would render perfect (i.e., free) good *impossible* in the world; on the other hand, God permits evil inasmuch as it is *possible* for His Wisdom to extract from evil a greater good or the greatest possible perfection" (p. 152). Possible for His Wisdom, not ours. What remains for us is faith and work. As Solov'ëv expressed it in his last words, "Hard is the work of the Lord" – our work, and it continues.[79]

---

[76] Walicki, *Legal Philosophies of Russian Liberalism*, pp. 195–196, 203–205. The subtitle of Walicki's chapter on Solov'ëv is "Religious Philosophy and the Emergence of the 'New Liberalism.'" Also see Valliere, "Vladimir Soloviev," pp. 560–562.

[77] Solov'ëv writes that in God there can be no process of becoming perfect, only "eternal and unchangeable" perfection (p. 150). This statement is difficult to square with Solov'ëv's overall philosophical approach. If an infinite perfection, one that transcends itself and increases in perfection, is greater than one that is "eternal and unchangeable," then that must be God (as the greatest possible perfection). Many of Solov'ëv's uses of the term "absolute" imply "infinite absolute," and the very concept of Godmanhood surely suggests that God is enriched in the process of our perfection. This problem may explain Solov'ëv's introduction of two poles into the absolute (see note 8). The logic of Godmanhood anticipates process theology.

[78] This was Sergei Bulgakov's view. See his essay "Basic Problems of the Theory of Progress" in Randall A. Poole (ed. and trans.), *Problems of Idealism: Essays in Russian Social Philosophy* (New Haven, CT: Yale University Press, 2003), p. 109.

[79] Quoted by Frank, *A Solovyov Anthology*, p. 27.

7

RUSSIAN PANPSYCHISM: KOZLOV, LOPATIN, LOSSKII

JAMES P. SCANLAN

Vladimir Solov'ëv was not the only Russian philosopher who revolted against materialism and positivism in the 1870s, nor was the religious thrust of his revolt the only direction taken by Russian thinkers who defended philosophy against incursions from the empiricists.

After the appearance of Solov'ëv's *Crisis of Western Philosophy* in 1874, another writer, also near the beginning of a distinguished philosophical career (though twenty-two years Solov'ëv's senior), published a sharply critical review of the work, calling it a reduction of philosophy to religion. "Religion is not philosophy," he insisted in conclusion. "Mr. Solov'ëv has based his dissertation on the false assumption that philosophy and religion have the same subject, and on the basis of that opinion he has... presented every philosophical movement as something unneeded."[1] The author of these lines was Aleksei Aleksandrovich Kozlov (1831–1901), one of a growing number of Russian philosophers who in the 1870s and later championed speculative philosophy as a discipline separate from both the natural sciences and religion.

Among these philosophical purists, Kozlov was the first of a subset who advanced a type of ontological idealism new to Russia, though its pedigree is traceable to the pre-Socratics and though it was developed in modern times by Leibniz. Although the outlook is sometimes loosely called "personalism" because of its focus on individual entities such as Leibniz's "monads," the established term for it (and the term Kozlov used) is *panpsychism* (in Russian, *panpsikhizm*). Most broadly, it holds that reality is composed of individual substances that are, in essence, not material but psychic. The mark of the psychic, for the panpsychist, is always *consciousness*, but the term is applied very broadly to various forms of what might better be called "awareness" – from full self-awareness (as in human beings), to sensory awareness (as in organisms

---

[1] A.A. Kozlov, "G. Vlad. Solov'ëv kak filosof," *Znanie*, no. 2 (February 1875), 29.

generally), and even to simple responsiveness to physical forces (as in inorganic objects).[2]

Panpsychism is still discussed by serious philosophers today because it offers intriguing answers to two troublesome questions concerning mind and matter. One is the age-old "mind–body" problem: if mind is immaterial and matter unthinking, as Descartes taught us, how can such diverse entities possibly act on one another? How can an ethereal "thought," such as my intention to raise my arm, move my physical, material arm? Another question, posed more recently, is this: how can mind, as evolutionists assume, have evolved out of unconscious matter? How can consciousness be produced by elements utterly devoid of consciousness? For the panpsychist, both questions are resolved, or at least rendered less problematic, by the recognition, first, that matter as such is *not* "unconscious" but is marked in every form of its existence by some level of awareness, however elementary; and, secondly, that the evolution of "mind" is not the production of something out of nothing but a gradual development of powers present in substances from the very beginning.

Kozlov, who taught at Kiev University, sought to build panpsychism into a comprehensive philosophical system, as did other Russian philosophers who subscribed to it. Two of them who, like Kozlov, deserve credit for the advancement of academic philosophy in tsarist Russia were Lev Mikailovich Lopatin (1855–1920) at Moscow University and Nikolai Onufrievich Losskii (1870–1965) at St. Petersburg University. The careers of these three thinkers span the brief history of the development and forced dissolution of a professional, primarily secular, university-based philosophical community in Russia during the last decades of the nineteenth century and the first decades of the twentieth. Not social activists and for the most part not markedly religious in their thinking (though all were professed Orthodox Christians and Losskii, in particular, grew closer to religion, especially after his exile in 1922), they were above all defenders of free speculative philosophy as an independent discipline.

ALEKSEI KOZLOV

Born in Moscow in 1831, Kozlov was the illegitimate son of a landowner named I.A. Pushkin (a distant relative of the poet) and an emancipated serf.[3] He

---

[2] On the history and current status of panpsychism, see T.L.S. Sprigge, "Panpsychism" in *Routledge Encyclopedia of Philosophy*, online version 1.0 (London and New York: Routledge, 1998); Galen Strawson *et al.*, *Consciousness and Its Place in Nature: Does Physicalism Entail Panpsychism?* (Anthony Freeman (ed.), Exeter: Imprint Academic, 2006).

[3] The best source on Kozlov's life is Sergei Askol'dov, *Aleksei Aleksandrovich Kozlov* (Moscow, 1912). "Askol'dov" was the pen name of Kozlov's son, the philosopher Sergei Alekseev (1879–1945); because Kozlov and Sergei's mother were never legally married, Sergei was prohibited by law from

was raised by his mother (who died, however, when he was 7) and an abusive stepfather, A.P. Kozlov. At the age of 13 he was rescued from a bleak future by his stepfather's sister, who financed his education at a Moscow secondary school and then at Moscow University. There, in the early 1850s, his philosophical interests were awakened not by formal study (the philosophy departments in Russian universities were closed by imperial order from 1850 to 1861) but by membership in student clubs and circles devoted to European intellectual developments. Like most other members of these circles, he was drawn particularly to radical thinkers such as Feuerbach and the French socialists. His formal study centered on economics; he graduated in 1854 and left the university in 1856, after having passed a candidate's examination with a thesis on Ricardo.

Suspect for his political sympathies, Kozlov drifted from one occupation to another for almost two decades. Only over the years 1870 to 1875 did he have the leisure to study philosophy independently (first Schopenhauer, then Kant and others), which led him to a decided shift toward idealism and a more conservative social outlook. He began to make a name for himself with a translation and exposition of Eduard von Hartmann's *Philosophy of the Unconscious* (*Philosophie des Unbewussten*),[4] and in 1876 he accepted a lectureship in philosophy at Kiev University. In 1880 he successfully defended a master's thesis on Plato. In 1884 he earned a doctorate from St. Petersburg University, whereupon he was named professor of philosophy at Kiev University.

Kozlov was introduced to panpsychism in the early 1880s when he chanced on an article by the German neo-Leibnizian Gustav Teichmüller (1832–1888), who taught for some years at Derpt (in German, Dorpat; now Tartu, Estonia) University. Further reading of Teichmüller and like-minded German thinkers convinced him of the truth of panpsychism, and in 1885 he founded the first Russian journal of philosophy, the *Philosophical Quarterly* (*Filosofskii trëkhmesiachnik*), as a vehicle for airing his views.

One year later, another chance event radically changed Kozlov's life. A stroke paralyzed his right side, leaving him permanently unable to hold a pen or walk without assistance. His philosophical output, however, increased once he retired from teaching and, writing by dictation, he devoted himself to making the case for panpsychism. After completing the fourth and final number of *Philosophical Quarterly* in 1887, he established another proprietary journal, *A Personal Word* (*Svoe slovo*), which was published in five issues over the years 1888–1898. His

---

bearing his father's surname. See also E. Bobrov, "Zhizn' i trudy A.A. Kozlova," *Filosofiia v Rossii. Materialy, issledovaniia i zametki*, no. 1 (Kazan', 1899), 1–24; and N. Losskii, "A.A. Kozlov i ego panpsikhizm," *Voprosy filosofii i psikhologii* 12, no. 3, bk. 58 (1901), 183–206.

[4] A.A. Kozlov, *Sushchnost' mirovogo protsessa, ili filosofiia bessoznatel'nogo E. fon Gartmana*, 2 vols. (Moscow, 1873–1875).

principal work in the second journal was "Conversations with the Petersburg Socrates," a serialized, five-part defense of panpsychism along Teichmüller's lines. It was cast in an engaging dialogue form, with a memorable cast of interlocutors, including characters from *The Brothers Karamazov*. Among his other noteworthy writings of the late 1880s and 1890s were a devastating critique of Lev Tolstoi as a philosophical thinker; an article on consciousness of God (1895) that Losskii called Kozlov's most important step beyond Teichmüller; and, in the last number of *A Personal Word* (1898), a lengthy discussion of contemporary philosophical movements that contained his final summary exposition of panpsychism.[5]

In 1891, Kozlov and his family moved to St. Petersburg, where he lived, writing and discussing philosophy, until his death from pneumonia in 1901.

In his 1898 summary, Kozlov describes panpsychism as the metaphysical theory in which "all being is regarded as psychic [*psikhicheskoe*] and (to however low a degree) conscious [*soznatel'noe*], or, in other words, in which absolutely unconscious being is denied."[6] By way of contrasting this outlook with the metaphysics of materialism, Kozlov goes on to formulate what he calls its "main theses": first, time and space are simply properties of our mental acts; what actually exists is non-temporal and non-spatial. Secondly, mental acts are not "epiphenomena" of a material brain but are "the real activity of our substances." Thirdly, the human body, "like all other bodies," exists not in reality but only, initially, as an image in the imagination and subsequently, as a concept created on the basis of that image (p. 132, emphasis omitted). Kozlov gives no indication that he thought of the less complex, less conscious bodies such as plants and electrons as in any sense "persons"; hence "personalism" is a misleading designation for the metaphysics of panpsychism as Kozlov conceived it. But human or not, no individual substances are "absolutely unconscious" or purely material. All are psychic in essence.

Individual psychic substances, Kozlov goes on, do not exist in isolation. Unlike Leibniz's monads, they are not "windowless"; they are directly aware of and influence each other as parts of "a single cosmic system." Just how this takes place, Kozlov never adequately explains (p. 159), though he does say that the "lesser substances" are linked by "a Supreme Substance, which mediates between them and which they, according to their type, reflect" (p. 131). Beyond this hint of creation in the image and likeness of God, Kozlov did little to

---

[5] For a list of Kozlov's principal publications, see Askol'dov, *Aleksei Aleksandrovich Kozlov*, pp. 37–41. For a much fuller bibliography, see Bobrov, "Zhizn' i trudy A.A. Kozlova," 89–105.

[6] A.A. Kozlov, "Mysli o nekotorykh filosofskikh napravleniiakh, preobladaiushchikh v sovremennoi russkoi literature i ob odnom vozmozhnom v budushchem," *Svoe slovo*, no. 5 (1898), 124 (emphasis omitted). Subsequent page references cited in text.

accommodate Christian theology in his metaphysical system, except to point out that all substances, as timeless and indivisible entities, are by definition indestructible – that is, immortal (p. 133).

Basic to Kozlov's epistemology, which was resolutely anti-mystical, is a distinction drawn by Teichmüller between primitive consciousness and thinking. Primitive consciousness is the immediate, pre-conceptual awareness of the content of a psychic experience, be it sensory image, emotional state, volitional impulse, or other datum. Such consciousness provides the building blocks of all knowledge, but in its primitive condition it is ineffable and must be conceptualized by the formation of ideas and the establishment of relations among them; the ideas of space and time, for example, arise as symbols of ordered relationships among data of consciousness. Consciousness gives us direct contact with reality but no knowledge of it; the thinking that produces knowledge requires mental effort and complex operations that can easily go wrong. Kozlov was convinced that humans have a primitive intuition of a supreme being; but he argued that the difficulties of conceptualizing this intuition and then forming knowledge of its object account for the broad diversity of religious beliefs among cultures.[7]

Although Kozlov's published works in philosophy were devoted almost exclusively to metaphysics and epistemology, he was not without strong convictions in other areas as well. Some of his more distinctive views were expressed only in conversation, reported by others. These conversations add essential elements to the complex picture of his worldview. Kozlov's private comments about religion, for example, provide an interesting counterweight to his public endorsement of a "Supreme Substance," immortality, and other articles of religious belief. From his son, Sergei Askol'dov, we learn that Kozlov was given to vocal "outbursts" against Christianity, that he never "clearly" returned to religion from his youthful atheism, and that he entirely excluded from his philosophical reflections "questions of miracles and the form of God's interaction with the world and with humanity."[8]

The principal importance of Kozlov's unwritten pronouncements, however, lies in what they reveal about his conception of human nature and its implications for ethics and society. His philosophical anthropology draws on his panpsychist metaphysics, with its emphasis on each individual substance as, to use his expression, "a whole individual world in itself."[9] There is an ontological self-centeredness in Kozlov's panpsychism that can, when carried over into the

---

[7] A.A. Kozlov, "Soznanie Boga i znanie o Boge," *Voprosy filosofii i psikhologii* 6, no. 4–5, bks. 29–30 (1895), 445–460, 558–567.

[8] Askol'dov, *Aleksei Aleksandrovich Kozlov*, pp. 182, 167, 183.

[9] Kozlov, "Mysli o nekotorykh filosofskikh napravleniiakh," 131.

world of personal, human substances, be developed in the direction of egoism – the direction Kozlov took.

Kozlov found in human beings no natural moral inclinations – no inborn conscience or sentiment of sympathy – and hence he saw no psychological foundation for any ethical system that demanded altruism or self-renunciation. He was particularly scornful of Tolstoi and others who preached "universal love," something he considered impossible not only psychologically but logically.[10] He urged philosophers to accept the fact that humans are immutably selfish.[11]

Kozlov never formally set down his conception of the *summum bonum*, but Askol'dov characterizes it as "the affirmation of life in its individual manifestations" and sketches it as follows:

Everything is permitted to a man as long as in his actions he elevates life, produces in it higher aesthetic and ideal values, attains greater intensity and complexity of vital manifestations. It is just this end to which moral duty should lead a person, quite independently of whether it coincides with the happiness [*blagopoluchie*] of one's own or another's "self."[12]

Particularly important to Kozlov was the development and expression of "superior powers" and the improvement of the human breed, for which reason Askol'dov speaks of Kozlov's individualism as not only "aesthetic" but "partly biological."[13]

Such emphasis on the development of the individual person might seem to qualify Kozlov as a personalist: not a metaphysical personalist (for, as we saw, that designation does not fit his panpsychist ontology) but an ethical personalist, or someone who locates the ultimate ground of value or worth in the individual person. The core of ethical personalism, however, is recognition of the equal worth of *all* persons, and in Kozlov's writings and recorded utterances we find no defense of human equality as either a fact or a value.

In conversations with Askol'dov and the young Nikolai Losskii, who lived in the Kozlov home as a boarder for three years, Kozlov often dwelled on the inequality of abilities among individuals, sexes, classes, and nations, and he contended that, through inheritance, these inequalities would inevitably increase.[14] As to *de jure* equality, there is no evidence that Kozlov ever affirmed universal dignity or worth as an ethical principle. On the contrary, Losskii

[10] For Kozlov's critique of Tolstoy's ethics, see especially A.A. Kozlov, "Pis'ma o knige gr. L.N. Tolstogo 'O zhizni,'" *Voprosy filosofii i psikhologii* 2, no. 4, bk. 8 (1891), 93–100.

[11] Askol'dov, *Aleksei Aleksandrovich Kozlov*, pp. 55, 197–198, 205; Losskii, "A.A. Kozlov i ego panpsikhizm," 203.

[12] Askol'dov, *Aleksei Aleksandrovich Kozlov*, p. 200.   [13] *Ibid.* p. 54.

[14] See also A.A. Kozlov, "Istoricheskie pis'ma P.L. Mirtova," *Znanie*, no. 2 (1871), 195; Askol'dov, *Aleksei Aleksandrovich Kozlov*, p. 45.

reports, Kozlov accepted the treatment of individuals as mere means when he argued that "mediocre" (*posredstvennye*) people may be used as "manure" (*navoz*) to promote the flowering of great men.[15] Askol'dov, too, conceded that Kozlov was "more a Nietzschean than a Kantian," adding that, on social questions generally, his views were comparable to those of his ultra-conservative compatriot, Konstantin Leont'ev.[16]

Both Askol'dov and Losskii point to signs of a moderation of Kozlov's egoistic stance in his later years, as he increasingly viewed the world as what Losskii called "an integral whole serving as the body of God."[17] "Not simply the development of life," Askol'dov explains, "but the coordination of one's acts with the world whole and its teleological development became for [Kozlov] the principal ethical demand." Askol'dov admits, however, that Kozlov did not succeed in indicating "the concrete path that flows from this demand."[18] Losskii is even less convinced that Kozlov's late focus on world unity in God succeeded in avoiding an inhumane egoism in practice. He contends that Kozlov continued to believe that power and even cruelty are required in order to achieve the unity of which he dreamed; Kozlov still thought that when individual substances deviate from God's purposes, "suffering is needed to bring them back to the true path"[19] – not an attitude characteristic of an ethical personalist. Kozlov's worldview, for all its focus on the individual substance as the ultimate unit of reality, cannot be called personalistic in either the metaphysical or the ethical sense.

LEV LOPATIN

In sharp contrast to Kozlov's humble beginnings and late introduction to philosophy, Lev Lopatin, the precocious son of a prominent Moscow jurist, M.N. Lopatin, read Hegel in German while still in high school. Within a decade of his 1881 graduation from Moscow University, Lopatin had published his magnum opus, *The Positive Tasks of Philosophy*, and was well on his way to becoming the central figure in Moscow's academic philosophical community, the largest and most vibrant in Russia.[20]

---

[15] Losskii, "A.A. Kozlov i ego panpsikhizm," 203.
[16] Askol'dov, *Aleksei Aleksandrovich Kozlov*, pp. 54, 200.
[17] Losskii, "A.A. Kozlov i ego panpsikhizm," 203.
[18] Askol'dov, *Aleksei Aleksandrovich Kozlov*, pp. 201–202.
[19] Losskii, "A.A. Kozlov i ego panpsikhizm," 203.
[20] For a concise systematic account of Lopatin's life and works (including works about him), see Randall A. Poole, "Lopatin, Lev Mikailovich (1855–1920)" in *Routledge Encyclopedia of Philosophy*, online version.

The Lopatin family's elegant house, in which Lev himself, who never married, lived to the end of his days, was a gathering place for Moscow's intellectual aristocracy. The elder Lopatins and the elder Solov'ëvs were close friends, and so, from early childhood, were their sons Lev and Vladimir, whose philosophical interests developed in tandem. The elder Lopatin hosted a weekly salon attended by notables from the legal and academic worlds. Thanks to his son, the guests came to include the leading philosophers of the day as well, men such as Nikolai Grot, the Princes Evgenii and Sergei Trubetskoi, and of course Solov'ëv. Evgenii Trubetskoi later wrote this nostalgic account:

Never in my entire lifetime was there a circle in Moscow richer in intellectual power . . . The center of the "intellectual conversations" was Mikhail Nikolaevich's study, paneled in white marble in Empire style, jammed to capacity and covered with clouds of tobacco smoke. From time to time, amid general laughter, Solov'ëv would declaim one of his humorous verses, [V.O.] Kliuchevskii would orate, or [L.I.] Polivanov would savor the latest novelty fresh from the pen of Lev Tolstoi.[21]

Lopatin would have been appointed to the philosophy faculty of Moscow University immediately upon graduation had it not been for the opposition of Professor M.M. Troitskii, whose attachment to British empiricism left him unsympathetic to the speculative idealism favored by Lopatin. By 1882, however, this objection was overcome and Lopatin was made a privatdotsent in philosophy. In 1886 he was awarded a master's degree for his dissertation, *The Sphere of Speculative Questions*, which was published as the first volume of *The Positive Tasks of Philosophy*; the second volume, published in 1891, consisted of his doctoral dissertation, *The Law of Causation as the Basis of Speculative Knowledge of Reality*.[22] He wrote no more books, but produced instead a multitude of articles elaborating on his outlook or examining the views of others.[23] At least as important as his writings in establishing Lopatin as the leader of Moscow's academic philosophical community was his lengthy tenure at the helm of the Moscow Psychological Society and the journal *Problems of Philosophy and Psychology*. Lopatin more than anyone else guided the work of both for the greater part of their existence.

As a metaphysician, Lopatin faced the same opposition that confronted Kozlov: opposition from empiricists, who favored materialism or positivism, and from thinkers such as the Slavophiles who looked to religion for their

---

[21] Evgenii Trubetskoi, *Iz proshlogo. Vospominaniia. Iz putevykh zametok bezhentsa. Umozrenie v kraskakh. Sofia, Vienna, Berlin, 1921–1926* (Newtonville, MA: Oriental Research Partners, 1976), pp. 180–181.

[22] L.M. Lopatin, *Polozhitel'nye zadachi filosofii*, 2 vols. (Moscow, 1886, 1891).

[23] Three collections of Lopatin's articles have been published: *Filosofskie kharakteristiki i rechi* (Moscow, 1911; new edn., 1995); *Aksiomy filosofii. Izbrannye stat'i* (Moscow, 1996); and *Stat'i po etike* (St. Petersburg, 2004).

fundamental convictions. He answered both in *The Positive Tasks of Philosophy*, arguing that reason, not the senses or faith, is the proper instrument for attaining truth about ultimate reality. He did not mean the "reason" of Kant or Hegel, however. Like Kozlov, he wished to go back further, to Leibniz, in whom he saw a true response to the Cartesian challenge to ground all beliefs on "clear and distinct" ideas. "We must discard every preconception," Lopatin wrote, "and build everything anew, relying on the clarity of reason, on what for reason is simple, clear, and indubitable."[24]

It was in this way, Lopatin believed, that Leibniz became the first thinker to discern "the universal, all-pervasive psychic character [*dukhovnost'*] of being" – in other words, the first principle of panpsychism.[25] Lopatin rarely used the term "panpsychism" for his outlook, preferring "spiritualism" (in Russian, *spiritualizm*), but that should not obscure its Leibnizian character or its essential identity with Kozlov's ontology. Lopatin's capsule description of "spiritualism" as the view that "all reality, both in us and outside us, is psychic [*dukhovna*] in its inner essence" would be equally acceptable to Kozlov as a brief definition of "panpsychism."[26]

One of the few points in metaphysics on which Lopatin and Kozlov disagreed was the nature of causality. Both accepted free will as an undeniable fact of immediate personal consciousness, but Lopatin believed that the determinism of the materialists was grounded in an impoverished understanding of causation. Drawing on Leibniz's identification of substance with activity and interpreting activity as the introduction of novelty, Lopatin concluded that not only acts of volition but *all* instances of causation are instances of creativity, in the sense that there is always something new in the effect, something not present in the cause.[27] In this way he could argue that "free will" is not a puzzling exception in an otherwise mechanistic world; it is, rather, the clearest case of the universal rule, whereas "determinism" is a misunderstanding stemming from our blindness to the novelty present in those causal transactions to which we have no immediate, intuitive access. Lopatin's admirers considered the idea of "creative causality" a

[24] L.M. Lopatin, "Otvetnaia rech' L.M. Lopatina," *Voprosy filosofii i psikhologii* 23, no. 1, bk. 111 (1912), 189.

[25] L.M. Lopatin, "Spiritualizm, kak monisticheskaia sistema filosofii," *Voprosy filosofii i psikhologii* 23, no. 5, bk. 115 (1912), 459.

[26] L.M. Lopatin, "Neotlozhnye zadachi sovremennoi mysli," *Voprosy filosofii i psikhologii* 28, no. 1, bk. 136 (1917), 23. The panpsychists tended to use interchangeably the three adjectives *dushevnyi* (mental, psychic), *dukhovnyi* (spiritual, inner), and *psikhicheskii* (psychic). Because "spiritual" in English has a religious connotation that I believe neither Kozlov nor Lopatin ordinarily intended (despite the latter's use of *spiritualizm*, a term borrowed from English), I have translated all three as "psychic" unless the context dictated otherwise.

[27] Lopatin's concept of "creative causality" is developed at length in his *Polozhitel'nye zadachi filosofii*, vol. 1, pp. 390–429, and vol. 2, pp. 248–376.

major contribution to metaphysics, but Kozlov was troubled by the notion of an effect having more "content" than its cause.[28]

Another distinctive feature of Lopatin's panpsychism is that he makes clear, in a way Kozlov did not, that the panpsychist metaphysician is typically relying on reasoning by analogy in his efforts to describe other beings and reality in general. Once we have posited that all substances are psychic in essence, it seems appropriate to describe them as having psychic features like our own – which are, after all, the only characteristics of spirit that are *directly* known to us, through introspection. Lopatin advocates this approach in what he called his "philosophical credo" in 1912: "[There is] only one road to real philosophical *understanding* of the world: being must be understood according to psychic analogies and in psychic categories. What is basic in our psyche . . . must lie at the basis of all other things as well."[29]

At the same time, Lopatin was aware of the dangers of anthropomorphism in such reasoning, though he never used that term. To justify the attribution of *human* features to non-human beings on the grounds of their likeness in other respects is surely an open invitation to anthropomorphism, and he warned against it, stressing our progressive inability to postulate likenesses as we move to increasingly distant levels of being:

The consistent proponent of the spiritualist conception of life must agree that of the greater part of the reality around us we have, and can have, only relative, symbolic knowledge . . . We know rather well the inner world of people like ourselves . . . [But] the psychic life of animals is a puzzle to us . . . and still more inaccessible to us is the inner subjective life of plants or crystals. Finally, a still greater fog envelops for us the subjective experiences of molecules, atoms, and electrons.[30]

Thus Lopatin gave us no ground for considering all individual substances as "persons," however psychic they may be in essence. As a corollary of panpsychism, even an electron must *have* subjective experiences, but we cannot say that they are the experiences of a *person*. Thus, like Kozlov, Lopatin granted the designation "person" to human beings only, and did not subscribe to metaphysical personalism in the strict sense.

But if Lopatin effectively resisted universal personalization with respect to *individual* substances, in viewing the cosmic order as a whole he appeared to ignore his own warning. He gave in to a grand burst of anthropomorphism, based again on purely analogical reasoning:

---

[28] This and other reservations about Lopatin's metaphysics are developed in A.A. Kozlov, "Poniatiia bytiia i vremeni. Po povodu knigi L. Lopatina *Polozhitel'nye zadachi filosofii*," *Svoe slovo*, no. 4 (1892), 131.

[29] Lopatin, "Otvetnaia rech'," 187.   [30] Lopatin, "Spiritualizm," 460–461.

What does the unprejudiced inner experience of the psyche reveal to us as most basic in itself? It reveals its unity, its self-determination, and thus its freedom, the creative character of all its processes, the purposeful direction of all its activity... Thus if the world is psychic in its inner essence, its being must be the expression of a unitary, free, creative force that leads everything created and generated by it toward its supreme goals.[31]

Thus, while denying that all individual substances are persons, Lopatin describes reality as a whole on the analogy of an individual human person.

Moreover, the effort to specify the "supreme goals" of the cosmos led Lopatin from ontology to axiology and eventually to an acceptance of *ethical* personalism. In 1890 he published one of his most influential essays, "The Theoretical Foundations of the Conscious Moral Life," in which he agrees with Kant that moral values are established by dictates of reason and that the categorical imperative expresses an absolute moral duty.[32] But he argues that Kant left the moral law unsubstantiated, because he gave no account of the dynamic world of reality in which the rational moral idea is embedded. By way of providing such an account, Lopatin describes the cosmic order as a temporal progression from chaos to harmony (p. 109):

The meaninglessness, strife, and formlessness of primitive chaos submits to the purposefulness, harmony, and order of successive creations. Teleology gradually approaches victory over nature. Is not this penetration of the elemental by reason the ultimate meaning of the cosmic process?... The ideal purpose of the world is the realization of the fullness of its being – that is, universal inner harmony along with the perfection of each individual link that makes it up.

It is universal harmony that reason morally obliges us to promote, according to Lopatin, and we do so by freely following the command to treat all people as ends rather than mere means, thereby recognizing the inherent worth of all individuals. "Our will coincides with the teleological law of the inner development of the world," he writes, "only when we acknowledge the equal value of spiritual substances" (p. 110). At first he seems to be asserting the "equal value" of *every* individual substance, human or nonhuman, but he soon singles out "the human soul" as an "*infinite value* in itself, before which the significance of everything else pales." Clearly, the "individual link" in the cosmic harmony that concerns him above all is the individual human being – the substance he also describes as having "incomparable supremacy... over everything else in nature" (p. 111).

---

[31] Lopatin, "Otvetnaia rech'," 187.

[32] L.M. Lopatin, "Teoreticheskie osnovy soznatel'noi nravstvennoi zhizni," in Lopatin, *Aksiomy filosofii*, pp. 84–124. Subsequent page references cited in text.

Though he seems never to have used the term "personalism," Lopatin is here subscribing to a personalist position in ethics. Evgenii Trubetskoi aptly characterized his attitude as "an ardent and unshakable conviction of the ineradicable individuality of the human spirit" and contrasted it with Solov'ëv's rejection of personal substantiality. Solov'ëv, Trubetskoi believed, was interested in the individual only as a member of a communitarian (*soborny*) whole, whereas Lopatin's thinking was imbued with "a sense of the individuality of spirit [and] an urge to defend it at all costs."[33]

Lopatin's faith in the triumph of reason and harmony was sorely tested by history in the first decades of the twentieth century. In his last comprehensive philosophical apologia, written in 1917, he laments the carnage of the World War, musing "and we seriously thought that we were standing at the bright summit of historical progress." The disappointment did not produce a fundamental rethinking of his worldview, however. Indeed, he argued that the "spiritualist" worldview is the only ray of hope for twentieth-century humanity, because "it alone has served as the inexhaustible source of the ideal demands of higher morality."[34]

The Bolshevik Revolution ended Lopatin's professional career. As a critic of materialism he aroused the ire of Lenin and was dismissed from his university positions.[35] The rigors of the civil war reduced his personal life to a struggle against hunger and cold in the same family home he had occupied all his life, though the brilliant salons of earlier days were now replaced by crowds of needy strangers whom Bolshevik authorities had forcibly settled there. At the height of the civil war in 1919, Lopatin wrote to a friend: "We are infinitely tired, terribly tormented, and dawn is nowhere in sight . . . [But] I am convinced that everything taking place is necessary, a painful, agonizing process of the rebirth of humanity."[36]

Still trusting in the grand march of reason, Lopatin succumbed to influenza in 1920 at the age of 65.

NIKOLAI LOSSKII

Nikolai Losskii was born into a petty nobility family in 1870 in the western province of Vitebsk.[37] Devout and patriotic as a young child, he tells us in

[33] Trubetskoi, *Iz proshlogo*, pp. 187, 195.   [34] Lopatin, "Neotlozhnye zadachi," 2, 21.

[35] V.I. Lenin, *Materialism and Empirio-Criticism: Critical Comments on a Reactionary Philosophy* (Moscow, n.d.), pp. 310–313.

[36] Quoted in I.V. Borisova, "Professor filosofii" in Lopatin, *Aksiomy filosofii*, p. 18.

[37] The best source on Losskii's life and thought is his autobiography: N.O. Losskii, *Vospominaniia. Zhizn' i filosofskii put'* (St. Petersburg: Izdatel'stvo S.-Peterburgskogo universiteta, 1994). Page

his autobiography (*Vospominiia. Zhizn'i filosofskii put'*) that by the age of 17 he had become so vocal a socialist and atheist that he was expelled from his gymnasium and stripped of the right to study in any other school in Russia. In search of educational opportunities, he went abroad, where his improbable adventures included a period of service in the French Foreign Legion (pp. 63–67). Returning to Russia in 1889 with the intention of learning a trade, he was unexpectedly granted permission to resume academic studies, whereupon he completed his gymnasium course and, in 1891, entered St. Petersburg University in the physics and mathematics department.

Losskii's circumstances in St. Petersburg could not have been more favorable for expanding his intellectual horizons. At the university he became friends with Aleksei Kozlov's son, Sergei Askol'dov, a fellow student who was living with his parents in their post-retirement home. In 1894, through that friendship, Losskii was welcomed into the Kozlov household as a boarder, putting him in daily contact for three years with one of the most noted philosophers in Russia. Kozlov, though severely crippled, was still full of enthusiasm for ideas. He "lived and breathed in the realm of philosophical thought," Losskii remembered. "He was like Socrates: every conversation involving him became a dialogue devoted to fundamental problems of philosophy" (pp. 91–92). Soon these dialogues not only turned Losskii onto the path of philosophy but set the tenor of his mature worldview: "Under the influence of the talks with Kozlov, I very quickly freed myself from materialism and moved to the opposite extreme – to *panpsychism*" (p. 92). Finally, through Kozlov Losskii met the many other leading figures who visited the housebound philosopher. Solov'ëv in particular took a liking to the adventuresome young former legionnaire and helped him with translations of Kant (pp. 104–106).

As a formal philosophy student Losskii worked primarily with the department head, the noted neo-Kantian Aleksandr Vvedenskii. Vvedenskii asked him to remain in the department to prepare for a professorship after his graduation in 1898; from that time until his exile in 1922, he was associated with the St. Petersburg (eventually Petrograd) University philosophy faculty. His master's dissertation defense with Vvedenskii in 1903 created some unpleasantness between them, as a result of which Losskii chose in 1907 to defend his doctoral dissertation (one of his most important works, *The Intuitive Basis of Knowledge*[38]) with his fellow panpsychist Lev Lopatin in Moscow (thereby losing still more

references cited in text. For a brief chronology of his life and an extensive bibliography compiled by his sons, Boris and Nikolai, see *Bibliographie des Oeuvres de Nicolas Losskii* (Paris: Institut d'Etudes slaves, 1978).

[38] N.O. Losskii, *Obosnovanie intuitivizma* (St. Petersburg, 1906). In English: *The Intuitive Basis of Knowledge: An Epistemological Inquiry* (N. Duddington (trans.), London, 1919).

favor with Vvedenskii). He was not named professor until 1916, just before the publication of another major work, *The World as an Organic Whole*.

Losskii's prolific writing continued unabated after his exile, with increasing attention to the religious dimension of human thought and experience. The thematic sweep of his work was impressive: among his thirty-four books are volumes in every major branch of philosophical thought except social and political philosophy. He taught until the age of 80, occupying positions successively at several universities in Czechoslovakia before emigrating to the United States in 1946. After teaching at St. Vladimir's Theological Academy in New York from 1947 to 1950 and becoming an American citizen, he resettled in France in 1961 and died near Paris in 1965 at the age of 94.

Losskii described his intuitivist epistemology (which he called alternatively "ideal-realism" or simply "intuitivism") as having flowed from a single moment of epiphany in which he sensed that, as he put it, "everything is immanent in everything."[39] For Losskii, this affirmation of a pervasive cosmic unity (Zenkovskii calls it the doctrine of "absolute immanentism"[40]) provided the route to overcoming the Cartesian gulf between subject and object: consciousness and its content are mutually immanent, with neither being divorced from or subordinate to the other. The cognized object *itself*, not a "copy" or other representation of it, is present in consciousness, and this is true of all objects of consciousness, of whatever sort. "The world of the not-self (the whole of that world, including God, if God exists)," he writes in *The Intuitive Basis of Knowledge*, "is known no less immediately than the world of the self."[41] By this time, of course, his retreat from materialism had long since included the decision that God *does* exist; his view that transempirical objects in general can be grasped immediately by intuition opened the way to an increasingly religious worldview.

In a later book, *Sensory, Intellectual, and Mystical Intuition* (1938), Losskii identifies three varieties of intuition, each with a different type of object. The object of sensory intuition is "real being," being with spatio-temporal existence. The object of intellectual intuition is "ideal being," which consists of abstract entities, conceived on the model of Platonic ideas. The object of mystical intuition, finally, is "metalogical being," such as the being of God, that transcends the logical laws of identity, non-contradiction, and excluded middle. Intuitions of all these types are legitimate grounds of knowledge; for Losskii there is

---

[39] N.O. Losskii, *Chuvstvennaia, intellektual'naia, i misticheskaia intuitsiia* (Paris: YMCA Press, 1938), pp. 156–157.

[40] V.V. Zenkovsky, *A History of Russian Philosophy*, 2 vols. (George L. Kline (trans.), New York: Columbia University Press, 1953), vol. 2, p. 668.

[41] Losskii, *Intuitive Basis*, p. 100.

no root difference, epistemologically, between sense perception and mystical contemplation.

That Losskii's epiphany showed him the way to a distinctive worldview is beyond question, but it did so by greatly loosening the restraints on metaphysical speculation. For the thesis of absolute immanence makes every object of consciousness a reality, not merely an image of a possible reality, which means that there is no longer any question of the correspondence of one's ideas with reality – the traditional criterion of truth. Losskii, echoing his mentor Kozlov's distinction between consciousness and knowledge, did make an effort to allow such operations as attention and discrimination to play a role, along with intuition, in the process of establishing knowledge; but in the end he cannot deny that the immanence principle makes every "intuition" presumptively true and never fundamentally false. He writes of mystical intuition, for example, that "*like the other types of intuition*, it cannot lead to ideas and concepts that are thoroughly mistaken."[42] In Losskii's epistemology, the troublesome question is not what makes a judgment true but how it is possible for a judgment to be false.

In any event, the immanence principle provided him with a license for speculative flights that critics found excessive. Lopatin, though he formally accepted Losskii's impressively erudite doctoral dissertation at Moscow University, published a review of it in which he expressed fundamental disagreement with Losskii's approach. "His whole work," Lopatin wrote, "is a long series of enigmatic, sometimes highly paradoxical propositions, concerning which even their logical conceivability is not shown."[43] Nikolai Berdiaev reacted wryly to Losskii's permissive epistemology: "The sphere of intuitive knowledge is narrower (by far) than Losskii thinks."[44]

The metaphysical structure that Losskii created in his roughly half-century of original work is equally provocative. Its foundation is an ontological dualism, expounded in his book *The World as an Organic Whole* (1917), that denies any comparability between the supernatural and natural orders.[45] The former is the realm of "metalogical being." It cannot be the "cause" of the natural order, because a causal relation requires some ontological likeness between its two terms. But because the natural world cannot be the ground of its own

---

[42] Losskii, *Chuvstvennaia*, p. 198 (emphasis added).
[43] L.M. Lopatin, "Novaia teoriia poznaniia. (Po povodu knigi N. Losskogo *Obosnovanie intuitivizma*)," *Voprosy filosofii i psikhologii* 18, no. 2, bk. 87 (1907), 201.
[44] N. Berdyaev, "Ob ontologicheskoi gnoseologii," *Voprosy filosofii i psikhologii* 19, no. 3, bk. 93 (1908), 435.
[45] N.O. Losskii, *Mir kak organicheskoe tseloe* (Moscow: Leman and Sakharov, 1917); republished in N.O. Losskii, *Izbrannoe* (Moscow: Pravda, 1991), pp. 338–483. In English: N.O. Losskii, *The World as an Organic Whole* (Natalie Duddington (trans.), London, 1928).

existence, there must be some "supracosmic principle" that grounds it, and we may postulate as this ground the metalogical being we encounter intuitively in religious experience and call "God."[46] This dualism is the principal feature that distinguishes Losskii's metaphysics from that of Vladimir Solov'ëv, with whom in other respects he eventually felt close kinship. Solov'ëv's concept of *vseedinstvo* (the unity of all) brought the divine and the natural together in what Losskii considered "a pantheistic current" in Solov'ëv's philosophy.[47]

The real substances of which the supracosmic principle is the ground are purely psychic individuals of varying degrees of complexity and development; Losskii called them all "substantival agents," and like Kozlov and Lopatin he viewed them as interacting, not "windowless." But unlike his Russian predecessors, who shied from extending the designation "person" to all substances, Losskii exercised no such restraint. For him, every "substantival agent," even a rock or a subatomic particle, is on a path of development toward human selfhood (is, in other words, at least a *potential* person) and on this ground he does not hesitate to endorse metaphysical personalism explicitly, qualifying it as "hierarchical personalism" in recognition of the fact that substantival agents exist at graduated levels of development.[48] In one bold passage he imagines a developmental scenario as follows:

The human self is an agent that perhaps led the life of a proton billions of years ago. Then, gathering around itself a few electrons, it took on the type of life of oxygen. Making its body still more complex, it then raised itself to the type of life of, for example, a droplet of water. After that it made the transition to the life of a unicellular animal. After a series of reincarnations – or better, a series of metamorphoses, to use Leibniz's term – it rose to the level of life of, say, a dog – man's friend – [and eventually] . . . a human being.[49]

Losskii's phrasing implies that the progress takes place at every step through purposeful decisions on the part of the agent. Far from shunning anthropomorphism, Losskii appeared determined to carry it as far as possible. For him even the most elementary "potential" person is already endowed with a remarkably advanced, essentially human set of psychic features, including not only free will and personal inclinations but, even more striking, the image of God and an awareness of good and evil. Indeed, Losskii contended that becoming a physical proton in the first place is the result of not only a choice but an *immoral* choice on the part of the substantival agent, which before that choice was a purely immaterial substance. The entire material world is, in fact, a product of such

---

[46] N.O. Losskii, *History of Russian Philosophy* (London: International Universities Press, 1952), pp. 257, 265.
[47] *Ibid.* p. 127.   [48] *Ibid.* p. 256.
[49] N.O. Losskii, *Bog i mirovoe zlo* (Moscow: Izd-vo Respublika, 1994; 1st edn. 1941), p. 340.

free, impious choices. God is not responsible for the presence of matter or of the space and time in which it exists. Rather, substantival agents assert their egoistic desire to rebel against the spiritual principle, to put themselves in place of God by materializing themselves. The material world is in effect the incarnation of evil.[50]

The ultimate goal of the teleological cosmic process for Losskii is victory over evil, which means nothing less than the complete elimination of matter. Already in his book *The World as an Organic Whole*, Losskii elaborated the distinction between what he called "the Kingdom of God," a spiritual realm devoid of "selfish isolation" and "mutual exclusivity," marked by the highest unity and perfect harmony; and "the Kingdom of Enmity," the material world, produced by evil self-assertion and full of strife (p. 74). Eventually, however, agents reach a "degree of spiritual development" at which they realize the futility of self-assertion and hence cease to "engage in the elementary processes of attraction and repulsion which create an impenetrable, i.e., a material body," whereupon their bodies disappear (p. 151). The whole material world, produced by the free choices of substantival agents, can and will be destroyed by such choices as the cosmic process moves relentlessly toward the Kingdom of God.

Losskii's clear interest in the moral dimension of personal life and his acceptance of the term "personalism" for his metaphysics suggest that his outlook on morality, too, might be considered personalistic, like Lopatin's. But here once more it is necessary to distinguish between metaphysical personalism and ethical personalism. Losskii did accept the former, as we have seen, but his attitude toward ethical personalism is conflicted at best.

On the one hand, when in *The World as an Organic Whole* Losskii takes up questions of value concerning the relation between the individual and the whole, he explicitly criticizes what he calls "extreme universalism" for ascribing value "only to the being of the Absolute . . . [and] regarding the existence of the individual as merely a means" (p. 185). He also describes all substantival agents as "unique" and "irreplaceable" (p. 188). In his personal life, too, we find opposition to the instrumental treatment of individuals; as a young man he was clearly disturbed by Kozlov's comments about lesser mortals as "manure," and at political meetings in 1917 he urged the preservation of "respect for the person of the capitalist."[51] At the same time, however, in the book he also criticizes "extreme individualism," the polar opposite of extreme universalism, for affirming that "the existence of each individual has absolute value." Such a position, he maintained, leads necessarily to subjectivism and relativism (p. 190).

---

[50] Losskii, *The World as an Organic Whole*, pp. 105–107. Subsequent page references cited in text.
[51] Losskii, "A.A. Kozlov," 203; Losskii, *Vospominaniia*, p. 221.

Losskii sought to avoid both extremes, but in doing so he lost the personalist's insistence on the equal dignity of all persons as ends. He argues that each individual substance has "a special destination" (p. 188), a part that "cannot be played by any other entity" (p. 192), and that in virtue of this unique role each individual has special significance. But, as he expresses it, it is the "super-individual" *role*, not the existence or the person of the individual as such, that has absolute value (p. 188). In support of his position he cites with full approval this passage from Fichte: "The highest moral act consists in the individual's mastering the special part assigned to him and not desiring to be anything different from what he, and only he, can be and ought to be in accordance with his higher nature, i.e., in accordance with the divine aspect of it" (p. 192). Such a statement is hardly an acknowledgment of individual dignity: to attribute value not to the individual but to the individual's "assigned" role in the whole, and to define morality as contentment with that role, are not ideas that would appeal to an ethical personalist. Are there not countless substantival agents in the cosmos whose "assigned role" appears to be precisely to act as an instrument?

Losskii's personal inclinations may have been squarely on the side of human dignity, but when it came to formulating his ethical position theoretically, he did not provide a coherent statement of ethical personalism. His very label "hierarchical personalism" raises questions, for it implies distinctions in personal status that seem incompatible with the assertion of the worth of all individuals. Losskii's highly anthropomorphized ontology was congenial to *metaphysical* personalism, but his developed conception of the organic cosmos made no room for *ethical* personalism. Of the three principal panpsychists, only Lopatin was avowedly an ethical personalist, only Losskii was a metaphysical personalist, and Kozlov was not a personalist at all.

In Losskii's writings, the rationalistic and individualistic panpsychism of Leibniz to which Kozlov and Lopatin subscribed gave way increasingly to a mystical and organicist outlook that had much in common with Solov'ëv's religiously-oriented monism. Losskii's intuitivist theory of knowledge, which legitimates mystical cognition; his organic conception of reality, which emphasizes the interconnectedness of individuals; his growing conception of the philosophical significance of religion in general and Christianity in particular – all these features of his thought help to account for the development in his later writings of further, more specific parallels between his and Solov'ëv's worldviews, such as his attraction to the doctrine of "Sophia," so important to Solov'ëv.[52] The irony, as Losskii himself noted in his autobiography, is that, starting out as an individualistic Leibnizian, distant from Solov'ëv, he should end up so close

[52] Losskii, *History of Russian Philosophy*, pp. 103–104, 131–132, 266.

to Solov'ëv in metaphysics – closer, Losskii claimed, than any other Russian philosopher.[53] Indeed by 1931 he explicitly rejected the term "panpsychism" for his views and called the metaphysics of Kozlov and Lopatin a one-sided mirror image of materialism.[54]

Other than the elaboration of Losskii's unique metaphysical system in his many later writings, there were no further developments in Russian panpsychism after the mass exile of 1922. None of the other exiles championed panpsychism as such. Most of its earlier adherents, of course, were dead. Among them were Pëtr Astaf'ev (1846–1893), a wealthy jurist and author of many works in philosophy and psychology, and Nikolai Bugaev (1837–1902), a mathematician, the father of the poet Andrei Belyi, who wrote an influential paper entitled "Basic Principles of Evolutionary Monadology."[55] Of the proponents of panpsychism who were still alive in 1922 but not exiled, none was able to remain active in teaching or writing. One of Kozlov's followers, Evgenii Bobrov (1867–1933), had been a student of Teichmüller in Derpt and had published translations of Leibniz and a short history of Russian philosophy; but he published nothing after 1916, and nothing is known of his situation in Russia between then and his death in 1933.[56] Kozlov's son, Sergei Askol'dov, could no longer work in philosophy; during the German occupation in 1941 he escaped to the West and died in Potsdam in 1945.

The original, secular panpsychism inspired by Teichmüller perished with the brilliant academic community that was destroyed by the Russian revolution. Kozlov and Lopatin were unpublished and forgotten, not only in the Soviet Union but in the West, and it was left to Losskii's religious, Solov'ëvian variant of panpsychism to represent the legacy of neo-Leibnizian individualism in Russian philosophy in emigration during the Soviet period.

[53] Losskii, *Vospominaniia*, pp. 106, 246.
[54] See N.O. Losskii, "Spiritualism and Panpsychism" in his *Tipy mirovozzrenii. Vvedenie v metafiziku* (Paris: Izdatel'stvo Sovremennye zapiski, 1931), ch. 5. Reprinted in Losskii, *Chuvstvennaia*, pp. 3–134.
[55] N.V. Bugaev, "Osnovnye nachala evoliutsionnoi monadologii," *Voprosy filosofii i psikhologii* 4, no. 2, bk. 17 (1893), 26–44.
[56] Bobrov, *Filosofiia v Rossii* (6 nos., 1899–1902).

PART III

HUMANITY AND DIVINITY IN RUSSIAN RELIGIOUS PHILOSOPHY AFTER SOLOV'ËV

8

A RUSSIAN COSMODICY: SERGEI BULGAKOV'S RELIGIOUS PHILOSOPHY

PAUL VALLIERE

Sergei Nikolaevich Bulgakov was born in 1871 in Orel Province in the Russian black-earth region. His father was an Orthodox priest; his mother also came from a priestly line. In later years Bulgakov liked to present himself as a "levite"; Evgenii Trubetskoi told him he was "born in a stole."[1] Not surprisingly, Bulgakov commenced his secondary education in Orel Theological Seminary. But in 1888 he transferred to a state gymnasium and two years later entered the law faculty of Moscow University, where he studied political economy. The levite had lost his Christian faith and joined the first generation of Russian Marxists.

THE MARXIST ECONOMIST

In his first book, *On Markets in the Capitalist Form of Production* (1897), Bulgakov introduced himself as a person who "shares the sociological point of view," by which he meant someone "who recognizes the regularity of the development of the forms of society, [a regularity] which cannot be eliminated by any concerted efforts on the part of 'critically minded individuals.'"[2] "Critically minded individuals" was a term from Russian populism, the dominant stream in Russian radicalism from the 1870s to the mid-1890s. The populists believed the achievement of social justice in Russia would be facilitated by enlightened individuals acting with and on behalf of the peasant masses to transform the political order. By the 1890s, this recipe for changing Russia had become stale. Young social activists were looking for a more organic grounding of social and political justice. Some, including Bulgakov, found it in Marxism, which combined passionate commitment to social justice with a putatively scientific analysis of history.

[1] S.N. Bulgakov, *Avtobiograficheskie zametki* (L.A. Zander (ed.), Paris: YMCA Press, 1946), pp. 25, 37.
[2] S.N. Bulgakov, *O rynkakh pri kapitalisticheskom proizvodstve: teoreticheskii etiud* (Moscow: Tipografiia A.G. Kol'chugina, 1897), p. 1.

Bulgakov's book contributed to a debate over capitalist markets. With England in mind, Marx had emphasized the need for "external" markets to sustain the economic expansion on which capitalism depends. But Russian capitalism was so weak that it was difficult to imagine Russian companies competing in the world market. The domestic peasant market would not contribute to economic expansion, either, for (according to Marx) capitalism was inexorably undermining the peasant economy. The populists believed the whole debate simply proved that capitalism had no future in Russia. Marxists, viewing capitalism as a necessary stage on the road to socialism, could not accept this conclusion.

Bulgakov argued that in applying a theory "it is necessary to pay attention to all the historical and social particularities of the development of a given country, which, if they are not in a position to shake the truth of an abstract law, can nevertheless introduce certain modifications in its factual realization."[3] This seemingly innocent observation led him to conclude that capitalist development can and does take place even in the absence of external markets in countries which are large enough, rich enough in natural resources, and economically diverse enough to fuel the capitalist engine from within. He invited his readers to compare the economies of England and the United States: a resource-poor manufacturing economy dependent on exports, and a resource-rich mixed economy comprising manufacturing and agricultural sectors with a large domestic market. Countries with an economy of the second type are less dependent on external markets. Since the Russian economy resembled the American type, at least potentially, Bulgakov concluded that "Russian capitalism has a vast and brilliant future."[4] His conclusion contradicted Marx's view of the necessity of external markets for capitalism.

Bulgakov discerned another problem in Marxist theory in his second book, *Capitalism and Agriculture* (1900). Noting the features of agricultural production that distinguish it from industrialism, Bulgakov came to believe that "in agriculture not only is concentration [of wealth] not going on, but decentralizing tendencies are advancing with extraordinary force."[5] If so, the relevance of the Marxist paradigm to the agrarian sector could be questioned, since for Marx concentration of wealth in the hands of a few and pauperization of the masses comprised the dynamic that would precipitate socialist revolution. Once again, Bulgakov's economics did not agree with his Marxism. His "sociological" view of the world was coming apart.

---

[3] *Ibid.* pp. 3–4. [4] *Ibid.* p. 225.
[5] S.N. Bulgakov, *Kapitalizm i zemledelenie*, 2 vols. (St. Petersburg: Tipografiia V.A. Tikhanova, 1900), vol. 2, p. 456.

FROM MARXISM TO IDEALISM

Three seminal essays of 1901–1902 form the dossier on Bulgakov's philosophical conversion from Marxism to idealism. "Ivan Karamazov as a Philosophical Type," "Basic Problems of the Theory of Progress," and "The Spiritual Drama of Herzen" all share "one and the same theme," namely, "the skeptical critique of the positivist theory of progress." Bulgakov wanted to know: "What really is the basis of the theory of progress and of the ethics and religion of humanity which are regarded as self-authenticating and solidly established in the eyes of the advocates of the positivist-humanist or 'egalitarian' worldview?"[6] Positivists claim their theories and values are scientific. But are they?

Bulgakov answered this question most systematically in "Basic Problems," the lead article in *Problems of Idealism* (1902), the first of the religious-philosophical anthologies (*sborniki*) of the Silver Age.[7] He begins with Auguste Comte. Comte presented positivism as the successor to the "theological" and "metaphysical" stages of human development, proclaiming the progress of humanity, not God or the soul, as the ultimate good. Of course, "humanity" did not denote individual human beings, since finite individuals cannot embody unlimited progress, so positivists located the ultimate human prospect in some future historical development, such as the *Zukunftstaat* of the Marxists or the victory of liberal democracy. Yet here the positivists pronounced an astonishing *non sequitur*: in the name of a scientific view of life, they pointed to ends which cannot possibly be verified. Far from being "positive," such ends have a metaphysical quality about them; indeed, according to Bulgakov, philosophical materialism itself is "entirely metaphysical." Positivism thus ironically vindicated "the universality and necessity of metaphysical thought."[8] Also, the power of historical myths in positivism demonstrated the "normal and irrepressible religious need" of human beings, even though positivist faith itself was "a faith that has crept in clandestinely, as contraband, without regal grandeur."[9]

In his essays on Ivan Karamazov and Aleksandr Herzen, Bulgakov probes the need for faith and a metaphysics vindicating the object of faith. Both essays depict idealists who longed to believe in God but could not do so because their scientific-materialistic worldview had excluded the option. The two protagonists achieved tragic nobility, however, by refusing to settle for the shallow values of positivism. Bulgakov admired Ivan's obsession with religious

---

[6] "Ot avtora" in S.N. Bulgakov, *Ot marksizma k idealizmu: sbornik statei (1896–1903)* (St. Petersburg: Tovarishchestvo "Obshchestvennaia Pol'za," 1903), p. xv.

[7] S.N. Bulgakov, "Basic Problems of the Theory of Progress" in Randall A. Poole (ed. and trans.), *Problems of Idealism: Essays in Russian Social Philosophy* (New Haven, CT and London: Yale University Press, 2003), pp. 85–125.

[8] "Basic Problems," pp. 87–90.   [9] *Ibid.* p. 96.

and metaphysical questions, and he seconded Ivan's protest against the historicist theodicies of nineteenth-century progressivism – the pictures of a glorious human future which was supposed to justify the agonies of the present. For Ivan, no happy future in this world or the next could justify the reduction of human beings to the status of tools for the implementation of a grand plan.

Bulgakov admired Herzen for doubting that modern bourgeois civilization constitutes the end of history. Herzen had abandoned his homeland for the bright shores of Europe. Once there, however, he experienced revulsion at European egoism and materialism. His despair prompted him to look back to Russia with renewed love, but it was too late. His positivist worldview blocked the way to spiritual rebirth, leading Herzen instead to embrace such dubious objects of veneration as the Russian peasant commune and a putative Russian socialism. Still, Bulgakov appreciated Herzen's idealism, if not his utopianism. Herzen was "a Prometheus who was chained, or better, who chained himself, to the barren cliff of positivism . . . *The philosophy of Herzen was less than the man himself.*"[10]

SYMPHONIC IDEALISM

By 1902 Bulgakov had completed the leap from Marxism to idealism. But what would be the substance of his idealism? Thus far, idealism simply meant openness to metaphysics and religious faith, but openness alone would not supply the content needed to make idealism concrete and productive. Neo-Kantianism was the most popular idealist option at the time, but it did not offer Bulgakov the sense of cosmic and intellectual wholeness he valued in Marxism.[11] He needed a holistic idealism.

He found it in Vladimir Solov'ëv, "Bulgakov's 'god-father' in his conversion 'from Marxism to idealism' and subsequent return to the Church."[12] In a 1903 essay Bulgakov asked, "What does the philosophy of Vladimir Solov'ëv give to the modern mind?" His answer was: "the positive unity of all" (*polozhitel'noe vseedinstvo*), Solov'ëv's distinctive formulation of the

---

[10] "Dushevnaia drama Gertsena" in *Ot marksizma k idealizmu*, p. 194.

[11] Bulgakov had recorded his aversion to the dualistic tendency of neo-Kantianism in a pair of early essays he wrote defending Marx against the criticisms of Rudolf Stammler: "O zakonomernosti sotsial'nykh iavlenii" (1896) and "Zakon prichinnosti i svoboda chelovecheskikh deistvii" (1897) in *Ot marksizma k idealizmu*, pp. 1–34 and 35–52.

[12] Aleksei Kozyrev, "Prot. Sergii Bulgakov. O Vl. Solov'ëve (1924). Iz arkhiva Sviato-Sergievskogo Bogoslovskogo Instituta v Parizhe" in M.A. Kolerov (ed.), *Issledovaniia po istorii russkoi mysli: ezhegodnik za 1999* (Moscow: O.G.I., 1999), p. 200.

Absolute of modern idealism.[13] Like all idealists, Solov'ëv saw the need for an all-embracing principle that would justify both reason and experience without the one-sidedness of either rationalism or empiricism. Post-Kantian idealists conceived of the Absolute as the identity of subject and object, an idea which Fichte elaborated by emphasizing the absoluteness of the thinking subject, Schelling by emphasizing the productive interaction between human beings and nature, and Hegel by emphasizing the absoluteness of thought itself. Of the three, Schelling's approach was the least stable but arguably the most creative. After repeated attempts to elaborate the theory of identity in a system that satisfied him, he abandoned system-building for more concrete projects, first in esthetics, eventually in philosophy of religion. Schelling rejected the results achieved by his more consistent colleagues: Fichte's radical subjectivism and Hegel's panlogism, an intellectualized form of pantheism. He continued to search for a "positive philosophy" that would do justice to God, man, and nature together and demonstrate the relationship of the three to each other in actual existence. He came to believe that philosophy could achieve this goal only through a "philosophy of revelation" uniting philosophy with religion.

Solov'ëv was a Schellingian, not in the sense of embracing the Schellingian system (for there was no definitive Schellingian system) but in the sense of pursuing the Schellingian project: the search for an all-embracing positive philosophy that vindicated the wholeness of things without annihilating the discrete and beautiful elements of the whole.[14] The key to achieving this outcome, as Schelling saw late in his career and Solov'ëv from the start, was to recognize the transcendence of the Absolute (its ecstatic, super-rational and super-essential character, its radical existence) while still acknowledging that we perceive the Absolute only through its relatedness to the actual world. The tension introduced by the transcendence of the Absolute is the reason why all attempts to capture the whole of things in a system fall short. But without that creative tension the world as we know it – a multiplicity-in-unity – would not exist.

To speak about the Absolute in this way was to acknowledge that our "intellectual intuition" of the Absolute is also an act of faith, for through it we come to recognize our radical dependence upon the Existing One for our own and the world's being.[15] The idealist's aspiration to do justice to rationalism and empiricism in a higher synthesis was thus complicated even as it was fulfilled. It was complicated because, alongside reason and experience, faith had

---

[13] "Chto daet sovremennomu soznaniiu filosofiia Vladimira Solov'ëva?" in *Ot marksizma k idealizmu*, p. 195.

[14] On the influence of Schelling on Russian philosophy see V.F. Pustarnakov (ed.), *Filosofiia Shellinga v Rossii* (St. Petersburg: Izdatel'stvo Russkogo Khristianskogo gumanitarnogo instituta, 1998).

[15] "Chto daet sovremennomu soznaniiu filosofiia Vladimira Solov'ëva?," p. 203.

entered the picture. A twofold synthesis had been transformed into a threefold symphony of formal reason, concrete experience, and mystical relatedness to the ground of being. Solov'ëv called such a symphony "free theosophy," the adjective denoting the intellectual independence he claimed for the enterprise.

The role of faith in idealism has a bearing on how idealism affirms the freedom and dignity of human beings. Faith in the sense of mystical connectedness to the super-essential ground of being is Solov'ëv's version of Schelling's understanding of human freedom. Schelling insisted on the translogical, abyss-like character of human freedom.[16] This point did not make it any easier for him to build a philosophical system, but it inspired him, and Solov'ëv after him, to resist the reductionism that submerges human beings in the world-process and so annihilates them.

Another feature of Solov'ëv's thought that attracted Bulgakov was Christian social conscience. Solov'ëv believed Christians were called to build a "free theocracy," that is, a just social and political order. During the 1880s and 1890s he wrote extensively on evils such as poverty, nationalism, capital punishment, and religious intolerance, eventually systematizing his ideas in a magisterial philosophy of practical reason, *The Justification of the Good* (1897). Solov'ëv's progressive Christianity provided an alternative to "police-state Slavophilism" and to the reduction of Christianity to a kind of "Islam [based on] submission and *resignation* before a higher power," namely the autocratic state.[17] According to Bulgakov, Solov'ëv's:

idea of Christian politics . . . liberates our understanding of Christian teaching from the monastic one-sidedness that interprets it exclusively as a teaching about the salvation of individual souls, an interpretation that coldly abandons "the world" to the powers of sin; and at the same time, [Solov'ëv's idea] unites the practical aspirations of modern progressivists, those Christians without Christ, with Christ's own teaching, not mechanically but organically.[18]

IDEAS IN ACTION

In 1901, Bulgakov and his family (he married Elena Tokmakova in 1898) moved to Kiev, where he taught political economy at the Kiev Polytechnical Institute. He remained there until 1906. These were the years when Russian neo-liberalism emerged not only as a philosophical tendency but as a political movement. In 1902, Pëtr Struve launched the political journal *Osvobozhdenie* (*Liberation*), and in 1903, a political organization, the Union of

---

[16] Most notably in *Philosophical Inquiries into the Nature of Human Freedom* (1809).
[17] "Chto daet sovremennomu soznaniiu filosofiia Vladimira Solov'ëva?," p. 256.   [18] *Ibid.* p. 246.

Liberation. Bulgakov took an active part in Struve's projects, associating himself with the reform agitation that would swell into the revolutionary tide of 1905–1906. He also collaborated with Nikolai Berdiaev in editing the religious-philosophical journal *Novyi put'* (*New Path*, 1903–1904) and its successor, *Voprosy zhizni* (*Questions of Life*, 1905), an alliance that linked the two together in the eyes of the intelligentsia as "the Siamese twins of idealism." In actuality, they were spiritual opposites. As Zinaida Gippius characterized them:

Bulgakov and Berdiaev – they are not just oil and water, but water and fire . . . Bulgakov has stopped with Solov'ëv and does not want to go any further, nor can he. Berdiaev seems like he is forever going somewhere, though in fact he just circles around in a monotonous orbit spinning on his own axis . . . The best thing they could do right now is to have a public intellectual duel to the death; perhaps Bulgakov's all-too-nice [*blagopoluchnyi*] monism would break up as it collided with Berdiaev's not-so-nice dualism.[19]

Bulgakov revised his social and political ideas in the light of his new philosophical convictions, but he did not discard the humanist values he had promoted in the 1890s. On the contrary, he believed that Christian idealism grounded humanism in a way that progressivist ideologies, because of their atheism and materialism, could not. He still shared the socialists' determination to overcome economic dependency, believing that this required a significant measure of state-supervised "economic collectivism" to neutralize the "personal dictatorship" of capitalists.[20] But he now believed that collectivism alone would not overcome dependency, especially in the agrarian sector. He strongly rejected the Marxist notion that promoting independent peasant proprietorship was reactionary because it strengthened investment in private as opposed to collective property. He argued that forms of labor and property are not goods in themselves but acquire ethical significance to the extent that they promote or retard "the ideal of freedom of the individual" (*ideal svobody lichnosti*) in a particular context. Bulgakov believed that independent proprietorship advanced this ideal in the agrarian sector just as moderate forms of collectivism advanced it in the industrial sector.[21]

Bulgakov had arrived at a social ideal which was neither pure liberalism nor pure socialism but a mixture of the two, concerned with human freedom *and* human dignity, the rights of individuals *and* the health of the social body. He rejected both egoistic capitalism and communist collectivism as "abstract

---

[19] Quoted in M.A. Kolerov, *Ne mir, no mech: russkaia religiozno-filosofskaia pechat' ot 'Problem idealizma' do 'Vekh' 1902–1909* (St. Petersburg: Izdatel'stvo "Aleteiia," 1996), p. 116.

[20] "O sotsial'nom ideale" in *Ot marksizma k idealizmu*, p. 305.

[21] S.N. Bulgakov, "Batrak ili muzhik?" in Kolerov (ed.), *Issledovaniia po istorii russkoi mysli*, pp. 234–244.

principles."[22] The term came from Solov'ëv, who employed it to denote the reduction of an antinomic whole into warring, absolutized opposites. The philosophic and Christian approach was to appreciate the coherence of the whole and accept its creative tensions. Bulgakov insisted that such an approach was in fact a kind of "realism."[23] After all, the real world is the greatest *coincidentia oppositorum* of all.

Bulgakov took the same approach to the evaluation of modern bourgeois civilization. The vast multiplication of goods and services achieved through capitalism had generated its own ethic, which Bulgakov called "hedonism" for lack of a better term. We call it consumerism. Spiritual elites, appalled by consumerist gluttony, preach salvation though renunciation of the physical world. But Bulgakov regarded ascetical rejection of wealth as one-sided. He saw consumerism and asceticism as abstract principles: "both take up one side of the truth and divorce it from its connection to the whole; and then, with the aid of this abstract principle, they set out to evaluate the whole. Thus both are wrong not in what they affirm but in what they deny; they are untrue precisely in their limitedness and their abstractness."[24] What was needed was an appreciation of the whole that justified the dignity of matter and spirit alike.

A point of social justice was also at stake. While rejecting consumerism, Bulgakov vigorously affirmed "the struggle against national poverty, helplessness and destitution." He reminded his readers that "to undertake a dispassionate study of the ascetic ideal of salvation and the seductive teaching of hedonism while the peasantry remains hungry and cold, while mothers of children are worked to death in our factories, while millions of people lead the lives of beasts of burden, with no joy, no light breaking in, would be criminal, savage, and hypocritical."[25] When the Russian public square burst into flame in 1905, Bulgakov took his own advice and threw himself into political activism.

On the political spectrum, Bulgakov stood closest to the Constitutional Democrats (Kadets), the left-leaning liberal party that won the most votes in Russia's first modern parliament, the First Duma (1906). Bulgakov himself won a seat in the Second Duma (1907) as an independent candidate from Orel Province. Practically speaking he was allied with the Kadets, but his refusal to join their party signaled an ideological gap between him and the Kadet mainstream. The difference had to do with religion. Most Kadet intellectuals were secular neo-Kantians, but Bulgakov, by contrast, envisioned an active role for

---

[22] "O sotsial'nom ideale," p. 306.   [23] *Ibid*. pp. 309–310.

[24] "The Economic Ideal" in Rowan Williams (ed.), *Sergii Bulgakov: Towards a Russian Political Theology* (Edinburgh: T&T Clark, 1999), p. 45. (*Ot marksizma k idealizmu*, p. 280.) I have changed a word in the translation.

[25] "The Economic Ideal," p. 46 (*Ot marksizma k idealizmu*, p. 281).

religion in politics. Already in 1905 he had published a plan for a "Union of Christian Politics" to promote Christian socialism in Russia.[26]

Bulgakov presented the Union of Christian Politics as a force that would mediate between the two extremes dominating Russian political life: atheist socialism and state-manipulated Orthodoxy. According to Bulgakov, socialism was rallying progressive forces so successfully that "materialism and socialism have become virtually synonymous," while the Orthodox Christian cause was identified with tsarist bureaucrats and reactionary Black Hundreds. The Union of Christian Politics challenged these perverse associations. Taking "as its governing principle the right to freedom and self-determination for every human person as a bearer of the image of God," the Union called on progressive Christians to promote "socialism not in the name of mangodhood but in the name of Godmanhood."[27]

The goals of Bulgakov's program were fairly radical, though he approached them in a pragmatic, non-violent spirit. He advocated the full panoply of rights and freedoms associated with liberal democracy. In economic policy, he proposed a gradualist path to socialism. He foresaw the eventual replacement of capitalism by socialism but insisted that the transition entail a long series of incremental reforms, such as the introduction of the eight-hour day, workers' insurance, and state-enforced safety regulations. In the agrarian sector he foresaw the eventual transfer of all land to the peasantry, but "in a gradual way, not rushing to destroy existing economic relationships too abruptly, which would be attended by all sorts of difficulties."[28] His program also called for the liberation of the Orthodox church from its subservience to the state. The church was "to receive full internal autonomy and the right to organize itself in accord with church canons."[29]

Bulgakov's Union of Christian Politics has been heralded as anticipating the Christian Democratic parties of twentieth-century Europe.[30] In his day, however, he failed to garner much support for the project. Even his own neo-liberal friends were critical. From left of center, Struve criticized Bulgakov for adopting too narrow an understanding of religion by emphasizing Orthodox Christianity rather than the "inner, subjective religiosity" which (Struve believed) underlies all religion and unites people of different faiths, including humanists. Struve also felt that Bulgakov had underestimated the damage that could be done to both

---

[26] "Neotlozhnaia zadacha (O Soiuze khristianskoi politiki)" in S.N. Bulgakov, *Khristianskii sotsializm* (V.N. Akulinin (ed.), Novosibirsk: "Nauka," Sibirskoe otdelenie, 1991), pp. 25–60.

[27] "Neotlozhnaia zadacha," pp. 54, 43.   [28] *Ibid.* p. 58.   [29] *Ibid.* p. 55.

[30] I.B. Rodnianskaia, "Introduction" to S.N. Bulgakov, *Sochineniia v dvukh tomakh*, 2 vols. (Moscow: Izdatel'stvo "Nauka," 1993), vol. 2, p. 6.

politics and religion by promiscuously combining the two.[31] Evgenii Trubetskoi criticized Bulgakov from the moderate right. Trubestskoi was a Christian idealist, and he agreed with Bulgakov that absolute values, including religious principles, had a role to play in politics. But he rejected the idea of a Christian political movement. "[Unconditional] values are not outside of politics, but they are outside of parties"; they represent "something common, something transcending parties, on which different parties can come together and which should serve as a foundation for their cooperation."[32]

The failure of the Union of Christian Politics, the one explicitly political initiative of Bulgakov's career, showed that politics was not his vocation. It also showed the difficulty of expressing Solov'ёvian wholeness in the political arena. Bulgakov would have gotten further politically if he had made his peace with the Kadets' "principle of principle-less-ness."[33]

Following his attempt at Christian politics, Bulgakov applied himself to the social scientific analysis of Christianity. His mastery of German gave him access to the best contemporary scholarship on the subject. In 1908, he drew on Adolph von Harnack, Rudolph Sohm and others in an essay on the social and political ideals of the early church, challenging the notion that early Christianity was a radical political movement subsequently diverted by reactionary ecclesiastics.[34] Bulgakov accepted the emerging scholarly consensus that early Christianity was a religious movement that naturally generated ecclesiastical and dogmatic concepts.

A year later, he drew on Max Weber's *The Protestant Ethic and the Spirit of Capitalism* (1904–1905) in an article on "National Economy and Religious Personality." Weber was virtually unknown in Russia at the time, and Bulgakov's "perspicacity" in recognizing his importance has been noted.[35] Weber's thesis concerning the role of spiritual factors in motivating economic activity was congenial to Bulgakov, for it united his two identities, the economist and the religious idealist. It also suggested a fresh approach to Russian economic development. Russians needed to recognize that "the national economy is not just a

---

[31] P.B. Struve, "Neskol'ko slov po povodu stat'i S.N. Bulgakova" in Akulinin (ed.), *Khristianskii sotsializm*, pp. 316–317.

[32] E.N. Trubetskoi, "Dva slova po povodu polemiki F. Lur'e i S.N. Bulgakova" in Akulinin (ed.), *Khristianskii sotsializm*, p. 318.

[33] S.N. Bulgakov, "Religiia i politika" (1906) in Akulinin (ed.), *Khristianskii sotsializm*, p. 62.

[34] "O pervokhristianstve (O tom, chto bylo v nem i chego ne bylo. Opyt kharakteristiki)" in S.N. Bulgakov, *Dva grada: issledovaniia o prirode obshchestvennykh idealov* (V.V. Sapov (ed.), St. Petersburg: Izdatel'stvo Russkogo Khristianskogo gumanitarnogo instituta, 1997), pp. 141–178.

[35] I.B. Rodnianskaia, "S.N. Bulgakov v spore s marksistskoi filosofiei istorii: ottalkivaniia i pritiazheniia" in *S.N. Bulgakov: pro et contra. Lichnost' i tvorchestvo Bulgakova v otsenke russkikh myslitelei i issledovatelei* (St. Petersburg: Izdatel'stvo Russkogo Khristianskogo gumanitarnogo instituta, 2003), pp. 886–887.

mechanism but also the energetic activity of human persons," and that religion "should also be counted among the important factors in the development of the national economy."[36]

Bulgakov's most important essay during this period was the piece he contributed to *Vekhi* (*Landmarks*, 1909), "Heroism and Asceticism."[37] *Vekhi* was a collection of essays on the Russian intelligentsia written in light of the failures of revolutionary activism in 1905–1906. The contributors included the leading lights of religious and neo-liberal philosophy in Russia, such as Nikolai Berdiaev, Pëtr Struve, Semën Frank, and Mikhail Gershenzon. While the *Vekhi* group was not monolithic, all contributors agreed that the failures of the Russian intelligentsia stemmed from its alienation from Russian national and religious values.

Bulgakov's essay was the longest in *Vekhi*. In it he contrasted the "heroic" revolutionary humanism of the secular intelligentsia with the Christian ethic of humble service and love of neighbor. The two ethics produce very different results. In revolutionary heroism, "maximal pretensions go hand in hand with minimal personal preparation in science as well as in practical experience and self-discipline." The Christian way, by contrast, is characterized by "maximalism in personal life, in the demands one makes upon oneself," combined with moderation in ends and means.[38] The revolutionary, living always for tomorrow, ends up doing violence to the present. The Christian, empowered by faith in Providence, ministers to the needs of today. The analysis recalled Bulgakov's assessment of Herzen's spiritual drama. What he had added was a robust affirmation of Christian spirituality as the antidote to utopian idealism. Bulgakov's word for asceticism, *podvizhnichestvo*, is the traditional Russian Orthodox term denoting spirituality of the monastic type, but he used the term in a wider sense to connote an ascetic engagement with the world, an *"innerweltliche Askese."*[39] Bulgakov's concept is thus as much Weberian as it is Orthodox. It presents an example of Solov'ëvian-style wholeness: Weber was Russianized while Orthodoxy was modernized.

PHILOSOPHY OF ECONOMY

One of the few areas where Bulgakov found Solov'ëv's thought wanting was political economy, which he called "the Achilles' heel of this philosopher."[40]

[36] "Narodnoe khoziaistvo i religioznaia lichnost'" in *Dva grada*, p. 125.
[37] "Geroizm i podvizhnichestvo" in *Vekhi: sbornik statei o russkoi intelligentsii*, 2nd edn. (Moscow: Tipografiia V.M. Sablina, 1909; reprint edn. Frankfurt: Posev, 1967), pp. 23–69.
[38] "Geroizm i podvizhnichestvo," p. 52.   [39] *Ibid.* pp. 54–55.
[40] "Chto daet sovremennomu soznaniiu filosofiia Vladimira Solov'ëva?," p. 249.

Bulgakov's passing comment may mark the moment when the idea of writing a Solov'ëvian "justification" of economy occurred to him. Moreover, because Bulgakov regarded economic enterprise as the paradigm of cultural creativity, *Philosophy of Economy* (1912) may also be read as a philosophy of culture, or, in Solov'ëvian language, as a "theurgy." Following Kant, Solov'ëv divided the life of the mind into three parts: whereas Kant spoke of pure reason, practical reason, and judgment, Solov'ëv spoke of theosophy, theocracy, and theurgy. *Philosophy of Economy* is the systematic theurgy Solov'ëv never wrote.

As an economics professor in an institution linked to the modern economy (the Moscow Commercial Institute, where Bulgakov taught after moving to Moscow in 1906), Bulgakov was well positioned to undertake a "philosophy of economy." His starting point was the unprecedented economic development of modern times. In Russia as elsewhere, the values associated with the new economy could be summed up in a single word: materialism. Marxists preached materialism without qualification, but capitalists were just as materialistic as socialists. "In practice, [all] economists are Marxists, even if they hate Marxism."[41] In short, everyone involved in the modern economy seemed to take materialism for granted. But the philosopher's job is to question what everyone takes for granted. Bulgakov wanted to know what economic activity is ultimately founded upon, its ontology. He compared his task to Kant's in *The Critique of Pure Reason*. Kant responded to the emergence of modern science. Science is so effective that its practitioners and beneficiaries rarely stop to ask what the whole enterprise is based on. But that was precisely the question Kant raised in the first critique: How is science possible? Bulgakov's question paralleled Kant's: "How is economy possible? What are its preconditions and foundations?"[42]

But if Bulgakov's question paralleled Kant's, his answer was Schellingian, as he explicitly stated.[43] Economy is possible, according to Bulgakov, because of a creative potency grounded in the relationship between human beings and nature, a potency which is repeatedly concretized in humano-cosmic products. The products might differ in complexity, from a field of grain to a masterpiece of literature. But ontologically they have equal status, since they all spring from the same glorious humano-cosmic economy. In them we see "nature as unconscious spirit and spirit as nature realizing itself."[44]

[41] S.N. Bulgakov, *Philosophy of Economy: The World as Household* (Catherine Evtuhov (ed. and trans.), New Haven, CT and London: Yale University Press, 2000), p. 41.
[42] "Filosofiia khoziaistva. Rech' na doktorskom dispute" in *Sochineniia v dvukh tomakh*, vol. 1, p. 301.
[43] *Philosophy of Economy*, pp. 93–94.   [44] *Ibid.* p. 84.

There is a moral as well as a metaphysical element in Bulgakov's vision. Following Kant, Bulgakov insisted that human beings should not be regarded merely as objects in the world; they are also agents of the world. *Homo economicus* is not an automaton. Economic activity involves creative initiative, a point that Weber's sociology had helped Bulgakov to grasp. The philosopher of economy must therefore look not just for the object of economy but for its subject. Yet the most obvious subjects, human beings, do not account for the economic process by themselves. The creative spark without which there would be no economy is not generated by human beings alone but by the friction between human beings and nature. One might describe the spark as coming either from above or from below; either way, it transcends the human subject. This "transcendental subject of economy" is the ground of creativity, forever inspiring human beings to undertake new initiatives or alter old ones. It has many names: world soul, demiurge, *natura naturans*, Sophia, among others. The last was Bulgakov's favorite. His "sophiology" began in *Philosophy of Economy*. Sophia, or Divine Wisdom, is the Muse of the cultural-economic enterprise.

Catherine Evtuhov has suggested that Bulgakov's "sophic" economy bears an affinity with the agrarian reforms instituted by the Russian Prime Minister Pëtr Stolypin. The reforms were designed to encourage the transfer of land from the peasant commune, with its ethic of collective responsibility, to independent farmers. Bulgakov's "economy" (*khoziaistvo*) resonated with the state's new emphasis on "proprietors" (*khoziaeva*). According to Evtuhov, "Bulgakov's instruction to the *khoziain* [peasant proprietor] is an ethic of labor infused with joy, for every stone he moves and every furrow he plows partakes of the divine Sophia and reproduces in microcosm the universal drama of Fall and Resurrection."[45] While Bulgakov's views distanced him from Stolypin politically, his economic thought clearly manifested a preferential option for the hard-working producer.

Bulgakov's philosophy of economy also derived from Solov'ëv's concept of "religious materialism." The concept was connected with Solov'ëv's project of justification of the world over against the world-denying monastic spirituality which many Russians took to be the essence of Christianity. The religious justification of the world, Solov'ëv insisted, was actually more in the Christian spirit than was world-denying spirituality. Most religions preach the existence of God, affirm a spiritual world, and advocate an altruistic morality. Christianity seconds these truths, but they are not its distinguishing characteristic. What makes Christianity special is the Incarnation: that is, not God per se,

45 Catherine Evtuhov, *The Cross and the Sickle: Sergei Bulgakov and the Fate of Russian Religious Philosophy* (Ithaca, NY and London: Cornell University Press, 1997), p. 155.

but the humanity of God, the Word made flesh in a concrete human being and the participation of all human beings as bearers of the image of God in that all-reconciling communion of natures. The Incarnation is what empowers Christians to affirm the physical world with a passion as great as that of the materialists, but without the latter's metaphysical nihilism.

Bulgakov's religious materialism owed much to the sacramental understanding of the material world in Orthodox Christianity. While Orthodoxy accommodates the monastic *virtuosi* of acosmic spirituality, in its worship the Orthodox church is profoundly cosmic. The Orthodox liturgy offers the fruits of the earth to God and receives them back again as sanctified gifts. The center of the liturgy, the eucharistic meal, is patterned on the most rudimentary exchange in human life: the consumption of food. Bulgakov emphasized the continuity between the supreme Christian sacrament and ordinary eating. Eating is "*natural communion* – a partaking of the flesh of the world.*" In eating, human beings experience both their oneness with the world and "the fatal duel raging between Life and Death" in the cosmos. The Christian meal sanctifies this exchange, transforming earthly nourishment into heavenly food, mortal consumption into immortal life.[46]

Sergei Horujy has noted that Bulgakov's sophiology manifests this liturgical vision of the world. Sophia embraces and elevates everything the Orthodox church blesses, which is to say all mortal life: not just its ideal aspects, but birth, reproduction, death, labor, economy, family, nation, the governing authorities and more.[47] The liturgical quality of Bulgakov's sophic economy makes it also a shalomic economy. In the Great Litany that opens the liturgy, the Orthodox pray in peace for the peace of the whole world. *Shalom*, which literally means "wholeness," is the *summum bonum* of the biblical faith in both testaments. Bulgakov's holistic, world-affirming vision of economy issues in a biblical, Hebraic religious humanism.

PHILOSOPHY OF REVELATION

Bulgakov's *The Unfading Light* (1917) forms a pair with *Philosophy of Economy*. Both books are Schellingian projects, *Philosophy of Economy* offering an updated philosophy of nature and culture, *The Unfading Light* a philosophy of revelation. The problematics of the two works are also related. *Philosophy of Economy* takes aim at the economic materialism of modern times; *The Unfading Light* targets

---

[46] *Philosophy of Economy*, pp. 101–105.
[47] S.S. Khoruzhii, *Posle pereryva: puti russkoi filosofii* (St. Petersburg: Izdatel'stvo "Aleteiia," 1994), pp. 85–86.

the "religious immanentism" of modern times, by which Bulgakov meant pre-scriptions for moral and spiritual fulfillment within the limits of the material world alone. According to Bulgakov, what modern materialism and religious immanentism have in common is the rejection of a transcendent God and of "contact with other worlds" (Dostoevskii). In *Philosophy of Economy*, Bulgakov rejected atheist-positivist materialism but affirmed religious materialism. Simi-larly, in *The Unfading Light* he cautioned his readers that "the pantheistic truth of 'immanentism' should not be rejected out of hand," as it is in traditional "transcendentism" and Manichaean dualism. On the contrary, "to know and to actually experience God in the world and the world in God . . . is the supreme task that the history [of religion] presents to religious consciousness."[48] This theocosmic unity resembles religious materialism in its vision of a symphonic whole transcending one-sided monisms. In a word, Bulgakov vindicates neither pantheism nor world-denying theism, but "panentheism," as he came to call it.[49]

Lev Zander did well to entitle his massive book on his mentor *God and the World*.[50] Bulgakov sought a modern world transformed by the Christian faith but also a Christian faith transformed by the freedom and creativity of the modern world. He did not underestimate the difficulty of this project: "Hard is the path through modernity to Orthodoxy and back again."[51]

Given the prevalence of religious immanentism in modern times, Bulgakov's first order of business in *The Unfading Light* was to vindicate the transcendence of God. This would be the first order of business in a critique of religious reason in any case, because religious faith begins in personal encounter with the transcendent one, the absolute other who confronts and addresses us. "Thou art" is "religion's synthetic *a priori* judgment," the absolute revelation of the Absolute.[52]

Given the problematization of the concept of God in modern times, many people ask for proof that God exists. Bulgakov knew he would disappoint them, for they are asking for something that does not engage the living God. One can prove something only if it stands in a logical or causal chain, making it possible to move from a known point in the chain to anterior or posterior points. But this approach does not work in theology because one cannot comprehend "the being of an absolute which transcends the relative and is free of causality." Living faith does not regress to the divine but begins with it. "Thou art" is

[48] "Ot avtora" in S.N. Bulgakov, *Svet nevechernii: Sozertsaniia i umozreniia* (Moscow: Izdatel'stvo "Respublika," 1994), pp. 5–6.

[49] S.N. Bulgakov, *Uteshitel'* (Paris: YMCA Press, 1936), pp. 232–233.

[50] L.A. Zander, *Bog i mir (Mirosozertsanie ottsa Sergiia Bulgakova)*, 2 vols. (Paris: YMCA Press, 1948).

[51] "Ot avtora" in *Svet nevechernii*, p. 3.   [52] *Svet nevechernii*, p. 19.

necessarily transcendent, since otherwise it would amount to a reflex of one's own subjectivity, a mode of "I am." But religion is so called (*religare*, "connect") because it connects us to an other – the absolute other.

The evidence for the reality of God is found in the history of religion, but these data are contingent. They do not prove the existence of God but respond to the Thou who is already believed in, trusted, feared, and loved. Those who have not experienced the presence of God on this aboriginal level will not evaluate positive religion as testimony to a transcendent reality. They will interpret religion in immanentist terms, at best valuing it for its contributions to worldly life, at worst seeing it as a web of deceit. Believers have no answer to immanentism except to bear witness to their faith. But a great cloud of witnesses through the ages have given such testimony. The mountains of data recorded in the annals of positive religion are the stuff that religious philosophy brings to light and arranges systematically. Taking these data seriously as revelatory of the Thou who addresses us (an approach Bulgakov calls "religious realism"[53]) is the business of philosophy of revelation.

The Unfading Light anticipates central themes in twentieth-century Orthodox theology. Foremost among these is apophaticism, or negative theology. The makers of the neo-patristic school of modern Orthodox theology, Georges Florovsky and Vladimir Lossky, promoted apophatism as part of their determined campaign against idealism and modernism in religion, a campaign directed against the Silver Age religious philosophers and Bulgakov in particular. So it is interesting to note that the first of the three parts of *The Unfading Light* bears the title "The Divine Nothing" and is given over almost entirely to apophatic theology. Rather than beginning with knowledge of God in creation, as a scholastic theologian might do, Bulgakov began with un-knowledge of God, or God's radical transcendence, drawing on Byzantine thinkers who were beginning to be recovered in his day, such as Maximus the Confessor and Gregory Palamas. But unlike the neo-patristic theologians, Bulgakov did not absolutize apophatic theology; he paired it with kataphatic or positive theology. Each mode has its own integrity, and both are needed to express the fundamental antinomy of our experience of God. The Divine Nothing of apophaticism paradoxically descends in a vast rain of positive revelations of God in creation, the human soul, history, culture, and the church. Neo-patristic thinkers, while not rejecting positive theology in principle, ignored or subordinated it in practice. Bulgakov's approach was more balanced and reconciling. For him, as we have so often noted, wholeness was everything.

---

[53] *Ibid.* p. 19.

The kataphatic side of *The Unfading Light* is the point where the project of philosophy of revelation connects with the philosophy of economy, since both are concerned with the religious significance of the created world and its humanization through the cultural process. In *The Unfading Light*, as in *Philosophy of Economy*, the "mythologem" of Sophia provided Bulgakov with a way of speaking about the cosmicizing force that keeps cosmic life cosmic and the humanizing force that keeps human life human.[54] Ranging far beyond the boundaries of traditional Orthodoxy, Bulgakov found resources for his sophiological presentation of the Christian faith in Platonism, Kabbalah, heterodox Christian mysticism and philosophical idealism. In his eclecticism, he typified the Russian Silver Age. But there was a guiding thread through the maze of sources he explored. Bulgakov was determined to show the pervasiveness of testimony to God in the world, which in turn implies the God-givenness of the world in all its freedom and diversity. *The Unfading Light* continues the Solov'ëvian project of justification of the world, or "cosmodicy," as Bulgakov called it.[55] The contrast with "theodicy" was intentional. In theodicy one seeks to justify the ways of God to those who speak for the world – sufferers, skeptics, scientists, and so on. In cosmodicy one seeks to justify the ways of the world to those who speak for God, such as the church, the ascetics, and other religiously-sanctioned authorities. Cosmodicy is a distinctively modern project in its affirmation of the freedom and dignity of the world.

Among other things, cosmodicy insists upon the freedom and dignity of religious faith. The philosophy of revelation seeks to vindicate religion against its cultured despisers and revisers – against Voltaire's scorn and Jefferson's deism, Kant's moralism and Hegel's paternalism, Comte's and Feuerbach's materialism, Marx's cynicism, Nietzsche's Prometheanism, and other forms of rejection. Bulgakov's case for the homely peasant proprietor in *Philosophy of Economy* is complemented by his case for the humble Orthodox believer in *The Unfading Light*.

THE END OF RELIGIOUS PHILOSOPHY

During the Russian Revolution of 1917–1918, Bulgakov got directly involved in public affairs as he had in 1905, only on this occasion the church, not the state, was the focus of his activism. Freed from its dependence on the tsarist autocracy, the Russian Orthodox Church convened a national church council in the fall of 1917 to work out structures of church government and ministry for a democratic Russia. Bulgakov was a leading member of the council and close

---

[54] Khoruzhii, *Posle pereryva*, p. 70.   [55] *Svet nevechernii*, p. 189.

adviser to Patriarch Tikhon. In spring 1918, Bulgakov entered the Orthodox priesthood. The levite had returned to his Father's house.

As civil war engulfed Russia in summer 1918, Bulgakov took refuge in Crimea, where he lived until he was expelled from the Soviet Union in 1922. These were his last years as a religious philosopher. In 1925 he found a secure position in exile as founding dean of the St. Sergius Orthodox Theological Institute in Paris, and there he launched a new career as a church theologian. From 1925 until his death in 1944, volumes of dogmatic theology poured from his pen.[56]

The most polished of Bulgakov's late religious-philosophical works is *At the Feast of the Gods* (1918), a historiosophical dialogue in the manner of Solov'ëv's *Three Conversations on War, Progress and the End of World History, with a Brief Tale of the Anti-Christ* (1899–1900). Bulgakov's interlocutors debate the future of Russia against the background of Bolshevik revolutionary government. The conversation accommodates a variety of viewpoints, from the secular Europeanism of a diplomat, through the Slavophilism of a writer, to the authoritarianism of a general who grudgingly accords the Bolsheviks a modicum of respect for their grasp of power politics. The debate culminates in the view that Russia can be renewed only "from a spiritual center,"[57] but opinions differ as to where that center might be found. A lay theologian believes it to exist already in the newly restructured Russian Orthodox Church, but a refugee from Poland argues that a more prophetic and ecumenical Christianity will be required to effect the necessary transformation of Russian and indeed European civilization. As in *Vekhi* a decade earlier, the need for spiritual rebirth among the intelligentsia is strongly emphasized. In the end, the refugee inspires all interlocutors except the diplomat to join him in affirming the mystical, if not yet palpable salvation of Russia. The dialogue ends with the Easter acclamation, "Christ is risen! He is risen indeed!"

In Crimea, Bulgakov wrote the greater part of two other philosophical works, *The Tragedy of Philosophy (Philosophy and Dogma)* and *Philosophy of Name*.[58] Composed without the benefit of libraries or professional colleagues, these books are not finished products but detailed laboratory reports exploring new horizons in religious philosophy. In *The Tragedy of Philosophy*, Bulgakov evaluated leading

---

[56] For surveys of Bulgakov's dogmatic theology see Paul Valliere, *Modern Russian Theology: Bukharev, Soloviev, Bulgakov – Orthodox Theology in a New Key* (Edinburgh: T&T Clark; Grand Rapids, MI: William B. Eerdmans Publishing Company, 2000), pp. 279–371; and Aidan Nichols, *Wisdom from Above: A Primer in the Theology of Father Sergei Bulgakov* (Leominster: Gracewing, 2005).

[57] *Na piru bogov* in *Sochineniia v dvukh tomakh*, vol. 2, p. 611.

[58] First editions: *Die Tragödie der Philosophie* (Darmstadt: Otto Reichl Verlag, 1927); *Filosofiia imeni* (Paris: YMCA Press, 1953).

continental philosophers since Descartes by comparing their systems to ancient Christian heresies. Schelling comes off best, although even in Schelling's thought Bulgakov detected a "bouquet of rationalism" which subverts its promise.[59] The point of *The Tragedy of Philosophy* is to underscore the dangers of dehumanization lurking in the failure to honor the "hypostatic" character of human persons, that is to say, their transcendence of any sort of unitary world-system. For Bulgakov, the surest foundation of personhood is the Triune God. Only Trinitarianism is cosmic enough and human enough to join God and the world together without fusion or confusion. But this conclusion points beyond religious philosophy to dogmatic theology.

In *Philosophy of Name*, Bulgakov undertook an evaluation of the religious significance of language, a project paralleling the linguistic turn of European thought after World War I. His interest in the subject was sparked by the quarrel over *imiaslavie* ("veneration of the name"), a pietistic movement in Russian Orthodox monasteries on Mt. Athos which was forcibly suppressed by Athonite and Russian authorities in 1913. Bulgakov's sympathies lay with the pietists, whom he regarded as Orthodox revivalists.[60] *Philosophy of Name* resembles *Philosophy of Economy*. Once again Bulgakov examined a concrete system of human exchange with the world (in this case, language) and sought its ontological foundation. Once again he resolved the ontological problem by appealing to the Incarnation, arguing that language, like labor, mediates a *meaningful* exchange with the world because it is a vehicle of divine-human communication, an actualization of the humanity of God.[61] Bulgakov's career as a religious philosopher thus ended as it began, with Solov'ëv's and arguably Christianity's grandest idea. The Word made flesh – made flesh in faith, in labor, in language, in social justice, in peace, in Israel, in Jesus – was Bulgakov's ultimate concern.

---

[59] *Sochineniia v dvukh tomakh*, vol. 1, p. 383.

[60] Bulgakov defended the name-venerators in "Afonskoe delo," *Russkaia mysl'*, no. 9 (1913), 37–46; reprinted in *S.N. Bulgakov: pro et contra*, pp. 292–304.

[61] For another way of contextualizing *Philosophy of Name* see I.B. Rodnianskaia, "Skhvatka S.N. Bulgakova s Immanuilom Kantom na stranitsakh 'Filosofii imeni'" in S.N. Bulgakov, *Pervoobraz i obraz: sochineniia v dvukh tomakh* (I.B. Rodnianskaia (ed.), Moscow: "Iskusstvo"; St. Petersburg, "Inapress," 1999), vol. 2, pp. 7–12.

9

PAVEL FLORENSKII'S TRINITARIAN HUMANISM

STEVEN CASSEDY

It would be difficult to find in the annals of any nation's cultural and intellectual history a figure so wide-ranging and at the same time so paradoxical as Pavel Aleksandrovich Florenskii (1882–1937).[1] Born into an educated family (his mother was artistic, while his father was an engineer descended from a line of Orthodox priests), Florenskii studied mathematics and philosophy at Moscow University, then went on to study at the Moscow Theological Academy, receiving his ordination to the priesthood in 1911. The range of subjects that he studied and on which he published is staggering: philosophy, theology, philosophy of language, mathematics, physics, electrical engineering, literature, art history, psychology, logic, botany, and others. He was equally at home discussing Kant's antinomies, the theory of perspective in art, the concept of divine Sophia in Russian Orthodoxy, mathematical discontinuity, Einstein's relativity, and Flaubert's *Temptation of Saint Anthony*. The footnotes in his scholarly works show a range of reading that boggles the mind.

TRINITY AND TRUTH

Florenskii first truly made a name for himself with the publication, in 1914, of what might be described as his *magnum opus*, a long book bearing the initially puzzling title *The Pillar and Ground of the Truth* and the equally puzzling subtitle *An Essay in Orthodox Theodicy in Twelve Letters*. In 1 Timothy (3:15), "the pillar

---

[1] I have drawn many of the ideas in this article from some of my other writings: "Pavel Florenskij's Philosophy of Language: Its Contextuality and Its Context," *Slavic and East European Journal* 35 (1991), 537–52; "Florenskij and Philosophy of Language in the Twentieth Century" in Michael Hagemeister and Nina Kaucisvilii (eds.), *P.A. Florenskii i kul'tura ego vremeni* (Marburg: Blaue Hörner Verlag, 1995), pp. 289–293; "P.A. Florenskii and the Celebration of Matter" in Judith Deutsch Kornblatt and Richard F. Gustafson (eds.), *Russian Religious Thought* (Madison, WI: University of Wisconsin Press, 1996), pp. 95–111; "The Idea, the Truth, and History: Florenskii's Dual Essentialism" in Norbert Franz, Michael Hagemeister, and Frank Haney (eds.), *Pavel Florenskij – Tradition und Moderne. Beiträge zum internationalen Symposium an der Universität Potsdam, 5. bis 9. April 2000* (Frankfurt am Main: Peter Lang, 2001), pp. 181–194.

and foundation of the truth" (or "pillar and ground of the truth," in the King James translation) refers to "the church of the living God," in a chapter on the proper conduct of bishops, women, and deacons in that church. *Theodicy*, meaning a justification of God and, more specifically, of his attributes, had been initially made famous by Leibniz's work of that title (in French, *Théodicée* (1710)). Leibniz used his book to prove God's qualities – his understanding, his power, his will – by the principle of sufficient reason.

But by the time *The Pillar and Ground of the Truth* came out, the word *theodicy* had occurred a bit more recently, in a passage far more relevant to the purposes of Florenskii: the final paragraph of Hegel's *Philosophy of History*. The paragraph, which concludes a long discussion of the process of development that is history, reads like this:

That world history is this process of development [*Entwicklungsgang*] and the actual becoming [*Werden*] of the mind/spirit [*Geist*], under the changing spectacle of its stories [*Geschichten*] – this is the true *theodicy*, the justification of God in history [*Geschichte*]. Only *this* insight can reconcile mind/spirit with world history and with reality – the insight that what has happened and what happens every day not only cannot be without God but essentially is the work of God himself.[2]

In Hegel, the term *theodicy* carries the meanings suggested not only by its component parts, *theos* ("god") and *dikē* ("justice"), but also by "in history"; it is thus inseparable from a revelatory process of development. The same is true in Florenskii, except that for him the justification of God emerges in not one but *two* revelatory processes: history, as in Hegel, but also the very argument that Florenskii presents in his own book. So Florenskii's title, *The Pillar and Ground of the Truth: An Essay in Orthodox Theodicy in Twelve Letters*, means something like this: "The church (broadly understood as God's living creatures), shown, through progressive revelation here, in this book, as the progressive revelation of and justification for God in history."

Florenskii's logic was in some ways modeled on Vladimir Solov'ëv's in the *Lectures on Godmanhood* (1878). The point of departure for that work is the observation that there are two worlds, one divine and one human. In Christ, or the Godman, the miracle of the Incarnation made possible a fleshly being embodying the divine and thus carrying both qualities. Nothing about these two thoughts is remarkable in most Christian theologies, but Solov'ëv extended the miracle of the Incarnation to include all of humanity, since in his view, man represents "a certain union of Divinity with material nature." The Russian philosopher further moved from the duality of the divinity–humanity

---

[2] G.W.F. Hegel, *Werke in zwanzig Bänden* (Eva Moldenhauer and Karl Markus Michel (eds.), Frankfurt am Main: Suhrkamp, 1970), vol. 12, p. 540.

opposition to a trinitarian scheme in man. The union of two qualities, he says, "presupposes in man three constituent elements; one divine, one material, and one properly human, connecting the other two."[3] Trinitarian thinking is pervasive in the *Lectures on Godmanhood*. In the seventh *Lecture*, Solov'ëv speaks of three "divine subjects" (spirit, mind, and soul), correlated with three "means of being" (will, representation, and feeling) as well as with three "ideas" (the good, truth, and beauty).[4]

Florenskii followed the same procedure in *The Pillar and Ground of the Truth*, arguing his way from duality to trinity. The first "letter" is entitled "Two Worlds"; in it he presents an essentially Kantian division between ordinary understanding and knowledge of the sort that would give us direct access to God. But rather than assert the power of faith as a faculty that would give us such access, Florenskii insists on the inaccessibility of God's truth. "God 'concealed' everything that uniquely may be called worthy of being known," he writes.[5] He goes on to speak about Christ, though he leaves it to the reader to surmise the relevance: Christ is the Godman and exists in both of the "two worlds" (*Stolp* p. 13).

The method by which Florenskii moved from this simple, dualistic model to trinity is ingenious and entirely unconventional. The second letter bears the title "Doubt," a concept that semantically and (in Russian and most other European languages) etymologically, implies duality (*so-mnenie*: "together-minds" or "two minds"). Here is a simplified version of his argument: the subject of the entire book is allegedly Truth (*Istina*). The question is how we arrive at truth, whether of the grandest sort (*Istina*, with an upper-case initial) or the ordinary sort (*istina*). Florenskii took the simplest example of what might be considered a truth statement: the identity proposition $A = A$. The use of the identity proposition makes particular sense in Russian, Florenskii reminds us, because the word for truth is etymologically connected with the form of the verb "to be" that is used as the copula: *est'*. Florenskii's controversial claim is that $A = A$ is not a truth statement for the even more controversial reason that when we say $A = A$, we're actually saying that A equals something *else*, some *not-A*, or some B. We thus find ourselves still in duality and, what's more, in an unproductive duality, since no truth can emerge from a proposition claiming that a certain thing *is* a certain other thing.

[3] V.S. Solov'ëv, *Sobranie sochinenii*, 2nd edn., 10 vols. (S.M. Solov'ëv and E.L. Radlov (eds.), (St. Petersburg: Prosveshchenie, 1911–1914), vol. 3, p. 166.

[4] *Ibid.* pp. 103–109.

[5] Pavel Florenskii, *Stolp i utverzhdenie Istiny: Opyt pravoslavnoi feoditsei v dvenadtsati pis'makh* (Moscow, 1914; reprinted Moscow: Izdatel'stvo "Pravda," 1990), p. 12. Cited in the text as *Stolp*. There is an English translation: Pavel Florensky, *The Pillar and Ground of the Truth: An Essay in Orthodox Theodicy in Twelve Letters* (Boris Jakim (trans.), Princeton University Press, 1997).

Then Florenskii proceeds to the critical claim. In order to arrive at truth, we need a third element to break the dualistic impasse of the identity statement. For reasons that quickly become obvious, he proves this claim by using the model of *persons*, as in grammar. "Through the *Thou*, the subjective *I* becomes an objective *He* and, in this *He*, has its affirmation, its objectiveness as an *I*" (*Stolp* p. 48). Why does Florenskii refer to grammatical persons? The answer immediately presents itself: truth is "the contemplation of Itself through an Other in a Third: Father, Son, Spirit" (*Stolp* p. 48). Truth is thus based in the Trinity, as Florenskii clearly asserts in the supplementary definition he gives. Paraphrasing the Athanasian Creed, he says, "Truth is one substance in three hypostases" (*hypostasis* meaning, in this case, a Person of the Trinity) (*Stolp* p. 49).

Florenskii has now established, at least to his own satisfaction, that Truth is intrinsically trinitarian and that it arises from an initial dualism. In the lengthy appendices to *The Pillar and Ground of the Truth*, he sought to show how pervasive the trinitarian concept is: three dimensions (in space); past, present, and future (in time); mind, will, and feeling (in *lichnost'*, the individual personality); thesis, antithesis, synthesis (in *razum*, reason). Even if these examples do not prove that *trinitarianism* is everywhere, they certainly show how frequently we run into the number three (*Stolp* pp. 593–599).

Florenskii thus regarded Truth as personalistic on three different levels (and in three slightly different senses). At the most basic level, the concept presented itself to him as built upon the three grammatical persons, regarded not purely as technical concepts but in truly *personal* terms in the most down-to-earth sense of *personal*: a real *I*, a real *thou*, and a real *he*. The concept operates at the level of the individual personality (*lichnost'*) in yet another triad of dimensions. And it operates at the level of the Christian Trinity, where the persons are the hypostases: God, the Son, and the Holy Spirit.

Truth bears an additional quality in Florenskii's formulation: it is *antinomic*. The sixth Letter in *The Pillar and Ground of the Truth* is entitled "Contradiction." According to this letter, truth is always based on an opposition between thesis and antithesis and thus incorporates a contradiction. Thesis and antithesis are related to one another dialectically. Florenskii echoed the language and style of Hegel, though he did not mention the name: "The unconditionality of truth on the formal side is expressed in the manner in which truth *in advance* implies and accepts its negation and answers any doubt concerning its truthfulness through the *acceptance* into itself of this doubt" (*Stolp* p. 147). But thesis and antithesis enjoy an "equal degree of convincingness," and thus the contradiction and truth itself may be described as antinomy (*Stolp* p. 147). To be sure, Florenskii did not set forth his antinomy in the classic format that Kant, in the *Critique of Pure Reason*, had used for *his* antinomies: parallel, side-by-side statement of thesis and antithesis, followed, underneath, by parallel, side-by-side proofs of thesis and antithesis. In fact, it is never clear precisely whether Florenskii understood the term "antinomy" as anything more than an opposition carrying with it some sort of paradoxical thought.

One of the most important manifestations of the trinitarian principle, especially given the centrality of *love* in Florenskii's work, is friendship. In Florenskii's view, friendship entails an *I* selecting a *thou*, which means an *other*, but it really begins for him only when there is a third member – God. Friendship consists in "the contemplation of Oneself through a Friend in God" (*Stolp* p. 438), "the seeing of oneself with the eyes of another, but before the person of a third, namely the Third [that is, God]" (*Stolp* p. 439). Once again, at the level of duality, before we reach the level of trinity, we have the model of contradiction and antinomy. In a characteristically convoluted passage, Florenskii explains: "But the friend is not only an *I* but also an *other I*, an *other* [person] for the *I*. The *I*, however, is unique [*edinstvennoe*], and everything that is *other* in relation to the *I* is already also non-*I*. The friend is [thus] an *I* that is not-*I*: the friend is a *contradictio*, and bound up into the very concept of it is an antinomy" (*Stolp* p. 439).

At the risk of gross simplification, we might say the logic that took Florenskii from duality to trinity with respect to truth, Truth, and friendship provided the motive force behind his understanding of practically everything that interested him in human experience. By itself the trinitarian concept does not provide this force. Instead, it is the duality that begins the process, the antinomic character of that duality (as best we can understand what Florenskii means by "antinomic"), and the final passage to trinity.

HISTORY

In the *Logic* (the first volume of the *Encyclopedia*), Hegel had shown that *becoming* (*das Werden*), and thus all historical development, derives from a dualistic opposition, namely that between *being* and *nothing*. "The truth of being, like that of nothing, is thus the *unity* of both; this unity is *becoming*," he wrote. "*Becoming* is the true expression of the result of being and nothing, as their unity; it is not only the *unity* of being and nothing, but *unrest* in itself – unity that exists within and against itself not just motionlessly as relation-to-itself, but through the difference between being and nothing that exists in becoming." "Becoming," he adds, "is the first concrete thought and therefore the first concept, while being and nothing are empty abstractions."[6] The model for the three-step logic that

[6] Hegel, *Werke in zwanzig Bänden*, vol. 8, pp. 188, 191–192.

gives rise to historical development was the same logic that operated at the level of the human spirit/mind (*Geist*) itself, as Hegel had shown in the *Phenomenology of Spirit*.

Florenskii uses a language blending the trinitarian with the explicitly Hegelian to describe the life of the individual mind and extend Hegel's concept of historical development. In his "Notes on Trinity," included in the appendix to *The Pillar and Ground of the Truth*, he wrote (*Stolp* p. 597):

And again, as we investigate more deeply the way man is constructed, we find everywhere the trinitarian principle, not only in the construction of his body but also in the life of his soul. The life of the mind [*razum*], in its dialectical development, pulsates with the rhythm of *thesis, antithesis,* and *synthesis,* and the law of the *three moments* of dialectical development is related not only to the mind but also to *feeling* and *will.*

In the chapter titled "The Comforter" (as the Holy Spirit is named in John 14:26), Florenskii shows that the path to Truth takes us through the Persons of the Holy Trinity, but he also shows that the path is historical as well as individual. Each Person, or hypostasis, corresponds to a stage in development of the human spirit, conceived (as in Hegel) in historical terms. The first Person, the Father, corresponds to the religion and life of antiquity; the second Person, the Son, corresponds to the religion and life of the new era; the third Person, the Holy Spirit, corresponds to the coming modern era, which renounces scientificity and yet, as Florenskii says in a conscious reference to Nietzsche (without, however, making clear what he has in mind), is inspired by the "gay science" (*Stolp* pp. 127–128).

Florenskii's pre-Hegelian model for the notion that the Trinity somehow drives history was the church father St. Gregory of Nazianzus (also called Gregory the Theologian, c. 330–c. 389). From the perspective of the fourth century CE, the logic was neat and clear. History is a process that follows the successive revelation of the three Persons: the Father in the Old Testament, the Son in the Gospels, and the Holy Spirit in the subsequent three-century life of the church. In his *Oration* on the Holy Spirit, St. Gregory divided history into discrete periods, separated by *changes* (Florenskii rendered the Greek *metathesis,* "change," as *preobrazovanie,* "transformation") or *earthquakes* (Greek *seismoi*): the change from the age of idols to the age of law in the Old Testament, and the change from the age of the law to the age of the Gospels. Gregory prophesied a third change: from this world (*enteuthen,* "from here") to the world beyond (*epi ta ekeise,* "to over there"), the world of "the immutable and unshakable" (*ta mēketi kinoumena, mēde saleuomena,* literally, "the no longer moved or shaken").[7]

---

[7] J.-P. Migne (ed.), *Patrologiae Cursus Completus: Series Graeca* (Paris, 1857–1866), vol. 36, pp. 160–161.

Though Florenskii's periods clearly do not line up precisely with St. Gregory's, the logic appears roughly the same, and the Holy Spirit in both instances refers to a coming age. And yet Florenskii provided a very odd commentary on this theory, one that reveals more about himself than about St. Gregory. "St. Gregory the Theologian," he wrote (*Stolp* p. 136):

is affirming the gradualness [*postepennost'*] of the historical appearance of the Spirit; but it is necessary to think of still another side – the discontinuity [*preryvnost'*] of [the Spirit's] transhistorical revelation, just as the Kingdom of God has both a gradual-historical and a discontinuous-eschatological appearance, neither of which is reducible to the other. Otherwise it is incomprehensible just how the final condition, the enlightening of [God's] creatures, the casting out of death, in a word, "the coming age," can be distinguished from the preliminary, waiting condition of "this age," in which death still reigns.

The history that Gregory presented is precisely *not* gradual: it *is* discontinuous. After all, he spoke of changes and earthquakes. But Florenskii appeared intent on introducing a concept that, as we will see shortly, was integral to his worldview: the idea of discontinuity (*preryvnost'*), understood in both its mathematical sense and the temporal sense in which he uses it here. The Trinity drives history and historical time, Florenskii suggested, but it leads, in the end, to a seismic break and a timeless "final condition," in which death is cast out.

Here, once again, we come back to Hegel. Toward the end of the *Encyclopedia*, in a section entitled "Revealed Religion," Hegel linked the Trinity with the final, timeless stage of the dialectical process he described: the stage of Absolute Spirit. The Notion (*Begriff*), which Hegel elaborated in the pages of the *Encyclopedia*, comprises three moments: the Universal, the Particular, and the Individual. Showing a *logical*, rather than a *temporal* connection between the moments, he asserted that the Father (as Universal) begets a Son, who (as finite and Particular) dies, resuming the character of the Father. From this contradiction and union, in the moment of the Individual, arises "the idea of the Spirit, eternal, yet *living* and present in the world."[8] For Hegel as for Florenskii, the final, absolute stage paradoxically, dialectically contains elements of the timeless (death is cast out for Florenskii, the Spirit is eternal for Hegel) and the worldly (Nietzsche's "gay science" for Florenskii, the Spirit that is "present in the world" for Hegel).

Thus, for Florenskii, history took its point of departure in the original tension between opposites – thesis and antithesis, I and Thou, *A* and *not-A*, Father and Son, "this" world and "that" world. But the pairs of opposites that appeared to fascinate him most of all are those modeled on the primary division between

---

[8] Hegel, *Werke in zwanzig Bänden*, vol. 10, pp. 375–376.

"this" world and "that" world – pairs, in other words, that include a component that is material, contingent, secular, temporal. It is worth noticing that, when he came to describe the "end-time," Florenskii resisted the terms commonly associated with the post-millennial condition, except for the casting out of death. Instead he emphasized "the enlightening of [God's] creatures" and Nietzsche's gay science. The term "creature" (*tvar'*) is especially remarkable, because, in dualistic schemes such as the one Florenskii introduced in "Two Worlds," the term is normally taken as the polar opposite of the divine.

The question is whether, in God's creatures, we emphasize the *creature*, as partaking of the profane material world, or whether we emphasize the *creature's origin* in God. Florenskii's preference seems to have been to emphasize the former, while keeping the latter firmly in mind. The presence of both elements, their coexistence and their conflict, appears to be what Florenskii meant by *antinomy*. Another way of putting this is to say that the spark of humanism remained inextinguishable everywhere this priest and author of a *theodicy* looked. It can hardly be an accident that, for the third and final period in history, the one corresponding to the Holy Spirit, Florenskii chose as an inspiration the force named in the title of the book where Nietzsche first proclaimed the death of God.

LANGUAGE

Philosophy of language lay close to the core of Florenskii's intellectual repertoire, even his worldview, and antinomy lies at the very core of his conception of language. Sometime in the mid-1920s, Florenskii wrote a document that he titled "Avtoreferat," a kind of brief intellectual self-description, written in the third person and intended as an encyclopedia entry (though the piece was not published till 1988). The heart of the "Avtoreferat" is the section entitled "Mirovozzrenie" (worldview). Here Florenskii presented what he saw as the fundamental division in his work and in his worldview:

Florenskii understands his life's task as laying a path toward a future integral worldview. In this sense, he may be called a philosopher. But in opposition to the methods and tasks established in modern times for philosophical thinking, he rejects abstract constructs and an exhaustive universe of problems understood schematically. In this sense, one ought rather to consider him an investigator [*issledovatel'* – literally, "seeker"]. Broad perspectives for him are always linked with concrete and closely designed investigations of individual, sometimes entirely specialized problems.[9]

[9] "P.A. Florenskii. Avtoreferat," *Voprosy filosofii*, no. 12 (1988), 113–119. The quoted passage appears on p. 114.

At the end of the entry, before the section listing his works, Florenskii referred to his studies of language (p. 116):

Rejecting the abstract logicality of thought, Florenskii sees the value of thought as lying in its concrete manifestation, like the revelation of individual personality [*lichnost'*]. Hence his interest in the stylistic investigation of the products of thought. In addition, rejecting the notion of non-verbal thought, Florenskii sees in the study of the word a significant tool for penetrating into the thought of another person and for the formation of one's own thought. Hence his studies in etymology and semasiology.

To what in Florenskii's actual work did these puzzling remarks refer? In 1918, Florenskii wrote a short piece titled "The Antinomy of Language." It was not published till many years after Florenskii's death but offers a valuable glimpse into the panopticon of his mind. Florenskii describes language as enjoying a dual status. It exists as both *veshchnost'* ("thingness") and *deiatel'nost'* ("activity"). In choosing these terms, Florenskii was attempting to render a distinction introduced by German philologist Wilhelm von Humboldt in the 1820s. Humboldt had written of two conceptions of language, one seeing it as *ergon*, the other as *energeia*. *Ergon* ("work") denotes language regarded as a ready-made, static, dead thing. *Energeia* ("energy," "action") denotes language regarded as a dynamic, living force, something that is constantly changing in fruitful ways. Humboldt, German Romantic that he was, writing in an era and intellectual context already dominated by Hegelian thought, favored the *energeia* conception, since it was consonant with his view of spirit and historical process as organic and evolving.

Florenskii characteristically refused to choose sides in the conflict between *ergon/veshchnost'* and *energeia/deiatel'nost'*, preferring instead to insist that language possesses both properties – thus the titular *antinomy* of language. But he also introduced an interpretation of the poles of the "antinomy" that Humboldt would not have recognized. The "thingness" of language means its material aspect and its immutable qualities, so we might initially think that Florenskii was referring simply to the nuts and bolts of a given language (its sound properties, its fixed forms) as it exists at a given moment in history. But instead, reverting to the two-worlds model that underlies so much of this thought, he linked the "thingness" of language with the divine and infinite – because "thingness," after all, is static, therefore unchanging, therefore like God. The "activity" of language means its mutable, contingent aspect. *This* is the aspect that corresponds to the earthly, finite pole of the two-worlds model, the pole that represents the world of God's creatures. If Florenskii thought the *veshchnost'–deiatel'nost'* opposition qualified as an antinomy, he must have viewed the two terms of that opposition as somehow equally valid. In a true antinomy, after all, thesis and antithesis not only directly contradict one another but also carry equal persuasiveness.[10]

In subsequent articles, Florenskii changed a number of positions he had taken in "The Antinomy of Language" – so much, in fact, that to claim that he came up with a single, coherent philosophy of language would be to strain credulity. But a remarkable pattern certainly emerges from his various writings in this field. As in his theological and historical musings, there is always a duality, a hesitation between the terms of the duality, and the sense that, as we face the duality, instead of choosing one term and rejecting the other, we position ourselves between them, adopting a series of intermediate perspectives. That was probably what Florenskii had in mind when he used the word "antinomy": not a true antinomy, as in Kant, but an opposition in which neither pole triumphs so completely over the other as to eliminate it.

In the end, it may not matter much if the theory that Florenskii presented in "The Antinomy of Language" differs from the one he presented in other related writings. The differences we find can easily be described as differences in emphasis or differences in intermediate positions between the poles of an opposition. What does matter, once again, in this allegedly religious thinker, this ordained Orthodox priest whose most important book is an 809-page "theodicy," is the insistent, invariable direction of his gaze at the realm of the mutable, material, historical, and worldly – whether or not in a particular instance he appears to be actually favoring that realm over the realm of the immutable, immaterial, timeless, and otherworldly.

SCIENCE AND MATHEMATICS

As a student in the Faculty of Physics and Mathematics at Moscow University, starting in September 1900, Florenskii attended lectures of Professor Nikolai Bugaev on mathematical discontinuity. To almost anyone but a Russian intellectual of this period, the name Bugaev conveys little. That Florenskii, after studying with Bugaev, titled the introduction to his dissertation "The Idea of Discontinuity as an Element of a Worldview" might also seem a mere curiosity. But Bugaev was an important figure, engaged in the late nineteenth-century debate between mathematicians who were primarily algebraists and those who promoted arithmology, specifically the theory of discontinuous functions. In Russia at the time, mathematical theories carried enormous moral, philosophical, even political weight. The larger idea behind this conflict, put very simply,

[10] P.A. Florenskii, "Antinomiia iazyka," *Studia Slavica Academiae Scientiarum Hungaricae* 32 (1986), 117–163.

was that conventional mathematics, like algebra, was based on causality and mechanism, and was therefore materialistic and deterministic. Discontinuous functions, however, suggested something altogether different. A discontinuous function is one (to put it in visual terms) whose graph is interrupted at one or more points, such that, if you were to imagine a point moving along the graph, that point would have to "jump" through empty space over the interruption. The interruptions in discontinuous functions suggested to philosophically-minded mathematicians like Bugaev the notion of freedom from mechanism, determinism, and materialism. And because the radical Left in Russia (whether "nihilist" or Marxist) was predominantly materialistic in outlook, arithmology and the theory of discontinuous functions came to be seen as an expression of opposition to revolutionary politics and support for traditional Russian institutions.[11]

What Florenskii appears to have learned from Bugaev was not so much the alleged political implications as the broader philosophical, even metaphysical implications of discontinuity. Frank Haney has recently claimed that discontinuity was the basis for Florenskii's very idea of truth and thus for his entire worldview. The principle, according to Haney, operates on at least two levels. First, Florenskii believed that modern science had shown reality itself to be riddled with breaks and interruptions. Secondly, his notion of truth (in other words, our mode of *knowing* that reality) was founded on antinomy, which implies contradiction and thus breaks and interruptions.[12]

Haney draws two important inferences from Florenskii's work in mathematics and science. The first is that mathematics and science served as the point of departure for *all* Florenskii's thought, even in fields seemingly quite remote from the mathematical and the scientific. "One might even go so far as to assert," Haney writes, "that [Florenskii] in his own theodicy was pursuing not so much requirements and questions internal to his theology as those that, in his view, were driving changes taking place in mathematics and the natural sciences from the end of the nineteenth to the beginning of the twentieth century" (pp. 51–52). Florenskii intently followed the latest developments in these fields: group and function theory in mathematics, quantum mechanics and relativity theory in physics. *The Pillar and Ground of the Truth*, Haney argues, is shot through with "mathematical-scientific argumentation," not because such argumentation serves a stylistic purpose but because "it follows organically from

[11] Alexander Vucinich, *Science in Russian Culture, 1861–1917* (Stanford University Press, 1970), pp. 351–354; Steven Cassedy, *Flight from Eden: The Origins of Modern Literary Criticism and Aesthetics* (Berkeley, CA: University of California Press, 1990), pp. 162–163.

[12] Frank Haney, *Zwischen exakter Wissenschaft und Orthodoxie: Zur Rationalitätsauffassung Priester Pavel Florenskijs* (Frankfurt am Main: Peter Lang, 2001), p. 202.

his entire understanding of the world" (p. 52). This first inference probably overstates the importance of discontinuous functions to Florenskii's worldview.

The second inference is that Florenskii was continually drawn to phenomena and conceptions that most powerfully defied conventional systems, by seeming to urge the investigator to abandon all hope of finding a neat, rational, and linear order in nature (whether or not the investigator was inclined to regard such an order as coming from God) and instead to accept the conclusion that nature – the entire universe, for that matter – displays a perverse inclination for the contradictory and the disorderly. Haney sees *antinomy* (always in the relatively loose sense associated with Florenskii) as another principle, like discontinuity, integral to Florenskii's worldview.

Florenskii also articulated another principle, *asymmetry*, and the related notion of *irreversibility*. On the basis of Einstein's theory of the curvature of space-time, Florenskii speculated that if we picture space-time as curved, then it must have a convex and a concave side. We customarily see reality from within, thus from the concave side of space-time. But our perspective would be entirely different if we were to approach space-time from the outside, that is, if we were facing the convex side. The conclusion? That all processes in reality are irreversible, and there is thus no such thing as a reversible process. "There are no symmetrical phenomena," he wrote in a letter to his son from prison camp in 1936. "It's not that by chance there aren't any; it's that, owing to the very essence of the matter, there can't be . . . *Being in space-time* is a synonym for *being irreversible and asymmetrical.*"[13]

Predictably, for Florenskii the perfect example of irreversibility from modern physics was the second law of thermodynamics, regarding entropy. Of course, the second law allows both for processes that are reversible and for processes that are irreversible; it doesn't claim that the entropy of *all* systems increases. But either Florenskii was unaware of this distinction, or it did not trouble him. What entropy meant to him was that the entire cosmos was following an irreversible process and that it was therefore asymmetrical.

HUMANITY AND HUMANNESS

Where do humanity and humanness fit in a worldview as wide-ranging but also as diverse and replete with contradictions as Florenskii's? In the fourth letter of *The Pillar and Ground of the Truth*, a letter devoted to "The Light of the Truth," there is a telling passage concerning love. Florenskii characteristically

---

[13] *Sochineniia v chetyrëkh tomakh* (Moscow: Izdatel'stvo "Mysl'," 1994–1998), vol. 4, pp. 426–427. Cited in Haney, *Zwischen exakter Wissenschaft und Orthodoxie*, p. 190.

approached love as a dualism that becomes trinitarian. "Love for another," he wrote (*Stolp* p. 90):

is the reflection onto *him* of truthful knowledge. But knowledge [*vedenie*] is the revelation, to the heart, of the Trihypostatic Truth Itself, that is, the dwelling, in the soul, of God's love for man: "If we love one another, God dwelleth in us, and his love is perfected in us" (1 John 4:12). We enter with Him not only into an impersonal/non-individual [*bezlichnoe*], providential-cosmic relation [*otnoshenie*] but also into a personal/individual [*lichnoe*], paternal-filial relationship [*obshchenie*].

Florenskii then spoke of love in terms he later employed in his discussion of friendship. "Rising above the logical, contentless-empty law of identity and identifying with the beloved brother," he wrote in a particularly convoluted passage (*Stolp* p. 92):

the *I*, by this very means, freely makes itself a non-*I* or, to use the language of sacred hymns, "empties," "emaciates," "ravages," "humiliates" itself (cf. Phil. 2:7), that is, voids itself both of the attributes that are necessarily given to it and inherent in it and of the natural laws of inner activity by the law of ontological egoism or identity . . . In this manner, the impersonal/non-individual *I* turns itself into a person, an *other I*, that is, a *Thou*. But in this "impoverishment," or "emaciation" of the *I*, in this "emptying" or "kenosis" of itself, a reverse renewal of the *I* takes place within the norm of being peculiar to itself. This norm, moreover, is not simply given but also justified, that is, it not only is present in a given place and moment but has a universal and eternal meaning.

It is not important to grasp every single word of this explanation. But a key concept is the one expressed by the Greek word *kenosis* and the string of verbs and verbal nouns associated with it. *Kenosis* means "emptying," and it refers to the passage Florenskii cites from Philippians. Literally translated from the Greek, that passage reads, "Who [Jesus], existing in the form of God, did not consider it plunder to be equal with God, but emptied himself, taking on the form of a slave, appearing in the likeness of men, and, being found in outward appearance like a man, humbled himself, becoming obedient unto death, even the death of the cross" (Phil. 2:6–8). The word "emptied" in Greek is *ekenōsen*, from the verb *kenoō*, "empty." The word *kenosis* is simply a noun derived from this verb, and it refers to the act by which Christ is said to have emptied himself, presumably of his divinity, in order to assume the appearance and the condition of a man – and not just any man but a particularly *humble* man, a slave.

The term *kenosis* was introduced to Russian religious thought by Mikhail Tareev, an Orthodox theologian who wrote a book under the forbidding title *The Temptations of the Godman as the Unique Redemptive Act of the Whole Earthly Life of Christ, in Connection with the History of Pre-Christian Religions and of the Christian Church* (1892). Tareev returned to the concept of *kenosis* in a later work, *The Humiliation of Our Lord Jesus Christ* (1901), which Florenskii cites in an endnote. The term *kenosis* had been used in German Protestant theology earlier in the nineteenth century to emphasize the earthly-human dimension of Jesus. In Tareev's work, it created a play of perspective that clearly appealed to Florenskii. When we consider the *kenosis*, by which Christ adopted human form to such an extent that he could die a human death on the cross, we find ourselves in a point-of-view position somewhere along a continuum between the two poles of divinity and humanity. Florenskii did not propose that we adopt a monophysite position and regard Christ as exclusively human, but he kept his eye fixed on Christ's human dimension. In "The Light of Truth," it became a necessary component of love, standing over against the divine.

Christ's humanity is, of course, the source of his connection with us in all other respects as well. The "kenotic" passage from Philippians occurs again in *The Pillar and Ground of the Truth*, in the ninth letter. The topic of this letter is *tvar'*, which may be translated variously as "creature," "creatures," or "God's creation." In this letter, Florenskii betrays what may well be the essence of his worldview: the notion that, even when faith leads us to believe in God, the world that God created originates in him, reflects his goodness, and therefore enjoys a kind of sanctity. Here is how Florenskii puts it in the letter (*Stolp* pp. 289–290):

Christ took the idea of God's humility to the ultimate limit: God, coming into the world, deposits there the image of His glory and takes on the image of His creatures (Phil 2:6–8), submits to the laws of creaturely life. He does not disturb the world's course, strike the world with lightning, or deafen it by thunder, as pagans supposed (think only of the myth of Zeus and Semele), but simply glimmers before it with a modest light, drawing to himself His sinful, troubled creatures, bringing them to reason but without chastising them. God loves His creatures and suffers for them, suffers on account of their sin. God stretches out his hands to His creatures, implores them, calls to them, waits for His prodigal son to come to Him. And, standing at the head of God's creatures, mankind is responsible to God for them, just as man is responsible to man.

At the end of the letter, Florenskii declares God's creatures to be "an eternal divine miracle" (*Stolp* p. 317).

So powerfully did Florenskii believe in the venerability of God's creation and specifically of humanity that, in the tenth letter of *The Pillar and Ground of the Truth*, he gave us a fourth Person of the Trinity to represent them. This person is the divine Sophia, whom he defines as "the Great Root of God's creation in its entirety... by which that creation enters into the inner-Trinitarian life and through which she [Sophia] receives unto herself Eternal Life from the One Source of Life; Sophia is the primordial nature of creation, the creative Love of God, 'which has been poured into our hearts through the Holy Spirit that has been given to us' (Romans 5:5)" (*Stolp* p. 326). In Florenskii's view, Sophia came to stand for creation itself: "If Sophia is all Creation, then the soul and conscience of Creation, Mankind, is chiefly Sophia. If Sophia is all Mankind, then the soul and conscience of Mankind, the Church, is chiefly Sophia" (*Stolp* p. 350).

If it is proper to speak of Florenskii's humanism, this would be its philosophical and theological underpinning. God reveals his divinity through his very creation. Through Christ's *kenosis*, he partakes of the world he created and of the creatures that inhabit that world. This means that God has humbled himself, but it also means he has exalted his creatures. As always for Florenskii, the heart of the matter lay in the play of perspectives arising from an initial dualism. If God's creation is one pole on a continuum whose other pole is God himself, then there can be no division between the two. As Florenskii saw it, in a world where this is true, to immerse oneself in the secular, to be a scientist, and, above all, to be a humanist is not to abandon faith but to embrace it.

Florenskii was arrested in 1933 and sentenced to ten years in a prison camp in Siberia. He did not serve out his full term. He was executed in August 1937. In Siberia, he continued his scientific work, producing, for example, sketches of local flora, one facet of God's creation. From camp he also wrote letters to his family. One letter addressed to his son some five months before Florenskii's death, included this self-reflective and retrospective passage: "What have I done my whole life? Examined the world as a whole thing, as a single picture and reality, but at every moment, or, more precisely, at every stage of my life, from a certain visual angle."[14] No words could better capture the essence of the vision that illuminated Florenskii's worldview, his humanism in particular.

[14] *Sochineniia v chetyrëkh tomakh*, vol. 4, p. 672. Cited on the cover of Michael Hagemeister and Nina Kaucisvilii (eds.), *P.A. Florenskii i kul'tura ego vremeni* (Marburg: Blaue Hörner Verlag, 1995).

10

SEMËN FRANK'S EXPRESSIVIST HUMANISM

PHILIP J. SWOBODA

To approach the philosophical thought of Semën Frank with a focus on his ideas concerning human dignity and self-realization is to view it from a perspective quite unlike the one from which it is generally viewed both in the standard histories of Russian philosophy and in recent Russian studies of his thought. The influential émigré historian Vasilii Zenkovskii, who considered Frank "the most outstanding among Russian philosophers generally," saw him primarily as the creator of a system of metaphysics founded on the notion of the world as a total unity (*vsëedinstvo*).[1] On the other hand, Piama Gaidenko, an acute contemporary Russian expositor of Frank, focused her attention on his epistemological theories, presenting him as a leading representative of the "turn to ontology," i.e., epistemological realism, in early twentieth-century European philosophy. This approach links him with such thinkers as Edmund Husserl, Max Scheler, Nicolai Hartmann, and Martin Heidegger.[2]

Without question, Frank's labors in the fields of metaphysics and theory of knowledge absorbed a large part of his energies as a philosopher, and called forth many of his most original insights. Yet I would maintain that Frank had no more compelling concern throughout his philosophical career than to vindicate a view of the human person as the earthly receptacle of divine spirit, and hence as a being of infinite worth. The theme of human dignity and individual rights surfaces again and again in Frank's writings, from the inception of his public activity to its very end. In this respect, as in many others, his deepest instincts were those of a convinced "Westernizer," unshakably committed to the fundamental values of modern European culture. His attachment to these

---

[1] V.V. Zenkovsky, *A History of Russian Philosophy*, 2 vols. (George L. Kline (trans.), New York: Columbia University Press, 1953), vol. 2, pp. 852–853. The term "total unity" (also translated "all-unity" or "unity of all") was given currency by Frank's elder contemporary Vladimir Solov'ëv. In consequence, Frank is often described in the literature as one of Solov'ëv's philosophical heirs (see, e.g., Zenkovsky, pp. 840, 853). In my view, the extent of Solov'ëv's influence on Frank has been much exaggerated.

[2] P.P. Gaidenko, "Metafizika konkretnogo vsëedinstva, ili Absoliutnyi realizm S.L. Franka," *Voprosy filosofii*, no. 5 (1999), 114–116.

values is evident not merely from his published works, but from many details of his biography, including his choice of philosophical allies and political associates.

In his writings, however, Frank chose to ground his belief in the transcendent dignity of the person and the right to free expression of his or her individuality on principles that were, in crucial respects, incompatible with the assumptions of liberal humanism. One of his most striking departures from the form of liberalism represented, for example, by the Russian legal philosophers was his pronounced ambivalence toward the concept of law, which manifested itself in a tendency to regard law not as a means to achieve human freedom and self-realization, but as their antagonist. Yet it is wholly impossible to classify him as an "illiberal" humanist either. On the contrary, he was one of the most acute and persistent critics of utopian thinking, particularly in its socialist version, that his era produced. There are grounds therefore for describing Frank as the upholder of a "third way" in twentieth-century Russian philosophy, founded on a "humanism" that was quite distinct both from the liberal humanism of the legal philosophers and from the illiberal humanism of Russia's various utopian visionaries. To define the specific character of this humanism is a major goal of this chapter.

BIOGRAPHY

Semën Liudvigovich Frank (1877–1950), the scion of an assimilated Jewish family of some wealth and status, grew up in Moscow and the provincial city of Nizhnii Novgorod.[3] During his final year at the Nizhnii gymnasium, he became an enthusiastic convert to Marxism. After graduating, he enrolled in the Law faculty of Moscow University, the faculty preferred by students of Marxist leanings, since political economy was taught under its auspices. Throughout his years at the university (1894–1898) he was involved with various revolutionary circles, though as time passed he grew increasingly disenchanted with the intellectual shallowness of his radical comrades. Nevertheless, he was arrested in 1899 for his role in a student protest, and, after his release, temporarily forbidden to reside in Moscow or any other university town. After taking his final examinations as an extern at Kazan' University, he left Russia to pursue further education at the University of Berlin.

---

[3] The biographical data that follows derives from the following sources: S.L. Frank, "Predsmertnoe: Vospominaniia i mysli," *Vestnik RSKhD*, no. 146 (1986), 103–126; *Sbornik pamiati Semëna Liud-vigovicha Franka* (Munich: Izdanie sem'i filosofa, 1954); *Biografiia P.B. Struve* (New York: Chekhov, 1956); Philip Boobbyer, *S.L. Frank: The Life and Work of a Russian Philosopher, 1877–1950* (Athens, OH: Ohio University Press, 1995).

Between 1899 and 1907, Frank spent much of his time abroad. During these years he first came to the notice of the Russian reading public as a left-wing social theorist, liberal publicist, and cultural critic. Though no longer a Marxist, Frank remained a radical "democrat" and an active opponent of the tsarist regime. He became the trusted collaborator of Pëtr Struve, another former Marxist who emerged after 1900 as the leading ideologist of pre-revolutionary Russian liberalism. Between 1902 and 1917, Frank contributed dozens of articles to the various underground newspapers, legal periodicals, and "thick journals" that Struve edited. Though some of these articles, particularly after 1907, were purely "philosophical" in content, in others Frank came forward as a passionate advocate of constitutional government and individual rights, and as a critic of the "anti-cultural" attitudes of educated Russian society.

Like other Russian liberals, Frank strongly supported the 1905 Revolution, and rapturously greeted the promises of constitutional reform extracted from the beleaguered tsar in October of that year. Frank persuaded himself that Russia was about to emerge as "the vanguard country of democracy."[4] During the following two years, as the hopes inspired by the events of 1905 came to seem increasingly illusory, Frank, under Struve's influence, came to blame the revolution's failure squarely on the faulty thinking and moral irresponsibility of the radical Left. He elaborated this critique in a number of articles, including his contribution to the symposium on the failings of the Russian intelligentsia published in 1909 under the title of *Landmarks* (*Vekhi*), undoubtedly his best-known piece of writing.[5] Frank also contributed articles to the two other article collections that defined the trajectory of liberal philosophy in Russia: *Problems of Idealism* (1902) and *Out of the Depths* (1918). During the final decade of the tsarist regime, Frank remained a moderate liberal and believer in constitutional government, but he ceased to play an active role in politics.

In 1908, Frank married Tatiana Bartseva, and began acquiring the necessary credentials to pursue a career as a university professor of philosophy. His new wife came of an Orthodox family, but she converted to Lutheranism to contract a legal marriage with Frank (Russian law forbade marriages between Jews and members of the established church of the empire). In 1912, Frank himself was baptized in the Orthodox church, which allowed his wife to return to her original faith, and enabled him to circumvent regulations against Jews holding professorships at Russian universities.[6] Later in the same year, Frank was

---

[4] "Molodaia demokratiia," *Svoboda i kul'tura*, no. 2 (10 April 1906), 77.

[5] "The Ethic of Nihilism" in *Vekhi (Landmarks): A Collection of Articles About the Russian Intelligentsia* (Marshall S. Shatz and Judith E. Zimmerman (trans.), Armonk, NY: M.E. Sharpe, 1994), pp. 131–155.

[6] Boobbyer, *Frank*, pp. 50–51, 53.

appointed an unsalaried lecturer at Moscow University. In 1915, he defended his master's thesis, a 500-page volume entitled *The Object of Knowledge*, which is arguably his most significant book.[7] This treatise laid down the fundamental principles of his mature metaphysical system, and remains the most detailed exposition and defense of his views on epistemology. In 1917, he published a second book, *Man's Soul*, an introduction to "philosophical psychology."[8]

Following the overthrow of the tsar, the Provisional Government appointed Frank the first dean of the newly-established humanities faculty at the University of Saratov. He and his family (the Franks had four children) endured the privations of the civil war in the Saratov region. Returning to Moscow in 1921 to take up a new teaching post, Frank was soon arrested by the Soviet authorities, and, on Lenin's express instructions, he was included among the dozens of "bourgeois" intellectuals and academics whom the Bolsheviks deported from Soviet Russia in 1922 as potential inspirers of ideological unrest. He spent the last three decades of his life in European exile, first in Germany, then in France, and finally in England. During the 1920s, he resided with his family in Berlin, where he was able to obtain some teaching work; but, following Hitler's rise to power in 1933, Frank, owing to his Jewish ancestry, could no longer find employment in Germany. He survived the next dozen years largely on the charity of friends.[9] In late 1937, he fled Germany for France. France's military defeat in 1940 had no immediate effect on his situation, since he was living at the time on the Riviera, which the armistice agreement assigned to the Vichy government. But once Vichy France was occupied by the German army late in 1942, Frank found himself in real danger of arrest and deportation to a death camp. To escape this fate, Frank spent the last year of the German occupation hiding out in a remote country district near Grenoble. At the end of the war he moved to London, where he died of lung cancer in 1950.

In emigration, Frank published five more books expounding his philosophical ideas.[10] Yet exile deprived Frank of the audience for specialized philosophical writing that he might have expected to enjoy had the Revolution not supervened and had he remained free to pursue his philosophical vocation in Russia. Much of his writing in emigration was therefore aimed at a less elite

---

[7] *Predmet znaniia: Ob osnovakh i predelakh otvlechënnogo znaniia* (Paris: YMCA Press, 1974, reprint).

[8] For a discussion of this neglected but strikingly original work, see my foreword to S.L. Frank, *Man's Soul: An Introductory Essay in Philosophical Psychology* (Boris Jakim (trans.), Athens, OH: Ohio University Press, 1993), pp. xi–xxx.

[9] Boobbyer, *Frank*, pp. 159–160, 179–180.

[10] Besides the books discussed below, these comprised *God with Us: Three Meditations* (Natalie Duddington (trans.), London: Jonathan Cape, 1946), a work of Christian apologetics, and *Reality and Man: An Essay on the Metaphysics of Human Nature* (Natalie Duddington (trans.), London: Faber and Faber, 1956), a final restatement of his main philosophical ideas.

audience than his first two books. He wrote lengthy articles on the spiritual meaning of the Russian Revolution, as well as studies of major figures in Russian and European literature. He also produced many essays for non-Russian periodicals aimed at explaining Russian culture to European readers. In the inter-war years Frank attempted to secure a place for himself in the world of European professional philosophy, but achieved only modest success. An abridged French translation of *The Object of Knowledge* appeared in 1937.[11]

Frank is often labeled a "religious philosopher," perhaps because in his émigré writings, as in the works of kindred thinkers such as Berdiaev, explicitly Christian themes enjoy a prominence rarely accorded them in twentieth-century western European or American philosophy. Yet at no time in his career did he regard himself as a practitioner of a special genre of thinking distinct from conventional philosophy. On the contrary, he was passionately convinced that genuine philosophy had always been "religious" – from Plato's time to the era of German Idealism.[12]

Frank's personal religious history was extremely complex, and his religious outlook altered radically more than once over the course of his lifetime. Raised in a pious Jewish household, he lost his belief in God in his gymnasium years and did not recover it, by his own testimony, until 1908.[13] He never returned, however, to the Judaism of his boyhood. His published writings shed little light on the motives for his formal conversion to Christianity in 1912. This step might have been prompted at least in part by family and career considerations. It is also likely that Frank saw Orthodox baptism as a symbolic way of asserting his membership in the Russian "nationality." Yet the philosophical system he elaborated during the next few years was arguably as remote from Christian orthodoxy as it was from Torah Judaism. The religious outlook revealed in his published works was of a pantheistic cast, nourished on Goethe, Plotinus, and the Upanishads, rather than on the Bible.

The trials of the revolutionary era appear to have deepened Frank's religious feelings and imparted to his faith a more definite Christian character. In European exile he emerged as a vigorous apologist for a generically "Christian" view of life. He took a particular interest in the spiritual welfare of émigré youth, and during the 1920s was one of the "ideological leaders" of the Russian Student Christian Movement.[14] Though he was emotionally attached to his church and its liturgy, Orthodox exclusivism was always completely alien to him, and his writings made limited use of concepts or language distinctive to the Orthodox theological tradition. To the end of his days, he took a contemptuous view of

[11] *La Connaissance et l'être* (Paris: Aubier, 1937).   [12] *Reality and Man*, p. xvii.
[13] *Shornik pamiati Semëna Liudvigovicha Franka*, p. 5.   [14] Boobbyer, *Frank*, p. 127.

the "theologizing" of professional theologians, which he saw as an irresponsible waste of time.[15] Theologians such as Zenkovskii returned the favor by questioning whether Frank's metaphysics of total unity (which Frank himself insisted on describing as "panentheistic" rather than "pantheistic") could be reconciled with the Christian doctrine of creation, which they understood to imply the existence of a more radical ontological gulf between divine and created being than Frank seemed prepared to acknowledge.[16]

PHILOSOPHICAL DEVELOPMENT

Standard accounts of Frank's philosophy tend to treat all his major books, starting with *The Object of Knowledge*, as expositions of a single system of ideas that underwent no significant modifications after 1915. There are some grounds for questioning the validity of this interpretation. Frank's efforts after 1922 to harmonize basic Christian doctrines with his own philosophical convictions forced him to wrestle with an array of questions that he had not previously addressed, and this intellectual struggle sometimes carried his thought in unexpected directions. Certainly the *tone* of the books he wrote in the 1930s and 1940s, after the rise of Stalin and Hitler, was strikingly different from that of his earlier writings. Anxious pessimism leavened with Christian hope succeeded calm confidence. On the whole, however, the basic structures of his thinking altered relatively little.

Any account of Frank's philosophical development must begin by noting his immense debt to German philosophy.[17] At the start of his career, he was powerfully influenced by neo-Kantianism, then the dominant philosophical trend in German universities. His first mentor in philosophy was the maverick neo-Kantian philosopher Georg Simmel, whose lectures Frank attended in 1899–1901 as a student at the University of Berlin; at roughly the same time, he came under the intellectual influence of Wilhelm Windelband. From the neo-Kantians, Frank derived not just particular doctrines but the whole framework of his early philosophical thinking; they taught him what the crucial problems of philosophy were, and what criteria a satisfactory solution to these problems would have to meet. It was not until 1908 that he began liberating his thought

---

[15] See, e.g., *The Light Shineth in Darkness* (Boris Jakim (trans.), Athens, OH: Ohio University Press, 1989), pp. xix–xxi.

[16] Zenkovsky, *A History of Russian Philosophy*, vol. 2, p. 862; for other criticisms of Frank's theological orthodoxy see p. 865 (Incarnation) and p. 867 (sin and evil).

[17] This discussion is based on material in the author's unpublished Ph.D. dissertation, *The Philosophical Thought of S.L. Frank, 1902–1915: A Study of the Metaphysical Impulse in Early Twentieth-Century Russia* (Columbia University, 1992).

from neo-Kantian assumptions. This process was never really complete, though in his émigré works Frank employs a philosophical vocabulary which tends to disguise the continuing hold on him of neo-Kantian ideas he had imbibed in his youth.[18] In his struggle to define his own philosophical path, he was greatly assisted by the writings of several contemporary German thinkers who stood outside the neo-Kantian mainstream (Wilhelm Schuppe, Wilhelm Stern, Edmund Husserl) as well as by *Lebensphilosophen* such as Friedrich Nietzsche and Henri Bergson. He benefited greatly from his intensive study of the history of philosophy, especially the Platonic tradition. In *The Object of Knowledge*, Frank declined to number himself among the adherents of any modern philosophical school; instead, he proudly proclaimed himself a "Platonist."[19] The primary reference of this label, which he continued to apply to himself to the end of his career,[20] was to an epistemological orientation. To be a Platonist was to affirm that the contents of our knowledge are eternal ideas. But the label also signaled Frank's sympathy with the mystical religiosity of such Platonic thinkers as Plotinus and Nicholas of Cusa, the latter of whom he once extravagantly described as his "only teacher in philosophy."[21]

Of the various non-Kantian influences on Frank's thinking, the first and arguably most important was Nietzsche. Frank fell under Nietzsche's spell in 1900, just at the time when he was ceasing to count himself a Marxist. The full intensity of his enthusiasm has only become evident with the recent discovery of a private spiritual diary Frank kept in 1901 and 1902.[22] Still eager to justify his break with his revolutionary friends, Frank was intoxicated by Nietzsche's vision of a lonely elite of "free spirits" set apart from the common herd by their pessimism about man as he is, by their capacity for suffering, and by their superiority to conventional moral norms.

Neo-Kantian and Nietzschean themes curiously intermingle in Frank's first published philosophical essay, his lengthy contribution to the *Problems of Idealism* symposium (1902).[23] The key idea in the essay derives from Simmel's book

---

[18] On this topic, see Philip J. Swoboda, "Windelband's Influence on S.L. Frank," *Studies in East European Thought* 47, nos. 3–4 (1995), 259–290.

[19] *Predmet znaniia*, p. vi.

[20] See, e.g., *The Unknowable: An Ontological Introduction to the Philosophy of Religion* (Boris Jakim (trans.), Athens, OH: Ohio University Press, 1983), p. x.

[21] *The Unknowable*, p. xi.

[22] S.L. Frank, *Saratovskii tekst* (Saratov: Izdatel'stvo Saratovskogo universiteta, 2006).

[23] "Fr. Nitsshe i etika 'liubvi k dal'nemy'" in S.L. Frank, *Filosofiia i zhizn': Etiudy i nabroski po filosofii kul'tury* (St. Petersburg: Izd. D.E. Zhukovskogo, 1910), pp. 1–71; "Friedrich Nietzsche and the Ethics of 'Love of the Distant'" in Randall A. Poole (ed. and trans.) *Problems of Idealism: Essays in Russian Social Philosophy* (New Haven, CT: Yale University Press, 2003), pp. 198–241.

The Philosophy of Money (1900), which had introduced Frank to the fundamentally neo-Kantian notion that there exist a range of "absolute" values. Such norms, which belong to a sphere (not further analyzable) of "the valuable and significant,"[24] present human beings with an incontrovertible moral claim to respect, whether or not we in fact respect them.[25] Frank mentions such values as "truth, justice, beauty, harmony, honor" as well as "the defense of truth, freedom, and human dignity."[26] He portrayed Nietzsche as the elaborator of an "aristocratic" moral "system" founded on uncompromising allegiance to such values (pp. 61–65). In his 1902 article, Frank employed this conception of morality to attack the Russian radical intelligentsia for renouncing the cultivation of these values in order to dedicate themselves single-mindedly to the service of the oppressed Russian masses. Frank asserted that the right to personal culture was one that the individual may not sacrifice to the welfare of the community (pp. 57–58). Thus the ultimate message of the essay was a principled rejection of altruistic morality in favor of a morality of individualistic self-dedication to absolute values (p. 64).

Through Nietzsche, Frank became acquainted with the tradition of ethical thinking that Charles Taylor has dubbed "expressivism."[27] His reading of Goethe, Wilhelm von Humboldt, the later Johann Fichte, and Friedrich Schleiermacher (all of whom Frank regarded at this time as "precursors" of Nietzsche), reinforced the young Russian thinker's conviction that the moral task of each individual was to develop his own unique spiritual content, to give expression to the "unique, unrepeatable, infinite, and self-enclosed spiritual universe" that lay within him. The corollary of this idea was a rejection of all universal norms or "abstract" rules of conduct that might constrain the "intimate self" [*intimnaia lichnost'*].[28] In a 1906 article which offers perhaps the most extreme expression of his hostility to such rules, Frank maintained that *moral* judgments are not concerned with actions at all, but with the fidelity of each individual to the urgings of his "intimate self." Since our inner "states of mind and feelings" are inaccessible and mysterious to others, there is no *action*, however heinous, that a person can commit that would authorize us to declare that *person* immoral. Frank did not deny that man's moral consciousness prescribes rules to govern the interrelations of individuals in society, or that

---

[24] Georg Simmel, *The Philosophy of Money* (Tom Bottomore and David Frisby (trans.), London: Routledge and Kegan Paul, 1978), pp. 67–68.

[25] "Fr. Nitsshe i etika 'liubvi k dal'nemy,'" pp. 33–34, where Frank quotes a long passage from Simmel, *The Philosophy of Money*, p. 239.

[26] "Fr. Nitsshe i etika 'liubvi k dal'nemy,'" pp. 35–36. Subsequent page references to this source are cited parenthetically in the text.

[27] Charles Taylor, *Hegel* (Cambridge University Press, 1975), p. 13 *et seq.*

[28] "K voprosu o sushchnosti morali" in Frank, *Filosofiia i zhizn'*, pp. 131–133.

these rules ought generally to be respected. What he did deny is that such rules are, strictly speaking, moral rules. What are usually classified as moral norms are in fact mere "norms of legal consciousness" (*pravosoznanie*). They cannot be allowed to hinder individuals from following their inner drive to self-realization wherever this drive might take them. "The living person," Frank concludes, "is in the final analysis more valuable than any law [*pravo*]."[29] As the last quotation suggests, the attitude toward norms expressed in Frank's article applied to *laws* as well as moral rules.

Frank's hostility toward the very idea of fixed universal norms reflected his passionate revulsion against the tyranny that public opinion can exert over the moral decision-making of individuals. All his life Frank retained bitter memories of the oppressive spiritual atmosphere that had prevailed in the revolutionary "circles" of his youth, of the cruel moral pressure they had exerted on their less resolute members, and of their scorn for "apostates" like himself.[30] This suspicion of formal norms, and his belief in the right of the individual to the unfettered expression of his unique inner content, was to color all of Frank's subsequent thinking about ethics, law, and society. In this sense, Nietzsche's impact on his mind was permanent and decisive, though Frank later ceased to entertain much respect for Nietzsche as a philosopher.

At this point in his career, Frank clearly perceived no contradiction between his negative attitude, as a moral philosopher, toward formal rules and his advocacy of "the rule of law" in the political sphere. In numerous essays and book reviews that Frank wrote for leading Russian periodicals in the era of the 1905 Revolution, he strongly affirmed his commitment to the ideal of a political community founded on the rule of law (*pravovoe gosudarstvo, Rechtsstaat*), and to the principle of legally guaranteed individual rights.[31] The most distinctive feature of Frank's thinking on this topic was his insistence on framing the defense of individual rights within a "philosophy of culture" that owed a great deal to the ideas of the neo-Kantians, especially Windelband and his school. Frank defined "culture" as "the totality of absolute values which have been or will be created by humanity." History has meaning as the process of "the gradual embodiment of the absolute ideal in the collective life of humanity."[32] The dignity of the human person (*lichnost'*) resides in the fact that he is the sole "creator and bearer of absolute values" in the world; the individual person

---

[29] *Ibid.* pp. 131–137.
[30] This aspect of Frank's psychology is discussed in Swoboda, *The Philosophical Thought of S.L. Frank*, chs. 2 and 3.
[31] See especially "Gosudarstvo i lichnost'," *Novyi put'* (November 1904), 308–317.
[32] "Ocherki filosofii kul'tury" (with P.B. Struve), pt. 1, *Poliarnaia zvezda* (22 December 1905), 110–111.

himself possesses "absolute value as the external envelope" through which "spirit, the supreme transcendental principle," manifests itself in the sphere of the actual. Accordingly, "the freedom of the person is the first and most essential condition of culture."[33]

In articles of this period, Frank spoke of man's creative task on earth as the "rationalization" or "humanization" of both external nature and human society itself.[34] Such language could be taken to imply a Promethean vision of humans' consciously reshaping the whole of their social and natural environment in accordance with a preconceived plan. Yet as the foregoing remark about "the freedom of the person" shows, this was not what Frank meant. If misused to justify "despotic" experiments in social engineering, "rationalization" was an "anti-cultural idea," since culture can develop only through an "unorganized ferment . . . a clash of spiritual forces and strivings."[35] By the time peace was restored to a Russia exhausted by two years of political violence, Frank's reservations about the idea of "rationalization" had been transformed into a bitter hostility to political "utopianism," particularly of the socialist variety – to the tempting but dangerous belief that a perfectly just society can be attained on earth by "earthly means" (i.e., by violence and coercion).[36]

METAPHYSICS AND EPISTEMOLOGY

Frank's early writings on ethics and the philosophy of value suffered, as we have seen, from an unresolved tension between the neo-Kantian and the Romantic or Nietzschean elements in his thought. Expressivist arguments representing morality as a matter of deeply personal "states of mind and feelings" sat very uncomfortably alongside a neo-Kantian conception of an "absolute," impersonal realm of values. The decisive turning-point in Frank's philosophical development may be said to have arrived when he found a way to bridge the gap between these two conceptions. To do so he jettisoned the transcendentalist presuppositions of neo-Kantianism, and adopted a resolutely metaphysical viewpoint, one that conceived values not as the contents of a free-floating consciousness-in-general, but as springing from the depths of absolute being. Frank's adoption of such a viewpoint was heralded in a series of journal articles

---

[33] "Ocherki filosofii kul'tury," pt. 2, *Poliarnaia zvezda* (30 December 1905), 170–171.
[34] "Problema vlasti" in Frank, *Filosofiia i zhizn'*, pp. 120–121; "Ocherki filosofii kul'tury," pt. 2, 174–175.
[35] "Ocherki filosofii kul'tury," pt. 2, 179.
[36] "Sotsializm i kantianstvo" in Frank, *Filosofiia i zhizn'*, pp. 353–354.

that he published from 1908 to 1910,[37] although it took him several additional years to work out the full implications of his new ideas. His new metaphysics was founded on the insight that the true center of our individual self lies beyond the limits of our separate personhood in the impersonal Absolute that is the ground of all being.[38] The Absolute, "Divinity," drives the individual's striving for moral self-realization and provides this striving with its content. Under those circumstances in which humans appear to assert themselves most radically as unique persons – in the utterances of scientific, artistic, and religious genius – they in fact give expression to truths arising from the depths of a reality that transcends, even as it grounds, individual personhood.[39] This ontological vision of the divinely grounded self was henceforth to serve as the supreme justification for Frank's belief in human dignity.

Frank's decision to embrace a positive doctrine of being closely coincided with the choice to devote himself professionally to philosophy. Since Frank had been reared in a neo-Kantian intellectual milieu where the priority of theory of knowledge among the philosophical sciences was taken completely for granted, he accepted that his first and most urgent duty as a philosopher was to construct an epistemological theory that would justify the bold metaphysical claims he now desired to advance. The outcome of his labors in this field was his first major book, *The Object of Knowledge*.

Ostensibly, Frank's treatise is an inquiry into the "grounds and limits" of "abstract knowledge," a term he employs to describe the kind of knowledge exemplified by science as well as by our common-sense picture of reality: a logically ordered system of determinate concepts.[40] By 1915, under the influence of vitalist thinkers such as Bergson and Wilhelm Stern, Frank had come to entertain serious reservations regarding the adequacy of the mechanistic world picture of nineteenth-century natural science, for which external nature was a concourse of dead atoms moving in accordance with inexorable physical laws. Notwithstanding his reservations about mechanism, however, Frank had no desire, either now or later, to repudiate the existing corpus of scientific knowledge, or to dispute the validity, in their proper sphere, of the methods by which it had been built up. On the contrary, he respected science as an essential component of "culture." Accordingly, in *The Object of Knowledge*, he appeared genuinely concerned to elucidate how valid scientific knowledge is possible.

---

[37] The most important of these were "Lichnost' i veshch'" and "K kharakteristike Gëte" in Frank, *Filosofiia i zhizn'*, pp. 164–217 and 355–366; and "Priroda i kul'tura," *Logos*, bk. 2 (1910), 50–89.
[38] *Man's Soul*, pp. 213–214; cf. *The Unknowable*, p. 171.   [39] *Man's Soul*, pp. 231–233.
[40] *Predmet znaniia*, p. 240. Subsequent page references to this source are cited parenthetically in the text.

In the course of his inquiry, however, Frank made it clear that the problem of abstract knowledge can be solved only in the framework of a valid *metaphysics*. To explain the possibility of any kind of knowledge, we must recognize that the *subject* of knowledge, the human knower, is grounded in absolute being.[41] Frank claimed that "abstract knowledge" is possible because we "possess" the object of knowledge in an indeterminate form prior to any specific act of knowing (pp. 241–242). Explicit knowledge, formulated in abstract concepts, is merely the actualization of a preexisting ontological relationship between the knower and the known (p. 97). But what is "known" in knowing, the true "object of knowledge," is not a single isolated thing but the Whole, the total unity of being of which we ourselves are part, in which we participate (p. 319). We acquire knowledge of particular truths through an intuitive encounter with this Whole, in the course of which we detach a particular content from the dark background of universal being and fix it in the form of a discrete logical judgment (p. 241). In intuition, the particular content to which we attend is "given" to us not in isolation, but in its inseparable connection with all the other elements of being (p. 304). This circumstance explains how it is possible for us to assemble a systematic corpus of knowledge out of many individual judgments, each of which captures only one of these connections. In successive acts of knowledge we progressively trace the manifold linkages that exist among the contents of the total unity. In this sense, the structure of our knowledge is given in advance: it is the structure of reality itself (pp. 203, 407–408, 417).

As a Platonist, Frank was convinced that our ordinary knowledge involves the subordination of the empirical material given in perception to concepts that are not themselves the product of experience, but "ideal" and, as such, timeless (pp. 103–104). He was strengthened in this conviction by the work of contemporary German philosophers such as Husserl, who assailed nineteenth-century "psychologism" – the attempt to reduce the logical relationship among concepts to a psychological relationship among mental contents (p. 149). Yet even as Frank insisted that abstract knowledge is valid knowledge, he argued that it is capable of capturing only one "layer" (*sloi*) of reality (pp. 318–319). On a deeper level, reality is more than a system of fixed elements: it is a concrete becoming in time. Abstract knowledge is incapable of grasping the living "flow" of being (p. 353). (Here Frank acknowledged the influence of Bergson on his thinking.) Because abstract knowledge isolates ideal contents from the living unity to which they belong, it constitutes a kind of frozen image of reality.[42] Fortunately, abstract knowledge is not the only form of knowledge of which human beings are capable. It is possible, Frank contends, for us to experience reality in its concreteness, to perceive the interconnections among

[41] *Ibid.* p. 154.   [42] *Ibid.* p. 312; cf. *The Unknowable*, p. 45.

things without the mediation of concepts. This higher form of knowledge Frank termed "living knowledge." Living knowledge is our sole avenue of access to knowledge of what is individual, including the mysteries of our own inner life and our moral impulses. The highest flights of human genius in art, in the study of history, and in science itself are founded on such knowledge. Yet even the ordinary person avails himself of the human faculty for grasping living reality in appreciating a work of art, or achieving a sympathetic understanding of another person's motives and feelings (pp. 425–426, 432–433).

The outstanding philosophical production of Frank's émigré period was his 1939 treatise *The Unknowable*. As its title suggests, this book, like its 1915 predecessor, approaches the crucial issues of metaphysics through an analysis of the limitations of human understanding. But the real interest of the volume lies in its treatment of a number of daunting religious-metaphysical issues that Frank had passed over in silence in *The Object of Knowledge*, but with which he could hardly avoid grappling once he chose to style himself a "Christian philosopher." These questions presented themselves with special urgency because Frank's metaphysics, like earlier monist systems (Spinoza's, for example) could be suspected of casting doubt on the very possibility of human freedom and autonomy. Frank discussed the ontological relationship of the divine principle to the universe of being that it sustains, the nature of freedom, and the problem of the existence of evil. For him, as for his philosophical predecessors, these questions were closely intertwined; he evidently believed that they could only be resolved through a more careful examination of the relationships among the various strata of reality than he had provided in his earlier book.

In *The Unknowable*, Frank uses the terms "unconditional being" or "reality" to designate the total unity that embraces everything.[43] Total unity is truly all-embracing inasmuch as it contains within itself both being and the *knowledge* of being. The total unity is being "illumined from within": in it, being as something "given" or "conceivable" is united with "subjectivity," with cognitive "possession" of itself. We are able to *know* because we *are* this being. Indeed, we "are conscious of ourselves only *through its self-revelation in us*" (p. 72). At the root of all being, animating it yet transcending it, lies what Frank calls the "primordial ground" (pp. 203–205). "God," for Frank, is precisely this primordial ground revealing itself to man as a "Thou" with whom we can enter into a personal relationship (p. 226). Unconditional being, in its turn, comprises two aspects: on the one hand, objective being (being as the potential object of abstract knowledge, as the manifold content which is capable of being determined by ideal concepts), and, on the other hand, a "substrate" of sheer

---

[43] *The Unknowable*, pp. 71–73. Subsequent page references to this source are cited parenthetically in the text.

actuality or "facticity." This substrate is wholly indeterminate; as such, it may be described as "existing potency" (p. 41) – Frank compares it to Aristotle's *prima materia* (p. 31). While objective being is illuminated from without by the light of knowledge which has its origin in the primordial ground, pure potentiality is "dark," eternally resistant to such illumination (p. 43). What renders reality "unknowable" is the presence in it of this dark, irrational element (p. 47). Yet it is just here, beyond the threshold of organized being, in the irrational sphere of elemental, restless potentiality (pp. 115–117) that Frank locates the womb of *freedom* (pp. 43, 46).

The idea of pure potentiality therefore has an important role to play in Frank's reflection on the problem of evil. The primordial ground, which grounds both truth and right, also in some sense enfolds the irrational substrate, which cannot, by definition, be "outside" the total unity of all. Given the presence of this substrate in objective being, the latter, taken in isolation from being as a whole, appears "ungrounded" (pp. 165, 265–266). Indeed, there is within it an element that "desires to be groundless" – and this is *evil* (p. 279). In other words, freedom and evil spring from the same primeval root, and are ontologically prior to any occasion of conscious, deliberate choice. Because evil is radically irrational, its existence can never be "explained" – which is why philosophy will never achieve its "ideal goal" of a complete explanation of reality (p. 280).

There is a certain resemblance between Frank's metaphysical account of evil and Jacob Boehme's speculations about the *Ungrund*. Frank was well acquainted with Boehme's ideas and with their elaboration by Schelling (p. 291). He was prepared to acknowledge that there was some value to these speculations, but he feared that they might have the unintended effect of "justifying" evil philosophically (p. 281). Moreover, Frank was unwilling to concede to pure potentiality the power to frustrate God's loving design for the universe which he fills. In the end, God triumphs over evil, for his love and power are stronger than the irrational (pp. 297–298). The freedom that is embodied in pure potentiality is a meaningless freedom (p. 115), since, in the strict sense, only the good can be chosen "freely." Only by complete submission to the urgings of the divine principle of being does man acquire autonomy (p. 247). In this state of true freedom, "law in the sense of universal norms or rules of behavior" is "overcome and completed by grace" (p. 254). As we shall see, the opposition between "law" and "grace" played a pivotal role in Frank's social philosophy.

SOCIAL PHILOSOPHY

By 1917, Frank had begun work on a book that would explain the relevance of the philosophical ideas he had expounded in *The Object of Knowledge* to the understanding of human life in society.[44] The exigencies of survival during the years of civil war, famine, and exile hindered the completion of this project. A first sketch of his new "social philosophy" can indeed be found in a short textbook that Frank published just before his expulsion from Soviet Russia, under the title *Outlines of a Methodology of the Social Sciences*.[45] But *The Spiritual Foundations of Society*, Frank's most systematic presentation of his social philosophy and social ethics, did not appear until 1930.[46] A number of the ideas put forward in this treatise were restated in a more theological guise in a second book that Frank began writing during World War II, published in 1949 as *The Light Shineth in Darkness*.

In emigration, Frank adopted a political standpoint to which he eventually gave the name of "liberal conservativism."[47] As a "liberal conservative," he extolled historical continuity, advocated the concentration of political authority in the hands of an "aristocracy" of culture, and defended a vigorous state power as indispensable for the maintenance of political stability while the masses were gradually raised to a higher cultural level. Yet he also retained a "liberal" commitment to "the principle of the spiritual independence of the person, of the non-intervention of the state in the sphere of spiritual culture," and to the maintenance of a "firm legal order" (*pravoporiadok*).[48] (In his émigré philosophical writings, however, as we shall see, Frank's affirmation of "legal order" was hedged with important qualifications.)

The point of departure of Frank's social theorizing was the same intuition that grounded his metaphysics generally: the intuition of the individual self as inwardly fused with the total unity of being. Social life is the outward expression of a primordial ontological unity among men which Frank labeled "the unity of 'we.'"[49] This unity finds expression in such objective phenomena as shared biological descent and language (pp. 52–55), as well as our feelings of communion with the various human groups to which we belong, from the family to the nation (pp. 60–62, 64). Most of the time, however, our consciousness is dominated by an awareness of ourselves as "subjects," and of other people as entities independent of us who pertain to the world of objective

---

[44] *Man's Soul*, p. xxxii.

[45] *Ocherk metodologii obshchestvennykh nauk* (Moscow: Bereg, 1922). The concept of "social philosophy" is introduced on pp. 101 and 109.

[46] *The Spiritual Foundations of Society: An Introduction to Social Philosophy* (Boris Jakim (trans.), Athens, OH: Ohio University Press, 1987).

[47] "Pushkin kak politicheskii myslitel'" in *Etiudy o Pushkine* (Munich, 1957), p. 47; *Biografiia P.B. Struve*, pp. 214, 216.

[48] "Pushkin kak politicheskii myslitel'," pp. 50–51.

[49] *The Spiritual Foundations of Society*, pp. 51–53. Subsequent page references to this source are cited parenthetically in the text.

being. This duality in our experience of society compels us, Frank maintained, to describe "social being" as consisting of two distinct layers or "strata," an outer and an inner (p. 55), corresponding to the two layers of being as a whole that he had distinguished in *The Object of Knowledge*. Like the superficial layer of being that "abstract knowledge" grasps, the "outer stratum" of society is characterized by "multiplicity," "separateness," and fragmentation (p. 100). We experience this outer layer in the free interactions among individual human wills that constitute life in "civil society," as well as in those circumstances where our individual will is constrained by the alien will of an organized collectivity in the guise of "power" and "law" (p. 56).

Frank's second basic postulate was that social life has an essentially moral character. A mere union of individuals becomes truly *social* only when its participants consciously or unconsciously serve some "social ideal" (p. 78). And man's capacity to live a life informed by "ideals" is the supreme proof of his "*divine-human* nature" (pp. 83–84). Through human activity, the "superhuman forces and principles that lie in the depths of man's being" achieve embodiment in the empirical world (p. 81). Ultimately, therefore, the "will" to which man subordinates himself as a member of society is not the will of any purely human collectivity, but the will of God (pp. 84, 86–87). In this sense, *every* society, even the most secularized, has a "theocratic" basis (pp. 87–88). It will be evident to the reader that Frank's post-revolutionary social philosophy is in many respects an elaboration of his pre-revolutionary philosophy of culture, a more detailed account of the means through which empirical reality is transformed by "spirit."

In his writings on social philosophy, Frank often sounds like a typical proponent of "positive liberty" in the sense given this term by Isaiah Berlin: one for whom the object of society is to establish the conditions under which humanity can rise above its "empirical" nature and actualize its "real self."[50] And indeed Frank explicitly rejected several of the core principles of liberal individualism in its classic nineteenth-century form. There are no "unshakably fixed individual rights" (p. 139). Freedom is not an end in itself; the object of society is not to protect the "negative liberty" of individuals to pursue whatever ends they choose (or, as Frank acidly put it, to indulge an "unrestrained individual willfulness" (p. 109)), but to "serv[e] . . . Divine *truth*" (p. 128). Yet several features of Frank's thinking mark it off from other theories proclaiming the value of "positive liberty." The first of these is Frank's intense awareness of the power of sin in human life, which led him to insist upon the irremediable imperfection of all human institutional arrangements (p. 124). The world of our empirical experience "lies in evil" (p. 99), and therefore represents a clouded medium for the manifestation of spirit. No fundamental alteration in the quality of human

---

[50] Isaiah Berlin, *Four Essays on Liberty* (London: Oxford University Press, 1969), pp. 132–133.

social relations is to be expected before the day when God brings history to an end (p. 124). Modest reforms and the elimination of a few crying abuses is the best that any generation can hope to achieve through its struggle to realize the truth in social life; regression to a lower spiritual level is an ever-present possibility. The failure to grasp this is the fatal flaw of every utopian vision of radical human liberation (p. 124).

Frank's social ethics is also distinguished from other doctrines of positive liberty by a kind of historicism. Consistent with the basic tenets of his epistemology, Frank believed that the divine will, like any other spiritual force welling up from the primordial ground, ultimately eludes conceptual thinking. We can define the ultimate social ideal only as the realization of "*all the fullness of divine truth* in social life," as "concrete total-unity" (p. 126). Human reason is incapable of grasping this "fullness," for the same reason that it is powerless to grasp total unity as such. Consequently, the "social ideal" that any age sets before itself is never more than an abstract and one-sided understanding of the fullness of divine truth, typically succeeded, in the next era of history, by an equally one-sided reaction (pp. 125–126). When Frank contended, therefore, that we are obliged to devote our lives in society to serving a moral purpose, he did not at all mean to imply that history is to be conceived in terms of humanity's continuous progress toward a fixed goal that can be apprehended in advance of its realization. The sequence of social ideals does not constitute a dialectical progression of ever higher manifestations of spirit. It is apparent, therefore, that the principle of the independence of spiritual culture that Frank identified as the core truth of liberalism is an indispensable component of his philosophy of history (pp. 151–152). Only the spontaneous creative activity of free individuals can give birth to new values capable of correcting the one-sidedness of a given society's social ideal. For this freedom to be fertile, however, it must be exercised in a framework of institutions that prescribe the general direction of social activity and function as the source of positive law (p. 171).

When he wrote *The Spiritual Foundations of Society*, Frank remained convinced, as he had been from the beginning of his career, that "essential morality" was not a matter of obedience to abstract norms, whether "moral" (in the Kantian sense) or legal. In the book, he recast his expressivist ethics in Christian terms. The essence of the moral life is "grace," "the presence of God in us . . . as a living substantial principle immanent in our being" (pp. 94–96). Grace subdues our rebellious nature and nourishes in us "the substantial forces of the good" (p. 98). We become fitted to serve as "conductors" of "the gracious powers of salvation" to other people.[51] In the sinful world in which we live, however, it

---

[51] *The Light Shineth in Darkness* (Boris Jakim (trans.), Athens, OH: Ohio University Press, 1989), p. 125.

is not enough for us to strive for inner moral perfection through obedience to the promptings of divine grace in our inmost self. We have a second duty. The ethics of love of neighbor demand that we participate in the humbler but equally urgent struggle to "protect the world from evil," to maintain that minimum level of order in empirical existence that will enable us and those around us to pursue the path of inner spiritual growth. The instrument of this task is law and morality in the form of fixed external norms, together with the coercive apparatus of power that is required to render these norms effective (p. 99).

In *The Light Shineth in Darkness*, however, Frank undercut this affirmation of the divine basis of law. There he argued that the radical imperfection of the world places us in a tragic moral predicament. While engaged in "protecting the world from evil," we must be ready to *violate* any fixed moral or legal norms, to "take the burden of sin upon our conscience," by adopting whatever means will be most effective in our battle against evil.[52] The Christian principle of "love of neighbor" compels us to shed any concern with preserving our personal moral "purity" should we arrive at a prudential judgment that the well-being of others requires it.[53] Such arguments, recalling earlier attacks on the Tolstoian principle of non-resistance to evil launched by Solov'ëv and Ivan Il'in, do not seem fully consistent with his depiction of law, in *The Spiritual Foundations of Society*, as an expression, albeit an "abstract," "external" one, of man's "inner, living, divine being" (p. 101).

CONCLUSION

The distinctive vision of life that we encounter in the writings of Semën Frank might be termed "expressivist humanism." It is a vision that affirms the infinite value of each human person as a potential vehicle for the manifestation of a unique spiritual content, a vehicle through which one facet of the infinite richness of the Absolute seeks expression. This vision received its classic formulation in the writings of various German thinkers of the age of Johann Herder, Goethe, and Schleiermacher, most of them products of a pietist religious milieu. Frank first made the acquaintance of these ideas via Nietzsche, and they never ceased to be tinged with the romantic spiritual elitism that Frank absorbed from him. The expressivist view of man also provided Frank with justification for his lifelong indignation over the tyrannical constraints that society imposes on the inner drives of the individual, an attitude that links him with other early twentieth-century rebels against Victorian moral rigidity. While a form of expressivism could be embraced by a rationalist such as Hegel,

[52] *Ibid.* pp. 137, 127, 129.   [53] *Ibid.* p. 130.

Frank's thought bore a closer affinity with the irrationalist vitalism of Bergson, owing to the Russian philosopher's conviction that the inexhaustible richness of divine reality cannot be captured in the categories of conceptual knowledge. When Frank's religious faith assumed a more definite Christian cast, his way of thinking proved readily adaptable to reformulation in Christian terminology, as when Frank drafted Pauline language regarding the opposition of "law" and "grace" into the service of his own ingrained antinomianism. In view of the pietist roots of expressivism, this adaptability should occasion no surprise. It is possible to make sense of much that is otherwise puzzling about Frank's thought if one recognizes that it represents a striking attempt to elaborate a system of philosophy, including a social philosophy, consistent with an expressivist view of the human person.

PART IV

FREEDOM AND HUMAN PERFECTIBILITY IN THE SILVER AGE

11

RELIGIOUS HUMANISM IN THE RUSSIAN SILVER AGE

BERNICE GLATZER ROSENTHAL

INTRODUCTION: RUSSIAN RELIGIOUS HUMANISM

In European history, "humanism" originally denoted an intellectual and cultural movement, based on the study of Latin and Greek texts, that began in the Renaissance. The term came to mean any system of thought that asserts the value and worth of man (individually and/or collectively) and focuses on human needs, interests, and values. There are secular humanists and religious humanists.

The religious philosophers of the Russian Silver Age were humanists. They foregrounded man's spiritual and psychological needs, raised issues of meaning and values, and exalted human agency and creativity. They wanted to sanctify this world, including "the flesh" (sex). Their philosophy incorporated aspects of Orthodox Christianity, such as anti-rationalism, the apotheosis of beauty, transfiguration, deification, and a holistic ontology. The last aspiration underlay their desire for "integral knowledge" in epistemology, "total unity" (*vsëedinstvo*) in metaphysics, and their social ideal – *sobornost'* (a free society united by love and common ideals whose members retain their individuality). By "individuality" they meant self-expression and personal development within a community, rather than apart from or against it. Several humanists exalted Sophia (divine wisdom or "the eternal feminine").

The most prominent religious humanists were (in alphabetical order) Nikolai Berdiaev (1874–1948), Sergei Bulgakov (1871–1942), Pavel Florenskii (1882–1937), Semën Frank (1879–1950), Zinaida Gippius (1869–1945), Viacheslav Ivanov (1866–1949), Dmitrii Merezhkovskii (1865–1941), Vasilii Rozanov (1856–1919), Sergei Trubetskoi (1862–1905), his brother Evgenii Trubetskoi (1863–1920), Lev Shestov (1866–1935), and the symbolist poets Andrei Belyi (1890–1934) and Aleksandr Blok (1880–1921).

They can be divided (roughly) into liberals and radicals. The liberals championed the rights of the individual, the rule of law, and parliamentary government. The radicals vehemently rejected "bourgeois" values and institutions, but they were apolitical until the revolution of 1905. Just about all religious humanists revised their views during and after it.

Throughout the period they responded to Solov'ëv, Dostoevskii, Nietzsche, and, to a lesser extent, Kant and Tolstoi. The nature of their responses changed over time.

Solov'ëv's basic principle was Godmanhood (*bogochelovechestvo*), the deification and salvation of all humanity. In its emphasis on human autonomy, agency, and perfectibility, Solov'ëv's thought was humanist in its very conception and decisively shaped the development of Russian religious humanism. Solov'ëv advocated an activist Christianity and positive work toward the establishment of the Kingdom of God on Earth. He asked his fellow Russians: "Which East do you want to be? The East of Xerxes or the East of Christ?"[1]

Godmanhood would transfigure the material cosmos, including "the flesh." Solov'ëv laid out his philosophy of sex in one of his most popular essays, *The Meaning of Love*, which had wide influence.[2] He separated procreation and sexual pleasure, sanctioning sex as a way of overcoming egoism. But he also maintained that the ideal human being is androgynous, "containing in itself all the fullness of eternal life."[3]

Also influential were Solov'ëv's aesthetics, his visions of Sophia and the erotic poems he wrote to her, and his eschatology. He believed that beauty is the incarnation of a spiritual or divine principle in matter, that art is a form of inspired prophecy, and that the lyric poet has a mission: to bring Sophia down from heaven and find forms to suit her essence. His visions of Sophia inspired Bulgakov, Florenskii, Ivanov, Belyi, and Blok. His poem "Pan-Mongolism" (written in 1894, published in 1905) and his "Tale of Antichrist" (1900) came to be seen as prophetic (see Judith Kornblatt in chapter 14).

Solov'ëv championed a liberalism that was based on personhood (rather than a social contract) and emphasized human dignity, human rights, and the rule of law. Russian liberals endorsed and developed these aspects of his thought. Russian radicals emphasized his erotic poems, his ideas on sex and gender, and his eschatology.

Dostoevskii's attack on secular ideologies and his psychological insights were appreciated by all the religious humanists. They interpreted his religious humanism in different ways but, by and large, agreed with his emphasis on inner faith

---

[1] S.M. Solov'ëv and E.L. Radlov (eds.), *Sobranie sochinenii Vladimira Sergeevicha Solov'ëva*, 2nd edn., 10 vols. (St. Petersburg: Prosveshchenie, 1911–1914; reprint, Brussels: Foyer Oriental Chrétien, 1969), vol. 12, p. 227.

[2] It is newly translated in Vladimir Wozniuk (ed. and trans.), *The Heart of Reality: Essays on Beauty, Love, and Ethics by V.S. Soloviev* (University of Notre Dame Press, 2003), pp. 83–133.

[3] Quoted by Olga Matich, *Erotic Utopia: The Decadent Imagination in Russia's Fin de Siècle* (Madison, WI: University of Wisconsin Press, 2005), p. 294.

(rather than external authority) as the essential condition of spiritual development. Some of them considered Dostoevskii and Nietzsche kindred spirits because they discussed the same issues, even though their answers were different.

The religious humanists perceived Nietzsche as a mystic and a prophet and appropriated his thought. They hailed his aestheticism, his attacks on rationalism and positivism, his belief that myth is essential to the health of a culture, his counterposition of the Apollonian and Dionysian impulses, and (in some cases) his Superman ideal. Nietzsche advocated smashing the "old tables of values" and writing "new values on new tables." The Christian humanists sought new Christian values. Unlike Nietzsche, they believed that there is an eternal truth, beyond the Dionysian flux. Nietzsche's announcement that "God is dead" and that Christianity promoted a slave morality spurred attempts to refute him.[4]

Solov'ëv was surprisingly receptive to Nietzsche's Superman ideal because it expressed a yearning to transcend human limitations.[5] He interpreted the Superman not in a biological or Darwinian sense, but as spiritual and psychological growth and as the ability to defeat death. For him, Jesus Christ was the authentic Superman.

Merezhkovskii fused Nietzsche and symbolism into a religion of art. When that religion failed him (it did not assuage his fear of death), he turned to Christianity – not "historical" Christianity, but a Nietzscheanized version. Ivanov argued that Dionysianism was a religious as well as an aesthetic and psychological phenomenon. He extolled loss of self-consciousness in cultic ecstasy and maintained that Dionysus "the suffering god" was a precursor of Christ.[6] Shestov concluded his study of Tolstoi and Nietzsche with the words: "Nietzsche has shown us the way. We must seek that which is higher than compassion, higher than the 'good'; we must seek God."[7] Florenskii drew on Nietzsche in his magnum opus, *The Pillar and the Ground of the Truth* (1914), and in his essays on icons, church ritual, and cults.[8]

---

4 See Bernice Glatzer Rosenthal (ed.), *Nietzsche in Russia* (Princeton University Press, 1986) and *New Myth, New World: From Nietzsche to Stalinism* (University Park, PA: Penn State University Press, 2002), ss. 1 and 2.

5 S.M. Solov'ëv, "The Idea of the Superman" in Vladimir Wozniuk (ed. and trans.), *Politics, Law, and Morality: Essays by V.S. Soloviev* (New Haven, CT: Yale University Press, 2000), pp. 255–263.

6 Viacheslav Ivanov, "Ellinskaia religiia stradaiushchego boga," *Novyi put'*, nos. 1, 2, 3, 5, 9 (1904); continued as "Religiia Dionisa," *Voprosy zhizni*, nos. 6, 7 (1905).

7 L. Shestov, "The Good in the Teaching of Tolstoy and Nietzsche: Philosophy and Teaching" in Bernard Martin and Spencer Roberts (eds. and trans.), *Dostoevsky, Tolstoy and Nietzsche* (Columbus, OH: Ohio State University Press, 1969), p. 146. This volume also contains Shestov's essay "Dostoevsky and Nietzsche: The Philosophy of Tragedy."

8 Details in Bernice G. Rosenthal, "Florenskii's Russification of Nietzsche" in Norbert Franz, Michael Hagemeister, and Frank Haney (eds.), *Pavel Florenskij: Tradition und Moderne* (Frankfurt am Main: Peter Lang, 2000), pp. 247–258.

Berdiaev asserted that "man has both a right and a duty to become a Superman because the Superman is the path from man to God."[9] In this instance, he used Nietzsche to supplement Kant. In other instances he faulted Kant's "middle-class [*meshchanskii*] morality" and his ignoring of the Dionysian aspects of the human psyche. Frank praised Nietzsche's concept of "love of the distant," interpreting it as love for a lofty ideal (personal freedom, equal rights, and so forth).[10] During the revolution of 1905, he advocated a "humanist individualism" that included property rights. Four years later, in his contribution to the symposium *Vekhi* (*Landmarks*, 1909), he declared that his position had evolved to "religious humanism."[11]

MEREZHKOVSKII'S SEARCH FOR A NEW FAITH

Dmitrii Sergeevich Merezhkovskii was a seminal thinker in the development of Russian religious humanism who posed many of its key themes.[12] He expressed his anguished search for a new faith in poems, historical novels, literary criticism, and the St. Petersburg Religious-Philosophical Meetings (1901–1903), which he co-founded. Catherine Evtuhov says that Merezhkovskii was "the first to give a definite shape to the intelligentsia's vague dissatisfaction with old forms," the first to "try to unite the intelligentsia and the church" and a "cultural arbiter."[13] Several religious humanists arrived at their views independently of Merezhkovskii and followed a different trajectory, but they responded to him and formulated their own answers to the questions he posed.[14]

In the 1890s, Merezhkovskii popularized symbolism and Nietzsche, advocated the creation of a new culture characterized by freedom and beauty, and reacquainted Russians with classical antiquity and the Renaissance. He translated *Antigone*, *Medea*, *Oedipus Rex*, and other Greek tragedies into Russian and

---

[9] N. Berdiaev, "The Ethical Problem in the Light of Philosophic Idealism" in Randall A. Poole (ed. and trans.), *Problems of Idealism: Essays in Russian Social Philosophy* (New Haven, CT: Yale University Press, 2003), p. 182 (translation slightly modified).

[10] S. Frank, "Friedrich Nietzsche and the Ethics of 'Love of the Distant'" in *Problems of Idealism*, pp. 198–241.

[11] S. Frank, "The Ethic of Nihilism: A Characterization of the Russian Intelligentsia's Moral Outlook" in Marshall S. Shatz and Judith E. Zimmerman (eds. and trans.), *Vekhi/Landmarks: A Collection of Articles about the Russian Intelligentsia* (Armonk, NY: M.E. Sharpe, 1994), p. 155.

[12] See Bernice Glatzer Rosenthal, *D.S. Merezhkovsky and the Silver Age: The Development of a Revolutionary Mentality* (The Hague: Martinus Nijhoff, 1975).

[13] Catherine Evtuhov, *The Cross and the Sickle: Sergei Bulgakov and the Fate of Russian Religious Philosophy, 1890–1920* (Ithaca, NY: Cornell University Press, 1997), pp. 52–53.

[14] For contemporary responses to Merezhkovskii, see D.K. Burlaka (ed.), *D.S. Merezhkovskii: pro et contra. Lichnost' i tvorchestvo Dmitriia Merezhkovskogo v otsenke sovremennikov* (St. Petersburg: Izdatel'stvo Russkogo Khristianskogo gumanitarnogo instituta, 2001). See also N. Berdiaev, *Novoe religioznoe soznanie i obshchestvennost'* (St. Petersburg, 1907).

explained their importance. In addition, he published essays about the Acropolis, Marcus Aurelius, and Pliny the Younger, poems with classical and Renaissance themes, and two historical novels, *Death of the Gods: Julian the Apostate* (1895) and *Rebirth of the Gods: Leonardo da Vinci* (published 1900–1901).[15] The novels were best-sellers.

In the first years of the twentieth century, Merezhkovskii interpreted Tolstoi, Dostoevskii, and Gogol as religious writers (the first literary critic to do so), attacked "historical Christianity," propounded a "new religious consciousness," and claimed that the Apocalypse was imminent. In 1901, he and his wife Zinaida Gippius began to convene a series of Religious-Philosophical Meetings in St. Petersburg. The meetings attracted soon-to-be-prominent poets and philosophers, and became the nucleus of a religious revival (see Robert Bird in chapter 13).

All his life, Merezhkovskii insisted that religious faith is the first and foremost human need, that it nourishes the soul, just as food nourishes the body. It endows life with meaning and purpose, fosters personal and social wholeness, and is the formative principle of a culture and society (in Nietzschean terms, its myth). He also insisted (contra the *intelligenty* who deemed boots "higher" than Shakespeare) that art is a necessity, that beauty is a link to the divine, and that all great art is inspired by religion. He believed that the choices made by his generation would determine the future, not only of Russia but all humankind.

Merezhkovskii's search for a new faith began in the late 1880s and was an outgrowth of his loss of faith in Russian populism. He sought a new faith that would quench his "religious thirst," reconcile all conflicts and contradictions, reunite the intelligentsia and *narod* (the people), guarantee personal immortality, and sanction the enjoyment of life. His lecture "On the Causes of the Decline and on the New Tendencies in Contemporary Russian Literature" (delivered in 1892, published in 1893, PSS 18:175–275), is considered the manifesto of Russian symbolism: challenging reason and science in general and "soulless" positivism and "materialistic" populism in particular, Merezhkovskii exalted art as the highest form of human activity, imagination as the highest human faculty, the poet as a seer, and symbolism as a theurgy that would lead to higher truths and, ultimately, to a new faith and a new culture. Indeed, "without faith in the divine principle, there is no earthly beauty, no justice, no poetry, and no freedom" (PSS 18:273).

[15] The essays first appeared in *Vechnye sputniki* (St. Petersburg, 1897) and are included in his collected works: D.S. Merezhkovskii, *Polnoe sobranie sochinenii*, 24 vols. (St. Petersburg, 1914), vol. 17, pp. 18–70. The novels, *Smert' bogov: Iulian Otstupnik* and *Voskreshenie bogov: Leonardo da Vinchi*, comprise vol. 1 and vols. 2 and 3, respectively, of Merezhkovskii's collected works, which will henceforth be cited parenthetically as PSS.

Merezhkovskii believed that his generation faced an entirely new situation. No other generation had needed religious faith as much, yet no other generation had the possibility of faith destroyed so completely (by reason and science). The mysticism of preceding centuries pales into insignificance, he claimed; his generation could not rely on the wisdom of the past. He and his contemporaries were free and alone. For salvation they needed entirely new truths, which would be revealed by symbolism. He believed that symbols reveal the "divine aspects of our spirit" and that they embody higher truths in aesthetic form (PSS 18:216). Symbolists plumbed the depths of the human soul and explored "other worlds than ours." They perceived eternal forms inaccessible to ordinary people.

Merezhkovskii concluded the lecture by urging Russian writers to campaign for a new culture. Even though many would fall in the attempt, others would continue the campaign over the bodies of their dead and wounded comrades. Ultimately, the divine spirit would sweep over the earth (PSS 18:274–275).

Only a year or so after giving the lecture, Merezhkovskii embraced a "pure" Nietzscheanism. Vehemently rejecting the Orthodox values of asceticism, altruism, and humility (which populists perpetuated in secular form), he expressed contempt for the rabble (the herd), advocated casting off all constraints (including sexual ones), and championed individualism, worship of beauty, and defiance of death. "For the new beauty," he proclaimed, "we will break all laws, trespass all limits."[16] In "Song of the Bacchantes" (1894), he glorified the Bacchanalian orgies, because the ecstatic revelers achieved oblivion and overcame their fear of death (PSS 22:45–46).

For much of the 1890s, symbolism was Merezhkovskii's religion. When its shortcomings became obvious, he tried to reconcile Nietzsche and Christ, or, as he put it, "the truth of the earth" (enjoyment of life) and the "truth of heaven" (personal immortality and love). According to Merezhkovskii, "two principles are locked in an eternal struggle for the human soul." History is the story of this struggle; it records the ascendancy of one or the other. But neither is sufficient in itself. Somehow, they must be reconciled. He described paganism as the principle of happiness on earth, and Christianity as the principle of personal immortality. He saw paganism as seeking the golden mean and as practical in orientation. Christianity focuses on the "limitless, measureless search for the eternal and endless," and scorns the very idea of impossibility. Paganism denies the soul while Christianity denies the body. Merezhkovskii thought it impossible to choose between paganism and Christianity, but also supposed

---

[16] "Deti nochi" (1896), in *Novye stikhtvoreniia* (St. Petersburg, 1896). Merezhkovskii deleted these lines from the poem published in PSS 22:171.

that choice is not necessary (PSS 18:130–131). Pushkin's life and work proved that a creative reconciliation of the two principles is possible. Pushkin reconciled the two principles unconsciously, but Merezhkovskii wanted a conscious reconciliation: he set out to find Pushkin's "secret." In 1899, Merezhkovskii "turned to Christ."

Dostoevskii's thought was a factor in this turn. In an 1897 essay, Merezhkovskii extolled Dostoevskii as the only modern writer with the courage and wisdom to identify the problems facing modern man. "He is us with all our thoughts and sufferings . . . he knows us . . . knows our most secret thoughts, the most criminal desires of our hearts" (PSS 18:67). Dostoevskii realized that freedom could be a curse; unchecked by faith and love, it could lead to all sorts of horrors. That is why, according to Merezhkovskii, Dostoevskii advocated a return to religion: in faith human beings can achieve inner wholeness and love. In a faith community, the individual is no longer alone.

Around 1900, Merezhkovskii embarked on a Nietzschean revaluation of all Christian values. The result was that he now embraced self-affirmation, enjoyment of life, and the liberation of instincts and passions repressed by "historical Christianity." He regarded traditional Christianity as obsolete because he believed that the Second Coming was imminent. Jesus Christ himself would grant humankind a Third Revelation that would reconcile all polarities – intelligentsia and people, flesh and spirit, East and West, religion and art, individual and community, spirit and dogma, Christianity and paganism, Godman and Mangod, Christ and Antichrist, Tolstoi and Dostoevskii.

In *L. Tolstoi and Dostoevskii* (1901–1902), Merezhkovskii compared the great writers to each other and to Nietzsche. He posited a polarity *within* Christianity, between the flesh and the spirit, symbolized by Tolstoi and Dostoevskii, respectively. Tolstoi was the "seer of the flesh," despite his preaching asceticism, because his characters are identified by a physical attribute, among other reasons. But Tolstoi's flesh, Merezhkovskii charged, is not the healthy pagan flesh, but an expression of a morbid preoccupation with death and dying.

Vehemently opposed to Tolstoi's rationalism and denial of Jesus's divinity, Merezhkovskii contended that Tolstoi was not a Christian at all, but an unconscious pagan in his art and a Buddhist in his religion whose real goal was Nirvana. Merezhkovskii preferred the unconscious pagan in Tolstoi to the false Christian. He faulted Tolstoi for ignoring the religious aspects of the struggle against Napoleon, and claimed that the great writer had no sense of history.[17] Merezhkovskii viewed history as God's plan, with a beginning,

---

[17] Details in Bernice Glatzer Rosenthal, "Merezhkovsky's Readings of Tolstoi" in James P. Scanlan (ed.), *Russian Thought After Communism* (Armonk, NY: M.E. Sharpe, 1994), pp. 129–131.

middle and end (the apocalypse), the opposite of the endless cycles of Buddhism.

In Dostoevskii's novels, by contrast, the flesh is infused with a new spirit, making it "holy flesh." Motivated by conviction, by the "passion of the intellect," his characters demonstrate how ideals can liberate man from the tyranny of the flesh. True, some are inhuman fanatics, but they show the harmful effects of the wrong ideal. Dostoevskii thought that in true Christian faith human beings become humane and loving.

Merezhkovskii frequently quoted Dostoevskii's statements that "Orthodoxy is paralyzed" and "beauty will save the world" because he believed that Dostoevskii was reaching toward a new apocalyptic faith. The Elder Zosima (in *The Brothers Karamazov*) articulated Dostoevskii's unconscious solution to the problems facing modern man. Zosima interprets Christianity as a religion of joy; he kisses the earth (in a symbolic rejection of Christian otherworldliness) and tells Alësha (his disciple) to leave the monastery, marry, and go out into the world, to speak to the peasants and "guide their hearts." Merezhkovskii regarded Zosima's kissing the earth as the equivalent of Zarathustra's injunction "Be true to the earth, my brothers" (PSS 12:46).

Merezhkovskii kept up his attack on "historical Christianity" in subsequent works. In his lecture "The Fate of Gogol" (1903) and his book *Gogol and the Devil* (1906), he attributed Gogol's ruin to the baleful influence of "historical Christianity," personified by Gogol's confessor Father Matvei (PSS 15:187–311). Merezhkovskii's studies of Tolstoi, Dostoevskii, and Gogol influenced younger writers, including Belyi and Blok.

Merezhkovskii was apolitical until 1904 when, outraged by the Holy Synod's decision to close the Religious Philosophical Meetings, he proclaimed that the Russian autocracy was from the Antichrist. He interpreted the revolution of 1905 as the beginning of the apocalypse that would usher in a New Heaven and a New Earth. He called Dostoevskii the "prophet of the Russian Revolution," declared that Jesus was a revolutionary (echoing Nietzsche), and advocated a "religious revolution" that would culminate in the destruction of the state, a total break with the Orthodox church, and the end of *meshchanstvo* (bourgeois philistinism) – "the most dangerous aspect of the Beast." He denounced *Vekhi* and, in a review of Boris Savinkov's novel *Pale Horse* (1909), waffled on the issue of terrorism (PSS 15:71–83, 23–31). Although he supported free speech, freedom of religion, and freedom of association, his ultimate goal was not rights-based liberalism but the abolition of law per se. In post-apocalyptic society, he thought, Jesus would be the only ruler and love the only law. Some religious humanists attacked Merezhkovskii's utopianism; others offered utopian visions of their own.

MEREZHKOVSKII'S CHRISTIAN HUMANISM

The major tenets of Merezhkovskii's Christian humanism were the need for religious faith, the concepts of personhood and Godmanhood, the inadequacy of surrogate religions, and a forthcoming Third Revelation. He defined religion as the "highest metaphysical limit of the physical feeling of self-preservation." Since he thought that religion begins when man realizes he is mortal, he saw personal immortality – the resurrection of the whole person (body, soul, and spirit) – as the essential concern of religion (PSS 9:5–6). Its other aspects are merely by-products of our search for eternal life.

Although he focused on immortality, Merezhkovskii did not think that religion should be otherworldly. In fact, he believed in bodily resurrection and that religion must meet the needs of the entire person: body, soul, and spirit. He argued that the effects of spiritual deprivation – despair, nameless fear, and loneliness – are just as real as hunger. Moreover, individuals live in a culture shaped by religious faith. When the faith fades, the culture becomes incoherent and individuals are left isolated and alone. Western civilization had been nourished by the sap of Christianity until rationalism drained that sap. Merezhkovskii thought that the current preoccupation with death and dying went beyond natural anxiety over mortality: it was western man's unconscious anticipation of his own doom (PSS 9:41–42).

Merezhkovskii's Christianity centered on the personhood of Jesus, rather than on moral laws or abstract concepts. He deemed belief in a personal God a metaphysical necessity, because an impersonal God renders prayer useless and leaves human beings without a model for their aspirations. Jesus, the Godman, was Merezhkovskii's model. He predicted that at the end of history everyone would achieve Godmanhood, but that outcome was not inevitable; it was contingent on human choice, and would involve struggle and sacrifice.

Merezhkovskii thought all surrogate religions doomed to failure, because they could not satisfy man's basic need – to defeat death. Of all surrogate religions, Merezhkovskii respected science the most, because of its dedication to truth. But science did not recognize the yearning for "other worlds than ours," or at least placed such yearning outside its own field of investigation. The impotence of science was all the more painful because science is the carrier of modern man's hopes. But Darwin destroyed the optimistic underpinnings of science; his world reenacted the horror of Chronos devouring his own children. In Darwin's cosmos, man is a species of animal, eternally battling other species for mere survival, and the fate of the individual is irrelevant. Merezhkovskii thought such a life not worth the struggle necessary to sustain it (PSS 13:8).

According to Merezhkovskii, the "religion of art" (symbolism in the 1890s) was equally futile. Beauty withers at the thought of death; tragic drama merely exacerbates man's anxieties. Tragedy depicts man as deprived of control over his own destiny and as helpless before amoral gods and inscrutable cosmic forces (PSS 13:7–8). In a 1916 essay, Merezhkovskii confessed that in the 1890s he had suffered from suicidal loneliness and despair, because a world predicated on the absence of God cannot have any meaning.[18]

Merezhkovskii also rejected the "religion of the family" (based on Rozanov's metaphysics of sex), because it eschewed the search for transcendent ideals. Sexual gratification in a happy family life reduced man to a creature of instinct and failed to recognize that children are no substitute for personal immortality. Besides, children will face the same metaphysical questions their parents did (PSS 13:8–9).

The "religion of society" (socialism) concentrated on the good of humanity. It had its own creed, heroes, martyrs, and history. Socialists typically dedicated their lives to a greater cause, hoping thereby to obviate their need for purely personal meaning and to avoid the burden of thought. Socialism promised to answer all of man's temporal needs, to provide him with prosperity and a sense of belonging. Its appeal, however, was not to man's mind, but to his instincts – to the very same elemental instinct which compels bees, ants, and cows to huddle together for security. The most dangerous of all false religions, socialism only appeared to relieve human anxiety and loneliness. Surrendering to instinct was not freedom, a temporal community was not the greater whole for which humanity yearned, and personal immortality could only be attained by choosing Christ (PSS 13:9–11).

Merezhkovskii argued that, in practice, socialists regarded society as the absolute and the individual as a means. Not believing in the sanctity of the individual, socialists were prepared to sacrifice the individual to a "greater good." Berdiaev made a similar point in "Socialism as Religion" (1906), but he advocated a Christian Socialism guaranteeing everyone the necessities of life.[19] Merezhkovskii ignored practical issues such as the standard of living. His point was that not only did socialism fail to solve the problem of "one and all" (individual and society), it required that humanity (or at least the present generation) forego both temporal happiness and eternal life (PSS 13:11). In his view, socialism was a secular faith that could not save people from what ailed them.

---

[18] D.S. Merezhkovskii, *Dve tainy russkoi poezii: Tiutchev i Nekrasov* (Petrograd, 1915), pp. 95–97.

[19] N. Berdiaev, "Socialism as Religion" in Bernice Glatzer Rosenthal and Martha Bohachevsky-Chomiak (eds.), *A Revolution of the Spirit* (Marian Schwartz (trans.), New York: Fordham University Press, 1990), pp. 107–133.

Only a "Christian Renaissance" could enable contemporary humanity to overcome despair and decadence. The present generation was destroying itself; it was the most "abandoned, craven, sick, and even absurd" generation of all time. Since it had come to the end of its road, an entirely new road would have to be carved out. People would have to develop a new Christianity based on the affirmation of life. Historical Christianity had emphasized death, self-denial, and suffering, but Jesus had overcome death. Christianity was based on the miracle of His resurrection (PSS 13:18–19). Merezhkovskii considered Jesus to be the Superman Nietzsche had sought in vain.

Merezhkovskii's prediction of a Third Revelation was, in part, an attempt to refute Nietzsche's critique of Christianity. Accordingly, Merezhkovskii claimed that Jesus was never an ascetic; his resurrection had demonstrated that Christianity accepts the body. Jesus had never advocated renouncing the world; his otherworldliness was a temporary expedient distinguishing his teachings from paganism and Judaism. By perpetuating asceticism and passivity, and by exalting suffering, historical Christianity had given credence to Jesus's detractors. Moreover, Jesus had not counseled passive resignation but active struggle against the powers of the ancient world. He had come to bring humankind "not peace but a sword" (Matthew 10:34; PSS 13:5). Nietzsche's charge that Jesus had embodied a passive slave morality, and Tolstoi's belief that Jesus had forbidden resistance to evil, were simply false, according to Merezhkovskii.

Nor was Jesus a leveler, as Nietzsche charged; Jesus's eradication of superficial differences had afforded greater scope for the expression of the "inner person." Equality before God did not make human beings into ants and bees (metaphors favored by Dostoevskii). Jesus was an individualist; respect for every person was the cardinal tenet of his teaching. He based his power on persuasion and love rather than force and enjoined all human beings (not just the strong and proud, but also the weak and humble) to develop their personality. Everyone could become a Christian individualist (PSS 11:143; 12:23–25). Nietzsche's "splendid blond beast" was a lion who devours living people; love is the divine means of self-affirmation.

Merezhkovskii thought that "historical Christianity" has fulfilled its function – keeping Jesus's memory alive and exalting the spirit – but that a greater truth was yet to come. The first Revelation (the Hebrew Bible) was from the Father; the second Revelation (the Christian Bible) was from the Son; the Third Revelation would be from the Holy Mother. She would reconcile Father and Son (as Merezhkovskii's own mother had done) and would unite divine spirit and earthly flesh. Through her, the "religious duality" now tormenting humankind would be ended. She would reveal that love is freedom

and would show humankind how to reconcile paganism and Christianity (PSS
12:17–18, 131; 13:128–129).[20]

The nature and role of the Holy Mother is the least developed aspect of
Merezhkovskii's theology. He was not clear as to whether the "Holy Mother,"
the "Holy Spirit," and the "eternal feminine" (a term he also used) were one
and the same; as to the manner of the Holy Mother's advent, or as to exactly who
would deliver the Third Revelation, the Holy Mother or Jesus. Also unclear is
whether the Holy Mother was Mary and/or the Woman Clothed in the Sun
who "pains to be delivered" (Revelation 12:1–2). Despite, or perhaps because of,
these problems, other poets and philosophers took up Merezhkovskii's attempt
to define the nature of the Holy Trinity.

MAIN THEMES OF EARLY TWENTIETH-CENTURY RUSSIAN RELIGIOUS HUMANISM

The religious humanists responded to Merezhkovskii, to one another, and
to Nietzsche, Dostoevskii, and Solov'ëv, each in his or her own way. All of
them emphasized what Merezhkovskii called the "inner man," the soul or
the psyche. Most of them emphasized personhood and Godmanhood, human
agency, creativity, beauty, sanctification of this world (including "the flesh"),
and eschatology.

Russian religious humanism was informed by Greek and Roman antiquity
and the Italian Renaissance. Their importance to Merezhkovskii has been noted
above. Ivanov concentrated on Greek antiquity, the cult of Dionysus in particular. In addition to his essay series "The Hellenic Religion of the Suffering
God" (1904),[21] he wrote poems on the subject, including "To Dionysus,"
"The Funeral Repast of Dionysus," and "The Maenad."[22] He also wrote two
tragedies, "Tantalus" (SS 2:23–73) and "Prometheus" (SS 2:105–155), and an
essay "Athena's Spear" (SS 1:727–733). He called his wife "Diotima," a priestess
from whom Socrates claimed, in Plato's *Symposium*, to have learned his theory
of love. Ivanov did not exalt the Renaissance; he preferred the late medieval
writers Dante and Petrarch. Florenskii regarded the Renaissance as the time

---

[20] See also C.H. Bedford, *The Seeker: D.S. Merezhkovskiy* (Lawrence, KS: University of Kansas Press,
1975), pp. 111–112.

[21] See note 6.

[22] The poems may be found in Viacheslav Ivanov, *Sobranie sochinenii*, 4 vols. (D.V. Ivanov and Olga
Deshart (eds.), Brussels: Foyer Oriental Chrétien, 1971–1987), vol. 1, pp. 538–551, 571–572,
vol. 2, pp. 227–228, respectively. Ivanov's collected works will henceforth be cited parenthetically
as SS.

when people fell away from God. Merezhkovskii eventually arrived at a similar view.

The "Inner Man"

Emphasis on the "inner man" went along with opposition to rationalism, positivism, and materialism, with an insistence on the reality of the soul and the psyche, and with a preference for "inner experience" or "living experience" over empirical evidence or abstract concepts. Radical religious philosophers rejected the constraints of reality, including the laws of nature. We recall Merezhkovskii's belief that Christianity scorns the very idea of impossibility. Ivanov extolled the "eros of the impossible" (SS 1:825). Neither paid any attention to economics.

Shestov traced the philosophies of Nietzsche, Tolstoi, and Dostoevskii to a defining personal experience. His own humanism began as a protest against inexplicable suffering and developed into a religious existentialism that drew on Judaism and Christianity. Throughout, his focus was on the suffering individual. Politically, Shestov was a liberal or a moderate socialist. Unlike other God-seekers, he was not a mystic, an aesthete, or an advocate of *sobornost'*.

Several religious humanists redefined "man." Ivanov said that man is "a religious animal," and "since ecstasy is the alpha and omega of religion, an ecstatic animal."[23] He foregrounded "mutual inner experience" and "direct religious experience," which included orgiastic experience, as in the Dionysian rites. He regarded politics as superficial and considered the (Dionysian) chorus, not the newly created Duma, to be the authentic voice of the people.

Florenskii called man a "liturgical animal," because he deemed ritual the heart of religion. Counterposing "living experience" to eclectic religiosity, vague mysticism, and abstract ideas, he wrote: "One cannot learn about Orthodoxy from books. One must immerse oneself in Orthodoxy, live in an Orthodox way."[24] Florenskii started out as a God-seeker. He honed his theology against what he considered the defects of the "new religious consciousness" (lack of concreteness, for example), but he retained a symbolist sensibility.

Personhood and Godmanhood

Christian humanists emphasized personhood as the foundation of human dignity, though some neglected the legal and political institutions necessary for its

---

[23] V. Ivanov, "Religiia Dionisa," *Voprosy zhizni*, no. 7 (1905), 127.

[24] Pavel Florensky, *The Pillar and Ground of the Truth: An Essay in Orthodox Theodicy in Twelve Letters* (Boris Jakim (trans.), Princeton University Press, 1997), p. 9. Subsequent page references are cited parenthetically in the text.

defense and development. Solov'ëv's many followers stressed the divine source and potential of human personhood – Godmanhood. Merezhkovskii maintained that human dignity requires a God who is a "He, not an It" (PSS 11:192). During the 1905 Revolution, Ivanov distinguished between the "empirical person," who asserted himself and claimed his rights, and the "mystical person," who sought union with others through love (eros, not agape), and envisioned a "new organic society" peopled by the latter.[25]

In the first years of the twentieth century, Berdiaev, Bulgakov, and Frank advocated a metaphysical liberalism based on the person rather than on a social contract. Emphasizing moral and existential issues, they regarded the individual person as the sole bearer of the moral law. Bulgakov challenged secular theories of progress, decried "atheistic humanism" and attacked "Feuerbach's religion of the man-god."[26] In *Philosophy of Economy* (1912), he emphasized the role of the person, rather than impersonal economic forces, and claimed that the economy is sobornal, i.e., the result of the action of individuals who remain part of a mystical whole. His close friend Florenskii regarded personhood as an Apollonian principle, Christianity's answer to the unbridled passions of Dionysianism.

Mikhail Gershenzon, one of the organizers of *Vekhi* and the author of its introduction, claimed that the "common platform" of the contributors was their "recognition of . . . spiritual life over the external forms of community. They mean by this that the individual's inner life is the sole creative force in human existence, and that this inner life . . . constitutes the only solid basis on which a society can be built."[27] In fact this "common platform" was not common to every contributor. Some (notably Bogdan Kistiakovskii) emphasized the importance of "external forms," law in particular.

Christian humanists counterposed the Godman Jesus to Dostoevskii's demonic mangod and/or Nietzsche's Superman. They believed that, since man is made in the "image and likeness of God," everyone can aspire to Godmanhood.

Human Agency and Creativity

Religious humanists counterposed "freedom" and "necessity." The radicals among them revolted against the "tyranny of reality." Ivanov advocated *bogoborchestvo* (theomachy, struggling with God), taking his cue from Ivan Karamazov's refusal to accept the world God created in the name of the world that ought

---

[25] Details in Bernice Glatzer Rosenthal, "The Transmutation of the Symbolist Ethos," *Slavic Review* 36, no. 4 (December 1977), 601–627.
[26] S.N. Bulgakov, "Basic Problems of the Theory of Progress" in *Problems of Idealism*, pp. 85–123.
[27] M. Gershenzon, in Shatz and Zimmerman (eds.), *Vekhi (Landmarks)*, p. xxxvii.

to be ("Ideia nepriiatiiaa mira," SS 3:79–90). Florenskii declared that "titanism" (theomachy or rebelliousness) is not a sin, but a virtue, the power of life and of existence itself, though it can lead to sin, the "sin" of self-affirmation. Most religious humanists advocated an activist Christianity, one that would really transform the world.

Many of them linked human agency with creativity. The symbolists championed "life-creation" (*zhiznetvorchestvo*), erasing the boundary between art and life by making one's own life a work of art. After the 1905 Revolution, the symbolists assumed that since art has theurgical powers, they could create a new society and a new world. Bulgakov believed that human creativity stems from the divine Sophia, who introduces a moral voluntarist aspect to the cosmos. One of his purposes was to encourage the growth of productive forces and personal initiative by sanctifying labor as a creative task.[28]

Berdiaev espoused a man-centered religion of creativity in *The Meaning of Creativity: A Justification of Man* (1916).[29] According to him (p. 110):

Creativeness is neither permitted nor justified by religion – creativeness is itself religion. Creative experience is a special kind of experience and a special kind of [path]; the creative ecstasy shatters the whole of man's being – it is an out-breaking into another world. Creative experience is just as religious as is prayer or asceticism . . . Christianity justified creativeness . . . [but] what matters is not to justify creativeness, *but by creativeness to justify life*. Creativeness is the final revelation of the Holy Trinity – its anthropological revelation.

For Berdiaev, man is creative because he is made "in the image and likeness of God." When Berdiaev said "man," he meant men. He considered "woman" generative but not creative.

In this book, Berdiaev called Nietzsche the "forerunner of a new religious anthropology, because he overcame humanism [which according to the Russian philosopher is based on necessity] for the sake of the superhuman. After Nietzsche, there can be no return to the old humanistic anthropology. Man himself must become a creator, a Godman" (p. 190). The Third Revelation (Merezhkovskii's term) would not come from on high; it would be the work of free men, a creative act. Christ would reveal Himself only to free men. Berdiaev counterposed creativity to obedience and proposed a cult of genius to complement the cult of saints. He considered lawlessness a sacred duty.

---

[28] Bernice Glatzer Rosenthal, "The Search for a Russian Orthodox Work Ethic" in Edith W. Clowes, Samuel D. Kassow, and James L. West (eds.), *Between Tsar and People: Educated Society and the Quest for Public Identity in Late Imperial Russia* (Princeton University Press, 1991), pp. 57–74.

[29] N. Berdiaev, *The Meaning of the Creative Act* (Donald Lowrie (trans.), New York: Harper, 1955). The English translation omits the subtitle. Page references are cited parenthetically in the text.

Berdiaev's religion of creativity was bound up with a mystique of sacrifice and suffering, hatred of "bourgeois" values and institutions, and apocalypticism. "The whole ancient social order and the entire old civilization (fully developed only in the twentieth century) must burn to ashes in order that the New Jerusalem should come down to earth from heaven. The way to the New Jerusalem is a way of sacrifice" (p. 294). He regarded the "idea of eternal bourgeois peace" an "evil, distorted, ungodly idea" and praised the Catholic Middle Ages as the "most military, least bourgeois, period of European history" (p. 291). He welcomed Russia's entry into the Great War. Berdiaev's humanism was not humane.

Aestheticism

To Merezhkovskii, as we have seen, the need for beauty was second only to the need for religious faith. Rozanov castigated Christian asceticism, but he found supreme beauty in the visage of Jesus and in Orthodox rituals. Bulgakov associated art with freedom, and economics with necessity. Convinced that art has theurgical qualities, he linked art with the transfiguration of the world and man. In *Unfading Light* (1917), he called art, not economics, the world transforming force.[30] Berdiaev wrote that "to live in beauty is the commandment of the new creative epoch" (*Creative Act*, p. 246). He regarded every creative act as a partial transfiguration. Florenskii referred to the "special spiritual beauty" of the saintly ascetics, "a beauty wholly inaccessible to the man of flesh," and said there is nothing more beautiful than Christ, the only sinless one (*Pillar*, p. 72).

In Florenskii's eyes, beauty was more important than kindness or morality. He called Kant "the great deceiver" because the German philosopher had made Christianity into an abstract conception, a "pedestrian morality," instead of posing the image of Jesus Christ, who was a real person, not an abstraction, as the precept of a new life and as the link between the visible and invisible worlds.[31] Apropos of morality, Florenskii declared that the holy is above "yes" and "no." Bulgakov and Berdiaev ended up rejecting Kant as well.

Wholeness

Living in a disintegrating society, religious humanists sought ontological and social wholeness and an all-encompassing worldview. For Merezhkovskii,

---

[30] S. Bulgakov, *Svet nevechernii* (Moscow: Put', 1917), pp. 353–417.
[31] P. Florenskii, "Kul't i filosofiia," *Bogoslovskie trudy* 17 (1977), 122.

wholeness had a personal psychological dimension, for in it he sought the end of the internal conflicts that tormented him. Belyi combined art, science, philosophy, and religion in an attempt to fashion a comprehensive theory of symbolism.

Bulgakov and Florenskii regarded Sophia as an agent of unification and transfiguration. Bulgakov believed that, through Sophia, the wholeness shattered by the Fall would be restored. He described her as the living link among God, man, and nature, endowing the created world with divine force, gathering chaos into cosmos, inspiring all human activities, and uniting people through love. Similarly, Florenskii regarded Sophia as the living link between God and creation. He posited a close connection between Sophia and the Mother of God.

Frank saw the world as a living whole: nothing exists in itself, utterly unconnected with everything else. The initial inspirations for his version of "total unity" were Spinoza and Goethe, not Solov'ëv, though he came to admire the Russian philosopher. Frank's "total unity" encompassed intuition and reason, being and consciousness, the intellectual and the artistic, and the individual and the absolute (God).[32]

Most Christian humanists advocated *sobornost'* as the way to integrate the individual into the community, but they disagreed on the degree of integration. Merezhkovskii envisioned a new church, a Church of the Holy Spirit, as a spiritual commune in which individuality is preserved. During and after the 1905 Revolution, he wanted to reconcile socialism and anarchism, but was closer to anarchism.

Ivanov predicted the end of "proud" individualism and the triumph of *sobornost'*. "The age of the epos has passed; let the communal dithyramb begin... He who does not want to sing the choral song should withdraw from the circle, covering his face with his hands. He can die, but he cannot live in isolation."[33] During the 1905 Revolution, he supported (with inner reservations) a doctrine called mystical anarchism, which purported to reintegrate Russian society by means of eros, myth, and sacrifice. Who or what would be sacrificed, and for what purpose, were never specified.

In 1907, Ivanov proposed a cultic version of *sobornost'* that induced self-forgetting in mystical/erotic ecstasy, to be achieved in a restored Dionysian theater devoted to myth-creation (*mifotvorchestvo*). There would be no separation between actors and spectators. Everyone would participate in creating the myth

---

[32] See Philip J. Swoboda in chapter 10 and Philip Boobbyer, *S.L. Frank: The Life and Work of a Russian Philosopher* (Athens, OH: Ohio University Press, 1995), pp. 90, 131, 171, 226–231.

[33] V. Ivanov, "The Crisis of Individualism" in *A Revolution of the Spirit*, p. 171.

and in "orgies of action" and "orgies of purification." He believed that a new myth (actually, a new formulation of an eternal myth) would engender a new cult, a new culture, and a new society.[34] In other writings, he called for "new barbarians" to revitalize a decadent culture.

Ivanov's humanism was no more humane than Berdiaev's. He knew that the original Dionysian rituals entailed human sacrifice, which he considered the purest form of sacrifice because it destroys the *principium individuationis*. In 1908, however, he concluded that "Dionysus in Russia is dangerous" (SS 3:126). In 1909, he proposed a specifically Christian *sobornost'* based on the "Russian Idea" (a term coined by Dostoevskii and adopted by Solov'ëv) as the way to end conflict and unite *narod* and intelligentsia. This version included an individuating Apollonian element but still extolled self-sacrifice.

Berdiaev regarded man as an organic member of a cosmic *sobornost'*. He opposed all earthly institutions as concessions to "necessity," denied the possibility of a Christian state, and condemned individualism as a "convulsion of the old Adam." Frank rarely used the term *sobornost'*, but he sometimes referred to "an all embracing divine consciousness" that had the potential for a philosophy of community as well as of the individual.

Florenskii advocated ecclesiality (*tserkovnost'*). The term had several layers of meaning, all of them related to the Holy Spirit, the invisible Church, and the unity of all believers in the mystic body of Christ (the original meaning of *sobornost'*). On one level, ecclesiality "is the beauty of a new life in Absolute Beauty – in the Holy Spirit" (*Pillar*, p. 234). On another level, ecclesiality was Florenskii's response to Ivanov's idea of a Dionysian theater temple. Loving union is possible only in a church, Florenskii claimed. He talked about the personal element in love (Dionysianism is impersonal) and claimed that boundaries and limits are necessary (Dionysianism dissolves them).

Sanctification of This World

That Christianity is a life-affirming and world-affirming religion was a major tenet of Christian humanism. Merezhkovskii insisted on it. Bulgakov argued that while Christianity teaches that the world lies in evil, it also teaches that God created the world and found it good. He praised Solov'ëv's "religious materialism" and referred to "sacred corporeality," "transfiguration of the flesh," and "holy flesh." He ruminated about the Sophian nature of the economy.

---

[34] Details in Bernice Glatzer Rosenthal, "Theater as Church: The Vision of the Mystical Anarchists," *Russian History* 4 (1977), 122–141.

Both Bulgakov and Florenskii believed that overcoming secular ideologies entailed developing a renovated Orthodoxy that sanctified life and endowed every human activity with religious meaning. Toward that end, Florenskii asserted the need for a non-positivist science. He believed that transfiguration applied to the material universe, not just "the flesh." Ivanov declared that mystical anarchism offered a "dazzling 'yes' to the world." He opposed the negativism of the Ten Commandments ("Thou shalt not").

The Flesh

Merezhkovskii extolled "holy flesh," talked about the "mystery of sex" in which two people become one, and described creation as a sexual union of Father Sky and Mother Earth (a borrowing from Slavic mythology). Rozanov extolled the holiness of sex and the family, praised Judaism's positive attitude to sex, and called Christianity a religion of death because it exalts virginity and celibacy. But he also claimed (as Florenskii did) that Jews murdered Christian children and used their blood in religious rituals.[35]

Ivanov praised the orgiasm of the Dionysian rites, and experimented with triangular sexual arrangements, which included same-sex arrangements. He was not a eudaimonist or hedonist, however. Rather, he believed that "mad" intoxication and oblivion were the outward manifestations of a state of ecstasy intimately connected with sacrifice and with suffering in an eternally self-renewing cycle of birth, death, and rebirth.

Florenskii accused proponents of the "new religious consciousness" of failing to distinguish marriage from lewdness. He claimed that love outside God is merely a physiological function, and he rejected Solov'ëv's view of sex as a way of overcoming egoism. Marriage is "two in one flesh," Florenskii wrote; friendship is "two in one soul," two separate and distinct relationships. He considered friendship between men superior to marriage and believed that a woman could not be a friend. His "church" was composed of male dyads; each one forming a molecule in the body of Christ. In a discussion of the Greek words for love, he downgraded eros and claimed that agape and philia are the Christian forms of love (*Pillar*, pp. 286–293). Florenskii traced contempt for the body to Gnosticism, not Christianity. He even posited three types of mysticism,

---

[35] V.V. Rozanov, *Oboniatel'noe i osiazatel'noe otnoshenie evreev k krovi* (St. Petersburg: Suvorin, 1914); reprinted V.V. Rozanov, *Sakharna. Oboniatel'noe i osiazatel'noe otnoshenie evreev k krovi* (A.N. Nikoliukin (ed.), Moscow: Respublika, 2001). Michael Hagemeiser, "Wiederverzauberung der Welt: Pavel Florenskys Neues Mittelalter" in Franz *et al.*, *Pavel Florenskij: Tradition und Moderne*, pp. 33–41.

each one connected to a part of the body (Christianity is connected to the heart), and related the seven sacraments to bodily processes.

Berdiaev associated sex with the natural order, which he wanted to overcome, so he advocated sublimation. His Sophia was an eternal virgin. Lamenting her replacement by Eve, the birth-giving woman, Berdiaev opposed procreation in the hope of breaking the endless chain of birth and death (Nikolai Fedorov's idea). His "new man" was an androgynous youth-maiden.

Some characters in Merezhkovskii's historical novels have masculine and feminine traits. He played with the idea of an androgynous Christ as a way of introducing a feminine principle into the godhead. He and Gippius inveighed against the hypocrisy of "legal marriage," had no children, and lived in a *ménage à trois* with Dmitrii Filosofov. Gippius wanted to abolish fixed gender roles, including the female position in sex, which she considered humiliating. She wore trousers (a rarity at the time) and signed some of her articles with a male pseudonym.

Berdiaev considered female emancipation a "symptom of the crisis of the race, the breakdown of sex now evident"; even so, he found female emancipation preferable to the hypocritical compulsion of the old family (*Creative Act*, pp. 202–203). Bulgakov's cosmology assumed masculine and feminine principles, the Logos and Sophia, respectively. He exalted femininity but opposed feminism.

Eschatology

Just about all religious humanists believed that they were living at the end of an era. Some believed that the fiery destruction of the old world was imminent and that the Kingdom of God on Earth would follow. Others envisioned the End, not so much as an event but as the culmination of an immanent process.

Their world did end with the Bolshevik Revolution. Rozanov called it *The Apocalypse of Our Time*.[36] Merezhkovskii labeled Soviet Russia the "Realm of the Antichrist." Berdiaev interpreted the Bolshevik Revolution as the beginning of a pan-European crisis, the end of the historical period that began with the Renaissance; he looked forward to a "new Middle Ages." Blok had been predicting the end of bourgeois civilization for over a decade. In "The Collapse of Humanism" (1919), he reiterated his conviction that bourgeois civilization was dead, that the reason and individualism that had dominated Europe since the Renaissance were doomed. He said that the intelligentsia must accept the

---

[36] V.V. Rozanov, *Apokalipsis nashego vremeni* (Sergiev Posad: Ivanov, 1917–1918).

Revolution or perish.[37] Ivanov maintained that humankind was returning to "the other side of humanism," to the Hellas of the pre-Socratics and Dionysus, i.e., to a different kind of humanism that he called "monanthropism," a movement toward one-man-ness or a feeling of one-man-ness (SS 3:368–382). He regarded individuation as the original sin.

CONCLUSION

The humanism of the Russian religious philosophers was expressed in their foregrounding of spiritual and psychological needs, their emphasis on meaning and values, their belief in human agency and choice, and their search for a new interpretation of Christianity that sanctifies this world. They posited new values (beauty, creativity, and self-expression), addressed issues of sexuality and gender, and speculated about Sophia and the "eternal feminine." Their metaphysics of personhood (encompassing body, soul, and spirit) situated the individual in a God-created cosmos, and, at a different level, in a new kind of society based on *sobornost'*. Their concept of Godmanhood provided a model for human aspirations and held out the possibility of human perfectibility.

The desire to create the Kingdom of God on Earth fostered a utopianism that led many religious humanists to ignore the economic requirements of human dignity and the need for legal rights to protect individuals from one another and from arbitrary state power. Berdiaev, Bulgakov, and Frank did acknowledge these factors in their liberal phase but, even then, they considered mass prosperity (as distinct from abolishing poverty) a bourgeois ideal. All three eventually lost interest in politics and economics.

Merezhkovskii, Ivanov, and Florenskii had never been interested in economics or in mundane politics. Their focus had always been on the "inner man" and on love as the mode of human connectedness. So intent were they on love that they substituted it for moral norms and Kantian ethics, inadvertently clearing a space for nihilism. Merezhkovskii and Ivanov rejected the laws of nature and the very idea of impossibility. Ivanov and Berdiaev (in *The Meaning of Creativity*) propounded a mystique of self-sacrifice and suffering that was profoundly inhumane. All too often, the faith that Russian religious humanists had in humanity's future rebirth involved contempt for humanity in its present state and an apocalypticism that fostered destructiveness. This type of utopianism was mainly characteristic of the radical humanists, but an argument can be made that, in Russia, liberalism itself was a utopian doctrine.

---

[37] A. Blok, "Krushenie gumanizma" in *Sobranie sochinenii v vos'mi tomakh* (Moscow-Leningrad: Gos. izdatel'stvo Khudozhestvennoi literatury, 1962), vol. 6, pp. 113–115.

12

RUSSIAN LIBERALISM AND THE PHILOSOPHY OF LAW

FRANCES NETHERCOTT

The five thinkers discussed in this chapter played a pivotal role in the development of Russian liberal thought after 1900. As public figures, Pavel Novgorodtsev, Pëtr Struve, Evgenii Trubetskoi, Bogdan Kistiakovskii, and Sergei Kotliarevskii campaigned for a state under the rule of law (*pravovoe gosudarstvo*), one based on recognition of human dignity, individual freedom, and civil or personal rights. All five were organizers of the Liberation Movement that culminated in the Revolution of 1905 and were founders of Russia's largest liberal party, the Constitutional Democratic (Kadet) Party. They played active roles in Russia's constitutional experiment until tsar and bureaucracy undermined the authority of the new parliament, the Duma, as an arena of open political debate. In the ten years between the dissolution of the Second State Duma in 1907 and the Revolution of 1917, they worked primarily as scholars committed to the ideals of *prosveshchenie* ("a culture of education"), through which they hoped to promote the broader cultural and social values of liberalism. Their neo-liberal worldview merits attention as a major contribution to the humanist tradition in Russian thought.[1]

The intellectual and career paths of these men present some interesting points of intersection that allow us to regard them as a clearly defined group. All were outstanding scholars in law, history, philosophy, economics, and the social sciences. Trubetskoi (1863–1920), Novgorodtsev (1866–1924), and Kotliarevskii (1873–1941) were law professors at Moscow University.[2] Novgorodtsev was also (from 1906 to 1918) director of the Higher Institute of Commerce in Moscow, which he made into one of the most successful private institutions of

[1] I have explored the Platonic origins of Russian humanist thought in my book *Russia's Plato: Plato and the Platonic Tradition in Russian Education, Science and Ideology (1840–1930)* (Burlington: Ashgate, 2000).

[2] They receive attention in David Wartenweiler, *Civil Society and Academic Debate in Russia, 1905–1914* (Oxford University Press, 1999), a valuable study of how these and other Russian scholars sought to promote liberal values through educational and cultural work. On Novgorodtsev in particular, see the masterful chapter devoted to him in Andrzej Walicki, *Legal Philosophies of Russian Liberalism* (Oxford University Press, 1987) and also the chapter on philosophy of law in my *Russia's Plato*.

higher education in Russia. He and Kotliarevskii were principal legal theorists of the Kadet party and deputies to the First State Duma. By signing the ill-fated Vyborg Manifesto (July 1906), which called for civil disobedience in response to the government's proroguing of parliament, Novgorodtsev and Kotliarevskii forfeited the right to membership in future Dumas.[3] Trubetskoi was one of the founders of the Kadet Party but resigned in January 1906 in protest over what he considered its radicalism. (He rejoined the party in 1917.) He opposed the Vyborg Manifesto, became a member of the Party of Peaceful Renewal, and advanced the party's moderate liberal program in the newspaper that he published with his brother Grigorii, *Moskovskii ezhenedel'nik* (*The Moscow Weekly*) (1906–1910), on which Kotliarevskii also collaborated.[4]

Kistiakovskii (1868–1920) came from a prominent Ukrainian family (his father Aleksandr was a highly regarded professor of criminal law) and was committed to securing both constitutional and national rights for all subjects of the Russian Empire.[5] In the 1890s, his interest in Marxism gradually gave way to neo-Kantianism, an intellectual affinity that deepened in Germany, where he studied under Georg Simmel and Wilhelm Windelband, and later collaborated with Max Weber.[6] In Russia, beginning in 1906, he taught at the Higher Institute of Commerce and other institutions. From 1912 to 1916 he edited *Iuridicheskii vestnik* (*Juridical Messenger*), the prestigious journal of the Moscow Juridical Institute. After the February Revolution he was appointed to the chair in law at Kiev University and in 1919 was elected to the Ukrainian Academy of Sciences.[7]

Struve (1870–1944), perhaps the best known of the group, was indisputably the practical arm of neo-liberalism.[8] His powerful, broad-ranging intellect made him a sort of latter-day "Enlightenment figure." By 1901, he had abandoned

---

[3] Novgorodtsev's major works are *Istoricheskaia shkola iuristov: Eë proiskhozhdenie i sud'ba* (1896); *Kant i Gegel' v ikh ucheniiakh o prave i gosudarstve: Dva tipicheskikh postroeniia v oblasti filosofii prava* (1901); *Krizis sovremennogo pravosoznaniia* (1909); and *Ob obshchestvennom ideale* (1917, 1918, 1921). Kotliarevskii's major studies are *Konstitutsionnoe gosudarstvo: Opyt politiko-morfologicheskogo obzora* (1907); *Pravovoe gosudartsvo i vneshniaia politika* (1909); and *Vlast' i pravo: Problema pravovogo gosudarstva* (1915).

[4] Trubetskoi's major works include *Religiozno-obshchestvennyi ideal zapadnogo khristianstva v V veke: Mirosozertsanie bl. Avgustina* (1892); *Religiozno-obshchestvennyi ideal zapadnogo khristianstva v XI veke: Ideia bozheskogo tsarstva v tvoreniiakh Grigoriia VII-go i ego publitsistov-sovremennikov* (1897); *Mirosozert-sanie Vl. S. Solov'ëva*, 2 vols. (1913); *Lektsii po entsiklopedii prava* (1916); *Metafizicheskie predpolozheniia poznaniia: Opyt preodoleniia Kanta i kantiantstva* (1917); and *Smysl zhizni* (1918).

[5] See Susan Heuman, *Kistiakovsky: The Struggle for National and Constitutional Rights in the Last Years of Tsarism* (Cambridge, MA: Harvard Ukrainian Research Institute/Harvard University Press, 1998) and Walicki, *Legal Philosophies of Russian Liberalism*, ch. 6.

[6] Kistinkovskii's doctoral dissertation, *Gesellschaft und Einzelwesen*, was published in 1899.

[7] His magnum opus is *Sotsial'nye nauki i pravo* (1916).

[8] The classic two-volume biography of him is Richard Pipes, *Struve: Liberal on the Left, 1870–1905* (Cambridge, MA: Harvard University Press, 1970) and *Struve: Liberal on the Right, 1905–1944* (Cambridge, MA: Harvard University Press, 1980).

revisionist Marxism for idealism and liberalism.[9] Late that year he went abroad and in July 1902 began publishing, with the editorial assistance of Kistiakovskii and others, his famous émigré journal *Osvobozhdenie* (*Liberation*), which was smuggled back into Russia and became the most important organ of the Liberation Movement. In July 1903, Struve, Novgorodtsev, Kotliarevskii, and Kistiakovskii were among the Russian constitutionalists who met in Schaffhausen, Switzerland, to plan the Union of Liberation. After his return to Russia in October 1905, Struve was elected (like Kotliarevskii) to the central committee of the Kadet Party. In 1907, he served as a deputy to the Second State Duma. After its dissolution in 1907, he spent the next ten years teaching economics and editing one of the leading "thick journals" of the era, *Russkaia mysl'* (*Russian Thought*), which he used as a vehicle to deepen his analysis of the reasons for the failure of Russia's fledging constitutional democracy.[10]

These five scholars were centrally interested in the fundamental problems of liberal political philosophy: personal autonomy and moral freedom, on the one hand, and law, state, and society, on the other. In dealing with these problems, they articulated nuanced responses to the revival of Kantianism and natural-law theory abroad. But their work also took shape in response to a powerful intellectual legacy at home: Boris Chicherin's Enlightenment, classical liberal view of individual freedom and the rule of law, and Vladimir Solov'ëv's religiously inspired vision of human perfectibility, which framed his "new liberal" conception of man's right to a dignified existence. During their lifetime, Chicherin's definition of right (*pravo*) as "external freedom defined by a universal law [*obshchii zakon*]," and Solov'ëv's formulation of law as the "minimum good" provoked some highly personalized polemics between the two men.[11] But for the Silver Age generation of legal thinkers, this double legacy offered rich intellectual reserves. Prior to 1905, it provided the broad framework within which Russian liberals refuted the materialist and positivist worldview that had dominated the 1880s and 1890s.

Novgorodtsev, who arguably spearheaded the revival of natural law in Russia, borrowed much of his conceptual apparatus from Kant's system as upheld by Chicherin. With Chicherin, he took the view, against Hegel, that "the true expression of the spirit is not formal and dead institutions, but the living person

---

[9] This intellectual evolution is traced in his collection of articles from 1893 to 1901, *Na raznye temy* (1902).

[10] In 1911 Struve published *Patriotica*, a collection of his essays from 1905 to 1910. His major study in economics is the two-volume *Khoziaistvo i tsena* (1913–1916).

[11] For Chicherin's definition, see his *Filosofiia prava* (Moscow, 1900), p. 84. For Solov'ëv's, see Vladimir Solovyov, *The Justification of the Good: An Essay on Moral Philosophy* (Natalie A. Duddington (trans.), Boris Jakim (ed. and annot.), Grand Rapids, MI.: William B. Eerdmans Publishing Company, 2005), pp. 318–320.

possessing consciousness and will."[12] Novgorodtsev praised Kant's theory of the autonomy of the will for opening up new horizons in social and political thought. But his priority to anchor the moral will more firmly in "real life circumstances" led him, again much like Chicherin (and also Solov'ëv), to qualify his acceptance of the Kantian paradigm. As Novgorodtsev saw it, Kant's formalism issued from the division he drew between the phenomenal realm of necessity and the noumenal realm of freedom. Kant placed the moral principle beyond the reach of the real world: it was a pure, unobtainable ideal. By contrast, Novgorodtsev argued that "the moral will seeks its realization in the world, through the establishment of harmony between the ideal and reality." In this "vital reciprocity" with the world, the moral will is strengthened and grows: "Such is the necessary passage from subjective to objective ethics, namely an ethics that endeavours to resolve the problem of the actual implementation of moral norms in view of real life circumstances."[13]

In a tribute to Solov'ëv's role as a philosopher of law shortly after his death in 1900, Novgorodtsev acknowledged the originality of the Solov'ëvian project, while also confirming its dependency on Kantian thought.[14] The Christian worldview that had shaped Solov'ëv's critique of classical liberalism suggested to Novgorodtsev how he might augment Kant's theory of the autonomous moral law with a moral law to be realized in human communities. As a "critique of abstract principles," Solov'ëv's approach vigorously challenged the formalism of Kant's practical philosophy. However, as Novogorodtsev recognized, it was vitally important for Solov'ëv to retain the fundamental principle of Kant's categorical imperative in his project to construct a social ideal: human beings are ends in themselves and ought never to be treated merely as means, even for the sake of the common good. "The guiding idea," in Andrzej Walicki's words, "is always the Kantian principle of the absolute significance of human dignity."[15] Whether appropriated in support of a theistic metaphysics or invoked in the more secular vein of transcendental idealism, this contention that human beings are "ends-in-themselves" and thus have absolute value was the undisputed first principle of Russian liberalism.

In the wake of the 1905 Revolution, these two aspects of Russian liberal thought – one privileging individual freedom and the rule of law, the other

[12] Chicherin, *Filosofiia prava*, p. 225; Walicki, *Legal Philosophies of Russian Liberalism*, pp. 291–292.

[13] P.I. Novgorodtsev, *Kant i Gegel' v ikh ucheniiakh o prave i gosudarstve* (Moscow, 1901), p. 102. The paradigm of "objective ethics" respected a long tradition in Russian philosophical thought going back to the Slavophiles, and refined by Solov'ëv.

[14] P.I. Novgorodtsev, "Ideia prava v filosofii Vl. S. Solov'ëva," *Voprosy filosofii i psikhologii* 12, no. 1, bk. 56 (1901), 112–129.

[15] Walicki, *Legal Philosophies of Russian Liberalism*, p. 195.

envisioning a social ethical project – prompted differentiated solutions to the "constitutional impasse" presented by the rapid restoration of autocratic rule. Forced to reposition the terms of their struggle for fundamental civil rights, most of the liberal theorists (Kistiakovskii being the exception) argued that the secular, rational concept of negative liberty needed to be supplemented by a religiously inspired view of man and culture. While remaining faithful to the idea of the rule of law for securing individual freedom, the philosophers acknowledged the force of Solov'ëv's appeal to the right to a dignified existence, which, by actively soliciting state involvement in the economic life of the community, constituted a radical departure from the classical *laissez-faire* economic model: "The *raison d'être* of society in relation to its members," wrote Solov'ëv, "is to assure for each not only a material livelihood, but also a *dignified* livelihood . . . Poverty beyond a certain threshold . . . is contrary to human dignity and therefore incompatible with true public morality."[16] During the long decade from 1905 to 1917, this idea was a powerful leitmotif in the philosophers' studies of social justice and welfare.

Three key collective volumes (*Problems of Idealism* (1902), *Landmarks* (1909), and *De Profundis* (1918)[17]) to which various permutations of the group contributed, are particularly significant for gauging the evolution of "classical" and "new" liberalism as Russia entered its age of revolution. Widely regarded as summations of the Silver Age mood, these seminal works also bring into focus the issues the liberal intelligentsia confronted in its bid to overcome the obstacles presented, on the one hand, by the tradition of autocratic rule, and by the lure of positive liberty and Bolshevik utopianism, on the other.

PROBLEMS OF IDEALISM

Problems of Idealism was conceived by Struve at the beginning of the Liberation Movement as a collective volume dedicated to the theme of freedom of conscience and its importance in the development of liberal thought. The

[16] "La question sociale en Europe" (1892), translated in Vladimir Wozniuk, *Politics, Law, and Morality: Essays by V.S. Soloviev* (New Haven, CT: Yale University Press, 2000), p. 34. In *Justification of the Good*, Solov'ëv reinforced this idea: "The moral point of view demands . . . that everyone should have the means of existence . . . and sufficient physical *rest* secured to him, and that he should also be able to enjoy *leisure* for the sake of his spiritual development." Solov'ëv, *The Justification of the Good*, p. 297.

[17] All three are available in English: Randall A. Poole (ed. and trans.), *Problems of Idealism: Essays in Russian Social Philosophy* (New Haven, CT: Yale University Press, 2003); Marshall S. Shatz and Judith E. Zimmerman (eds. and trans.), *Vekhi (Landmarks): A Collection of Articles about the Russian Intelligentsia* (Armonk, NY: M.E. Sharpe, 1994); William F. Woehrlin (ed. and trans.), *Out of the Depths (De Profundis): A Collection of Articles on the Russian Revolution* (Irvine, CA: Charles Schlacks, 1986).

volume was intended to represent a "common platform" with contributions by established academics in fields (e.g., philosophy, law, and religion) that were clearly germane to a broadly conceived liberalism. After Struve went abroad in December 1901, editorial responsibilities fell to Novgorodtsev. The volume was published in November 1902 by the Moscow Psychological Society, the most important center of Russian philosophy in this period. Thus, *Problems of Idealism* was ostensibly an academic undertaking presenting a number of theoretical divisions with respect to idealism. Certain authors worked within the bounds of Kantian transcendental idealism. Others professed a more religiously inspired idealism that guided their engagement with transcendent reality. As a whole, *Problems of Idealism* was a robust, if eclectic, defense of neo-idealism as a theory of liberalism. It was a disavowal of the materialist and positivist worldviews that had dominated the intelligentsia scene in the closing decades of the nineteenth century and which calculated individual well-being as a by-product of social, economic, and historical contingency.

As editor, Pavel Novgorodtsev provided the book's "mission statement." "Social and political circumstances today," he wrote, "no longer represent the simple demand of expediency, but the categorical imperative of morality, which gives primary importance to the principle of the absolute significance of personhood (*lichnost'*)."[18] In spite of Novgorodtsev's rallying call, the contributions themselves offered little positive cohesion: authors put forward different conceptions of idealism and engaged in arcane polemics in their own fields. Novgorodtsev's chapter, for example, was framed by his quarrel with the historical school of law. He directed attention to ancient Greek philosophy as an avenue of escape from nineteenth-century historicism and sociologism. In Novgorodtsev's opinion, Plato and Aristotle taught that abstract principles of equality and freedom must be applied in the concrete circumstances of social life and that social justice must infuse abstract legal principles with moral content.[19] Evgenii Trubetskoi defended natural law by criticizing the main premises of Marxism.[20] His contention that the human mind is irreducible to "economic or other causes" touched on a line of inquiry (the theory of causation) that Struve and Kistiakovskii developed in their respective critiques of Nikolai Mikhailovskii, whose theory of "subjective sociology" had gained considerable purchase with the populist movement in the 1870s and 1880s. Struve's rebuttal of natural causation employed the Kantian terminology of "is" and "ought," relating to the

[18] P. I. Novgorodtsev, "Foreword to the Russian Edition" in *Problems of Idealism*, p. 83 (translation slightly modified).
[19] P.I. Novgorodtsev, "Ethical Idealism in the Philosophy of Law" in *Problems of Idealism*, pp. 274–324.
[20] E.N. Trubetskoi, "Toward Characterization of the Theory of Marx and Engels on the Significance of Ideas in History" in *Problems of Idealism*, pp. 124–142.

separate and irreducible realms of the phenomenal and noumenal, in order to demonstrate the simplistic and flawed equation that positivists drew between these realms. Deriving "what ought to be" from "what is" constituted, in Struve's eyes, the monstrous idea of "scientific ethics."[21] Kistiakovskii's chapter made much the same point. "The Russian sociologists," he wrote, "take pride in introducing an ethical element into the understanding of social phenomena, and in bringing about recognition that the social process cannot be examined apart from the ideas of the good and of justice that inspire this process. But of what value is an ethical element for which the highest criterion is possibility?"[22] Mikhailovskii's ethical relativism, according to Kistiakovskii, made moral values dependent on subjective choice instead of seeing them as objective and obligatory.

Through its multifaceted critique of materialist and positivist worldviews, *Problems of Idealism* represented a concerted attempt to rehabilitate the "complex questions of life" and encourage "a general aspiration towards moral renewal."[23] But while the authors convincingly exposed the shortcomings of empirical, positivist theories of man and progress, and powerfully advanced the principle of personhood, they were almost reticent in their definitions of the state and socio-legal order: "Raising the question of the organization of society necessarily takes us into the sphere of public policy and law," Novgorodtsev wrote. "Natural law takes its starting points, its highest principles, from moral philosophy, and thus the first line of defining it follows the abstract demands of the moral law. But this is only the first line: further it is necessary to study concrete conditions and to construct the ideal that most closely matches them."[24]

CONCEPTIONS OF THE (CONSTITUTIONAL) STATE

Although Novgorodtsev's comments clearly hinted that the imperatives of natural law demand a constitutional system,[25] in 1902 open debate on "rule of law" and constitutionalism was still quite rare. But as the country edged towards

---

[21] P.B. Struve, "Toward Characterization of Our Philosophical Development" in *Problems of Idealism*, p. 148. Poole suggests that Struve's essay was in fact a "profession de foi" of sorts, charting a "self-evaluation of his evolution from Marxism to idealism." See the Editor's Introduction, p. 31.

[22] B.A. Kistiakovskii, "The 'Russian Sociological School' and the Category of Possibility in the Solution of Social-Ethical Problems" in *Problems of Idealism*, p. 352.

[23] Novgorodtsev, "Foreword to the Russian Edition" in *Problems of Idealism*, pp. 82, 83.

[24] Novgorodtsev, "Ethical Idealism in the Philosophy of Law," pp. 312–313.

[25] Indeed he was quite explicit: "Natural law is the expression of the autonomous, absolute significance of the person, a significance that must belong to it in any political system. In this respect natural law is more than a demand for better legislation: it represents the protest of the person against state absolutism, reminding us of the unconditional moral basis that is the only proper foundation of society and the state." Novgorodtsev, "Ethical Idealism in the Philosophy of Law," p. 313.

revolution, that began to change. In 1904, in the midst of Russia's damaging campaign with Japan, Novgorodtsev published an article expressing his hopes for a "self-limiting" state (*gosudarstvennoe samoogranichenie*) grounded in natural law. Only such a state, he believed, is committed at its inception to respect the freedom and equality of its citizens. The "natural-law state" (*estestvenno-pravovoe gosudarstvo*) must conform to the higher moral norms from which it derives its legitimacy and principles of governance. In Novgorodtsev's view, the state is an instrument of law, not its creator. Of course, the state determines the form of law (*pravo*) in the sense that it devises legal structures, ensures the separation of the branches of government, and so forth, but the content of law is "directly determined by life, and finds its highest sanction in moral consciousness."[26] Thus, the state is a law-giver, not a law-maker.

For all the Russian neo-liberal theorists, the state, however understood, was a positive value. It provided not only the necessary ("negative") guarantees of individual freedom but also a framework for political community.[27] As Novgorodtsev, Kotliarevskii, and Trubetskoi suggested, it imparted a sense of solidarity: a willingness to subordinate one's private interests to the common good, which, in turn, would prevent the assertion of individual rights from degenerating into anarchy.[28] Whether conceived as a guarantor of social welfare, a "cooperative unity of the people," or even in the spirit of Chicherin's conservative-liberal call for a "strong hand" (*tverdaia ruka*) combined with "liberal measures," the idea of the state as an organizing principle ensuring the liberty and well-being of all its members distinguished Russian liberal thought from west European *laissez-faire* politics and individualism.[29] Almost from its inception, Russian liberalism moved beyond the classical liberal separation of public and private spheres toward a conception of law and freedom emphasizing "positive freedom" and broad

---

[26] P.I. Novgorodtsev, "Gosudarstvo i pravo," *Voprosy filosofii i psikhologii* 15, no. 5, bk. 75 (1904), 510–511.

[27] See Judith E. Zimmerman's pioneering essay, "Russian Liberal Theory, 1900–1917," *Canadian-American Slavic Studies* 14, no. 1 (Spring 1980), 1–20, especially 17–18.

[28] E.N. Trubetskoi, "Filosofiia prava Prof. L. I. Petrazhitskogo," *Voprosy filosofii i psikhologii* 12, no. 2, bk. 57 (1901), 30–33; S.A. Kotliarevskii, "Predposylki demokratii," *Voprosy filosofii i psikhologii* 16, no. 2, bk. 77 (1905), 104–128; P.I. Novgorodtsev, *Krizis sovremennogo pravosoznaniia* (Moscow, 1909), pp. 367–391.

[29] Andrzej Walicki has aptly likened the Russian liberal activist conception of the state to the modern welfare state, beginning with the *Rechtsstaat* liberalism of Bismarck's Germany. See *Legal Philosophies of Russian Liberalism*, pp. 202–204, and his essay "Nravstvennost' i pravo v teoriiakh russkikh liberalov kontsa XIX – nachala XX vekov," *Voprosy filosofii* 8 (1991), 25–40. On the distinctive features of the intellectual origins of Russian liberalism, also see, e.g., Charles Timberlake (ed.), *Essays on Russian Liberalism* (Columbia, MO: University of Missouri Press, 1971); I.N. Sizemskaia, "'Novyi liberalizm': uchenie o pravakh cheloveka i gosudarstvennoi vlasti" in V.V. Shelokhaev (ed.), *Russkii liberalizm: Istoricheskie sud'by i perspektivy* (Moscow: Rossiiskaia polit. entsiklopediia, 1999), pp. 209–216; G.P. Aksenov, "Lichnost' kak osnova liberal'noi idei" in *ibid.* pp. 217–225.

state responsibility for promoting justice under law. Struve, for example, held
that the state, by representing the broader community, could help break down
divisions of class and nationality.[30] For Novgorodtsev, the state was not merely
about "government" or "power": it was a "cooperative unity of the people as
a whole." He thought that "to safeguard . . . the state – in the highest and most
profound sense of this word – is simultaneously to safeguard the living human
person: it is an affirmation of, and a means of caring for, the man and citizen
within each and every individual."[31] In other words, human dignity should be
assured by positive state action, and the state, ideally, should be the bearer of
egalitarian principles.

Few Russian legal thinkers, especially those who counted themselves among
Solov'ëv's successors, willingly endorsed the Enlightenment legacy of rational individualism as such. It was neither relevant to Russia's political tradition
of *proizvol* (arbitrary exercise of state power) that they were combating as an
immediate priority, nor did its cultural legacy, which they typically perceived as
narrow bourgeois morality, private property, and the marketplace, fit with their
view of personhood.[32] Historically, Russia's impoverished legal culture made it
unwise to rely on fundamental legal norms alone as the basis for society. Thus,
Novgorodtsev's bid to ground the state in the principle of personhood should
also be understood within this broader context of Russian legal history. He
wanted to curb the stubborn tendency among Russians to regard the relation
between state and the population in terms of an insurmountable "us"/"them"
opposition. Time and again throughout his career he argued for a closer reciprocity between government and society by stressing that "society is a union of
individuals [*litsa*]" and that its significance is wholly determined by their level
of moral and legal consciousness. If we deprive even one individual of moral
value, he wrote, "we deprive the totality of individuals of the same moral value,
and, conversely, in recognizing the moral value of individuals, we must also
recognize the moral value of the union of individuals."[33]

LIBERAL PHILOSOPHY, POLITICS, AND REVOLUTION

In the immediate pre- and post-revolutionary years, when a form of constitutional rule was still seen as an attainable goal, Russian liberal theorists discussed current West European parliamentary practices with a clear view to their

---

[30] For this point see Zimmerman, "Russian Liberal Theory, 1900–1917," 18.

[31] Novgorodtsev, "Gosudarstvo i pravo," 535.

[32] See Laura Engelstein, "Combined Underdevelopment: Discipline and Law in Imperial and Soviet
Russia," *American Historical Review* 98, no. 2 (1993), 338–353.

[33] P.I. Novgorodtsev, *Vvedenie v filosofiiu prava* (Moscow, 1922), p. 66.

practical implementation at home. In this spirit, they analyzed efforts to improve representative government through such mechanisms as electoral laws, referendums, initiatives, and interest groups.[34] In the run-up to the 1905 Revolution, the Kadet Party, led by Struve and Pavel Miliukov, acquired enough momentum to gain majority representation in the first two Dumas, but the ensuing government backlash, together with continuing acts of subversion by radical and terrorist elements, quickly undermined hopes of simple political solutions to the long-term problems of the country's liberal development. Inversely, however, the liberal theorists' short-lived experience in politics demonstrates that they were less concerned with narrow political gains than with the more ambitious, yet somehow less tangible, goals of securing social justice and human welfare. Thus, Novgorodtsev and Kotliarevskii pressed for the inclusion of a statement in the 1906 Kadet Party program guaranteeing a decent human existence and the right to work. As they saw it, granting civil rights was a straightforward formal matter and, in any event, a basic requirement of a constitutional state, but ensuring the social right to a dignified existence depended on the general cultural and economic level of society.[35] In other words, they conceived politics through the prism of a social ideal that was anchored in a moral-religious worldview. It was not enough to ensure equality before the law for all citizens; the purpose of the constitutional system was to encourage, and provide the necessary means for, the realization of the full potential of the individual.[36]

The experience of revolution and Duma politics reinforced Novgorodtsev's misgivings regarding what he called an "exaggerated respect" for juridical and political means. Good political practice required more than defining citizens' rights and duties; it entailed raising their political, legal, and civic awareness. Novgorodtsev regretted that, in some quarters, the constitutional experiment had merely reinforced legal nihilistic tendencies (he was thinking of Lev Tolstoi's anarchic dismissal of law), and he took this as proof that law needed to be complemented with new principles. "The lawful state [*pravovoe gosudarstvo*]," he wrote, "is not the crown of history or the final ideal of moral life; it is no more than an auxiliary element in the larger configuration of moral forces. It follows that law, compared to the plenitude of moral demands, is an insufficient and crude instrument, inadequate to the task of embodying the purity of moral principles."[37]

---

[34] Zimmerman, "Russian Liberal Theory, 1900–1917," 9. She refers to a number of punctual studies and articles by Novgorodtsev, Kotliarevskii, and Kistiakovskii addressing these topics.

[35] Zimmerman, "Russian Liberal Theory, 1900–1917," 13, referring to S.A. Kotliarevskii, *Vlast' i pravo: Problema pravovogo gosudarstva* (Moscow: Mysl', 1915), p. 347, and Novgorodtsev, *Krizis sovremennogo pravosoznaniia*, p. 342.

[36] Zimmerman, "Russian Liberal Theory, 1900–1917," 11.

[37] Novgorodtsev, *Krizis sovremennogo pravosoznaniia*, p. 16.

These words introduce one of Novgorodtsev's major works, *The Crisis in Modern Legal Consciousness* (1909), in which he placed the problems of Russian constitutional development in a wider European context.[38] Drawing extensively on French debates since Rousseau, he traced developments in modern European social and legal philosophy and concluded that radical claims of popular sovereignty in reaction to state authority betrayed an anachronistic faith in the (failed) promises of the Enlightenment. For Novgorodtsev, this tendency constituted a European-wide "crisis" in legal consciousness which neither outmoded claims to state supremacy nor the demands of popular sovereignty could resolve. Instead, echoing Solov'ëv, he called for a renewed "justification of law" (*opravdanie prava*) as a precondition of moral progress. True solidarity, he maintained, rested on the moral foundation of personhood.[39]

The publication of this work coincided with one of the most heated polemics in the history of the Russian intelligentsia, the appearance of *Vekhi* (*Landmarks*) in 1909. Although Novgorodtsev himself scarcely referred to the "Russian question," the theoretical arguments he advanced concerning relations between the individual and society, and his stress on the progressive cultural impact of education as a means to achieve justice and the rule of law,[40] had an immediate resonance for his fellow Russian liberals as they tried to confront the devastating social-cultural consequences of the 1905 Revolution.

THE *VEKHI* EPISODE

The initial idea for what is now widely regarded as the second "landmark" of the Silver Age, *Vekhi*, came from Mikhail Gershenzon, a literary historian and collaborator on Kistiakovskii's journal, *Kriticheskoe obozrenie* (*Critical Survey*). In autumn 1908, Gershenzon contacted a number of leading non-Marxist philosophers, asking them to reflect on the deeper meaning of the revolution and its failure. Both Struve and Kistiakovskii contributed essays. As "Westernizers" in temperament and outlook, they were understandably critical of the residual Slavophilism that colored the views of some of the other contributors. But their desire to protect political and social institutions as potential forces for mobilizing civic awareness (they ranked among the few Kadets prepared to work with the compromised gains of the October Manifesto and Fundamental Laws) made them willing participants in this bitter truth-telling venture. Struve pursued much the same line of argument regarding the absolute value of the person as he had done in 1902, only now the immediate frame of reference was

---

[38] This work was originally serialized in *Questions of Philosophy and Psychology* between 1906 and 1908.
[39] Novgorodtsev, *Krizis sovremennogo pravosoznaniia*, p. 243.   [40] *Ibid.* pp. 233–244.

the psychology of the intelligentsia, its blind commitment to acts of heroism, and its doctrinal approach to politics. The intelligentsia's practice of self-denial for the sake of revolutionary change "does not necessarily imply recognition of the idea of personal responsibility as a principle governing private and public life."[41] Similarly, Struve echoed the argument he had developed in his critique of Mikhailovskii's essentially utilitarian ethics to expose the conceptual flaws underlying the revolutionary mentality: "While reducing politics to the external organization of life – which it is from the technical point of view – the intelligentsia simultaneously viewed it as the alpha and omega of its own and the people's entire existence . . . Thus, a limited means was turned into an all-embracing end – an obvious, though in human affairs, extremely common distortion of the relationship between means and ends."[42]

Kistiakovskii gave a comprehensive critique of the lamentable state of the nation's legal culture, deploring not just the intelligentsia's legal nihilism and false ethics, but also bureaucratic coercion and the casuistry of the codified laws. Together these phenomena obstructed the development of the ideal of the *legal* person: "Both aspects of this ideal, the person disciplined by law and by a stable legal order, and the person endowed with all rights and freely enjoying them, are alien to our intelligentsia's mentality."[43] It is true that, historically, Russian legal practice gave the intelligentsia strong grounds to ignore law in its pursuit of absolute ideals of social harmony, but what troubled Kistiakovskii was the intelligentsia's stubborn refusal to differentiate between law as a normative principle (*pravo*) and codified laws (*zakon*), "those external, lifeless rules that fit so neatly into the articles and paragraphs of a written statute."[44] This refusal explained the intelligentsia's failure to grasp that, in the first instance, law is conducive to social discipline: "Only law creates social discipline, and a disciplined society is identical to a society with a well-developed legal system."[45]

Politically, Kistiakovskii was on the left of the liberal spectrum. Intellectually, though, he was more attached to Chicherin, the conservative liberal. Like Chicherin, Kistiakovskii was critical of legal philosophies that drained *pravo* of moral content (in the positivist "struggle for law" tradition of Jhering, for example), and, like Chicherin, he was critical of the tendency to treat law as an ethical minimum (Jellinek abroad, Solov'ëv at home). If, as Kistiakovskii acknowledged, Solov'ëv "gave irrefutable proof of the moral character of law in its genuine essence," his self-proclaimed successors betrayed its theoretical

---

[41] P.B. Struve, "The Intelligentsia and Revolution" in *Vekhi (Landmarks)*, p. 124.
[42] *Ibid.* p. 127.
[43] B.A. Kistiakovskii, "In Defence of Law: The Intelligentsia and Legal Consciousness" in *Vekhi (Landmarks)*, p. 96.
[44] *Ibid.* p. 104. [45] *Ibid.* p. 91.

core: "Some teach that law contains a minimum of moral commands that are compulsory for everyone; others go so far as to argue that anything in existing legal orders conflicting with moral commands is not law; a third group teaches that law and morality will attain full harmony only through the process of cultural development, in the deepening of self-awareness and in the creation of new social forms."[46] While he may have sympathized with the goals of Novgorodtsev, Trubetskoi, and Kotliarevskii as characteristic of the third group, Kistiakovskii's immediate concerns were far more prosaic, namely, to remind his readers that the substantive content of law is external, relative freedom – a necessary precondition for inner, absolute spiritual freedom – and that the distinctive property of law, as a formal value, is preeminently social, instilling social discipline.

CULTURAL ENDEAVOR AND THE RELIGIOUS ROOTS OF RUSSIAN LIBERALISM

Concluding his *Vehki* essay, Struve wrote: "Of course, we do need persistent cultural work." During the decade between revolutions, as Duma politics were increasingly affected by assertive right-wing forces, liberal theorists began to prioritize cultural endeavour (*prosveshchenie*) as a means to address issues of social justice and welfare. They understood that, by itself, political reform could not provide justice, for achieving justice is a cultural task: "We need ideas, and the creative struggle of ideas."[47]

Superficially, the liberal focus on social cohesion overlapped with the Social Democratic pledge to fight for social justice. Indeed, both camps exploited the terms *prosveshchenie* and *vospitanie* (education/upbringing) in their campaigns to raise social and political consciousness. But contrary to the radical intelligentsia's instrumentalist view of education, cultural endeavor in the liberal lexicon implied promoting spiritual values rooted in religious awareness. Struve emphasized the fundamental differences between the two camps:

Our concept of education has nothing to do with the "organization" of the social environment and its pedagogical effect on the personality. This is the "socialist" idea of education, and it has nothing in common with the idea of education in the religious sense. The latter is completely alien to socialist optimism. It believes not in organization

---

[46] B.A. Kistiakovskii, "Metodologicheskaia priroda nauki o prave" in *Sotsial'nye nauki i pravo* (Moscow: Izd. M. i S. Sabashnikovykh, 1916). Quoted from A.P. Al'bov *et al.* (ed.), *Russkaia filosofiia prava: Filosofiia very i nravstvennosti* (St. Petersburg: Izd-vo "Aleteiia," 1997), p. 321.

[47] Struve, "The Intelligentsia and Revolution," p. 129. Also see S.A. Kotliarevskii, "Politika i kul'tura," *Voprosy filosofii i psikhologii* 17, no. 4, bk. 84 (1906), 353–367, and Zimmerman, "Russian Liberal Theory, 1900–1917," 11.

but only in creation, in a person's positive labor on himself, in his inner struggle for the sake of creative tasks.[48]

Cultural endeavor, by harnessing genuine spiritual values, was thus indispensable for raising civic awareness, and, by extension, for promoting economic development. In short, it was crucial to providing the type of life consistent with human dignity that Solov'ёv had identified as a fundamental right.

Struve returned to this point on several occasions in his popular articles. His aim was to recover the original Christian premises on which liberalism, historically, had been built, but which liberalism had squandered in the modern process of secularization.[49] Thus, just as Novgorodtsev hoped to rehabilitate law as an integral part of more complex "moral forces," Struve hoped for the resurgence of an authentic religious worldview combining the traditional Christian motifs of moral self-sacrifice (*podvig*) and duty with the modern idea of individual freedom, conceived as "creative autonomy": "Man as the repository of personal creative deeds within the cosmos – herein lies the central idea which, whether calmly or impetuously, slowly or with great speed, shall take hold of humanity, take hold of it in a religious sense, infusing our deadened private and public life with new energy. This is my belief."[50]

The themes of human dignity, justice, and cultural endeavor also drove the arguments that Sergei Kotliarevskii developed in his major work, *Power and Law* (1915). His overall philosophical approach was clearly idealist. "The dignity of the human person," he wrote, "has no grounding in the finite scientific-empirical worldview; it is uniquely in our religious consciousness that man appears as the crown of nature, as an intermediary between two worlds."[51] Kotliarevskii shared with Novgorodtsev the view that law is a pathway of sorts to morality, but his main intellectual inspiration was Solov'ёv, whose "justification of the good" he reconfigured as a type of justification for the rule-of-law state:

Power should be limited by law in the name of justice, and justice should be completed by active charity, which, in a sense, is higher justice, stemming from the dignity of the human person and consciousness of cosmic and moral unity. The higher level encompasses the lower and bestows it with true meaning. However, society cannot ascend directly to the higher level, and it is here that the rule-of-law state acquires its fundamental justification. Not only is there no contradiction between it and higher forms in the moral-cultural sense, rather, it is the path leading to them. The rule-of-law

---

[48] Struve, "The Intelligentsia and Revolution," p. 127.
[49] P.B. Struve, "Religiia i sotsializm," *Russkaia mysl'* (August 1909), reprinted in his collection *Patriotica: Politika, kul'tura, religiia, sotsializm* (1910). Cited from the recent edition compiled by V.N. Zhukov and A.P. Poliakov (Moscow: Respublika, 1997), pp. 325–334.
[50] *Ibid.* p. 334. [51] Kotliarevskii, *Vlast' i Pravo*, p. 395.

state is, so to speak, on the *threshold* of a community which, to the degree possible, harmonizes with the spiritual requirements of the individual.[52]

Personhood was thus the integral link between normative law and a higher moral justice predicated on charity, compassion, love, and forgiveness. In practice, as Kotliarevskii noted, the emergence across European society of inchoate measures of fundamental justice, such as charitable work with the mentally ill, was an important indication of this shift in contemporary social political thought.[53]

AGAINST UTOPIA

Kotliarevskii used his theory of the rule-of-law state to counter arguments (which were not uncommon among utopian thinkers of the Russian Silver Age) in favor of theocracy. To his mind, theocracy (in whatever guise) was incompatible with modern legal consciousness in two main respects: theocracy's coercive nature threatened the principle of individual freedom, and theocracy debased the religious ideal by identifying it too closely with the temporal world.[54] But like Trubetskoi and Novgorodstev, Kotliarevskii believed that the liberal values of dignity, equality, and freedom required a theistic, specifically Christian, metaphysics. Solov'ëv's concept of "Godmanhood" best answered their concern to emphasize man's active participation as a free and autonomous being in the process of salvation. By unifying the divine and human, while preserving their distinct eternal and temporal natures, Godmanhood was, for these liberal-idealists, the most powerful affirmation of human value and human freedom as self-determination. As Trubetskoi put it in his profound meditation, *The Meaning of Life* (1918), "The justification of freedom consists precisely in the fact that, without it, *partnership* [*druzhestvo*] between God and creation would be impossible. Deprived of freedom, that is, the possibility of self-determination, His creation [*sushchestvo*] could not be a free collaborator [*sotrudnik*] with God, a co-participant in His creative acts."[55]

The tonality of Trubetskoi's religious philosophy was wholly consistent with the beliefs he held as a liberal thinker and public figure. Indeed, tested by war and revolution, his vigorous defense of human freedom acquired even greater

---

[52] *Ibid.* pp. 403–404.
[53] *Ibid.* p. 401. On Kotliarevskii, see Randall A. Poole, "Sergei Kotliarevskii and the Rule of Law in Russian Liberal Theory," *Dialogue and Universalism* 16, nos. 1–2 (2006), 81–104.
[54] Kotliarevskii, *Vlast' i Pravo*, p. 413.
[55] E. Trubetskoi, *Smysl zhizni* (Moscow: Sytin, 1918). Cited from the recent edition compiled by A.P. Poliakov and P.P. Apryshko (Moscow: Respublika, 1994), p. 81 (see also pp. 49, 69, and 80). On Trubetskoi, see Randall A. Poole, "Religion, War, and Revolution: E.N. Trubetskoi's Liberal Construction of Russian National Identity, 1912–1920," *Kritika: Explorations in Russian and Eurasian History* 7, no. 2 (Spring 2006), 195–240, here, 229.

urgency as an attempt to salvage the "meaning of life." Similarly, Novgorodtsev's seminal study of utopianism in modern European thought served as an occasion to reassert the crucial importance of freedom and individual self-determination as starting-points for the attainment of the common good. Originally written as a series of articles for *Questions of Psychology and Philosophy* (1911–1916), *On the Social Ideal* was a timely critique of Bolshevik revolutionary utopianism. Novgorodtsev's message was resoundingly clear: there was no possibility of realizing the Golden Age of Communism or any other earthly paradise. Taking up the biblical motif of "render unto Caesar," he conveyed, with remarkable clarity, the essential tenets of liberal social thought:

Render unto Caesar what is Caesar's and unto God what is God's – this ancient commandment remains in force today. It recognizes the autonomy of spiritual and political affairs: each sphere has its own distinct paths and tasks, and each should preserve its importance for man. But the starting and end point in both is man and his moral vocation. Thus, *rather than faith in a terrestrial paradise*, which is, in essence, unobtainable, the task before us should be *faith in human action and moral obligation*. *Not the Promised Land, rather the stalwart [nepreklonnaia] person* – this should be our ultimate mainstay. The person, unrelenting in her moral aspirations, drawing strength from steadfast faith in the absolute ideal of the good as she traverses the twists and turns of history – this is what we should be fighting for as the basis for a social construction.[56]

A year later, however, as the Bolsheviks claimed Kadet members as their first victims in the civil war, Novgorodtsev would write that their utopian dreams betokened less a romantic maximalism in the spirit of Hegelian or even Marxian thought than an extreme form of rationalist reductionism with appalling consequences for spiritual freedom.[57]

CODA: *DE PROFUNDIS*

In spring 1918, Struve returned from the relative safety of the provinces to Moscow, where he contacted former *vekhovtsy* with the idea for a follow-up volume. Novgorodtsev and Kotliarevskii were among the other contributors he invited.[58] By summer, as the Bolsheviks unleashed the Red Terror and

---

[56] P.I. Novgorodtsev, *Ob obshchestvennom ideale* (A.V. Sobolev (ed.), Moscow: Izd-vo "Pressa," 1991), p. 44.

[57] P.I. Novgorodtsev, "On the Paths and Tasks of the Russian Intelligentsia" in *Out of the Depths (De Profundis)*, pp. 175–190.

[58] Former *Vekhovtsy* who did not contribute to *De Profundis* were Kistiakovskii (who, by 1918, had returned to his native Ukraine) and Gershenzon (with whom Struve had quarrelled following the publication of *Vekhi*). E. Trubetskoi, a contributor to *Problems of Idealism*, was also absent from this new collection.

War Communism, Struve managed to put together a collection of reflections exploring the deeper significance of the events the authors were witnessing first-hand. Never published in Russia during the Soviet era (although a small handful of printed copies survived), the collection became known, quite fortuitously, in the West in the late 1960s. Since then it has become widely regarded as the concluding instalment of a "trilogy" of works, preceded by *Problems of Idealism* and *Vekhi*, charting the closing stages of liberal and religious social thought in the pre-revolutionary era.

Out of the Depths offers a reasoned explanation of the authors' hostility to Bolshevism, which they perceived as the culmination of an iniquitous worldview that they had been fighting against for the past two decades. Echoing the critique they had launched in *Vekhi*, they attacked the premises of Bolshevism – its anti-statism, atheism, and internationalism – which were being aggressively forced on Russian culture and society. They saw these premises as artificial postulates lacking any objective foundation. But the pathos of this collection, as its title suggests, lies in the fact that it was a tacit valediction to an era of thwarted liberal ideals. In his short opening preface to the book, Struve identified these ideals with religious consciousness. Irrespective of their choice of subject matter, he wrote: "equally inherent and dear to all the authors is the conviction that the *positive* principles of social life *are rooted* in the depths of religious consciousness, and that the rupture of this essential bond is a misfortune and a crime. The unprecedented moral and political collapse that has befallen our people and state is, they sense, such a rupture."[59]

Whether condemning Bolshevism as the logical outcome of an intel-ligentsia tradition predicated on an exaggerated "moralizing subjectivism" (Kotliarevskii), or blaming the autocracy for not introducing constitutional reform earlier and for its disastrous disposition of the "peasant question" (Struve), all the authors in the collection expressed vain hope for the restoration of the spiritual tradition that they had helped foster as part of their endeavors to promote legal culture. Novgorodtsev called for the work of enlightened minds to repair the damage caused by Bolshevism, which, as a product of the radical intelligentsia, assumed "that evil and suffering may be conquered by human rea-son in a perfect social order." Instead of rationalistic utopianism, he advocated religious care for the people, "but only on the condition that it does not create an idol out of the people... Only in that case will the progressive thought of the intelligentsia acquire its true and sound content, and will national life be consolidated on the solid foundation of organic construction."[60]

---

[59] P.B. Struve, "Preface" to *Out of the Depths (De Profundis)*.
[60] Novgorodtsev, "On the Paths and Tasks of the Russian Intelligentsia," pp. 188, 185.

In a sense, the overriding affirmation of religious values shared by the contributors to *Out of the Depths* attested to a tradition of Russian thought reaching back to the Slavophiles. As I have suggested, in prioritizing the idea of law over politics as a means to ensure the common good, most of the Russian liberals discussed in this chapter both adhered to and went beyond the tenets of classical liberalism. Their quest to construct a social philosophy that answered Russia's specific needs as a largely agrarian, commune-based nation required an account of human dignity that classical liberalism alone could not supply. And, if the outcome of the October Revolution prevented these liberal thinkers from realizing their social and political goals, it seemed to confirm their demands for spiritual integrity, demands which they (especially those who spent their remaining years in emigration) increasingly traced to the Slavophiles' original demands of freedom of thought and association. As successors, then, to Russia's "first liberals," they sought to perpetuate an indigenous intelligentsia tradition beyond her borders.

13

IMAGINATION AND IDEOLOGY IN THE NEW RELIGIOUS CONSCIOUSNESS

ROBERT BIRD

From the terrifying distance there sounds a voice of hope – not the hope of a single life, but a universal hope for the potential salvation of humanity from the ugliness and vulgarity of life by means of true, inspired beauty. Then I look out the window of my monastic cell onto this noisy Petersburg, with its innumerable smoking chimneys, with its damp streets along which crowds rush, and I wonder: where is this ferment of young, still vital forces leading? What road will it find? Will victory be had by the elements that turn the life of the capital into an insufferable soulless turmoil, or will those elemental forces finally prevail which found expression in the prophetic works of the best Russian artists and which periodically glimmer in the moods of individual people who thirst for the highest truth? O, I believe that this inner force will conquer; I believe, I believe.[1]

Akim Volynskii (1861–1926) in 1899

VOLOGDA, 1902

An unlikely debate club forms, made possible by the tsarist authorities' questionable policy of allowing internally exiled political opponents to congregate in a single provincial town, where they have little to do save carry on their partisan polemics. Among the Social Democrats gathered here are Nikolai Berdiaev (1874–1948), Aleksandr Bogdanov (1873–1928) and Anatolii Lunacharskii (1875–1933); the Socialist Revolutionaries include writer Aleksei Remizov (1877–1957) and budding terrorist Boris Savinkov (1879–1925). Though the Vologda exiles follow the debates in metropolitan journals and correspond with their comrades by post, in the hothouse atmosphere the ideological battles heat up and sparks fly. Debates on the admissibility of terrorist action lead to a split between Savinkov and the more humanistic Remizov, depicted in the latter's novel *The Clock* (1908). The Social Democrats' debates focus on the polemics between the realists (Bogdanov and Lunacharskii) and

---

[1] Akim Volynskii, *Dostoevskii* (St. Petersburg: Akademicheskii proekt, Izdatel'stvo DNK, 2007), p. 101.

idealists (Berdiaev). Though most Russian intellectuals continue to share an almost obsessive concern with the divide between the educated classes (*intelligentsiia*) and the "people" (*narod*), the idealists (following the Slavophiles) propose to bridge it by accepting the "eternal need" and "active life of the spirit," which some begin to see reflected in the people's religious traditions, that is, the church.[2]

The idea of Russian intellectuals opposing radical ideology in the name of religious tradition was still quite novel in 1902, and it is no surprise that these apostates from radicalism made slow headway against the prevailing trends. One participant in the Vologda club later recalled: "The idealists, represented by Nikolai Berdiaev, were usually defeated, but they did not seem perturbed by this in the least; beaten on earth by means of science and logic, they escaped to the heavens (to borrow a phrase from Aleksandr Bogdanov), into the realm of the transcendent, and there – where the methods of science and logic don't apply, they of course remained undefeated."[3] Bogdanov dismissed the idealist wing as harbingers of what he called the "new Middle Ages."[4] Widely derided as "God-seekers," the idealists did not seem to present a serious alternative to radical materialism.

Still, the realists departed Vologda having imbibed the idealist bug. Bogdanov and Lunacharskii were soon to be found at the forefront of an opposition to Leninist orthodoxy within the Bolshevik party, painting in the theoretical outline of revolutionary struggle with the colors of collective action. Bogdanov's brand of Marxism in particular relied on compelling images of future society as a single super-human being: "Man has not yet arrived," Bogdanov wrote, clearly under the sway of Nietzsche's *Uebermensch*, "but he is nearby, and his silhouette shows clearly on the horizon."[5] Bogdanov imagined revolution as a victory of mind over matter, less the destruction of the old world than its thorough reorganization on the basis of scientific reason. Like so many thinkers of the age, both realist and idealist, Bogdanov sought a monistic explanation of the world, which often found expression in attempts to describe or depict reality as a single world-image: he admitted that "we, people of an imbalanced and disharmonious development, cannot imagine this kind of life in fullness and clarity," but he nonetheless asserted that "we have vague presentiments of

[2] [P.I. Novgorodtsev], "Predislovie" in *Problemy idealizma* (Moscow: Modest Kolerov, "Tri kvadrata," 2002), p. 236.
[3] I.E. Ermolaev, "Moi vospominaniia" (1923), as cited in A.A. Ermichev (ed.), *N.A. Berdiaev: Pro et contra. Antologiia* (St. Petersburg: Izdatel'stvo Russkogo Khristianskogo gumanitarnogo instituta, 1994), p. 32.
[4] A.A. Bogdanov, "Novoe srednevekov'e" in *N.A. Berdiaev: Pro et contra*, pp. 120–145.
[5] Quoted from Robert C. Williams, *The Other Bolsheviks: Lenin and His Critics, 1904–1914* (Bloomington and Indianapolis, IN: Indiana University Press, 1986), p. 39.

it in moments of ecstatic contemplation or thought," such as those provided in visual and narrative art.[6] Bogdanov's most compelling exposition of his ideas was arguably neither his three-volume study *Empiriomonism* (1904–1906) nor his two-volume *Tectology* (1913–1922), but his science-fiction novels *Red Star* (1908) and *Engineer Menni* (1913), which use Mars as a polygon for his philosophical and political theories. For his part, Lunacharskii reformulated Marxism as a "religion of humanity," positing the ultimate goal of revolution as the abolition of death. Lenin (1870–1924) condemned his comrades' abandonment of materialism or adoption of metaphysical language for the gritty business of revolution, though for the sake of Bolshevik unity he refrained from turning the polemic into outright schism.

The Vologda discussions of 1902–1903 manifested the broader confluence of Marxism and modernism in Russian intellectual culture. Confident in their scientific knowledge of the physical universe and emboldened by artistic images of its creative transformation, both Marxists and modernists deployed a totalizing discourse that frequently culminated in exhortations to "overcome" empirical limits, of time and even of death, whether in an act of revolution or transcendence, by transforming knowledge into action, economics into justice, and humanity into super-humanity. The result (as seen in Judith Kornblatt's chapter 14) was a discourse dominated by apocalyptic images of the end, frequently indifferent to the means of its achievement and to the complexities of historical process. Across the political spectrum ideas ceded authority to images, by means of which cultural agents sought to intervene in the social consciousness directly, without recourse to political or philosophical discourse.

ST. PETERSBURG, 1903

Leaving Vologda, the idealists are drawn to Petersburg where since 1901 many of the issues that concern them have been discussed at a regular series of Religious-Philosophical Meetings. Initiated by religious-minded intellectuals like secular theologian Valentin Ternavtsev (1866–1940) and philosopher Vasilii Rozanov (1856–1919), and approved by Ober-Procurator Konstantin Pobedonostsev (1827–1907), the Meetings gather a broad coalition of churchmen (including future patriarch Sergii Stragorodskii (1867–1944)) and modernists. In addition to the major participants, the Meetings are followed with interest by everyone from symbolist poet Aleksandr Blok (1880–1921) to the "World of Art" painter Alexandre Benois (1870–1960). By common

---

[6] A. Bogdanov, *Novyi mir (Stat'i 1904–1905)* (Moscow: Izdanie S. Dorovatovskogo i Charushnikova, 1905), p. 86.

acclamation the lead role belongs to Dmitrii Merezhkovskii (1865–1941) and Zinaida Gippius (1869–1945), who beginning in 1903 also publish the proceedings in their journal *Novyi put'* (*The New Path*), the main print organ of the idealist movement.

Hitherto the only comparable forum for free discussion among Russian intellectuals had been the Russian School of Social Sciences in Paris, founded by sociologist Maksim Kovalevskii (1851–1916), which was dominated by radical thinkers but had also featured some young modernists. In 1903, Vladimir Ul'ianov (aka Lenin) was lecturing there under the pseudonym V. Il'in, while down the hall (one imagines) Viacheslav Ivanov (1866–1949) was holding forth on "The Hellenic Religion of the Suffering God." The Petersburg group paid close attention, inviting Ivanov to publish his lectures in *Novyi put'* and eventually drawing him to Petersburg, albeit after the demise of the Meetings.

Concerning the first informal discussions at Rozanov's apartment, Merezhkovskii later recalled that the Religious-Philosophical Meetings brought together:

> the most radical reactionaries and equally radical revolutionaries, if not in a political then in a philosophical and religious sense, professors of the seminary, Synodal bureaucrats, priests, monks, and real "underground men," meaning anarchists and decadents. Between these two sides there arose apocalyptic conversations, as if taken directly out of [Dostoevskii's] *Demons* or *The Brothers Karamazov*. Of course nowhere else in modern Europe had such conversations been heard. This was a reflection in the highest layer of society of what was happening in . . . the depths of the common people [*narod*].[7]

Merezhkovskii coined the phrase "new religious consciousness" to denote a mindset capable of overcoming intractable social conflicts and rigid ideological divides. Participants debated the relation between faith and reason and the need for legal guarantees of freedom of conscience, especially in the wake of Lev Tolstoi's excommunication in February 1901. With especial reverence for the legacy of Vladimir Solov'ëv (1853–1900) and Nikolai Fëdorov (1829–1903), participants in the Religious-Philosophical Meetings sought to transcend politics through art and metaphysics. The effect, as had become customary in Russia, was that philosophy and even theology became a means of political contention by another name, while political ideas took quite fanciful form.

Common to these cultural actors was the sense of being on the cusp of a new historical period that would require its own truths and own forms. In his first presentation to the Religious-Philosophical Meetings in 1902, Vasilii Rozanov argued:

---

[7] D.S. Merezhkovskii, *Ne mir, no mech: K budushchei kritike khristianstva* (St. Petersburg: Izdanie M.V. Pirozhkova, 1908), p. 109.

Christianity is truth drawn in pencil, in the best case painted in watercolors, but by no means painted in oils. I repeat, of course, truth remains truth and I don't dispute it; I simply point to the fact that it has not been imbued with blood and juice... Why should religion be a *concept*, not a *fact*? [In Slavonic translation] the Book of Genesis is the Book of *Being*, not the book of "*thoughts*"; that is how the old theology began [i.e., with Being]. "In the beginning was the Word": this is how the new theology began. The *word* has diverged from *being*; the "word" is the province of the clergy, while society has "being"; but this "word" is bloodless, while this being is not divine.[8]

Adapting ancient Christian speculations, Merezhkovskii spoke of a "third testament" that would supplement the books of the Father and the Son with a new "revelation of the Spirit." Dostoevskii, in particular, was for Merezhkovskii and others the chief herald of this third testament, which would reconcile the worlds of body and spirit with the revelation of "holy flesh"; at times, Merezhkovskii and Gippius seemed to be creating their own sect. Much of this rankled with church representatives, who disputed the very notion of dogmatic development in Orthodoxy. Even Father John of Kronstadt, later canonized in the Russian Orthodox Church, took notice, questioning the need for a *new* religious consciousness: "This journal [i.e., *Novyi put'*] has set itself the task of seeking God, as if the Lord had not appeared to people and not revealed to us the true path. They will find no other path than in Christ Jesus, our Lord... It is Satan who reveals these new paths."[9] This harsh judgment has been cited as a reason why the ecclesiastical authorities decided to withdraw permission for the Meetings in April 1903.[10] In the end, the modernists shared with the churchmen merely an openness to religious discourse; the latter were bound to take exception to the modernists' tendency to ascribe greater religious authority to artistic inspiration than to church doctrine and tradition (much as Lenin objected to the imaginative schemes of Bogdanov). By contrast, the differences among the modernists (decadents, idealists, and realists) were less substantial than their shared faith in the image and the imagination.

Across the ideological spectrum, the modernists focused their social teachings on images of the future projected through artistic media. From Nikolai Chernyshevskii's *What Is to Be Done?* (1862–63) to Vladimir Solov'ëv's *Three Conversations* (1899–1900) and Dmitrii Merezhkovskii's trilogy of historical novels *Christ and Antichrist* (1896–1904) from Aleksandr Blok's *Poems to the Beautiful Lady* (1904) to Lev Bakst's monumental canvas *Ancient Terror* (1908), the idealists relied heavily on the attractive power of the image

[8] Vasilii Rozanov, *Okolo tserkovnykh sten* (Moscow: Respublika, 1995), p. 476.
[9] "Otzyv o. Ioanna Kronshtadskogo o 'Novom puti,'" *Novyi put'* (March 1903), 253.
[10] S.M. Polovinkin, "Religiozno-filosofskie sobraniia v Sankt-Peterburge v 1901–03 gg." in *Russkaia filosofiia: Malyi entsiklopedicheskii slovar'* (Moscow: Nauka, 1995), pp. 439–442.

to imprint theoretical discourse in sensible form. Of all the elements of Solov'ëv's legacy, none was more pervasively influential than the prophetic role he accorded to art as the physical manifestation of truth and the good; and of all the prophetic artists, Dostoevskii and Tolstoi (who remained an acute if detached observer until his death in 1910) were preeminent in the minds of modernists. In 1904, Akim Volynskii, a critic who first broached many of the characteristic ideas of Russian modernism, called for a "higher reconciliation...a synthesis of the ideas of Tolstoi and Dostoevskii." He expressed hope that "the Russian nation will become worthy of its artistic geniuses and will create, so to speak, social flesh to match their spirit."[11]

The emphasis on the imagination in Russian modernism reflected an interest in the reaction against rationalism in western philosophy, evident in such diverse thinkers as Friedrich Nietzsche and Henri Bergson, both of whom attracted the especial attention of the Russian modernists. Nietzsche received an unusual, religious reading. Viacheslav Ivanov, for instance, depicted Nietzsche's frenzy of negation as an act of self-sacrifice akin to that of Christ. In the lectures he published in *Novyi put'*, Ivanov adapted Nietzsche's dichotomy of Dionysus and Apollo, seeing the former as the mystical source of religious knowledge and the latter as its visual and verbal formalization. Like Merezhkovskii's theory of the "third testament," Ivanov's Dionysianism became common currency in Russian modernism.

The Russian modernists' interest in questions of sexuality was most closely associated with Vasilii Rozanov, who tirelessly promoted an earthy and sometimes bawdy family ideal.[12] The dominant tendency, however, stemmed from Solov'ëv's idea that physical sex should be transcended in higher forms of interaction, with procreation ceding to creativity in the spiritual, not the physical realm.[13] Berdiaev contended that, "Love by its nature is tragic; its thirst is empirically insatiable; it always leads man out of the given world onto the border of infinity, revealing the existence of other worlds."[14] Berdiaev argued passionately against the concept of the family, which confined the infinite sexual drive within a proto-institutional unit: "Family-oriented sexual love is a seeming, illusory overcoming of the difference of the sexes; unified and full, perfected

[11] Volynskii, *Dostoevskii*, p. 433.
[12] On Rozanov, see Olga Matich, *Erotic Utopia: The Decadent Imagination in Russia's Fin de Siècle* (Madison, WI: University of Wisconsin Press, 2005), ch. 7; Edith W. Clowes, *Fiction's Overcoat: Russian Literary Culture and the Question of Philosophy* (Ithaca, NY: Cornell University Press, 2004), ch. 6; Laura Engelstein, *The Keys to Happiness: Sex and the Search for Modernity in Fin-de-Siècle Russia* (Ithaca, NY: Cornell University Press, 1992), ch. 8.
[13] Eric Naiman, *Sex in Public: The Incarnation of Early Soviet Ideology* (Princeton University Press, 1997), pp. 27–78.
[14] N.A. Berdiaev, *Novoe religioznoe soznanie i obshchestvennost'* (Moscow: Kanon+, Reabilitatsiia, 1999), p. 224.

and eternal individuality is not achieved in it."[15] For all his rhetoric about the flesh, Merezhkovskii's eroticism was of a similarly arid variety. Berdiaev approvingly commented that "Rozanov reveals the sanctity and divinity of sex and amorous passion as if before the beginning of the world, wanting to return us to the paradisic state before the fall; Merezhkovskii reveals the same but after the end of the world, appealing to the passionate and holy feast of the flesh in the world transfigured, redeemed and resurrected. Merezhkovskii is correct, because he looks forwards, not backwards."[16] Mystical (i.e., childless and sometimes even sex-less) marriages were all the rage, for instance between Gippius and Merezhkovskii, Nikolai and Lidiia Berdiaev (1871–1945), and Aleksandr Blok and Liubov' Mendeleeva (1882–1939); it was not unusual for these and other married couples to expand into threesomes, sometimes with earnest theoretical and even mystical designs ("where two or three are gathered . . ."). Intersecting with some of these erotic experiments was an exploration of homoerotic behavior and homosexual partnerships. It is a trivial but indicative fact that, of all the figures discussed in this chapter, Rozanov was practically the only one with children.

The tendency of the modernists to regard history as a narrative leading inexorably to an imaginable future outcome inevitably generated fantastic political schemes. Following Solov'ëv and Dostoevskii, some projected the image of a state founded on principles of Christian brotherhood. Though it originated as a rather conservative ideology, over time this vision became increasingly radical and even anarchistic. Writing in 1905, Merezhkovskii argued: "For us who are entering the Third Testament, the Third Kingdom of the Spirit, there is not and cannot be any positive religious principle in state power. For us, between the state and Christianity there can be no collusion, no reconciliation; 'a Christian state' is a monstrous absurdity."[17] In a discussion of the anarchist Mikhail Bakunin (1814–1876), Merezhkovskii proclaimed that the coercive power of the state would yield to the power of love, and that "the power of love is no longer power but freedom."[18] This political vision, in the words of James Scanlan, predicted that "[h]istory itself will come to an end, and a sanctified humanity will enter upon the 'superhistorical' stage of eternal blessedness in an anarchistic theocracy."[19] The actual political shape of this vision was not of the essence; as Arkadii Dolinin commented: "In order to enter the ranks

---

[15] Berdiaev, *Novoe religioznoe soznanie i obshchestvennost'*, p. 221.

[16] N.A. Berdiaev, *Opyty filosofskie, sotsial'nye i literaturnye* (Moscow: Kanon+, Reabilitatsiia, 2002), pp. 400–401.

[17] D.S. Merezhkovskii, "Novoe religioznoe deistvie," cited in *N.A. Berdiaev: Pro et contra*, p. 149.

[18] D.S. Merezhkovskii, *Bol'naia Rossiia* (Leningrad: Izdatel'stvo Leningradskogo Universiteta, 1991), p. 26.

[19] James P. Scanlan, "The New Religious Consciousness: Merezhkovskii and Berdiaev," *Canadian Slavic Studies* 4, no. 1 (Spring 1970), 19.

of the radical intelligentsia Merezhkovskii had no need to re-build his entire worldview. His synthesis used to sanctify autocracy. Now the same synthesis sanctifies revolution. The synthesis is not affected. Black or red paint, it doesn't matter; no paint sticks to it. The incorporeal shadows of abstraction are always colorless."[20]

The politics of the new religious consciousness resembled the "political romanticism" defined by Carl Schmitt, dwelling on antitheses in the phenomenal realm (subject/object, man/nature) only as "occasions" for the manifestation of some third, absolute power (community, God), in which "the concrete antithesis and heterogeneity disappear."[21] Since political romantics see the activity of this "third" element in art, manifest conflicts become occasions merely for the experience or "mood" of the individual artist, for his personal "activity and productivity": "The assent of the romantic occasionalist weaves a web for itself that is not touched by the real external world, and thus it is not refuted either."[22]

The contrast between the modernists' grandiose schemes and the actual course of events was conspicuous. Of Russia's military defeat by Japan in 1904 Rozanov later wrote: "When I think of the young sailors . . . I think that I would curse or revile anyone who said: 'So what? The sailors have passed on, but we're alive; let's discuss the issue of theocracy and the roles of the High Priest and Emperor.'"[23] With such acute social problems the "people" proved to have more urgent concerns. Rozanov argued that the entire "new religious consciousness" had passed largely unnoticed by the increasingly secularized population: "*obedient to the rites* and *formally belonging* to the Church, they had basically flown off, as if on Count Zeppelin's airships, far from the *mainland* and from these and any such religious themes, no longer knowing fundamentally what Christianity or paganism were."[24] Amidst the ever-broadening social crisis the idealists were obliged to take the measure of reality, but few if any rose to the task.

PETERSBURG–MOSCOW–PARIS, 1905

In one of the clearest demonstrations of their political romanticism the "idealist" philosophers and poets find themselves playing at revolution alongside some of the "realists" amidst widespread social tumult. After troops fire upon a column

[20] A. Dolinin, "Dmitrii Merezhkovskii" in S.A. Vengerov (ed.), *Russkaia literatura XX veka (1890–1910)*, 2 vols. (Moscow: XXI vek – Soglasie, 2000), vol. 1, pp. 231–232.

[21] Carl Schmitt, *Political Romanticism* (Guy Oakes (trans.), Cambridge, MA: MIT Press, 1986), p. 89.

[22] *Ibid.* pp. 96, 103. The radical critic N.K. Mikhailovskii compared Berdiaev's idealism to that of Novalis, who is also a central example of political romanticism for Schmitt.

[23] V.V. Rozanov, *Okolo narodnoi dushi* (Moscow: Respublika, 2003), p. 286.   [24] *Ibid.* p. 360.

of petitioners, led toward the Winter Palace by the enigmatic Father Georgii Gapon (1870–1906), Gippius, Merezhkovskii, and Andrei Belyi (1880–1934) set off to demand the closure of the theatres. They end up in a hall where, standing atop a chair, Belyi comes close to heeding Gapon's call to arms. Merezhkovskii and Gippius retreat home, while Belyi rushes back to Moscow to man the barricades.

Perhaps more surprising than the revolutionary convergence between ideal-ists and realists was the difference that quickly emerged between Petersburg and Moscow beginning in 1905. Gippius and Merezhkovskii quickly lost interest in political events. They left Petersburg for Odessa and then for Paris. Gippius later admitted that the couple "lived amidst different interests."[25] They ceded control of their journal to their rivals Berdiaev and Sergei Bulgakov (1871–1944), who rechristened it *Voprosy zhizni* (*Questions of Life*) and brought it more squarely into the ideological mainstream.[26] In 1907, Bulgakov was elected an independent deputy to the Second State Duma on a Christian Socialist platform. Meanwhile in Paris, where they remained for over two years, Merezhkovskii and Gippius wrote prolifically but ever more abstrusely on political subjects. They also dallied with radicals, even establishing close relations to a terrorist cell of the Socialist Revolutionary Party led by Boris Savinkov. Not only did the writers play at being revolutionaries, revolutionaries also played at writing. Gippius was liter-ary advisor for Savinkov's novel *Pale Horse* (published 1909), which provided an apocalyptic dramatization of the events of 1905, including the paradoxes of provocation and betrayal symbolized by the terrorist and police informer Evno Azef (1869–1918), who in 1906 had allegedly engineered the murder of Father Gapon (among other crimes). Merezhkovskii felt that Savinkov's fictional method was of crucial importance: "The religious question concerning violence can be answered not by reason, but by the 'something extra' that is more than reason."[27] By the same coin, Savinkov's practical experience transformed the fiction into "something extra": "the difference between Dostoevskii and *Pale Horse* is the same as between the chemical formula of an explosion and the explosion itself." [28] The revolutionary here was *artiste extraordinaire*, and vice versa.

Belyi retreated to Moscow where the modernists were intent on transforming their visions into concrete political practice. One radical political group, the Christian Brotherhood for Combat, was led by Vladimir Ern (1882–1917) and

[25] Zinaida Gippius, "Dmitrii Merezhkovskii" in *Zhivye litsa: Vospominaniia* (Tbilisi: Merani, 1991), p. 244.
[26] On this see especially the memoirs of the editorial secretary for *Novyi put'* and *Voprosy zhizni*: Georgii Chulkov, *Gody stranstvii* (Moscow: Ellis Lak, 1999).
[27] Merezhkovskii, *Bol'naia Rossiia*, p. 133.   [28] *Ibid.* p. 134.

the enigmatic Valentin Sventsitskii (1871–1931). Together with Pavel Florenskii (1882–1937), Ern and Sventsitskii represented a second generation of idealists to be dissatisfied with the polite academic reasoning of Bulgakov and his peers; they tried to act out its conclusions.[29] A student at the Moscow Seminary at Sergiev Posad, on March 12, 1906 Florenskii delivered an impassioned sermon protesting the execution of Lieutenant Pëtr Schmidt (1867–1906). Standing before an icon of the Crucifixion, Florenskii called to mind lurid images of Christ's suffering at the hands of the authorities, which images he then proceeded to compare to the actions of the Russian state:

Under the guise of "pacification" peaceful peasants and workers are being beaten. People who lack a crust of bread are being shot by one who lives on account of their labours . . . Christ was executed and people were silent, failing to defend him. His Body is being tortured and once again we are immersed in a shameless, self-loving acquiescence of murderers and rapists . . . Do you not realize that every shot is aimed at Christ's Body?[30]

What was most startling here was not Florenskii's urgent sense of injustice but the very notion that the state's repressive acts were first and foremost a matter for the church, which for 200 years had been a compliant instrument of state power. About this time Florenskii broke off relations with the Merezhkovskiis, to whom he wrote that "without a doubt there is a chasm between Sergiev Posad and Petersburg, between the home of the Venerable One [i.e., St. Sergius of Radonezh] and the city of the Emperor."[31] The idea of "ecclesiastization" (*otserkovlenie*) became a central element in Florenskii's work, most notably in his 1914 magnum opus *The Pillar and Ground of the Truth*. After a brief fascination with revolution, Florenskii, Sventsitskii, and Bulgakov (in addition to several lesser-known denizens of their milieu) accepted ordination as priests.

For their parts, Merezhkovskii and Gippius were unflagging in their criticism of the Muscovites' move towards the church. Gippius commented that "Christianity is not of the Church, but it is a path to the Church, the path of self-immersion in a solitary, personal faith."[32] Proceeding along this path, she continued, "one must look not backwards but forwards."[33] Merezhkovskii discounted Ern's dream of restoring authentic Orthodoxy, arguing that, like

[29] George F. Putnam, *Russian Alternatives to Marxism: Christian Socialism and Idealistic Liberalism in Twentieth-Century Russia* (Knoxville, TN: University of Tennessee Press, 1977), especially pp. 72–78.

[30] P.A. Florenskii, "Vopl' krovi," quoted from Sergei Golubtsov, *Moskovskaia Dukhovnaia Akademiia v revoliutsionnuiu epokhu* (Moscow: Martis, 1999), pp. 91–92.

[31] P.A. Florenskii, undated letter draft, from E.V. Ivanova (ed.), *Pavel Florenskii i simvolisty: Opyty literaturnye. Stat'i. Perepiska* (Moscow: Iazyki slavianskoi kul'tury, 2004), p. 515.

[32] Zinaida Gippius, *Dnevniki* (Moscow: Intelvak, 1999), vol. 1, p. 340.   [33] *Ibid.* vol. 1, p. 342.

Old Belief, Orthodoxy was first and foremost a matter of custom. Instead of "reformation," which would be tantamount to restoration, Merezhkovskii held to his program of revolution.[34]

The Muscovite response to the social crisis also found expression in nascent institutions of civil society. The Vladimir Solov'ëv Religious-Philosophical Society was founded in 1905 with the close participation of Berdiaev, Bulgakov, Florenskii, and Evgenii Trubetskoi (1863–1920). The Society attracted large and diverse crowds, including (in Ern's glowing account) "sectarians, Tolstoians, priests, young ladies, students, workers and the representatives of radical parties."[35] From 1910 it was closely associated with the publishing house *Put'* (*The Path*), named as if in polemical homage to the earlier Petersburg journal. From 1913, when Florenskii became editor of *Bogoslovskii Vestnik* (*Theological Herald*), members of the society gained a louder voice within the church. In retrospect, for the Muscovites 1905 turned out to be less about political ideology than about the church. For them the main result of 1905 was not the institution of the Duma in 1906 but the convocation of a church council in 1917, the first in over 300 years, in which religious philosophers like Trubetskoi and Bulgakov were leading lay participants.

ST. PETERSBURG, 1907

In the aftermath of 1905 intellectuals have gone from a revolutionary optimism to a feeling of profound malaise. Prime Minister Pëtr Stolypin (1862–1911) has begun a harsh crack-down on radicals, and intellectual disputes have retreated into private quarters. Most Wednesdays Russia's intellectual and cultural elite gather at Viacheslav Ivanov's apartment, which coincidentally but rather pointedly overlooks the Tauride Palace, where Duma sessions were held. Ivanov's cenacle is described by British historian Sir Bernard Pares who stays there in March 1907 while observing the Second State Duma:

The Ivanovs' flat was known as the Tower, and served as a meeting-place for a number of the most distinguished writers of the time. Here I met Alexander Blok, a young Apollo and the greatest poet of his generation; the dreamy-looking Andrey Bely; the bearded religious thinker, Nicholas Berdiayev; and the eccentric novelist, [Mikhail] Kuzmin, who lived in the flat. Kuzmin was a wonderful musician, and about three o'clock in the morning he would play the Appassionata of Beethoven on a fine piano, only just on the other side of a door in my room, against which lay my bed; but it would have been quite

[34] See D.S. Merezhkovskii, "Reformatsiia ili revoliutsiia?" in *V tikhom omute: Stat'i i issledovaniia raznykh let* (Moscow: Sovetskii pisatel', 1991), pp. 85–93.
[35] Vladimir Ern, quoted from Evgenii Gollerbakh, *K nezrimomu gradu: Religiozno-filosofskaia gruppa "Put'" (1910–1919) v poiskakh novoi russkoi identichnosti* (St. Petersburg: Aleteiia, 2000), p. 20.

impossible to have been anything but grateful to him. The family and their friends used to sit up all night, reading out to each other from their latest works, as yet unpublished, and criticising them in common. They begged me not to sing when I was in my bath in the morning, because that was the time when they were just going to bed. It was an exceptional and in some ways an eccentric environment, but it served admirably to balance the eccentric environment which filled the life of the poor Second Duma.[36]

This intimate atmosphere of artistic and intellectual experimentation found a distinctive, though controversial, expression in Georgii Chulkov's doctrine of mystical anarchism, which advocated social renewal through the intensification of individual spiritual experience. Revolution and religion, it seemed, had both gone indoors.

One of the first Wednesdays, on December 7, 1905, featured a dispute on Eros, featuring presentations by Berdiaev "The Metaphysics of Gender and Love" and Ivanov's own contribution "On a Love that Dares."[37] Berdiaev later recalled:

It became a real symposion, and speeches about love were delivered by such different people as the host Viacheslav Ivanov, Andrei Belyi who had travelled up from Moscow, the elegant professor Thaddeus Zieliński, Anatolii Lunacharskii, who saw the modern proletariat as the reincarnation of ancient Eros, and a materialist who recognized nothing apart from physiological processes.[38]

Eros provided these thinkers with a means of imagining social unity without compromising ideological difference. Berdiaev's presentation, published as "The Metaphysics of Sex and Love," underscored the objective significance of intimate experience: "People of the new mystical experience and new religious consciousness demand that from now on the most intimate things be brought out onto the universal historical path, that they be revealed in this path and that they determine it."[39] In their practical application these theoretical views could on occasion be taken to an absurd extreme. A case in point is the ritual Ivanov instigated on May 2, 1905 at the Petersburg home of modernist poet-philosopher Nikolai Minskii (1856–1937) and his wife Liudmila Vil'kina (1873–1920), who were both Jewish. Minskii's wife "donated" her blood, which the guests then passed around in a chalice. This supremely decadent rite, apparently intended as a proto-ecumenical bonding ceremony, succeeded only in creating a scandal for its almost self-parodic esotericism and

[36] Bernard Pares, *My Russian Memoirs* (London: Jonathan Cape, 1931), p. 132.
[37] Andrei Shishkin, "Simposion na peterburgskoi bashne v 1905–1906 gg." in *Russkie piry* (St. Petersburg: Kanun, 1998), pp. 273–352.
[38] Nikolai Berdiaev, "Ivanovskie sredy" in Vengerov (ed.), *Russkaia literatura XX veka (1890–1910)*, vol. 2, p. 235
[39] Berdiaev, *Novoe religioznoe soznanie i obshchestvennost'*, pp. 214–215.

anti-Semitic overtones.[40] Berdiaev recalled the incident with "an unpleasant feeling," simply because "like many phenomena of the time . . . everything was very literary, theatrical, and essentially frivolous."[41] The prevalence of intimate societies and anarchistic social teachings was symptomatic of a broad crisis of authority in Russian intellectual institutions. By 1907, some of the same figures had initiated a new Religious-Philosophical Society in St. Petersburg under the leadership of Berdiaev, Bulgakov, and Rozanov, but with the growing influence of Merezhkovskii, Gippius, and Ivanov, among others.

The abiding unity of the Russian modernist discourse is evident in its presentation for foreign readers. Noting a rise in interest in religion, "une sorte d'effervescence," in April 1907 the Paris-based journal *Mercure de France* began publishing the answers it had solicited to the question, "Are we witnessing a dissolution or evolution of the religious idea and religious feeling?" The question had been sent to a broad range of Europeans who provide a snapshot of intellectual life at the time, from Henri Bergson to H.G. Wells. The seven Russian respondents (of 141 in all), who were asked especially to comment on "the hostility of autocratic Orthodoxy towards liberalism,"[42] also provide a representative sample of intellectual opinion at a crucial historical juncture. Evgenii de Roberti (1843–1915), an academic philosopher and sociologist from the Russian School in Paris, voiced the still-dominant view of materialist science. He stated that religion as such was in terminal decline thanks to the spread of knowledge and "the contagious example of elites" who had long since ceased to believe; the religious problem was merely the social problem in disguise.[43] A similar answer was provided by the Bolshevik Georgii Plekhanov (1856–1918), who suggested rephrasing the question to read: "Isn't the dissolution of the religious idea a necessary condition of its evolution?"[44] Indifferent to the fate of religion as such, Plekhanov merely expressed his concern that morality be successfully detached from outmoded beliefs.

The materialists were outnumbered by idealists who predicted that the future would bring a new kind of religion. Ivan Novikov (1877–1959), a writer with links to the Petersburg modernists, admitted that since the "idea of God is an anthropomorphic error of the human spirit," the only "true religion [is]

---

[40] See Vasilii Rozanov's wicked account of the evening: V.V. Rozanov, *Sakharna* (Moscow: Respublika, 1998), pp. 336–339; cf. L.A. Il'iunina, *Russkoe revoliutsionnoe dvizhenie i problemy razvitiia literatury. Mezhvuzovskii sbornik* (Leningrad: Izd-vo Leningradskogo Universiteta, 1989), pp. 178–180.

[41] N.A. Berdiaev, *Samopoznanie (Opyt filosofskoi antropologii)* (Moscow: Kniga, 1991), p. 157.

[42] Frédéric Charpin, "La Question religieuse: Enquête internationale," *Mercure de France* no. 236 (April 15, 1907), 37, 38.

[43] Eugène de Roberty, in *Mercure de France* no. 239 (June 1, 1907), 437–438.

[44] Georges Plékhanoff, in *Mercure de France* no. 236 (April 15, 1907), 617.

religion without God";[45] in this sense traditional religion was doomed by the spread of education. Nonetheless, Novikov suggested, as a source of distinct comfort and even pleasure religious ritual will always remain. More radical was Merezhkovskii who, affirming his characteristic Hegelian model of dialectical revolution instead of evolution, felt that modernity was witnessing a critical moment akin to the birth of Christianity which would result in a grand apocalyptic synthesis: "The pre-Christian religions are the thesis; Christianity is the antithesis; the religion of the Spirit is the synthesis."[46] Merezhkovskii anticipated that the Spirit "will give humanity the new name of the Son of God, Divine Humanity."[47] Elsewhere at the time Merezhkovskii predicted that, joined in their common sacrifice, "all the martyrs of the revolutionary and religious movements in Russia" would "merge into one," marking Russia's transition "from the Orthodox Church and autocratic state into the universal church of the Single High Priest and the universal kingdom of the Single King – Christ."[48] Merezhkovskii anticipated that theocracy would look like anarchism from the outside and like socialism from the inside, manifesting "a perfect synthesis of endlessly free personality and endlessly loving society."[49] In his response to the questionnaire, Berdiaev affirmed that religion would continue to develop in the sense of "the truth concerning humanity, the truth of its redemption on earth": "history is moving towards a free theocracy that will be equally distant from the Catholic caesarism of the popes and the Orthodox papism of the tsars."[50]

Most curious was the response of Nikolai Minskii, who combined radical politics with speculative metaphysics:

The fundamental character of mystical ideas and feelings is that they are absolutely desirable and at the same time *meonic*, that is to say, absolutely opposed to our entire experience ([based on the Greek] *me on*, non-existent). But this is not the opposition of a miraculous phenomenon (as is always the God of believers), but that of an ideal that is ever inaccessible.[51]

Minskii's "meonism" reconciled the "two divine principles – absolute existence and absolute non-existence," represented by western and eastern religions respectively, in the assertion of existence as a potential that humanity strives to

[45] J. Novicow, in *Mercure de France* no. 240 (June 15, 1907), 648, 649.

[46] Dmitry Merejkowsky, in *Mercure de France* no. 237 (May 1, 1907), 69. Earlier in the year *Mercure de France* had issued a collection of essays by Merezhkovskii, Gippius, and Dmitrii Filosofov: *Le Tzar et la révolution* (Paris, 1907).

[47] Dmitry Merejkowsky, in *Mercure de France* no. 237 (May 1, 1907), 71.

[48] D.S. Merezhkovskii, *Ne mir, no mech*, pp. 116–17.   [49] Merezhkovskii, *Ne mir, no mech*, p. 38.

[50] Nicolas Berdaieff, in *Mercure de France* no. 241 (July 1, 1907), 38.

[51] [Nikolai] Minsky, in *Mercure de France* no. 239 (June 1, 1907), 444–445. For Minskii's most succinct summation of his ideas, see [N.M. Minskii], "'Meonizm' N.M. Minskogo v szhatom izlozhenii avtora" in Vengerov (ed.), *Russkaia literatura XX veka (1890–1910)*, vol. 1, p. 340–444.

fulfill: "According to meonism, divinity is conceived as absolute Unity which, out of love for the world of multiplicity, dies voluntarily, sacrifices itself continually for the universe and revives in the universe's aspiration for absolute Unity."[52] The result, for Minskii, is a unitary religion of disinterested love and sacrifice, eminently reconcilable to radical socialism.

The idealists' attempt to synthesize revolution and religion continued to resonate on the radical Left, as is shown by the response of Maxim Gor'kii (1868–1936), a writer with radical political views who was exiled from Russia after 1905. Gor'kii conceded the death of "the idea of God as a supernatural being directing the destinies of the universe and of men," but confidently predicted the transformation of religion through the human "creative process": "The religious sentiment as I understand it must exist, develop and make man perfect."[53] This idea of God as a political project, shared by Lunacharskii, Aleksandra Kollontai (1872–1952), and others, became known as "God-building" (*bogostroitel'stvo*). Informed by George Sorel's syndicalism and Joseph Dietzgen's "religion of socialism," God-building continued the collectivist revision of Bolshevism pioneered by Bogdanov and became the latest idealist heresy for Lenin to combat in the Bolshevik ranks.[54]

Responding to these developments on the Left, Viacheslav Ivanov proposed a union between the modernist "God-seekers" and Marxist "God-builders" on the basis of their shared faith in the people (*narod*) as the ultimate source of a new social order in Russia. The authority of the people, in turn, was based on the fact that, for Ivanov, Russians were a nation of mystics:

The Russian soul instinctually thirsts for the absolute, instinctually renouncing all that is conditional. It is barbarically noble, i.e. profligate and recklessly broad like the empty steppe, where the snowstorm covers nameless graves. It unconsciously rebels against all that is artificial and all that is artificially raised to the status of value and idol, taking its tendency to devalue to the extreme of insulting the human image and humiliating the personality, which just an instant before was so proud and uncontrollable; to the extreme of distrusting everything in man that carries the divine seal, whether in the name of God or of no one. It carries this tendency to the extreme of the intoxicated soul's suicidal impulses, to all kinds of theoretical and practical nihilism . . . Only among Russians can one observe a true will for organic universality.[55]

---

[52] [Nikolai] Minsky, in *Mercure de France* no. 241 (July 1, 1907), 55. In this postscript to his original response Minskii focuses on his debt to German philosopher Philipp Mainländer (1841–1876).

[53] Maxime Gorki, in *Mercure de France* no. 236 (April 15, 1907), 594, 595.

[54] Williams, *The Other Bolsheviks*, pp. 85–102.

[55] Viacheslav Ivanov, "On the Russian Idea" in Michael Wachtel (ed.), *Selected Essays* (Robert Bird (trans.), Evanston, IL: Northwestern University Press, 2001), p. 139; on Russia as "millions of mystics," see p. 131.

Instead of sending his answer to the *Mercure de France*, Ivanov published it as a separate essay entitled "Thou Art," in which he described how, at the very depths of negation, the human soul discovers the divine in an event of "orgiastic frenzy" or "ecstasy."[56] Ivanov presents this birth of religion as a gendered event: the feminine soul accepts the masculine spirit as a bride accepts her bridegroom; thus Ivanov joins religious (and, specifically, Christian) mysticism to erotic ecstasy.

Ivanov's essay "Thou Art" marks one of the most gloriously esoteric moments of Russian modernism, where the movement overlaps with theosophy and anthroposophy, seeming to abandon any meaningful philosophical or social relevance. In a "Postscriptum" Ivanov calls the essay a "continuation" of his work on mystical anarchism, which, as one of the most influential attempts to provide a social transcription of the impulses animating Russian culture at the time, had recently been written up in *Mercure de France*.[57] Across the ideological spectrum one encounters faith in the untapped potential of human imagination. The need to mediate intimate and public concerns allowed a leading role in ideological and even philosophical discourse to be played by artistic images and narratives. As a result, to a greater degree perhaps than anywhere else, intellectual culture in Russia overlapped with the development of a modern image culture.

MOSCOW, 1915

On April 16, the religious-philosophical elite gather in the rain at Novodevichii Monastery for the funeral of composer Aleksandr Scriabin (1872–1915), who has passed away suddenly from an acute infection two days earlier. Even before the funeral his friends establish a society in Scriabin's memory, featuring, in addition to the most prominent composers, musicians, and music critics of the day, poets and philosophers like Ivanov and Bulgakov. Amidst the hardships of war and the intensification of revolutionary struggle one might expect the event to mark the symbolic burial of the modernist imaginary. Remarkably, this is not the case.

Since its founding in 1905, the Vladimir Solov'ëv Religious-Philosophical Society had gradually shifted to the right. After the outbreak of World War I, the Society hosted many patriotic events, including Vladimir Ern's impassioned and infamous speech "From Kant to Krupp" (delivered October 6, 1914),

---

[56] See especially the first publication of this essay: Viacheslav Ivanov, "Ty esi," *Zolotoe runo*, no. 7 (1907), 100–102.

[57] E. Séménoff, "Le Mysticisme Anarchique," *Mercure de France* (July 16, 1907), 361–364.

where he drew a direct line from Kant's analytical rationalism to the German war machine. Ern thought that Russian statehood, by contrast, expressed the spiritual ideal of the church, which was now withstanding "with great spiritual power and under the protection of the Most Pure Mother of God" the worst excesses of European modernity in an apocalyptic struggle.[58] Elsewhere, Ern drew on the example of St. Sergius of Radonezh, who had blessed Russian forces before their victory over the Mongols on Kulikovo Field in 1380.[59] For Ern, "Holy Russia is not a concept of popular ideology or a Kantian 'regulative' idea of the national Russian consciousness, but an absolutely concrete, mystically real sanctuary of the nation's noetic labour and its spiritual being."[60] After the February Revolution of 1917, several members of the Society took leading parts in the All-Russian Church Council that elected Patriarch Tikhon. In all of these contexts the Society diligently distinguished itself from the decadents of the 1900s; those Petersburgers who relocated to Moscow, like Ivanov in 1913, seemed immediately immersed in the atmosphere of traditional Orthodoxy and drifted to the Right. However, many members of the Society, notably Florenskii, Bulgakov, and Ivanov, remained in the thrall of the aesthetic image and indeed saw reality itself as an image.

For his part, Scriabin had gradually transformed himself from a virtuosic pianist-composer à la Chopin into an exceptionally ambitious experimenter. His 1910 work *Prometheus* included for the first time notation for colour projection to accompany the music. Subsequently, Scriabin conceived of a massive multimedia extravaganza called *Mysterium* which, after a conversation with the composer, Ern described as something "in which there won't be spectators, but all will be participants, in which there will be a partial synthesis between the arts: music, dance and light effects."[61] As the project developed, Scriabin came to feel that a successful performance of the *Mysterium* might well lead to a cosmic event, possibly even to the apocalypse. For better or for worse, Scriabin's sudden demise prevented him from realizing his conception; he left behind only sketches of a *Preliminary Act*, which he had begun on his friends' advice as a kind of run-up to the *Mysterium*. Still, Scriabin's unwritten music long reverberated in the minds of the Moscow religious philosophers, to whom it extended a path of direct intervention in the fabric of reality, without mediation in the realm of ideological discourse and political action.

The religious philosophers were attracted by Scriabin's realization that, having been derived from ritual, art could only achieve its potential by once again

---

[58] V.F. Ern, *Sochineniia* (Moscow: Pravda, 1991), p. 318.   [59] *Ibid.* pp. 297–298.   [60] *Ibid.* p. 398.
[61] V.I. Keidan (ed.), *Vzyskuiushchie grada. Khronik chastnoi zhizni russkikh religioznykh filosofov v pis'makh i dnevnikakh* (Moscow: Iazyki russkoi kul'tury, 1997), p. 603.

becoming a form of direct religious action, what Vladimir Solov'ëv had termed *theurgy*. Berdiaev, with his typical emphasis on the individual actor, stressed the heroic, Promethean aspects of Scriabin's theurgic task: "In his frenzied creative impulse Scriabin sought not a new art, not a new culture, but a new earth and a new heaven. He had a sense of the end of the old world and wanted to create a new cosmos."[62] Others, most notably Ivanov, stressed the cosmic sweep of Scriabin's project, seeing it as "direct evidence of a turning point that is coming to pass in the consciousness of humanity":

Scriabin's break with the entire musical past was the break of a modern genius with humanism in music. His harmony leads beyond the limits of a humanly secure, studied, and well-formed circle, such as Bach's tempered clavier. The canon, and not only the aesthetic canon, but also the essentially ethical one, is based on the idea of the unity of the normative activity of the human spirit. The rejection of the canon is musical trans-humanism, which must seem to every right-thinking humanist not even "native" chaos, which "gives birth to a star," but "a horrible cry of insanity, that shakes the soul," a paean of frenzy and destruction.[63]

Not everyone, even among the Moscow religious philosophers, was persuaded by Scriabin's intellectual pretensions. Vladimir Ern reflected: "He is not simply a musician by God's grace, 'singing as the birds sing,' but a philosopher who sets his music philosophical tasks, and these tasks are spiritually flawed."[64]

Immediately after Scriabin's death, Ivanov set to work on a "lyrical trilogy" of immense size and complexity, which eventually became the "melopeia" or narrative poem *Chelovek* (*Man*), a literary transcription of Scriabin's *Mysterium*. In *Chelovek*, Ivanov tells the story of creation as the fall of Lucifer (the principle of "I am") from divine being ("I AM"). Derived from Lucifer, cut off from God, man struggles to assert himself until he recognizes within himself the imprint of God and says to Him "Thou Art." Linked to Ivanov's 1907 essay on the future of religion, *Chelovek* was first read on March 30, 1916 at a meeting of the Religious-Philosophical Society, eliciting a lively debate in the press. Critics complained that, at least for the Moscow religious philosophers, instead of becoming ritual, modern art was in danger of becoming theology.

One of the last acts of the original Scriabin Society was Ivanov's lecture "Scriabin and the Spirit of Revolution," read on October 24, 1917, the very eve of the Bolshevik take-over in Petrograd. Ivanov argued that Scriabin's apocalyptic ideal was a more authentic revolution than that envisioned by the Bolsheviks, but strangely enough Bolshevik cultural authorities shared this affinity for Scriabin's

---

[62] N.A. Berdiaev, *Filosofiia tvorchestva, kul'tury i iskusstva* (Moscow: Iskusstvo, Liga, 1994), vol. 2, p. 396.
[63] *Selected Essays*, pp. 211, 171. [64] *Vzyskuiushchie grada*, p. 603.

theomachic spirit. As early as July 30, 1918, Lenin ordered a monument erected to the composer. Scriabin's *Prometheus* was then performed at a gala concert on the eve of the first anniversary of the October Revolution, November 6, 1918, with Lenin in attendance and with a speech by Lunacharskii. Lunacharskii later called Scriabin's music "the supreme gift of musical romanticism to the revolution."[65] A Scriabin Museum was opened on July 17, 1922, and as late as 1930, Lunacharskii was writing that "Scriabin is still quite close and kindred to us, and . . . the musicians who will be creating the new music of the epoch when we will approach the realization of socialism can learn very much from Scriabin."[66] Scriabin's *Mysterium* culminated in the mass festivals promoted by the Bolshevik authorities in 1919–1921 and again in the late 1920s (after which they quickly turned into closely orchestrated parades). Ivanov even collaborated with Lunacharskii and others in providing the theoretical basis for these festivals. Thus, despite the death and exile of many of the original decadents and idealists, the mass festivals and Scriabin celebrations of the early Soviet era once again testified to the ability of the Russian modernists of all ideological stripes to unify around grand aesthetic projections.

The Bolshevik Revolution put paid to the modernists' political schemes, largely because the modernists failed in their utopian attempts to delineate a rival concept of power to those embodied by the autocratic state and the revolutionary conspirators. However, in significant respects the Bolshevik Revolution actually represented the victory of the modernist, "idealist" imagination. Like Russian modernism, early Bolshevik culture was based on the search for a new ritual that would produce images projecting a new society. Thus, the most influential ideological groupings, whether materialist or idealist, shared the notion that history can be imagined as a totality and reshaped through aesthetic activity.

---

[65] A.V. Lunacharskii, "Taneev i Skriabin" in *V mire muzyki: Stat'i i rechi* (Moscow: Sovetskii kompozitor, 1971), p. 140.

[66] A.V. Lunacharskii, "Znachenie Skriabina dlia nashego vremeni" in *A.N. Skriabin i ego muzei* (Moscow: MONO, 1930), p. 14.

14

ESCHATOLOGY AND HOPE IN SILVER
AGE THOUGHT

JUDITH DEUTSCH KORNBLATT

> Panmongolism! Although the word is wild
> It caresses my ear,
> As though full of the portend
> Of God's great fate.   Vladimir Solov'ëv, 1894

It is only natural that this chapter should begin with an epigraph from a poem by Vladimir Solov'ëv (1853–1900), arguably the figure most influential for the modernist thinkers in Russia's pre-revolutionary period. That this particular poem, "Panmongolizm" ("Panmongolism," 1894, published 1905), should have pride of place is also no accident. These four lines, the first of a nine-stanza paean to a mysterious Asiatic force bent on the destruction of holy Moscow, preface Solov'ëv's own "Kratkii povest' ob Antikhriste" ("Short Tale of the Antichrist," 1899), published the year before he died. Two of the lines also serve as epigraph to the poem "Skify" ("The Scythians," 1918) by the symbolist poet Aleksandr Blok (1880–1921), thus in many ways bracketing the two-decade period known as the Silver Age of Russian culture. Between the two appeared a number of other poems, essays, and stories about an apocalyptic invasion from the East, most notably "Griadushchie gunny" ("The Coming Huns," 1904–1905) by Valerii Briusov (1873–1924). The juxtaposition of these three poems serves as a door into the spiritual and philosophical preoccupations of an entire generation of intellectuals as they anticipated the demise of Russian autocracy.[1]

---

[1] I would like to thank Melissa Miller for her invaluable assistance with all aspects of research for this chapter. I would also like to thank the late Robert A. Maguire, who first suggested to me the links between these three poems. The three poems have previously been considered in combination by Ettore Lo Gatto in "*Panmongolismo* di V. Solov'ëv, *I Venienti Unni* di V. Brjusov e *Gli Sciti* di A. Blok" in Morris Halle et al., *For Roman Jakobson: Essays on the Occasion of his Sixtieth Birthday* (The Hague: Mouton & Co., 1956), pp. 295–300. The poems are also juxtaposed, although much more briefly, in Renato Poggioli, "Qualis Artifex Pereo! Or Barbarism and Decadence," *Harvard Library Bulletin* 13, no. 1 (Winter 1959), 135–159. See also O.A. Ovcharenko, "Stikhotvorenie A. Bloka 'Skify' i traditsii russkoi literatury," *Vestnik Moskovskogo Universiteta*, series 9, *Filologiia*, no. 5 (1990), 12–20; and Boris Thomson, "Blok and Belyi: Divergent Readings of the Poetry of Vladimir

The anxiety permeating the Silver Age centered in large part on a perceived tension between individual and whole, between the ethically autonomous *lichnost'* and the amorphous masses, and thus concerned the very meaning of humanity. As a number of chapters have already shown, a preoccupation with the relationship of the one and the many was inherited by late-imperial intellectuals from early in the nineteenth century. This chapter suggests that the tension took on new meaning as revolutionary fervor – and fears – grew in the first two decades of the last century. The dangers, even evil, of choosing empty individualism over moribund totality (or vice versa) were often expressed in terms of West and East: the West imagined as the rampant egoism in a disintegrating Europe, the East representing undifferentiated oneness. Russia (or rather the evocative concept of ancient and holy Rus') sat uncomfortably between the two, as the country had historically, "absorbing" the Mongol invasion of the thirteenth to fifteenth centuries. In this prevailing view of a Russia poised between West and East, the Russian people were fated to transfigure western fragmentation and eastern absolutism into a new age of integration.[2]

The creative interaction between one and many paralleled another tension, also raised by Solov'ëv and preoccupying his heirs in the next generation: the uneasy coexistence of faith in salvation and a pervading fear of the dramatic ending toward which the modern world seemed to be hurtling. I argue here that Solov'ëv's writings, while recognizing the palpable existence of evil in the world, nonetheless successfully integrated hope with recognition of the potential end to Russian hegemony through his repeated emphasis on the role of active human participation in our own salvation. Solov'ëv's continued faith in humanity's salvific power led him to focus on the responsibility of the individual for the creation of civil society and to recognize the value of rational struggle in promoting social progress.[3] As he wrote in 1897, let the seeker of the future "struggle to carry the sacred burden of the past across the real flood of history... *He who saves shall be saved.* That is the secret of progress – there is and will be no other."[4] Over the course of two decades following his death and

Solov'ëv" in *Symbolism and After: Essays on Russian Poetry in Honour of Georgette Donchin* (London: Bristol Classical Press, 1992), pp. 39–57.

[2] See Solov'ëv's 1877 essay "Tri sily" in V.S. Solov'ëv, *Polnoe sobranie sochinenii i pisem v dvadtsati tomakh*, 3 vols. (Moscow: Nauka, 2000–2001), vol. 1, p. 207.

[3] For an excellent analysis of Solov'ëv's transformation of the church's doctrine of salvation, see Richard F. Gustafson, "Soloviev's Doctrine of Salvation" in Judith Deutsch Kornblatt and Richard F. Gustafson (eds.), *Russian Religious Thought* (Madison, WI: University of Wisconsin Press, 1996), pp. 31–48.

[4] "Taina progressa" in S.M. Solov'ëv and E.L. Radlov (eds.), *Sobranie sochinenii Vladimira Sergeevicha Solov'ëva*, 2nd edn., 10 vols. (St. Petersburg: Prosveshchenie, 1911–1914), vol. 9, pp. 85, 86. Subsequent citations to this source indicated as *SS*.

leading up to the Russian Revolution, Solov'ëv's modernist heirs continued to articulate their mentor's belief in the active integration of opposites, but became increasingly irrational in their faith in progress. As they grappled with the meaning of evil and the chaos that multiplied around them, they ultimately welcomed the inhuman masses from their imagined Orient, not in the spirit of hope, but of despair.

The focus on three poets in this chapter by no means ignores the contribution to the related themes of eschatology, hope, and apocalypse in other Silver Age writers. A cursory perusal of titles alone confirms the preoccupation of modernist writers with the end of civilization. Note, for example, an essay by symbolist writer and friend of Blok, Andrei Belyi (pseudonym of B.N. Bugaev, 1880–1934), called "The Apocalypse in Russian Poetry" (1905) that begins, like Blok's "The Scythians," with an epigraph from "Panmongolism." Belyi's novel *Petersburg* (1916, 1922) is replete with apocalyptic imagery. Indeed, eschatological thinking was everywhere among the creative intelligentsia.[5] Consider, for example, the comment of L.A. Tikhomirov, quoted in one of Belyi's prose collections: "Apocalypse is the latest fashion."[6] Dmitrii Merzhkovskii, already discussed in this volume, wrote frequently of the coming end, of the Antichrist, and of the hoped for Second Coming of Christ, most notably in his trilogy of historical novels referred to as *Christ and Antichrist* (1896–1905) and in his survey of Russian literature, *Christ and Antichrist in Russian Literature: Tolstoi and Dostoevskii* (1901–1903). Vasilii Rozanov (1856–1919) in *The Apocalypse of Our Time* (1917–1918), published toward the end of the Silver Age, builds on the theme as well. Other writers who focused on the tension between hope and eschatology include the maverick existentialist Lev Shestov (1866–1938), the innovative modernist author Aleksei Remizov (1877–1957), and members of the "Scythian" movement, especially R.V. Ivanov-Razumnik (1878–1946). As the symbolist poet and theoretician Viacheslav Ivanov (1866–1949) claimed once in the presence of Blok, "The period of crisis and of the Last Judgment is beginning."[7]

---

[5] A. Belyi, *Petersburg* (St. Petersburg, 1916, 1922). For a definition of the "creative intelligentsia" as distinct from the political intelligentsia of the pre-revolutionary period, see Maria Carlson, *"No Religion Higher Than Truth": A History of the Theosophical Movement in Russia, 1875–1922* (Princeton University Press, 1993), p. 7.

[6] *Nachalo veka* (Moscow and Leningrad: GIKhl, 1933), p. 140; also cited in Sergei Hackel, *The Poet and the Revolution: Aleksandr Blok's "The Twelve"* (Oxford: Clarendon Press, 1975), p. 2.

[7] Cited in *ibid.* p. 2. Robert Bird in chapter 13 mentions other apocalyptic texts of the time. Although the two adjectives technically have different meanings, I use "eschatological" and "apocalyptic" largely interchangeably as did the modernist thinkers. Apocalypse refers more narrowly to a series of texts in Jewish and early Christian tradition (most notably the Book of Daniel and the Revelation of John) that narrate a specific struggle between good and evil using esoteric symbolism to describe a

SOLOV'ËV'S "ESCHATOLOGICAL" TALE

We return now to the epigraph to this chapter from Solov'ëv's "Short Tale of the Antichrist" in *Tri razgovora* (*Three Conversations*), a set of three dialogues with the subtitle *O voine, progresse i kontse vsemirnoi istorii* (*War, Progress, and the End of History,* 1899). With an explicit, if left-handed bow to Plato (see *SS* 10, p. 92/tr. p. 30),[8] Solov'ëv used the dialogue form to direct his readers toward an interpretation of his subtitle. Despite the prevalent dramatic genre, Solov'ëv also embedded a lengthy prose story within the text. Paul Valliere concludes about both Solov'ëv's and Plato's dialogues (*Gorgias* and *Republic* specifically): "In the end, however, the philosopher must resort to an eschatological parable to cap his justification of the good."[9] Solov'ëv's goal was indeed a "justification of the good," the title of an almost contemporaneous work (*Opravdanie dobra,* 1894–1898; *SS* 8, pp. 1–516). The juxtaposition of Solov'ëv's two works (one a lengthy philosophical treatise, the other three dramatic dialogues) reminds us that the drawing room conversations between a Lady, a Prince, a General, a Politician, and a character named only Mr. Z are not only a fictional portrayal about war at the end of history, as the title of the embedded story suggests, but also a hybrid discussion about the possibility of good within history. Examined as a whole, *Three Conversations* turns out to imagine neither good nor evil alone, but rather to dramatize the active interaction of the two opposing poles. Furthermore, evil for Solov'ëv was not fiction, not the mere absence of good. He regarded evil as a force that must be actively confronted to save both the world and the saviors themselves. Solov'ëv saw humanity as destined to reconcile the end of time with hope in salvation, as Russia was destined to reconcile West and East.

Why, though, in this popular work written just one year before his untimely death, did Solov'ëv have to "resort to" a short story featuring the Antichrist, an "eschatological parable," as Valliere declares? Solov'ëv himself tried to explain (*SS* 10, p. 88/tr. pp. 21–22):

hidden disclosure about a time after the end of time. In this future, usually revealed to the prophet in a dream, evil will be defeated and only the chosen few will remain. In common parlance, however, "apocalyptic" has come to describe a time near to or coincident with the "eschatological" end, when mass destruction will lead to God's Final Judgment. For more on apocalypsis in this period, see Frank Kermode, "Apocalypse and the Modern" in Saul Friedlander, Gerald Holton, Leo Marx, and Eugene Skolnikoff (eds.), *Visions of Apocalypse: End or Rebirth* (New York: Holmes and Meier, 1985), pp. 84–106.

[8] All citations from *Three Conversations* will be cited from *SS*, followed by reference to the translation of Vladimir Solovyov, *War, Progress and the End of History: Three Conversations Including a Short Story of the Anti-Christ* (Alexander Bakshy (trans.), Thomas R. Beyer, Jr. (rev.), Hudson, NY: Lindisfarne Press, 1990). I have modified the translation slightly when necessary.

[9] Paul Valliere, *Modern Russian Theology: Bukharev, Soloviev, Bulgakov, Orthodox Theology in a New Key* (Edinburgh: T&T Clark and Grand Rapids, MI: Eerdmans, 2000), p. 219.

At first I treated this subject in the form of a dialogue, as I had treated the other parts, and with a similar sprinkling of jocularity. But friendly criticisms convinced me that this method of exposition was doubly unsuitable; first, because the interruptions and interpolations required by the form of dialogue tended to weaken the interest in the story; and second, because the colloquial and particularly the jocular character of conversation did not accord with the subject's religious importance. I recognized the justice of these criticisms and, accordingly, altered the form of the Third Conversation, introducing in it the reading from a manuscript left by a monk after his death and containing an independent "Short Story of the Antichrist."

Thus Solov'ëv signaled the significance of the short story form (supposedly uninterrupted in form and serious in tone) for a complete reading of his work on the "end of history."

The following reading of *Three Conversations* is revisionist,[10] for virtually all scholars have followed the more pessimistic and apocalyptic readings of Solov'ëv's Silver Age heirs who are the focus of the remainder of this chapter. They tended to see only a narrative of destruction in "Short Story of the Antichrist," missing its overriding hope. Indeed, immediately upon publication, readers began to claim that Solov'ëv had repudiated his earlier faith in humanity. According to Evgenii Trubetskoi, "In his new understanding, we no longer find that earthly completion of progress that earlier seemed so necessary to the philosopher."[11] In more dramatic terms, the critic Konstantin Mochul'skii claimed: "Solov'ëv castigated himself as well... That is why the tone of *Three Conversations* rises to tragic passion; Solov'ëv could not have died without writing it. It is his repentance."[12] Later, Dmitrii Stremooukhoff wrote that Solov'ëv had recognized at last that "theocracy will not be realized in history."[13] When the Antichrist appeared for twenty pages or so, readers concluded that violent apocalypse was the dominant genre of the entire "justification of good."

Instead, Solov'ëv quite openly asks us to note that the larger frame of the third philosophical dialogue includes a piece of deliberately creative fiction, embedded, as it were, in a manuscript itself replete with puns, interpolated poems and stories, and general attention to words and genres. Furthermore, the story itself breaks off before completion, drawing attention to itself and its form.

[10] Also see two of my previous essays: "Soloviev on Salvation: The Story of the 'Short Story of the Antichrist'" in Kornblatt and Gustafson (eds.), *Russian Religious Thought*, pp. 68–87; and "The Truth of the Word: Solovyov's *Three Conversations* Speaks on Tolstoy's *Resurrection*," *Slavic and East European Journal* 45, no. 2 (2001), 301–321.
[11] E.N. Trubetskoi, *Mirosozertsanie Vl.S. Solov'ëva*, 2 vols. (Moscow: Tovarishchestvo tipografii A. Mamontova, 1913), vol. 2, p. 302.
[12] Konstantin Mochul'skii, *Vladimir Solov'ëv: Zhizn' i uchenie*, 2nd edn. (Paris: YMCA Press, 1951), p. 256.
[13] Dmitrii Stremooukhoff, *Vladimir Soloviev and His Messianic Work* (Philip Guilbeau and Heather Elise MacGregor (eds.), Elizabeth Meyendorff (trans.), Belmont, MA: Nordland, 1980), p. 331.

The clearly fictional author, we are told, bequeathed an incomplete manuscript
to Mr. Z, who, now as editor, reads it to yet other invented characters, as well
as to the implied reader as we eavesdrop on the created scene and the fanciful
narration. All of these tried and true literary tropes (the inherited manuscript,
the focus on words and wordplay, indeed the existence of an epigraph itself)
suggest that we must attend to *how* the story is *narrated*, that is, to its literary
aspects, as much as or more than to its "simple" meaning.[14]

As Solov'ëv informs the reader of *Three Conversations*, "All took their seats,
and Mr. Z began to read his manuscript" (*SS* 10, p. 193/tr. p. 159). The short
story relates how an Emperor-Superman took advantage of a grand struggle
between the "Panmongol" East and the "European" West to rise up and offer
himself as benefactor to humanity. Like Dostoevskii's Grand Inquisitor, who
was clearly one of the inspirations for the character, the Emperor offers security
in exchange for total subservience.[15] That the Superman gained his power from
"a strange figure gleaming with a dim phosphorescent light" whose "two eyes
pierced his soul with their painful penetrating glitter," and that the voice of
this strange figure emerges "from inside or outside him – he could not tell
which" (*SS* 10, p. 200/tr. p. 168), should leave no doubt that the Emperor-
Superman is a rather melodramatic incarnation of the Antichrist himself. The
story continues with the triumph of the Emperor over virtually all the world,
while a few helpless representatives of the three major Christian denominations
escape into the desert to await the Second Coming. A woman "clothed in the
sun with the moon beneath her feet and a wreath of twelve stars on her head"
(see Revelation 12:1) appears to lead them to find divine assistance at Mt. Sinai
(*SS* 10, p. 218/tr. p. 190). Thus, "The Short Story of the Antichrist" as written
appears to narrate the triumph of evil in the world and ends on an apocalyptic
vision dependent upon divine intervention. This reading seems to deny the
possibility of salvific human action. It is no wonder that critics sensed a change
of tone in this work toward capitulation and tragedy, rather than the faith in
salvation that Solov'ëv exhibited throughout his earlier career.

Most readers forget, however, that "here the reader stopped," as the written
text again self-consciously informs us. With some cajoling from the other
characters, Mr. Z agrees to narrate the rest of the story that he "remembers
only in its main outlines" (*SS* 10, p. 218/tr. p. 191). In the oral completion,

---

[14] On the illusion of simplicity, see an analysis of Solov'ëv's polemic with Tolstoi's novel *Resurrection*
in Kornblatt, "The Truth of the Word."

[15] See Marina Kostalevsky, *Dostoevsky and Soloviev: The Art of Integral Vision* (New Haven, CT: Yale
University Press, 1997) for an excellent discussion of the friendship between Dostoevskii and the
much younger Solov'ëv.

the Jews rise up to confront the Emperor, since they "unexpectedly discovered that he was *not even circumcised*." This "army of Jews, one million strong, soon took Jerusalem and locked up the Anti-Christ" (*SS* 10, p. 219/tr. p. 192). The ensuing fight includes an earthquake, volcano, and streams of fire (all reminiscent of divine or demonic manipulation in other apocalyptic tales) but the supernatural magic of the Emperor proves of no avail against the newly invigorated human host. The remaining Christians ultimately emerge from the desert, unite with the Jews, and "for a thousand years, they lived and reigned with Christ." Although Christ appears at the end of the oral story "with the wounds from the nails in his outstretched hands" (*SS* 10, p. 220/tr. p. 193), salvation from the Antichrist's evil intentions in fact comes from the all-too-human efforts to overcome evil by the otherwise lowly Jews, not from any kind of belated divine intervention. Not apocalypse, but faith in human salvation triumphs at the true end of the story, when both its written and oral parts are taken together. Humanity survives in Solov'ëv's rendition of the seemingly supernatural struggle between good and evil because of humanist values and human actions.

Let us now look more closely at the epigraph from "Panmongolism," at its position in *Three Conversations*, and at the full text of the poem from which the inscription is taken. As we saw, with all the characters seated around him, Mr. Z takes up the manuscript of a tale allegedly written by an acquaintance, the monk Pansophius. The name of the supposed author is significant, as it is a pun on two of Solov'ëv's most important ideas: "pan" for all-unity (*vsëedinstvo*) and "sophius" for Sophia, the integrator of the divine and the human, and presumably the subject of Solov'ëv's own mystical visions.[16] As the manuscript deals with the "end," it is no coincidence that Pansophius qua Solov'ëv bestows it on his friend on the occasion of his own end, that is, as he lay on his deathbed having reached only the halfway point in his story. Mr. Z, whose name stands out from the surrounding Cyrillic text by the letter that ends the Latin alphabet, reads aloud the title, "Short Tale of the Antichrist," followed by the first four lines of "Panmongolism." The Lady immediately interrupts to ask the source of the epigraph, and Mr. Z answers just as immediately: "I think that the author of the story wrote it himself." However, as quickly as the Lady interrupts "the uninterrupted reading of a 'short tale of the Antichrist,'" supposedly "left by a monk after his death" (*SS* 10, p. 88/tr. p. 22), Solov'ëv just as immediately

---

[16] Sophia in its/her many forms is perhaps the single most important concept, image, and topic of Solov'ëv's poetic and philosophical *oeuvre*. See Judith Deutsch Kornblatt, *Divine Sophia: The Wisdom Writings of Vladimir Solovyov* (Ithaca, NY: Cornell University Press, 2009).

disrupts the illusion of a found manuscript, since he, himself, is obviously the author of this widely circulated, if still not published verse. We are forewarned, then, that the tale to follow is no more a true and inevitable historical account than it is uninterrupted and undisturbed. It is in fact a literary artifice that amply borrows the esoteric symbolism of earlier apocalyptic texts (see *SS* 10, p. 88/tr. p. 22). Thus Solov'ëv cautions us to listen to the tale with our literary antennae fully extended. He directs us to interpret, indeed grapple with his symbolism not as historical prediction, but as a complicated embodiment in art of the truth and goodness of human interaction.

"PANMONGOLISM" BY VLADIMIR SOLOV'ËV

In "Panmongolism,"[17] the speaker of the poem directly addresses Russia: "O Rus'! Forget your former glory." The term Rus' evokes for the reader both the mythic origins of the current Russian empire and the self-proclaimed holy status of Moscow as the "Third Rome" of Christendom. Just as the "Second Rome" (Constantinople) came to an end in 1453 when the "spurned Messiah" raised an "unknown and alien nation from the East" (i.e., Islam) to destroy Byzantium, the poem informs us that now "hordes of His soldiers," "from eastern islands," "like countless locusts," are amassing to march on Russia. This terrible vision of a future when Russia is laid waste and "yellow children" are given "tatters of your standard" as toys is told in the present tense. To further horrify, the "yellow" "Panmongol" force is inhuman; it is an insatiable, undifferentiated mass (*t'my*) with "alien" or even "otherworldly power" (*nezdeshnei siloiu*); it is an insect-like swarm (*roi*) that overcomes with an inevitable fatal blow the individual "flatterers of Russia." Those modern men who could, each in his own way, "forget the testament of love," will have no option but to "submit in trembling and fear" to the alien, subhuman mass, as "the Third Rome lies in dust, and a fourth there shall not be."[18] The present tense rendering of a future vision, the closing of the circle of history with a repetition of the invasion of biblical hordes of locusts that helped spur the creation of the people of Israel in Exodus (compare Exodus 10:12–15 and Revelation 9:1–12), and the utter absence of salvation might seem to lend this poem a sense of eschatological

---

[17] The manuscript of this poem can be dated to October 1, 1894, but was not published until 1905 in *Voprosy zhizni* no. 8, p. 27, when it was read as a direct prediction of Russia's disastrous loss in the Russo-Japanese War. For the complete poem, see *SS* 12, p. 95.

[18] Note the similarity of the ending to the poem and the ending of Solov'ëv's essay "The Secret of Progress" already quoted: "That is the secret of progress – there is and will be no other." For an interesting look at the idea of Moscow as Third Rome, see Daniel B. Rowland, "Moscow: The Third Rome or the New Israel?," *Russian Review* 55 (October 1996), 591–614.

despair. Yet, the speaker welcomes this apocalypse in the opening lines: the word "Panmongolism" "caresses my ear." This "wild word" (*slovo diko*) from the East in fact is also the Word of God: *Slovo*, Logos, Christ. Panmongolism, the Word, is "full of the portent of God's great fate." A closer look at the poem mediates the apparent despair it evokes.

Solov'ëv's 1890 poem, "Ex Oriente Lux" (*SS* 12, p. 27), helps explain the speaker's paradoxical embrace of the predicted end of humanity. "The Light from the East" of the poem's title refers not only to the destructive fires of Thermopylae,[19] as described in the poem, but also to the light of Christ shining westward through Orthodox Russia toward Europe. If a vengeful God will sweep away the false flatterers of contemporary Russia in "Panmongolism," and if "Ex Oriente Lux" similarly condemns the haughty with a familiar "you" (*ty*) engrossed by "proud thoughts," the latter poem nonetheless gives hope that a collective "you," as Rus', might make the right decision when the fateful question is posed: "Which East then do you want to be, the East of Xerxes or of Christ?" The speaker of "Panmongolism" is pleased to hear the incarnated "Word" of God that brings an eschatological end to today's individualistic and egoistical pride, but not as a paean to destruction qua final judgment. Instead, the word "soothes the ear" of the poet who hears not ending, but salvation.

Solov'ëv's answer to the insect-like plague he evokes was the social responsibility preached by the Word in the Gospels. As he wrote in the years between the penning of "Panmongolism" and *Three Conversations* (*SS* 5, p. 421):

The commandment for moral perfection is given to us for eternity in the Word of God. It is obvious that it is given not so that we should repeat it like parrots or splinter it into pieces with our own individual chatter, but so that we might do something to realize it in our very midst. In other words, the moral principle must, without fail, be incarnated in social action.

These words, from Solov'ëv's essay "The Russian National Ideal" (1891) in the second volume of his *Natsional'nyi vopros v Rossii* (*National Question in Russia*), could have appeared eight years later as part of Mr. Z's critique of the Prince's pacifism (and passivity) in the face of evil. As is well recognized, the Prince is a thinly veiled representative of the ideas of the novelist Lev Tolstoi who, according to Solov'ëv, merely mimicked the moral teachings of the Gospel about "doing good," missing the message of the Resurrection, denying

[19] In the Battle of Thermopylae, an alliance of Greek states held off the much more powerful Persian army of Xerxes for three days.

the real incarnation of Christ the Word, and thus failing to combat evil in any way.[20]

When Mr. Z reads the opening of "Panmongolism" as though it were the epigraph to Pansophius's "Short Tale of the Antichrist," Solov'ëv raises the specter of an evil force, imaged as a destructive clash of West and East, individual and mass. Since Pansophius did not complete the manuscript, however, and Mr. Z fills in an almost humorous oral story about the consequent destruction of the evil destroyer at the hands of the otherwise stereotypically helpless Jews, Solov'ëv moves from pessimism about the end to optimism about the future. His approach to the philosophical question of the existence of evil is neither to ignore it nor dwell on it, but to suggest how best to respond to it. Instead of wielding the Word of Jesus Christ in a more expected way, however, the Jews inadvertently preserve humanity from the evil forces of the Antichrist by strict adherence to an ancient and very physical Judaic rite: circumcision. Thus, salvation comes from a surprising corner, transforming an ancient instrument of social life – the circumciser's knife – into a military tool to overcome evil and save the world.

Individual responsibility for salvation in the story is thus found in the collective persons, the *lichnosti*, who take responsibility for completing the tale. "*He who saves shall be saved,*" Solov'ëv observed in "The Secret of Progress" (*SS* 9, p. 86). In Solov'ëv's dialogue, Mr. Z is the primary symbol of *lichnost'*, for he finishes the story of the Antichrist with the Jewish victory. In fact, Mr. Z is the only character in *Three Conversations* referred to by a name, even if the name is only an abbreviation. The other characters have only abstract titles: Prince, Lady, Politician, General. Mr. Z's oral conclusion about the humorously powerful Jews comes at the end of the story to remind us of the power of the individual who interacts with the whole. Likewise, in "Panmongolism," Solov'ëv juxtaposes the voracious masses of the primitive past ("Asia" and "the East") with the powerless individuals of the Europeanized, western present, both equally at fault if they "forget the testament of love." Only through an active embrace of the words, the story (the true Word of human responsibility, not the empty reading of the Gospels preferred by the Prince with his false or simplistic goodness) can humanity (here oxymoronically represented by the activist Jews, as well as by the story-teller Mr. Z) overcome the despair facing the complacent "flatterers" who simply repeat platitudes and neglect their responsibility to fight for a better world. "East" must *actively* meet "West," the human must confront the fateful insect-like hordes, faith must contemplate the

---

[20] See Solov'ëv's parable of the "Hole Worshippers" in the preface to *Three Conversations* (*SS* 10, pp. 83–86/tr. pp. 16–20).

end, and all must interpenetrate in the "wild word" to bring on the ultimate transfiguration of humanity.

"THE COMING HUNS" BY VALERII BRIUSOV

In this poem,[21] the symbolist poet Briusov refers not to the thirteenth-century Mongol invasion that Solov'ëv evokes, but to the Huns, an even earlier horde from the East. These Eurasian tribes, most notoriously led by Attila (434–453 CE), moved from Central Asia as far as Europe in the fourth and fifth centuries, where they ultimately founded the state of Hungary. Briusov's epigraph, from Ivanov's 1904 poem "Kochevniki krasoty" ("Nomads of Beauty"), evokes the Hun's destruction of the supposedly civilized, European world: "Trample their paradise, Attila."[22]

Where Solov'ëv addresses his own people in "Panmongolism," Briusov addresses the barbarians, literally welcoming them into his own vulnerable territory: "But you, who will annihilate me,/ I greet with a welcoming hymn." Russia, for its part, presents no resistance, for it is a "decrepit carcass," inhabited by "wise men and poets" who are now the helpless guardians of faith. Like the Christian leaders in "Short Story of the Antichrist," they will slink off "to catacombs, to deserts, and to caves" in the face of the coming threat.

Apocalypse was clearly on Briusov's mind, as it was on those of his fellow Silver Age writers. His 1903 poem "Kon' bled" ("Pale Steed") begins with an epigraph from Revelation 6:8: "And I saw, and behold, a pale horse, and its rider's name was Death." In the poem, the apocalyptic horseman called Death appears amidst the "Deafening din, speech, and rumble of carriages" of the western city, and its hooves will trample, like those of Attila's horses. Only Mary Magdalene and a Hebrew prophet welcome the destruction: "Crying, she kissed the horse's hooves."[23] If we note that one of Solov'ëv's many names for the Emperor-Superman in his short story is "griadushchii chelovek" (the "coming man" or "man of the future," *SS* 10, p. 203/tr. p. 171),[24] we cannot help but read

---

[21] The manuscript bears the dates fall 1904 and July 30–August 10, 1905. It was first published in *Voprosy zhizni* no. 9 (1905), 203, the issue immediately after the publication in the same journal of Solov'ëv's "Panmongolism." For the complete poem, see Valerii Briusov, *Stikhotvoreniia i poemy* (A.A. Ninov (ed.), Leningrad: Sovetskii pisatel', n.d.), pp. 278–279.

[22] "Topchi ikh rai, Attila, – / I nov'iu pustoty / Vzoidut tvoi svetila, / Tvoikh stepei tsvety!" Viacheslav Ivanov, *Stikhotvoreniia i poemy* (P.E. Pomirchii (ed.), Leningrad: Sovetskii pisatel', 1978), pp. 140–141.

[23] Briusov, *Stikhotvoreniia i poemy*, pp. 283–284.

[24] See Valliere, *Modern Russian Theology*, p. 214; and David M. Bethea, *The Shape of Apocalypse in Modern Russian Fiction* (Princeton University Press, 1989), p. 113.

Briusov's Huns as a collective Antichrist.[25] Like Solov'ëv's Panmongol locusts, Briusov's annihilators form a swarm or cloud. Although they are "iron," the collective force is still organic, elemental: "like a drunken horde," with "waves of fiery blood." Something has changed, however, since the earlier rendition; history has caught up with Solov'ëv's predictions. Russia's humiliating defeats in the Russo-Japanese War of 1904–1905, a war that all of Europe expected Russia to win, provoked, in part at least, the first Russian Revolution, in 1905. The standard reading of "The Coming Huns" understands Briusov to be as fearful of the revolutionaries as the Europeans were of the eastern threat. According to the critic Renato Poggioli: "The date of the poem itself, '10 August 1905,' testifies that it was written in trembling and fear, at the climax of a double catastrophe: the downfall of Russia's arms in distant seas and lands, under the onslaught of an alien race, and the breakdown of her social fabric through an inner upheaval that in retrospect was to be named both a 'little revolution' and a 'dress rehearsal' for the greater one."[26] Yet much of the poem was probably written a year earlier, in 1904.[27] Contra Poggioli, the poem is less a specific response to the 1905 Revolution or even the war with Japan, and more a widely repeated expression of the modernist's reaction to the general turmoil of the period, his ambivalence about the place of the individual in relationship to the threatening masses, and about the relationship of the one and the many, imaged here as the decrepit West and the iron-clad hordes of the East.

Whatever the historical context, Briusov ultimately took a step away from Solov'ëv's optimistic humanism, and in this poem could not fully reconcile the one with the many. The individuals of the poem, the "wise men and poets," retreat to the catacombs, and no one remains to counter the massive, inhuman evil of the modern-day Huns. The poets have become mere "guardians of mystery and faith," rather than contemporary practitioners like Solov'ëv's Jews who are willing to take up the struggle for freedom and humanity. Briusov's remnant, righteous or otherwise, does nothing but "greet with a welcoming hymn" those "who will annihilate me."

---

[25] Russian literature, and symbolist poetry especially, is highly referential. Merezhkovskii's not coincidentally named essay "Griadushchii kham" ("The Coming Scoundrel," 1906) refers to the Briusov poem, and declares: "The Chinese are perfect yellow-faced positivists; the Europeans for the time being are still imperfect white-faced Chinese." D.S. Merezhkovskii, *Polnoe sobranie sochinenii* (St. Petersburg, Moscow: Izdanie M.O. Vol'f, 1911), vol. 40, p. 7. A clear intertextual reference for Blok's later poem "The Scythians" is another with that title by Briusov ("Skify," 1900).

[26] Poggioli, "Qualis Artifex Pereo!," 142.

[27] According to the Soviet editors, "The poem 'The Coming Huns' repeats the conception of the revolutionary socialist movement as a destructive, barbaric elemental force." Briusov, *Stikhotvoreniia i poemy*, p. 779. They also point out that Briusov reworked the theme of the poem in 1906 in the story "The Last Martyrs."

Yet the welcoming hymn (*gimn*) of the last line itself refers phonically back to the Huns (*Gunny*) of the first, reminding us of Solov'ëv's wild word that caresses the ear in his opening lines. Despite his apprehension about the bloody upheaval he predicts, the speaker might ultimately be the one to integrate passive individual and active collective, "wise man" and horde, those who "submit to trembling and fear" and those who can embrace and sing of the future. The "end" might mean hope as much as despair.

"THE SCYTHIANS" BY ALEKSANDR BLOK

In "The Scythians,"[28] written just after the 1917 Revolution, Blok explicitly returned to Solov'ëv with an epigraph from "Panmongolism": "Panmongolism! Although the name is wild/It caresses my ear." A small change in the epigraph from the original (the substitution of "name" for "word" (*imia* for *slovo*)) might be a mere mistake,[29] but could also have been a move away from, or paradoxically an attempt to underline, Solov'ëv's association of the "light from the East" with Christ the Word. Instead of Solov'ëv's Mongols or Briusov's Huns, Blok evokes an even older people, the Scythians. And instead of warning his fellow Russians about the Mongols, as Solov'ëv did, or addressing the Huns as a Russian waiting for them, as did Briusov, Blok has the "I" of his poem speak directly from the Scythian camp. By the end of the Silver Age, "we" the Russians on the eastern edge of Europe, have become "you" the eastern invaders poised to devastate that same Europe it once had saved.

As in the earlier poems, the West is a collection of individual elements, unable to unite into an active force, and the East (now equated with Russia) is uncountable and amorphous: "You are millions. We are hordes, and hordes, and hordes." The Russians are voracious, Asiatic, drenched in black blood, with animal mugs rather than human faces. Yet the "eastern" Russians are also different from the merely destructive Antichrist of "The Coming Huns," for they are not only a monolithic subhuman mass. Instead, they are "all" or, to use Solov'ëv's language, "all-unity," the union of East and West, with their love

---

[28] The poem's manuscript bears two dates: January 29 and 30, 1918. Its composition, then, was only a few short months after the October Revolution in 1917 and coincides with the composition of his more famous poem "Dvenadtsat'" ("The Twelve"). For the original, see A.A. Blok, *Polnoe sobranie sochinenii i pisem v dvadtsati tomakh* (Moscow: Nauka, 1999), vol. 5, pp. 77–80 (henceforth Blok, *PSS*).

[29] According to Thomson, "Blok and Belyi," p. 39, "quotations from Solov'ëv's poetry are particularly indicative, since they are almost always made from memory." Blok added the epigraph after the poem was first published, and could have taken it from a variant of Solov'ëv's poem. See also Blok, *PSS* 5, p. 477.

of cold statistics *and* their irrational, divine visions: "We love it all – the heat of cold statistics,/And the gift of holy visions."

In his 1918 essay "The Intelligentsia and Revolution," Blok evoked a similar sensibility: "All I hear around is: 'Russia is perishing,' 'Russia is no more,' 'May Russia's memory live on.' But before me is . . . Russia. I see the Russia dreamt of by our great writers in their frightening and prophetic dreams; I see the Petersburg envisioned by Dostoevskii, the Russia which Gogol' called a rushing troika. Russia is a storm."[30] The Russia that pessimists said was perishing was merely the Russia in imitation of the West; the rushing troika, however, was full of the elemental energy of the East, the hordes, the hurricanes. The following year, as the Silver Age seemed to be drawing to a close and the Soviets began their bloody march toward power, Blok distinguished between civilization – the legacy of the supposedly all-powerful individual – and culture – the inherent, if sometimes threatening energy of the masses, imaged in the spirit of music ("The Collapse of Humanism," 1919):[31]

It is not possible to civilize the masses, but it is also not necessary. If we are going to talk about the coming together of humanity with *culture*, then it isn't clear who has the greater right to do the joining: civilized people or the barbarians or vice versa. Civilized people have become weak and lost their cultural integrity. In times like these, the fresher barbarian masses have become the unwitting defenders of culture.[32]

As Europe became more and more fragmented, Blok tells us, it lost its right to call itself "humanist," despite the origins of philosophical and artistic human-ism in the European Renaissance. The West became devoid of the "spirit of wholeness, of musical cohesion" and, "having lost the right to the name [*imia*], civilization clung ever more tightly to that name, as a degenerating aristocrat clings to his title."[33] In this emphasis on the "name" of humanism, Blok brings us back to the epigraph to "The Scythians": "Although the name is wild/It caresses my ear." Good, true, and beautiful ("musical") humanism retains the wild, barbarian, and sometimes threatening energy of the whole.

Now, in war and revolution, Blok welcomes a "new music,"[34] much like Solov'ëv's new word and Briusov's hymn. And like the invasions described in the poems, it is a "stormy whirlwind," a "snowy storm," a "worldwide cyclone."[35] But in this "stormy flood that carries away the splintered remnants of civilization" we can already distinguish "a new role for the person (*lichnost'*), a new human breed": "The goal of this movement is no longer the ethical,

[30] Aleksandr Blok, *Sobranie sochinenii v shesti tomakh* (Leningrad: Khudozhestvennaia literatura, 1982), vol. 4, p. 229 (henceforth Blok, *SS*).
[31] Blok, *SS* 4, pp. 327–247.   [32] *Ibid.* p. 333.   [33] *Ibid.* p. 334.
[34] *Ibid.* p. 231.   [35] *Ibid.* p. 232.

political, or humane human being, but the *human-artist*; he and only he will be able to *live avidly and to act* in the looming era of whirlwind and storm, into which humanity has irrepressibly rushed."[36]

CONCLUSION

These three poems taken together show us a confusion of we, you, and they; a confusion of past, present, and future. Solov'ëv speaks *to* the Russians *about* an eastern, swarming, uncountable threat; Briusov speaks instead directly *to* the eastern threat, this time *about* Russian false "wise men and poets," and ends on a hymn for the Huns. Blok for his part speaks in the other geographic and metaphysical direction, *to* the Europeans, with the voice of the Russians who have now become like the eastern threat itself. Yet he asks Europe to be "wise" (*premudryi*, like Solov'ëv's Divine Wisdom, Sophia), and ends his poem playing an oxymoronic barbaric lyre that paradoxically invites the enemy to a brotherly banquet. The scholar Ovcharenko has claimed that Blok "took the words 'Scythians' and 'barbarians' that had been thrown to him and turned them on their head."[37] Instead of this dualistic reading, however, I would argue that Blok participated in the Silver Age tradition of integration begun by Solov'ëv. He grappled with the juxtaposition of the opposites of one and many, East and West, hope and eschatology, looking for a way to unite them into a new and musical whole.

Blok wrote "The Scythians" in the same creative burst as his more famous narrative poem about the Revolution, "Dvenadtsat'" ("The Twelve," 1918).[38] The latter poem describes a group of twelve revolutionaries walking through the defeated imperial capital of Petrograd. It ends on a curious note – Christ marching in advance of the ragtag soldiers: "In front – with a bloody banner / . . . / Wearing a white crown of roses – / In front was Jesus Christ."[39] Exactly in the manner of Solov'ëv's defense of his use of a short story within the dialogues, Blok claimed that he had not initially intended for Christ to appear: "I wanted the end to be different. When I finished, I too was surprised: Why Christ?" and "It's not that the Red Army soldiers are 'unworthy' of Jesus who walks before them. It's just that it is precisely He who is marching with them. It needed to be the Other."[40] Perhaps Blok "had to" have Christ the Word lead the new world order, as the "wild word" leads Solov'ëv's defense of humanity.

[36] *Ibid.* p. 347.   [37] Ovcharenko, "Stikhotvorenie A. Bloka," 18.
[38] See the lengthy commentary to "The Twelve" in Blok, *PSS* 5, pp. 301–381.
[39] Blok, *PSS* 5, p. 20.
[40] See A. Blok, *Stikhotvoreniia*, Biblioteka poeta series (Leningrad: Sovetskii pisatel', 1955), p. 773.

Or, as the recent critic Boris Zaitsev has argued, it is the "Other," the Antichrist who is revealed behind Christ.[41] Blok's rendition is equivocal.

Let us return again to Solov'ëv's "Ex Oriente Lux," this time as it was used by Merezhkovskii in a "Speech delivered on 14 November 1916, at an evening dedicated to the memory of V.S. Solov'ëv."[42] "Why," asks Merezhkovskii, "at this moment, is a memorial service for V.S. Solov'ëv so timely?" The answer, he tells us immediately, is found in the rise of nationalism as exemplified in the current World War, a rise that demonstrates "the profane assertion of one's people as absolute, as God." Merezhkovskii calls the war "an absolute war," that is, "the fruit of absolute nationalism." And, he continues, "you can conquer the absolute of nationalism only by confronting it with a true absolute (*absoliut istinnyi*)."[43] What is this "true absolute," Merezhkovskii asks, since it is neither the monolith of eastern hegemony nor the jingoistic patriotism of the separate European states? It is God, the Good, True, and Beautiful Absolute, not the false amassing of individuals under one nationalist flag.

Here, Merezhkovskii's use of the last four lines of Solov'ëv's poem "Ex Oriente Lux" takes on a new meaning that can refocus our discussion of the one versus the many and hope versus eschatology in the immediately pre-revolutionary period:

> Oh Rus'! Proud thoughts
> Engross you with exalted foresight;
> Which East would you like to be:
> The East of Xerxes or of Christ?

With this poem, Merezhkovskii looked back a full decade before *Three Conversations*, with its tale of the Antichrist and its epigraph from "Panmongolism," to Solov'ëv's so-called utopian period,[44] when he repeatedly preached the establishment of a theocracy based on the integration of the western priestly principle, the eastern kingly principle, and the prophetic principle of the Jews, themselves the unifying people between Catholic Poland and Orthodox Russia. The 1880s were also the years when Solov'ëv spoke out repeatedly against totalizing nationalism, both in his two collections of essays called *The National Question in Russia* and in his several works on the Jews, especially *Evreistvo i khristianskii vopros (Jewry and the Christian Question*, 1884). What is

---

[41] B. Zaitsev, "Dinamika razmezhevanii i skhozhdenii: Tipy tvorchestva" in L.N. Dar'ialova (ed.), *Russkaia literatura XX veka posle Oktiabria* (Kaliningrad: KGU, 1998), p. 45; cited in Blok, *PSS* 5, p. 381.

[42] See D.S. Merezhkovskii, "Rech', skazannaia 14 noiabria 1916 goda na vechere v pamiat' V.S. Solov'ëva" in B. Averin and D. Bazanova (eds.), *Kniga o Vladimire Solov'ëve* (Moscow: Sovetskii pisatel', 1991), pp. 472–474.

[43] *Ibid.* p. 472.   [44] See Trubetskoi, *Mirosozertsanie VI.S. Solov'ëva*, vol. 1, p. 419 *et seq.*

it that makes the Jews special, the birth family of Jesus, he asks in that latter work? It is the fact that they are both particular and universal, both individual and embedded in the divine whole.[45] Even earlier, in his *Chteniia o Bogochelovechestve* (*Lectures on Divine Humanity*, 1878), Solov'ëv claimed that the Jewish people in the period of the prophets were free of "national exclusivity and egoism" and exhibited both "true patriotism" and "true universalism" (*SS* 3, p. 80). Jews of the Orient, the family of Jesus, thus rejected national egoism, but also rejected the tyranny of the masses. That is why the light comes from the East. Xerxes, like the Mongols, the Huns, and the Scythians, brought destruction to the West, but the elemental force of the Orient also contained the potential for a renewed wholeness, one that accepted humanity not as a fragmented, degenerating individual, but as a true *lichnost'*, suffused with the integrating power of the all, what Merezhkovskii called the "true absolute."

Modifying his own earlier apocalypticism, Merezhkovskii recognized here, just as Solov'ëv did before him, that East and West, old and new, poet and warrior, must not stand apart. Evil lay not in one or the other, but in the inability to reconcile the opposites of the world. Yet faith in integration became more and more difficult to sustain as Solov'ëv's relatively stable nineteenth century gave way to the upheavals of war and revolution that inaugurated the twentieth. Solov'ëv's Silver Age heirs inherited a hope for active integration, but succumbed more and more to the despair of disintegration, the dangers of exclusive nationalism, and obsession with the end of time.

[45] See Solov'ëv, *SS* 4, pp. 132–185.

PART V

RUSSIAN PHILOSOPHY IN REVOLUTION AND EXILE

15

RUSSIAN MARXISM

ANDRZEJ WALICKI

The history of Russian Marxism is inseparable from ideas of human freedom and dignity. It combined the real desire to alleviate the misery and degradation of the laboring masses with the Marxian dream of the total realization of collective human potential, envisioning a totally regenerated human species of the future. As a whole it utterly failed to appreciate that individual human beings are absolute values in themselves who ought never to be sacrificed as means for ostensibly higher (and remote) purposes. In this, Russian Marxism proved deeply inimical to its own humanist ideals.

MARXISM IN PRE-REVOLUTIONARY RUSSIA

The emergence of Russian Marxism was preceded by the reception of Marx's and Engels's ideas in the populist movement.[1] The Russian populists saw Marxism as the last word in the socialist theory of capitalism, that is, of the "bourgeois stage" of social evolution. Unlike earlier, "utopian" forms of socialism, Marxism assumed the necessity of capitalist development but had no illusions about its painful consequences for the broad masses of the population. The necessity of capitalism was grounded in the general Marxist theory of the "objective laws of history," independent of human will and consciousness. The dire consequences of capitalist development for the welfare of the people were part of its historical task, which consisted in the expropriation of direct producers (peasants and artisans) and their transformation into property-less proletarians in order to pave the way for the concentration of capital, which was seen as a necessary condition of socialism. In the developed countries of the West, capitalism had already fulfilled its mission and, therefore, the harmonious socialist future was

---

[1] For the populist reception of Marxism, and Marx's and Engels's reactions to the ideas raised by the Russian populists, see A. Walicki, *The Controversy Over Capitalism: Studies in the Social Philosophy of the Russian Populists* (Oxford: Clarendon Press, 1969; University of Notre Dame Press, 1989).

close; Russia, however, and the underdeveloped countries in general, had to embark first on the long and painful "capitalist path."

The impatient populist socialists did not wish to accept this conclusion. They shared the Marxist analysis of capitalism but rejected the theory of the necessary laws of history, setting against it their so-called "subjective sociology" which stressed the decisive role of "subjective factors," such as human will and conscious choice of values. They fully accepted Marx's view of the cruelty and essential unreformability of capitalism, but staunchly opposed Marxist historical determinism as intellectually controversial and morally unacceptable.

The "father of Russian Marxism," Georgii Plekhanov (1856–1918), a former populist who in 1883 founded in Switzerland the first organization of Russian Marxists, the Emancipation of Labor Group, gave Marxism a somewhat Hegelian flavor, interpreting it as scientific knowledge of the rational necessity of historical processes. Such knowledge was, in his view, an invaluable instrument of human freedom – not "merely negative," liberal freedom, which exposed individuals to the mercy of chance, but rational, positive freedom, which consisted in the "understanding of necessity" and thus entailed the ability to rationally master one's own fate. In his *Development of the Monistic View of History* (1894), Plekhanov described this liberating science as "dialectical materialism," presenting it as the crowning achievement of the intellectual history of modern Europe: the definitive overcoming of the "abstract rationalism" of the Enlightenment and of subsequent positivistic scientism, which reduced people to the role of mere objects of evolutionary processes. Philosophically, "dialectical materialism" was to be a synthesis of Marx's historical materialism (as a method and theory of history) with a Hegelian-inspired conception of dialectical laws governing the entire universe (first outlined by Friedrich Engels in his *Anti-Dühring*, 1878). To Plekhanov, the special value of dialectical materialism was the combination of the understanding of (and submitting to) necessity with the capacity to change the world. Plekhanov explained this as follows:

Dialectical materialism says that human reason could not be the demiurge of history, because it is itself the product of history. But once that product has appeared, it must not – and in its nature it *cannot* – be obedient to the reality handed down as a heritage by previous history; of necessity it strives to transform that reality after its own likeness and image, *to make it reasonable.*[2]

To properly understand these words, we must remember that Plekhanov, as a true Marxist, saw the subject of rational freedom not in the individual but in the human species as a whole. He conceived human liberation as a long, cruel

[2] G. V. Plekhanov, *Selected Philosophical Works* (Moscow: Progress Publishers, 1974), vol. 1, pp. 666–667.

historical process in which entire generations and classes have to be ruthlessly sacrificed for the sake of the unfettered development of the species in the socialist future.

In his first Marxist books, *Socialism and Political Struggle* (1883) and *Our Differences* (1885), Plekhanov launched a passionate attack on the populist idea of "skipping the capitalist stage" of social development in Russia. Russian Marxism was in his eyes a continuation of Russian Westernism; the great mission of the Russian workers was to complete the work of Peter the Great. A seizure of power by revolutionary socialists would only hinder the realization of this end and bring about a great historical regression. He thought true socialism impossible without a high level of economic development and an equally high level of class consciousness among the workers. Revolutionaries attempting to enforce socialism on a backward country "would have to seek salvation in the ideals of patriarchal and authoritarian communism," with a socialist caste in place of the "Peruvian Children of the Sun" and their officials. To prevent this outcome, Russian socialists should choose rather the longer but safer capitalist way: political struggle by means of agitation among workers, in close cooperation with liberals and all progressive forces of society. Socialist revolution should be separated from political revolution (i.e., the overthrow of autocracy) by a period of time sufficiently long to achieve the maximum degree of capitalist industrialization and to educate the working class in the school of the rule of law and political freedom. This period could be shorter than in the West but it should not be *too* short – otherwise it would not lead to the desirable results.

In Plekhanov's arguments we can discern two lines of reasoning: sometimes he argued that European, capitalist development was simply the best choice for Russia, but more often he referred to an alleged "historical inevitability," claiming that there were no other choices, that his program for Russia was based upon scientific knowledge of the "objective laws of history." He was obviously inclined to universalize the western type of historical development, unconsciously differing in this from Marx who, in the last years of his life, under the influence of Russian populists, embraced the view that backward countries, and especially Russia, could achieve a "direct transition to socialism."[3]

In his philosophical views Plekhanov claimed to be simply an orthodox Marxist. In reality, however, he offered a dialectical and extremely "necessitarian" interpretation of Marxism. Necessitarianism was, of course, a common feature

---

[3] In his letter to Vera Zasulich (a Russian revolutionary from Plekhanov's group) of March 8, 1881, Marx explicitly endorsed the populist view that Russia could achieve the transition to socialism on the basis of the peasant commune. In the three drafts of this letter he developed this idea in detail. See K. Marx, *Selected Writings* (David McLellan (ed.), Oxford University Press, 1977), pp. 576–580.

of the prevalent positivistic model of Marxism, canonized by the "pope" of the
Second International, Karl Kautsky. In Plekhanov's case, as already mentioned,
there was also an admixture of Hegelianism, providing additional arguments
against populist "subjectivism." For Plekhanov, historical necessity was not
reducible to the laws of evolutionary adaptation: it was a meaningful, *rational*
necessity, embodying the Hegelian Reason of History. Understandably, the Bolshevik Revolution was in his eyes a violation of the laws of history, caused by
an irresponsible relapse into the populist dream of "by-passing capitalism" and
threatening Russia with catastrophic consequences.

The Russian controversy over capitalism reached its climax in the 1890s, with
the emergence of "legal Marxism." The leading figure in this influential movement was Pëtr Struve (1870–1944), whose *Critical Notes Concerning the Economic
Development of Russia* (1894) contained the famous phrase: "We must concede
that we lack culture and go to the school of capitalism." After Struve's book,
"legal Marxism" became an important current of economic thought, supporting Finance Minister Sergei Witte's program of capitalist industrialization. It
had its own periodicals and representatives in universities and other institutions of higher education (Mikhail Tugan-Baranovskii, Aleksandr Skvortsov,
and others). Among the most important members of Struve's group were
the future leading figures of the Russian religious-philosophical renaissance:
Nikolai Berdiaev (1871–1944), Sergei Bulgakov (1874–1948), and Semën Frank
(1877–1950).

In fact, the "legal Marxists" were not genuine Marxists but rather liberals,
interested above all in economic growth and constitutional freedom, and treating
socialism as a question of the remote future. Even in their theoretical constructions they were, from the very beginning, rather far from Marxist orthodoxy.
Struve anticipated in his *Critical Notes* some of the crucial ideas of Eduard Bernstein's revisionism. He openly stated that Marxism, though the most scientific
theory of social development, lacked as yet a proper philosophical foundation.
About 1900, the majority of Struve's group finally broke with Russian Social
Democracy and joined the ranks of the emerging liberal movement.

In addition to the Emancipation of Labor Group and the "legal Marxists,"
there also existed in the 1890s a third variant of Russian Marxism: revolutionary
Marxism, with Vladimir Ul'ianov (1870–1924) – Lenin – as its unquestionable
leader and main theorist. Unlike Plekhanov's group, it developed not in exile
but inside Russia and continued in many respects the tradition of revolutionary
populism. Many members of the revolutionary circles of the 1880s and early
1990s, especially in the Volga region, represented in their views a blend of
Marxism, the cult of populist revolutionaries from the "People's Will," and a
populist commitment to the idea of a direct transition to socialism. A typical

representative of this semi-Marxist, semi-populist intellectual formation was Lenin's elder brother, Aleksandr Ul'ianov (1866–1887), who was executed in 1887 for an abortive attempt on the life of the tsar.

Already in his early work *The Economic Content of Populism and its Criticism in P. Struve's Book* (1895), Lenin set forth his own version of Marxism. He distanced himself from "objectivism," keenly observing that it might easily degenerate into justification of existing conditions, and set against it the spirit of *partiinost'* (the party principle), that is, the obligation to stand up simply and openly for the standpoint of a definite social class. He interpreted Marxism not so much as a variant of historical determinism, which stressed the principal role of the development of productive forces, but rather as a theory of class struggle. Hence history was for him not an "objective" process whose driving force was impersonal necessity, but a battlefield, a scene with human actors whose participation implied conscious or unconscious identification with a specific class and therefore the conscious or unconscious choice of certain values. In the light of this conception, the antithesis between the "objective course of events" (stressed by Plekhanov and the "legal Marxists") and the conscious will of the individuals (i.e., the "subjective factor," stressed by the populists) lost its significance: no objective course could be conceived other than in terms of the actions of human beings, and conscious will could not be divorced from its social determinants.

Equally original was Lenin's position in the controversy over Russian capitalism. He claimed that capitalism had to be defined not as a system of highly developed productive forces in conditions of "bourgeois freedom" but as a naked system of class exploitation of hired labor, existing without any patriarchal embellishment. From this point of view capitalism was not Russia's future but Russia's present, "something already and definitely established,"[4] sufficiently ripe to justify waging a relentless war against it. This argument, first expressed in the polemic with Struve and developed in detail in *The Development of Capitalism in Russia* (written between 1896 and 1899), was initially directed against the populists but also ran counter to the views generally accepted among the Russian Marxists, who conceded that capitalism in Russia had entered its first stage, but who also took pains to stress that it could not become "definitely established" until after the political defeat of autocracy.

The distinctive features of Lenin's Marxism were further developed in his seminal work *What Is To Be Done?* (1902), written for the Second Congress of the Russian Social Democratic Labor Party (held in Brussels and London, July–August 1903). The work dealt with the so-called "organizational

[4] V.I. Lenin, *Collected Works*, 45 vols. (Moscow: Progress Publishers, 1960–1970), vol. 1, p. 495.

question," arguing that the workers' movement needed a hierarchically organized, disciplined vanguard party of professional revolutionaries; otherwise, left to the operation of spontaneous forces, it would degenerate into mere trade-unionism, adapting itself to market forces. The vanguard party had to be equipped with an iron will and a "correct theory" to shape the class consciousness of the workers. Thus, class consciousness had to be brought to the workers *from without*. The view that it should develop *from within* was radically wrong, since "the spontaneous development of the working-class movement leads to its subordination to bourgeois ideology."[5]

On the face of it, this theory seemed close to the views of Kautsky and Plekhanov, who also believed in the importance of "scientific theory," which could not be produced by uneducated workers. Because of this, Plekhanov's first reaction was to support Lenin. However, it soon became clear that Lenin had in mind not Marxist intellectuals, who needed autonomy for scholarly research, but professional revolutionaries, organized in an utterly centralized illegal party, struggling with all possible means for political power and imposing its will without the slightest scruples on the rank-and-file members of the social democratic mass movement. Having realized this, Plekhanov changed sides and joined Lenin's opponents, the "Mensheviks" (from the Russian word *menshinstvo*, minority; Lenin's followers, who prevailed at the Congress, called themselves "Bolsheviks," i.e., members of the majority).

Deep differences between Plekhanov and Lenin were reflected also in their respective theories of "bourgeois revolution." Before 1917, Lenin shared in principle Plekhanov's view that a socialist revolution against capitalism must be preceded by a bourgeois-democratic revolution against the autocracy. He did not share, however, Plekhanov's conviction that the practical consequence of this diagnosis must be a revolutionary alliance between the workers' party and the liberals, as two forces interested in capitalist modernization. His habit of seeing everything through the prism of class conflict made obvious for him that much more natural would be an alliance between the workers and the poor peasantry, as two parts of the exploited masses. From his perspective the liberals, represented by the Constitutional-Democratic Party (the Kadets), appeared as the most reliable ally of the old regime and the most dangerous enemy of a plebeian revolution. In the revolutionary years 1905–1906, this estimate laid the foundation for the theory that the "bourgeois-democratic" revolution in Russia must be leveled against all privileged classes, including the bourgeoisie, and take the form of a "revolutionary dictatorship of the proletariat and the peasantry."

[5] Robert C. Tucker (ed.), *The Lenin Anthology* (New York: W.W. Norton, 1975), p. 29.

A similar view was offered by Leon Trotskii (Lev Bronshtein, 1879–1940) in his theory of overcoming economic backwardness through "permanent revolution." In his reflections on the first Russian Revolution (1905–1906) he set forth the view that, in conditions of a highly developed capitalist world market, economic backwardness is rarely total: as a rule, it consists in a juxtaposition of the very old and the very new, which results in "uneven and combined development," skipping, or telescoping, the developmental stages and by-passing social forms characteristic of the classical western model. This was precisely the Russian case. Like Lenin, Trotskii concluded that the Russian Revolution had to combine the anti-feudal revolution of the peasantry with the anti-capitalist proletarian revolution. He also asserted that the chief enemy of revolutionary forces was the reactionary alliance of the land-owning nobility with the liberal bourgeoisie under the aegis of autocracy.

However, in contradistinction to Lenin, Trotskii (at this stage) did not champion the idea of a revolutionary dictatorship of an elitist vanguard party. He accused the Bolshevik party of "substitutionalism," by which he meant substituting for the working class a narrow group of political elites, instead of allowing workers to speak for themselves. From Lenin's point of view, Trotskii was guilty of an unpardonable concession to the theory of "spontaneity." But from Trotskii's point of view, Lenin's insistence on centralization and ruthless discipline was a dangerous manifestation of Jacobinism, threatening a new reign of terror.

An especially disturbing element of Lenin's theory of revolutionary dictatorship was its ideocratic aspect: its stress on the need for a "single, correct theory" and monolithic ideological unity. The vivid interest of some members of the Bolshevik Party in modern philosophical trends, such as empiriocriticism, caused Lenin to undertake an effort to silence the dissenting philosophical voices by providing the party with an obligatory philosophical *credo*. He did so in a lengthy book *Materialism and Empiriocriticism: Critical Comments on a Reactionary Philosophy*, published in March 1909 under the pen name V. Il'in.

The entire history of philosophy, Lenin argued, consists, as Engels had shown, in the relentless struggle between two parties, materialism and idealism. The progressive camp in philosophy is materialism; philosophical idealism leads always to fideism and clericalism, thus serving the cause of the exploiters and oppressors. The partisan principle deeply permeates all non-empirical sciences; "neutrality" is either a conscious fraud or a naive illusion. In fact, professors of economics are nothing but learned salesmen of the capitalist class, while professors of philosophy are learned salesmen of the theologians.[6]

---

[6] Lenin, *Collected Works*, vol. 14, pp. 342–343.

In Lenin's view, materialism is incompatible with any doubts about the cognizability of the world. Agnosticism leads inevitably to subjective idealism and finally to solipsism, bound up with reactionary fideism. In the materialist theory of knowledge, the only legitimate position is the "copy theory," treating our sensations as "copies, photographs, images" of the objectively existing extrahuman world. All knowledge is class-bound, but in the case of Marxism the class standpoint fully coincides with objective truth. Hence, a truly Marxist party has a monopoly on truth and cannot tolerate any relativizing pluralism of opinions. The most efficient and most hateful ideological tool of reactionaries, according to Lenin, is religion, not only institutionalized religion but non-denominational religious feeling as well.[7]

No wonder that most Russian philosophers found Lenin's philosophical position too primitive to deserve serious discussion. After the October Revolution, however, Lenin's book became a Holy Bible for communist philosophers. The only way of making Lenin's philosophy more sophisticated was to stress his interest in Hegelian dialectics, reflected in his *Philosophical Notebooks*. But it is undeniable that Lenin until the end of his life remained above all a crude, violently anti-religious materialist. His "philosophical testament" was the article "On the Significance of Militant Materialism" (1922), proclaiming the urgent need for "untiring atheist propaganda."

Interestingly, the author of the most comprehensive criticism of *Materialism and Empiriocriticism* was the chief theorist of an alternative current within Bolshevism, Aleksandr Bogdanov (1873–1929).[8] As a philosopher who tried to combine Marxism with empiriocriticism (a synthesis he called "empiriomonism"), he was one of the main targets of Lenin's attacks. In turn, he forcefully exposed Lenin's fanatical intolerance, showing its deep roots in a pre-capitalist, authoritarian structure of thought.[9]

The main feature of Bogdanov's philosophy was a resolute rejection of the concept of "objective truth" and the corresponding notion of an objectively existing world, independent of the knower. In his view, the real world (that is, the world *known to us*, as opposed to metaphysical "things-in-themselves") was a product of human collective praxis. The difference between the spiritual and the material, or "subjective" and "objective," boiled down, he claimed, to the difference between individually and socially organized experience. Therefore, he had to reject both Lenin's "vanguardism," which endowed the revolutionary

---

[7] *Ibid.* vol. 35, pp. 121–122.
[8] See R.C. Williams, *The Other Bolsheviks. Lenin and His Critics, 1904–1914* (Bloomington and Indianapolis, IN: Indiana University Press, 1986).
[9] See A. Bogdanov, "Vera i nauka" in *Padenie velikogo fetishizma* (Moscow, 1910), pp. 145–223.

elite with superior, infallible knowledge, and Plekhanov's version of historical determinism. The very notion of objective, irrevocable laws of social development was for him not a scientific explanation of the human world but, rather, something to be explained in historical and social terms.

In ancient and feudal societies, Bogdanov argued, thinking was based on authority; it was marked by a dualism of "spirit" and "matter," a result of the separation of the organizational from the executive function, and by the manner of conceiving causality as an action (command) of authority, that is, conceiving regularities as if they were external or transcendent to the universe. At the next stage, in the society of individualized commodity producers, the authoritarian kind of causality gives way to an "abstract causality," that is, to the notion of "necessity," combined with the phenomenon of "social fetishism." The concept of "necessity" involves considering the regularities in phenomena as immanent forces, impersonal and independent of human will. Hence, the relationships within the processes of cooperation appear to people as laws of an "objective course of things," and the entire world of collective human experience comes to be perceived as alien to human beings, uncontrollable and ruled by abstract, impersonal forces.

Bogdanov did not maintain that capitalism had completely eliminated "authoritarian causality." On the contrary, he saw it as a transitional system in which authoritarian relationships prevail in the inner organization of each factory while "abstract necessity" rules in the sphere of global production and exchange. Because of this, proletarian ideology in the first stages of its formation was also tinged with fetishistic imagery. The theorist of empiriomonism hoped, however, that in its further development the proletarian worldview would overcome both authoritarian dualist and abstract necessitarianism, and thus make possible a "monist organization of experience," which, in turn, would eliminate in human beings the sense of their alienation in the universe and society. "Abstract causality," he predicted, will give way to a "causality of labor" – a projection of the method employed in the technology of complex mechanical production. It will endow people with a higher, collectivistic consciousness and with an ability to transform the world in accordance with freely chosen, non-authoritarian plans.[10]

The consequences of this imminent change will be truly miraculous. The distinction between individually-organized and socially-organized experience will wither away, human beings will liberate themselves from the narrow cages of their individual selves, and the social world, even the natural world, will cease to be felt as an alien, reified, and hostile force. There will be no room for

[10] A. Bogdanov, "Ideal poznaniia" in *Empiriomonizm*, 2nd edn. (Moscow, 1905), vol. 1, pp. 5–63.

a chaotic pluralism of conflicting ideals and values. All individual experiences will be harmonized by "a single society with a single ideology."

In 1909, Bogdanov's group organized itself under the name "Vperëd" ("Forward"), presented its philosophical ideas in a collective book *Outlines of the Philosophy of Collectivism*, and founded a school for revolutionaries on Capri. Apart from Bogdanov, the leading theorist of the group was the literary critic Anatolii Lunacharskii (1875–1933).

Lunacharskii tried to derive from Marxism a heroic, Promethean ethics, combining an action-oriented interpretation of Marxism with strong inspiration from Nietzsche. He saw in Nietzsche a philosopher of the "tragic intensification of will" and was enthusiastic about his claim for the "will to power." He believed that both Marxism and Nietzscheanism were based on the idea of a maximum growth of the power of the human species; hence in both cases the will to power had primacy over justice, and the Christian maxim "love thy neighbor" was replaced by "love the remote," by the readiness to sacrifice the present on the altar of the future. Moreover, the views of Marx and Nietzsche were convergent in their rejection of individualism, seen as the morality of the weak, for the sake of "ultra-individualism," i.e., the aspiration to identify oneself with humankind as a whole. This ultra-individualism led both Marx and Nietzsche to "collectivism" in Bogdanov's sense. Lunacharskii did not hesitate to proclaim that the realization of this collectivist utopia would lead to the emergence of an entirely new man – the Nietzschean "Superman," representing the full actualization of the divine potencies of the human species.

In his two-volume book *Religion and Socialism* (1908), Lunacharskii set forth a grandiose vision of "god-building" and of transforming Marxism into a new, truly universal religion. His vision was a secularized version of Christian millenarianism, with the working class as the Messiah, the proletarian revolution as the act of salvation, and communist society as the Kingdom of God on Earth.[11]

MARXIST THOUGHT BETWEEN THE REVOLUTIONS OF 1917 AND THE CONSOLIDATION OF STALINISM

The two Russian Revolutions of 1917 (the democratic February Revolution and the Bolshevik October Revolution) changed the entire spectrum of ideological positions in Russia. The greatest change, unexpected even in Bolshevik headquarters, was Lenin's decision, in April 1917, to remove the adjective "Social Democratic" from the name of his party, to call it instead the Communist Party

[11] A. Lunacharskii, *Religiia i sotsializm* (St. Petersburg, 1908), vol. 1, pp. 101–102.

(retaining the word "Bolshevik" in brackets), and to call for a new revolution, with the aim of a direct transition to socialism. It was to replace the "bourgeois state" by the dictatorship of the proletariat, involving the abolition of the police, the army, and the bureaucracy.

The program of this revolution was carefully thought out, based upon a systemic study of all Marx's and Engels's texts about the dictatorship of the proletariat and the socialist society of the future, especially Marx's *Critique of the Gotha Program*, his writings on the Paris Commune, and Engels's vision of the imminent victory of scientific socialism. Lenin expounded the program in a surprisingly utopian treatise, *State and Revolution*, written on the eve of the Bolshevik seizure of power. The utopian dimension of this text, totally neglecting realistic, tactical considerations, reflected Lenin's wish to leave a political testament, which in the case of defeat would explain his intention to future generations and rekindle the flame of revolution.[12]

The most characteristic feature of Lenin's utopia is the tension between the idea of a direct workers' democracy and the Marxist commitment to rational planning, presupposing the strictest control of economic conduct. Following Marx's scheme from *Critique of the Gotha Program*, Lenin distinguished two phases of communism: the lower phase (which he called "socialism"), in which the state would exist in the form of the dictatorship of the proletariat, and the higher phase of communism proper, in which the state apparatus would wither away and the principle "to each according to his work" would be replaced by the highest communist principle, "from each according to his ability, to each according to his needs." In the interpretation of the proletarian dictatorship he differed from Marx, since he was not prepared (as Marx was) to tolerate the existence of multiple workers' parties: he strongly stressed that the workers' will had to be embodied in a single party, and he saw tolerance of political pluralism as the greatest mistake of the first form of the proletarian dictatorship, the Paris Commune. But he did not deviate from classical Marxism in emphasizing that embarking on socialism had to involve from the very beginning the abolition of the market. Like Marx and Engels, he saw the market economy as the despotic rule of blind economic forces, totally incompatible with the ideal of rational self-mastery.

It is useful to remember that the ideal of the complete elimination of the market and the organization of society along the model of a single big factory was also an inseparable part of the Erfurt Program (1891) of the Social Democratic Party of Germany. The deradicalization of German Social Democracy began shortly after Engels's death and led to the gradual abandonment of these ideas,

[12] See A. Ulam, *The Bolsheviks* (New York: Macmillan, 1968), pp. 348–349.

making the party less and less communist. Lenin saw this process as a shameful retreat and in 1917 committed his party to the realization of the final goal of the Marxist movement – to the accomplishment (as Engels put it) of the "leap from the kingdom of necessity to the kingdom of freedom."[13]

Lenin's policy in the first three years after the October Revolution, known in the literature as War Communism, was characterized by the belief that a combination of ideological mobilization with brutal, physical coercion could realize the communist project of a totally marketless economy. Most characteristic of this "heroic period" of Bolshevism are three books published in 1920: *The ABC of Communism* by the well-known Bolshevik theorist Nikolai Bukharin (1888– 1938) and the economist Evgenii Preobrazhenskii (1886–1937), Bukharin's *Economics of the Transition Period*, and Trotskii's *Terrorism and Communism*. The first of these books, enjoying for some time greater currency and authority than the works of Lenin, offers an incredibly naive and extreme utopianism. The authors had no doubt that producing everything in accordance with a "general plan," with all details thought out beforehand, would bring about the total regeneration of humanity. Children will no longer belong to their parents but to "the collective," the household will be seen as a barbaric vestige of the past, and "the strictest mutual control" will have a singularly ennobling effect on people. Thus, for instance, the "new man" of the communist epoch will be completely free from the harmful habit of drunkenness, artificially implanted in the workers by the bourgeoisie; the demand for vodka will be replaced by the demand for culture.[14]

The other two books contain apologias for coercion as an alternative to material labor incentives. Bukharin claimed that under the dictatorship of the proletariat, coercing workers does not contradict their freedom, inasmuch as undisciplined individuals are subject to the will of their own class. He even declared that proletarian coercion, "beginning with shootings and ending with labor conscription," is a means of "gathering humanity together," "a method of forging communist mankind out of the human material left by the capitalist epoch."[15] Trotskii put forward a program for the greatest intensification of state coercion, arguing that the future dying-out of the state had to be preceded by "the most merciless dictatorship." He demanded the universal militarization of

---

[13] For a comprehensive history of Marxism as communism see A. Walicki, *Marxism and the Leap to the Kingdom of Freedom: The Rise and Fall of the Communist Utopia* (Stanford University Press, 1995).

[14] N. Bukharin and E. Preobrazhensky, *The ABC of Communism*, preface and introduction by Sidney Heitman (Ann Arbor, MI: University of Michigan Press, 1966), pp. 32, 234.

[15] N.I. Bukharin, *Selected Writings on the State and the Transition to Socialism* (R.B. Day (ed. and trans.), Armonk, NY: M.E. Sharpe, 1982), p. 80.

labor, pointing out that the army provides the best model of social discipline, based on a vertical command structure.[16]

All the terrible sacrifices of the transition period were seen, of course, as necessary to pave the way for the fullest realization of the magnificent potential inherent in the human species. Trotskii, like Lunacharskii before him, described the "new man" of the communist future in terms strongly reminiscent of the Nietzschean "Superman": "Man will become immeasurably stronger, wiser and subtler." "The average human type will rise to the heights of an Aristotle, a Goethe, or a Marx. And above this ridge new peaks will arise."[17]

A peculiar feature of communist ultra-radicalism was the unique combination of a strong penchant for authoritarianism with equally strong anarchic leanings, expressing themselves in outbursts of class hatred and the will to destroy all vestiges of the old world. In the years of militant communism these powerful passions gave rise to an eruption of symbolic vandalism in the villages and to iconoclastic wars against the old culture of the literary intelligentsia. Especially provocative was the rhetoric of the Futurists, headed by Vladimir Maiakovskii, who expressed a truly nihilistic attitude toward the great artistic traditions of the past. Similar radicalism flourished in the Proletarian Culture (Proletcult) movement, headed by Bogdanov. This was a truly mass movement, reaching half a million participants in 1919, with thirty-four journals and about 300 organizations.[18]

An especially destructive form of leftist ultra-radicalism was so-called "legal nihilism." The first legislative act of Bolshevik power was the decree "On Courts" (December 7, 1917), which abolished all existing legal institutions. The old courts were replaced with new, popular courts, composed of elected and "freely revocable" judges, who were to be guided not by any formal rules but by the dictates of the revolutionary legal consciousness of the working people. This decision was provided with good arguments by Mikhail Reisner (1868–1928), a sociologist and legal theorist who already before the revolution (in his book *The Theory of Leon Petrazhitskii: Marxism and Social Ideology*, 1908) tried to reconcile Marxism with Petrażycki's conception of legal consciousness and intuitive law:[19] he agreed with Petrażycki that law was in fact a form of

---

[16] L. Trotskii, *Terrorism and Communism: A Reply to Karl Kautsky* (Westport, CT: Greenwood Press, 1986), pp. 141, 169–170.

[17] L. Trotskii, *Literature and Revolution* (Ann Arbor, MI: University of Michigan Press, 1966), pp. 254–256.

[18] R. Stites, *Revolutionary Dreams: Utopian Vision and Experimental Life in the Russian Revolution* (New York and Oxford: Oxford University Press, 1989), pp. 70–71. Also see Z.A. Sochor, *Revolution and Culture: The Bogdanov-Lenin Controversy* (Ithaca, NY: Cornell University Press, 1988).

[19] On Leon Petrażycki (1867–1931), the leading figure in pre-revolutionary Russian jurisprudence, see A. Walicki, *Legal Philosophies of Russian Liberalism* (Oxford: Clarendon Press, 1987; University of Notre Dame Press, 1992), pp. 213–290.

consciousness, adding, of course, that for Marxists the binding power of law was to be found in the intuitive legal consciousness of workers.

Obviously, this system provided ample room for arbitrariness. From Lenin's point of view, however, popular judges proved to be too lenient toward their class enemies. Because of this, popular courts soon gave way to a highly repressive centralized system, directly subordinate to the commands of the party leadership.

The entire period of "War Communism" can be described as a peculiar outcome of the operation of three factors: the utopian blueprint of the vanguard party, anarchic impulses of the radical masses, and the increasingly autonomous role of state terrorism. It was a complete fiasco. In March 1921, Lenin was forced to proclaim the so-called New Economic Policy (NEP), opening the way to a market sector of petty commodity producers.

The economic results of NEP were quick and good, but Lenin had very mixed feelings about its success. In fact it was an utterly humiliating experience for him. At the Eleventh Party Congress (March–April 1922) he defined the situation as the total defeat of the proud dream of consciously directing the course of history. The communists, he said, "are not directing, they are being directed." They had made the greatest revolution in the world but had proved to be culturally inferior to the politically defeated and had let victory slip through their fingers.[20]

In the intellectual sphere, the positive influence of NEP was most visible in the philosophy of law. The main theorist of NEP legal culture was Evgenii Pashukanis (1891–1937), the only Soviet legal philosopher to win significant recognition outside the Soviet Union. His *General Theory of Law and Marxism* (1924) maintained that law was neither a form of class power nor simply a command by the holders of state power: it was above all a product of market relationships, constituted by the exchange of goods. Therefore, only bourgeois civil law (i.e., law regulating the relationships between separate individuals, subjects of egoistic interests) was law in the true sense of the term. On the other hand, Pashukanis was faithful to the view that the existence of law was incompatible with the communal spirit. He firmly believed that, after the abandonment of NEP, the construction of socialism should entail the realization of the Marxist vision of the future withering away of law and the state.[21]

In philosophy, the situation was complicated and unstable. In fall 1922, on Lenin's personal order, the most outstanding non-communist philosophers (as

---

[20] *The Lenin Anthology*, pp. 522–527.
[21] Since this was not Stalin's intention, Pashukanis was declared to be an ideological "wrecker" and, despite his severe self-criticism, fell victim to the great purge of the 1930s. Pashukanis's works are available in English: *Selected Writings on Marxism and Law* (Piers Beirne and Robert Sharlet (eds.), London: Academic Press, 1980).

well as some other prominent representatives of the humanities) were forcefully banished from Russia. This act of violence was accompanied by the establishment of the first Soviet philosophy journal, *Under the Banner of Marxism*, and by heated discussion on its pages of the role of philosophy after the Revolution.

At the outset this discussion was dominated by views reminiscent of the nihilistic radicalism of the pre-NEP period. Sergei Minin (1882–1962), a militant atheist, published in the journal a programmatic article "Philosophy Overboard!" It argued that philosophy as such was a bourgeois ideology, in the same way that religion was a feudal one, and that the working class needed only exact sciences. After a while, however, the discussants agreed that Marxist philosophy did also exist and needed to be developed. This agreement was immediately followed by the emergence of two philosophical schools: the "mechanists" and "dialecticians." The "mechanists," represented by Bukharin, Bogdanov, and Liubov' Aksel'rod (1868–1946), stressed the paramount importance of the scientific approach, which led them to rigid determinism, materialistic reductionism, and the denial of qualitative leaps in development. The "dialecticans," headed by Abram Deborin (1881–1963) and having in their ranks talented historians of philosophy like Valentin Asmus (1894–1975) and Ivan Luppol (1897–1943), saw their main task as a materialist reworking of Hegelian dialectics, which offered more room for philosophical imagination. Political differences between the two schools were not always clear, but on the whole the "mechanists," because of their commitment to scientific caution and gradualism, were seen as a "Right" deviation, whereas the "dialecticians" were associated with "Left" deviationism, accused of philosophical idealism and an unrealistic approach to practical matters.

For some time the "mechanists" seemed to prevail. The most representative and widely used handbook of Marxism remained Bukharin's *Historical Materialism: A System of Sociology* (1921, 1925), a book totally neglecting Marxist dialectical philosophy and for this reason strongly criticized by the famous Italian Marxist, Antonio Gramsci.[22] However, the process of the gradual abandonment of NEP undermined Bukharin's position and gave the Deborinites the upper hand. Their triumph proved to be very short-lived. In March 1930, a group of Stalinist activists, headed by Mark Mitin (1901–1987), announced a "battle on two fronts in philosophy," accusing both schools of extremely harmful errors. Predictably, the "mechanists" were represented as Bukharinites and the "dialecticians" as alleged allies of Trotskii. These accusations, sanctioned by a June 1930 article in *Pravda*, put an end to toleration of relative pluralism in

---

[22] See A. Gramsci, *Selections from the Prison Notebooks* (Quintin Hoare (ed.), New York: International Publishers, 1971), pp. 426–448.

philosophy, firmly establishing the position of Stalin as the highest arbiter in Marxist theory.

Let us return to the Soviet Union under NEP. Lenin's premature death (January 21, 1924) left the party with the feeling that it was ideologically bound to put an end to the concessions of NEP. But it was deeply divided on how far to go in the new "communist offensive." The Left, associated with Trotskii, defended the view that communism demands organizing agricultural production in large collective farms strictly controlled by the state. In economic terms, collectivization was strongly recommended by Preobrazhenskii, one of the authors of *The ABC of Communism*. Bukharin, his co-author, was seen as the leader of the "Right": without defending NEP capitalism, he stood firmly against the expropriation of the peasantry and was therefore perceived as an ideologist of the "kulaks" (peasant proprietors). Stalin, representing the center, was initially closer to Bukharin, with whom he also shared the idea of "socialism in one country" (in opposition to Trotskii's position). However, in 1928–1929, he embarked upon his "revolution from above," consisting, above all, in forcible collectivization. The Left initially saw collectivization merely as a practical solution to the grain procurement crisis. In fact, the procurement crisis was only a pretext. The deepest reason for Stalin's decision was his will to subject the peasantry (the majority of the population) to the strictest political control, securing thereby the safety of "socialism in one country" and enormously strengthening his own personal dictatorship.

Stalin's revolution was successfully implemented, at the cost of enormous suffering, borne most of all by the peasants. By early 1932, the pace of revolutionary mobilization had slowed. Two years later, the Seventeenth Party Congress (January–February 1934), the so-called "Congress of Victors," proclaimed that the "revolution from above" had been completed. Stalin's next step was to undertake a thorough purge of the party, cleansing it of "Lenin's old guard" (as capable of opposing Stalin's will) and replacing it by young party activists, mostly from the provinces, who owed the new leader their entire careers and, therefore, unbounded personal loyalty. This upheaval was accompanied by a policy of controlled "normalization" in other spheres of life, aimed at stabilization and directed against communist radicalism. Trotskii called it a "Soviet Thermidor" and a "betrayal of the revolution": for him Stalin's rehabilitation of traditional values – especially his defense of the family (putting an end to easy divorce and abortion), restoration of social hierarchy and inequality, and appeal to patriotism (visible, for instance, in the demotion of Mikhail Pokrovskii's revolutionary school of historiography and elevation of a more traditional approach to teaching Russian history) – was a "great retreat," the end of the revolutionary process in Russia and the beginning of the "transition to normality," which had to include the gradual but inevitable return to elements of a market economy. Many émigré Russian scholars (such as the sociologist Nikolai Timasheff, author of *The Great Retreat: The Growth and Decline of Communism in Russia*) shared this diagnosis but gave the term "retreat" a positive meaning.[23]

The Stalinist stabilization was symbolized in the Constitution of 1936 which adopted with great ceremony the general principles of democracy. Of course, as the Moscow show trials of the time demonstrated, these principles were not to be taken seriously. Nevertheless, many western observers, including Russian émigrés like Timasheff, pointed out that even a hypocritical adoption of the principles of a law-based state could have positive value for the future.

Legalism, however, was never meant to replace ideological cohesion. To ensure this, it was necessary to prepare a manual of basic ideology, popular enough to be studied by all citizens and to be treated as binding for all of them. This project materialized in 1938 as the *History of the Communist Party of the Soviet Union (The Bolsheviks): A Short Course*. Its most important theoretical part, the chapter on "Dialectical and Historical Materialism," was written by Stalin himself, and for this reason was immediately proclaimed to be a work of genius and the cornerstone of the entire edifice of communist education.

Unlike Bukharin or Trotskii, Stalin was not an original Marxist theorist. He had, nevertheless, a considerable capacity for simplified popularization combined with suggestive didacticism. His account of Marxism was based entirely on the Engelsian conception of materialist dialectics, Plekhanov's necessitarian version of historical materialism, and Lenin's "copy theory of knowledge." It stressed that Marxism is scientific knowledge of the "objective laws" of nature and history. This approach provided Stalin with a primitive but powerful legitimating device. It was an attempt to demonstrate that the activity of the party was grounded in the innermost structure of the universe, that it accorded with the universal laws of nature and history, and that those who possess scientific knowledge of these laws (as Stalin obviously did) could not possibly be wrong. His emphasis on the laws of dialectics as the most general laws of the material universe created the impression that the decisions of the party leadership had not only a historical sanction, but a cosmological sanction as well. Thus, for instance, Stalin's determination to crush the deviations within the party was consistent with the so-called law of uncompromising struggle between opposites, while Bukharin, who contradicted this law in his "theory of equilibrium" and his

---

[23] N. Timasheff, *The Great Retreat: The Growth and Decline of Communism in Russia* (New York: E.P. Dutton and Co., 1946).

idea of the peasantry gradually growing into socialism, was rightly condemned and sentenced by the tribunal of history.

A striking feature of Stalin's Marxist catechism was its conspicuous silence on the communist future. There was not a single word on the problems raised in Lenin's *State and Revolution*!

The reasons for this silence are obvious: the Soviet dictator wanted to legitimize his power by deriving it from objective necessities, but did not want to become dependent on ideological "final goals" in whose name he might conceivably be opposed. His last work, *Economic Problems of Socialism in the USSR* (1952), shows that he did not forget about these "final goals" and fully realized that socialism (the lower stage that was already in existence) was to be replaced by the higher stage of communism proper. But he wanted to use the concept of objective, necessary laws of development not only against the enemies of communism but also against impatient communist radicals, who might be willing to destabilize the state in the name of communist eschatology.

Thus, the teleological legitimization of communist totalitarianism, prevalent under Lenin, was replaced by a *necessitarian* legitimization. The totalitarianism of the revolutionary movement, trying to create an entirely new world and new man, gave way to the totalitarianism of the state, no longer committed to the vision of changing human nature (hence its "rehabilitation" of the traditional family, inequality, and so forth) but striving to control everything for the sake of increasing its unrestricted power. Communist mythology was still needed as a part of the legitimizing tradition, but its inner vitality was bound to inevitable routinization and erosion. Ideology remained utterly important as a means of *ideocratic* rule, which sought to control not only the external conduct of people but also their minds and consciences, but it lost its importance as a vivid force and inspiration to change the world.

The best analysis of Stalinism from a Marxist standpoint was Trotskii's book, *The Revolution Betrayed* (1936). Trotskii wrote it from a safe distance, because in 1928 he had been forced into exile. A few years later, however, on August 20, 1940, he was murdered in Mexico City by a Stalinist agent.

As already mentioned, Stalin's retreat of the 1930s was seen by Trotskii as the Thermidorian phase of the Russian Revolution. Stalin became the leader of the state bureaucracy and in this capacity "conquered the Bolshevik party," transforming it into the "political organization of bureaucracy."[24] But this betrayal of the revolution did not result in a total dismantling of the existing system; the ruling bureaucratic stratum transformed the remnants of the workers' state into

---

[24] L. Trotsky, *The Revolution Betrayed: What is the Soviet Union and Where is It Going?* (New York: Pathfinder, 1972), pp. 93–94.

a *totalitarian* regime standing halfway between capitalism and socialism. In fact, the transformation had been a gradual process: in Trotskii's view, the Soviet regime "had become 'totalitarian' in character several years before this word arrived from Germany."[25]

The socialist side of the regime was a planned economy based on the nationalization of the means of production; its capitalist side was the replacement of planned distribution (i.e., ration cards) by trade, accompanied by conscious support of inequality. Hence, the Soviet government was a transitional regime characterized by a deep contradiction between socialist norms of production and bourgeois norms of distribution. As such, it could develop in either direction, depending on the relative strength of its social forces. It could slip back into capitalism, which would be to the advantage of its upper stratum, or it might give rise to a new proletarian revolution.[26]

Trotskii's view that the "degenerated workers' state" of the Soviet Union could slip back into capitalism seemed at the time to be a fantasy, but as we now know it proved to be prophetic. It had to be so because the communist vision of a totally planned, marketless economy was simply unrealizable, irrespective of the wishes of the ruling bureaucracy.

Another sound insight of Trotskii's book was its description of the Stalinist regime as totalitarian, similar to fascist states in its demand for unconditional obedience and absolute personal loyalty to the leader. It has been largely forgotten that the author of *The Revolution Betrayed* was a pioneer in developing the concept of totalitarianism (as distinct from revolutionary dictatorship, which he continued to advocate). His particular contribution to the explanation of Stalinist totalitarianism was the stress on unprecedented, incomparable ideological control and unspeakable spiritual oppression.[27]

Soon after the publication of Trotskii's book the accuracy of his description of the tragic fate of independent Marxists under Stalin was confirmed by the 1938 trial and execution of Bukharin. Bukharin, a devout communist and Stalin's personal friend, publicly confessed at the trial that he had committed unpardonable counter-revolutionary crimes. He did so as a "last service to the party," believing that in the light of history, the party could never be wrong. Bukharin endorsed the concept that opposing the party's leadership was tantamount to "objective guilt and objective treason." Trotskii, who himself believed for a long time that "one cannot be right against his own party,"[28] understood this

---

[25] *Ibid.* p. 100.   [26] *Ibid.* pp. 254–255.   [27] *Ibid.* pp. 181–184.
[28] Trotskii's words at the Thirteenth Party Congress (May 1924), quoted in R. Medvedev, *Let History Judge* (New York: Columbia University Press, 1989), p. 127.

very well. And the ex-communist writer, Arthur Koestler, in his classic novel *Darkness at Noon* (1941), paid a powerful literary tribute to Bukharin's "logic."

RUSSIAN MARXISM AND "POSITIVE FREEDOM"

The entire story of Marxist communism in Russia (the "legal Marxism" of the liberals was, of course, something different) can be seen as motivated by the idea of "positive freedom" in Isaiah Berlin's sense of the term.[29] There existed different understandings of the Marxist interpretation of this idea, but in all of them freedom meant not individual freedom here and now, under the rule of law, but collective freedom in the communist future; not "negative freedom" from external compulsion, but freedom as the positive capacity for collective self-realization.

In the simplest sense, prevalent in the language of class struggle, freedom was understood as the social emancipation of the working class. For Plekhanov, who was a patriot and a Westernizer, it meant at the first stage Russia's liberation from autocracy, which he understood as a precondition of the country's participation in the common European endeavor of the movement toward communism. However, despite his readiness to cooperate with the liberals, Plekhanov identified freedom with Hegelian "rational necessity" and explicitly proclaimed the need to sacrifice human individuals on the altar of history.

The Bolsheviks were much more radical. For Lenin, the liberation of the workers through the dictatorship of the proletariat, leading to universal human emancipation, was the only acceptable meaning of the word "freedom." In his eyes, liberal "bourgeois" freedom was either a conscious fraud or total illusion.

The more philosophical Marxists, like Bogdanov, Lunacharskii, and Trotskii, gave freedom a Promethean dimension, defining it (after Marx) as rational mastery over human collective fate and describing the transition to communism as the leap from the kingdom of necessity (i.e., the domination of blind economic forces) to the truly human "kingdom of freedom." Thus, they were concerned not merely with the social emancipation of the oppressed masses, but also, and above all, with creating the conditions for the freest and fullest development of the human species. Hence, they were fascinated with the image of the powerful, magnificent Man of the Future, and often supported this vision with references to the Nietzschean Superman. According to some American scholars (George Kline and Bernice Glatzer Rosenthal, in particular) this quasi-Nietzschean motif was an important part of the ideological rationale for heroic efforts and unlimited sacrifices in building communism.

---

[29] Isaiah Berlin, "Two Concepts of Liberty" in *Four Essays on Liberty* (Oxford University Press, 1969).

Under Stalinism, the idea of rational mastery over collective fate was conveniently reduced to the view that comprehensive social planning, a necessary means for overcoming humiliating dependence on blind economic forces, required total control of all spheres of human life. In this way, the idea of positive freedom as rational self-control was transformed into a powerful justification of the totalitarian state as an omnipresent controlling agency, and of the leader of the party-state as the supreme controller. And the idea that true freedom could be achieved only at the highest stage of communism, that is, not now, but in the ill-defined future, helped to justify the obvious unfreedoms, egregious violations of human dignity, and other multiple deprivations of the present.

16

ADVENTURES IN DIALECTIC AND INTUITION: SHPET, IL'IN, LOSEV

PHILIP T. GRIER

INTRODUCTION

Three of the most remarkable, and remarkably independent, Russian philosophers of the early twentieth century each developed an approach to philosophy that apparently combined significant elements of Hegelian dialectic and Husserlian intuitionism. That aim is perhaps most clearly manifested in the self-proclaimed "dialectical phenomenology" of Losev. However, Shpet's development of a Husserlian phenomenology was explicitly set within an Hegelian framework, and Il'in's interpretation of Hegel was notable for its insistence that Hegel's dialectical method should be understood as an earlier version of the very same intuitionist intellectual procedure that Husserl came to call "phenomenology."

Since Hegel and Husserl do not at first glance appear to have been engaged in parallel modes of inquiry, why did their philosophical projects loom so large in the thinking of these three very different Russian philosophers? In all three cases the Russians' interest in Hegel and Husserl went directly to the question of *method* – a focus that places us immediately at the heart of each of their visions of the philosophical project, illuminating crucial contrasts and comparisons among them. Moreover, in stipulating their attitudes toward Hegel and Husserl, each of these philosophers inevitably revealed something of his understanding of the relation of Russian philosophical thought to the western tradition as a whole.

The fact that these three philosophers were very nearly of the same generation,[1] that they all lived in Moscow during the period when these projects took shape, that they were all connected with Moscow University, that they knew each other personally, and that they participated in a number of the same intellectual societies, lends biographical plausibility to the supposition that they might have been linked by some broadly shared intellectual outlook. Yet

---

[1] Shpet was four years older than Il'in, and Il'in, in turn, ten years older than Losev.

they were fiercely independent thinkers, each pursuing his own project with extraordinary courage and stubbornness, inspired by radically distinct visions of what the times, and Russia, required. That, of course, makes it all the more curious that they should have apparently agreed on this particular point: that Hegel and Husserl together should be taken as the major touchstones of contemporary philosophical method.

Husserl himself had a notorious blind spot where Hegel was concerned, and nothing on the surface of Husserl's writings would be likely to conduct the reader back to Hegel. In his famous programmatic essay of 1911, "Philosophy as Rigorous Science," Husserl complained that the emergence of Hegelianism, which he termed "romantic philosophy," had disrupted the vital project of a critique of reason to which German philosophy had been previously committed in the figures of Kant and Fichte. According to Husserl, "Only with romantic philosophy does a change occur. However much Hegel insists on the absolute validity of his method and his doctrine, still his system lacks a critique of reason, which is the foremost prerequisite for being scientific in philosophy."[2] Husserl seemed entirely oblivious to the fact that Hegel's *Science of Logic* was the most radical, thorough, and systematic critique of reason attempted by any German Idealist philosopher, and offered a more fundamental critique of it than any conceived by Kant or Fichte. Husserl instead ineptly presented his own work as an attempt to *revive* the Kantian/Fichtean project of a fundamental critique of reason that had been *derailed* by Hegel and his followers.

These Russian philosophers were ahead of their time in extricating Hegel from a half-century of neglect and uncomprehending criticisms and in restoring him to the philosophical pantheon. Still more significantly, the choice of Hegel and Husserl as the major touchstones of contemporary philosophical method arguably represented the crossing of an historic threshold for Russian philosophical thought. If the ideal of pure or genuine philosophical inquiry is complete methodological self-consciousness, or, alternatively, approaching as closely as possible an ultimately presuppositionless form of inquiry, the two philosophers in the modern period most conspicuously committed to such an ideal are surely Hegel and Husserl. In adopting these two philosophers as their primary exemplars of contemporary philosophical method, Shpet, Il'in, and Losev each revealed their professional sense of the most exacting standards applicable to the philosophical enterprise.

---

[2] E. Husserl, "Philosophy as Rigorous Science" in Peter McCormick and Frederick A. Elliston (eds.), *Husserl: Shorter Works* (University of Notre Dame Press, 1981), p. 168. Husserl continued in the same passage, "In this connection it is clear that this philosophy, like romantic philosophy in general, acted in the years that followed either to weaken or to adulterate the impulse toward the constitution of rigorous philosophical science."

THREE PHILOSOPHICAL PROJECTS

Gustav Gustavovich Shpet

Gustav Shpet (1879–1937) was born and educated in Kiev, finishing St. Vladimir University with a prize-winning study of causality in Hume and Kant. He moved to Moscow in 1907, and began teaching at Moscow University in 1910. He was well versed in the neo-Kantian projects of his day, and knew the details of their derivations through the various schools of nineteenth-century German philosophy. Shpet traveled in Europe during the summer terms of 1910 and 1911, spending some time in Göttingen. He spent the academic year 1912–1913 (his official *stazhirovka*) in Göttingen, where he developed close personal relations with Husserl, who regarded him as one of his most exceptional students. Returning to Moscow, Shpet wrote *Appearance and Sense* (1914), a defense of Husserl's transcendental phenomenology, immediately establishing his reputation as Russia's leading phenomenologist. Yet Shpet's independence of mind soon led him beyond Husserl's formulation of the phenomenological project (as Shpet then understood it) toward a hermeneutical phenomenology of social being, focused upon the logic of history, language, and of art, which he developed in a series of important publications from 1916 to 1927.

In 1922, Shpet's name was apparently placed on the list of "irreconcilables" who were to be exiled by the Bolsheviks on the "philosophers' steamship." He pleaded with his friend Lunacharskii to have his name removed, and succeeded in remaining in Soviet Russia. In an *Essay on the Development of Russian Philosophy* (1922), he announced his belief in the possibility of a Russian "Renaissance" to be brought about through the revolution.[3] The new Russia would require a new intelligentsia with a new ideology, as yet unformed. Shpet appeared to think that he could contribute to the formation of the new ideology and thus to a new culture. He believed that philosophy, conceived "as knowledge, not as morality, not as preaching, not as 'worldviews,'" would be a crucial element of the Russian Renaissance, and that Russian philosophy was just beginning to reach the stage of objective knowledge.[4] As for the relation of a national philosophical tradition to philosophy in general, Shpet claimed that questions, once posed, do not have "national" answers, only objective ones. National traditions of philosophical inquiry can be reflected only in the distinctive questions they

---

[3] *Ocherk razvitiia russkoi filosofii*, republished in A.I. Vvedenskii, A.F. Losev, E.L. Radlov, G.G. Shpet, *Ocherki istorii russkoi filosofii* (B.V. Emel'ianova and K.N. Liubutina (eds.), Sverdlovsk: Izd. Ural'skogo universiteta, 1991), pp. 217–578, here p. 221.

[4] Shpet, *Ocherk razvitiia russkoi filosofii*, p. 218.

pose.[5] Shpet seemed to regard himself as an avatar of the new "scientific" philosophy, philosophy conceived as objective knowledge; hence his enthusiastic welcome of Husserl's conception of philosophy as "rigorous science."

Ivan Aleksandrovich Il'in

Ivan Il'in (1883–1954) was born in Moscow and educated in the Faculty of Law at Moscow University from 1901 to 1906. Inspired by Pavel Novgorodtsev and Evgenii Trubetskoi, he developed a solid grasp of the history of philosophy and of legal philosophy. He followed his mentors in rejecting the reigning positivist legal theory in favor of a version of natural law. In late 1910, Il'in went abroad, primarily to Germany, for his academic *stazhirovka* in legal philosophy. Studying with Husserl in Göttingen in summer 1911, he came to view Husserl's phenomenology as a major development in the history of philosophy, but he nevertheless devoted most of his research abroad to Hegel's philosophy. On returning to Moscow, he wrote a major two-volume commentary, *Hegel's Philosophy as a Theory of the Concreteness of God and Humanity* (1918),[6] intended as his master's thesis. Over the next few years he also continued writing and publishing on legal theory. As Russia's misadventure in World War I unfolded and anarchy threatened the tsarist state, Il'in turned to political activities. During the October Revolution, he became an outspoken opponent of Bolshevism. He was arrested by the Cheka six times between 1918 and 1922. Evidently on two of these occasions he was saved from the Cheka through the personal intervention of Lenin, who admired his commentary on Hegel.[7]

In May 1918, Il'in managed to schedule the defense of his master's dissertation. In recognition of the extraordinary breadth and depth of his work on Hegel, he was awarded not only the master's degree but a doctorate as well. Il'in's name was also placed on the list of those intellectuals to be exiled in 1922, and, given his political attitudes, there was no possibility of reprieve. The remainder of his life was spent in exile, in Germany until 1938, then in Switzerland until his death in 1954. While in exile, Il'in produced an extraordinary number of writings in a variety of fields, including moral philosophy, political commentary, legal theory, aesthetics, cultural history, and religious thought. He remained perhaps the emigration's most uncompromising, outspoken, and hardened ideological opponent of Bolshevism. He advocated a visionary renewal of

---

[5] *Ibid.*

[6] I.A. Il'in, *Filosofiia Gegelia kak uchenie o konkretnosti Boga i cheloveka*, 2 vols. (Moscow: Izd. G.A. Lemana i S.I. Sakharova, 1918; St. Petersburg: Nauka, 1994; Moscow: Russkaia kniga, 2002). See my translation (Evanston, IL: Northwestern University Press, 2010).

[7] See "Biograficheskii ocherk" by V.A. Tomsinov in I.A. Il'in, *Teoriia prava i gosudarstvo* (Moscow: Zertsalo, 2003), pp. 26–27.

traditional Russian cultural, social, religious, and political institutions, in a future post-communist Russia, which simultaneously amounted to a severe critique of the historical actuality of these institutions in pre-revolutionary Russia.[8]

Il'in's writings in legal theory developed a conception of law and state authority as grounded in a consciousness and recognition of right (*pravosoznanie*). In the area of applied law, Il'in tried to imagine the details of a possible post-communist system of law for Russia. He championed a future state grounded in the authority of law and in mutual recognition of rights and duties by government and citizenry. He rejected the conception of the state all too common in Russian history as simply an organ for the assertion of power. He envisaged a society in which individual citizens develop a level of spiritual dignity, autonomy, and respect for others such that the rule of law emerges as an organic and integral aspect of national life.[9] In recent years, specialists have come to regard Il'in as the most important and original twentieth-century Russian theorist of law and the state. His contributions are increasingly widely discussed in the literature.[10]

Aleksei Fëdorovich Losev

Aleksei Losev (1893–1988) was born in Novocherkassk and educated at Moscow University from 1911 to 1915 in the Faculty of History and Philology. At an early age he developed extraordinary erudition in the philosophy and literature of ancient Greece; he soon expanded his interests to the Neoplatonists and to eastern and western patristic literature. Losev was a keen student of the history of modern philosophy, including Hegel and Husserl. He was also a passionate devotee of the arts, with an exceptional knowledge of music and a deep love of theatre. Before 1920 Losev embarked upon a series of far-reaching investigations into ancient Greek and late Hellenistic philosophy, inspired above all by the Christian Neoplatonist writings of Pseudo-Dionysius the Areopagite.[11] His research focused on Plato and on Neoplatonic derivations of the cosmos from the One, the philosophy of the name (*imiaslavie*),[12] music, artistic

---

[8] For a somewhat fuller account of Il'in's life and intellectual biography, see my "The Complex Legacy of Ivan Il'in" in James P. Scanlan (ed.), *Russian Thought After Communism: The Recovery of a Philosophical Heritage* (Armonk, NY: M.E. Sharpe, 1994), pp. 165–186.

[9] See *O sushchnosti pravosoznaniia*, esp. chs. 15, 17, 19, in Il'in, *Teoriia prava i gosudarstvo*.

[10] See, e.g., William E. Butler, *Russian Law*, 3rd edn. (New York: Oxford University Press, 2009).

[11] Aza Takho-Godi, quoted in Viktor Troitskii, *Razyskaniia o zhizni i tvorchestve A.F. Loseva* (Moscow: Agraf, 2007), p. 172.

[12] *Imiaslavie* (onomatodoxy) is the much-contested doctrine that "the name of God is in its essence holy and is God himself." A.F. Losev, "Imiaslavie," accessed 23 April 08 at www.ccel.org/contrib/ru/Other/Losev/ONOMATOD.HTM, p. 3.

form, Neoplatonic number theory, symbolism, and myth, culminating in the publication of eight remarkable books between the years 1927 and 1930.[13] An important source of inspiration for Losev in these years was Vladimir Solov'ëv's platonic metaphysics and sophiology. In the course of several of these studies, Losev developed an elaborately detailed dialectical schema of principles and categories, paralleling the derivation of the cosmos from the One through the hypostases of Plotinus and Proclus; he interpreted the fundamental triad in terms of an expanded tetrad and pentad, by the addition of two supplementary principles.[14]

Though the Bolsheviks' ideology of official atheism made it dangerous for Losev to reveal the true intent of much of his work, he sought to develop and defend a version of Russian Orthodox theology. In 1929, he was secretly tonsured as a monk, taking the name Andronik, while his wife became the nun Afanasiia; these events were revealed only after Losev's death. One of the specific, though necessarily disguised, motives of his early work was to make a philosophically precise defense of *imiaslavie* against widespread accusations of pantheism.[15]

Another deep motive of Losev's work, connected with the first, was to reinterpret and defend hesychasm, with its apophatic theology, originally grounded in a distinction between the *energeia* and the *ousia* (essence) of the Divine, holding out the possibility of a mystical union with the Divine energy of God. The possibility of human participation in the Divine energy was spelled out in Losev's philosophy of the name. According to Losev's doctrine, the name originates not in human language, but in the self-manifestation of the Divine in relation to meonic other-being (not to be confused with other-being within the created world), in Divine self-understanding of its own essence. Only that which has personhood can possess a name; for a name to be created it must necessarily manifest itself actively in meaning and personhood. This sovereign Divine self-manifestation is directed outward as an energy that everywhere reveals or communicates as a living symbol that which is named.[16] According to

[13] *The Ancient Cosmos and Contemporary Science* (1927), *The Philosophy of the Name* (1927), *Music as an Object of Logic* (1927), *The Dialectic of Artistic Form* (1927), *The Dialectic of Numbers in Plotinus* (1928), *Aristotle's Criticism of Platonism* (1929), *Essays in Ancient Symbolism and Mythology* (1930), and *The Dialectics of Myth* (1930). Only the last is available in English translation: *The Dialectics of Myth* (Vladimir Marchenkov (trans.), London: Routledge, 2003).

[14] For an excellent summary account of this schema of principles and categories, see Troitskii, *Razyskaniia o zhizni i tvorchestve A.F. Loseva*, pp. 270–297.

[15] See the very useful summary of Losev's intellectual biography by L. Gogotishvili on the website of the Losev Library at http://losev-library.ru (accessed on 11 March 2008).

[16] Losev, *Veshch' i imia* in his *Bytie, imia, kosmos* (A.A. Takho-Godi and I.I. Makhan'kova (eds.), Moscow: Mysl', 1993), p. 840.

Losev, "The energy of the essence of God is inseparable from God himself and is God himself... The name of God is God himself, but God himself is not a name."[17] Divine energy is manifest in the created world in the form of *communication*, of *meaning* present in *symbol*, understood not conventionally, as a stand-in for something not present, but rather as itself the living presence of the divine within the created world, apprehended as the *name* of God. Apprehension of the divine name from within the created world is Losev's interpretation of the "mystical union" of the divine and human in traditional hesychast doctrine.[18] Losev's defense of the orthodoxy (i.e., the non-pantheistic nature) of hesychasm and *imiaslavie* in the context of his own reformulation of Christian Neoplatonist thought is viewed by many as the culmination of a distinctively Russian philosophical tradition. On this account Losev is sometimes called "the last Russian philosopher."

The culminating idea in *The Dialectics of Myth* (1930), the last of Losev's famous eight early works, is Absolute Mythology, "the only possible picture of the world."[19] It was to be elaborated in a subsequent work which Losev was never allowed to write; the task of *The Dialectics of Myth* was merely to define "myth" in a manner leading up to the idea of Absolute Mythology, which could only be sketched there in terms of a few defining categories. The first of these was personalism. Losev claimed that the dialectical structure of myth consists in the triad of person, history, and word. According to him, "every real mythology contains (1) the doctrine of the primordial luminous being or simply of the primordial essence; (2) a theogonic and, generally speaking, historical process; and finally, (3) the primordial essence that has reached self-consciousness of itself in other-being."[20] Losev conceived the cosmos itself as essentially personalistic. The primordial essence was God in Losev's Orthodox Christian conception, and his conception of the cosmos was an irreducibly religious one.

SEARCHING FOR METHOD: DIALECTIC AND INTUITION

Somewhat improbably, Shpet, Il'in, and Losev all characterized their central methodological approaches in terms of some combination of Hegelian dialectic and Husserlian phenomenological intuition. In this section I will attempt to delineate, in necessarily brief and highly condensed form, the respective roles of dialectic and intuition in each project.

[17] From a letter to P.A. Florenskii (January 30, 1923), quoted in L. Gogotishvili, "Religiozno-filosofskii status iazyka" in Losev, *Bytie, imia, kosmos*, p. 910.
[18] See L. Gogotishvili's essay on Losev on the website of the Losev Library.
[19] Losev, *The Dialectics of Myth*, p. 189.   [20] *Ibid.* pp. 182–183.

Shpet's Attitudes toward Hegel and Husserl

The most strikingly Husserlian project in early twentieth-century Russian philosophy is Gustav Shpet's *Appearance and Sense*,[21] published barely one year after Husserl's *Ideas I*, in which he provided an exposition and defense of the method of phenomenological reduction, first applied systematically by Husserl in that work. Interestingly, from the outset Shpet employs a Hegelian framework for the exposition of Husserl's thought. Shpet begins by delineating a contrast between "negative" and "positive" philosophy, locating Husserl's project within the latter. For Shpet, "negative" philosophy is essentially characterized by the assumption that the aim of philosophy must be "to determine the limits of reason or of knowledge" (p. 3); thus, negative philosophy regularly calls into question the achievement of all previous philosophy, as requiring some foundation that was not, or could not be, supplied. On the other hand, "positive" philosophy stands within the tradition, always taking as its ultimate problem that of "knowing what is *real in all* its forms and types" (p. 3). Elaborating on this distinction, Shpet identifies the central concern of negative philosophy in its modern form as "not the study of cognizable being, but of the cognizing subject itself, yet again not in its *being*, as a cognizing subject, but only in its cognitive forms," i.e., the project of "theory of knowledge" (p. 9).

Having chosen to set up the initial problem in these terms, Shpet then moves to an exposition and defense of Husserl's project of establishing "the fundamental philosophical science" (p. 5). This way of setting out the motivation for Husserlian phenomenology was apparently drawn more or less verbatim from Hegel's famous "Introduction" to the *Phenomenology of Spirit*. Shpet makes repeated use of the metaphor of "not getting into the water until we have learned how to swim" (Hegel's metaphorical representation of the "negative" project of a "theory of knowledge," e.g., pp. 51, 70).[22] As Shpet notes, the metaphor comes from section 10 of Hegel's *Encyclopedia Logic*, which is a brief restatement of the central argument against the Kantian "epistemological" project (and all similar projects) given in the "Introduction" to the *Phenomenology*. Since this is the context in which Shpet introduces the distinction between negative and positive philosophy, Kant thereby becomes the exemplar of negative philosophy in the modern period, and Hegel, by implication, of positive philosophy, and thus the crucial predecessor of Husserl's project (Husserl's own view of Hegel notwithstanding).

[21] *Iavlenie i smysl* (Moscow: Germes, 1914). Available in English translation as *Appearance and Sense* (Thomas Nemeth (trans.), Dordrecht: Kluwer, 1991). Parenthetical page citations in the text are to the translation.

[22] Also see G.G. Shpet, *Istoriia kak problema logiki* (V.S. Miasnikova (ed.), Moscow: Pamiatniki istori-cheskoi mysli, 2002), p. 35.

This fundamental distinction between negative philosophy and positive philosophy remained central for Shpet throughout his work. In his view, negative philosophy tended to lead to skepticism and relativism, calling into question the possibility of any knowledge of objective reality. The project of negative philosophy in the modern period was synonymous with the "theory of knowledge," which Shpet consistently treated as a regrettable mistake to which many of his contemporaries remained committed. Kant, Kantians, and neo-Kantians all fell under Shpet's condemnation.[23] Conversely, throughout his career Shpet maintained a consistently positive evaluation of Hegel's philosophical accomplishment.[24] He treated Hegel and Husserl as the most important representatives in the modern period of the "positive" tradition that began with Plato and Plotinus, and ran through Descartes, Spinoza, and Leibniz. In this light it is understandable that Shpet's final scholarly undertaking should have been a masterful translation of Hegel's *Phenomenology of Spirit.*[25]

In his overall estimation of Husserl's accomplishment, Shpet took an approving but carefully circumscribed attitude. In his view, Husserl's transcendental phenomenology was a project holding great promise as a step forward in the development of positive philosophy, yet in its current form that project had generated at least as many questions as answers. In *Appearance and Sense,* Shpet declared that "the distinctive feature of phenomenology as contained in Husserl's exposition lies in the fact that *for the time being* he does not so much solve problems as *pose* them. This fact alone reveals the great productivity of the phenomenological method" (p. 145).

Indeed, Shpet expressed several of his own problems with Husserl's phenomenology. Chief among them was the difficulty of formulating the *social* dimension of human existence as an object of phenomenological investigation. In Husserl, he wrote, "a particular species of empirical being is left out, namely *social* being, which . . . must have its own peculiar datum and its own peculiar mode of cognition" (p. 100). In the social realm, "things continuously appear before us as signs. Language, art, any social object at all, organisms, people, etc., etc. always appear as signs and with their own inner intimate sense." In the social context, the sense of things is connected with their purposes, their uses, their *"entelechies"* (p. 159). This sense is most often *bestowed* upon things

---

[23] For example, "The epidemic of neo-Kantianism spread with lightning speed; and did many of the philosophically inclined representatives of our generation escape this more or less acute contagion?" *Istoriia kak problema logiki,* p. 35. For a more measured and careful exposition of his objections to Kant's philosophical project, see in the same work, pp. 550–568.

[24] See, e.g., George L. Kline, "Gustav G. Shpet as Interpreter of Hegel," *Archiwum Historii Filozofii i Myśli Społecznej* 44 (1999), 181–190.

[25] Published posthumously as vol. 4 of the Soviet edition of Hegel's works.

through acts of interpretation, *hermeneutical acts* (pp. 154–155). The paradigm instances of such hermeneutical acts occur in *communication*. When someone instructs us in something, or we read something in a book, there is a *presentative moment* which is neither an inference on our part, nor an originary "seeing" of the object itself, but some sort of an intellectual intuition whereby we acquire the sense of the thing.

Shpet concluded that Husserlian phenomenology, in its 1913 form, could not supply a grounding for such hermeneutical acts.[26] And yet our very being as individuals is constituted through continuous immersion in such a web of communication. "*Absolute social solitude, 'solitary confinement,' is the destiny not of the individual, as such, but only of the insane. To forfeit the faculty of intelligible intuition, of comprehension . . . means to go mad – the sole means of escape from the social union*" (p. 160). Shpet appeared thus firmly committed to an extension or development of the phenomenological enterprise in order to accommodate an explicit focus upon the social dimension of being; at the same time he admitted that he could not see a way to accomplish this within the confines of Husserlian phenomenology as it stood in 1913. In Shpet's subsequent work, three fields of inquiry loom large – history, language, and art – all of which are dimensions of social being. To pursue these topics in the spirit of Husserl's phenomenology, seeking to delineate the fundamental objectivities presented to intuition within each of these phenomena, required Shpet to move beyond the bounds of Husserlian phenomenology, as he then understood it, in the direction of a hermeneutical phenomenology.

Shpet's next major publication was his master's dissertation, *History as a Problem of Logic* (1916). This book, comprising over 500 pages, was intended as the first part of a four-volume study; it was the only part published in his lifetime. Shpet also completed the second part; it was published for the first time in 2002.[27] This second volume makes clear that he was still pursuing the Husserl-inspired project of a fundamental philosophical science. For example, he claimed to be working out the possibility of objective intuition into "historical actuality" rather than following a more standard inquiry into the "logic of historical science."[28] Shpet maintained that actuality is accessible through various forms of intuition which are *fundamental* or *pure* in that what is

---

[26] Shpet did not have access either to Husserl's subsequent published work, nor, of course, to the voluminous archival materials that were to be assembled later. After the outbreak of war with Germany in 1914, scholarly communications between the two nations were essentially cut off. Thus Shpet would have had no possibility of learning of Husserl's later turn toward "genetic" phenomenology, nor generally of Husserl's own strong interest in these very issues, solutions to which Shpet found lacking in Husserl's work.

[27] Shpet, *Istoriia kak problema logiki*.   [28] *Ibid.* p. 574.

given for them is directly presented as an objectivity ("givenness") without pre-
supposition, without theory, hence as *phenomena* in the Husserlian sense. "Thus
there remains only phenomenology, and the phenomenologically established
object . . . Phenomenology offers a pre-theoretical investigation of the object,
and therefore can serve as the foundation for any theoretical study of it; in this
sense, then, it is the universal fundamental science."[29] At the same time, Shpet's
preoccupation with an overarching dialectic of the historical and the logical in
this work appeared to reflect an essentially Hegelian frame of reference.

Shpet's more detailed treatment of the interconnection of dialectic and intuition arises in the context of his hermeneutical investigation of discourse (*slovo*),
especially in Part II of the *Aesthetic Fragments* (1922–1923) and in *The Internal
Form of the Word* (1927).[30] In Part I of *Aesthetic Fragments*, he makes a number
of suggestive remarks on the state of social being in contemporary Russia, such
as: "The revolution devoured yesterday's actuality." "When actuality becomes
an illusion, there exist only empty *forms*." "We do not know actuality now, but
in order to cognize it, we must find it asserted." "And the artist doesn't create
actuality, doesn't produce [it]; what he produces is art, and not actuality – he
imitates and reproduces. But he asserts actuality *sooner* than the philosopher,
because intuition goes before all cognition."[31]

If actuality (in the form of social being) can be "devoured," "become an
illusion," and be "asserted" in a new form by the artist before being subsequently
cognized by the philosopher, then we must conclude that social being must be
inseparable from its own history. And if it must be asserted, then the primary
mode of social being must be *discourse*; that is, the specific words, images,
symbols, etc. that comprise the existing culture of a specific people. If, at the
same time, social being is indeed a mode of *actuality*, then the web of discourse
comprising it must somehow be constitutive of the actual. Its elements, relations,
and laws must constitute objectivities which in their givenness are ultimate
phenomena for philosophical intuition. But these elements, relations and laws
must equally be dynamic, subject to development, capable of having a history.
Part II of the *Aesthetic Fragments*, and especially *The Internal Form of the Word*,
are devoted above all to working out some of the details of such an account of
our intuitions of discourse.

Inspired by Humboldt, Shpet developed an account of the "internal form"
of the word as the key to the problem. The internal form of the word

---

[29] *Ibid.* p. 577.
[30] *Esteticheskie fragmenty*, 3 parts, and *Vnutrenniaia forma slova: etiudy i variatsii na temy Gumbol'ta*, both
     in Gustav Shpet, *Iskusstvo kak vid znaniia* (Tat'iana Shchedrina (ed.), Moscow: Rosspen, 2007).
[31] *Esteticheskie fragmenty*, Pt. 1, pp. 192, 193, 198.

(discourse) is a dimension lying *between* what Shpet identified as the morphological ("external") forms and the ontic ("pure") forms of the word.

Shpet's notion of "morphological" form poses no special difficulties; it involves the familiar notions of phoneme, morpheme, etc., that is, the idea of discriminable differences presented through sensuous intuition that enable us to identify discrete units of speech or language. However, the ontic ("pure") and internal forms of the word, both grasped through *intellectual* intuitions, present the greatest initial obscurities. The differences between these two forms of intellectual intuition may be approached in terms of Shpet's distinction between the object (*predmet*, the ontic form, given to abstractly rational intuition), and the thing (*veshch'*, the internal form, given to rational intuition). The object is the concept, or logical schema, required for successful communication concerning things in the world, but the object is itself merely an abstraction, a necessary subcomponent of the process.

If nothing but these "pure" or "ontic" forms were involved in our grasp of a word, we would be able to "conceptualize" the object, to grasp the relevant concept, but not to "understand" the meaning of the term in its full intended usage. For the listener to comprehend that I am speaking about *this* thing, and not merely the class of all possible such things in general, a further form of logical intuition is required, one capable of grasping things in their concrete individuality, in their content as well as in their form, namely concretely rational (*razumnaia*) intuition. According to Shpet, reference to an individual thing (*veshch'*) can be achieved only when meaning has been established, when the pure concept has been filled out, provided with content. These content-filled forms of concrete individual things, grasped through rational intuition, constitute the *internal form* of the word.

At this point Shpet explicitly invokes Hegel in order to distinguish the two forms of logical intuition as abstractly rational (*rassudochnaia*) and concretely rational (*razumnaia*).[32] Rational intuition grasps the given concretely; Kant notwithstanding, rational intuition is capable of providing content as well as form, according to Shpet. Form and content are correlative terms; one does not occur without the other. "The correlativity of the terms form and content signifies not only that neither of these terms is thinkable without the other, and likewise that form on a lower level is content for a higher level, but also that the more we seize upon form, the less there is of content, and conversely. In idea one can even say: *form and content are one*."[33]

---

[32] "Hegel has already shown this with unobscurable clarity." *Esteticheskie fragmenty*, Pt. 2, p. 238.
[33] *Ibid.* p. 246.

Moreover, according to Shpet, to grasp things concretely, through rational intuition, is to see them dynamically, in terms of their dialectical development. Meaning is thus constituted dynamically, dialectically, "and always carries within itself, so to speak, the history of its composition," he writes. "Meaning is also the historical, more precisely the dialectical accumulator of thoughts, always ready to transmit its charge of thought to a fitting receiver. All meaning whatever hides within itself a long 'history' of changes of sense (*Bedeutungswandel*)."[34]

Whereas abstractly rational intuition grasps things formally, conceptually, and only in their isolated separateness, concretely rational intuition grasps them "in their connectedness, in their streaming, in their *coursing*," in other words, as discourse.[35] In sum, to grasp the "inner forms" of the words comprising discourse is to grasp their *meanings* as given to rational intuition in their concreteness, interconnectedness, and dialectical development, and also as exhibiting the historical traces of that development. According to Shpet, such rational intuition provides direct access to actuality: "The greatest penetration of the intuitions of reason lies not in the fact that they supposedly convey us to a 'new' world lying beyond the bounds, but in the fact that, having penetrated through all the piled-up ontic, logical, sensuous and non-sensuous forms, they place us directly before the most real actuality."[36]

Shpet went so far as to claim that his doctrine of the internal form of the word would supply "the ground for a radical reform of all of logic."[37] This conviction that he was on the threshold of uncovering a new dialectical logic manifested in (determining?) the development of culture was affirmed in the following lines:

Such a dialectic, in distinction from the Platonic dialectic of hypostasized ($\varepsilon\iota\ \acute{\varepsilon}\sigma\tau\iota\nu\ \ldots\ \varepsilon\iota\ \mu\eta\ \acute{\varepsilon}\sigma\tau\iota\nu$, Parm. 136b) ideas, in distinction from Kantian empty (*bloss*) ideas (*nur eine Idee!*), in distinction from the Hegelian dialectic of objectivized concepts, is a real dialectic, a dialectic of the realized cultural meaning, and may be called – keeping in mind the methods of formation of the element of culture, the word-concept – *an expounding and interpreting dialectic*, or, embracing the material and formal tasks, and the unity present in them, *a hermeneutic dialectic*.[38]

Looking back over Shpet's various invocations of Hegel and Husserl, we arrive at something like the following picture. First of all, the viability of Shpet's fundamental distinction between negative and positive philosophy in the modern period presupposes his continuing dependence upon the success of Hegel's *Phenomenology of Spirit* in criticizing Kant's epistemological project. At the same

[34] *Ibid.* p. 240.   [35] *Ibid.* p. 238.   [36] *Ibid.* p. 242.
[37] *Vnutrenniaia forma slova*, p. 403.   [38] *Ibid.* pp. 416–417.

time, Shpet remained committed to Husserl's project of philosophy as a fundamental and rigorous science of phenomena as given in pre-theoretical intuition. Shpet's investigations of social being, of the objectivities presented to intuition by discourse, or culture, were a projection of his understanding of Husserlian method. However, in attempting to extend Husserl's method into the sphere of language as a form of social being so as to construct a *hermeneutic phenomenology*, Shpet once again turned to Hegel (this time to the *Logic*) for crucial elements of that account, which turned out to be not simply a hermeneutic phenomenology, but more precisely, a *hermeneutic dialectic*.

One of the enduring challenges of Shpet interpretation is to explain the relative ease with which he felt one could shift back and forth between Husserlian and Hegelian perspectives, or rather combine them in a single inquiry. Shpet's conviction that these two projects of phenomenology were essentially congruent still presents intriguing puzzles for further investigation. Interestingly, we find an analogous conviction in the work of Il'in.

Il'in's Husserlian Interpretation of Hegel

Ivan Il'in's first serious engagement with Husserlian phenomenology took place during the summer academic term of 1911 in Göttingen. He perceived the core of Husserl's method to revolve around the "philosophical act" within which the object of philosophical intuition is framed, inspected, and analyzed. The "philosophical act" described by Il'in is a deliberately cultivated *experience* of a richly complex content that can be rendered objective by leaving aside one's theories and biases concerning the content of the experience, as well as the role of one's own consciousness as the medium in which the experience occurs. Such experiences are constructable (involving the creation of more complex experiences out of more elementary ones);[39] repeatable (in subsequent philosophical acts by the same thinker); duplicable (in the experience of like-minded thinkers); susceptible of imaginative variation; and corrigible (by the original thinker alone, or with the assistance of others). Through all of these exercises it is possible for more than one thinker to arrive at an experience of essentially one and the same content. When the "philosophical act" is properly carried out, the resulting content is something *given*, open to *intuitive contemplation* (intuition, inspection). According to Il'in, philosophical analysis takes place only following the enactment of the experience through the philosophical act, and its intuitive contemplation as something given. Hence he understood the philosophical act

---

[39] "Constructable" here certainly does not mean that the object, the content of the experience, is produced by consciousness. Neither Husserl nor Il'in would have accepted any such implication. Husserl spoke rather of the object "constituting itself."

as taking place in three stages: first, the framing of the object in experience; secondly, the intuiting of its content; and thirdly, the rational analysis of that content.

Apart from the notion of the "philosophical act," which is certainly a theme in Husserl's earlier works (though not treated in precisely the way Il'in uses it), Il'in appeared to restrict his appropriation of Husserlian phenomenology primarily to the doctrine of eidetic intuition and the concomitant exercise of eidetic variation. This borrowing amounts only to a preliminary step toward the full doctrine of the phenomenological reduction in Husserl, and thus one can question whether Il'in can properly be described as a serious follower of Husserl.

Yet Il'in was quite serious in concluding that Husserlian phenomenology was a new and more precise articulation of a method that was "as old as philosophy itself," and that Hegel had in fact pursued a version of the same method under the title "speculative thinking." Drawing out the further implications of this conclusion, Il'in declared that Hegel's method must therefore be understood to be intuitive and not dialectical, contrary to the usual view:

> If by "method" is meant the "type and mode" of cognizing subjectively practiced by the philosopher, then one may regard Hegel as a "dialectician" only in a completely superficial, abstractly-rationalistic sense. He neither "searches" for contradictions in concepts nor "strives" to reconcile them afterward; he doesn't think "analytically" and then "synthetically." He continuously intuits in a concentrated way and intensively describes the changes taking place *in the object itself:* he intuits by means of thought. In this consists his "subjective" method of cognizing. It is *not he* who practices "dialectic" but *the object.*[40]

Though he did not speak of it in such terms, Il'in's "reinterpretation" of Hegelian dialectic along the lines of Husserlian intuition amounted in truth to the core of a hermeneutic theory: in order to truly comprehend another thinker, one must reproduce for oneself the philosophical act of that thinker. On the "Husserlian" account of the philosophical act that Il'in supplied, this reproduction should always in principle be possible. The essence of his explanation of the general failure of at least two generations of previous philosophers to comprehend or adequately expound Hegel was that they had failed to master the appropriate hermeneutic method. The notion of the "philosophical act" thus served a double purpose for Il'in: it enabled him to give an account

---

[40] I.A. Il'in, *Filosofiia Gegelia kak uchenie o konkretnosti Boga i cheloveka* (Moscow: Russkaia kniga, 2002), vol. 1, ch. 6, pp. 155–156. See also Il'in's opening remark in the "Literary Appendix" for that chapter: "It can be considered that the age of overestimation of the significance of the dialectical method in Hegel's philosophy is past" (p. 373).

of his understanding of the fundamental method of philosophical inquiry (a method which Il'in employed where appropriate throughout his own intellectual career), and it also supplied an account of sound hermeneutical procedure for interpreting the works of other philosophers.

Losev's "Dialectical Phenomenology"

Losev made declarations concerning his philosophical method in numerous places. Two of the earliest and most detailed occur in the opening pages of *The Philosophy of the Name* and *The Ancient Cosmos and Contemporary Science* (1927). In the first he declared that, "The sole correct and complete method of philosophy . . . is the *dialectical* method. All my work, if it has any relation at all to philosophy, is a result of my dialectical thought." But he also wrote, "there are those points where my method never diverges from the methods of pure phenomenology or pure transcendentalism."[41] The phenomenology he had in mind was Husserlian, and the doctrine that attracted his attention was that of the *eidos*. According to Husserl, *eide* are essences that can be given primordially in pure intuition;[42] they are to be distinguished from facts which are given in empirical intuition concerned with individual things as existing in space and time.[43] Losev had exhaustively investigated Plato's use of the term *eidos* and connected Husserl's use with Plato's (more freely than did Husserl himself).

However, Losev immediately set about qualifying his acceptance of Husserlian phenomenology. Despite declaring that, "I accept both the doctrine of the *eidos*, and the doctrine of pure description, and in general, phenomenology in its entirety,"[44] he complained in *Ancient Cosmos* that phenomenology "stops with the static recording of the statically given meaning of a thing."[45] Whereas Husserl believed that the task of phenomenology was merely to describe and not to explain (because the task of explanation properly belonged to the naturalistic approach), he failed to understand that "an eidetic explanation of the *eidos*, as opposed to a naturalistic one, is possible, that a purely eidetic placing of the *eidos* in a system of other *eide* . . . is possible."[46] Note that "a purely eidetic

---

[41] *Filosofiia imeni*, in Losev, *Bytie, imia, kosmos*, pp. 617, 615.

[42] E. Husserl, *Ideas* (Boyce Gibson (trans.), New York: Collier Books, 1962), p. 7. According to Husserl: "The essence (Eidos) is an object of a new type. Just as the datum of individual or empirical intuition is an individual object, so the datum of essential intuition is a pure essence" (p. 49).

[43] *Ibid.* pp. 46–47.   [44] Losev, *Filosofiia imeni*, p. 615.

[45] *Antichnyi kosmos i sovremennaia nauka*, in Losev, *Bytie, imia, kosmos*, p. 72.

[46] *Ibid.* p. 72. For a fuller discussion of Losev's departures from Husserlian phenomenology, see Alexander Haardt, *Husserl in Rußland* (Munich: Wilhelm Fink, 1993), pp. 226–230, and S.S. Khoruzhii, "A Rearguard Action" in *Russian Studies in Philosophy* 40, no. 3 (Winter 2001–2002), 36–38, 45.

placing of the *eidos* in a system of other *eide*" would seem to imply that *eide* contain their own logical forms and are capable of developing into concrete wholes on their own. In other places, however, Losev held to the view that the dialectic had the ability to explain the generation of one *eidos* from another, and the emergence of systems of *eide* making up complexes of meaning. "I am accustomed to think that 'explanation' is not necessarily naturalism, that there is 'explanation' that is not psychological, not metaphysical, but purely in terms of meaning. *And that explanation in terms of meanings I see in dialectic.*" More specifically, the dialectic explained "meaning in all its connections, in all its structural inter-connections and self-generation. *It is necessary to explain one category by means of another category*, so that it is clear how one category *generates* the other, and how all together generate each other – not naturalistically, of course, but eidetically, categorially, remaining within the sphere of meaning." Losev thought that "dialectic is the sole method capable of grasping living actuality as a whole."[47]

Nevertheless, when we look more closely at Losev's account of dialectic, which he generally connected with Hegel, several puzzles emerge. Losev claimed that "genuine dialectic is always immediate knowledge," and he referred to Hegel's *Encyclopedia Logic* (paragraphs 63–77). But in those passages Hegel was actually concerned to deny that genuine knowing could be merely immediate; true knowing, he thought, is always both immediate and mediate. On the other hand, if we bear in mind that Losev elsewhere characterized the dialectic as "the logical construction of the *eidos*,"[48] his claim may make more sense. The *eidos* is initially apprehended through an act of intuition and is therefore immediate in some sense.[49] If being manifests itself through the *eidos*, and the *eidos* is grasped in its immediacy, then the dialectic, as the form of knowing in which the truth presents itself, might be conceived as immediate knowing (ignoring some of the other problems that such a claim might pose).

Losev also insisted that dialectic itself is necessarily abstract and also dead.[50] The claim that dialectic must be abstract seems to presuppose a straightforward dualism of thought and being: all thought is intrinsically abstract; being alone is concrete. But the succession of categories within Hegel's *Science of Logic* constitutes stages of a development from the abstract to the concrete, so no simple binary opposition of abstract and concrete could adequately reflect the

[47] Losev, *Filosofiia imeni*, pp. 616–617.

[48] Losev, *Antichnyi kosmos i sovremennaia nauka*, p. 69.

[49] However, we must note that the entire issue of "mediated" and "immediate" may be significantly altered when the "immediate" apprehension is not of sensuous particulars or of transient states of feeling, but of an *eidos* (an essence) or of an intuited concept which exhibits the capacity for dialectical self-development.

[50] Losev, *Filosofiia imeni*, pp. 622, 623.

argument of that *Logic*.[51] Whatever final judgments one may reach concerning these puzzles, it appears that, despite frequent references to Hegel, Losev's conception of the dialectic was not very closely related to Hegel's. This outcome seems to be unavoidable in view of Losev's attempt to marry the *eidos* with the dialectic. A similar conclusion was reached by Sergei Khoruzhii in his path-breaking article on Losev's early work:

> Upon closer examination, it is easy to see that the two components of this methodology still cannot be brought into full harmony and that Hegel and Husserl interfere fatally with each other. (This should be no surprise, if we recall that the phenomenological conception was created precisely in reaction against the absolutized dialectic in order to affirm the meaning-*eidos* as in principle indissoluble and nondeductible.) Losev's method, of course, does not implement fully the principles of phenomenology, for it openly rejects a most important part of them, the principle of pure descriptivity, and introduces what from the standpoint of phenomenology is a deliberate naturalism and arbitrary metaphysical speculation. But it does not implement fully the principles of the dialectic either.[52]

More recently, another philosopher, Andrei Tashchian, in a multifaceted analysis of the relation of *eidos* and *logos* in Losev, came to a similar set of conclusions. He points out that in *The Ancient Cosmos and Contemporary Science*, Losev "calls *logos* as well as *eidos* a fundamental concept." "However," argues Tashchian, "only one of them really can be a substantial form. Otherwise, the house of thought, divided against itself, would not stand. Therefore, in the final analysis, Losev always subordinates *logos* to *eidos*, making the former an aspect of the latter."[53] After identifying a substantial number of difficulties, obscurities, and puzzles into which Losev's various attempts to specify the relation between *eidos* and *logos* become entangled, Tashchian concludes that "phenomenology is relative, while dialectics is absolute":

> But dialectics in the Russian philosopher is logic and therefore it exists in *logoi*. This means that absolute knowledge, that is, the dialectics, is possible only through *logoi*, through *concepts* (διά λόγων), not through *eide*. Precisely for this reason concept, not *eidos*, is the absolute intelligible form. And precisely *eidos* is an aspect of *logos*, not vice versa.[54]

In short, Losev's attempt to combine a phenomenology of the *eidos* with a dialectical *logos* falls victim to an intimidating number of difficulties and possible confusions.

---

[51] On this point see my "Abstract and Concrete in Hegel's Logic" in George di Giovanni (ed.), *Essays on Hegel's Logic* (Albany, NY: SUNY Press, 1990), pp. 59–75.

[52] Khoruzhii, "A Rearguard Action," 45.

[53] Losev, *Antichnyi kosmos i sovremennaia nauka*, p. 68. Andrei Tashchian, "Eidetics and Logic in Losev's Methodology," *Russian Studies in Philosophy* 44, no. 1 (Summer, 2005), 45.

[54] *Ibid.* p. 57.

CONCLUSION

Amid all the many complexities and divergences of the three philosophical enterprises outlined above, it would be easy to overlook some important convergences that should be viewed as milestones in the development of Russian philosophy. Four will be indicated here.

First, all three philosophers, but especially Il'in and Shpet, should be credited with a very great advance in the understanding of Hegel. All three were well ahead of most of their western European contemporaries in grasping the centrality of Hegel's contribution to the development of modern philosophy and in setting aside most of the standard misrepresentations and confusions that had been common intellectual currency for several decades. Shpet was particularly scathing about the first generation of Russian "Hegelians" whose caricatures of Hegel's system as sacrificing individual personality on the altar of the Absolute (no matter how widely believed) were little more than a testimony to their incomprehension of the texts.[55] And Il'in's very extensive commentary on Hegel's philosophy in some important respects still stands up to scrutiny in the light of the latest scholarship, some nine decades removed.[56]

Secondly, all three of these philosophers lived through the Bolshevik Revolution, but spurned its Marxist-Leninist ideology as undermining the values of individual freedom (Shpet), the rule of law (Il'in), and the sacredness of individual personality, grounded in an Orthodox personalistic cosmology (Losev). Shpet's most striking pronouncements on the fundamental value of individual freedom occurred in his *Herzen's Philosophical Worldview* (1921).[57] Il'in's most important work on the rule of law was *On the Essence of Legal Consciousness* (1956), while the outlines of Losev's theological position can be grasped from his *Dialectic of Myth*.

A third important conclusion to be drawn is that, despite the vagaries that affected their respective understandings of the philosophical methods of Hegel and Husserl, all three seem to have rightly comprehended that these two philosophers above all merited their closest attention as exemplars of pure philosophical inquiry.

---

[55] See G.G. Shpet's "K voprosu o gegel'ianstve Belinskogo," *Voprosy filosofii*, no. 7 (1991), 115–176, and especially James Scanlan's discussion of it in "The Fate of Philosophy in Russia: Gustav Shpet's Studies in the History of Russian Thought" in Galin Tihanov (ed.), *Gustav Shpet's Contributions to Philosophy and Cultural Theory* (W. Lafayette, IN: Purdue University Press, forthcoming).

[56] See the Introduction to my translation of Il'in's *Filosofiia Gegelia kak uchenie o konkretnosti Boga i cheloveka*.

[57] *Filosofskoe mirovozzrenie Gertsena* (Petrograd: Kolos, 1921). Again, for an excellent discussion see Scanlan, "The Fate of Philosophy in Russia: Gustav Shpet's Studies in the History of Russian Thought."

Finally, all three philosophers exhibited a marked tendency to suppose that the methods of Hegel and Husserl were in some fundamental sense congruent. That shared conviction still presents numerous puzzles for contemporary interpreters, because, though not obviously false, it is by no means widely accepted, and the issues involved have yet to be thoroughly explored in the literature.

17

NIKOLAI BERDIAEV AND THE PHILOSOPHICAL
TASKS OF THE EMIGRATION

STUART FINKEL

Is the Russian emigration aware of its mission? This mission cannot be limited to a haughty awareness of one's superiority over those who have remained within Russia, in the cultivation of feelings of malice and vengeance, in petty political rivalries, based on fictions. This mission lies first and foremost in spiritual tasks, in the gathering and forging of spiritual forces, in the spiritual overcoming of a malicious, vengeful attitude toward the ordeals God has sent them.

"Spiritual Tasks of the Russian Emigration,"
from the editors of *Put'* (*The Path*), 1925

Man fell from the heights and can ascend to the heights.
Nikolai Berdiaev, *The Destiny of Man*, 1931[1]

Paradoxically, Russian philosophy of the Silver Age experienced a final renaissance during and immediately after the grueling years of the Russian Civil War. Despite difficult material conditions, government censorship, ideological and political estrangement, and significant emigration, philosophy flourished in universities, public societies, *kruzhki* ("circles") and resurgent thick journals and monographs. As before the Revolution, neo-idealist religious thought predominated, and there was significant cross-fertilization among philosophy, literature, religion, and *obshchestvennost'*, the distinctly Russian intellectual sense of public duty.[2] This renaissance ended abruptly in 1922 with the expulsion of most of Russia's most prominent philosophers, the elimination of traditional philosophy departments at the most important universities, and the closure of non-Marxist philosophical societies.[3]

---

[1] [N. Berdiaev], "Dukhovnye zadachi russkoi emigratsii. (Ot redaktsii)," *Put'* (1925), no. 1, 3–8. N.A. Berdiaev, *O naznachenii cheloveka* (Moscow: Respublika, 1993), p. 51 (1st edn. Paris: Sovremennye zapiski, 1931); translated by Natalie Duddington as *The Destiny of Man* (London: G. Bles, 1937).

[2] On the concept of *obshchestvennost'*, see inter alia Catriona Kelly and Vadim Volkov, "*Obshchestvennost'*, *Sobornost'*: Collective Identities" in Catriona Kelly and David Shepherd (eds.), *Constructing Russian Culture in the Age of Revolution, 1881–1940* (Oxford University Press, 1998), pp. 26–27.

[3] See my *On the Ideological Front: The Russian Intelligentsia and the Making of the Soviet Public Sphere* (New Haven, CT: Yale University Press, 2007).

Once abroad, the expelled philosophers had to determine their mission: what was the proper role of a Russian philosopher in exile? Several of them, including Nikolai Aleksandrovich Berdiaev (1874–1948), resolved to reconstruct the institutions (journals, societies, even universities) they left behind in Russia so as to preserve an authentic Russian philosophical tradition in what Marc Raeff called "Russia Abroad."[4] Most of these philosophers continued to pursue the broader programmatic questions that had traditionally engrossed the Russian intelligentsia, but now adapted their inquiry to the conditions of exile: "What is to be done?" became "What is the task of the Russian emigration?" There were thinkers like Pëtr Struve (1870–1944) and the Hegelian scholar Ivan Il'in (1883–1954) who believed that the evils of Bolshevism had to be combated directly and that the emigration should dedicate itself to no other task. But Berdiaev, Semën Frank, and others rejected the idea that the emigration should or even could openly challenge the Soviet regime; they recommended a *Vekhist* philosophy of inner spiritual development and self-perfection as indispensable preconditions for genuine political change. While offering a devastating criticism of the intellectual milieu and mentality that they believed had led directly to the October Revolution, veterans of the *Vekhi* collective and other religious philosophers thus retained the traditional notion that *intelligenty* had a specific role to play in the service of Russia and its people, something to which their "public work" (*obshchestvennaia deiatel'nost'*) both within Soviet Russia and Russia Abroad clearly attests.

THE *BAB'E LETO* (INDIAN SUMMER) OF RUSSIAN IDEALIST-RELIGIOUS PHILOSOPHY

The post-revolutionary revival of Silver Age thought in Moscow and Petrograd would be remembered with great nostalgia. Writing from Dresden in 1934, the philosopher and sociologist Fëdor Stepun (1884–1965) recalled:

In a very short time great spiritual and cultural intensity developed. In the years 1919 to 1921 the entire cultural life of anti-Bolshevik Russia was concentrated in the free philosophical society and the "house of authors" in Petrograd, and in the religio-philosophical society in Moscow. When one thinks back, in the peace and comfort even of the agitated Europe of today, to Soviet Russia in the first years, it seems hard to believe that half-starving men could assemble in great numbers several times a week in

---

[4] It is Raeff's argument that the emigration, despite its political bickering, did succeed in creating an alternative Russia and preserving its cultural heritage. Marc Raeff, *Russia Abroad: A Cultural History of the Russian Emigration, 1919–1939* (New York: Oxford University Press, 1990), especially pp. 3–5.

badly lighted and unheated rooms, to debate philosophical problems for three or four hours and listen to poems.[5]

Evidence of what Lenin and his colleagues sourly termed the "renaissance of bourgeois ideology" abounded at this time: the resuscitation of the Petrograd philosophical journal *Mysl'* (*Thought*); the appearance of significant scholarly monographs and almanacs; the feverish activity of publishers in Petrograd (Academia and Nauka i Shkola) and Moscow (Bereg); and the revival of several prominent philosophical societies and circles. Works issued just in 1922 included Frank's *Study in the Methodology of Social Sciences*, Lev Karsavin's *Noctes Petropolitanae*, and Nikolai Losskii's *Logic*.[6] More or less formal groupings emerged to provide fora for like-minded thinkers, including the *Vol'naia filosofskaia assotsiatsiia* (Free Philosophical Association or Vol'fila) in Petrograd and Berdiaev's *Vol'naia akademiia dukhovnoi kul'tury* (Free Academy of Spiritual Culture) in Moscow. The Philosophical Society at Petrograd University, the Moscow University Institute of Scientific Philosophy, and the venerable Moscow Psychological Society provided more "academic," but to the Bolsheviks no less objectionable, settings for philosophical discussions.

Berdiaev's Free Academy was perhaps the most prominent of these groups. It was structured around a set of "courses," including Frank's "Introduction to Philosophy," Belyi's "Philosophy of Spiritual Culture," Stepun's "Life and Creativity," Pavel Muratov's "Art of the Renaissance," Father Vladimir Abrikosov's "Stages of the Mystical Path," and Berdiaev's "Philosophy of History," "Philosophy of Religion," and "Dostoevskii." Frank, Berdiaev, Stepun, Boris Vysheslavtsev, Iulii Aikhenval'd, and others, lectured on subjects such as the crisis of culture, the crisis of philosophy, Christian freedom, theosophy and Christianity, Russia and Europe, and Hindu mysticism.[7] Perhaps the most controversial and popular cycle of lectures was devoted to Oswald Spengler's recently translated *Decline of the West*, out of which would come a collection of articles that contributed directly to Lenin's decision to deport the philosophers.[8]

---

[5] Fëdor Stepun, *The Russian Soul and Revolution* (Erminie Huntress (trans.), New York: Charles Scribner's Sons, 1935), pp. 150–151.

[6] S.L. Frank, *Ocherk metodologii obshchestvennykh nauk* (Moscow: Bereg, 1922); N.O. Losskii, *Logika* (Petrograd: Nauka i shkola, 1922); L. Karsavin, *Noctes Petropolitanae* (Petrograd: [A.S. Kagan], 1922). On the Bolshevik campaign against Idealism see Roger Pethybridge, "Concern for Bolshevik Ideological Predominance at the Start of NEP," *Russian Review* 41, no. 4 (October 1982), 445–453, and S.A. Fediukin, *Bor'ba s burzhuaznoi ideologiei v usloviiakh perekhoda k NEPu* (Moscow: Nauka, 1977), pp. 36–39.

[7] "Vol'naia Akademiia Dukhovnoi Kul'tury v Moskve" in N.A. Berdiaev (ed.), *Sofiia. Problemy dukhovnoi kul'tury i religioznoi filosofii* (Berlin: Obelisk, 1923), pp. 135–136.

[8] Fëdor Stepun, *Byvshee i nebyvsheesia* (New York: Chekhov Publishing House, 1956), vol. 2, pp. 75–79; and A. Lavretskii, "Iz auditorii. Zakat Evropy. (Lektsiia F.A. Stepuna)," *Narodnoe prosveshchenie*, no. 92 (December 10, 1921), 13.

The flourishing of intellectual life during this time perhaps occurred because philosophers sensed that the very survival of Russia was in doubt. The question remained, however, whether there was a directly political solution to the crisis. "Russia is seriously ill," Berdiaev declared in early 1918. "This illness has as its material symptoms the disintegration of the state and social organism. But at root this illness is spiritual, not physical."[9] For Berdiaev, Russia's turmoil was not surprising: indeed, since 1909 the *Vekhi* authors had been warning of impending catastrophe. They claimed that only an inner spiritual regeneration could combat the materialism that had corrupted the Russian intelligentsia. Berdiaev's own early philosophical trajectory, and those of other former "legal Marxists" like Struve, Frank, and Sergei Bulgakov, testified to the primacy of the spiritual over the material, to the belief that the intelligentsia had made a disastrously misguided turn when it became obsessed with politics, positivism, and historical materialism.[10] In Berdiaev's view, human beings could not be elevated through improving political or material conditions, but only by transcending material reality by means of creative moral activity.[11] This was precisely what he prescribed in 1918 for the spiritual illness afflicting revolutionary Russia. "Russia's recovery presupposes first of all the return to health [*ozdorovlenie*] of the spiritual basis of the life of the Russian people and the leading circles of the Russian intelligentsia."[12] Russia's recovery, he asserted, must come not from an obsession with social equality, but from inner transformation – a turn to free personality (*lichnost'*) and ethical creativity.[13]

Berdiaev was not alone in diagnosing Russia's spiritual illness. Shortly after the Bolshevik coup, Struve solicited essays for a sequel to *Vekhi*, entitled *Iz glubiny* (*Out of the Depths*). The essays were written and the volume published in late summer 1918, but, with the open proclamation of the Red Terror

---

[9] Nikolai Berdiaev, "Ozdorovlenie Rossii" in *Sobranie sochinenii* (Paris: YMCA, 1990), vol. 4, p. 242. Originally published in *Nakanune*, no. 6 (1918).

[10] For two recent summaries of Berdiaev's life and work, see James P. Scanlan's entry on him in Edward Craig (ed.), *Routledge Encyclopedia of Philosophy* (London: Routledge, 1998), vol. 1, pp. 726–732, and Olga Volkogonova's in Donald M. Borchert (ed.), *Encyclopedia of Philosophy*, 2nd edn. (Detroit, MI: Macmillan Reference USA, 2006), vol. 1, pp. 558–561. Two early, admiring biographies are Donald Lowrie, *Rebellious Prophet: A Life of Nikolai Berdyaev* (New York: Harper, 1960) and Michael A. Vallon, *An Apostle of Freedom: Life and Teachings of Nicolas Berdyaev* (New York: Philosophical Library, 1960). More recent explorations include Aleksandr Vadimov [Tsvetkov], *Zhizn' Berdiaeva: Rossiia* (Oakland, CA: Berkeley Slavic Specialties, 1993), covering the period up to his expulsion in 1922, and O.D. Volkogonova, *N.A. Berdiaev: Intellektual'naia biografiia* (Moscow: Izd-vo Moskovskogo universiteta, 2001). For a thorough bibliography see Tamara Klépinine, *Bibliographie des oeuvres de Nicolas Berdiaev* (Paris: YMCA Press, 1978).

[11] The summation of these views may be found in his important pre-revolutionary works, *Filosofiia svobody* (*Philosophy of Freedom*, 1911) and *Smysl tvorchestva* (*The Meaning of Creativity*, 1916).

[12] Berdiaev, "Ozdorovlenie Rossii," p. 242. [13] *Ibid.* p. 247.

and civil war, it could not be distributed in Soviet Russia.[14] *Iz glubiny* rang with bitter recriminations against those who had ignored earlier prophecies of doom; the authors again blamed the intelligentsia's spiritual poverty for Russia's catastrophe. Positivism and materialism were false gods, the chasing of which had undone the moorings not just of socialists, but of liberals and conservatives as well.[15] At the same time, the biblical reference in the volume's title already suggested the possibility – even the inevitability – of a national rebirth, and this theme was reflected in several of the key essays.

In the titular essay "*De Profundis*," Semën Frank lamented in scriptural terms the complete destruction of Russia, after a prolonged "moral illness." "If even several years ago anyone had foreseen the depths of the abyss into which we have now fallen, and in which we flounder helplessly, not one person would have believed him. The gloomiest pessimists never went so far in their predictions, nor approached in their imaginations that final brink of hopelessness to which fate has led us." Yet Frank looked to the possibility, even to the inevitability of a fantastic rebirth: "If Russia is destined yet to be reborn – a miracle in which, despite everything, we want to believe, more than that, in which we are *obliged* to believe, while we still live – then this rebirth now can be only a genuine resurrection, a rising from the dead with a new soul to an entirely different, new life." The necessary first step in this hoped-for rebirth, Frank asserted, was a true understanding of what had caused the current calamity (in particular the "diabolical hallucinations" of the intelligentsia) and a reinforcement of the "organic inner-spiritual forces of social being."[16]

Berdiaev, in his contribution, "Spirits of the Russian Revolution," focused on how Dostoevskii had prophetically foretold the Russian catastrophe:

He did not remain on the surface of social-political ideas and formations, but penetrated into the depths, and he revealed that Russian revolutionism is a metaphysical and religious phenomenon, and not a political and social one. Thus he succeeded in grasping religiously the nature of Russian socialism. Russian socialism is preoccupied with the

---

[14] Printworkers tried, unsuccessfully, to sell the warehoused copies of *Iz glubiny* at the time of the Kronstadt rebellion. See William F. Woehrlin, "Introduction (Voices from Out of the Depths)" in W.F. Woehrlin (ed. and trans.), *Out of the Depths (De Profundis): A Collection of Articles on the Russian Revolution* (Irvine, CA: Charles Schlacks, Jr., 1986), pp. xxiii–xxiv, citing S.L. Frank, *Biografiia P.B. Struve* (New York: Chekhov Publishing House, 1956), p. 121.

[15] For a detailed explication of Struve's essay in *Iz glubiny*, see Jane Burbank, *Intelligentsia and Revolution: Russian Views of Bolshevism, 1917–1922* (New York: Oxford University Press, 1986), pp. 132–137.

[16] S.L. Frank, "De Profundis" in *Iz glubiny. Sbornik statei o Russkoi revoliutsii*, 2nd edn. (Paris: YMCA Press, 1967), pp. 311–313, 319, 326. (I have, with a few minor changes, followed William Woehrlin's translations in *Out of the Depths*, pp. 219–234.) See also Phillip Boobbyer, *S.L. Frank: The Life and Work of a Russian Philosopher, 1877–1950* (Athens, OH: Ohio University Press, 1995), pp. 117–119.

question of whether or not there is a God, and Dostoevskii foresaw how bitter the fruits of Russian socialism would be.

Dostoevskii had revealed, most notably in the character of Ivan Karamazov, that the atheism, materialism, and nihilism predominant in the Russian intelligentsia precluded true human love. "Ivan's pathos is not love, it is rebellion. He has a false sensitivity, but not love. He rebels because he does not believe in immortality, because for him everything is encompassed in this meaningless empirical life filled with suffering and grief."[17] Berdiaev expanded on this analysis in a series of lectures that eventually developed into *Dostoevskii's Worldview* (1921), the publication of which in Russia was forestalled.[18] In his view, Dostoevskii had foreseen the inner nature of Russia's revolutions: "He saw in them a mighty spirit of the Antichrist, the ambition to make a god of man." Dostoevskii's (and Berdiaev's) critique centered on the intelligentsia's diabolical striving to perfect the external world. "Revolution is not conditioned by outward causes and circumstances but is determined interiorly: it is an indication of a disastrous alteration of man's original relationship with God, with the world, and with his fellows."[19]

The publication of Spengler's lugubrious *Decline of the West*, heralding the end of the thousand-year reign of western civilization, provided another opportunity for those who viewed the October Revolution and Civil War as evidence of apocalypse, and who saw, perhaps, the potential for national and spiritual rebirth from out of the rubble. In a series of public debates out of which emerged a controversial collection of essays, Frank, Berdiaev, Stepun, and the economist Iakov Bukshpan saw in Spengler's dark pessimism a verification of their own sentiments concerning the destruction they had witnessed.[20] With Spengler they distrusted an excessive focus on the material to the detriment of the spiritual, on "civilization" to the detriment of "culture." Yet, just as several of the despairing contributions to *Out of the Depths* had concluded with the hope that out of complete destruction would come renaissance and renewal, so, too, in their *Zakat Evropy* (*Twilight of Europe*) Spengler's Russian commentators added a note of optimism to his grim prophecy, of hope that out of the ashes

---

[17] Nikolai Berdiaev, "Dukhi russkoi revoliutsii" in *Iz glubiny*, pp. 79–80 and 84 (Woehrlin's translations are in *Out of the Depths*, pp. 41, 45.) See also Burbank, *Intelligentsia and Revolution*, pp. 195–198.

[18] Both this book and his *End of the Renaissance*, also prohibited by the censor, were prepared by the Petrograd-based Epokha in 1921 (Klépinine, *Bibliographie*, p. 31; and "Izdatel'stvo 'Epokha,'" *Novaia russkaia kniga*, no. 1 (1922), 35). The Dostoevskii volume was published abroad in 1923 and translated into eight languages.

[19] Nicholas Berdyaev, *Dostoevsky* (Donald Attwater (trans.), London: Sheed & Ward, 1934), pp. 135–137.

[20] *Osval'd Shpengler i Zakat Evropy* (Moscow: Bereg, 1922).

the Phoenix would rise. Post-revolutionary Russia, the ultimate realization of Spengler's ominous warnings of Europe's collapse, might become the site of its resurrection.[21] Berdiaev noted that in Russia the turn away from the spiritual to the material had reached its apocalyptic conclusion and thus had cleared the way for a spiritual rebirth. "In Russia there is hidden a secret, at which we ourselves cannot fully guess," he concluded. "Our hour has not yet come."[22]

The *Twilight of Europe* volume infuriated Lenin, who denounced it as a "literary cover for a Whiteguard organization."[23] Despite the Bolsheviks' fundamental concurrence with Spengler's central proposition that bourgeois European civilization was bankrupt, Spengler challenged one of the main tenets of Marxism, namely the teleological-progressive conception of history.[24] Lenin, alarmed by the "renaissance of bourgeois ideology," was livid that the book had been published. The GPU placed all four contributors, including, at first, the otherwise inoffensive Bukshpan, on the list of intellectuals slated for deportation. In mid-1922 the newly formed central censorship organ, Glavlit, mobilized itself to prevent future publications of idealist philosophical thought.

At the same time, the Commissariat of Enlightenment ousted non-Marxist philosophy from the universities. At the end of the 1920–1921 school year, the philosophy department at Moscow University was disbanded, its professors shuffled to other units.[25] Berdiaev's short teaching career ended, as did Il'in's. The Petrograd University philosophy department was also dismantled that fall, with Losskii, Ivan Lapshin, and other instructors relieved of their teaching duties.[26] Because the regime's primary concern was the threat these professors posed to the minds of impressionable youth, they were often, as the sociologist

---

[21] These are ideas that Berdiaev developed extensively in his own philosophy of history, especially in *Smysl istorii* (*The Meaning of History*) and *Konets Renessansa* (*The End of the Renaissance*), and after his deportation in *Novoe srednevekov'e* (*The New Middle Ages*). See Christian Gottlieb, *Dilemmas of Reaction in Leninist Russia: The Christian Response to the Revolution in the Works of N.A. Berdyaev, 1917–1924* (Odense: University of Southern Denmark, 2003), pp. 134–144, 146–149.

[22] Nikolai Berdiaev, "Predsmertnye mysli Fausta" in *Osval'd Shpengler*, pp. 71–72. Semën Frank similarly suggested that through a spiritual, religious rebirth Russia (and Europe) could still be saved from the current catastrophe. S.L. Frank, "Krizis zapadnoi kul'tury" in *Osval'd Shpengler*, pp. 49–51, 53–54. Boobbyer, *S.L. Frank*, pp. 113–114.

[23] Lenin to Gorbunov, March 5, 1922, *Polnoe sobranie sochinenii*, 5th edn., 55 vols. (Moscow, 1958–1965), vol. 54, p. 198.

[24] For one "official" response, see P.F. Preobrazhenskii, "Osval'd Shpengler i krushenie istiny. (Stranitsy iz istorii gibeli odnoi kul'tury)," *Pechat' i revoliutsiia*, no. 4 (1922), 58–65.

[25] List of professors and instructors, Moscow University social science faculty, June 18, 1921, Tsentral'nyi Munitsipal'nyi Arkhiv goroda Moskvy [TsMAM] f.1609, op.5, d.73, l.51–55.

[26] Materials of the State Academic Council, March–May 1921, Gosudarstvennyi Arkhiv Rossiiskoi Federatsii [GARF] f.298, op.2, d.29, l.175, 184 and d.15, l.55–55ob.; and N.O. Losskii, *Vospominaniia. Zhizn' i filosofskii put'* (St. Petersburg: Izdatel'stvo S.-Peterburgskogo Universiteta, 1994), pp. 232–233.

Pitirim Sorokin noted, "removed to the Research Institute, where they would not be harmful to students."[27] Even this shuffling did not initially stop those determined to teach; after the disbanding of the philosophy department, the Moscow University Institute of Scientific Philosophy attempted to organize temporary courses for continuing majors (instructors included Frank and Il'in).[28] Lectures in conjunction with the independent philosophical societies continued to be very well attended. Berdiaev and Frank even established a "Faculty of Philosophy and Humanities" under the auspices of the Free Academy of Spiritual Culture. In 1922, the exasperated Bolshevik leadership put a stop to this illicit instruction by shutting down these societies and deporting their leaders.[29]

BANISHMENT AND RENEWAL: PHILOSOPHY ABROAD

The Russian philosophical revival did not end with the "philosophers' steamboats" so much as it underwent an involuntary relocation abroad. Losskii, Karsavin, Lapshin, A.S. Izgoev, and the publisher A.S. Kagan were expelled from Petrograd; Il'in, Berdiaev, Frank, Stepun, and S.E. Trubetskoi were deported from Moscow; and Sergei Bulgakov left via the Crimea. Their departure marked the end of autonomous philosophy in Soviet Russia. The Moscow University and Petrograd University philosophy departments had been replaced; Glavlit had shut down the journal *Mysl'* and leading publishers of philosophical monographs, such as Bereg and Petropolis; other philosophical and religious societies were either immediately disbanded or gradually liquidated over the next several years.[30]

It did little good for the arrested intellectuals to assure the GPU that their ideological disagreements with the Bolsheviks should not be confused with political opposition. Stepun attempted in vain to distinguish between his "loyal" political attitude toward the government and his philosophical conviction that

---

[27] Pitirim Sorokin, *Leaves from a Russian Diary* (New York: E.P. Dutton, 1924), p. 247.

[28] Gustav Shpet as Director of the Institute to the Moscow University Presidium, September 28, 1921, TsMAM f.1609, op.5, d.77, l.23–230b.; and L.A. Kogan, "Neprochitannaia stranitsa (G.G. Shpet – direktor Instituta nauchnoi filosofii: 1921–1923)," *Voprosy filosofii*, no. 10 (1995), 95–117.

[29] Nikolai Berdiaev, *Samopoznanie* (Moscow: Eksmo-Press; Khar'kov: Folio, 1997), pp. 482–486; Boobbyer, *S.L. Frank*, pp. 112–113; and Stepun, *Byvshee*, vol. 2, pp. 272–279.

[30] The NKVD summarily rejected the efforts of B.A. Griftsov to maintain the Free Academy after Berdiaev's expulsion, while Vol'fila was abolished in 1924. GARF f.393, op.43a, d.1817a, l.16–160b. and d.1822, l.462–710b; Aleksandr Galushkin, "Posle Berdiaeva: Vol'naia akademiia dukhovnoi kul'tury v 1922–1923 gg." in *Issledovaniia po istorii russkoi mysli. Ezhegodnik za 1997 god* (St. Petersburg: Aleteiia, 1997), pp. 237–244; and V.G. Belous, *Petrogradskaia Vol'naia Filosofskaia Assotsiatsiia (1919–1924). Antitotalitarnyi eksperiment v kommunisticheskoi strane* (Moscow: Magistr, 1997), pp. 29–30.

Bolshevism was a "grave illness of the popular spirit."[31] Berdiaev distanced himself from class-based ideologies but critiqued elementary egalitarianism. "My personal ideology I consider aristocratic," he stated, "not in the estate sense, but in the sense of the rule of the best, the smartest, the most talented, the most educated, the most noble. I consider democracy a mistake, because it depends on the rule of the majority."[32] Il'in, ever the Hegelian scholar, declared that he considered the Soviet regime "a historically inevitable processing of a great social-spiritual ailment which has been ripening in Russia over the course of the last several centuries."[33] On his way out of Russia, Losskii pointed out that his very expulsion contradicted dialectical materialism: "And so, I am banished from Russia, as a year ago they banished me from Petrograd University, having been found guilty only for my religious-philosophical ideology. This means that my opponents themselves secretly admit that the following thesis is true: being is determined by consciousness, the spirit rules over matter."[34]

Stymied in their efforts to participate in the Soviet public sphere, the deportees eagerly involved themselves in the vibrant network of émigré institutions that was meant to serve as an alternative Russian *publicum*. Where institutions did not already exist, the expelled intellectuals formed their own, often mimicking the ones they had been forced to leave behind in Russia. With the assistance of the YMCA, Berdiaev, Stepun, and others formed the Russian Religious Philosophical Academy, whose instructors included Berdiaev, Il'in, Karsavin, and Aikhenval'd, to continue the work of the defunct Free Spiritual Academy.[35] The program for the Religious-Philosophical Academy explicitly encapsulated Berdiaev's mantra of internal spiritual renewal: "Only religious rebirth can save Russia and heal Europe and the whole world. All political forms and all social organizations are impotent and fruitless, unless they are filled with content and subordinated to the spiritual aims of life."[36] These views were further articulated in a companion volume entitled *Sofiia: Problemy dukhovnoi kul'tury i religioznoi filosofii* (*Sophia: Problems of Spiritual Culture and Religious Philosophy*), which featured the writings of Berdiaev, Karsavin, Losskii, Il'in, and Frank,

[31] Stepun, *Byvshee*, vol. 2, pp. 417–418.
[32] A.V. Velidov, "Nikolai Berdiaev – arest i vysylka," *Sovershenno sekretno*, no. 8 (1991), 2.
[33] I.A. Il'in, *Sobranie sochinenii*, suppl. vol. 1, *Dnevnik, Pis'ma, Dokumenty (1903–1938)* (Iu. T. Lisitsa (ed.), Moscow: Russkaia kniga, 1999), pp. 433–434.
[34] "Zapisi pod chertoi," *Novyi zhurnal*, no. 40 (1955), 269–274.
[35] See, inter alia, "Russkaia religiozno-filosofskaia akademiia pri Amerikanskom Khristianskom Soiuze Molodykh liudei," *Dni* (November 16, 1922), 4, and "Russkaia literaturnaia i nauchnaia zhizn' za rubezhom," *Novaia Russkaia kniga*, nos. 11–12 (1922), 27.
[36] Burbank, *Intelligentsia and Revolution*, p. 206, citing "Religiozno-filosofskaia akademiia v Berline" in Berdiaev, *Sofiia*, p. 136.

and similarly emphasized the primacy of internal spiritual transformation over external political developments.[37]

A plethora of newspapers and journals replaced the publications that had been shut down in Soviet Russia, and émigré publishers allowed the deportees to put out a multitude of works they had been unable to issue at home.[38] More informal *kruzhki* also emerged. In Berlin, "it was not unusual in 1922 to find four or five separate literary gatherings or poetry readings going on simultaneously on a given evening."[39] In 1923 and 1924, the emigration began to shift from Berlin to Prague and Paris; by the mid-1920s, cafes in Montparnasse were filled with Russians debating philosophy, art, and politics. Religious-philosophical groupings, including Sergei Bulgakov's Brotherhood of St. Sophia, arose as well. In the Prague suburb of Zbraslav, a lively and extremely diverse circle of intellectuals, including Lapshin and Losskii, met on Fridays in the garden of a local restaurant.[40]

Philosophers also helped establish scholarly and educational establishments. The Russian Scientific Institute in Berlin, whose initiators included Berdiaev and Karsavin, aimed to provide a first-rate Russian education for émigré youth, to assist scholars in research and publication, and to present public lectures and discussions. As the political situation and living conditions worsened in Germany, however, many scholars took part in an exodus from Berlin to Prague, which would become the center of Russian émigré scholarly life until the late 1930s. The Czech government's generous "Russian Action" plan helped establish an impressive set of institutions, including the Russian Law Faculty and the Russian Popular University.[41] This set of educational institutions, created in

[37] Robert C. Williams, *Culture in Exile: Russian Émigrés in Germany, 1881–1941* (Ithaca, NY: Cornell University Press, 1972), pp. 251–252. While *Sofiia* was initially intended to be a periodical, only one volume was issued. Berdiaev would assign a very similar mission to *Put'*, launched two years later.

[38] Philosophy publishers included Obelisk and Kagan's re-formed Petropolis in Berlin, and the YMCA Press in Paris, run by Berdiaev until his death in 1948. L. Fleishman, R. Hughes, and O. Raevsky-Hughes (eds.), *Russkii Berlin, 1921–1923* (Paris: YMCA Press, 1983), p. 252; Lowrie, *Rebellious Prophet*, p. 184; Raeff, *Russia Abroad*, p. 73.

[39] Williams, *Culture in Exile*, pp. 131–132.

[40] Robert H. Johnston, *New Mecca, New Babylon: Paris and the Russian Exiles, 1920–1945* (Montreal and Kingston: McGill-Queen's University Press, 1988), p. 27; Raeff, *Russia Abroad*, pp. 91–92; Boobbyer, *Frank*, p. 125; Valentin Bulgakov, "Kak prozhita zhizn'," [memoirs] Rossiiskii Gosudarstvennyi Arkhiv Literatury i Isskustva [RGALI] f.2226, op.1, d.61, l.117–70; S.P. Postnikov, *Russkie v Prage, 1918–1928* (Prague: [Volia Rossii], 1928), pp. 141–143; and Losskii, *Vospominaniia*, p. 249.

[41] "Russkaia literaturnaia i nauchnaia zhizn' za rubezhom," *Novaia russkaia kniga*, no. 1 (1923), 36, and no. 2 (1923), 39; Catherine Andreyev and Ivan Savický, *Russia Abroad: Prague and the Russian Diaspora, 1918–1938* (New Haven, CT: Yale University Press, 2004), pp. 80–116; Williams, *Culture in Exile*, pp. 130–131; Raeff, *Russia Abroad*, pp. 61–64; and Postnikov, *Russkie v Prage*, pp. 36–41, 54–58, 69–100.

adverse circumstances, attested to the desire of émigré scholars to pass knowledge down to a younger generation of Russians abroad.

THE SPIRITUAL TASKS OF THE RUSSIAN EMIGRATION

Despite their critique of the intelligentsia for having paved the way to political catastrophe, émigré philosophers retained a sense of civic duty to the Russian nation, a key element in the traditional *intelligent* mentality. How intellectual and spiritual energies should be spent, however, was a matter of great dispute. A split soon developed among philosophers over whether they should oppose the Soviet regime directly or focus on inner spiritual regeneration. Immediately on arriving in Berlin, Berdiaev wrote his old colleague Struve that he was anxious over how much their views might now differ.[42] He felt uneasy among the émigrés, sensing that the Whites were generally no less hostile to the idea of freedom than were the Bolsheviks. In a subsequent letter to Struve, Berdiaev articulated his core view of the task of philosophers in emigration:

I consider my mission as much as I can to draw Russians abroad away from furious politics and petty political intrigues and to focus their awareness on spiritual life and spiritual interests. Russia's soul is gravely ill and can be saved only by means of a spiritual healing and strengthening, and not by external politics. Russia's political recovery will come only by means of spiritual sources. Bolshevism is a secondary phenomenon, of the reflexes, and only a symptom of the spiritual illness of the people. And one ought not to exaggerate the significance of "Bolshevism," just as one ought not to have exaggerated the significance of "autocracy." What is most important is what sort we ourselves are (*kakovy my sami*). The brute force that has pressed us, like a nightmare, is only an expression of our own spiritual weakness, a retribution for our own sins.[43]

Berdiaev rejected open political or military struggle and any resumption of civil war; he made quite clear that the institutions and journals that he helped launch would address only matters of spiritual renewal.[44]

While Struve agreed with the need for a spiritual regeneration, otherwise he saw matters quite differently, stressing the importance of a continued struggle against Bolshevism. Rather than quiescently accepting that "an epoch may be loathsome," he urged that "we need to fight it."[45] That these differences were irreconcilable quickly became evident at a gathering of philosophers in

---

[42] Berdiaev to Struve, October 14, 1922, in M.K. [M.A. Kolerov] (ed.), "Piat' pisem N.A. Berdiaeva k P.B. Struve (1922–1923)" in *Issledovaniia po istorii russkoi mysli. Ezhegodnik za 2000 god* (Moscow: OGI, 2000), p. 298.

[43] Berdiaev to Struve, November 6, 1922, in *ibid.* p. 299.

[44] See, e.g., his letter to Struve of December 17, 1922, in *ibid.* pp. 303–307.

[45] Cited in Nikolaj Plotnikov, "Revolution and the Counter-Revolution: The Conflict over Meaning between P.B. Struve and S.L. Frank in 1922," *Studies in East European Thought* 46 (1994), 193.

Berdiaev's apartment. In vain Izgoev and Frank attempted to persuade Struve of the need to come to terms with existing political realities; after Il'in, whose views were similar to Struve's, gave what the others viewed as a rambling nationalist speech, Berdiaev was apoplectic.[46] Berdiaev soon broke entirely with Struve, enraged by what he saw as the unforgivable arrogance of his old colleague's assertion that Russian spiritual life continued to exist only among the emigration. Berdiaev placed his hopes for regeneration in the spiritual thirst of the Russian people.[47]

Even Struve's close friend Frank fell out with him over the advisability of armed conflict, echoing Berdiaev's call for a spiritual regeneration in the spirit of *Vekhi*. Frank saw a terrible logic in the unfolding of the catastrophic events of the Revolution, and even in the horrors of Bolshevism. "The Bolshevik regime," Frank explained, using terms similar to Berdiaev's, "is only the scum and foam of the revolution, and not its essence; it is only a symptom of the infection (in its turn, of course, this symptom exacerbates the illness and impedes its treatment)."[48] He rejected calls for direct struggle with the Bolsheviks and for "heroism," and he dismissed Struve's criticism of those who would "kowtow to the facts" (*faktopoklonstvo*). Political change was irrelevant, Frank held, if it did not address Russia's inner malady; acknowledging the fact of the revolution was thus a necessary step on the path toward moral recovery.[49] Like Berdiaev, he also took exception to Struve's implication that those émigrés who had fought directly against the Bolsheviks were more representative of the real Russia than those still there. "Although the Kremlin is occupied by the Bolsheviks, the heart of Russia remains in Moscow, not in Prague."[50]

At least one of the deported philosophers shared Struve's view that reliance on a nebulous spiritual regeneration smacked of quietism and acquiescence to evil: the Hegelian scholar Ivan Il'in. As Frank wrote Struve, "Of our group – that is, those of like mind to you who have been living and are living in Russia – only Il'in approaches your mood."[51] Il'in, one of the few unequivocal

---

[46] Frank, *Biografiia P.B. Struve*, pp. 131–132, and Berdiaev, *Samopoznanie*, p. 495.

[47] Berdiaev to Struve, December 17, 1922, in "Piat' pisem," pp. 304–306.

[48] Frank to Struve, October 18, 1922, in "Ispytanie revoliutsii i kontrrevoliutsii: Perepiska P.B. Struve i S.L. Franka (1922–1925)," *Voprosy filosofii*, no. 2 (1993), 123.

[49] Boobbyer, *Frank*, pp. 134–137; Frank, *Biografiia P.B. Struve*, pp. 123–147; Plotnikov, "Revolution and Counter-Revolution," 187–196; and their correspondence in "Ispytanie revoliutsii i kontrrevoliutsii," 115–139.

[50] Frank to Struve, November 4, 1922, in "Ispytanie revoliutsii i kontrrevoliutsii," 127.

[51] Frank to Struve, October 21, 1922, in *ibid*. 125. Frank did not think very highly of Il'in: "But Il'in . . . is in his personal moral relations far from the purest and disinterested among us – by his ideas completely driven and devastated by the pride of moral denunciation and morally-based hate, and in this mood is alien to us."

defenders of the White movement among the deported philosophers,[52] developed a close relationship with Struve after his exile. He became an active contributor both to Struve's newspaper *Vozrozhdenie (Rebirth)* and his journal *Russkaia mysl' (Russian Thought)*, and he shared Struve's conviction that the emigration should not reconcile itself to the Soviet state and indeed should renew attempts to overthrow it by means of armed intervention.[53] The publication of Il'in's *O soprotivlenii zlu siloiu (On the Resistance to Evil by Force, 1925)* was a controversial event that divided émigré philosophers. Il'in argued that Lev Tolstoi's doctrine of non-resistance naively placed the honest and righteous man in the position of passively accepting and therefore condoning evil, thus weakening his principles and character. In certain situations, he asserted, if the enemy were truly wicked and the warrior truly righteous, force was not only justified but a moral imperative. Il'in's book, then, amounted to a theological-philosophical justification of armed struggle against the Bolsheviks.[54]

Berdiaev regarded Il'in's book as an appalling example of the kind of moral self-righteousness that had led him and Frank to quarrel so fiercely with Struve, and he published a lengthy excoriation of it in his journal *Put'*. "I have rarely had to read such a nightmarish and torturous book as I. Il'in's *On the Resistance to Evil by Force*. The book is capable of inducing a revulsion to 'good'; it creates an atmosphere of spiritual suffocation; it plunges into the torture chamber of moral inquisition."[55] Berdiaev pointed to the fallacy at the root of Il'in's proposition, namely, that it assumed the author's own moral purity and superiority. Il'in, whose book on Hegel Berdiaev admired, had now given up philosophy to act like a judge in a military tribunal. "A 'Cheka' in the name of God is even more repugnant than a 'Cheka' in the name of the Devil." Berdiaev considered the hate and vengeance that had given birth to the Bolsheviks the central

---

[52]   Frank, *Biografiia P.B. Struve*, pp. 131–132.

[53]   Il'in's extensive correspondence with Struve after his deportation is in Il'in, *Sobranie sochinenii*, suppl. vol. 2, *Dnevnik. Pis'ma. Dokumenty (1903–1938)*, pp. 115–209. Despite his conservative views, Il'in advised Struve to disassociate himself from *Vozrozhdenie* as it became openly reactionary, and he contemptuously rejected the Black Hundreds, while refusing Nazi demands that he teach anti-Semitism. Richard Pipes, *Struve: Liberal on the Right, 1905–1944* (Cambridge, MA: Harvard University Press, 1980), pp. 390–391; and Philip T. Grier, "The Complex Legacy of Ivan Il'in" in James P. Scanlan (ed.), *Russian Thought after Communism: The Recovery of a Philosophical Heritage* (Armonk, NY: M.E. Sharpe, 1994), pp. 167, 184 n. 12.

[54]   I. Il'in, *O soprotivlenii zlu siloiu* (Berlin: [Tipografiia Ob-va "Presse"], 1925). On the polemics around this book, see "O soprotivlenii zlu siloi: Pro et contra. Polemika vokrug idei I.A. Il'ina" in Il'in, *Sobranie sochinenii*, vol. 5, pp. 289–556; N. Poltoratskii, *I.A. Il'in i polemika vokrug ego idei o soprotivlenii zlu siloi* (London, ON: Zaria, 1975); and N. Poltoratskii, *Ivan Aleksandrovich Il'in: zhizn', trudy, mirovozzrenie. Sbornik statei* (Tenafly, NJ: Hermitage, 1989), pp. 120–131.

[55]   Nikolai Berdiaev, "Koshmar zlogo dobra. (O knige I. Il'ina 'O soprotivlenii zlu siloiu')," *Put'*, no. 4 (June–July 1926), 103.

illness of modern times, no matter what form it took or in what ideology it cloaked itself. Rather than serving as a philosophical justification of force, Il'in's book was proof that its author shared the spiritual ailment of modernity. "Il'in has been infected with the poison of Bolshevism, which possesses the ability to act in the most various, most seemingly contradictory forms. He internalized it as a bloody nightmare; he did not find the spiritual strength to resist it."[56]

As evidence of what Berdiaev held to be the simplistic misapprehension that drove Il'in's thesis, he noted that Il'in's logic could easily be accepted by the Bolsheviks, who "consider themselves to be the bearers of absolute good and in its name resist by force that which they consider to be evil." Il'in (and Berdiaev certainly also had in mind the many émigrés who shared Il'in's mentality) was a mirror image of Bolshevism. He had lost sight of the fundamental Christian truth that all of humanity is pierced by original sin, that human beings are not divided between those who are good and those who are evil. Il'in's book, Berdiaev declared, "is permeated with a sense of pharisaic self-righteousness. Anyone who considers himself the bearer of absolute good and who judges and chastises others in the name of this absolute good is doomed to this pharisaism. In such bearers of absolute good, a false pose of heroism and uncompromising bellicosity easily develop." Il'in's concept of the "Good" never left the realm of abstraction, and neither did his "Spirit."[57]

Semën Frank had made a similar sweeping critique of contemporary Russian political movements in "De Profundis":

The most noteworthy and tragic fact of contemporary Russian political life, which points to a very deep and general feature of our national soul, is the internal affinity of the moral character of the typical Russian conservative and revolutionary: an identical lack of understanding of the organic spiritual foundations of society, an identical love for the mechanistic measures of external violence and drastic reprisals, the same combination of a hatred for living people with a romantic idealization of abstract political forms and parties.[58]

It was this perverse echo of Bolshevik maximalism – its justification of any means, including violence and terror, to achieve the desired end – that Berdiaev found so appalling. While Frank was made uneasy by what he saw as a Christianized Nietzscheanism in Berdiaev's metaphysics, he was in full agreement with the "political" tenor of Berdiaev's critique of Il'in, and he entirely shared Berdiaev's conviction that the emigration should strive for spiritual regeneration,

---

[56] *Ibid.* 104. [57] *Ibid.* 104, 107, 112.

[58] Frank, "De Profundis," p. 323, cited in Philip Boobbyer, "The Two Democracies: Semen Frank's Interpretations of the Russian Revolutions of 1917," *Revolutionary Russia* 6, no. 2 (1993), 203.

not military intervention.[59] As Philip Boobbyer has noted, for Frank, as for Berdiaev, "the dividing line between good and evil lies not between political parties or races, but within human hearts."[60] What was necessary, then, was not the triumph of one or another political program or party, but a return to moral principle. This could only be achieved, as both men had insisted from *Vekhi* onward, through spiritual renewal.

Fëdor Stepun, who largely shared Frank and Berdiaev's views, rejected the idea that the only two possibilities at hand were open war with or submissive reconciliation to the Soviet regime. He thought the task of the emigration lay "not in the restoration of the past, but in the conservation for the future of the eternal character of Russia."[61] Such a task was precisely what Berdiaev and his collaborators hoped to achieve through the academies, societies, and journals they had founded as arenas for public activity. These goals were stated explicitly in the introductory editorial remarks to the journal *Put'*, which, published from 1925 to 1940, proved to be perhaps the most enduring of these ventures. This introduction, entitled, with characteristic Berdiaevan immodesty, "The Spiritual Tasks of the Russian Emigration," acknowledged the world-historical significance of the current diaspora. "It is hard to imagine a greater historical tragedy, than that which the Russian people have lived through," he wrote. But true Christians should not think that the trials and tribulations they have endured are meaningless or accidental; deprived of external good, they could recover their inner spiritual vitality. And (echoing his earlier disputes with Struve, and anticipating his revulsion to Il'in), he declared that émigrés themselves were neither blameless nor innocent: they must realize that, while Bolshevism truly represented the negation of Christian truth, Russia's spiritual illness had not begun and would not end with Bolshevism.[62]

For Berdiaev, turning inward to spiritual tasks did not at all signify passivity. "On the contrary, this is a call to the greatest spiritual activism [*aktivnost'*], which will lead also to civic [*obshchestvennoi*] and historical activism. But civic activism is fruitless and empty if it does not spring from spiritual activism."[63] Proving himself to be firmly rooted in the Slavophile-populist traditions of the Russian intelligentsia (despite his own trenchant critiques of intelligentsia traditions),

---

[59] Frank to Berdiaev, March 28, 1926, Bakhmeteff Archive (New York), Berdiaev Collection, Box 1, and Metropolitan Anastasii to Frank, June 3/17, 1926, Bakhmeteff, Frank Collection, Box 6. Frank did not review Il'in's book publicly, but he "was known to have privately opposed Il'in at the time." Grier, "Complex Legacy," p. 179, and N.K. Gavriushin, "Antitezy pravloslavnogo mecha," *Voprosy filosofii*, no. 4 (1992), 79–83.

[60] Boobbyer, "Two Democracies," 203.

[61] Fëdor Stepun, "Mysli o Rossii. (O 'Vozrozhdenii' i vozvrashchenstve)," *Sovremennye zapiski*, no. 28 (1926), 365–392.

[62] "Dukhovnye zadachi," 3–4.   [63] *Ibid.* 4.

Berdiaev spoke of the spirituality of the Russian people who remained (trapped) in Soviet Russia and warned the emigration not to allow itself to remain cut off from the *narod* (common people). "The schism between the emigration and the Russia remaining under Bolshevism must be overcome. On this depends the future of the Russian people." But this reunification had nothing to do with political movements, at least not directly. The overcoming of this terrible schism "must be first and foremost spiritual, religious. Overcoming it means the overcoming of émigré psychology," of the political bickering and militarist fantasies of overthrowing Bolshevism. "Only by means of a religious movement will Russians in Russia and Russians abroad come to constitute a united spiritual organism."[64]

The exigency of inner spiritual evolution had a central place in Berdiaev's mature philosophical output. In *O naznachenii cheloveka* (*The Destiny of Man*, 1931), he insisted on a creative Christian ethics, divorced from politics and the state. Man was elevated not through perfecting the realm of Caesar, but through a painstakingly cultivated everyday spiritual sensitivity. Christ's gospel was not a simple prescription that merely replaced Mosaic law, but rather a turn to a more nuanced and sophisticated form of spirituality. It was not for good to struggle against evil in the temporal world; it could never succeed fully and would inevitably be corrupted in the process. The "fundamental paradox of the struggle of good and evil" was that "struggle with evil continually generates new evil – intolerance, fanaticism, violence, cruelty, evil feelings. The 'good' in their struggle with those who are 'evil' are often themselves evil."[65] The human personality (*lichnost'*) was not lifted by participating in political struggle; just the opposite was true, even and especially when fighting in the name of freedom, or of the good in a more general sense. What was called for instead was a steady devotion to the ethics of redemption, and, even more, the ethics of creativity: the understanding that man was constantly called upon to employ Christ's message in new situations, imaginatively and energetically.

The tasks that Berdiaev assigned the emigration (and which would be pursued in *Put'* and other organs) were a religious–spiritual variant on the traditional intelligentsia mission to enlighten and serve. The rebirth, for which Berdiaev hoped he and his *Put'* colleagues might serve as midwives, was to occur as individual Russians in emigration turned away from petty politics and vengeful spite, the main symptoms of the modern epochal disease. Most important were the émigré youth, already coalescing into Christian student groups, who would be the source of the renaissance and would guide the process, eventually reconnecting with Russians in Russia. "In Russia first of all there lies ahead

---

[64] *Ibid.* 5. [65] Berdiaev, *O naznachenii cheloveka*, p. 142.

a colossal job of spiritual education and enlightenment of the popular masses, who have fallen away from the old ways and been mobilized into frenetic movement. For this [education] one needs to spiritually prepare. And with this is connected the primary task of the emigration." Émigrés needed to abandon their reactionary goals, Berdiaev wrote, and not limit their Christianity to personal salvation, which constituted "a rejection of a creative relationship to questions of the life of all mankind and the entire world."[66] It was the self-appointed task of the editors of *Put'* to initiate the process of creative spiritual work.

Paradoxically, Berdiaev and Frank, who were such effective and relentless critics of the faults and failures of the Russian intelligentsia, presented their calls to inner spiritual rebirth entirely within the framework of traditional intelligentsia *obshchestvennost'*, a sense of public duty. It was their goal to assist the people (including, but not limited to, the wayward *intelligenty*) to see their way toward spiritual rebirth. For Frank, the monastic separatism that characterized Russian Orthodoxy had kept it from being a beacon to ordinary people: "Long ago the Russian religious spirit stopped strengthening the people in their daily working life, stopped nourishing their earthly economic and legal relations with moral agency."[67] The task of the religious philosopher, then, was to guide the people along the path (*put'*) to a spiritual rebirth that could eventually transform Russia as a whole. Berdiaev's relentless energy in establishing institutions and publications to propagate these views, from the Free Academy of Spiritual Culture in Moscow, to *Sofiia* and the Religious-Philosophical Academy, to *Put'*, was directed quite explicitly at educating all who would listen concerning the way toward this hoped-for renaissance.

[66] "Dukhovnye zadachi," 5, 7.
[67] Frank, "De Profundis," cited in Boobbyer, "Two Democracies," 204.

18

EURASIANISM: AFFIRMING THE PERSON
IN AN "ERA OF FAITH"

MARTIN BEISSWENGER

Eurasianism, an intellectual movement among Russian émigrés in central and western Europe during the 1920s and 1930s, is not usually associated with the defense of human dignity or with concern for the person (*lichnost'*). On the contrary, critics of the movement have compared its precepts to authoritarianism, fascism, or even totalitarianism.[1] The focus of scholarly attention has hitherto been on Eurasianism's abstract speculations that geographically, culturally, and historically Russia was a country *sui generis*, neither a part of Europe, nor of Asia, but a self-contained "continent" in between and a synthesis of both – Eurasia.[2] Rather than examining the Eurasianists' conceptualization of the individual person, many historians of the movement have studied its bold historiosophical declarations and "geopolitical" statements, often instrumentalized as justifications of Russian neo-imperialist intentions.[3] Other scholars have scrutinized Eurasianist efforts to solve imperial Russia's nationality problem by inventing a "supra-national" Eurasian nationalism that would encompass all the country's nationalities, transcending traditional Russian ethnic nationalism.[4] In view of the movement's sweeping generalizations about historical developments

---

[1] For example, Fëdor Stepun called Eurasianism "Russian fascism": F.A. Stepun, review of *Evraziiskii vremennik* 3 (Berlin, 1923), *Sovremennye zapiski*, no. 21 (1924), 404; Nikolai Berdiaev identified the Eurasianist "ideocracy" and its "utopian state absolutism" as an example of the "total state": Nicolai Berdjajew, "Zur Kritik des Eurasiertums," *Orient und Occident*, no. 17 (1934), 35–36. Roman Bäcker claimed that Eurasianism "evolved from a specific nationalism towards a not finally crystallized totalitarianism": R. Bekker, "Mezhdu revoliutsionnym konservatizmom i totalitarizmom. Dilemmy otsenki mezhvoennogo evraziistva," *Slavianovedenie*, no. 5 (2001), 17–18.

[2] N.V. Riasanovsky, "The Emergence of Eurasianism," *California Slavic Studies* 4 (1967), 39–72; O. Böss, *Die Lehre der Eurasier. Ein Beitrag zur russischen Ideengeschichte des 20. Jahrhunderts* (Wiesbaden: Otto Harrassowitz, 1961); S. Wiederkehr, *Die eurasische Bewegung. Wissenschaft und Politik in der russischen Emigration der Zwischenkriegszeit und im postsowjetischen Russland* (Cologne: Böhlau, 2007).

[3] A recent example is V.G. Makarov, "'Pax rossica.' Istoriia evraziiskogo dvizheniia i sud'by evraziitsev," *Voprosy filosofii*, no. 9 (2006), 102–117.

[4] The post-imperial and post-colonial context of the movement has been emphasized by M. Laruelle, *L'Idéologie eurasiste russe ou Comment penser l'empire* (Paris: L'Harmattan, 1999) and S. Glebov, "Science, Culture, and Empire: Eurasianism as a Modernist Movement," *Slavic and East European Information Resources*, no. 4 (2003), 13–31.

over the *longue durée* and its interest in large political and national collectives and geographical units, it is not surprising that scholars have neglected the attention that Eurasianists gave to the individual and its defense.

Yet concern for the "person," understood as a divine creation "in the image and likeness of God," was at the very center of Eurasianism. This concern was a direct consequence of the movement's profound religiosity and its effort to create a new Russian ideology on the basis of Orthodoxy.[5] Stimulated by the catastrophic *Zeitgeist* of the Great War, Russian Revolution, and Civil War, leading Eurasianists embraced the spirituality of the pre-war Russian religious renaissance. From its origins in 1921 until the early 1940s, Eurasianism gradually came to affirm the sanctity of personhood and of personal rights vis-à-vis the collective. Initially, Eurasianism was highly ambiguous about the safeguarding of the individual person against social collectives, asserting the "absolute value" of both individual and collective. Only after the rise of totalitarian states and ideologies in the late 1920s and early 1930s did Eurasianism's ambiguity in this respect gradually dissolve. While some Eurasianists chose to support the collectivism of the Soviet Union, others explicitly denounced totalitarian states and ideologies and demanded the defense of the individual person.

Analysis of Eurasianism's ambiguous personalism makes clear the movement's essentially religious foundation, reveals the ideological heterogeneity of its members, and shows that Eurasianism was not a static set of "canonical" ideas, but a dynamic ideology that continuously changed in response to social and political events.

ANTICIPATING EURASIA'S RELIGIOUS MISSION

Eurasianism emerged as an intellectual movement in 1921 with the publication of the almanac *Iskhod k Vostoku* (*Exodus to the East*). It contained contributions by the economist P.N. Savitskii (1895–1968), the ethnographer and linguist N.S. Trubetskoi (1890–1938), the musicologist and art critic P.P. Suvchinskii (1892–1985), and the historian and theologian G.V. Florovskii (1893–1979).[6] The collection's powerful preface set the general tone for the movement's emerging ideology. The authors were united by their experience of a historical catastrophe but also by their sense of what Aleksandr Herzen called the plasticity and

[5] Surprisingly, there is only one explicit study of Eurasianism's attitude to religion: Iu. K. Gerasimov, "Religioznaia pozitsiia evraziistva," *Russkaia literatura*, no. 1 (1995), 159–176.

[6] The emergence of Eurasianism as a movement was preceded by Trubetskoi's pamphlet *Evropa i chelovechestvo* (Sofia: Rossiisko-Bolgarskoe knigoizdatel'stvo, [1920]) and Savitskii's review of it: "Evropa i Evraziia (Po povodu broshiury kn. N.S. Trubetskogo 'Evropa i chelovechestvo')," *Russkaia mysl'*, nos. 1–2 (1921), 119–138.

openness of history. They anticipated an imminent "migration and regeneration of culture," the decline of Europe, and the rise of a Eurasian Russia that would "reveal to the world an all-human truth." The Eurasianist authors acknowledged their debt to the Russian Slavophile tradition, yet rejected their predecessors' populism, their idealization of the peasant community's collectivism, and their identification with Slavic ethnicity. The Eurasianists recognized the importance of creative individuals and praised Russia as a multi-ethnic empire, where non-Russian nationalities were in close contact with the Russian people as active participants in the building of Russian culture, based on an "affinity of souls" and mutual economic interests. The Eurasianists rejected communism, yet interpreted the Russian Revolution as an elemental national act of resistance against forced Europeanization.[7]

The Eurasianist writings of the early 1920s were animated by a profound religiosity, by the anticipation of an "era of faith," and by the desire to defend Russian Orthodoxy as the only true confession of Christianity. All the Eurasianists advocated a holistic spirituality and rejected the secularist trends of imperial Russia and the alleged materialism of western Europe. At the same time, individual Eurasianists approached Russia's past, present, and future from their own perspective, often based on their field of professional expertise. Throughout the first half of the 1920s, the leading Eurasianists (Trubetskoi, Suvchinskii, and Savitskii) formed an ideological "troika." Although other authors contributed to various Eurasianist publications, the ideas of the "troika" were decisive and influenced Eurasianism throughout its existence.[8]

For Nikolai Trubetskoi, Eurasianism's apologist of nationalism, cultural diversity was an essential element of the divinely sanctioned world-order.[9] He perceived the multiplicity of human languages and cultures as God's punishment for human hubris symbolized in the construction of the Tower of Babel, an example of "blasphemous self-exaltation" and pure technical progress that had lost its religious purpose. According to Trubetskoi, genuine cultural diversity was a precondition for satisfying the spiritual and material needs of human societies. A homogeneous universal culture, Trubetskoi cautioned, can encompass only those elements common to all human beings, that is, their "material needs" rather than their tastes, beliefs, religion, ethics, and aesthetics. The inevitable result of cultural homogeneity would be "intensive

---

[7] *Iskhod k Vostoku. Predchuvstviia i sversheniia. Utverzhdenie evraziitsev* (Sofia, 1921), pp. iii–viii.

[8] G.V. Florovskii had left the movement already in 1923 because of its gradual politization. On him see A. Blane (ed.), *Georges Florovsky: Russian Intellectual and Orthodox Churchman* (Crestwood, NY: St. Vladimir's Seminary Press, 1993).

[9] On Trubetskoi see N.S. Trubetzkoy, *The Legacy of Genghis Khan and Other Essays on Russia's Identity* (Anatoly Liberman (ed.), Ann Arbor, MI: Michigan Slavic Publications, 1991).

scientific and technical development" accompanied by "spiritual and moral degeneration."[10]

National cultures, Trubetskoi argued, are highly original, "noble in their incomprehensibility and immense complexity and at the same time complex harmony."[11] Trubetskoi classified Russian popular culture as genuinely "Eurasian" and considered it a perfect example of such "complex harmony." It was neither European, nor purely Slavic, but permanently in touch with the "East."[12] In this sense, Trubetskoi's "Eurasia" was a particular "cultural-historical type," similar to those established half a century earlier by the Russian Panslavist thinker Nikolai Danilevskii (1822–1885) in his *Russia and Europe* (1871).[13]

Pëtr Suvchinskii argued that Eurasian culture was based on the Orthodox religion as an all-embracing spiritual system.[14] His call for the total sacralization and ritualization of life, society, and culture was Suvchinskii's main contribution to Eurasianism. Inspired by the Russian symbolist idea of "creating life" (*zhiznetvorchestvo*), he located Russia's vital spiritual forces not in the bureaucracy of the state-dominated church, but in the practice of Orthodoxy in everyday life. Here, spirituality was ritualized, performatively experienced as art, as the "confession of everyday life" (*bytovoe ispovednichestvo*), where the "mundane and the religious are synthesized in an inseparable unity." In his opinion, the Russian people's performative religiosity fundamentally differed from the consciously-dogmatic approach to religion characteristic in the West.[15] Russians practiced an "Eastern" religiosity that embodied the divine wholeness of life. Suvchinskii was convinced that "only constant, persistent and habitual memory of God can direct consciousness toward true understanding of the divine lawfulness of the world and the entire process of life."[16]

Pre-revolutionary Russia's intelligentsia and government, he complained, had largely ignored the "confession of everyday life." Unfulfilled popular religious longings ultimately triggered the revolution, which Suvchinskii viewed as a spiritual awakening during which the country had become aware of its "cultural

[10] N.S. Trubetskoi, "Vavilonskaia bashnia i smeshenie iazykov," *Evraziiskii Vremennik* 3 (1923), 109–111.

[11] *Ibid*. 119.

[12] N.S. Trubetskoi, "Verkhi i nizy russkoi kul'tury" in *Iskhod k Vostoku*, pp. 86–103.

[13] N. Danilevskii, *Rossiia i Evropa*, 5th edn. (St. Petersburg: Izd. N. Strakhova, 1895; reprint, New York: Johnson Reprint Corporation, 1966).

[14] On Suvchinskii see Alla Bretanitskaia (ed.), *Petr Suvchinskii i ego vremia* (Moscow: Izdatel'skoe ob''edinenie "Kompozitor," 1999) and Sergey Glebov, "Le frémissement du temps: Petr Suvchinskii, l'eurasisme et l'esthétique de la modernité" in *Pierre Souvtchinski, cahiers d'étude* (Éric Humbertclaude (ed.), Paris: L'Harmattan, 2006), pp. 163–223.

[15] P.P. Suvchinskii, "Inobytie russkoi religioznosti," *Evraziiskii Vremennik* 3 (1923), 82–86.

[16] *Ibid*. 103–104.

and political particularity," had returned to its genuine foundations, and had begun to search for its religious mission.[17]

The theme of Russia's religious mission was further elaborated by Pëtr Savitskii, who added to Trubetskoi's and Suvchinskii's ideas an economic and geographic dimension.[18] A comprehensive knowledge of Russia's particular Eurasian nature, he argued, was the key for Russia's successful accomplishment of its divine mission: the economic transformation of Eurasia and the "East" into a prospering "Garden of Eden." Russia's experience of incomparable suffering under the Bolshevik regime was a sure sign of the country's divine selection. In its vibrant religiosity, Savitskii explained, Russia had shown its close connection with the "East." Russian art and life had always been affected by other cultures, and without the Turanic and Mongolian influences Russian statehood could not have emerged. Now it was Russia's mission to raise the economically languishing East, where the "era of faith" had never ended, to new prosperity.[19]

Russia-Eurasia, uniquely situated between Europe and Asia, could reconcile the scientific achievements of the West with the spiritual legacy of the East. Far from denying scientific progress or economic prosperity per se, Savitskii rejected western European culture because of its "enslavement of the spirit by the fetishes of technical 'progress,' its neglect of the Heavenly Kingdom (*Grad Nezdeshnii*) . . . and its excessive concern for the Earthly Kingdom (*Grad Zdeshnii*)."[20] And in this new era Russia-Eurasia would be the leader, uniting the constitutive principles of the West and the East: "economy and religion, knowledge and faith."[21]

The Eurasianists did not limit themselves to contemplative religious anticipations and philosophical speculations: although initially they had rejected politics and declared the "primacy of culture," after 1923 many of them became committed to changing the politics of the Russian émigré community and, more importantly, of Soviet Russia. One of the driving forces behind this activism was Pëtr Arapov (1895–1930s), a former officer of the Imperial Guard, who joined the movement in 1922. He wanted Eurasianism to be "not only an academic current," but also a "potentially effective force" politically. For him this meant the energetic propagation of Eurasianist ideas within the Soviet

---

[17] P.P. Suvchinskii, "K preodoleniiu revoliutsii," *Evraziiskii vremennik* 3 (1923), 32–36.

[18] On Savitskii see S. Glebov, "A Life with Imperial Dreams: Petr Nikolaevich Savitsky, Eurasianism, and the Invention of 'Structuralist' Geography," *Ab Imperio*, no. 3 (2005), 299–329, and Martin Beisswenger (ed.), *Petr Nikolaevich Savitskii (1895–1968): A Bibliography of his Published Works* (Prague: Slavonic Library, 2008).

[19] P.N. Savitskii, "K obosnovaniiu evraziistva," *Rul'*, no. 349 (January 10, 1922), 2–3.

[20] P.N. Savitskii, "Khoziaistvo i vera," *Rul'*, no. 295 (November 5, 1921), 1–2.

[21] Savitskii, "K obosnovaniiu evraziistva," 2.

Union.[22] The decisive stimulus in shifting Eurasianism's focus from philosophical ideas to political deeds was its collaboration, starting in 1923, with the so-called "Trest," allegedly an underground anti-communist resistance group but, in fact, a bogus organization set up by the OGPU to control and manipulate the Russian emigration.[23] Assured by "Trest" of their popularity within the Soviet Union, Eurasianists significantly increased their publication activities and soon transformed themselves into a political party. The financial means for such large-scale operations were provided in 1924 by Arapov's friend and fellow officer P.N. Malevskii-Malevich (1891–1974), who had received £10,000 from the English philanthropist Henry Norman Spalding (1877–1953) "for the Russian cause."[24] The Eurasianists' new "political" character had decisive consequences for their theoretical writings. In order to overthrow the communist regime and replace it with a Eurasianist one, it was not enough to enthusiastically predict Eurasia's mission in the East, to affirm a genuinely multinational Eurasian nationalism, or to advocate the sacralization of everyday life. What was needed was a pragmatic, systematic, and explicitly political declaration. This program required a firm organizing principle – a principle the Eurasianists found in the "affirmation of the person."

AFFIRMATION OF THE PERSON

The concept of the person was the Eurasianists' principal instrument for translating their general religious expectations of Russia's "era of faith" of the early 1920s into a political program. It emerged between 1925 and 1927 in intensive discussions among the movement's leaders. Besides the "troika" (Savitskii, Suvchinskii, and Trubetskoi), the leadership by then included the former officers Arapov and Malevskii-Malevich as well as the historian and philosopher L.P. Karsavin (1882–1952). Together these six men formed the "Eurasianist Council." Some aspects of Eurasianism's personalism were developed in their private correspondence; other aspects were elaborated in programmatic booklets and articles.[25] Despite all the efforts to forge a common understanding,

---

[22] Gosudarstvennyi arkhiv Rossiiskoi Federatsii (GARF), fond 5783 (fond P.N. Savitskii), op. 1, ed. khr. 444, ll. 1–1 verso, protocol of meeting Arapov, Savitskii, and Suvchinskii in Berlin, March 1923.

[23] On "Trest" see Lazar Fleishman, *V tiskakh provokatsii. Operatsiia "Trest" i russkaia zarubezhnaia pechat'* (Moscow: Novoe literaturnoe obozrenie, 2003).

[24] GARF, f. 5783, op. 1, ed. khr. 359, ll. 94–95 ob., letter Suvchinskii to Trubetskoi, October 29, 1924.

[25] Some archival materials on the internal discussions were published (in excerpts and with several inaccuracies) by B. Stepanov, "Spor evraziitsev o tserkvi, lichnosti i gosudarstve (1925–1927)" in M.A. Kolerov (ed.), *Issledovaniia po istorii russkoi mysli: Ezhegodnik za 2001–2002 gody* (Moscow: Tri kvadrata, 2002), pp. 74–173.

Eurasianism's concept of the person remained for the time being ambiguous and contradictory. Although all the Eurasianists agreed on the fundamental importance of Orthodoxy for their ideology, each had different ideas about the relationship between the individual person and so-called "collective persons," such as the state, the nation, culture, the economy, and the church. The difficulty was that the Eurasianists explicitly confirmed the "absolute value" of the individual, while claiming the same value for collective persons of a "higher order," such as the state or the nation.

The main protagonist of Eurasianism's programmatic efforts was Lev Karsavin, who was introduced to the movement in April 1924 by Suvchinskii.[26] Karsavin was ideally suited to synthesize the diverging views of the individual Eurasianists into a programmatic booklet.[27] Already in 1923 he had welcomed Eurasianism's religious interpretation of the Russian Revolution and of the new "era of faith," yet he also criticized the lack of a coherent philosophical analysis that would rationally prove the movement's claims.[28] Moreover, starting in 1923 Karsavin had worked on a comprehensive summary of the principles of Christianity that he now could "apply" to the Eurasianist program.[29] Inspired by the Slavophile thinker Aleksei Khomiakov's ecclesiological tract *The Church is One* (1844–1845), Karsavin introduced the concept of the "symphonic" or "conciliar" (*sobornaia*) person, his most important contribution to Eurasianism, as a means to understand the hierarchical relationship among the individual, the state, culture, and the church.[30] This concept was based on the individual's relationship to the divine and modeled on the example of the church. The ambiguity of the "church" as an "absolute" and also an "empirical" phenomenon could cause a confusion of these two spheres. Karsavin tried to solve this problem by calling upon the empirical to become sacred: he desired an "ecclesiastization" (*otserkovlenie*) of the state and of the world in general. Ultimately, however, the attempt to transfer categories describing the relationship of the individual person with God and the church to the secular sphere of the social and political remained highly problematic.

Karsavin made it clear that individual human beings are persons only by virtue of partaking of the divine, since, in the Christian understanding, personhood was

---

[26] GARF, f. 5783, op. 1, d. 359, l.74 verso, letter Suvchinskii to Trubetskoi, April 11, 1924.

[27] [L.P. Karsavin], *Evraziistvo. Opyt sistematicheskogo izlozheniia* ([Paris]: Evraziiskoe knigoizdatel'stvo, 1926). On Karsavin see S.S. Khoruzhii's Introduction to L.P. Karsavin, *Religiozno-filosofskie sochineniia* (S.S. Khoruzhii (ed.), Moscow: Renessans, 1992), vol. 1, pp. v–lxxiii, and Iu.B. Melikh, *Personalizm L.P. Karsavina i evropeiskaia filosofiia* (Moscow: Progess Traditsiia, 2003).

[28] L.P. Karsavin, "Evropa i Evraziia," *Sovremennye zapiski*, no. 15 (1923), 297–314.

[29] L.P. Karsavin, *O nachalakh* (A.K. Klement'ev (ed.), St. Petersburg: YMCA Press, 1994).

[30] Khomiakov's tract was reprinted with Karsavin's introduction and notes: A.S. Khomiakov, *O tserkvi* (L.P. Karsavin (ed.), Berlin: Evraziiskoe knigoizdatel'stvo, 1926).

first of all a divine principle, connected with the Holy Spirit. As material beings, human beings are not yet persons, and they become so not through their own efforts alone, but through God. Thus, by themselves individuals are neither fully self-determined nor entirely free; they become self-determining and free persons in "communion" with God through the church as the ultimate sacral sphere. The relationship between the individual and God is mediated by the church, which Karsavin considered, in its ideal and metaphysical essence, a perfect, "all-united" (*vsë-edinaia*) community of faithful individuals. Standing between the ideal church and the individual there were other collective persons, not perfectly "all-united," but "conciliar" or "symphonic" – in Karsavin's words, "a hierarchy of persons with a decreasing degree of conciliarity (*sobornost'*) ranging from the united Church itself to individuals." Although these social entities were hierarchically higher than the individual person, Karsavin denied that such collective persons would restrict the freedom of individual persons, explicitly declaring that "all persons are equal in value."[31] Since both collective and individual persons depend on each other, he thought that one could not exist without and beyond the other. He meant that the individual could not exist as a person independent of other individuals or collectives; indeed, each individual "specifically expresses and realizes the whole in his very own and particular way." Similarly, collective persons could not exist outside their manifestations in individuals or "*otherwise than as their free unity.*"[32]

Yet this free and harmonious relationship between individual and collective persons, Karsavin admitted, was possible in all its perfection only in the absolute sphere of the church. In the empirical sphere things were different. Here the imperfect and sinful individual strove not toward harmony with others but acted egoistically. For the sake of the individual and the whole, it was therefore necessary to restrict the individual's egoistic self-interest, because otherwise he would not only harm the collective and other individuals, but ultimately destroy himself. In practice, the limitation of the individual can be realized by one or more collective entities: family, the social group, or the nation. Each of these collectives was held together by some leader or spokesperson, who stood in a certain power relationship vis-à-vis other members of the collective.[33]

The problems with Eurasianist political ideas reveal themselves most clearly in Karsavin's definition of the state and its function. The state, he claimed, was of principal significance, because only through and within the state could the "unity of all spheres" constitute itself as an "externally unified culture"

---

[31] L.P. Karsavin, *Tserkov', lichnost' i gosudarstvo* (Paris: Evraziiskoe knigoizdatel'stvo, 1927), pp. 6–8.

[32] L.P. Karsavin, "Osnovy politiki," *Evraziiskii vremennik* 5 (1927), 189. Original emphasis.

[33] Karsavin, *Evraziistvo*, p. 39; "Osnovy politiki," 191 and 193–194.

and the symphonic collective subject "acquire genuine personal existence." The state was the form alone through which a given culture gained its "personal existence and personal realization [*kachestvovanie*]."[34] In Karsavin's view, culture and the state were so closely interrelated as to be virtually identical: "In principle the state is culture itself in its unity and by its capacity to bring unity out of diversity – that is, in principle, the state encompasses all spheres of life."[35] Yet Karsavin cautioned that it was wrong to worship the state, which, after all, was only an empirical entity, and therefore as "sinful" as an individual human being.[36] Ultimately, Karsavin claimed, state and culture would become the church in the broadest and absolute sense – they would undergo full and complete "ecclesiastization."[37] Although Karsavin's concepts of "all-unity" and "conciliar" or "symphonic persons" of various hierarchical rank allowed for a certain ideological flexibility, he blurred the distinctions between the metaphysical and the material, the "absolute" and the "empirical," between the individual person and his rights, on the one hand, and the collective "persons" on the other. In the end, Karsavin's political writings remained vague, making it impossible to determine precisely the exact distribution of power and authority between the state and the individual or between the state and other collective entities.

Each of the other prominent Eurasianists shared some of Karsavin's ideas, in particular his notion of "symphonic persons," but they rejected others. Each of them had different views on the relationship of the individual to the collective. While Arapov and Malevskii-Malevich demanded the predominance of the collective, in particular the state, over the individual, Savitskii defended the rights of individual persons in the economic sphere. Trubetskoi's position was somewhere in between.

More than any other Eurasianist, Arapov emphasized the primacy of collectives over the individual, and he demanded that the state organize society, for without it neither culture nor true religion was possible. Arapov's ideas (his fierce rejection of nationalism, his call for a dominant state as a precondition for cultural creativity, and his fascination with contradictions and paradoxes) betrayed the strong influence of the Russian diplomat and conservative thinker K.N. Leont'ev (1831–1891).[38] In order to create a strong Eurasian state, Arapov claimed, it was essential to reject modern, ethnic "nationalism" in favor of a pre-modern supra-national concept of authority resting firmly on the ruling

---

[34] Karsavin, "Osnovy politiki," 207.   [35] Karsavin, *Evraziistvo*, p. 40.
[36] Karsavin, "Osnovy politiki," 207.   [37] Karsavin, *Evraziistvo*, p. 26.
[38] On Leont'ev see K. Leont'ev, *Vostok, Rossiia i Slavianstvo: Filosofskaia i politicheskaia publitsistika. Dukhovnaia proza (1872–1891)* (G.B. Kremnev (ed.), Moscow: Respublika, 1996).

power.[39] He conceded that individual national cultures could function within an over-all Eurasian culture, but only if Eurasian culture were truly supra-national and committed to "cultural tasks of a universal nature."[40] The promotion of creativity and culture was the main task of the state, an "apparatus of coercion" ruled by an ideologically unified group of people, who were "forcibly realizing all means for fostering the creativity, development and diffusion of this culture."[41] But cultural activity was not an end itself: ultimately it served religious and eschatological purposes. By organizing the environment and creating a new culture, the Eurasian state would raise life to a higher plain of existence, closer toward Transfiguration. This transformation, Arapov claimed, was "a perpetually on-going process, never to be concluded" that needed to be undertaken "without taking into account the happiness or suffering of the people."[42]

Vis-à-vis the lofty goals of state and culture Arapov gave little agency to the individual. Acknowledging the existence of the human person not as "a dot or an atom" but as a "system of qualities," he explicitly claimed the primacy of culture "as a system" over the individual. As a "system of qualities" all persons were "functionally" interconnected with each other, and each individual was determined through his or her participation in the system (*sistemnost'*).[43] Ultimately, Arapov declared, "the rights of the individual person must be limited by the cultural goals that are realized by the state."[44]

Arapov's outlook was shared by Malevskii-Malevich, who saw the individual's duty in spiritual and religious service alone. Like Arapov and Karsavin, he rejected an independent, self-determined individual, arguing that "the meaning of human existence does not lie in the egoistic self-assertion of the individual, but in his service to God and man." He made it clear that "from a moral point of view" the individual possessed only one "absolute right": "*to have the opportunity of serving this great purpose in the best possible way, without obstacles to impede his work of service.* All other rights are derived from this and are correlative to definite duties."[45]

Not all Eurasianists agreed with Karsavin's and Arapov's definition of the state and culture as "symphonic persons" or regarded them as principal agents

[39] GARF, f. 5783, op. 1, ed. khr. 410, l. 45, letter Arapov to Council of Seven, September 7, 1925.
[40] GARF, f. 5783, op. 1, ed. khr. 411, l. 68, letter Arapov to Trubetskoi, October 5, 1925.
[41] GARF, f. 5783, op. 1, ed. khr. 411, l. 50, letter Arapov to Council of Seven, September 17, 1925.
[42] GARF, f. 5783, op. 1, ed. khr. 411, l. 81, letter Arapov to Trubetskoi, December 4, 1925.
[43] GARF, f. 5783, op. 1, ed. khr. 411, ll. 67–68, letter Arapov to Trubetskoi, October 5, 1925.
[44] GARF, f. 5783, op. 1, ed. khr. 411, l. 50, letter Arapov to Council of Seven, September 17, 1925.
[45] P.N. Malevskii-Malevich, *A New Party in Russia* (London: Routledge, 1928), pp. 80–81. Original emphasis.

within the empirical sphere. Trubetskoi, for example, regarded Karsavin's and Arapov's views as "state-worshipping," a typical western, rather than Eurasian phenomenon. Trubetskoi gave more recognition to the agency of individual persons than did Karsavin, Arapov, and Malevskii, yet his views about the person were vitalist and highly elitist. Still, the starting point of his Eurasianism was "the affirmation of the person, . . . created in the image and likeness of God." In this respect, he claimed, the human person resembles God: the person "is never just a dot or an atom, but is always a system or a council of certain qualities. God himself. . . is a 'Council of the Father, the Son and the Holy Spirit,' and every individual human person is also conciliar." The "conciliarity" of God inscribed on every human person was, in Trubetskoi's opinion, also inscribed on the nation as a human collective. In sharp contrast to Karsavin and Arapov, Trubetskoi did not describe state and culture as "persons," for they were not created by God but were "the creation of human hands." As such, they represented a relative value, whereas the value of persons, individual and collective (the nation), was absolute.[46]

This did not mean, however, that all human beings were identical or equal. Although every human being possessed certain "volitional fluids" (*volevye fliuidy*), only those individuals with the most active "fluids" should make up the "ruling stratum" and government.[47] United by a common ideology and by a "single unitary party," these individuals alone were genuinely devoted to the people's needs. In such an "ideocracy," the rulers would express the will of the nation more organically than could professional politicians in a democracy, where public opinion and national culture were manipulated by "private capital and the press."[48] Countering Arapov's critique of nationalism, Trubetskoi advanced the idea that, precisely in a supra-national Eurasia, a whole system of nations could form yet another collective person of an even higher order, even as individual nations and their "ruling stratum" preserved certain particularities.[49]

Trubetskoi's vitalist and "ideocratic" understanding of the state and society also affected his views of the church, whose task he saw exclusively in the

---

[46] GARF, f. 5783, op. 1, ed. khr. 408, l. 338 and ll. 340–341, letter Trubetskoi to Arapov, undated (late September 1925). On the scientific implications of Trubetskoi's views on the person see N.S. Trubetskoi, "Ot avtora" in *K probleme russkogo samopoznaniia: sobranie statei* ([Paris]: Evraziiskoe knigoizdatel'stvo, 1927), pp. 3–9, and Patrick Sériot, *Structure et totalité: les origines intellectuelles du structuralisme en Europe centrale et orientale* (Paris: Presses Universitaires de France, 1999).

[47] GARF, f. 5783, op. 1, ed. khr. 312, l. 42 verso, "Soobrazheniia N.S. T[rubetskogo] po povodu zapiski L.P. K[arsavina] 'O Tserkvi, lichnosti i gosudarstve.'"

[48] N.S. Trubetskoi, "O gosudarstvennom stroe i forme pravleniia," *Evraziiskaia khronika*, no. 8 (1927), 5.

[49] GARF, f. 5783, op. 1, ed. khr. 408, ll. 339–340, letter Trubetskoi to Arapov, undated (late September 1925).

salvation of the "soul of the person – individuals and nations." Since the state lacked a soul, the church should not attempt to directly interfere with politics, but should rather pursue the "ecclesiastization" of individual persons. Trubetskoi distinguished between the church's deep commitment to the individual ("for the Church every person possesses absolute value, regardless of his earthly role in the life of the state") and its necessary moderation in the political sphere.[50]

Although Savitskii welcomed the idea of the "symphonic" person in principle, his own affirmation of the person focused more on the individual.[51] His ideal of personhood was the integral yet relatively self-determined person, the "master" (*khoziain*), who through labor elevated and spiritualized his material environment. Here, Savitskii built upon Sergei Bulgakov's attempt in *Philosophy of Economy* (1912) to spiritualize the material, empirical sphere and to transcend positivism and materialism.[52] Yet as an economist with a strong interest in economic geography, and as a student of the liberal economist Pëtr Struve, Savitskii was more interested in the empirical and pragmatic applications of Eurasianism than were some of his fellow Eurasianists. In his understanding, the "master" was God's earthly counterpart and assistant, firmly embedded in a hierarchy of individual and collective persons, actively striving "to become like the Supreme Master of the world."[53] In contrast to the capitalist "entrepreneur" (*predprinimatel'*), Savitskii's "master" embodied the spiritual essence of the economy. The entrepreneur, Savitskii argued, cared only for his enterprise as the source of the highest possible net profit. Not so the "good master." His relationship to the economy was holistic and respectful. For him the goal of earning maximal profit was only one among others, such as manifesting a responsible and caring attitude to employees and equipment, preserving the natural environment, and promoting sustainability.[54]

Savitskii's praise of the personal element in the economy was no apology for economic liberalism. In accordance with the Eurasianist teachings that established a system of individual and collective persons on various levels, the individual "master" was to be complemented by the state – a "collective master" enforcing social justice. Only the interplay of individual and collective initiatives could provide for economic progress, technological innovation, and social justice.[55] Although Savitskii's concept of the "master" did not amount to an

---

[50] GARF, f. 5783, op. 1, ed. khr. 312, ll. 42 verso and 43, "Soobrazheniia N.S. T[rubetskogo] po povodu zapiski L.P. K[arsavina] 'O Tserkvi, lichnosti i gosudarstve.'"

[51] GARF, f. 5783, op. 1, ed. khr. 337, l. 45, undated note (1926?) by P.N. Savitskii.

[52] S.N. Bulgakov, *Filosofiia khoziaistva* (V.V. Sapov (ed.), Moscow: Nauka, 1990).

[53] P.N. Savitskii, "Khoziain i khoziaistvo," *Evraziiskii vremennik* 4 (1925), 426.

[54] *Ibid.* 408–412.

[55] P.N. Savitskii, "K voprosu o gosudarstvennom i chastnom nachale promyshlennosti. (Rossiia XVIII–XX vekov)," *Evraziiskii vremennik* 5 (1927), 308.

unconditional defense of the individual human person and his rights, it nevertheless effectively affirmed the individual person in principle, even if only in the economy.

CRITIQUE, TENSIONS, AND SOLUTIONS

Until the late 1920s, the Eurasianists' definitions of individual and collective persons and their attempt to situate them relative to each other remained complex and contradictory. Despite its seeming coherence, Karsavin's hierarchical system of "symphonic" and individual persons and his call for an "ecclesiastization" of the empirical sphere towards an absolute "all-unity" raised several crucial problems, as contemporary critics were quick to point out.

The most insightful responses among the many reactions to Eurasianism's political ideology belonged to the historian and literary critic P.M. Bitsilli (1879–1953), the philosopher Nikolai Berdiaev (1874–1948), and Georgii Florovskii, all of whom in one way or another had been affiliated with the Eurasianist movement during the 1920s, sympathized with some of its ideas, yet sharply rejected its political implications. Bitsilli did not see how the Eurasianists could reconcile their demand for a "single unitary party" for the future Eurasian "ideocracy" with the establishment of corporative bodies and councils on lower levels. The Eurasianists, he claimed, had to make a crucial choice: "either syndicalism or fascism, either freedom or dictatorship." If the Eurasianists chose to base their political program upon the absolute truth of Orthodoxy, the result would be reactionary extremism – not "a party of unity," but a new "Union of the Russian People." Bitsilli considered a "Eurasianist Orthodox Party" an oxymoron. "Orthodoxy" and "Eurasia" were divergent spheres, since the Orthodox church transcended the "Eurasian continent."[56]

In a similar vein, Berdiaev considered Eurasianism an ideology based more on "necessity" than on "freedom," one in which the individual was subordinated to the collective and political decisions were to be devoid of moral evaluations.[57] He saw the cause of Eurasianism's danger in its "naturalist monism and optimism," features that led to a "utopian etatism." In advocating the "ecclesiastization" of the state, Berdiaev explained, the Eurasianists conceived the state as a function of the church and erased the "fundamental dualism of the two orders." Such monism, he wrote, "leads to the absolutization of the state, to the understanding of the state as an earthly embodiment of the truth, of the true ideology." Eurasianism's "ideocracy," in Berdiaev's opinion, was nothing

---

[56] P.M. Bitsilli, "Dva lika evraziistva," *Sovremennye zapiski*, no. 31 (1927), 425–428.
[57] N.A. Berdiaev, "Utopicheskii etatizm evraziitsev," *Put'*, no. 8 (1927), 141–144.

but Plato's utopian "perfect state" – an "absolute tyranny." Eurasianism had confused the earthly and the heavenly: "Monism is possible only in the kingdom of God, in the transfigured and deified (*obozhennyi*) world, on a new earth and new heaven." Until then, the dualism between the secular and the sacred must be retained in order to protect freedom, "the individual person, and the distinction between what is and what shall be." After all, Berdiaev confirmed, "the human being is higher than the state."[58]

Florovskii shared Berdiaev's concerns for the freedom of the individual. Florovskii was also seriously alarmed by the consequences Eurasianism's ambiguities might have for the church and the individual's relationship to God. According to Eurasianism, "created subjects" (*tvarnye sub"ekty*) acquired their personhood only through "communion" with God. Given the Eurasianist hierarchical system of individual and collective persons, Florovskii concluded, this would logically entail that "nations and individual 'conciliar' persons of lower rank," such as the "Eurasianist party," would also be in communion with God. This realization led him to fear that the "Eurasianist party" might become a self-proclaimed "church," imperiously standing above the real church. Florovskii emphatically defended the transcendental character of the Orthodox church against Eurasianist attempts to employ it for earthly purposes. "The Church neither creates nor realizes itself in the process of earthly cultural construction. Culture is not a stage in the emergence of the Church . . . Not everything is a part of the Church, much, all too much, remains outside its threshold . . . The Eurasianists burden the Church with too much of the worldly and earthly. Flesh and blood do not inherit eternal life."[59]

The tensions among the Eurasianists over individual and collective persons and over the sacred and the secular soon led to a rupture in the movement. In late 1928, the newly established Eurasianist newspaper, *Evraziia*, published in the Parisian suburb Clamart by Arapov, Suvchinskii, Karsavin, Malevskii-Malevich, Sergei Efron (1893–1941), and D.P. Sviatopolk-Mirskii (1890–1939), openly embraced Marxism, thus opting for the collective over the individual and the secular over the sacred. This programmatic and political "evolution" provoked a serious ideological conflict with the other Eurasianists, prompting Trubetskoi's resignation from the leadership of the movement and, in early 1929, a "schism" that seriously weakened the movement. However, the new "Marxist" brand of Eurasianism in Paris soon disintegrated. Many of its members accepted the Soviet Union as the genuine and legitimate executor of Russia's spiritual mission in Eurasia. Some of them, such as Arapov, Efron, and Sviatopolk-Mirskii, even returned to the Soviet Union only to perish in prisons and camps.

[58] *Ibid.*   [59] G.V. Florovskii, "Evraziiskii soblazn," *Sovremennye zapiski*, no. 34 (1928), 340–342.

The remaining members of the movement also underwent a programmatic reorientation leading to a more pragmatic focus on the empirical sphere. Yet the experience of the schism, ideological competition with Marxism, Stalin's rise to power in the Soviet Union, and the darkening of the political horizon in Europe, all left their mark. In early September 1931, the First Eurasianist Congress in Brussels announced a new political program.

This new program was more secular and pragmatic than Eurasianism of the 1920s. It defined the status of the individual person in a more liberal fashion, yet still emphasized the role of the state and other "collective" persons. The Eurasianists now attached "exceptional significance to the concept and phenomenon of the person." They saw genuine human relations as possible only on the basis of "faith in the Divine," and if "permeated by the spirit of love and an unswerving care for the personal dignity of the human being." They did not want to turn freedom "into an idol" as had happened, they believed, in the West. They saw freedom as a neutral ideal that needed to be filled with the "good." Eurasianists remained hostile to a "one-sided cult of the animalistic human"; they noted that deification of the individual in the West and in the Soviet Union had led to "materialist individualism and materialist collectivism."[60]

The Eurasianism of 1932 also contained clear statements about safeguarding individual rights against the state, against social collectives, and against religious intolerance. In the future Eurasianist state, the right to "self-determination" was guaranteed "for social groups, nationalities, professions, unions and societies, and for individual persons." These individual and collective rights were "inalienable" and protected by the state.[61] The individual was also to be protected against complete "socialization," whereby the person "becomes deprived of the freedom to vote and becomes mere material" for the realization not of his own goals, but those of state and society.[62] The sphere of religious convictions was now declared a sphere of "absolute freedom." Although Eurasianists still attached "paramount significance" to Orthodoxy, they admitted that Eurasianists "belonging to other confessions of Russia-Eurasia" could approach common tasks "from the depths of their own religious convictions."[63] This explicit statement on religious freedom was a significant step away from the absolutization of Orthodoxy in the Eurasianism of the 1920s.

Mobilized by the change in Europe's political climate throughout the 1930s, some Eurasianists acknowledged even more explicitly the individual person's need to be safeguarded against domination by the collective, especially by the

---

[60] *Evraziistvo. Deklaratsiia, formulirovka, tezisy* ([Prague]: Izdanie evraziitsev, 1932), p. 11.
[61] *Ibid.* pp. 15–16.   [62] *Ibid.* p. 19.   [63] *Ibid.* p. 3.

state. During the 1920s it had been easy to speculate about "ideocracy," when, with the exception of fascist Italy and the NEP-era Soviet Union, there were no other examples of "ideocratic" regimes. By the early 1930s, however, with Stalin's brutal dictatorship, forced industrialization and violent collectivization in the Soviet Union, and the rise to power of National-Socialism in Germany, "ideocracy" had plainly revealed its dark sides. No doubt, the transformation of ideocratic states into "totalitarian" ones, as Eurasianists now called them, contributed to the Eurasianists' questioning of their own ideology and to the clarification of their political goals.

By 1934, even Karsavin, a former adherent of the pro-Soviet Clamart group, had revised his views. Although he continued fiercely to criticize radical democracy and party politics and to advocate the need for an organic theory of society, where the individual person was harmoniously interconnected with numerous collective persons on various levels, he also made it explicitly clear that Italian fascism and German National-Socialism were unacceptable totalitarian regimes. He now refrained from ascribing potential divinity to the state and dealt exclusively with the empirical and secular state. He found a remedy against both the state's totalitarian aspirations and individual license in the self-organization of society into non-governmental groups. Rather than depending on a "disorganized herd of voters who are convened from time to time" the state should rely on "living social groups . . . , on practical self-government, on professional and agrarian associations." He suggested the establishment of a "congress of representatives" of each of these groups as an almost grass-roots basis for civic life. The best example of such an organization of state and society Karsavin found, somewhat surprisingly for a former Eurasianist, in the United Kingdom, which "grew out of self-government and to the present day rests upon it," and where individuals still knew "how to relinquish their egoistic aspirations for the sake of the interests of society."[64]

Strikingly similar ideas were put forward in 1938 by another Eurasianist, the legal scholar N.N. Alekseev (1879–1964), who had joined the movement in 1926. With unprecedented frankness he rejected both liberal democracies and totalitarian regimes, because both disregarded the dignity of the human person as a spiritual being and in essence supported collectivism. In such regimes the highest value was the "physical collective, regardless which – race, the secular state, or communist society of the future." In Alekseev's view, communism and democracy shared the same false concept of the person as an egoistic and hedonistic individual. This concept led to an atomization and secularization of society and produced an individual "cut off from his social ties" and interested

---

[64] L.P. Karsavin, "Gosudarstvo i krizis demokratii," *Novyi mir*, no. 1 (1991), 193.

in "material pleasures" only.[65] Alekseev strongly rejected the communist or fascist state's "totalitarian pretensions, its aspirations to impose the obligatory confession of one single ideology, which is tantamount to the suppression of the freedom of the human spirit and human thought." In sharp contrast to earlier Eurasianist statements, he renounced the very idea of a "single unitary party," which he now considered "a more terrible thing than the democratic multi-party system." Alekseev's alternative model for an ideal state remained rather general. He demanded that the authority of the state be based on the people, and that the supreme political authority be exercised by a permanent ruler under the constant control of the people and other state organs. The rights of the individual would be safeguarded by law and independent courts. Like Karsavin, Alekseev praised the Anglo-Saxon political model, in which "professional associations" rather than political parties dealt with "various current and organizational questions of state life."[66]

Between 1921 and the mid-1930s, Eurasianism had moved from the proclamation of Russia as a world apart to expressing certain sympathies for the political system of the United Kingdom. Initially, the Eurasianists had anticipated a new era of faith, in which religion would again take center stage, and Russia would resurrect the world; by the mid-1920s, Eurasianism had discovered the individual person and its defense as the crucial element of its mission.

The Eurasianists' bold historiosophical claims and passionate assertions in the early 1920s of Russia's religious mission were by-products of an emotional and speculative reaction to the experience of the Great War, the Russian Revolutions, and the Civil War. They believed only a new ideology, based on Orthodoxy and conscious of Eurasia's geographical, historical, and cultural character, could save Russia from uncritically imitating "the West," which they blamed for causing the revolutions. After the mid-1920s, however, the movement's religious pathos transformed itself slowly into a political program, finding its conceptual focal point in the affirmation of the person. The Eurasianists were convinced that only a state and society based on a genuine spiritual foundation could provide its citizens a dignified existence and allow them to express their God-given individuality without being exploited by an unbridled economy or the secular state and society. In western European liberal democracies, the individual was merely a depersonalized atom, deprived of originality. Moreover, the Eurasianists claimed that the individual person's spiritual potential could be fully realized only within larger collectives. Only as part of a higher "symphonic" person –

[65] N.N. Alekseev, "O budushchem gosudarstvennom stroe Rossii," *Novyi grad*, no. 13 (1938), 100–101.
[66] *Ibid.* 105–107.

such as the nation, culture, state, or the church – could the individual find proper orientation and full freedom in his environment, thus escaping atomization, realizing his spiritual potential, and becoming a full-fledged integral person.

This demand for "intermediate" collective persons, the centerpiece of the Eurasianist "ideocratic" political system of thought, seemingly brought Eurasianism into close proximity with other contemporary organic ideologies, such as communism or fascism, which also tied the individual's value to the value of the collective. In fact, however, Eurasianism's religiously motivated "affirmation of the person" prevented the movement from explicitly depriving individual persons of their human dignity and from unambiguously subordinating them to the unqualified domination of collective persons. Furthermore, late in the 1920s, Eurasianists had begun to clarify their previously ambiguous ideas in this respect. After the rise of Stalin to power in the Soviet Union and the establishment of the National-Socialist dictatorship in Germany in 1933, individual Eurasianists distanced themselves not only from parliamentary democracy, as they had done before, but from totalitarianism as well.

The complex history of the religious foundations of Eurasianism and the movement's ambiguous defense of the person and human dignity constitute a fascinating episode in Russian intellectual history, an episode that attests to the richness and productive power of the concept of the person in the history of Russian thought.

Afterword

ON PERSONS AS OPEN-ENDED
ENDS-IN-THEMSELVES

(THE VIEW FROM TWO NOVELISTS AND
TWO CRITICS)

CARYL EMERSON

If Russian philosophy is at heart a human story, one more resembling a quest for "integral worldviews" than an abstract system or set of logical propositions, can the great Russian novelists be said to practice a type of homeland philosophy? The idea has long intrigued readers. In 2002, James Scanlan published his controversial *Dostoevsky the Thinker*, which presented its subject as an anthropocentric theist probing the "mystery of man" (and the existence of God) by routes more compatible with Kant than with Russian Orthodox mysticism.[1] Lev Tolstoi, during his final decades, experimented with a vast array of fictional, memoiristic, and journalistic genres to communicate with his readership persuasively, intimately, in utmost sincerity – and his contribution to secular and religious philosophy has been a node of dispute and inspiration ever since.[2] But this close overlap, almost a palimpsest, between literary creativity and philosophy proper is of a special sort. It is not only that Russian novelists also wrote polemical treatises, the way Vladimir Solov'ëv "also wrote poems" and Sergei Bulgakov also produced insightful literary criticism. Rather, the very stuff of Russian fiction, its created heroes and worlds, has been recruited wholesale and reclassified *as* philosophy without changing a word, by later readers and even by the authors themselves.

[1] James P. Scanlan, *Dostoevsky the Thinker* (Ithaca, NY: Cornell University Press, 2002). For an alternate view stressing the paradoxical, antinomic, ultimately idealistic nature of Dostoevskii's faith, see Steven Cassedy, *Dostoevsky's Religion* (Stanford University Press, 2005). Two other perspectives on Dostoevskii's treatment of conversion, healing, and the challenge of a Living God are also highly valuable: Robin Feuer Miller, *Dostoevsky's Unfinished Journey* (New Haven, CT: Yale University Press, 2007) and Rowan Williams, *Dostoevsky: Language, Faith, and Fiction* (Waco, TX: Baylor University Press, 2008).

[2] Three indispensable and very different treatments of Tolstoian philosophy are Donna Tussing Orwin, *Tolstoy's Art and Thought, 1847–1880* (Princeton University Press, 1993); Richard F. Gustafson, *Leo Tolstoy: Resident and Stranger* (Princeton University Press, 1986); and Inessa Medzhibovskaya, *Tolstoy and the Religious Culture of his Time: A Biography of a Long Conversion, 1845–1887* (Lanham, MD: Lexington Books, 2008).

Examples are legion. Part One of Dostoevskii's "Notes from Underground" routinely turns up in textbooks on the foundations of Existentialism. Tolstoi endows his Ivan Il'ich, Prince Nekhliudov (from *Resurrection*) and Konstantin Levin (from *Anna Karenina*) with lengthy chunks of intellectual argument straight from the Maker's mouth that only the genius of Tolstoi could integrate persuasively without self-parody. Writers can even exercise this license against one another. Tolstoi did not approve of *The Brothers Karamazov*, but he loved its homiletic Book Six, "The Russian Monk," and petitioned Dostoevskii's widow (unsuccessfully) to allow him to extract and republish it as a pamphlet on spiritual education, cleansed of its dissolute, distracting novelistic frame.

These great writers succeed at being philosophers, I believe, because philosophy defined as "a quest for one's own worldview" naturally structures itself as a thickly-populated thought experiment. Such quests are best conducted with subjects who *see* one another, respond verbally or behaviorally to what they see, and thus accrue specific interpersonal responsibilities. This "other" is not an abstract static norm but a developing human being presumed to possess dignity – a word much favored in this volume that we might define here in yet one more way. Persons possess dignity when they are perceived, both by themselves and others, as *open-ended* ends-in-themselves, subjects optimally realized not by their conquest of solitary "civil rights" for themselves but by their affirmation of the unique relationships that bind them to other persons.[3] The strongest students of the Russian novel, sensing the ethical implications of this dynamic, tend to be philosophically ambitious themselves. In this brief afterword, I discuss Dostoevskii and Tolstoi as transformed into humanist thinkers by two of their most gifted twentieth-century interpreters, Mikhail Bakhtin (1895–1975) and Lydia Ginzburg (1902–1990). The humanism that Bakhtin and Ginzburg detect in these creative writers resonates with the three qualities highlighted in this volume: *tsel'nost'* or wholeness (unity that is neither homogenous nor uniform but restlessly dynamic); *lichnost'* or personhood (individuality that is neither autonomous nor necessarily guaranteed by law); and *organichnost'* or "organicity" (an energy inherent in living things that is both intuitive and transfigurative, but because organisms must respond uninterruptedly to the outside world, this energy is neither arbitrary nor blind). None of these four (the two novelists and their two critics) is a liberal humanist. Nor could we call them illiberal humanists. Each defends selfhood in a distinctively Russian fashion. Impersonal

---

[3] That novels can be "philosophy by other means," see the Introduction to Martha C. Nussbaum, *Love's Knowledge: Essays on Philosophy and Literature* (New York: Oxford University Press, 1990).

political power is despised and if possible ignored; communal support and em-
pathy (which in its intimate form we recognize as love) is a matter of desperate
importance; and human perfectibility is for each a binding article of faith.

Let us begin with Bakhtin, the better-known case. He always considered
himself a philosopher (or better, "thinker"), not a literary critic. Literature was
simply safer to pursue, and Bakhtin's opening maneuver in *Problems of Dostoevsky's Poetics* (1929, revised 1963) reflects this caution.[4] Mindful that Maksim
Gor'kii had placed Dostoevskii under ban as an unhealthy influence well before
the Revolution, Bakhtin begins formalistically: he will investigate this great
novelist not for his ideology but for his insight into the craft of literature. Like
all writers, Dostoevskii deploys "devices" that an astute critic can tease out.
His cardinal device, or "dominant," is human consciousness. The more discrete
selves, or integrated self-aware consciousnesses, a novelist can put into play, the
more polyphonic the novel. Such an aesthetic program lays special strain on the
conventional narrator.

In the traditional novel, so Bakhtin argues, the author (or his narrative surrogate) sits at the center of his emerging Creation like the Greek god Zeus, passing
out bits of consciousness piecemeal to characters and controlling the "surplus"
space between them. This narrator calculates in advance the value and propor-
tional weight of each attitude, action, and character trait. In Bakhtin's view,
Dostoevskii replaces this authoritative paradigm, modeled on royal caprice or
rigid Law and thus filled with "voiceless slaves" (p. 6), by a more reciprocal,
answerable New Testament scenario, where the authorial function (in the spirit
of Christ) enters the fictive field already incarnated (that is, delimited) and thus
spatio-temporally equal to the characters, literally at their eye level. Delimited beings are not only contained physically; they are in transition, vulnerable,
answerable. By default they constitute their own end. They are free, not "fixed
elements in the author's design" (p. 7), and thus they will err in unforeseen ways.
Logic is powerless to save such a being from perdition; only concrete love, fitted
irrationally to the contours of the individual, will work. "Dostoevsky's world
is profoundly personalized," Bakhtin writes (p. 9). But the major Dostoevskian
personalities do have an ideological mission, which is where philosophy proper
comes in.

Bakhtin insists, controversially, that "plot" itself is not crucial to Dostoevskii.
One big blunt event (murder, suicide, conspiracy, concealed sexual abuse) is
sufficient to fuel the novel's action. What matters are the moral dilemmas and
verbal debates that arise around this event. To this end Dostoevskii designs

---

[4] Mikhail Bakhtin, *Problems of Dostoevsky's Poetics* (Caryl Emerson (ed. and trans.), Minneapolis, MN:
University of Minnesota Press, 1984), ch. 1.

each of his major heroes as an idea-person (*ideia-chelovek*): an idea that uses a hero as its carrier to realize its potential as a developing force in the world. By definition, such heroes cannot be vanquished by death. As Bakhtin says of the Elder Zosima and other righteous idea-people: "Personality [*lichnost'*] does not die. Death is a departure . . . The person has departed, having spoken his word, but the word itself remains in the open-ended dialogue" (p. 300). Bakhtin, like Dostoevskii, was a practicing (if idiosyncratic) Russian Orthodox Christian. But Bakhtin's commitment to polyphonic voicing, in and outside literature, requires neither an afterlife nor a personal Savior; all that is needed is faith in "Great Time," an unfinalized interval where every utterance will eventually find its sympathetic interlocutor.[5] Bakhtin advises us to read Dostoevskii in that capacious sense, not as the "novel-tragedies" envisioned by Viacheslav Ivanov and not as treatises unfolding dialectically toward a preordained end (Bakhtin considered Hegel's dialectic "monological").[6] Everywhere Bakhtin senses in Dostoevskii's worldview a *de*-centering of authorship and simultaneous heightening of individual responsibility.

Heightened individuality does not promise to solve the human riddle, however – a point stressed by Randall Poole in his essay "The Apophatic Bakhtin."[7] "The mystical union of self and other in God is not an idea congenial to Bakhtin's thought," Poole writes. But complete and fully articulated self-knowledge is also uncongenial: "a corollary of the unknowability of God is the unknowability of man" (p. 159). Dostoevskii linked this apophatic idea with humility and placed it at the core of his concept of human freedom. His horror at the transparent Crystal Palace, at the inert corpse of Christ in Hans Holbein's painting, at arithmetical charts or Inquisitional largesse that would exchange uncertainty and suffering for the satisfaction of some finalized value, all exemplify Dostoevskii's principled rejection of any cognitive stopping-point, which for him was more than a dead end: it was death. Poole's account of Bakhtin's apophatic method can help us to understand the spiritual dimensions of novelistic dialogism. In Bakhtin's rather rosy reading of the novelist (and for this he has been much criticized) Dostoevskii does not thirst after radical, self-annihilating freedom. Or rather, Dostoevskii as polyphonic writer defines freedom as an unfinalizable loophole made possible by the innate, "intuitive idealism" of the human spirit. This idealism can become creative only if it is plural. Since my self is not a natural given and I do not coincide with myself,

---

[5] See "Toward a Methodology for the Human Sciences" in M.M. Bakhtin, *Speech Genres and Other Late Essays* (Vern W. McGee (trans.), Austin, TX: University of Texas Press, 1986), p. 167.

[6] On Ivanov, see Bakhtin, *Problems of Dostoevsky's Poetics*, p. 11; on Hegel, Bakhtin, "Toward a Methodology," p. 162.

[7] Randall A. Poole, "The Apophatic Bakhtin" in Susan M. Felch and Paul J. Contino (eds.), *Bakhtin and Religion: A Feeling for Faith* (Evanston, IL: Northwestern University Press, 2001), pp. 151–175.

I am always inadequate when taken on my own terms; I need you to gaze on me and complete me from your outside perspective. Sonia Marmeladova provides this painful service for Raskolnikov, Alësha Karamazov for his two brothers. Dostoevskii never provides it definitively for anyone. Beneath that authorial strategy lies the conviction that although I need you, we will never know each other completely – and not because my mystery, or your mystery, is a matter of transcendence or esoteric inaccessibility, but because our placements in time and space are each non-transferably unique. My uniqueness brings with it responsibilities that only I can discharge or deny. It follows that the loving gaze of another will not necessarily bring justice or relief; its purpose is largely ethical, to help me *not turn away* from the obligations of my unique time and place. If, in the Bakhtinian model, there is a need for God and a diversified Trinity (three-dimensional outsideness), the reasons are more human than Divine.

The Tolstoian dynamic begins elsewhere, and Bakhtin did not approve of it. In his book on Dostoevskii, he claims that Tolstoi's voice is "monolithically naive," and that a "second autonomous voice (alongside the author's voice) does not appear in Tolstoi's world."[8] Spying and eavesdropping on everyone, Tolstoi does not allow his heroes to speak out on their own except under his panoptic gaze. If, Bakhtin intimates, the decentralizing Dostoevskii admires complexity and unknowability in the human personality, then the great simplifier Tolstoi tells you straight out what is true, what is false, and insists that we all could discriminate between the two if only we cleansed our minds of propaganda and our bodies of intoxicants (liquor, caffeine, meat, violence, lust). Anyone who loves Tolstoi will find a great deal wrong with Bakhtin's position, which has been admirably refuted by American scholars using an array of Bakhtin's own critical tools.[9] The most provocative Russian defense of Tolstoi, however, is by Lydia Ginzburg. A literary historian and philosopher of poetics, she defends Tolstoi against Bakhtin not on the turf of the word but of the psyche.

Born in 1902, only seven years after Bakhtin, Ginzburg was sixteen at the time of the Bolshevik Revolution. But those half-a-dozen years (as we have seen elsewhere in this volume) make an enormous difference. Unlike Bakhtin, who attended university courses during the twilight years of the tsarist regime and considered the symbolists his elder contemporaries, Ginzburg was entirely the product of a Soviet education. Like Bakhtin, she was for many years marginalized, emerging from obscurity only in the 1970s. Her writing career lasted

---

[8] Bakhtin, *Problems of Dostoevsky's Poetics*, p. 56. On why Bakhtin was so mean to Tolstoi, see David Sloane, "Rehabilitating Bakhtin's Tolstoy: The Politics of the Utterance," *Tolstoy Studies Journal* 13 (2001), 59–77.

[9] See Andrew Baruch Wachtel, *An Obsession with History: Russian Writers Confront the Past* (Stanford University Press, 1994), ch. 5; and Gary Saul Morson, *Hidden in Plain View: Narrative and Creative Potentials in "War and Peace"* (Stanford University Press, 1987), pp. 186–189.

sixty-six years; she was published for six. As a student of literary genre, Ginzburg specialized in the professional working methods of novelists, especially Tolstoi and Proust. Her analytic mind (following her formalist mentors Boris Eikhenbaum and Iurii Tynianov) was intrigued by Tolstoi's bold literary experimentation with what she came to call "in-between genres": diaries, memoirs, working notebooks, personal correspondence. Ginzburg classified these literary forms as "human documents" and studied them throughout her life.[10] Human documents exist on the boundary between the real-life self and a fictional (or real-life) other. What are the benefits of interaction on this border?

Bakhtin, we recall, holds this zone to very high standards. His self–other boundary separates two mutually accessible, but unjoined, consciousnesses. Each is open and curious about the other. No threats, no border guards, but also no sentimental fusion of souls – or as he put it late in life, "benevolent demarcation and only then cooperation."[11] For either side to begin to speak, there must be a presumption of trust. And finally, from my perspective on this side of the line, "the other side" presents me with a human voice or face – not a mass, not a collective, not a political party or indirectly elected parliament, not a set of social conventions. None of those entities or procedures can obligate us, and obligation is key. For Bakhtin, responsibility accrues when two faces confront one another, unimpeded and unmediated, and each acknowledges the radical primacy of the other: "Thou Art" ("*Ty esi*").[12]

Ginzburg's understanding of the intergeneric interhuman border was different. As a self-avowed atheist, she was alien to the religious or Christological overtones of "Thou Art." Equally alien was the possibility that values were grounded in any potentially divine Absolute. In her view, what compels us to experiment with "in-between" genres is not "*Ty esi*" (a confession of faith in the presence of an Other) but rather the *lack* of a loving interlocutor, and the shame and embarrassment of having to conceal that need. An unspeakably difficult reality "beyond the border" might even require me to bifurcate my creative and judging self. This is not the pathological gesture of a disillusioned mind, as in Dostoevskii's novel-tragedy *The Double*, but a rational self-distancing (*samootstranenie*) undertaken in imitation of Tolstoi, who aesthetically shaped his anxiety and awkwardness into a human document that allowed him to stand outside of it and create.[13]

---

[10]   Lydia Ginzburg, *On Psychological Prose* (Judson Rosengrant (ed. and trans.), Princeton University Press, [1977] 1991).

[11]   "From Notes Made in 1970–71" in Bakhtin, *Speech Genres and Other Late Essays*, p. 136.

[12]   Bakhtin invokes this Biblically inflected formulation in connection with Viacheslav Ivanov's Dostoevskii criticism; see *Problems of Dostoevsky's Poetics*, p. 10.

[13]   Emily Van Buskirk, "Writing the Immanent Self: Self-distancing and Moral Evaluation" in *Reality in Search of Literature: Lydia Ginzburg's In-Between Prose* (Ph.D. dissertation, Harvard University, September 2008), ch. 1.

On Psychological Prose, Ginzburg's most sustained treatment of Tolstoi, does not target Bakhtin's Tolstoi-phobia directly. But its entire argument demonstrates that she is not persuaded by polyphony, nor by Bakhtin's claim that the texture of a Tolstoian novel is more single-voiced than a Dostoevskian one. Dostoevskii specialized in crisis-ridden, melodramatic, idea-laden narratives, which for Ginzburg invite psychologically crude treatment which obscures actual people confronted with life's obligations in everyday time. She considers Dostoevskii's major heroes symbolic, cerebral, self-contained creations. They do not talk with one another as much as test their ideas out on one another. But this was to be expected. A "novel of ideas" always runs the risk of becoming selfish, insulated, ideal – and thus monologic. Tolstoi's worlds, in contrast, are always embedded in the socially and economically real.

Ginzburg admits that the Tolstoian narrative voice has its authoritarian moments. But the fictional characters Tolstoi creates are motley, multifaceted, hard to predict, and difficult to define. Since they live such "socially-sensitized" lives, they present one side of themselves to one interlocutor, another to a second or a third, and each of these witnesses brings out, or contributes to, a different aspect of the hero's authentic, non-reducible person. The fact that Tolstoian heroes cohere, while not being predictable in their actions or "articulatable" in any stable ideology, is the great miracle of Tolstoian psychology. We recognize major Tolstoian heroes *not* through an "idea" (their ideas are usually a mess) but through the variegated pattern of others' responses to their confused personalities, bodies, behaviors, and utterances as they try to do the right thing and get through the day. That index is less available for Dostoevskian heroes, who aren't bothered much by hierarchy or convention. Few of them fit in anyway, or care about fitting in. Eccentricity and scandal are the *norm*. There is no dialogic social fabric governing their worlds, little scheduled everyday work to be done. "Of course," Ginzburg remarks pointedly in *On Psychological Prose*, "it is more interesting to conceive of yourself in Dostoevskian terms, since then you can focus all your attention on yourself."[14]

The charge is astute, and one would love to know Bakhtin's response to it. Ginzburg claims that Tolstoi is more alert to the pain and embarrassment of real dialogue than Dostoevskii could ever be, precisely because Tolstoi is so excruciatingly aware of social norms, collapses in communication, failures to be accepted by a desirable group – to what she calls *obuslovlennost'*, or our inevitable *conditioned-ness* by our social surroundings. Precisely because Tolstoi admitted our psychological need for social structure did he resent its power so deeply and work so hard to manage its painful fallout. It is considerably more difficult to start a dialogue than Bakhtin thinks. Ginzburg insists that the verbal utterance

[14] Ginzburg, *On Psychological Prose*, p. 243.

is more lonely, needy, and less secure than sturdy, well-loopholed Dostoevskian polyphony might suggest. She understood the interpersonal word as vulnerable and dependent. What confronts me on the far side of the boundary, in her view of things, is most likely *not* another singular loving face curious to listen to me but a fabric of social expectations, public roles, hierarchies, pressing work tasks, to which I wish to contribute and where I desperately want to fit in.

Much in Ginzburg's personal and professional life fed in to this need. A marginally employed intellectual in the 1930s and survivor of the Siege of Leningrad, she was also a woman, a Jew, and a lesbian prone to passionate, long-term, unrequited attachments. To survive a dead-ended or abortive communication act and make it productive, Ginzburg worked out (on the human document of her own personality) her self-distancing mechanisms, to some extent as formalist devices but far more fragile than those confident constructs. *Samootstranenie* bears some relationship to Bakhtin's *vnenakhodimost'* or outsideness. By the act of "stepping outside," both subjects gain access to the vision of a larger whole not available to the isolated author. But Bakhtin's author steps outside to generate a surplus of vision that facilitates the hero's free development; this "love-laden distancing of oneself [*ustranenie*] from the life-field of the hero" is permeated by composure, close attention to detail, and an abundance of trust.[15] Ginzburg's self-distancing is a more agitated survival device, necessary to preserve one's identity when the environment has lost all ethical orientation and yet no moral Absolute exists. A life-saving "outlet from the self" did exist, however. It was not in the direction of a loving other (of whose existence she could never be sure) but in one's own activity of service (in Russian, not state or church service (*sluzhba*) but the process of serving, *sluzhenie*). We should note that Ginzburg's recourse here to "serving" is firmly in the tradition of the Russian philosophical intelligentsia. Exemplary is Nikolai Berdiaev, whose two-pronged commitment to a-political spiritual regeneration and renewed civic activism became even more intense after the deportations of 1922.

Ginzburg's most wry and bittersweet discussion of the concept of service comes in a jotting from 1934, "The Stages of Love" ("Stadii liubvi"), an anatomy of erotic non-reciprocity.[16] At the first stage, "desire finds an object." Then comes the "decisive moment" when love becomes a concept – but the beloved

[15] "Author and Hero in Aesthetic Activity" in M.M. Bakhtin, *Art and Answerability* (Michael Holquist and Vadim Liapunov (eds.), Vadim Liapunov (trans.), Austin, TX: University of Texas Press, 1990), p. 14. Translation adjusted.

[16] "Stadii liubvi" [1934], *Kriticheskaia massa*, no. 1 (2002), 34–38 (predislovie i publikatsiia Denisa Ustinova). See Emily Van Buskirk, "Making Love Literary: Sexuality and the Third Person in the Prose of Lydia Ginzburg" in *Reality in Search of Literature*, ch. 4, pp. 313–387.

is already losing interest, so the love-concept quickly shifts into the cooler, face-saving category of "concern" (*zabota*). We can serve the indifferent beloved for some time in this stage, but eventually even concern becomes a burden and "catastrophe" arrives, after which the desire is replayed, distanced, and turned into a biographical definition ("my great unhappy love"). Although Ginzburg considers intellectuals poorly equipped to succeed in acts of love, the pain of this sequence can send the unrequited lover-thinker out on the path of more general service. Along this path (one long dreary quest for erotic substitutes) there can be "service upward" toward God (an option for believers) and "service downward" toward children (in her meditations on same-sex love, Ginzburg wrote frankly about her envy of biological motherhood). But such gratifying alternatives are not everyone's fate. There is something Tolstoian about this tormented trajectory, both intensely private and outward-seeking; as in Tolstoi there are absolutely no systematic solutions and no respect for rhetorical display.

Ginzburg's "Stages of Love" serve to remind us how very remarkable is Bakhtin's theory of love and how strange his devotion to it alongside a passion for Dostoevskii.[17] Bakhtinian love is so full of the warmth of human sympathy, the tolerance of heteroglossia, the interchangeably joyous physical embraces of carnival where no one is repulsive or repelled, and so devoid of the envious, possessive heat of Eros. Overall, "love" in Bakhtin is more a category of cognition than of desire. When we love, we return again and again to the site of the beloved and attend to every contour of intonation, shape, need, finding more of interest on each visit.[18] Nothing is wrong with this – indeed, everything is right with it – but it only applies (as does so much in Bakhtin) in reciprocal scenarios. The beloved must want to be loved. In the absence of such reciprocity, Ginzburg seeks acceptance within a larger human pool. Against Freud but in the spirit of Alfred Adler, she insists that social self-affirmation, not libido per se, is the driving force behind the behavior that others see.[19]

Both Tolstoi and Dostoevskii were humanists in the Renaissance sense outlined in the Introduction to this volume. For each, "the ability to pose ideals and realize them" was grounds for "faith in divine reality" as well as human dignity. Neither, in my view, entertained utopian constructs in his fiction in any sustained way. Revelatory moments, yes, but not utopia: from Raskolnikov's lengthy, gradual, uncertain rebirth announced in the Epilogue of *Crime and*

---

[17] For Bakhtin's theory of love, see *K filosofii postupka* (1919?): M.M. Bakhtin, *Toward a Philosophy of the Act* (Vadim Liapunov (trans.), Austin, TX: University of Texas Press, 1993), p. 64.

[18] *Ibid.* p. 62.

[19] Andrei Zorin, "Proza L.Ia. Ginzburg i gumanitarnaya mysl' XX veka," *Novoe literaturnoe obozrenie* 76 (2005), 45–68. Zorin notes the non-Freudian moments and draws parallels with the social psychology of Alfred Adler, Valentin Voloshinov, and George Herbert Mead.

Punishment to Levin's tentative recommitment to incremental self-improvement at the end of *Anna Karenina*, these two novelists document the tenacity of human error and the unpredictability of our ascent. How did our two exemplary twentieth-century critics interpret this triumph in literary terms? For Bakhtin, Dostoevskii the novelist avoided the utopian trap by insisting on the "loophole," that open-ended supplement in every addressed word inviting a response that would modify it. Ginzburg's Tolstoi resists utopian solutions by building his worlds from the ground up, out of finely concrete human documents rather than ideas, which assures that the residents of those worlds will not cohere fraudulently around a mere abstraction. Dignity, of course, is not guaranteed in either novelistic cosmos. That is never a given, forever a task.

BIBLIOGRAPHY

This selective bibliography is intended as a guide to further reading. It concentrates on the figures and topics considered in this volume, on book-length studies in English, and on English translations of Russian philosophical texts. No attempt has been made to include Russian editions of the works of Russian philosophers.

HISTORIES OF RUSSIAN PHILOSOPHY

Bobrov, Evgenii. *Filosofiia v Rossii: Materialy, issledovaniia i zametki*, 6 vols. (Kazan': Tipolitografiia Imperatorskogo Universiteta, 1899–1902)

Chamberlain, Lesley. *Motherland: A Philosophical History of Russia* (London: Atlantic Books, 2004)

Copleston, Frederick C. *Philosophy in Russia: From Herzen to Lenin and Berdyaev* (University of Notre Dame Press, 1986)

Craig, Edward (ed.). *Routledge Encyclopedia of Philosophy*, 10 vols. (London and New York: Routledge, 1998; print and online versions). Extensive coverage of Russian philosophy (Aileen M. Kelly, subject editor)

Evgrafov, V.E. *et al. Istoriia filosofii v SSSR*, 5 vols. (Moscow: Nauka, 1968–1988)

Goerdt, Wilhelm. *Russische Philosophie: Zugänge und Durchblicke* (Freiburg and München: Verlag Karl Alber, 1984)

Iakovenko, B.V. *Ocherki russkoi filosofii* (Berlin: Russkoe universal'noe izd-vo, 1922; Moscow: Respublika, 2003)

Kuvakin, Valery A. (ed.). *A History of Russian Philosophy*, 2 vols. (Amherst, NY: Prometheus Books, 1993)

Levitskii, Sergei A. *Ocherki po istorii russkoi filosofskoi i obshchestvennoi mysli*, 2 vols. (Frankfurt-am-Main: Posev, 1968, 1981)

Lossky, N.O. *History of Russian Philosophy* (New York: International Universities Press, 1951)

Masaryk, Thomas Garrigue. *The Spirit of Russia: Studies in History, Literature and Philosophy*, 2nd edn., 2 vols. (Eden and Cedar Paul (trans.), London: George Allen and Unwin, 1955)

Maslin, M.A. (ed.). *Russkaia filosofiia: Entsiklopediia* (Moscow: Algoritm, 2007)

Stolovich, L.N. *Istoriia russkoi filosofii: Ocherki* (Moscow: Respublika, 2005)

Vvedenskii, A.I., A.F. Losev, E.L. Radlov, and G.G. Shpet. *Ocherki istorii russkoi filosofii* (B.V. Emel'ianova and K.N. Liubutina (eds.), Sverdlovsk: Izd. Ural'skogo universiteta, 1991). This edition includes two classic histories: Radlov, *Ocherk istorii russkoi filosofii* (St. Petersburg, 1912) and Shpet, *Ocherk razvitiia russkoi filosofii* (Petrograd, 1922)

Walicki, Andrzej. *A History of Russian Thought from the Enlightenment to Marxism* (Hilda Andrews-Rusiecka (trans.), Stanford University Press, 1979)

Zarys myśli rosyjskiej od oświecenia do renesansu religijno-filozoficznego (Cracow: Wydawnictwo Uniwersytetu Jagiellońskiego, 2005)

Zenkovsky, V.V. *A History of Russian Philosophy*, 2 vols. (George L. Kline (trans.), New York: Columbia University Press, 1953)

GENERAL COLLECTIONS OF TRANSLATED TEXTS

Edie, James M., James P. Scanlan, and Mary-Barbara Zeldin (eds.), with the collaboration of George L. Kline. *Russian Philosophy*, 3 vols. (Chicago, IL: Quadrangle Books, 1965; Knoxsville, TN: University of Tennessee Press, 1976)

Kohn, Hans (ed.). *The Mind of Modern Russia: Historical and Political Thought of Russia's Great Age* (New York: Harper Torchbooks, 1962)

Leatherbarrow, W.J. and D.C. Offord (eds. and trans.). *A Documentary History of Russian Thought: From the Enlightenment to Marxism* (Ann Arbor, MI: Ardis, 1987)

Raeff, Marc (ed.). *Russian Intellectual History: An Anthology* (New York: Harcourt, Brace and World, 1966)

Shein, Louis J. (ed.). *Readings in Russian Philosophical Thought* (The Hague: Mouton, 1968)
    Readings in Russian Philosophical Thought: Logic and Aesthetics (The Hague: Mouton, 1973)
    Readings in Russian Philosophical Thought: Philosophy of History (Waterloo, ON: Wilfred Laurier University Press, 1977)

HISTORICAL-CULTURAL CONTEXT

Billington, James H. *The Icon and the Axe: An Interpretive History of Russian Culture* (New York: Random House, 1966)

Figes, Orlando. *Natasha's Dance: A Cultural History of Russia* (New York: Henry Holt and Co., 2002)

Hosking, Geoffrey. *Russia: People and Empire, 1552–1917* (Cambridge, MA: Harvard University Press, 1997)

Meyendorff, John. *Byzantine Theology: Historical Trends and Doctrinal Themes* (New York: Fordham University Press, 1979)

Pipes, Richard. *Russia under the Old Regime* (New York: Scribner, 1974)

Raeff, Marc. *Understanding Imperial Russia* (Arthur Goldhammer (trans.), New York: Columbia University Press, 1984)

Treadgold, Donald W. *The West in Russia and China: Religious and Secular Thought in Modern Times*, vol. 1, *Russia, 1472–1917*. (Cambridge University Press, 1973)

NINETEENTH-CENTURY RUSSIAN THOUGHT

Texts

Annenkov, P.V. *The Extraordinary Decade: Literary Memoirs by P.V. Annenkov* (Arthur P. Mendel (ed.), Irwin R. Titunik (trans.), Ann Arbor, MI: University of Michigan Press, 1968)

Belinskii, V.G. *Selected Philosophical Works* (Moscow: Foreign Languages Publishing House, 1956)

Belinskii, V.G., N.G. Chernyshevskii, and N.A. Dobroliubov. *Belinsky, Chernyshevsky, and Dobrolyubov: Selected Criticism* (Ralph E. Matlaw (ed.), Bloomington and Indianapolis, IN: Indiana University Press, 1976)

Bird, Robert and Boris Jakim (eds. and trans.). *On Spiritual Unity: A Slavophile Reader* (Hudson, NY: Lindisfarne Books, 1998)

Chaadaev, Peter. *The Major Works of Peter Chaadaev* (Raymond T. McNally (trans. and commentary), University of Notre Dame Press, 1969)

    Philosophical Letters and Apology of a Madman (Mary-Barbara Zeldin (trans.), Knoxville, TN: University of Tennessee Press, 1969)

Chernyshevskii, N.G. *Selected Philosophical Essays* (Moscow: Foreign Languages Publishing House, 1953)

    What Is To Be Done? (Michael R. Katz (trans.), William G. Wagner (annot.), Ithaca, NY: Cornell University Press, 1989)

Dobroliubov, N.A. *Selected Philosophical Essays* (Moscow: Foreign Languages Publishing House, 1956)

Gershenzon, Michael. *A History of Young Russia* (James P. Scanlan (trans.), Irvine, CA: Charles Schlacks, 1986)

Herzen, Alexander. *From the Other Shore, and The Russian People and Socialism, an Open Letter to Jules Michelet* (Moura Budberg and Richard Wollheim (trans.), with an Introduction by Isaiah Berlin, London: Weidenfeld and Nicolson, 1956)

    Selected Philosophical Works (Moscow: Foreign Languages Publishing House, 1956)

    My Past and Thoughts: The Memoirs of Alexander Herzen, 4 vols. (Constance Garnett (trans.), Humphrey Higgens (rev.), London: Chatto and Windus, 1968)

    Letters from France and Italy, 1847–1851 (Judith Zimmerman (ed. and trans.), University of Pittsburgh Press, 1995)

Lavrov, Peter. *Historical Letters* (James P. Scanlan (ed. and trans.), Berkeley and Los Angeles, CA: University of California Press, 1967)

Pisarev, D. I. *Selected Philosophical, Social, and Political Essays* (Moscow: Foreign Languages Publishing House, 1958; Westport, CT: Hyperion Press, 1981)

Studies

Acton, Edward. *Alexander Herzen and the Role of the Intellectual Revolutionary* (Cambridge University Press, 1979)

Berlin, Isaiah. *Russian Thinkers*, rev. 2nd edn. (Henry Hardy and Aileen Kelly (eds.), London: Penguin, 2008)

Billington, James H. *Mikhailovsky and Russian Populism* (Oxford: Clarendon Press, 1958)

Bowman, Herbert E. *Vissarion Belinski: A Study in the Origins of Social Criticism in Russia* (Cambridge, MA: Harvard University Press, 1954)

Brown, Edward J. *Stankevich and His Moscow Circle, 1830–1840* (Stanford University Press, 1966)

Byrnes, Robert F. *Pobedonostsev: His Life and Thought* (Bloomington, IN: Indiana University Press, 1968)

Christoff, Peter K. *An Introduction to Nineteenth-Century Russian Slavophilism: A Study in Ideas*, 4 vols. (The Hague: Mouton, 1961–1991)

Gerstein, Linda. *Nikolai Strakhov: Philosopher, Man of Letters, Social Critic* (Cambridge, MA: Harvard University Press, 1971)

Gleason, Abbott. *European and Muscovite: Ivan Kireevsky and the Origins of Slavophilism* (Cambridge, MA: Harvard University Press, 1972)

    Young Russia: The Genesis of Russian Radicalism in the 1860s (New York: Viking, 1980)

Gratieux, Albert. *A.S. Khomiakov et le mouvement slavophile*, 2 vols. (Paris: Éditions du Cerf, 1939)

Ivanov-Razumnik, R.V. *Istoriia russkoi obshchestvennoi mysli*, 3rd edn., 2 vols. (St. Petersburg: M.M. Stasiulevich, 1911)

Kelly, Aileen M. *Mikhail Bakunin: A Study in the Psychology and Politics of Utopianism* (New Haven, CT: Yale University Press, 1987)
  Toward Another Shore: Russian Thinkers between Necessity and Chance (New Haven, CT: Yale University Press, 1998)
  Views from the Other Shore: Essays on Herzen, Chekhov, and Bakhtin (New Haven, CT: Yale University Press, 1999)
Kindersley, Richard. *The First Russian Revisionists: A Study of "Legal Marxism" in Russia* (Oxford University Press, 1962)
Koyré, Alexandre. *La philosophie et le problème national en Russie au début du XIX-e siècle* (Paris: Champion, 1929)
  Études sur l'histoire de la pensée philosophique en Russie (Paris: J. Vrin, 1950)
Lampert, Evgenii. *Studies in Rebellion* (London: Routledge and Kegan Paul, 1957)
  Sons against Fathers: Studies in Russian Radicalism and Revolution (Oxford: Clarendon Press, 1965)
Lukashevich, Stephen. *Ivan Aksakov, 1823–1886: A Study in Russian Thought and Politics* (Cambridge, MA: Harvard University Press, 1965)
MacMaster, Robert E. *Danilevsky: A Russian Totalitarian Philosopher* (Cambridge, MA: Harvard University Press, 1967)
Malia, Martin. *Alexander Herzen and the Birth of Russian Socialism, 1812–1855* (Cambridge, MA: Harvard University Press, 1961)
McNally, Raymond T. *Chaadayev and his Friends: An Intellectual History of Peter Chaadayev and his Russian Contemporaries* (Tallahassee, FL: Diplomatic Press, 1971)
Mendel, Arthur P. *Dilemmas of Progress in Tsarist Russia: Legal Marxism and Legal Populism* (Cambridge, MA: Harvard University Press, 1961)
Paperno, Irina. *Chernyshevsky and the Age of Realism: A Study in the Semiotics of Behavior* (Stanford University Press, 1988)
Pereira, N.G.O. *The Thought and Teachings of N.G. Černyševskij* (The Hague: Mouton, 1975)
Pipes, Richard. *Russian Conservatism and Its Critics: A Study in Political Culture* (New Haven, CT: Yale University Press, 2005)
Pomper, Philip. *The Russian Revolutionary Intelligentsia* (New York: Crowell, 1970)
  Peter Lavrov and the Russian Revolutionary Movement (University of Chicago Press, 1972)
Pozefsky, Peter C. *The Nihilist Imagination: Dmitrii Pisarev and the Cultural Origins of Russian Radicalism (1860–1868)* (New York: Peter Lang, 2003)
Quénet, Charles. *Tchaadaev et les Lettres philosophiques: contribution à l'étude du mouvement des idées en Russie* (Paris: Lib ancienne Honoré Champion, 1931)
Randolph, John. *The House in the Garden: The Bakunin Family and the Romance of Russian Idealism* (Ithaca, NY: Cornell University Press, 2007)
Riasanovsky, Nicholas V. *Russia and the West in the Teaching of the Slavophiles: A Study of Romantic Ideology* (Cambridge, MA: Harvard University Press, 1952)
  Nicholas I and Official Nationality in Russia, 1825–1855 (Berkeley, CA: University of California Press, 1959)
  A Parting of Ways: Government and the Educated Public in Russia, 1801–1855 (Oxford University Press, 1976)
Schapiro, Leonard. *Rationalism and Nationalism in Russian Nineteenth-Century Political Thought* (New Haven, CT: Yale University Press, 1967)
Terras, Victor. *Belinskij and Russian Literary Criticism: The Heritage of Organic Aesthetics* (Madison, WI: University of Wisconsin Press, 1974)
Tschižewskij [Chizhevskii], Dmitrij. *Gegel'v Rossii* (Paris: Dom knigi and Sovremennye zapiski, 1939)

Hegel bei den Slaven, 2nd edn. (Darmstadt: Wissenschaftliche Buchgesellschaft, 1961)
Russian Intellectual History (Martin P. Rice (ed.), John C. Osborne (trans.), Ann Arbor, MI: Ardis, 1978)
Utechin, S.V. *Russian Political Thought: A Concise History* (New York: Praeger, 1964)
Venturi, Franco. *Roots of Revolution: A History of the Populist and Socialist Movements in Nineteenth-Century Russia* (Francis Haskell (trans.), University of Chicago Press, 1960)
Vucinich, Alexander. *Social Thought in Tsarist Russia: The Quest for a General Science of Society, 1861–1917* (University of Chicago Press, 1976)
Walicki, Andrzej. *The Controversy over Capitalism: Studies in the Social Philosophy of the Russian Populists* (Oxford: Clarendon Press, 1969; University of Notre Dame Press, 1989)
The Slavophile Controversy: History of a Conservative Utopia in Nineteenth-Century Russian Thought (Hilda Andrews-Rusiecka (trans.), Oxford: Clarendon Press, 1975; University of Notre Dame Press, 1989)
Woehrlin, William F. *Chernyshevskii: The Man and the Journalist* (Cambridge, MA: Harvard University Press, 1971)
Wortman, Richard. *The Crisis of Russian Populism* (Cambridge University Press, 1967)
Zimmerman, Judith E. *Midpassage: Alexander Herzen and European Revolution, 1847–1852* (University of Pittsburgh Press, 1989)

RUSSIAN IDEALIST AND RELIGIOUS PHILOSOPHY

Bibliographies

Baranoff, Nathalie. *Bibliographie des oeuvres de Léon Chestov* (Paris: Institut d'Études slaves, 1975)
Bibliographie des études sur Léon Chestov (Paris: Institut d'Études slaves, 1978)
Bird, Robert (ed.). *A Bibliography of Russian Idealist Philosophy in English* (Carlisle, PA: The Variable Press, 1999)
Frank, Vasily. *Bibliographie des oeuvres de Simon Frank* (Paris: Institut d'Études slaves, 1980)
Groberg, Kristi. "Vladimir Sergeevich Solov'ev: A Bibliography," *Modern Greek Studies Yearbook* 14/15 (1998–1999), 299–398
Klementiev, Alexandre. *Bibliographie des oeuvres de Lev Karsavine* (Paris: Institut d'Études slaves, 1994)
Klépinine, Tamara. *Bibliographie des oeuvres de Nicolas Berdiaev* (Paris: YMCA Press, 1978)
Lossky, Boris and Nikolai. *Bibliographie des oeuvres de Nicolas Lossky* (Paris: Institut d'Études slaves, 1978)
Naumov, Kliment. *Bibliographie des oeuvres de Serge Boulgakov* (Paris: Institut d'Études slaves, 1984)

Texts

Berdiaev [Berdyaev], Nikolai. *The End of Our Time* (Donald Attwater (trans.), London: Sheed and Ward, 1933)
Freedom and the Spirit (Oliver Fielding Clarke (trans.), London: Geoffrey Bles, 1935)
The Meaning of History (George Reavey (trans.), London: Geoffrey Bles, The Centenary Press, 1936)
Solitude and Society (George Reavey (trans.), London: Geoffrey Bles, The Centenary Press, 1938)
Leontiev (George Reavey (trans.), London: Geoffrey Bles, The Centenary Press, 1940)
Slavery and Freedom (R.M. French (trans.), New York: Charles Scribner's Sons, 1944)

Spirit and Reality (Oliver Fielding Clarke (trans.), London: Geoffrey Bles, 1946)

The Divine and the Human (R.M. French (trans.), London: Geoffrey Bles, 1949)

Dream and Reality: An Essay in Autobiography (Katherine Lampert (trans.), London: Geoffrey Bles, 1950)

The Beginning and the End (R.M. French (trans.), London: Geoffrey Bles, 1952)

The Realm of Spirit and the Realm of Caesar (Donald A. Lowrie (trans.), New York: Harper & Row, 1953)

Truth and Revelation (R.M. French (trans.), London: Geoffrey Bles, 1954)

The Meaning of the Creative Act (Donald A. Lowrie (trans.), New York: Harper & Row, 1955)

The Destiny of Man (Natalie Duddington (trans.), New York: Harper & Row, 1960)

The Origin of Russian Communism (R.M. French (trans.), Ann Arbor, MI: University of Michigan Press, 1960)

The Fate of Man in the Modern World (Donald A. Lowrie (trans.), Ann Arbor, MI: University of Michigan Press, 1961)

Christian Existentialism: A Berdyaev Anthology (Donald A. Lowrie (ed. and trans.), London: George Allen & Unwin, 1965)

The Russian Idea (R.M. French (trans.), Christopher Bamford (rev.), Hudson, NY: Lindisfarne Press, 1992)

Bulgakov, Sergei. *A Bulgakov Anthology* (James Pain and Nicolas Zernov (eds.), London: SPCK, 1976)

Karl Marx as a Religious Type: His Relation to the Religion of Anthropotheism of L. Feuerbach (Virgil R. Lang (ed.), Luba Barna (trans.), with an Introduction by Donald W. Treadgold, Belmont, MA: Nordland, 1979)

The Orthodox Church (Donald A. Lowrie (ed.), Elizabeth S. Cram (trans.), Lydia Kesich (rev.), Crestwood, NY: St. Vladimir's Seminary Press, 1988)

Sophia, The Wisdom of God: An Outline of Sophiology (Hudson, NY: Lindisfarne Press, 1993)

The Holy Grail and the Eucharist (Boris Jakim (trans.), with an Introduction by Robert Slesinski, Hudson, NY: Lindisfarne Books, 1997)

Sergii Bulgakov: Towards a Russian Political Theology (Rowan Williams (ed.), Edinburgh: T&T Clark, 1999)

Philosophy of Economy: The World as Household (Catherine Evtuhov (ed. and trans.), New Haven, CT and London: Yale University Press, 2000)

The Bride of the Lamb (Boris Jakim (trans.), Grand Rapids, MI: William B. Eerdmans Publishing Company, 2002; Edinburgh: T&T Clark, 2002)

The Friend of the Bridegroom: On the Orthodox Veneration of the Forerunner (Boris Jakim (trans.), Grand Rapids, MI: William B. Eerdmans Publishing Company, 2003)

The Comforter (Boris Jakim (trans.), Grand Rapids, MI: William B. Eerdmans Publishing Company, 2004)

The Lamb of God (Boris Jakim (trans.), Grand Rapids, MI: William B. Eerdmans Publishing Company, 2008)

Florensky, Pavel. *Iconostasis* (Olga Andrejev and Donald Sheehan (trans.), Crestwood, NY: St. Vladimir's Seminary Press, 1996)

The Pillar and Ground of the Truth: An Essay in Orthodox Theodicy in Twelve Letters (Boris Jakim (trans.), Princeton University Press, 1997)

Frank, S.L. *La Connaissance et l'être* (Paris: Aubier, 1937)

God With Us: Three Meditations (Natalie Duddington (trans.), London: Jonathan Cape, 1946)

Biografiia P.B. Struve (New York: Chekhov Publishing House, 1956)

Reality and Man: An Essay on the Metaphysics of Human Nature (Natalie Duddington (trans.), London: Faber and Faber, 1956)

The Unknowable: An Ontological Introduction to the Philosophy of Religion (Boris Jakim (trans.), Athens, OH: Ohio University Press, 1983)

The Spiritual Foundations of Society: An Introduction to Social Philosophy (Boris Jakim (trans.), Athens, OH: Ohio University Press, 1987)

The Light Shineth in Darkness: An Essay in Christian Ethics and Social Philosophy (Boris Jakim (trans.), Athens, OH: Ohio University Press, 1989)

Man's Soul: An Introductory Essay in Philosophical Psychology (Boris Jakim (trans.), Athens, OH: Ohio University Press, 1993)

Frank, S. L. (ed.). *Iz istorii russkoi filosofskoi mysli kontsa XIX i nachala XX veka: Antologiia* (Washington, DC: Inter-Language Literary Associates, 1965)

Losskii [Lossky], N.O. *The Intuitive Basis of Knowledge: An Epistemological Inquiry* (Natalie Duddington (trans.), London: Macmillan, 1919)

The World as an Organic Whole (Natalie Duddington (trans.), London: Oxford University Press, 1928)

Freedom of Will (Natalie Duddington (trans.), London: Williams and Norgate, 1932)

Novgorodtsev, P.I. (ed.). *Problems of Idealism: Essays in Russian Social Philosophy* (Randall A. Poole (ed. and trans.), New Haven, CT: Yale University Press, 2003)

Schmemann, Alexander (ed.). *Ultimate Questions: An Anthology of Modern Russian Religious Thought* (New York: Holt, Rinehart and Winston, 1965)

Shatz, Marshall S. and Judith E. Zimmerman (eds. and trans.), *Vekhi/Landmarks: A Collection of Articles about the Russian Intelligentsia* (Armonk, NY: M.E. Sharpe, 1994)

Shestov, Lev. *Athens and Jerusalem* (Bernard Martin (ed. and trans.), Athens, OH: Ohio University Press, 1966)

Potestas Clavium (Bernard Martin (trans.), Athens, OH: Ohio University Press, 1968)

Kierkegaard and Existential Philosophy (Elinor Hewitt (trans.), Athens, OH: Ohio University Press, 1969)

A Shestov Anthology (Bernard Martin (ed.), Athens, OH: Ohio University Press, 1970)

In Job's Balances: On the Sources of the Eternal Truths (Camilla Coventry and C.A. Macartney (trans.), with an Introduction by Bernard Martin, Athens, OH: Ohio University Press, 1975)

All Things are Possible, and Penultimate Words and Other Essays (with an Introduction by Bernard Martin, Athens, OH: Ohio University Press, 1977)

Speculation and Revelation (Bernard Martin (trans.), Athens, OH: Ohio University Press, 1982)

Shpet, Gustav. *Appearance and Sense* (Thomas Nemeth (trans.), Dordrecht: Kluwer, 1991)

Solov'ëv [Solovyov, Soloviev], Vladimir. *God, Man and the Church: The Spiritual Foundations of Life* (Donald Attwater (trans.), London: James Clarke, 1938)

Russia and the Universal Church (Herbert Rees (trans.), London: Geoffrey Bles, 1948)

A Solovyov Anthology (S.L. Frank (ed.), Natalie Duddington (trans.), London:. SCM Press, 1950; London: St. Austin Press, 2001)

"Foundations of Theoretical Philosophy" (Vlada Tolley and James P. Scanlan (trans.)) in James M. Edie, James P. Scanlan, and Mary-Barbara Zeldin (eds.), with the collaboration of George L. Kline, *Russian Philosophy* (Chicago, IL: Quadrangle Books, 1965; Knoxville, TN: University of Tennessee Press, 1976), vol. 3, pp. 99–134

War, Progress, and the End of History: Three Conversations. Including a Short Story of the Anti-Christ (Alexander Bakshy (trans.), Thomas R. Beyer, Jr. (rev.), Hudson, NY: Lindisfarne Press, 1990)

Lectures on Divine Humanity (Peter P. Zouboff (trans.), Boris Jakim (ed. and rev.), Hudson, NY: Lindisfarne Press, 1995)

The Meaning of Love (Jane Marshall (trans.), Thomas R. Beyer, Jr. (rev.), Hudson, NY: Lindisfarne Press, 1995)

The Crisis of Western Philosophy (Against the Positivists) (Boris Jakim (ed. and trans.), Hudson, NY: Lindisfarne Press, 1996)

Politics, Law, and Morality: Essays by V.S. Soloviev (Vladimir Wozniuk (ed. and trans.), New Haven, CT: Yale University Press, 2000)

The Heart of Reality: Essays on Beauty, Love, and Ethics by V.S. Soloviev (Vladimir Wozniuk (ed. and trans.), University of Notre Dame Press, 2003)

The Justification of the Good: An Essay on Moral Philosophy (Natalie A. Duddington (ed. and trans.), Boris Jakim (annot.), Grand Rapids, MI: William B. Eerdmans Publishing Company, 2005)

Enemies from the East? V.S. Soloviev on Paganism, Asian Civilizations, and Islam (Vladimir Wozniuk (ed. and trans.), Evanston, IL: Northwestern University Press, 2007)

Freedom, Faith, and Dogma: Essays by V.S. Soloviev on Christianity and Judaism (Vladimir Wozniuk (ed. and trans.), Albany, NY: State University of New York Press, 2008)

The Philosophical Principles of Integral Knowledge (Valeria Z. Nollan (trans.), Grand Rapids, MI and Cambridge: William B. Eerdmans Publishing Company, 2008)

Divine Sophia: The Wisdom Writings of Vladimir Solovyov (Judith Deutsch Kornblatt (ed. and trans.), Ithaca, NY: Cornell University Press, 2009)

Vysheslavtsev, B.P. *The Eternal in Russian Philosophy* (Penelope V. Burt (trans.), Grand Rapids, MI: William B. Eerdmans Publishing Company, 2002)

Studies

Amelina, E.M. *Problema obshchestvennogo ideala v russkoi religioznoi filosofii kontsa XIX–XX vv.* (Kaluga: Eidos, 2004)

Bercken, Wil Van Den, Manon de Courten, and Evert Van Der Zweerde (eds.). *Vladimir Solov'ëv: Reconciler and Polemicist* (Leuven: Peeters, 2000)

Bohachevsky-Chomiak, Martha. *Sergei N. Trubetskoi: An Intellectual Among the Intelligentsia in Prerevolutionary Russia* (Belmont, MA: Nordland Publishing Co., 1976)

Boikov, V.F. (ed.). *Vl. Solov'ëv: Pro et Contra (Lichnost' i tvorchestvo Vladimira Solov'ëva v otsenke russkikh myslitelei i issledovatelei)*, 2 vols. (St. Petersburg: Izdatel'stvo Russkogo Khristianskogo gumanitarnogo instituta, 2000)

Boobbyer, Philip. *S.L. Frank: The Life and Work of a Russian Philosopher, 1877–1950* (Athens, OH: Ohio University Press, 1995)

Burchardi, Kristiane. *Die Moskauer "Religiös-Philosophische Vladimir-Solovyov-Gesellschaft" (1905–1918)* (Wiesbaden: Harrassowitz, 1998)

Cioran, Samuel D. *Vladimir Solov'ev and the Knighthood of the Divine Sophia* (Waterloo, ON: Wilfred Laurier University Press, 1977)

Copleston, Frederick C. *Russian Religious Philosophy: Selected Aspects* (University of Notre Dame Press, 1988)

Dennes, Maryse (ed.). *Gustave Chpet et son héritage: aux sources russes du structuralisme et de la sémiotique*, Slavica Occitania, vol. 26 (Toulouse: Département de slavistique de l'université de Toulouse II and Le Mirail, Centre de recherches Interculturalité et monde slave, 2008)

Evtuhov, Catherine. *The Cross and the Sickle: Sergei Bulgakov and the Fate of Russian Religious Philosophy, 1890–1920* (Ithaca, NY: Cornell University Press, 1997)

Florovsky, Georges. *Ways of Russian Theology*, 2 vols. (Robert L. Nichols (trans.), Belmont, MA: Notable and Academic Books, 1979, 1987)

Franz, Norbert, Michael Hagemeister, and Frank Haney (eds.). *Pavel Florenskij – Tradition und Moderne. Beiträge zum internationalen Symposium an der Universität Potsdam, 5. bis 9. April 2000* (Frankfurt am Main: Peter Lang, 2001)

Gaidenko, P.P. *Vladimir Solov'ëv i filosofiia Serebrianogo veka* (Moscow: Progress–Traditsiia, 2001)

Gollerbakh, Evgenii. *K nezrimomu gradu: Religiozno-filosofskaia gruppa "Put'" (1910–1919) v poiskakh novoi russkoi identichnosti* (St. Petersburg: Aleteiia, 2000)

Hagemeister, Michael. *Nikolaj Fedorov: Studien zu Leben, Werk und Wirkung* (Munich: Verlag Otto Sagner, 1989)

Kamenskii, Z.A. and V.A. Zhuchkov (eds.). *Kant i filosofiia v Rossii* (Moscow: Nauka, 1994)

Khoruzhii [Horujy], S.S. *Posle pereryva. Puti russkoi filosofii* (St. Petersburg: Izdatel'stvo "Aleteiia," 1994)

Mirosozertsanie Florenskogo (Tomsk: Vodolei, 1999)

O starom i novom (St. Petersburg: Aleteiia, 2000)

Opyty iz russkoi dukhovnoi traditsii (Moscow: Parad, 2005)

Kline, George L. *Religious and Anti-Religious Thought in Russia* (University of Chicago Press, 1968)

Kolerov, M.A. *Ne mir, no mech': russkaia religiozno-filosofskaia pechat' ot 'Problem idealizma' do 'Vekh' 1902–1909* (St. Petersburg: Aleteiia, 1996)

Kornblatt, Judith Deutsch and Richard F. Gustafson (eds.). *Russian Religious Thought* (Madison, WI: University of Wisconsin Press, 1996)

Kudishina, A.A. *Ekzistentsializm i gumanizm v Rossii: Lev Shestov i Nikolai Berdiaev* (Moscow: Akademicheskii proekt, 2007)

Losev, A.F. *Vladimir Solov'ëv i ego vremia* (Moscow: Progress, 1990)

Lowrie, Donald. *Rebellious Prophet: A Life of Nikolai Berdyaev* (New York: Harper, 1960)

Mochul'skii, Konstantin. *Vladimir Solov'ëv: Zhizn' i uchenie*, 2nd edn. (Paris: YMCA Press, 1951)

Motroshilova, N.V. *Mysliteli Rossii i filosofiia Zapada: V. Solov'ëv, N. Berdiaev, S. Frank, L. Shestov* (Moscow: Respublika, 2006)

Nethercott, Frances. *Une rencontre philosophique: Bergson en Russie (1907–1917)* (Paris: L'Harmattan, 1995)

Russia's Plato: Plato and the Platonic Tradition in Russian Education, Science and Ideology, 1840–1930 (Burlington, VT: Ashgate, 2000)

Nichols, Aidan. *Wisdom from Above: A Primer in the Theology of Father Sergei Bulgakov* (Leominster: Gracewing, 2005)

Putnam, George F. *Russian Alternatives to Marxism: Christian Socialism and Idealistic Liberalism in Twentieth-Century Russia* (Knoxville, TN: University of Tennessee Press, 1977)

Read, Christopher. *Religion, Revolution and the Russian Intelligentsia, 1900–1912: The Vekhi Debate and its Intellectual Background* (London: Macmillan, 1979)

Scherrer, Jutta. *Die Petersburger religiös-philosophischen Vereinigungen. Die Entwicklung des religiösen Selbstverständnisses ihrer Intelligencija-Mitglieder (1901–1907)* (Wiesbaden: Harrassowitz, 1973)

Shein, Louis J. *The Philosophy of Lev Shestov (1866–1938): A Russian Religious Existentialist* (Lampeter, NY: E. Mellen Press, 1991)

Slesinski, Robert. *Pavel Florensky: A Metaphysics of Love* (Crestwood, NY: St. Vladimir's Seminary Press, 1984)

Solovyov, Sergey M. *Vladimir Solovyov: His Life and Creative Evolution*, 2 vols. (Aleksey Gibson (trans.), Fairfax, VA: Eastern Christian Publications, 2000)

Stremooukhoff, Dmitrii. *Vladimir Soloviev and his Messianic Work* (Philip Guilbeau and Heather Elise MacGregor (eds.), Elizabeth Meyendorff (trans.), Belmont, MA: Nordland, 1980)

Sutton, Jonathan. *The Religious Philosophy of Vladimir Solovyov: Towards a Reassessment* (New York: St. Martin's Press, 1988)

Tihanov, Galin (ed.). *Gustav Shpet's Contributions to Philosophy and Cultural Theory* (West Lafayette, IN: Purdue University Press, 2009)

Vadimov [Tsvetkov], Aleksandr. *Zhizn' Berdiaeva: Rossiia* (Oakland, CA: Berkeley Slavic Specialties, 1993)

Valevičius, Andrius. *Lev Shestov and his Times: Encounters with Brandes, Tolstoy, Dostoevsky, Chekhov, Ibsen, Nietzsche, and Husserl* (New York: Peter Lang, 1993)

Valliere, Paul. *Modern Russian Theology: Bukharev, Soloviev, Bulgakov: Orthodox Theology in a New Key* (Grand Rapids, MI: William B. Eerdmans Publishing Company, 2000)

Vallon, Michael A. *An Apostle of Freedom: Life and Teachings of Nicolas Berdyaev* (New York: Philosophical Library, 1960)

Volkogonova, O.D. *N.A. Berdiaev: Intellektual'naia biografiia* (Moscow: Izd-vo Moskovskogo universiteta, 2001)

Young, George M., Jr. *Nikolai Fedorov: An Introduction* (Belmont, MA: Nordland, 1979)

Zander, L.A. *Bog i mir (Mirosozertsanie ottsa Sergiia Bulgakova)*, 2 vols. (Paris: YMCA Press, 1948)

Zernov, Nicolas. *The Russian Religious Renaissance of the Twentieth Century* (New York: Harper & Row, 1963)

RUSSIAN PHILOSOPHY, LITERATURE, AND LITERARY CRITICISM

Bibliographies

Egan, David R. and Melinda A. Egan. *Leo Tolstoy: An Annotated Bibliography of English Language Sources to 1978* (Metuchen, NJ: Scarecrow Press, 1979)

   Leo Tolstoy: An Annotated Bibliography of English Language Sources from 1978 to 2003 (Lanham, MD: Scarecrow Press, 2005)

Leatherbarrow, William J. *Fedor Dostoevsky: A Reference Guide* (Boston: G.K. Hall, 1990)

Texts

Bakhtin, M.M. *The Dialogical Imagination: Four Essays by M.M. Bakhtin* (Michael Holquist (ed.), Caryl Emerson and Michael Holquist (trans.), Austin, TX: University of Texas Press, 1981)

   Problems of Dostoevsky's Poetics (Caryl Emerson (ed. and trans.), Minneapolis, MN: University of Minnesota Press, 1984)

   Speech Genres and Other Late Essays (Vern W. McGee (trans.), Austin, TX: University of Texas Press, 1986)

   Art and Answerability: Early Philosophical Essays by M.M. Bakhtin (Michael Holquist and Vadim Liapunov (eds.), Vadim Liapunov (trans.), Austin, TX: University of Texas Press, 1990)

   Toward a Philosophy of the Act (Vadim Liapunov and Michael Holquist (eds.), Vadim Liapunov (trans.), Austin, TX: University of Texas Press, 1993)

Berdyaev, Nicholas. *Dostoevsky* (Donald Attwater (trans.), London: Sheed & Ward, 1934)

Ginzburg, Lydia. *On Psychological Prose* (Judson Rosengrant (ed. and trans.), Princeton University Press, 1991)

Ivanov, Viacheslav. *Freedom and the Tragic Life: A Study in Dostoevsky* (Norman Cameron (trans.), London: Harvill Press, 1952; New York: Noonday Press, 1952; reprinted, with an Introduction by Robert Louis Jackson, Wolfeburo, NH: Longwood Academic, 1989)

Roberts, Spencer E. (ed. and trans.). *Essays in Russian Literature – The Conservative View: Leontiev, Rozanov, Shestov* (Athens, OH: Ohio University Press, 1968)

Rozanov, V.V. *Dostoevsky and the Legend of the Grand Inquisitor* (Spencer E. Roberts (trans.), Ithaca, NY: Cornell University Press, 1972)

Shestov, Lev. *Dostoevsky, Tolstoy and Nietzsche* (Bernard Martin and Spencer E. Roberts (eds. and trans.), Columbus, OH: Ohio State University Press, 1969)

Studies

Bethea, David M. *The Shape of Apocalypse in Modern Russian Fiction* (Princeton University Press, 1989)

Cassedy, Steven. *Flight from Eden: The Origins of Modern Literary Criticism and Aesthetics* (Berkeley, CA: University of California Press, 1990)

Dostoevsky's Religion (Stanford University Press, 2005)

Clark, Katerina and Michael Holquist. *Mikhail Bakhtin* (Cambridge, MA: Harvard University Press, 1984)

Clowes, Edith W. *The Revolution of Moral Consciousness: Nietzsche in Russian Literature, 1890–1914* (DeKalb, IL: Northern Illinois University Press, 1988)

Fiction's Overcoat: Russian Literary Culture and the Question of Philosophy (Ithaca, NY: Cornell University Press, 2004)

Emerson, Caryl. *The First Hundred Years of Mikhail Bakhtin* (Princeton University Press, 1997)

The Cambridge Introduction to Russian Literature (Cambridge University Press, 2008)

Felch, Susan M. and Paul J. Contino (eds.). *Bakhtin and Religion: A Feeling for Faith* (Evanston, IL: Northwestern University Press, 2001)

Frank, Joseph. *Dostoevsky*, 5 vols. (Princeton University Press, 1976–2002)

Gustafson, Richard F. *Leo Tolstoy: Resident and Stranger* (Princeton University Press, 1986)

Knapp, Liza. *The Annihilation of Inertia: Dostoevsky and Metaphysics* (Evanston, IL: Northwestern University Press, 1996)

Kostalevsky, Marina. *Dostoevsky and Soloviev: The Art of Integral Vision* (New Haven, CT: Yale University Press, 1997)

Masing-Delic, Irene. *Abolishing Death: A Salvation Myth of Russian Twentieth-Century Literature* (Stanford University Press, 1992)

Medzhibovskaya, Inessa. *Tolstoy and the Religious Culture of his Time: A Biography of a Long Conversion, 1845–1887* (Lanham, MD: Lexington Books, 2008)

Mihailovic, Alexandar. *Corporeal Words: Mikhail Bakhtin's Theology of Discourse* (Evanston, IL: Northwestern University Press, 1997)

Miller, Robin Feuer. *Dostoevsky's Unfinished Journey* (New Haven, CT: Yale University Press, 2007)

Morson, Gary Saul. *Hidden in Plain View: Narrative and Creative Potentials in "War and Peace"* (Stanford University Press, 1987)

The Boundaries of Genre: Dostoevsky's Diary of a Writer and the Traditions of Literary Utopia (Austin, TX: University of Texas Press, 1981; Evanston, IL: Northwestern University Press, 1988)

Anna Karenina in Our Time: Seeing More Wisely (New Haven, CT: Yale University Press, 2007)

Morson, Gary Saul and Caryl Emerson. *Mikhail Bakhtin: Creation of a Prosaics* (Stanford University Press, 1990)

Orwin, Donna Tussing. *Tolstoy's Art and Thought, 1847–1880* (Princeton University Press, 1993)

Consequences of Consciousness: Turgenev, Dostoevsky, and Tolstoy (Stanford University Press, 2007)

Paperno, Irina. *Suicide as a Cultural Institution in Dostoevsky's Russia* (Ithaca, NY: Cornell University Press, 1997)

Pattison, George and Diane Oenning Thompson (eds.). *Dostoevsky and the Christian Tradition* (Cambridge University Press, 2001)

Scanlan, James P. *Dostoevsky the Thinker* (Ithaca, NY: Cornell University Press, 2002)

Williams, Rowan. *Dostoevsky: Language, Faith, and Fiction* (Waco, TX: Baylor University Press, 2008)

THE RUSSIAN SILVER AGE

Bibliographies

Davidson, Pamela. *Viacheslav Ivanov: A Reference Guide* (New York: G.K. Hall, 1996)

Kalb, Judith E. and J. Alexander Ogden, with I.G. Vishnevetsky (eds.). *Russian Writers of the Silver Age* (Detroit, MI: Gale, 2004)

Texts

Belyi [Bely], Andrei. *Selected Essays of Andrei Bely* (Steven D. Cassedy (ed. and trans.), Berkeley, CA: University of California Press, 1985)

Ivanov, Viacheslav. *Selected Essays* (Michael Wachtel (ed.), Robert Bird (trans.), Evanston, IL: Northwestern University Press, 2001)

Peterson, Ronald E. (ed. and trans.). *The Russian Symbolists: An Anthology of Critical and Theoretical Writings* (Ann Arbor, MI: Ardis, 1986)

Proffer, Carl and Ellendea Proffer (eds.). *The Silver Age of Russian Culture: An Anthology* (Ann Arbor, MI: Ardis, 1975)

Rosenthal, Bernice Glatzer and Martha Bohachevsky-Chomiak (eds.). *A Revolution of the Spirit: Crisis of Value in Russia, 1890–1924* (Marian Schwartz (trans.), New York: Fordham University Press, 1990)

Rozanov, V.V. *The Apocalypse of Our Time, and Other Writings* (Robert Payne (ed.), Robert Payne and Nikita Romanoff (trans.), New York: Praeger, 1977)

  Four Faces of Rozanov: Christianity, Sex, Jews, and the Russian Revolution (Spencer E. Roberts (trans.), New York: Philosophical Library, 1978)

Studies

Bedford, C.H. *The Seeker: D.S. Merezhkovskiy* (Lawrence, KS: University of Kansas Press, 1975)

Bird, Robert. *The Russian Prospero: The Creative Universe of Viacheslav Ivanov* (Madison, WI: University of Wisconsin Press, 2006)

Bowlt, John E. *The Silver Age: Russian Art of the Early Twentieth Century and the "World of Art" Group* (Newtonville, MA: Oriental Research Partners, 1982)

  Moscow and St. Petersburg in Russia's Silver Age, 1900–1920 (London: Thames & Hudson, 2008)

Carlson, Maria. *"No Religion Higher than Truth": A History of the Theosophical Movement in Russia, 1875–1922* (Princeton University Press, 1993)

Engelstein, Laura. *The Keys to Happiness: Sex and the Search for Modernity in Fin-de-Siècle Russia* (Ithaca, NY: Cornell University Press, 1992)

Grossman, Joan Delaney and Ruth Rischin (eds.). *William James in Russian Culture* (Lanham, MD: Lexington Books, 2003)

Matich, Olga. *Erotic Utopia: The Decadent Imagination in Russia's Fin de Siècle* (Madison, WI: University of Wisconsin Press, 2005)

Pachmuss, Temira. *Zinaida Hippius: An Intellectual Profile* (Carbondale, IL: Southern Illinois University Press, 1971)

Paperno, Irina and Joan Grossman (eds.). *Creating Life: The Aesthetic Utopia of Russian Modernism* (Stanford University Press, 1994)

Poggioli, Renato. *The Poets of Russia, 1890–1930* (Cambridge, MA: Harvard University Press, 1960)

Pyman, Avril. *A History of Russian Symbolism* (Cambridge University Press, 1994)

Ronen, Omry. *The Fallacy of the Silver Age in Twentieth-Century Russian Literature* (Amsterdam: Harwood Academic Publishers, 1997)

Rosenthal, Bernice Glatzer. *D.S. Merezhkovsky and the Silver Age: The Development of a Revolutionary Mentality* (The Hague: Martinus Nijhoff, 1975)
  New Myth, New World: From Nietzsche to Stalinism (University Park, PA: Penn State University Press, 2002)
Rosenthal, Bernice Glatzer (ed.). *Nietzsche in Russia.* (Princeton University Press, 1986)
  The Occult in Russia and Soviet Culture (Ithaca, NY: Cornell University Press, 1997)
Wachtel, Michael. *Russian Symbolism and Literary Tradition: Goethe, Novalis, and the Poetics of Vyacheslav Ivanov* (Madison, WI: University of Wisconsin Press, 1994)
West, James D. *Russian Symbolism: A Study of Vyacheslav Ivanov and the Russian Symbolist Aesthetic* (London: Methuen, 1970)

RUSSIAN LIBERALISM: HISTORY AND PHILOSOPHY

Texts

Chicherin, Boris. *Liberty, Equality, and the Market: Essays by B.N. Chicherin* (G.M. Hamburg (ed. and trans.), New Haven, CT and London: Yale University Press, 1998)
(Also, under Russian Idealist and Religious Philosophy above, see in particular Solov'ëv, *Politics, Law, and Morality*; *The Justification of the Good*; Novgorodtsev (ed.), *Problems of Idealism*; and *Vekhi/Landmarks*)

Studies

Clowes, Edith W., Samuel D. Kassow, and James L. West (eds.). *Between Tsar and People: Educated Society and the Quest for Public Identity in Late Imperial Russia* (Princeton University Press, 1991)
Crisp, Olga and Linda Edmondson (eds.). *Civil Rights in Imperial Russia* (Oxford: Clarendon Press, 1989)
Emmons, Terence. *The Formation of Political Parties and the First National Elections in Russia* (Cambridge, MA: Harvard University Press, 1983)
Fischer, George. *Russian Liberalism: From Gentry to Intelligentsia* (Cambridge, MA: Harvard University Press, 1958)
Glushkova, S.I. *Problema pravovogo ideala v russkom liberalizme* (Ekaterinburg: Izd-vo Gumanitarnogo universiteta, 2001)
Hamburg, G.M. *Boris Chicherin and Early Russian Liberalism, 1828–1866* (Stanford University Press, 1992)
Heuman, Susan. *Kistiakovsky: The Struggle for National and Constitutional Rights in the Last Years of Tsarism* (Cambridge, MA: Harvard Ukrainian Research Institute and Harvard University Press, 1998)
Hosking, Geoffrey A. *The Russian Constitutional Experiment: Government and Duma, 1907–1914* (Cambridge University Press, 1973)
Leontovitsch, Victor. *Geschichte des Liberalismus in Russland* (Frankfurt am Main: V. Klostermann, 1957)
Miliukov, Paul. *Russia and Its Crisis* (London: Collier-Macmillan, 1962)
Nethercott, Frances. *Russian Legal Culture Before and After Communism: Criminal Justice, Politics, and the Public Sphere* (London: Routledge, 2007)
Offord, Derek. *Portraits of Early Russian Liberals: A Study of the Thought of T.N. Granovsky, V.P. Botkin, P.V. Annenkov, A.V. Druzhinin and K.D. Kavelin* (Cambridge University Press, 1985, 2009)

Osipov, I. D. *Filosofiia russkogo liberalizma XIX–nachalo XX v.* (St. Petersburg: Izd-vo S.-Pëterburgskogo universiteta, 1996)

Pipes, Richard. *Struve: Liberal on the Left, 1870–1905* (Cambridge, MA: Harvard University Press, 1970)

Struve: Liberal on the Right, 1905–1944 (Cambridge, MA: Harvard University Press, 1980)

Roosevelt, Priscilla Reynolds. *Apostle of Russian Liberalism: Timofei Granovsky* (Newtonville, MA: Oriental Research Partners, 1986)

Rosenberg, William G. *Liberals in the Russian Revolution: The Constitutional Democratic Party, 1917–1921* (Princeton University Press, 1974)

Schapiro, Leonard. *Russian Studies* (Ellen Dahrendorf (ed.), New York: Viking, 1987)

Stockdale, Melissa Kirschke. *Paul Miliukov and the Quest for a Liberal Russia, 1880–1918* (Ithaca, NY: Cornell University Press, 1996)

Timberlake, Charles (ed.). *Essays on Russian Liberalism* (Columbia, MO: University of Missouri Press, 1971)

Vasil'ev, B. V. *Filosofiia prava russkogo neoliberalizma kontsa XIX–nachala XX veka* (Voronezh: Voronezhskii gosudarstvennyi universitet, 2004)

Walicki, Andrzej. *Legal Philosophies of Russian Liberalism* (Oxford: Clarendon Press, 1987; University of Notre Dame Press, 1992)

Wartenweiler, David. *Civil Society and Academic Debate in Russia, 1905–1914.* (Oxford University Press, 1999)

Wortman, Richard S. *The Development of a Russian Legal Consciousness* (University of Chicago Press, 1976)

RUSSIAN MARXISM AND RUSSIAN PHILOSOPHY IN REVOLUTION AND EXILE

Bibliographies

Zernov, Nikolai (ed.). *Russkie pisateli emigratsii: Biograficheskie svedeniia i bibliografiia ikh knig po bogosloviiu, religioznoi filosofii, tserkovnoi istorii i pravoslavnoi kul'ture, 1921–1972* (Boston: G.K. Hall, 1973)

Texts

Kline, George L. (ed. and trans.). *Spinoza in Soviet Philosophy: A Series of Essays* (London: Routledge, 1952)

Losev, A.F. *The Dialectics of Myth* (Vladimir Marchenkov (trans.), London: Routledge, 2003)

Stepun, Fëdor. *The Russian Soul and Revolution* (Erminie Huntress (trans.), New York: Charles Scribner's Sons, 1935)

Vinkovetsky, Ilya and Charles Schlacks, Jr. (eds.). *Exodus to the East: Forebodings and Events – An Affirmation of the Eurasians* (Marina del Ray, CA: Charles Schlacks, Jr., 1997)

Woehrlin, William F. (ed. and trans.). *Out of the Depths (De Profundis): A Collection of Articles on the Russian Revolution* (Irvine, CA: Charles Schlacks, 1986)

(For émigré writings of Russian philosophers, see texts above under Russian Idealist and Religious Philosophy. The writings of the Russian Marxists exist in various editions that need not be cited here.)

Studies

Andreyev, Catherine and Ivan Savický. *Russia Abroad: Prague and the Russian Diaspora, 1918–1938* (New Haven, CT: Yale University Press, 2004)

Bakhurst, David. *Consciousness and Revolution in Soviet Philosophy: From the Bolsheviks to Evald Ilyenkov* (Cambridge University Press, 1991)

Baron, Samuel. *Plekhanov: The Father of Russian Marxism* (Stanford University Press, 1963)

Besançon, Alain. *The Rise of the Gulag: Intellectual Origins of Leninism* (Sarah Matthews (trans.), New York: Continuum, 1981)

Blane, Andrew (ed.). *Georges Florovsky: Russian Intellectual and Orthodox Churchman* (Crestwood, NY: St. Vladimir's Seminary Press, 1993)

Burbank, Jane. *Intelligentsia and Revolution: Russian Views of Bolshevism, 1917–1922* (Oxford University Press, 1986)

Chamberlain, Lesley. *Lenin's Private War: The Voyage of the Philosophy Steamer and the Exile of the Intelligentsia* (New York: St. Martin's Press, 2006)

Finkel, Stuart. *On the Ideological Front: The Russian Intelligentsia and the Making of the Soviet Public Sphere* (New Haven, CT: Yale University Press, 2007)

Haimson, Leopold. *The Russian Marxists and the Origins of Bolshevism* (Cambridge, MA: Harvard University Press, 1955)

Hardeman, Hilda. *Coming to Terms with the Soviet Regime: The "Changing Signposts" Movement among Russian Émigrés in the Early 1920s* (DeKalb, IL: Northern Illinois University Press, 1994)

Johnston, Robert H. *New Mecca, New Babylon: Paris and the Russian Exiles, 1920–1945* (Montreal and Kingston: McGill-Queen's University Press, 1988)

Kniazeff, Alexis. *L'Institut Saint-Serge: De l'académie d'autrefois au rayonnement d'aujourd'hui* (Paris: Beauchesne, 1974)

Kolakowski, Leszek. *Main Currents of Marxism*, 3 vols. (P.S. Falla (trans.), Oxford University Press, 1978)

Lowrie, Donald A. *Saint Sergius in Paris: The Orthodox Theological Institute* (London: SPCK, 1954)

Poltoratskii, N.P. *Rossiia i revoliutsiia: Russkaia religiozno-filosofskaia i natsional'no-politicheskaia mysl' XX veka (Sbornik statei)* (Tenafly, NJ: Hermitage, 1988)

Ivan Aleksandrovich Il'in: zhizn', trudy, mirovozzrenie (Sbornik statei) (Tenafly, NJ: Hermitage, 1989)

Raeff, Marc. *Russia Abroad: A Cultural History of the Russian Emigration, 1919–1939* (New York: Oxford University Press, 1990)

Scanlan, James P. *Marxism in the USSR: A Critical Survey of Current Soviet Thought* (Ithaca, NY: Cornell University Press, 1985)

Scanlan, James P. (ed.). *Russian Thought After Communism: The Recovery of a Philosophical Heritage* (Armonk, NY: M.E. Sharpe, 1994)

Sochor, Zenovia A. *Revolution and Culture: The Bogdanov-Lenin Controversy* (Ithaca, NY: Cornell University Press, 1988)

Walicki, Andrzej. *Marxism and the Leap to the Kingdom of Freedom: The Rise and Fall of the Communist Utopia* (Stanford University Press, 1995)

Wetter, Gustav A. *Dialectical Materialism: A Historical and Systematic Survey of Philosophy in the Soviet Union* (Peter Heath (trans.), New York: Praeger, 1958)

Williams, Robert C. *Culture in Exile: Russian Émigrés in Germany, 1881–1941* (Ithaca, NY: Cornell University Press, 1972)

The Other Bolsheviks: Lenin and his Critics, 1904–1914 (Bloomington and Indianapolis, IN: Indiana University Press, 1986)

INDEX

CPSIA information can be obtained at www.ICGtesting.com
Printed in the USA
LVOW05s1655100214

373092LV00004B/955/P